PROJECT MANAGEMENT HANDBOOK

SECOND EDITION

Edited by

David I. Cleland
Professor
Engineering Management
School of Engineering
University of Pittsburgh

William R. King
University Professor
Katz Graduate School of Business
University of Pittsburgh

VNR VAN NOSTRAND REINHOLD
—————————————— New York

Copyright © 1988 by Van Nostrand Reinhold

Library of Congress Catalog Card Number 87-23151

ISBN 0-442-22114-2

Printed in the United States of America

Van Nostrand Reinhold
115 Fifth Avenue
New York, New York 10003

Van Nostrand Reinhold International Company Limited
11 New Fetter Lane
London EC4P 4EE, England

Van Nostrand Reinhold
480 La Trobe Street
Melbourne, Victoria 3000, Australia

Nelson Canada
1120 Birchmount Road
Scarborough, Ontario, M1K 5G4, Canada

16 15 14 13 12 11 10 9 8 7 6 5 4

Library of Congress Cataloging-in-Publication Data

Project management handbook.
   Includes index.
   1. Industrial project management. I. Cleland,
David I. II. King, William Richard
HD69.P75P75   1988   658.4′04   87-23151
ISBN 0-442-22114-2

Preface

When the first edition of this handbook was honored with the Institute of Industrial Engineer's Book-of-the-Year Award, we as editors felt that we had accomplished our objective, ". . . to provide project managers and those individuals concerned with project management in both public and private organizations a reference guide for the fundamental concepts and techniques of managing projects."

However, in the fast-moving field of project management, there is a need for continuing updating as new techniques, tools, understandings and experiences are developed. Hence, this second edition has been fashioned to build on the strengths of the first edition and to add insights that were unavailable when the first editon was published.

Like all good handbooks, this is a reference source for practical how-to-do-it information. A manager or professional who has a problem with project management can turn to this handbook and find the help needed to solve the problem.

However, there are other important uses to which this handbook can be put. The field of project management has been growing so rapidly in recent years that anyone who wishes to learn more about the discipline is faced with an abundance of published information. The handbook is organized so that it can be used either as a reference or for sustained study.

Thus, in such a rapidly developing field, even experienced project managers are faced with the challenge of keeping up with current developments and selecting those concepts and techniques that are most appropriate for their needs, will find it to be useful.

Those who are not experienced project managers, but who must play a role in the process of project management—functional managers, general managers, project team members and support staff—have an even more difficult task, for they must "keep up" in a rapidly expanding field that is not their special area of expertise. So, the *Project Management Handbook* is also addressed to their needs.

Students of project management may use the *Handbook* as a self-study aid, for it has been organized to facilitate an overall program of learning about the field as well as to provide a quick reference source on specific topics.

The *Project Management Handbook* seeks to provide guidance for all varieties of projects—from the largest and most complex systems development efforts, to the personal "research project." Its emphasis, however, is organizational in the sense that much of the material deals with the integration of projects into an overall managerial framework.

In addition to serving the needs of those who are directly concerned with project management, this book will be useful to top managers who wish to motivate and establish a philosophy of project management within their organizations. There are different types of project management, ranging from the simplistic use of expediters to sophisticated multiproject organizational approaches; the high-level manager who believes that one of these forms will be useful will find the *Handbook* to be a sound guide for planning for the evolution of project management in the organization.

The handbook provides information on both the theory and practice of project management. While primary emphasis is on the pragmatic aspects of managing projects, this pragmatism is casted in a sound, theoretical framework of managerial thought.

In the editors' opinion, the proportion of project participants who require access to a handbook in this field is greater than for any other managerial group. This is because of the relative newness of the field, the lack of adequate training programs, and the general awareness that, unlike some other disciplines, there is a practical body of knowledge which can serve to support all aspects of the project management process.

As one leafs through the pages of the *Project Management Handbook,* the number and variety of the factors and forces with which the project manager must deal become clear. Their very number appears at first to make it impossible for one individual to master the art and science of managing projects. However, in reading further one becomes aware of the creativity and ingenuity which the authors have brought to bear on project management. For most of the problem situations that a project participant will face, this handbook has information that can be of help. Certainly, no one would claim that the state-of-the-art of this field has stabilized. Further evolution will continue. Nevertheless, the reader will find that there are workable solutions to the situations that arise in project management.

This handbook is the result of the cooperative efforts of a large number of people. The qualifications of the individual contributors are clear from the biographical sketch given on the title page of each article. The topic content of the handbook is broadly designed to be relevant to the general organizational contexts in which project management is found. Accordingly, some of the parochial subjects of project management in specific industries are not included. For example, configuration management and value engineering—two key concerns of project managers in the aerospace industry—are not treated. The editors believe that the parochial interests of a particular industry's project manager's needs can be best served by studying the literature of that industry.

Whatever its value to the reader, the *Project Management Handbook* reflects the experiences and considered judgments of many qualified individuals about the pivotal factors and forces surrounding project management. Eight interdependent areas of project management are developed:

1. *An Overview of Project and Matrix Management.* The framework of practice and theory in which contemporary project and matrix management is found.
2. *The Project Organization.* The alignment of resources to support project objectives, particularly in terms of the matrix organization.
3. *Organizational Strategy and Project Management.* The deployment of resources to support broader organization missions, objectives, and goals.
4. *Life Cycle Management.* The management of projects as they fit into broader and longer-range organizational cycles.
5. *Project Planning.* Planning to include the development of goals, strategies, and actions to allocate project resources.
6. *Project Implementation.* The actions and constraints that are relevant to getting the project that has been planned actually carried out.
7. *Project Control.* The means to determine the harmony of actual and planned cost, schedule, and performance goals, including the use of computers.
8. *Behavioral Dimensions and Teamwork in Project Management.* The development of a climate whereby the project people work together with economic, social, and psychological satisfaction.
9. *The Successful Application of Project Management.* An examination of what counts for success in project management.

We thank the contributing authors who have given so importantly and unselfishly through their practical how-to-do-it presentations of the forces and factors involved in project management.

The editors are deeply indebted to Claire Zubritzky, who managed the administration involved in the development and production of this handbook. We are also indebted to Olivia Harris, whose contributions, both to the *Handbook* and to the milieu in which we work, were substantial. Karen Bursic's efforts on the index and Ellen Hufnagel's proofreading are also appreciated.

We thank the late Dr. Albert G. Holzman, former Chairman of the Industrial Engineering Department, Dr. Harvey Wolfe, the current chairman, Dr. Charles A. Sorber, Dean of the School of Engineering, and Dr. H. J. Zoffer, Dean of the Katz Graduate School of Business, all of the University of Pittsburgh, who provided us with the environment to pursue this effort.

DAVID I. CLELAND
WILLIAM R. KING
Pittsburgh, PA

Contents

Section I
Overview of Project and Matrix Management

This introductory section of the handbook presents an overview of project and matrix management. Project management is viewed as a powerful tool that is particularly useful in terms of the management of the many interfaces that exist within an organization, and between an organization and its environment.

However, despite the power of the concept and its history of successful application, project management is not presented as a panacea. Rather, it is a tool which, *when properly used under appropriate circumstances,* can aid the organization in the achievement of its major goals.

In the first chapter, Robert D. Gilbreath demonstrates how rapid change has created a need for project management. He distinguishes the modern project environment from the traditional "operations" of continuous repetitive processes.

In Chapter 2, Peter W. G. Morris explains the need for project and matrix management in an insightful chapter on "interface management." He discusses project and matrix management in conceptual terms and provides, as well, numerous real-world illustrations and prescriptions for the successful management of interfaces.

In the third chapter, Linn C. Stuckenbruck discusses project integration in the matrix organization by emphasizing the proactive nature of integration; that it does not just happen, but must be made to happen. He discusses how a project management system can be implemented in the organization and what the project manager must do to properly begin the project.

1. Working with Pulses, not Streams: Using Projects to Capture Opportunity

Robert D. Gilbreath*

The phenomena of rapid social, economic, technological, and political change have revised our view of business activity, destroyed the viability of accepted business models, and led to new definitions of ourselves and our effect. Although our products or our services may be similar to those of the past, how we bring them about and how reliable that effect can be are no longer taken for granted. A greater understanding and more intelligent response to change forces us to reconsider the very foundations of our work, our contribution to it, and its place in the realm of business. Change is reshaping the nature and meaning of work.

Nowhere is this more pronounced than through the *"projectization"* of work, its centering in unique, temporary packets of effort. Whereas industrial production and all its social and cultural spin-offs relied upon linear, sequential arrays of highly specialized and synchronized effort (i.e., the automobile assembly line), this new, change-directed concept of work involves parallel, unsynchronized, and generalized effort not tied to or dependent upon any established tools or techniques.

If the concept of work dominant in the past has been symbolized by a *line,* the new representation of work is more apt to be a *circle*—a circle that encloses a comprehensive interaction of concurrent, temporary, and accomplishment-oriented tasks. If the old term for work was *"operations,"* the new term is *"projects."*

In times of change the project orientation dominates all operational frameworks. The logic supporting this conclusion is inescapable, and we see it manifested with great frequency by business examples all about us. Perceptive managers know, then, that in times of change, for today and tomorrow, they will more often than not be managing *projects.*

* Robert D. Gilbreath advises corporations on new management perspectives and evolving executive issues. He is the author of *Managing Construction Contracts* and *Winning At Project Management* (John Wiley & Sons, 1983, 1986). This chapter is excerpted with permission from his third management book *Forward Thinking: The Pragmatist's Guide to Today's Business Trends* (McGraw-Hill Book Co., Copyright 1987).

3

We cannot simply count the growing number of efforts our companies now designate as *"projects"* and hold this increase up as the sole result of a projectization phenomenon. Much more is happening to change the nature of our work and our perception of our role in it. Subtle, project-influenced changes are even taking place in operational settings. Most of all, operationally oriented managers are beginning to understand the unique aspects and condition of project assignments. Here are some other signposts indicating a widespread turn toward projects.

SIGNPOSTS OF CHANGE

- *Adaptation of the "project manager" designation.* Once regarded as an organizational oddity, the project manager is now invading even the most nonproject-oriented companies. In a future dominated by change, every manager, at one time or another, will be a project manager.
- *More temporary, results-directed organizations.* The days of the concrete, tiered organization are gone. We now view all organizations as temporary, goal-directed contrivances—necessary evils rather than structures of intrinsic beauty. Projects cannot be managed by pyramids. They demand clusters of people gathered around a challenge.
- *More common use of outsiders (consultants, subcontractors, joint ventures, temporaries, etc.) for specific efforts.* Organizations are being built and destroyed on the bases of risk and pragmatism. The old notions of insiders and outsiders don't fit anymore. We'll use whichever players we need, regardless of what uniforms they wear.
- *More local and perishable procedures, plans, standards.* Standards don't work well in times of flux. Like organizations, they will be disposable, situationally responsive, and full of room for discretion.
- *Emphasis on "people skills" among management.* Project management is, first, people management. To coalesce disparate interests, transcend goal conflicts, and create binding mutuality, we will need those who hold people skills.
- *Constant creation and dismantling of management scaffolding.* Procedures, policies, reports, information systems, and progress measurements are all elements of managerial scaffolding. When everything remains static, the scaffolding can be built of steel and anchored in bedrock. In times of change, it must be as temporary and mobile as a tent.
- *Devaluation of tradition, of "what worked last time."* In the world of projects, there simply is no "last time." This is the world of change—the phenomenon that mocks the past.

- *The emergence of pragmatism and resourcefulness over perfection and compliance as favorable management attributes.* We will need scroungers, tinkerers, masters of the extemporaneous, and those who can make it happen, regardless of the rules, the odds, or the inevitable second guess. Project positions are contribution-based and need-justified. Our position and authority will be functions of what we *are doing,* not what we *have done* or *who we are.*

ILLUSTRATING THE DISTINCTIONS*

One must clearly understand and fully appreciate the bold and fine differences between *operations* and *projects* in order to comprehend the powerful influence of change on business. By shifting our needs from operationally-achieved work to work accomplished through projects, change has exerted one of its most observable and profound effects. Its impacts reach our notion of work itself, our roles in work, the needs and limitations of management—affecting both our senses of identity and our value systems.

As we draw and give examples of some of the many distinctions between these two approaches to work, we will not only be depicting differences in work orientations but also describing the particular nature and far-reaching impact of change. To understand the differences between operations and projects is to understand the differences between a changeless and a changing world—that is, to understand change itself.

WHY OPERATIONS AND PROJECTS DIFFER

There are countless differences between operations and projects as ways to organize and manage business effort, and they include concept, context, intent, and application. Rather than defining each and every difference, our approach will be to point out the most significant differences and those which most directly illustrate the effect of change.

Operations are based on the concept of *using* existing systems, properties, processes, and capabilities in a continuous, fairly repetitive fashion. If our business is automobile production, our operational base is comprised of physical plant (the factory), tools, equipment, information and control systems, knowledge, and production skills. Our operational objective is to use this fixed potential as efficiently and effectively as possi-

---

* In this chapter I draw from some distinctions made in my earlier book, *Winning At Project Management: What Works, What Fails, and Why* (Wiley, New York, 1986), not to identify all project aspects but to present only those that illustrate business responses to change.

ble. Operations are aimed at making the best use of what exists, over and over again.

FEWER PRESUMPTIONS

Projects, in contrast to operations, presuppose no fixed tools, techniques, or capability. They seek to create a limited impact through temporary and expedient means. The design and construction of an automobile assembly plant is a good example. As such, this "project" is unique and apart from any other undertaken. We produce one "product," the plant, rather than a series of similar products (the cars that will result from operation of the finished plant). Uniqueness of effort and result are the hallmarks of project situations. Consistency and uniformity are typical of operations.

Operations are geared to maintain and exploit, while projects are conceived to create and make exploitation available. Projects, therefore, typically precede operations in the normal business cycle.

Projects are temporary and expedient exercises, while operations are more sustained and continuous, and therefore more amenable to optimization. Economies of scale help to optimize operations, as do trial and error, but given the temporary and unique world of each project, neither of these approaches is very useful in a project. If a successful operation can be imagined as a continuous, uninterrupted *stream* of effort yielding a predictable collection of similar results, we must view each project as a temporary *pulse* of activity yielding a unique, singular result.

Projects represent, then, one-time-only configurations of resources, people, tools, and management expectations, while operations presuppose continuity of the conversion process well into the future. We seldom consider the end of an operation, but we always consider the end of a project as soon as we conceive of its initiation. We expect projects to be completed, to be finished, and, like cruise missiles, to be self-consuming once their singular purposes have been accomplished. Operations may outlive their results, but projects expire when their result is achieved.

FREE VARIABLES AND SOFT LINKS

In order to exploit induced change, operations rely on circumstances in which most variables are fixed and the rest are manipulated. Working conditions are fairly constant; we are usually enclosed in a factory, office, or shop; and our resources are of like nature and consistent in appearance and quality. Project work, though, is hostage to many free variables, few of which are presumed to be fixed. The fixing of free variables must take place every time a project is initiated, as when staffs are hired, organizations are created, procedures are adopted, plans are made, and lines of communication are strung. Most of these variables are fixed and already in place by the time operational work begins.

Since synchronization is essential to any effort involving more than one participant, both operations and projects need to meet the challenge of synchronization. They differ in how the challenge is met, though. With operations, the links connecting serial work steps are usually "hard" or mechanical, inherent in the equipment, line, material, or techniques used. If metal must be rolled before stamping, we simply position the rollers in advance of the stamping press in the production line. This is a *"hard link,"* designed into the operation and therefore difficult to avoid or circumvent.

With project work, activity cannot be so easily synchronized. We often must depend on forced, artificial, or human linkage, the so-called soft links that tie otherwise disparate work elements together. Soft links include contract terms and conditions ("All steel shall be rolled before stamping"), written procedures, management inspection, and supervision. Soft links require constant enforcement and monitoring, for they may be easily bypassed or ignored. They are much less dependable as guarantees of synchronicity. Again, with project work less is fixed (or fixable) and less can be taken for granted.

Most astute executives understand the tension between process and product-dominated business approaches and have seen how a product-oriented effort better fits changing conditions. This also applies to a project effort, where we begin with an expected set of results and seek to find or build a collection of processes to bring it about (*result drives process*). With operations the reverse is true. We begin with a process (factory, plant, refinery, line, etc.) and search for materials to feed it and markets in which to discharge the result (*process drives product*).

Project work is also amenable to the pressure change exerts toward generalization and away from specialty restrictions. Project work, by its nature, begins with nothing and relies on synthesis to proceed. It requires coalescence: bringing elements together and creating mutuality among them. Operations tend to divide labor and its contribution into discrete, incremental stages. In fact, division of labor is a hallmark of the industrial revolution.

CHANGE SENSITIVITY OR DEFIANCE

Because of their fixed conditions, hard links, stationary components, and hard-wired process steps, most operational efforts are rightly classified as insensitive to change or defiant of it. They shield themselves as much as possible from incurred change and stick to their original goals, methods, and results. Project work cannot be so shielded. It is conceived, born, lives, and expires in change. It evolves continuously, because of both induced and incurred change. It takes a different approach to the challenge of change immunity; it opts for disposability or adaptation rather than durability.

Finally, we must recognize that operations take time, money, and a great deal of effort to establish, long before the first product rolls off the end of the line. All the capital investment, design, hard wiring, and variable fixing they employ must precede their use. Once erected, operational apparatus cranks out a great deal of product at lower and lower unit cost. The question is, "Do we have the time to spend and the resources to sink before the first stream of products starts to flow?" Unless we exist in a relatively static environment, the answer is, "No, we have neither."

When conditions are in a state of flux, opportunities are fleeting, and our businesses must seize the moment, the rapid deployment of a project effort is much more suitable. If the targets of opportunity remain similar and stationary for long periods of time, if they are unthreatening and fixed, we can design and erect a very efficient method of shooting them down. This is the operational solution. If instead we are running through a jungle of beasts, some pursued and some pursuing, the ability to quickly access and deploy *any* weapon is much more important to us. Selecting the *available,* albeit not often *ideal,* weapon is the project solution. Changing conditions favor the pragmatic.

THE PROJECT ANOMALY

Projects are a special type of business anomaly. They often evolve, change shape, and resist definition (as force waves, for example, do), but then again, they are always composed of discrete items such as people, resources, and conversion processes (as are particles of mass). And we can never point to, look at, or "see" a project (as we can never see subatomic matter). We can see project activity and results, and we can see project managers and production workers doing their work. But even when considered all together, these factors do not actually make up the project model; they are simply parts of it. Projects follow the concept of *holism* or *synergy* in that each is a collection of entities or objects that can generate a larger reality not analyzable in terms of the components themselves.

The best way to model a project is not to use a visual representation at all. A project is a *mutual effort,* using a collection of resources in an orchestrated way to achieve a joint goal. As such, projects are like "waves"—forces and bundles of energy moving through time—each with its own identity, culture, methods of conversion, and contrived cohesion. Upon accomplishment of the project goal, this contrived cohesion no longer serves to bind the project together (thus making it an anachronism); instead, it dissolves the project—dissipating the project wave upon the beach of success.

It's easy to identify project work in architecture or engineering, for the physical result symbolizes the project itself. A new power plant, a factory, a shopping mall, and an aircraft carrier are examples. But the project model applies to many other fields and to efforts most of us are involved with at one time or another. Here is a partial list of other efforts that might fit the definition of "project":

Performing a heart transplant
Designing a new weapons system
Producing a stage play
Developing a strategic business plan
Researching and writing a book
Conducting a political campaign
Renovating an antique automobile
Producing a motion picture
Establishing a small business
Throwing a party
Introducing a new product
Taking a vacation trip
Designing and installing a computer network
Creating an occupational training program

There is subtle commonality in all these examples. They each involve (1) working with few existing standards, (2) the need for creativity and synthesis, (3) a temporary pulse of effort, and (4) a keen sense of, if not reliance on, the phenomenon of change.

THE DIRECTION OF CHANGE

Each element characterizing a project, and differentiating it from operations, can be seen as a change-directed quality. Projects are the perfect response to change. They are no less than change-responsive bundles of effort. Because they more closely represent waves, and not incompressible particles, projects can expand; shrink; bend; accelerate and slow down; change shape and direction; and escape the burdens of capitalization, process addiction, and hardness. While operations try to withstand the impacts of change, projects ride along with it: business waves upon the sea of time.

FORCES AND FACTORS FAVORING PROJECT ORIENTATIONS

Once we understand the project concept and couple it with what we know about change, it's easy to see why projects are becoming more and more the accepted context of work. Here we should briefly mention why this is true.

Rapid creation and deployment allow project efforts to respond quickly to changed conditions. Their independence from capital burdens lets our work flex with or dodge unforeseen changes in technology or process methodology. The fleeting nature of opportunity gives its rewards only to the most adaptive, mobile pursuer. Project orientations provide that mobility; we can move our effort to the opportunity rather than attempt to entice it into our operating environment, in terms of space and time.

This explains the sudden and successful emergence of *entrepreneurism* in today's business culture. Entrepreneurs succeed where large, static organizations fail—because of their flexibility, mobility, and pursuit. Entrepreneurs are lean and responsive, able to quickly detect and pursue the opportunities that change strews all about. Even with the most expensive, powerful mechanism, a large supertanker needs miles of space and huge amounts of time to execute a complete 180-degree turn, whereas a small speedboat can turn on a dime.

Changing markets, resources, prices, and needs do not allow us the benefit of time or of the fixed variables that operations presuppose. Project work is amenable to dynamic conditions, while operations demand static ones. The tendency of change to emphasize purpose over process also runs counter to the operational premise (process in search of purpose) and diminishes the value of pursuing process enhancements.

If change serves to make any given method or technique less lasting and more perishable, then it also devalues fixed versions of processes and operations. If an operation is dependent on technique and that technique is made obsolete through change, the operation becomes obsolete. Project work has few dependencies, and those it suffers are seldom exclusive.

THE CONTRIBUTION OF BUSINESS MEGACHANGE

Megachanges in the business world itself, each caused partly by recognition of the power of change, also seem to be running in the project direction. These are (1) *variation* in enterprise among megacompanies, (2) *diversification* of risk and assets, (3) use of more *distributed* information and effort (outsourcing, subcontracting, joint ventures, prefabrication elsewhere, containerization, process packaging, etc.), and (4) *decentralization* of business authority and management effect.

Each of these megachanges should have had and has had a tremendous effect on our reevaluation of work and how we relate to it. And each favors the project orientation. Whether they are effects of change or causes of change itself, they signal a new business culture, more cognizant of and more responsive to change. It we are going to manage in the future, we are going to have to manage in this culture—this culture which is impacted by change and in which work is more often than not "projectized."

THE NEW BUSINESS CULTURE

The emergence and proliferation of the project model of work, of work as integrated pulses rather than a continuous line, is helping to define a new and very different business culture. This culture will be dominated by a need to generalize, to spread awareness and ability over large spaces and times, rather than to focus both on ever-narrowing fields of specialty. If generalization represents the prevailing condition of the new business culture, then *synthesis* represents the activity that will bring it about. The ability to synthesize—to coalesce or bring together the forces and resources needed to equip a project effort—is quickly becoming the critical ability of the future. "Synthesis" and "adaptation" are fast replacing "optimization" as the watchwords of today's management.

Management in change will more often be judged by its results than by its inherent sophistication, complexity, or level of detail. A business culture ruled by pragmatism will tend to value accomplishment over refinement, attainment of goals over perfection of a limited ability to attain them. To be truly adaptive, we will embrace independence of any certain set of plans, tools, techniques, or conversion processes. We will view such factors as simply means to an end, and means of temporary and utilitarian value. No business will transcend time and change totally intact, for no business is immune to these forces.

If we are to adapt, our methods and scaffolding must be malleable, disposable, and expedient. We can no longer shackle our companies to any given feature, no matter how well it has served us in the past or how attached or dependent upon it our managers have become. Managers in change are independent managers, serving not technique or tool but higher principles which do transcend momentary changes. These principles are pragmatism, expediency, reason, adaptability, independence, and human value.

We will no longer treasure managers who continue to divide, to separate, and to polarize. Instead, our new leaders will be *integrators,* skilled in human synthesis and mutuality of intent and effort. Only integrators will achieve mutually beneficial results.

The new business culture is evident among entrepreneurial companies today, where flexibility and maneuverability dominate fixity and stead-fastness. Other companies that learn from entrepreneurs will quickly trim their concepts and scaffolding to increase their capabilities. Entrepreneurs aren't successful because they have the best ideas or the greatest intelligence, but because they possess the agility to pursue fleeting opportunity and are lean enough to survive the chase. They can succeed because they are not tied to the legacy of the past: massive capital investment, ingrained management approaches, and obsolete tools and techniques. Their efforts are almost always new, and because they are new they have been created to embody the new culture and to treasure the new values. These are the efforts most aligned with the concept of change, for they are being forged in the white-hot furnace of business-change: today's business climate.

In this climate we will continue to take less and less for granted. Fixed variables are the relics of the past, and nostalgia is beneficial only when it sharpens our awareness of the difference between the past and the present. Because less will be taken for granted, our managers will have to more frequently contrive "mental gathering points," selected reference points at which all members of a project team are allowed to regroup, synchronize their intentions, and recognize a set of mutual accomplishments and goals. Project managers need to coalesce the raw material of their efforts not only at the beginning of a project, but periodically throughout the life of the project, and they need to align not only forces and things but also concepts, energy, and understandings. Again, project managers must be creators and ensurers of *sustained mutuality*.

The new business culture will also favor the quick, the rapid, and the immediate. This increases our dependence on the project mode of work, for projects surpass operations in this regard. They can be marshalled almost instantaneously and implemented with little cost and a minimum amount of time.

Project orientations allow us to *capture* opportunity, while subsequent operations allow us to *exploit* what we have captured. As exploitation times become shorter with change, and capture becomes dependent on alert and mobile management, the abilities to listen and to move quickly become more valuable. The business culture of tomorrow, then, will involve more frequent and more urgent pursuit. And the project, the *energy pulse*, is ideally created to meet that need.

As change becomes more apparent and active, and as company managements recognize the impetus change gives to project efforts and skills, we will see more managers shifting from operations to projects. Even the most operationally entrenched managers will have to encounter and accomplish project tasks more frequently than ever before. The line between projects and operations will begin to blur, and the distinctions will eventually evaporate, for most work will be viewed as project work. As work becomes "projectized," so shall managers.

This being the case, it is best to become acquainted with project skills and project management tenets, no matter what our present alignment may be. We will all need them. If you are going to profit in change, you will profit as some sort of project manager.

The essence of project managers is cohesion. Project managers provide this by acting as organizational "glue," and they exert a strong directing influence upon what they help to bind together. This includes the frequent use of and referral to plans, benchmarks, standards of accomplishment, and temporary achievements, as well as those "mental gathering points" that ensure periodic synchronicity. *Cohesion* and *direction* will replace the old operational needs of *drive* and *efficiency*.

Project managers must be the guardians of plans and of the integrity of objectives, while operationally oriented counterparts are needed to safeguard the productive capacity: the machines, line, or process. The new manager will most often exhibit irreverence for scaffolding, technique, and tradition, whereas the manager in the past defended and reinforced these qualities. In each project experience, the new manager will seek to quickly find and harness the affective essence of the project combination. In contrast, the essence of an operation is fairly obvious to its managers, who seek only to squeeze more and more incremental value from it (to achieve optimization).

The position of project manager is by its nature both tenuous and demanding. No project manager has value without a project, and each demonstrates no strengths except through the project effort. Moreover, project managers cannot hide behind a particular process, concept, or technique. The position of project management is perishable and must be constantly renewed. With operations, management value is embedded in the operational process once synchronization and optimization are attained. The project manager, tomorrow's manager, will have value embedded only in himself or herself. To the degree that this confidence is deserved, it will be acknowledged.

Project managers will seek to create their own policies and rules, to create their own procedures and methods, rather than to comply with those established by others. Project-oriented managers, because of their twin drives for expediency and pragmatism, will value only methods that contribute, that work. They will shun the rest as burdens or obstacles. They should be judged by their resourcefulness and adaptation, in contrast to operational managers of the past, who were punished when they exhibited these traits but rewarded for strict compliance.

In the end, project managers will reap the rewards or penalties of their own embedded capital and that which they nurture in others. They will not be able to depend on fixed assets or scaffolding, or to cherish attached capital, as is so often done in operational settings. Their challenge will be to transcend differences and limitations rather than to depend on presumed fixity. If they do this successfully, they will become the magicians of the new business world: the project-oriented world of work.

DEVELOPING CONTRASTS

To enhance our appreciation of the fundamental differences between projects and operations, we can contrast their expectations—what they require of us as a price for our allegiance:

Operations Demand That We:	Projects Demand That We:
Use them repetitively	*Create and abandon them at will*
Bring opportunity to them	*Use them to pursue opportunity*
Harness similarity	*Harvest diversity*
Let them define expectations	*Let them achieve expectations*
Steer the phenomenon of change	*Steer through or around the phenomenon of change*
Wrap the work around the tools	*Wrap the tools around the work*
Chain people to the process	*Chain the process to people*

THE PRICES AND RISKS OF MANAGING PROJECTS, NOT OPERATIONS

Nothing in this chapter should be construed to diminish the principles of operational management or to suggest that these will no longer be needed. Operational orientations and skills have created the business climate and bounty which most industrialized nations now enjoy, and they will be needed far into the future. What is implied, however, is that, given the nature and emerging awareness of change, the significance of operational models and behavior will diminish, and that of project-oriented approaches will increase.

People who agree with the notion of project suitability and strength in times of change should be aware of the cultural changes it brings and the management ramifications involved. Most of these have been presented in this chapter. In terms of risk and price, however, a few need amplification.

One price, at least to some managements, of a shift to project work is the constant state of organizational flux it requires. We cannot simply reorganize one time and hope this will change our company from a functional, operating organization to a project-sensitive one. Project organizations need to be constantly created, modified, and destroyed. This is often done in concert with modifications and reorganizations on the functional side of the company, where operations occur. Reshaping of project organizations is not done in a vacuum, for it commonly involves movement of people and groups across project-operations borders. Although various forms of matrix organizations have been contrived to facilitate this transition, "tension" is still the best word we can use to describe it.

Process-dependent, technique-addicted, or specialty-limited managers will not be comfortable with the new project environment, just as they are uncomfortable with other aspects of change. Most of the demands of this environment will run counter to their skills and proclivities. Managers who cannot make the attitudinal shift to the new business culture will have to be reassigned to scarcer operational settings, or they will become handicaps to our adaptability.

Executive managers will need to sharpen their own project-related skills—to enhance their ability to harness and nurture strong personalities, independent managers, and creative and innovative pragmatists. Such people are extremely difficult to orchestrate, and simple reliance on procedures or convention will never suffice. Project managers, we must remember, love to create and hate to comply. They will not follow unless they are led. To harvest the bounties they bring, our executive management must reshape its own values and abilities in view of change. Sometimes this price is too high for them.

Project work requires *agility of pursuit* and *agility of perspective* as well. This means we must constantly shift our attention, focus our vision, tune our listening, and most importantly, reshape our understanding. Frequent reestablishment and modification of view and attitude is difficult for many of us. By our natures, we prefer fixity. Unfortunately, change does not allow us this luxury.

Projects require unique views as well as unique efforts. They exist in and for change, and change affects not only our conversion processes and our particular company attitudes and cultures, but the entire fabric of business enterprise, the culture of the business world. The emergence of projects is but one aspect of this new culture. It affects not only that which surrounds us, but ourselves as well, our group and individual identities and values. To some, this reshaping is painful and frightening. To managers attuned to change, it is exciting, challenging, and very rewarding.

2. Managing Project Interfaces— Key Points for Project Success

Peter W. G. Morris*

One of the most important qualities of a project manager is a mature understanding of the way projects develop. This allows the nature of project activities to be better understood, problems to be seen in perspective, and needs to be assessed ahead of time.

To some extent this understanding of project development is intuitive, though it clearly also depends upon specialist knowledge of the project's technology and industry. It can, however, also be acquired in large part from formal study of the development process of projects, since all projects, regardless of size or type, follow a broadly similar pattern of development.

The organizational framework underlying a project's development is the subject of this chapter. The intent of the chapter is to illustrate the types of issues that are normally encountered as a project develops and to suggest ways in which these issues should be handled. The extent to which these issues can be related to project success is then discussed.

THE SYSTEMS PERSPECTIVE AND PROJECT MANAGEMENT

The most pervasive intellectual tradition to project management, whether in organization, planning, control, or other aspects, is without doubt the systems approach.

---

* Dr. Peter Morris is Director of the Major Projects Association, a member of Oxford University's Faculty of Physical Sciences and an Associate Fellow of Templeton College, the Oxford Centre for Management Studies, Oxford, England. He undertook research into project management at Manchester University, England, in the late 1960s, gaining his Ph.D. in 1972. He has worked both as a manager and as a consultant on a variety of projects around the world ranging from telecommunications and petrochemical projects in the Mideast, North Africa, and Europe; steel projects in Latin America; and construction, MIS, and aerospace projects in North America and Europe. Prior to returning to England in 1984, he was responsible for the international business of the Arthur D. Little Program Systems Management Company, Cambridge, Massachusetts. He is the co-author of *The Anatomy of Major Projects,* published by John Wiley & Sons Ltd., 1987.

A system is an assemblage of people, things, information, or other attributes, grouped together according to a particular system "objective." Thus, one has an electrical system, the digestive system, a high-pressure weather system, an air conditioning system, a weapons system, a system for winning at cards.

A system may be logically broken down into a number of subsystems, that is, assemblages of people, things, information, or organizations required to achieve a defined system *sub*objective, like the switching, outside plant, building, transmission, and subscriber subsystems in a telephone system. The subsets of each subsystem may then be identified—cables, poles, microwave, and transmission and distribution equipment for the transmission subsystem—thereby creating sub-subsystems. Subsets of these subsets may then be identified, and so on.

Properly organized and managed, the overall system acts in a way that is greater than the sum of its parts. The systems approach emphasizes treating the system as a whole.

The systems approach has its origin in the late 1920s and 1930s. Biologists noticed similarities in the way that living organisms interacted with and controlled their environments. At the same time, similar patterns were observed by Gestalt psychologists in the way the human mind organized sensory data. Both the mind and living organisms have to adapt to changes in their environment. Systems of this type are known as "open" systems. Before long it was seen that all social systems operate as open systems.[1]

During the 1950s, work in economics, psychology, sociology, anthropology, and other disciplines developed these open-system ideas by elaborating such concepts as self-organization, purposive systems, the importance of goals and objectives, the hierarchical classification of systems and subsystems, and the importance of systems' boundaries and interfaces (2)*. At the same time, this "systemic" view of the world was enriched by a parallel (but initially separate) set of disciplines which had their origin in the industrial and military applications of the scientific method during and immediately after World War II. This was the essentially numeric set of disciplines, such as cybernetics, control theory, oper-

---

[1] Open systems are "open" to the effects of their environment. On the other hand, closed systems, which are the other major system type (including, for example, much of physical chemistry and many types of machines), operate independently of their environment. In open systems, events rather than things are structured; there is a constant energy and information exchange between the system and its environment; the system organizes to minimize entropic decay; equilibrium with the environment is achieved through a process known as homeostasis; and there is a tendency towards differentiation. Closed systems operate in almost exactly the opposite manner (1).*
* Numbered references are given at the end of this chapter.

ations research, systems analysis, and systems engineering, concerned with modeling real-life situations so that complex behavior could be more accurately described and forecast. Slowly both streams merged, encouraged greatly by the enormous growth in the ability of the computer to apply these systems ideas with powerful effectiveness, so that the systems approach is now an established and vigorous influence on management and research.

The systems perspective has contributed substantially to the development of project management. Firstly, the systems emphasis on viewing a system as a whole has frequently been behind the recognition of the need for an across-the-board integrating role—that is, for project management itself (3).[2]

Secondly, systems thinking has shown how projects should work as successfully regulated organizations, for example, the need for clearly defined objectives, the recognition that projects are organizations in constant change, and the need to define and manage major subsystems and their interfaces. A third important contribution is that the dynamic control needs of projects are now better understood—the importance of feedback, the progressive development of information and multilevel project control. And a fourth contribution is the widespread use of systems techniques—systems analysis, systems engineering, work breakdown structures, and simulation models.

Interface Management, as it is used in project management today,[3] is an outgrowth of the first two of these influences of systems thinking on project management. Interface Management identifies the following:

- The subsystems to be managed on a project,
- The principal subsystem interfaces requiring management attention,

---

[2] The development of project management by the U.S. military is an illustration: the systems ideas developed initially for technical purposes were adapted to generate the organizational flexibility and control missing in the existing military bureaucracy. This can be seen in each of the steps in the U.S. military's development of project management—the development of the USAF and Navy program management practices (4), particularly for the ICBM programs (5) and for Polaris (6) around 1952–1955; Peck and Scherer's study of the U.S. and Soviet weapons procurement processes in the late 1950s (7); the development of PERT on Polaris in 1958; the introduction of project organizations in the Navy, Air Force, and Army in the late 1950s/early 1960s; McNamara's extensive study and implementation of program management and project control techniques in the early 1960s; and Laird's and Packard's process-oriented focus on the needs of the total project life cycle in the late 1960s/early 1970s (8).

[3] Interface Management is generally used now in a broader sense than it was ten or twenty years ago. In the 1960s and early 1970s Interface Management generally referred simply to ensuring that system interfaces matched (i.e., had the same specifications, were not missing any equipment, data, etc.). Today it is used in the sense of defining systems—organizational, managerial, and technical—and of actively managing their interrelationships. The term "interface management" is relatively common in high-technology projects, such as information systems and aerospace; it is much rarer on construction projects.

- The ways in which these interactions should be managed successfully.

The emphasis on identifying key interfaces and on focusing on interface performance has grown as it has been increasingly realized that all projects share a common pattern of interfaces derived from a common pattern of subsystem interaction. This is true no matter what the type of project, be it a theater production, an aid program, an election or a major capital investment program.

There are three sets of subsystems on any project: those deriving from the project's life cycle, its management levels, and its operational characteristics.

PROJECT LIFE CYCLE[4a]

Project management teaches that to achieve the desired project objective one must go through a specific process. There is no exception to this rule. The process is known as the project "life cycle."

Projects (like people) have a life cycle that involves a gradual buildup as definitions are established and working characteristics developed, a full-bodied implementation as the work is accomplished, and a phasing out as the work is completed and the project winds down. While there are various definitions of the project (or program) life cycle (Figure 2-1), the essential sequencing is invariant, although (as with people) sometimes not fully recognized or respected.

A project starts as an incipient idea which is explored for financial and technical feasibility in the *Prefeasibility/Feasibility Stage.* Capacity is decided, locations chosen, financing arranged, overall schedule and budget agreed, and preliminary organizations set up. At the end of this phase there should be a formal "go/no-go" decision. In the next phase, *Design,* the work is organizationally and managerially similar to the first phase only it is more comprehensive and detailed. The technical definition of the project is expanded (albeit generally still at a fairly strategic level); schedule, budget, and financing are reappraised; contracting strategy is defined; permits are sought; and infrastructure and logistics systems are defined.

---

[4] Note that an interface is technically defined as the space between interacting subsystems. Even though there might be a common set of subsystems on all projects, this does not necessarily mean there will be a common set of interfaces. The extent that there is depends on the commonality of subsystem interaction. This chapter will show that subsystem interaction does in fact follow a common pattern on most projects.
[4a] The implications of the life cycle are treated in greater detail in Chapter 9.

Kelley's model [9] is essentially that of a program life cycle. He differentiates product control from project control, product control being concerned with the definitions of the end product parameters and project control being concerned with the process of making that product.

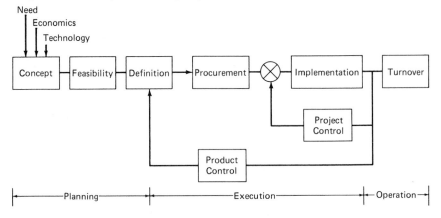

Wearne's model [10] is typical of industrial projects. "The nature and scale of activities change at each stage but the stages usually overlap." Of particular interest are the Demand and the Use, Maintenance, and Records & Experience stages, since these are often overlooked in project management. Iteration within and between the early stages is not unlikely.

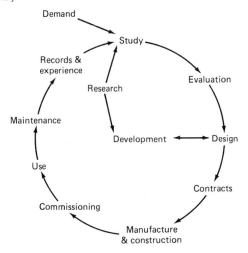

Figure 2-1. Views of the project/program life cycle.

In phase three, *Manufacture, Construction, and Installation* (or *Production*), equipment is procured, civil work is undertaken, and equipment and facilities are installed. This phase differs dramatically from the previous two. First, whereas the *Design* and *Feasibility* phases were organic and evolutionary in character, the *Production* phase is highly mechanistic

Morris' [11] concentrated on the feasibility-design-implementation phases to make several points about the nature of work within and between phases. The design phase is basically "organistic," for example, while the production phase is more "mechanistic." Crossing the design-production interface, with the letting of implementation contracts, is a major transition point in the project life cycle.

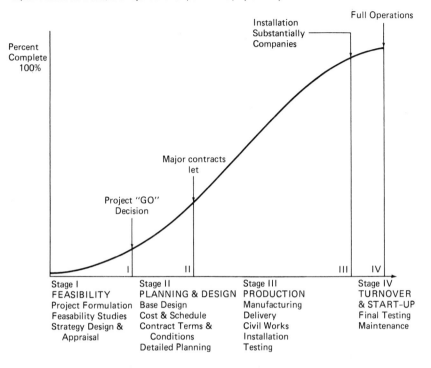

Stage I	Stage II	Stage III	Stage IV
FEASIBILITY	PLANNING & DESIGN	PRODUCTION	TURNOVER
Project Formulation	Base Design	Manufacturing	& START-UP
Feasability Studies	Cost & Schedule	Delivery	Final Testing
Strategy Design &	Contract Terms &	Civil Works	Maintenance
Appraisal	Conditions	Installation	
	Detailed Planning	Testing	

Kerzner's diagram [12] illustrates the financial life of a product development program (me). Kerzner comments on the way the life cycle varies between systems, projects and products; apart from differences in terminology, a major difference is in the overlapping of phases.

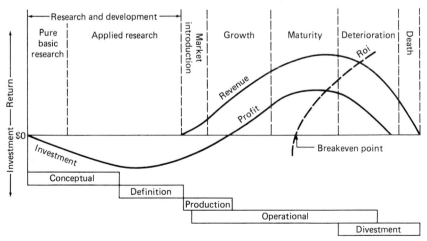

Figure 2-1. (*continued*)

(13). The aim is not to develop new technical options but to build as efficiently as possible the thing which has been defined in the *Design* phase. Second, there is a large—sometimes vast—expansion in organization (whereas there may have been only dozens or hundreds of persons active in the first two phases, there may be thousands or even tens of thousands involved in this third phase.) And third, the characteristic mode of control changes from one of "estimating" costs and durations to one of tight "monitoring" of quality, schedule, and cost to keep actual performance within the target estimates.

The fourth and final phase, *Turn-Over and Start-Up,* overlaps the third phase and involves planning all the activities necessary for acceptance and operation of the project. Successfully synchronizing phases three and four can prove a major management exercise. The cost of capital locked up in the yet uncommissioned plant, and the opportunity costs of both underutilized operating systems such as sales, operating plant, personnel, etc., and a possible diminishing strategic advantage while competitors develop rival products, can prove enormous.

Between each of these life-cycle phases there are distinct "change points" (what shall later be called "dynamic project interfaces"):

- From *Prefeasibility/Feasibility* to *Design:* the "go" decision.
- From *Design* to *Production.*
- From *Production* to *Turn-Over & Start-Up.*

The project on either side of these change points is dramatically different—in mission, size, technology, scale, and rate of change—and these differences create their own particular different characteristics of work, personal behavior, and direction and control needs. Thus, importantly, the management style of each of the four main life-cycle phases is significantly different.

PROJECT MANAGEMENT LEVELS

The four phases have a set and important managerial relation to each other. The work of the *Prefeasibility/Feasibility* stage is highly "institutional" (top management) in kind—decisions taken in this phase will later have an overriding impact on the health of the investing enterprises. In *Design,* the work is of a "strategic" nature, laying the axes upon which the detailed, "tactical" work, of the third, *Production* phase will rest. Interestingly, the fourth phase, *Turn-Over & Start-Up,* exhibits a mixture of all three managerial levels of work: institutional, strategic, and tactical.

These three levels of management activity have been recognized as distinct levels of management since at least the time of Talcott Parsons, the eminent American sociologist. Parsons made the point that each of the three levels has an essential role to play in any successfully regulated enterprise: the technical/tactical level (III) manufactures the product; middle management (II) coordinates the manufacturing effort; at the institutional level (I) top management connects the enterprise to the wider social system (14). Each of these three management levels has a fundamental role to play in the management of every project (although it is true that the levels tend to become more blurred on the smaller projects). Yet surprisingly, most project management literature deals only with Levels II and III. There is little in the literature that treats such Level I issues as: the role of the owner and his financer; relations with the media, local and federal government, regulatory agencies, lobbyists, and community groups; the sizing and timing of the project in relation to product demand and the cost of finance—all issues that became crucially important during the 1970s and are particularly so in the 1980s.[5]

The distinction between Levels II and I is quite critical since it is essentially the distinction between the project and its outside world (Figure 2-2). Levels II and III deal almost exclusively with such familiar project activities as engineering, procurement, installation, testing, and start-up—Level III providing the technical input, Level II providing both a buffer from the outside world and guidance in how to avoid external pitfalls. But no project exists in isolation from outside events. Level I provides the coordination of the project with outside events and institutions. Level I actors typically include the project owner and his finance team, government agencies, community groups, very senior project management, and one or two special project executives specifically charged with external affairs, such as Public Relations and Legal Counsel.

The involvement of each of these Levels is different during each of the major phases of the project life cycle. During the *Prefeasibility/Feasibility* stage, the owner and his team (Levels I and II) have to make crucial decisions about the technical performance and business advantages they are to get for their investment—and indeed, whether the project should "go" at all. Once the decision to go ahead is taken the weight of the work moves to the design team (Levels II and III). During *Production* engineering reaches a detailed level. Both project management (Level II) and technical staff (Level III) are now at full stretch, while top management (Level I) takes a more reduced "monitoring" role. Finally, during *Turn-Over and Start-Up,* all three Levels are typically highly active as engi-

---

[5] Such "institutional" project management issues are preeminently the concern of the UK Major Projects Association (15). They are treated in this handbook in Chapters 8, 13, 18, and 22.

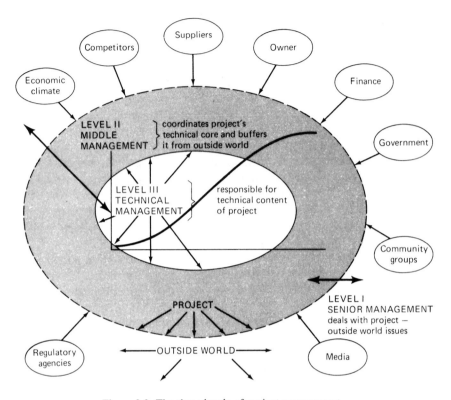

Figure 2-2. The three levels of project management.

neering work gets completed (Level III), often under intense management pressure (Level II), while high-level coordination is required at the owner level in coordinating the initiation of Start-Up activities.

The responsibilities of these Levels thus focus on two main areas of activity: Levels II and III on the technical and middle management work within the project, and Level I on the senior management work at the project/outside world interface.

PROJECT OPERATIONAL SUBSYSTEMS

The work of these two essentially distinct levels of project management activity tends to follow a pattern which is similar on many projects.

At the project/outside world level, the concern is to ensure that the project is commercially viable and, as far as possible, is provided with the conditions and resources necessary to succeed. The principal areas of work at this level are

- Ensuring satisfactory *Project Definition* (which includes both technical content, cost and schedule requirements)
- Preparing for *Operations & Maintenance*
- Preparing for *Sales & Marketing*
- Ensuring appropriate *Organization* structures and systems, both for the project and for operations
- Facilitating relations with important *Outside Groups* such as government and community groups, financial institutions, and the media
- Ensuring appropriately skilled *Manpower* for both the project and future operations
- Ensuring that the total enterprise is *Commercially Sound* and "adequately financed."

Work within the project, on the other hand, focuses more on accomplishing the tasks within the strategic parameters developed and managed by senior management. At the intra-project level, the principal subsystems are

- Realizing the desired *Project Definition*—i.e., assuring that the project is produced to technical specification, on time, and in budget
- Creating the *Organization* needed to execute the project—this includes both the formal organization structures, contractual relationships, systems of information flow and control procedures, and also informal patterns of working relationships and communication
- Minimizing external disruptions from the *Environment*—by, for example, acquiring adequate materials inventory to provide buffer stocks against delivery disruptions, handling union negotiations, obtaining necessary regulatory approvals, or warning top management of future financing needs[6]
- Providing adequate *Infrastructure and Logistics* to accomplish the project (facilities, transportation, communication, utilities).

---

[6] The effects of environment on a project can be profound, and continue to provoke keen theoretical analysis and discussion. Of particular interest is the problem of how organizations behave in a constantly and rapidly changing environment. Theorists describe such environments as turbulent and call the type of systems that operate in such environments "multistable" (16). Large or complex projects in particular suffer many of the consequences predicted for multistable systems, such as large subsystem interaction, continuous objectives redefinition, rich internal feedback processes, high impact of external factors (often causing the subsystems to have to act in an apparently less-than-rational way), and substantial organizational change, often of a step-function size. These characteristics can be found on major projects such as the Concorde and North Sea Oil projects, nuclear power projects, and many defense projects (17).

STATIC AND DYNAMIC INTERFACES

The likely existence of these subsystems in a project, no matter how it unfolds, enables us to categorize certain interfaces as on-going or "static"—they are not a function of the way the project develops but represent relationships between on-going subsystems (like engineering and procurement, or Level I and Level II). There is another group of interfaces, however, which arise only as a function of the pattern of activity interdependencies generated by the way the project develops. These we may identify as life-cycle or "dynamic" interfaces.

Dynamic interfaces between life-cycle (or activity) subsystems are of the utmost importance in project management, first because of the continuous importance of the clock in all projects, and second because early subsystems (like *Design*) have a managerially dominant role on subsequent ones (like *Manufacturing*). Dynamic interrelationships require careful handling if minor mistakes in early systems are not to pass unnoticed and snowball into larger ones later in the project.

Boundaries should be positioned where there are major discontinuities in technology, territory, time, or organization (18). Major breakpoints in the project life cycle—as, for instance, between each of the four major phases, and also between activity subsystems within each phase (for example between manufacture, inspection, delivery, warehousing, installation, and testing)—provide important dynamic interfaces. These serve as "natural" check points at which management can monitor performance.

Most major dynamic interfaces are in fact used in this way: for example, the Project Feasibility Report, the initial Project Technical Design, the formulation and negotiation of the "Production" contracts, and Testing and Hand-Over. Review points such as design-freeze points, estimates-to-complete, and monthly progress reports may also be introduced for purely control purposes without there being any "natural" discontinuity. Each in its own way represents a response by project management to control the project's momentum across its dynamic interfaces.

Whereas the important dynamic interfaces are relatively sharply defined for Level II and III management, at Level I they are less distinct. Level I management is certainly partly driven by the anatomy of the project's internal development, but it also has its own dynamic interfaces for each of its own principal subsystems. Operation, Sales, many of the Outside Groups, Manpower, and Finance and Commercial issues each have their own often distinct life cycles. (For example: the process of recruiting and training manpower; preparing annual financial plans.) Thus at Level I, dynamic interfaces do not become less important; rather they become more varied and less clearly defined. They are still crucial to the project's success.

Static interfaces too are less clearly defined at Level I than at Levels II and III, partly due to the wider scope of concern of Level I (which gives rise to much multifacted subsystem interaction, as, for example, between Operations, Sales, Manpower, and Finance) and partly due to the disruptive effect of the outside environment.

Figure 2-3 sketches the three principal sets of project subsystems which have now been identified: the three levels of management, static subsystems, and dynamic subsystems.

PROJECT INTEGRATION

Some interfaces are clearly larger and more important than others. Organization theorists describe the size of an interface not in terms of, for instance, a small change point or a major one, but in terms of the degree of *differentiation* between subsystems. Typical measures of differentiation include differences in

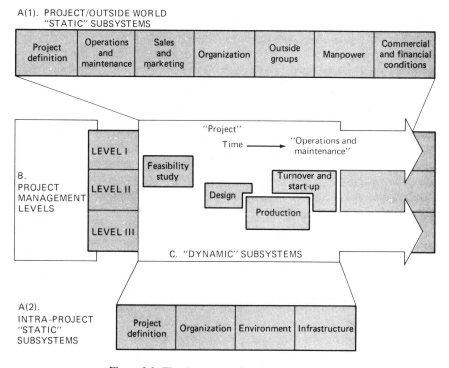

Figure 2-3. The three sets of project subsystems.

- Organization structure
- Interpersonal orientations
- Time horizons
- Goals and objectives (19).

Thus, a mechanized infantry brigade can be differentiated clearly from a local community opposition group on all dimensions. The R&D wing of a company can be similarly differentiated from the marketing wing. The architect on a building project can be differentiated from the building contractor.

A mechanized infantry brigade will go to some lengths to avoid having to integrate with a local opposition group but R&D has to integrate with marketing quite frequently, and it is inevitable that architects must integrate with contractors. Why? Because the activities of the groups create certain technical, organizational, and environmental *interdependencies*. These interdependencies may be almost accidental or may be deliberately organized. *Integration* becomes important when the degree of organizational interdependence becomes significant. Research has shown that tighter organizational integration is necessary when

- The goals and objectives of an enterprise bring a need for different groups to work closely together
- The environment is complex or changing rapidly
- The technology is uncertain or complex
- The enterprise is changing quickly
- The enterprise is organizationally complex (20).

The amount of integration actually required at an interface depends both on the size of differentiation across the interface and on how much "pulling together" the interfacing subsystems need.

Certain project subsystems can be differentiated from one another quite markedly. For example, the project/outside groups interface is marked by very strong differences in time horizons, goals and objectives, interpersonal orientations, and structure—this is why the conflict over many environmental and regulatory issues is so drastic on many large projects: the aims and mores of the environmentalists are far, far removed from those who are trying to build the project. The design group often functions quite differently from the construction group—the former's interest might be elegant engineering, time might not be money, and quality might be paramount; the construction crew might be of less elitist thinking, have strong incentives not to waste time, and might often work in a tougher organizational milieu. Similarly, there are major differences in perspective between operations and project personnel, between the project finance team and project engineering, between a construction manager and project management, and so on. It is, in short, possible to establish the degree of differentiation between each one of the project's interacting subsystems, and in so doing thereby establish which are the principal project interfaces (21).

Despite the insights of management theorists, choosing the degree of integration—the amount of "pulling together"—required across an interface still calls for considerable judgment. This is inevitable. There is no easy answer to the question, "How much management is enough?" There are some pointers, however. James D. Thompson, in a classic book (22), observed that there are three kinds of interdependency, each requiring its own type of integration. The simplest, "pooled," only requires that people obey certain rules or standards. The second form, "sequential," requires that interdependencies be *scheduled*. "Reciprocal" interdependence, the most complex kind, requires *mutual adjustment* between parties (Figure 2-4). In project terms, subsystems which are in continuous

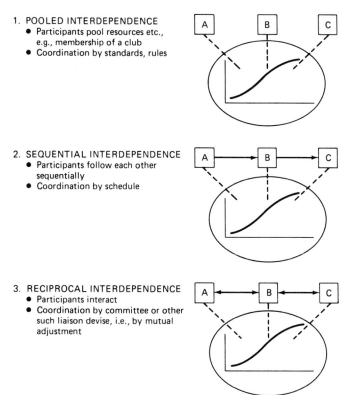

1. POOLED INTERDEPENDENCE
   - Participants pool resources etc., e.g., membership of a club
   - Coordination by standards, rules

2. SEQUENTIAL INTERDEPENDENCE
   - Participants follow each other sequentially
   - Coordination by schedule

3. RECIPROCAL INTERDEPENDENCE
   - Participants interact
   - Coordination by committee or other such liaison devise, i.e., by mutual adjustment

Figure 2-4. The three types of interdependence.

interaction require liaison in order to achieve the necessary integration, whereas those that just follow on from one another can follow plans and schedules.

There is a range of devices which can be used to achieve liaison (23):

- Liaison positions
- Task forces
- Special teams
- Coordinators (or permanent integrators)
- Full project management
- Matrix organizations.

Each of these options provides stronger integration than the last.

The primary function of *liaison positions* is to facilitate communication between groups. Other than this, the liaison position carries no real authority and little responsibility. *Task forces* are much stronger. Task forces provide mission-oriented integration: a group is formed specifically for a particular task and upon completion of the task the group disbands. *Special teams* are like task forces but attend to regularly recurring types of problems rather than specific issues. A *coordinator,* or permanent integrator, provides a similar service as a liaison position but has some formal authority. He exercises this authority over the decision-making processes, however, not over the actual decision makers themselves. This is a subtle point, but an important one, and it often causes difficulties in projects. The coordinator cannot command the persons he is coordinating to take specific actions. That authority rests with their functional manager. He can, however, influence their behavior and decisions, either through formal means such as managing the project's budget and schedule, approving scope changes, etc., or through informal means such as his persuasive and negotiating skills. The full *project manager* role upgrades the authority and responsibility of the integration function to allow cross-functional coordination. The integrator—the project manager—now has authority to order groups directly to take certain actions or decisions. *Matrix organizations* are, by general consent, considered about the most complex form of organization structure. Matrix structures provide for maximum information exchange, management coordination, and resource sharing (24). Matrixes achieve this by having staff account simultaneously to both the integrating (project) managers and the functional managers whose work is being integrated. Both project managers and functional managers have authority and responsibility over the work, albeit there is a division of responsibility: the functional manager is responsible for the "what" and "by whom"; the project manager decides the

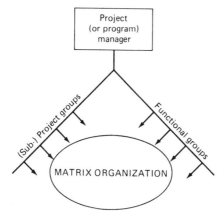

Figure 2-5. Typical use of the project management and matrix organizations simultaneously.

"when" and "for how much." Unfortunately the person who often comes off the worst in the matrix is the poor soul (at Level III) who is actually doing the work. He reports to two bosses—his project manager and his functional manager—which is not in itself necessarily a problem except when, as often happens, the project manager and functional manager are themselves in conflict (for instance, over how much should be spent on the project). Matrix structures generate considerable conflict and suffer from constantly changing boundaries and interfaces (25).

The relative merits of the matrix organization vis-à-vis the full-fledged project organization is one of those hardy perennials of project management. Various writers at various times have offered all kinds of reasons why one or other form is better. Three points seem to stand out, however. First, the full project management role—with a project manager in overall command of the project—does offer stronger leadership and better unity of command.[7] It is better for achieving the big challenge. Second, the matrix organization is more economical on resources. For this reason alone it is often almost unavoidable on large or complex projects. Third, it is quite common to find a full-fledged project manager sitting on top of a matrix structure (Figure 2-5)—the two forms are not incompatible but in fact fit rather well together: the top project manager (Level I) providing

[7] Note, then, that if one were to list the integrating devices in terms of ascending project management authority, the last three forms would change order to become "project coordinator, matrix organization, full project form" (26).

the leadership and ultimate decision-making authority, the matrix providing maximum middle management (Levels II and III) integration.

The challenge in moving through this range of liaison devices is very clear. Achieving greater integration requires increased attention to interfacing parties. Interfaces tend to become increasingly difficult to manage as one moves through the continuum. Let us look now at some experience of managing project interfaces.

MANAGING PROJECT INTERFACES

Interface Management is not, it must be admitted, a well-developed theory of management well supported by a tight body of research and experience. It is more a way of looking at project management which is particularly useful especially on large, complex, or urgent projects. The insights which are offered below are therefore illustrative rather than comprehensive in their exposition of Interface Management.

Keep Static Interfaces Clearly Defined

On projects, problems require solutions within short time frames, organizational conflicts abound, and compromises are inevitable. In such an environment, boundaries can blur. It is therefore a fundamental principle of Interface Management to maintain the static interfaces clearly defined.

In the Apollo program there was a constant need to reinforce organizational boundaries. When General Phillips was appointed director of the Apollo program in 1963, he found that the program was organized entirely along project grounds: one group for the Lunar Excursion Module, one for the rocket, and so on. This created a number of problems, particularly with the wide geographic dispersion of the program. The program was therefore reorganized to stress its functional and geographic needs as well as its project requirements. Five functional divisions were created—systems engineering, checkout and test, flight operations, reliability and quality assurance, and program control—with project offices in Houston, Huntsville, and Cape Canaveral. A matrix organization was thus created which reported to a strong but small program office in Washington, D.C. (Figure 2-6). This office, of only about 120 persons, managed a program which consisted at times of upwards of 300,000 persons. It did so by very clearly defining lines of responsibility and authority and program interface relationships, and by insisting that work be delegated and accounted for strictly in accordance with these lines and procedures (27).

Organizational checks and balances also help keep organization interfaces clearly demarcated. There are four groups which must always be

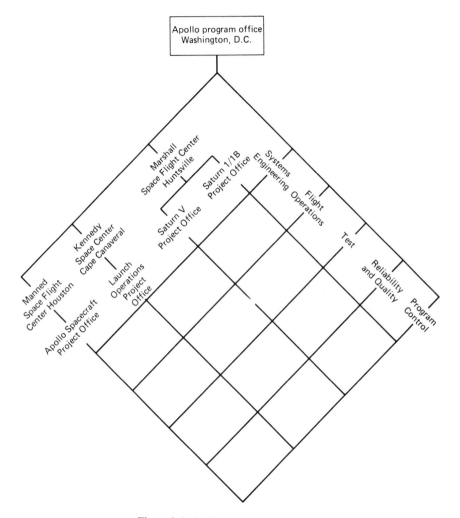

Figure 2-6. Apollo program organization.

organizationally distinct on projects: project management, project control, the functional groups, and subprojects. Project management should be separate since its role as an integrator requires it to maintain an independent viewpoint and power base. The Project Control Office should be independent since its job is to report accurate and objective data on project progress. If positioned as part of another group, say project management or construction, there will be a tendency to downplay poor performance because management will inevitably hope that things will improve. Functional groups—engineering, contracting, production, testing, reliability, contracts, etc.—represent the "engine room" of the project: the place where technical progress is accomplished. On a large project or program which is divided into subprojects there is usually a number of important schedule interlinkages and competition for scarce resources between the subprojects. Often budget and personnel are swapped between the subprojects. Subproject boundaries should be clearly defined and their interfaces closely monitored by senior management if subproject performance is to be properly controlled.

The organization structure used for the $3.5 billion Açominas steel mill project shows these four principal groups very clearly (Figure 2-7), as does the Apollo organization shown in Figure 2-6. (The Açominas case is described in more detail below.)

Early Firm Control of Technical Definition Is ESSENTIAL to Project Success.

Research has shown that time and again projects fail because the technical content of the program is not controlled strictly enough or early enough (28).

Software development projects (particularly large, complex ones) are extremely difficult to manage at the best of times since their work content (residing for most of the project in the project team's heads) is not as tangible as in other projects. Unless the system design is very carefully defined and communicated, the system often ends up technically inadequate, late, and very costly. The software development life cycle consists of five basic phases: concept definition, design, development, evaluation, and operation. The first phase involves problem definition and feasibility study; the second, specification of user functions and technical system design; the third, coding, integration testing, user documentation, etc.[8] Many software projects rush the first two phases and move too quickly into coding. Subsystem interfaces are then wrongly designed and code is inappropriately written. Project management techniques are now being increasingly applied to software projects. Configuration management is being used to help specify the technical content of the system as it develops and to control all changes as they arise. Software development techniques are also now emphasizing the careful, top-down evolution of the system's design and programming.

Figure 2-8 shows a model of the building process life cycle (29). Interestingly, in most building projects there is in practice no obvious checkpoint at the interface between Sketch Design and Detailed Design. There

---

[8] An "expanded" version of the information systems development life cycle is treated in Chapter 12.

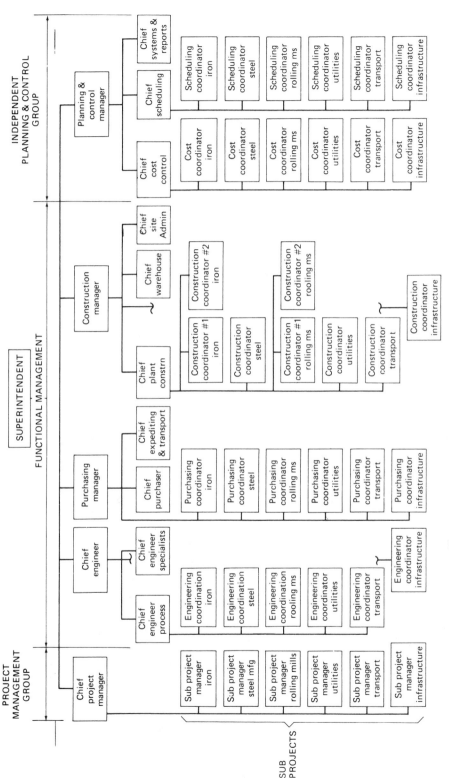

Figure 2-7. The four principal project groups on the Açominas project.

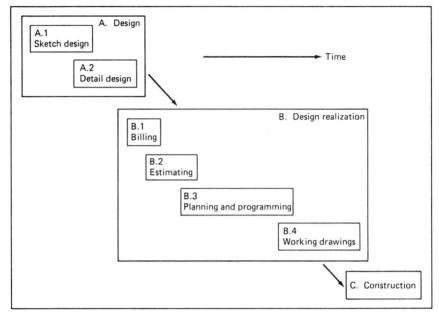

Figure 2-8. Model of the "official" British building process.

are no clearly recognized discontinuities in either technology, territory, or time at this interface,[9] nor are there any major organizational changes. Yet the outline design developed in the Sketch Design phase determines the character of the building, and thus lays the foundations for many of the technical problems which may subsequently arise during the project. If this dynamic interface is not properly controlled—and sadly, often it is not—the danger of design errors cropping up unexpectedly later in the project is high (31).

Churchill Falls is often lauded as an example of a successful project. The praise invariably centers on its tight control of design. An ambitious project in northern Canada, the project consisted of retaining the flow of the Churchill River through a series of vast reservoirs and dams over a 2500-square-mile basin in Upper Labrador. The project was begun in earnest in 1966 for a budget of $550 million and was completed eight and a half years later on budget and ahead of schedule. The project was marked by an early and very intense coordination between project management, engineering, construction management, and finance (including insur-

---

[9] Miller has shown that boundaries should be formed where there are discontinuities in time, technology, or territory (30).

ance)—each of which was conducted by quite separate companies. At the time of arranging project financing the state of project documentation was such that there were "virtually no questions unanswered" (32). Following this exhaustive initial design there was continuous close review by construction management of the engineering design as it developed, and intensive engineering to achieve cost savings wherever possible.

One way of achieving firm control of design is through configuration management. Configuration management documents the technical design of the project, ensures regular design reviews, rigorously checks the technical cost and schedule impact of all changes before approving them, and ensures that all parties working on the project are using up-to-date documentation. Configuration management has been used primarily in the U.S. aerospace and information systems sectors; it is only slowly being applied to other types of projects. It is not used in the building and civil engineering industries, for example, though its potential applicability on the larger and more complex of such projects is quite strong.

The Skills Required in Managing Dynamic Interfaces Vary Depending on the Management Level and Stage of the Project

The Trans Alaskan Pipeline (TAPS) remains one of the largest and most ambitious of recent major projects. Although constructed in the three years between 1974 and 1976 (at a cost of approximately $8 billion), the project had in fact been on and off since 1968. Senior management was required to concentrate on a series of strategic issues of startling variation: firstly, on engineering (how to prevent hot oil damaging the Alaskan permafrost and how to design for seismic damage), and then moving through political support (the project manager actually moved to Washington, D.C. to advise the political effort that eventually resulted in the 1973 TAPS Act), infrastructure development (transportation, camps, equipment supply, and union negotiations), organization issues (the development of a highly decentralized matrix organization once construction began), environmental regulations, and finally, engineering and construction again. The sequence of issues is interesting: firstly, achieve agreement on the technical concept and political support for the project; secondly, assure adequate infrastructure and organization; thirdly, resolve environmental, construction, and engineering issues as the project is built. This is essentially the institutional, strategic, and tactical sequence already noted as typical for all projects. At the middle management level, however (where managers were responsible for anything up to $4 billion of work!), activity centered either on resolving engineering and construction problems or on issues of organization and leadership. Nowhere was the organizational concern more clearly evident than in the change at about 15% of the way through construction from a 9-tiered, centralized, functional organization to a 4-tiered, decentralized, matrix organization (Figure 2-9). The result was a highly flexible construction organization relying, like Apollo, on a small cadre of senior managers (33). Emphasis was on leadership, horizontal and informal communication, simple structures, and tight reporting relationships—and getting the job done.

The TAPS pipeline matrix organization tells of an experience very simi-

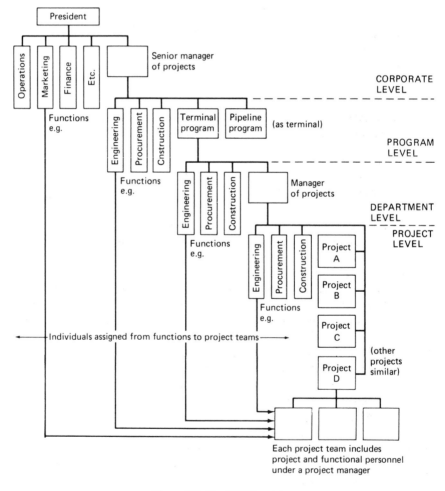

Figure 2-9. The TAPS matrix.

lar to that of Apollo and Açominas. Açominas is a steel plant recently completed at a cost of over $7.5 billion in central Brazil. Initially, the project schedule was, like TAPS and Apollo, tight. The project staff, numbering about 400, were organized on a matrix basis, operating simultaneously at three distinct levels (Figure 2-10). Like TAPS, Açominas was initially organized along primarily functional lines. Functional managers took the lead in developing the engineering design, planning the project, and negotiating the contracts. As contracts were signed and the project moved into the production phase, however, responsibility was delegated

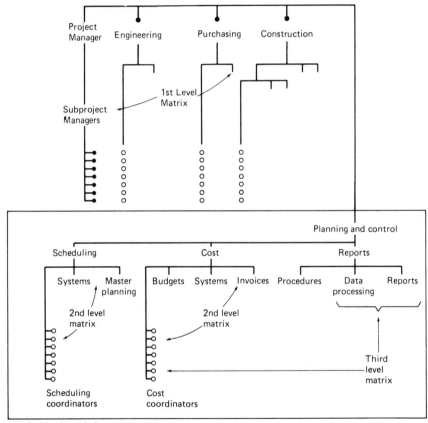

The 2nd level matrix in
planning and control
— Other management
  groups have similar
  second level matrices.

Figure 2-10. The multilevel Açominas matrix.

to the project management teams: as the project moved from its design phase to production, there was a "swing" of the matrix towards a greater "project orientation (34).

The TAPS/Acominas organization development leads to three important observations about the development of projects.

1. **Typically, Large Projects Require a Decentralized Organization During Production with Centralization Before and After.** Both projects exhibited the same pattern of centralization—decentralization—centralization. (The final centralized phase during *Turn-Over and Start-Up* has not been discussed here.) The initial, design phase requires unified strategic decision making. During production the volume of work becomes so great that responsibility must be delegated: the organization becomes decentralized under the project and functional matrix control. Finally, at *Turn-Over*, the volume of work decreases while the need for unified integration with Operations' *Start-Up* creates the need for centralization once again.

2. **The Project Organization Must Change According to the Needs of the Project's Size, Speed, and Complexity.** The Açominas matrix was planned to change at the onset of production—about one and a half years after it was set up, which fits with the time it usually takes to "grow" a matrix (35). Research suggests that while the timing of the organization change is a function of the project's schedule, the severity of the change depends on the project's size, speed, and complexity (36).

3. **Once Decentralized, Projects Require a Substantial Management Superstructure to Effect the Necessary Coordination.** Projects decentralize, essentially, to ease the pressure on decision making. Once decentralized, informal controls and communication tend to proliferate and there is a rapid growth in the number of meetings and committees. With this growth in informal decision making there is more need than ever for careful configuration management and budgetary and schedule control. Formal reporting will clearly lag actual events considerably, but in an informal organization there is a danger of assuming that things are happening when in fact they may not be. (Also, informal reporting will tend to concentrate on strategically important items only; formal reports should provide a regular update on all aspects of project progress.) It is, therefore, vital to ensure full, regular reporting during this decentralized phase.

The character of a project thus varies both at different stages of its development and at different levels of management. The skills which are required in managing the project's evolution vary depending on the level of management and stage of the project.

Each Major Project Change Point Requires Its Own Distinctive Total Management

Changing from one major life-cycle phase to another—from *Prefeasibility/Feasibility* to *Design, Design* to *Production,* and *Production* to *Turn-Over and Start-Up*—is a major event. The *Prefeasibility/Feasibility–Design* transfer is economically the most important step in the project's life. Major federal acquisitions have long placed great importance on the need for very thorough feasibility studies. Thorough agency needs-analysis and exploration of alternative systems is now mandatory federal practice. Yet while the importance of a thorough feasibility study is now generally recognized, it is surprising how many projects do become committed to and move into *Design* on the basis of a totally inadequate feasibility study. Two of the most notorious of recent projects exhibit this clearly. Concorde was conceived almost entirely by the British aircraft establishment, largely on the wings of technological fascination with only the minimum of financial analysis (37). The proposal was championed ardently by one or two senior British ministers who effectively resisted Treasury pressure to review the financial assumptions. Once the French government joined the project the political momentum became virtually unstoppable. Final commitment to the project was made on the basis of a twenty-page report which was "little more than a sketch" (38). At this stage the research and development was estimated to cost £150 million to £170 million; the final cost is some £2 billion. Likewise, the Sydney Opera House was committed to on the basis of a totally sketchy design backed by strong political support. New South Wales' prime minister, John Cahill, saw the Opera House as an imaginative political act (39). A design competition was held and Utzon's design was selected as winner. The design was, however, little more than diagrammatic. There was little evidence of structural feasibility and no cost estimate. A quantity surveyor was therefore asked to prepare one, which he did "under duress in a few hours" (40) arriving at a figure of $A 7 million. The final cost, after drastic redesign (resulting in so reducing the scenery space that opera cannot be fully staged in the building) was $A 102 million.

The transition from *Design* to *Production* is less clear-cut than that from *Prefeasibility/Feasibility* to *Design.* It is also much broader in scope and involves much fuller management attention. At this interface, management must be fully active in all the major project subsystems: project definition, organization, environment, and infrastructure. The overriding preoccupation should be that the strategic parameters are properly set as the interface is crossed, since once *Production* begins the scale and pace of events increase dramatically. So important is this interface to project implementation success that it requires "total" management attention: planning, organizing, directing, and controlling. Contracting—the key interface activity in fact—offers a good example. The contracting process must be supported by project management through integrated planning, thorough negotiating, and through close monitoring. Often contracting is not managed but just happens, thus swamping the project with work and delaying it considerably. (Açominas had to sign 400 contracts during an 18–24-month period. Accomplishing this was a major management achievement in its own right.)

Turn-Over and Start-Up probably receives considerable non-project planning and control but generally from places other than within the project team. The meshing of the two important phases of project construction and operations is complex and has large cost implications. All Level I subsystems must be complete and activated as soon as *Turn-Over* occurs. Despite the obvious importance of smoothly transitioning from *Production* to *Turn-Over,* it appears rare, especially in the construction industries, that a project planning group prepares and monitors integrated plans for crossing this interface. This might be partly because of the substantial differences in *Start-Up* between aerospace programs and large new capital expansion facilities (factories, telecommunication systems, ports, etc.) which may have depressed the evolution of defense/aerospace program management ideas on this important area of work.

Planning Must Be Phased to the Stage of the Project Life Cycle

The differing nature and requirements of the various project life-cycle phases require that different issues be addressed as the project unfolds. Project planning cannot be done comprehensively, once and for all, at the beginning of the project. The uncertainty during the early stages of a project is too great. Instead, planning must be incremental (41). Initial planning must concentrate on building viable planning bases for each principal subsystem, detail being added later in phase with the project schedule (Figure 2-11).

The Apollo Mission's "Phased Project Planning" explicitly recognized this (42)—major life-cycle phases being identified and planning review checkpoints positioned along the life cycle (Figure 2-12)—as have subse-

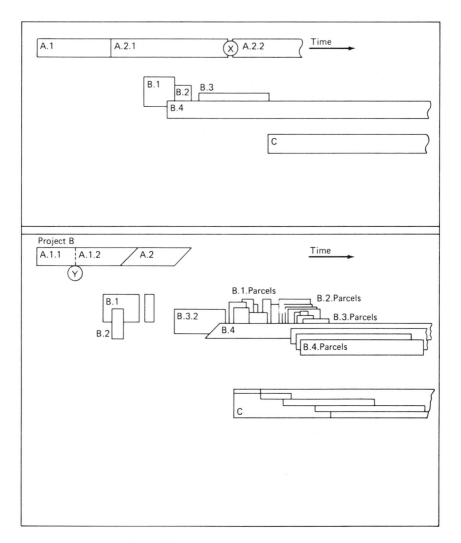

Figure 2-11. Project planning development.

quent U.S. aerospace manuals (e.g., DOD 3200.9, DOD 5000.1, AFSC 800-3, to mention just three).

Apollo was fortunate in that it had nearly a decade for NASA to develop its systems and program planning. Many projects are less fortunate. Early North Sea oil projects, for example, were implemented with great urgency, and made worse by the short summer weather window for towing and positioning platforms in the North Sea. Oil companies found

PLANNING SYSTEM \ PLANNING STAGE	FEASIBILITY	PROJECT STRATEGY	DESIGN	PRODUCTION	TURN-OVER & START-UP
ECONOMIC EVALUATION	• Benefits • Risk	• Continue Appraisal with View to Changing Project Specifications if Necessary	• Impact on other Business Functions Assessed • Adjustments Made as Necessary		• Assess Project Cost for Product Pricing Purposes
PROJECT DEFINITION	• System Specs • Base Technology • $ Estimate • Project Schedule	• Outline Design • Configuration Definition • Budget by Major Areas • Milestone Schedule • Detailed "Planning" Schedule	• Futher development of Outline Design, Schedule and Budget	• Detailed Contract Specs and Drawings • Overall Schedule Requirements • Detailed Budget/Contract Bids	• Operating Manuals • Training • Primary Materials Preparation • Hand-over Schedules • Test Schedules • Move
FINANCE	• Potential Sources	• Principal Sources • Major Payments Schedule	• Detailed Sources • More Detailed Cash Requirements	• Detailed Payments Schedule by Creditors & Currency	• Annual Financial Operating Plan
ENVIRONMENT	• Initial Impact Assessment	• Definition of Environmental Impact Statement • National & Local Government Support Assessed • Local Population Attitude Assessed • Supplier Situation Assessed	• Schedule of Approvals Required • Government or Community Support Groups Identified	• Permit Expediting System • Expediting Schedules • Pubic Relations	• Marketing • Personnel • Inventory Planning • Safety Procedures • Outstanding Legal Issues

ORGANIZATION & SYSTEMS	• Initial Project Outline	• Overall Concepts for: —Contractor Strategies —Design Fabrication, Construction —Labor & Materials Sources • Principal Responsibilities Determined • Major Information Systems Identified • Key Personnel Identified	• Contract Negotiating Plan • Some Major Contracts Signed • Union Discussions • Possibly Some Long Lead Materials Ordered • Responsibilities Matrix • Manpower Plan • Systems Design Schedule	• Contract Terms and Conditions • Owner Organization Detailed • Detailed Staffing Plans	• Operations Organization Development and Start-up • Project Organization Phase-out • Wind-down of project personnel
INFRASTRUCTURE & SUPPORT	• Assess Extent of Support Required	• Preliminary Plans for: —Labor Relations —Camps —Logistics	• Further Definition of: —Labor Relations —Camps —Administration —Transport, Logistics & Warehousing • Support Organization Outlined • Permits Requested	• Detailed Definition of: —Labor Relations —Camps —Transport, Logistics, etc. • Construction Schedules/Contracts for Camps, Power, Transport, etc. • Service Contracts Identified • Support Organization Defined	• Wind-down and sell-off of project camps, etc. • Plan for housing, transport, physical & social welfare of operating personnel

Figure 2-12. Apollo's phased program planning.

themselves having to develop a new generation of rigs, which involved the use of new technology, working in a harsh and poorly documented environment, without adequate codes of practice or regulations—all within a very tight schedule. A slippage of just a few weeks could result in the delay of the whole program for nearly a year. To speed up the program, projects were often sanctioned on the basis of preliminary design data and manufacturing was overlapped with design as much as possible. While these early projects could probably have been managed more efficiently if there had been a longer start-up time to acquire environmental design data, develop codes, and put project management systems and procedures in place (as has been suggested (43)), the economic pressure on distributing North Sea oil as soon as possible effectively precluded this option. In these projects, the project life cycle not only determined the sequence and degree of planning appropriate at a given stage, it set an absolute limit on the time available for planning.

Ensure Full Working Out of the Static Subsystems at Each Stage of the Project Life Cycle

"Static" project subsystems (technical definition, organization, environment, and infrastructure) must be fully worked out at each phase of the project's life cycle. Unfortunately this does not always happen, often because the habits of an industry or organization have institutionalized a culture of neglecting certain "essential" subsystem considerations.

Movie productions are notorious, for example, for overrunning budget. The most common reason for their doing so is that there is a culture of allowing the director to work out how the film will develop as he shoots it—there is neither "design" nor "schedule." (No one on the set, including the director, knew how *Casablanca* was going to end until the end of shooting; Francis Ford Coppola did not have the ending of *Apocalypse Now* worked out even as he entered the editing room.)

Sometimes, the effects of urgency are so great that it is not possible to work out fully the static subsystems before moving on to the next phase. Many defense projects cannot avoid modifying their performance requirements (because of a changed Threat Analysis) yet must still keep to schedule (44). This is the situation known as concurrency (45): there is a substantial body of knowledge available showing that concurrency is invariably associated with difficulties and overruns (46). Concurrency has proved unavoidable on several occasions in the nuclear power industry, basically when changes have been required at an advanced stage of construction or during commissioning because of regulatory changes or technical problems (47).

The tendency for architectural design to dominate the building process has already been commented upon. Figure 2-13 compares two basically well managed, large, complex building projects (48). The first (A) was managed by architects working under the RIBA's Plan of Work (49). Since the Plan of Work assumes competitive bidding by the main contractor, it does not mention the use of any form of construction management advice prior to construction bidding. Thus the architects did not schedule the project or seek any form of production advice during the early design phases. Project B, however, used a large U.S. A/E firm which was familiar with project management practice and employed both systems design techniques and a management contractor. As a result there was early project scheduling and production advice so that the technical definition subsystem was fully worked out early in the project.

Control Needs Vary Depending on the Level of Control and Stage of the Project

As the tasks of the different levels of project management vary, so do their control needs. Level III management uses frequent, often daily, control of key performance factors such as earth moved, concrete poured, pipe laid, vessels installed, tests completed, together with basic cost data. At Level II further data are required in addition to the Level III "key drivers": for example, inventories, drawing approvals, transporta-

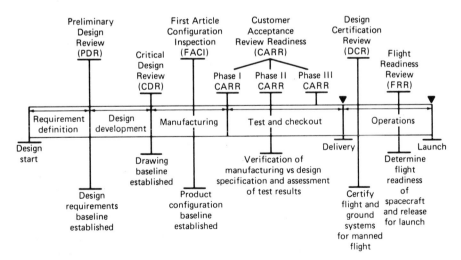

Figure 2-13. Comparison of two British building projects. (For Subsystem Coding refer to Figure 2-8.)

tion, camp capacity, security, accidents, contract management, changes pending and approved, contingency reserves. These are data not needed on such a frequent basis as the "key drivers" data. Level I interests are broader still: exception reporting on progress (i.e., report problems and poor trends only), interface relationships with other subsystems (e.g., between subprojects, between operations planning and project progress), training, cash flows, etc. (50).

"Control" has a meaning which is greater than merely monitoring. It is used in the broader context of setting standards, monitoring, and correcting for deviations between actual and planned performance. This more complete interpretation of control is the one used in cybernetics. (The word "cybernetics" itself derives from the Greek "to steer".) The nature of control during *Prefeasibility/Feasibility* and *Design* is different from that during *Production* and *Turn-Over*. As has been already noted, the need during the early stages of a project to plan, design, and estimate correctly is very large. The costs during these early phases are small compared with the total project cost, and so the need to monitor them (at least from a project as opposed to design point of view) is correspondingly small. Later, during *Production,* the crucial control need is the monitoring of performance to ensure that quality is being achieved and resources are being deployed on schedule and in budget. Hence the nature of control changes during the project life cycle from predicting to monitoring.

"Control" in this broader sense also varies depending upon the interests and objectives of the persons doing the controlling. Different groups, with their different interests, will have different control needs. A project owner, for example, will want to monitor the economic worth of the project as much as its technical, cost, and schedule performance. A contractor might be particularly concerned with cash flow control.

Personnel Issues Will Vary, Again Depending on the Level of Control and the Stage of the Project

Conflict is inherent in every project, not least since the primary project objectives—quality, cost, and schedule—are themselves in conflict. Quality costs money and requires time; working more quickly costs money. Also, projects often engender contractual and community conflict.

Studies in the mid-1970s (51) have shown that the pattern of conflict varies during the project life cycle (Figure 2-14): schedule and priorities dominate the early phases, with technical issues coming to the fore later (and with cost as a consistently low-conflict item). One should not assume that this pattern applies for all projects, however—one would normally

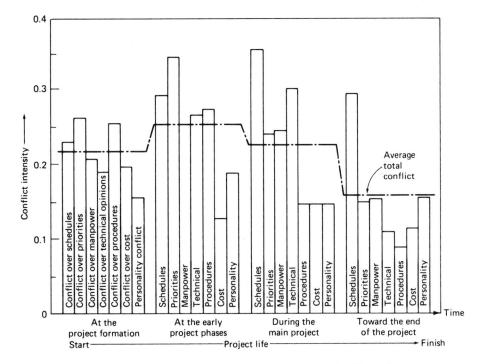

Figure 2-14. Relative intensity of conflict over the project life cycle.

expect greater conflict over technical issues earlier in the project; the conflict pattern might vary by type of project (and contract type); cost pressures may be generally more dominant than they were on the projects studied; and personal issues are probably stronger on matrix and overseas projects. Despite such necessary caveats, the findings are extremely valuable: they provide solid evidence that the type of conflict varies according to the stage of the project life cycle.

Similar research (52) has also studied how the factors which are (a) most important and (b) most inhibiting to project success vary with the life-cycle stage (Figure 2-15). It too has shown that personal issues vary with the stage of project life cycle.

The nature of conflict also differs according to the level of management. All the research on project conflict undertaken to date either concentrates on Level II/III management or has been in the aerospace industries, which have typically been more sheltered from external pressures. Conflict at Level I is usually totally different, requiring other modes of resolution. Most of the behavioral work in projects to date assumes a normative, mechanistic view of the world: a world where people make rational

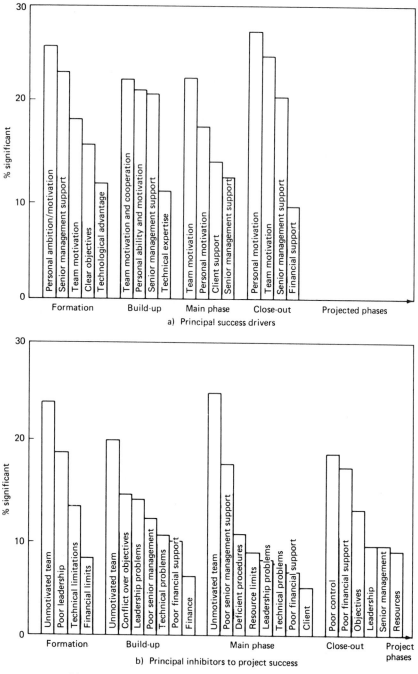

Figure 2-15. Behavioral drivers during the project life cycle.

decisions based on trade-offs of costs and benefits, and where open dialogue between men of goodwill leads to amicable solutions. While this approach is largely valid for most intra-project conflict and behavioral issues, it is often inappropriate for dealing with outside-world issues. The Level I manager will as often as not find himself having to deal with people having completely different value systems from those of the project's. Hence, while the more mechanistic approach to personal issues is appropriate to Levels II and III, Level I often requires a more political approach.

Many practitioners comment on the importance of leadership to project success. Strangely, however, the research evidence on this is at best skimpy (53). There would appear to be little doubt, however, that leaders' abilities are associated with success or failure, although it is generally difficult to isolate the effect of leadership from other factors such as top management support and authority.

Leaders have a particularly important role to play in creating the context for success. Leaders create climates: their personality can sway the ability to evaluate a project objectively; they can often negotiate or communicate things which otherwise would not be agreed. These abilities are particularly important at Level I in working with outside parties.

RELATION TO PROJECT SUCCESS

To what extent are these findings relevant to that most important issue, the question of project success? The first point to note in addressing this question is that the notion of project success is, as has already been observed, relative. In recent research on this question, I used four distinct measures: functionality—does the project function in the way the sponsors expected?; project management—was the project completed on schedule, in budget, to technical specification?; contractors' long-term commercial success; and, where appropriate, termination efficiency (54). This said, there would seem to be considerable evidence that several of the issues raised in this chapter bear strongly on the chances of success.

Firstly, the discipline of Interface Management itself was seen to be important where there is significant interdependence on projects (55). Organizational issues have been shown to relate to project success (56). Issues of design management, concurrency, and planning have a potentially enormous impact on projects if not accomplished effectively. The evidence on the relationship between human factors and project success is, by comparison, considerably softer, as was just noted (57).

Insofar as Interface Management relates to clear planning and the orderly management of relevant project systems and dimensions, it is almost self-evident that it must contribute to project success. The insights related in this chapter are, almost without exception, proved through quoted experience or academic research to have an effect on the final outcome of a project. The twist, however, is that the definition of success varies from individual company to individual company; and that as one moves from Level III to Level I, the diversities and uncertainties of the many groups operating in the project's environment are likely to make judgments about the causes and effects of project success increasingly difficult to make.

REFERENCES

1. Katz, D. and Kahn, R. L. *The Social Psychology Of Organizations* (Wiley. New York, 1966), pp. 14–29.
2. Kast, F. E. and Rosenzweig, J. E. *Organization and Management. A Systems Approach* (McGraw-Hill. New York, 1970).
3. Lorsch, J. W. and Lawrence, P. R. *Studies In Organization Design* (Irwin Dorsey. Homewood, Ill., 1970).
4. Putnam W. D. "The Evolution of Air Force System Acquisition Management," RAND, R-868-PR, Santa Monica, Calif., 1972.
5. Beard, E. *Developing the ICBM* (Columbia University Press. New York, 1976).
6. Sapolsky, H. *The Polaris System Development: Bureaucratic and Programmatic Success in Government* (Harvard University Press. Cambridge, Mass., 1972).
7. Peck, M. J. and Scherer, F. M. *The Weapons Acquisition Process; An Economic Analysis* (Harvard University Press. Cambridge, Mass., 1962).
8. Acker, D. D. "The Maturing of the DOD Acquisition Process." *Defense Systems Management Review*, Vol. 3(3) (Summer, 1980).
9. Kelley, A. J. "The New Project Environment" in *New Dimensions of Project Management* (Lexington Books. Lexington, Mass., 1982).
10. Wearne, S. H. *Principles of Engineering Organization* (Edward Arnold. London, 1973).
11. Morris, P. W. G. "Interface Manage—An Organization Theory Approach to Project Management." *Project Management Quarterly,* Vol. 10(2) (June, 1979).
12. Kerzner, H. *Project Management: A Systems Approach to Planning, Scheduling and Controlling* (Van Nostrand Reinhold. New York, 1982).
13. The organistic/mechanistic classification of organization types was developed by Burns, T. and Stalker, G. M. in *The Management of Innovation* (Tavistock. London, 1961).
14. Parsons, T. *Structure and Process in Modern Societies* (Free Press. Glencoe, Ill., 1960).
15. Morris, P. W. G. and Hodgson, P. "The Major Projects Association and Other Macro-Engineering Societies: Their Activities and Potential Contribution to the Development of Project Management," in *8th World Congress on Project Management* (Internet. Rotterdam, 1985).
16. See, for example: Metcalf, J. L. "Systems Models, Economic Models and the Causal Texture of Organizational Environments: An Approach to Macro-Organizational Theory." *Human Relations,* Vol. 27 (1974), pp. 639–663. Also, Emery, F. E. and Trist, E. L. "Sociotechnical Systems," in *Systems Thinking,* ed. Emery, F. E. (Penguin. Harmondsworth, 1969), pp. 241–257.
17. Morris, P. W. G. and Hough, G. H. *Preconditions of Success and Failure in Major Projects* (Major Projects Association, Templeton College. Oxford, September, 1986).

18. Miller, E. J. "Technology, Territory and Time: The Internal Differentiation of Complex Production Systems." *Human Relations,* Vol. 12(3) (1959), pp. 270–304. Also, Miller, E. J. and Rice, A. K. *Systems of Organization, The Control of Task and Sentient Boundaries* (Tavistock. London, 1967).

19. Lawrence, P. R. and Lorsch, J. W. *Organization and Environment; Managing Differentiation and Integration* (Harvard University Press. Cambridge, Mass., 1967).

20. Morris, P. W. G. "Organizational Analysis of Project Management in the Building Industry." *Build International,* Vol. 6(6) (1973), pp. 595–616.

21. Ibid.

22. Thompson, J. D. *Organizations in Action* (McGraw-Hill. New York, 1967).

23. This list is based on Galbraith, J. R. *Organization Design* (Addison-Wesley. Reading, Mass., 1973).

24. Davis, P. and Lawrence, P. R. *Matrix* (Addison-Wesley. Reading, Mass., 1977).

25. Ibid.

26. Youker, R. "Organizational Alternatives for Project Management." *Project Management Quarterly,* Vol. 8(1) (1977), pp. 18–24.

27. See for instance Baumgartner, J. S. "A Discussion with the Apollo Program Director, General Sam Phillips," in *Systems Management,* ed. Baumgartner, J. S. (The Bureau of National Affairs. Washington, D.C., 1979).

28. Alexander, A. J. and Nelson, J. R. "Measuring Technological Change: Aircraft Turbine Engines" Rand Corporation, R-1017-ARPA/PR, Santa Monica, Ca (June 1972); Cochran, E. G., Patz, A. L. and Rowe, A. J. "Concurrency and Disruption in New Product Development" *California Management Review* (Fall, 1978); Department of Energy, "North Sea Costs Escalation Study" (Her Majesty's Stationery Office, London, 1976); General Accounting Office, "Why Some Weapons Systems Encounter Production Problems While Others Do Not: Six Case Studies" GAO/NSIAD-85-34, Washington DC, 24 May 1985; Harman A. J. assisted by Henrichsen S "A Methodology for Cost Factor Comparison and Prediction" Rand Corporation, R-6269-ARPA, Santa Monica, Ca (August 1970); Marshall, A. W. and Meckling, W. H. "Predictability of the Costs, Time and Success of Development" Rand Corporation, P-1821, Santa Monica, Ca (December, 1959); Merrow, E., Chapel, S. W. and Worthing, C. A. "A Review of Cost Estimation in New Technologies: Implications for Energy Process Plants" Rand Corporation, R-2481-DOE, Santa Monica, Ca (July, 1979); National Audit Office "Ministry of Defence: Control and Management of the Development of Major Equipment", report by the Comptroller and Auditor General (Her Majesty's Stationery Office, London, 12 August 1986); Murphey, D. C., Baker, B. N. and Fisher, D. "Determinants of Project Success," National Technical Information Services, Springfield, Va.; Myers, C. W. and Devey, M. R., "How Management Can Affect Project Outcomes: An Exploration of the PPS Data Base," RAND, N-2106, Santa Monica, Calif., 1984; Perry, R. L. et al. "System Acquisition Experience" Rand Corporation, RM-6072-PR, Santa Monica, Ca (November, 1969); Pugh, P. G. "Who Can Tell What Might Happen? Risks and Contingency Allowances." Royal Aeronautic Society Management Studies Group, 1985.

29. Royal Institute of British Architects, *Plan of Work, Handbook of Architectural Practice and Management* (RIBA. London, 1963).

30. Miller, E. J., op. cit. (18).

31. Morris, P. W. G. "Systems Study of Project Management." *Building,* Vol. CCXVI(6816 and 6817) (1974), pp. 75–80 and 83–88.

32. Warnock, J. G. "A Giant Project Accomplished—Design Risk and Engineering Management," in *Successfully Accomplishing Giant Projects,* ed. Sykes, A. (Willis Faber. London, 1979), pp. 31–61.

33. Moolin, F. P. and McCoy, F. "The Organization and Management of the Trans Alaskan Pipeline: The Significance of Organizational Structure and Organization Changes." *Proceedings of the Project Management Institute Conference, Atlanta, 1980* (Project Management Institute. Drexel Hill, Pa., 1980).
34. Reis de Carvalho, E. and Morris, P. W. G. "Project Matrix Organizations, Or How To Do The Matrix Swing." *Proceedings of the Project Management Institute Conference, Los Angeles, 1979* (Project Management Institute. Drexel Hill, Pa., 1979).
35. See, for instance Davis, P. and Lawrence, P. R. *Matrix,* op. cit. (24) Also, Whitmore, K. R. *Matrix Organizations in Conventional Manufacturing-Marketing Companies,* M.S. Thesis (Sloan School of Management, MIT. Cambridge, Mass., 1975).
36. See Reis de Carvalho, E. and Morris, P. W. G., op. cit. (34).
37. Hall, P. *Great Planning Disasters* (Weidenfeld and Nicolson. London, 1980), pp. 87–108; Morris.
38. See Hall, P., op. cit. (37); and Edwards, C. E. *Concorde: Ten Years and a Billion Pounds Later* (Pluto Press. London, 1972).
39. Kouzmin, A. "Building the New Parliament House: An Opera House Revisited?" *Human Futures,* Vol. 3(1) (Spring 1980), pp. 51–74.
40. Hall, P., op. cit. (37), p. 141.
41. Horwitch, M. "Designing and Managing Large-Scale, Public-Private Technological Enterprises: A State of the Art Review." *Technology in Society,* Vol. 1 (1979), pp. 179–192.
42. Seamans, R. and Ordway, F. I. "The Apollo Tradition: An Object Lesson for the Management of Large Scale Technological Endeavors." *Interdisciplinary Science Review,* Vol. 2 (1977), pp. 270–304.
43. Department of Energy, op. cit. (28).
44. Morris, P. W. G. and Hough, G. H., op. cit. (17).
45. Acker, D. D., op. cit. (8); also Harvey, T. E. "Concurrency Today in Acquisition Management." *Defense Systems Management Review,* Vol. 3(1) (Winter, 1980), pp. 14–18.
46. Cochran, E. G., Patz, A. L. and Rowe, A. J. op. cit. (28); General Accounting Office, ibid; Patz, A. L., *Innovation Pitfalls and Management Solutions in High Technology Industries* (University of Southern California. Los Angeles, Calif., 1984).
47. Kutner, S. "The Impact of Regulatory Agencies on Superprojects," in *Planning, Engineering and Constructing the Superprojects,* American Society of Civil Engineers' Conference, Pacific Grove, 1970 (ASCE. New York, 1978); Monopolies and Mergers Commission, *Central Electricity Generating Board, A Report on the Operation of the Board of Its System for the Generation and Supply of Electricity in Bulk* (Her Majesty's Stationery Office. London, 1981).
48. Morris, P. W. G. op. cit. (20, 31).
49. Royal Institute of British Architects, op. cit. (29).
50. Morris, P. W. G. "The Use and Management of Project Control Systems in the 80's." *Project Management Quarterly,* Vol. XI(4) (December, 1980), pp. 25–28.
51. Thamhain, H. J. and Wilemon, D. L. "Conflict Management in Project Life-Cycles." *Sloan Management Review* (Summer, 1975).
52. Dugan, H. S., Thamhain, H. J. and Wilemon, D. L. "Managing Change Through Project Management." *Proceedings of the Project Management Institute Conference, Atlanta, 1980* (Project Management Institute. Drexel Hill, Pa., 1980).
53. Gemmil, G. and Thamhain, H. J. "Project Performance as a Function of the Leadership Styles of Project Managers." *Project Management Institute Conference, 1972* (Project Management Institute. Drexel Hill, Pa.); Honadle, G. and Van Sant, J. *Implementation*

for Sustainability. Lessons from Integrated Rural Development (Kumarian Press. West Hartford, Conn., 1985); Murphy, D. C. et al., op. cit. (28); Myers, C. W. and Devey, M. R., ibid; Rubin, I. M. and Sellig, W. "Experience as a Factor in the Selection and Performance of Project Managers." *IEEE Transactions on Engineering Management,* Vol. EM-131(35) (September, 1967), pp. 131–135; Ruskin, A. M. and Lerner, R. "Forecasting Costs and Completion Dates for Defense Research and Development Contracts" *IEEE Transactions on Engineering Management,* Vol. EM-19(4) (November, 1972), pp. 128–133.

54. Morris, P. W. G. and Hough, G. H., op. cit. (17).
55. Ibid.
56. Paulson, B. C., Fondahl, J. W. and Parker, H. W. "Development of Research in the Construction of Transportation Facilities." 'Technical Report No. 223, The Construction Institute, Department of Civil Engineering, Stanford University, Stanford, Ca., 1977.
57. Gemmil, G. and Thamhain, H. J., op. cit. (53).

3. Integration: The Essential Function of Project Management

Linn C. Stuckenbruck*

INTRODUCTION

Project management has achieved almost universal recognition as the most effective way to ensure the success of large, complex, multidisciplinary tasks. The success of project management is based on the simple concept that the sole authority for the planning, the resource allocation, and the direction and control of a single time- and budget-limited enterprise is vested in a single individual. This single-point authority and responsibility constitutes the greatest strength of project management, but it also constitutes its greatest weakness. The pressures for the completion of an often almost impossible task must of necessity be focused on how effectively the project manager carries out his or her job (20).

Therefore, project management is not a panacea, and unfortunately it does not always work. Its use does not guarantee the success of a task; rather, it takes a great deal more. It takes great dedication and considerable effort on the part of an experienced and talented project manager leading an equally experienced and talented project team to ensure that a project will be a success. However, even these proven ingredients are not always enough—projects occasionally fail.

Determining the real or basic cause or causes of project failure can be a frustrating experience. It can be very difficult to pin down the basic causes because they are seldom simple or clear-cut. The problems will be numerous, extremely complex, very much interrelated, and often deeply hidden. It is all too easy to pick a scapegoat, and the project manager is usually the handiest person. Of course the project manager may not be at

* Dr. Linn C. Stuckenbruck is with the Institute of Safety and Systems Management at the University of Southern California where he teaches project management and other management courses. Prior to this he spent seventeen years with the Rocketdyne Division of Rockwell International where he held various management positions. He holds a Ph.D. from the State University of Iowa, and is the author of the book *The Implementation of Project Management—The Professional's Handbook,* published by Addison-Wesley Publishing Company.

fault, but there are definitely any number of things that project managers can do wrong. Among the many pitfalls that the unwary or inexperienced project manager can fall into is a failure to completely understand some of the basic aspects of the job.

Project management can, of course, be perceived as just another job requiring an experienced and conscientious manager. But, is just any experienced manager prepared for the job of project management?

It is a management axiom that the overall job of every manager is to create within the organization an environment which will facilitate the accomplishment of its objectives (11).

Certainly the job of the project manager fits this role very well. In addition, all managers, including project managers, are responsible for the universally accepted managerial functions of planning, organizing, staffing, directing, and controlling. It can then be asked whether project management is really significantly different from management in general. An old management cliche states, "A manager is a manager," or putting it another way, "A good manager can manage anything." This statement implies that there is little real difference between the job of the project manager and that of any line or disciplinary manager. However, there is one extremely important, very real, and significantly different aspect of the job of the project manager which makes it different from general management.

By definition projects are complex and multidisciplinary tasks; therefore, project managers must of necessity be very much aware of or even in some cases completely preoccupied with the problem of integrating their projects. This problem, which is of major importance to all but the simplest projects, seldom confronts line managers. This chapter will discuss this essential function of project integration and indicate the various actions that are necessary to achieve a fully integrated project.

SYSTEMS INTEGRATION

The term systems integration is usually applicable to most projects because inevitably a project is a system. This term is used to indicate the process of integrating any system being utilized or developed, whether it is hardware, software, an organization, or some other type of system. This process of systems integration has been identified as an important management function which has been described by Lawrence and Lorch. They pointed out that with the rapid advances in technology and the increased complexity of systems to be managed, there is an increased need both for greater specialization (differentiation) and for tighter coordination (integration) (13). An effective manager has a need for both; however, since these two needs are essentially antagonistic, one can usually be achieved only at the expense of the other (14). It can be described as a trade-off between these two needs as shown in Figure 3-1.

Referring to Figure 3-1, it has been suggested that the ideal high-performance manager falls on the arrow midway between differentiation and integration, and probably is typical of high-performance top management. It is also true that line or discipline management usually falls closer to the differentiation arrow, and that the truly effective project manager falls closer to the integration arrow. This model emphasizes the importance of the project manager's role as an integrator.

Systems integration is related to what Koontz and O'Donnell call "the essence of management-coordination, or the purpose of management is the achievement of harmony of individual effort toward the accomplishment of group goals" (12). However, doesn't every manager have this function? Yes, but the project manager has to be preoccupied with it. The project manager's major responsibility is assuring that a particular system or activity is assembled so that all of the components, parts, subsystems and organizational units, and people fit together as a functioning, integrated whole according to plan. Carrying out this responsibility comprises the function of systems integration.

INTEGRATING THE PROJECT

Every project is a system in that it consists of many interrelated and interconnected parts or elements which must function together as a "whole." Projects vary greatly in size, complexity, and urgency; however, all but the simplest projects have a common element in that they

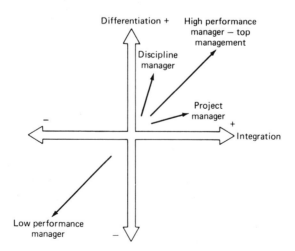

Figure 3-1. Measuring managerial performance.

must be integrated. Project integration can then be described as the process of ensuring that all elements of the project—its tasks, subsystems, components, parts, organizational units, and people—fit together as an integrated whole which functions according to plan. All levels of management ascribe to this goal, but project managers must be preoccupied with it since they have the direct responsibility to ensure that it occurs on every project. These project elements will not automatically come together; the project manager must make a concerted effort and take a number of specific actions to ensure that integration occurs.

The principal precaution that the project manager must take is to make certain that adequate attention is given to every element of the project system. It is easy to be trapped into thinking of the project as consisting entirely of the hardware or other system being designed, developed, or constructed. Many elements of the project may have little direct relationship to the system being worked on, but they may be critical to ultimate project success. Most projects involve a number of different organizational units, many only in a service or support capacity, and an infinite variety of people may be stakeholders in some aspect of the project. The total project system consists of everything and everyone that has anything to do with the project. The diversity of the project system is indicated in Figure 3-2.

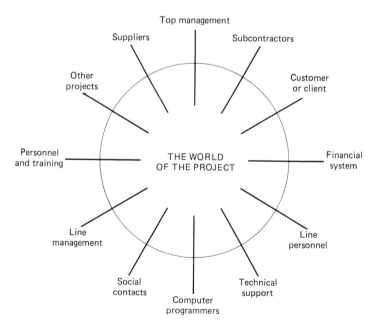

Figure 3-2. The total project system.

INTEGRATION IN THE MATRIX

The job of project integration is most important and most difficult when the project is organized in the matrix mode. The matrix is a complex organizational form that can become extremely complicated in very large projects. The matrix is complex because it evolved to meet the needs of our increasingly complex society with its very large problems and resulting very large projects. The conventional hierarchical functional management structure usually finds itself in difficulty when dealing with large projects. The pure project organization is a solution when the project is very large, but it is not always applicable to smaller projects. Therefore, management, in an effort to obtain the advantages of both project and functional organizational forms, has evolved the matrix, which is actually a superimposition of project organizations upon a functional organization. The matrix is not for everyone (23). It should only be utilized if its advantages outweigh the resulting organizational complexity.

Why is systems integration difficult in the matrix organization? What is so different about the matrix? Since the matrix is such a complex organizational form, all decisions and actions of project managers become very difficult, primarily because they must constantly communicate and interact with many functional managers. The project manager discovers that the matrix organization is inherently a conflict situation. The matrix brings out the presence of conflicting project and functional goals and objectives. In addition, the project manager finds that many established functional managers who must contribute to the project feel threatened, and continual stresses and potential conflicts result.

The matrix organization has evolved to cope with the basic conflict inherent in any large organization—the needs of specialization versus the needs of coordination (18). These divergent needs in the hierarchical organizational structure lead to inevitable conflict between functional and top management, and often lead to nonoptimizing decisions. All major decisions must be made by top management who may have insufficient information. The matrix organization was a natural evolution growing out of the need for someone who could work problems through the experts and specialists. The project manager has assumed the role of "decision broker charged with the difficult job of solving problems through the experts" (18), all of whom know more about their particular field than he or she.

The role of the project manager in the matrix organization has been analyzed by Galbraith (8, 9), Lawrence and Lorsch (13, 14, 15, 16), and Davis and Lawrence (5). They point out that the horizontal communication in a matrix organization requires an open, problem-solving climate. However, as pointed out by Galbraith (8, 9), when the subtasks in an organization are greatly differentiated a matrix structure may be required to achieve integration. The integrator coordinates the decision processes across the interfaces of differentiation. The project manager must function as an integrator to make the matrix work.

Problem solving and decision making are critical to the integration process since most project problems occur at subsystem or organizational interfaces. The project manager is the only person in the key position to solve such interface problems. The project manager provides "1. a single point of integrative responsibility, and 2. integrative planning and control" (2). The project manager is faced with three general types of problems and with the subsequent necessity for decision making:

1. Administrative problems involving the removal of roadblocks, the setting of priorities, or the resolution of organizational conflicts involving people, resources, or facilities.
2. Technical problems involving the making of decisions, and scope changes; making key trade-offs among cost, schedule, or performance; and selecting between technical alternatives.
3. Customer or client problems which involve interpretation of and conformance to specifications and regulatory agency documents.

Matrix organizations will not automatically work, and an endless number of things can go wrong. Recognizing that the matrix is a complex organizational form is the first step. The next step is getting this complex organization to function. Its successful operation, like that of any management function, depends almost entirely on the actions and activities of the various people involved. In a matrix, however, the important actions and activities are concentrated at the interfaces between the various organizational units. The most important of these interfaces are between the project manager and top management, and between the project manager and the functional managers supporting the project. Moreover, most matrix problems occur at the interfaces between the project manager and functional managers. Project managers must effectively work across these interfaces if they are going to accomplish their integrative function.

Project managers carry out their function of project integration primarily by carefully managing all of the many diverse interfaces within their projects. Archibald indicates that "the basic concept of interface management is that the project manager plans and controls (manages) the points of interaction between various elements of the project, the product, and the organizations involved'' (1). He defines interface management as consisting of identifying, documenting, scheduling, communicating, and monitoring interfaces related to both the product and the project (1).

The complexity that results from the use of a matrix organization gives the project manager even more organizational and project interfaces to manage. These interfaces are a problem for the project manager, since whatever obstacles he or she encounters, they are usually the result of two organizational units going in different directions. An old management cliche says that all the really difficult problems occur at organizational interfaces. The problem is complicated by the fact that the organizational units are usually not under the direct management of the project manager, and some of the most important interfaces may even be completely outside of the company or enterprise.

Types of Interfaces

There are many kinds of project interfaces. Archibald divides them into two types—product and project—and then further divides them into subgroups, of which management interfaces are a major division (2). The problem of the overall project/functional interface is thoroughly discussed by Cleland and King, who point out the complementary nature of the project and the functional or discipline-oriented organization. "They are inseparable and one cannot survive without the other" (3).

Another way of describing the various interfaces that the project manager must continually monitor for potential problems is (a) personal or people interfaces, (b) organizational interfaces, and (c) system interfaces (2). In other words, project management is more than just management interfaces; it involves all three of the above types.

1. Personal Interfaces—These are the "people" interfaces within the organization whether the people are on the project team or outside it. Whenever two people are working on the same project there is a potential for personal problems and even for conflict. If the people are both within the same line or discipline organization, the project manager may have very limited authority over them, but he or she can demand that the line supervision resolve the personal problem or conflict. If the people are not in the same line or discipline organization, the project manager must play the role of mediator, with the ultimate alternative of insisting that line management resolve the problem or remove one or both of the individuals from the project team. Personal interface problems become even more troublesome and difficult to solve when they involve two or more managers.

2. Organizational Interfaces—Organizational interfaces are the most troublesome since they involve not only people but also varied organizational goals, and conflicting managerial styles and aspirations. Each organizational unit has its own objectives, its own disciplines or specialties, and its own functions. As a result of these differences, each organizational unit has its own jargon, often difficult for other groups to understand or appreciate. It is thus apparent that misunderstandings and conflict can easily occur at the interfaces. These interfaces are more than purely management interfaces since much day-to-day contact is at the working level. Purely management interfaces exist whenever important management decisions, approvals, or other actions that will affect the project must be made. Organizational interfaces also involve units outside the immediate company or project organization such as the customer, subcontractors, or other contractors on the same or related systems.

3. System Interfaces—System interfaces are the product, hardware, facility, construction, or other types of nonpeople interfaces inherent in the system being developed or constructed by the project. These will be interfaces between the various subsystems in the project. The problem is intensified because the various subsystems will usually be developed by different organizational units. As pointed out by Archibald (1), these system interfaces can be actual physical interfaces existing between interconnecting parts of the system, or performance interfaces existing between various subsystems or components of the system. System interfaces may actually be scheduled milestones involving the transmission of information developed in one task to another task by a specific time, or the completion of a subsystem on schedule.

Management Interfaces

Each of the three types of interfaces that have been described pose important problems. Problems become particularly troublesome when personal and organizational interfaces are combined into what may best be called management interfaces (17). Management interfaces have personal aspects because normally two individuals are concerned, such as a project manager and a particular functional manager. Management interfaces, however, also have organizational aspects because the respective managers lead organizations which probably have conflicting goals and aspirations.

There is a great difference between the conventional organization chart (whether it be hierarchical or matrix) and the actual operation of a real-world organization. The conventional hierarchical organization charts or matrix organization charts clearly show many of the management interfaces, such as superior/subordinate and project management/worker relationships. However, conventional management charts only suggest some of the other really important interfaces. These important interfaces, as shown by the double-ended arrows in Figure 3-3, consist of project manager/functional manager interfaces, project manager/top management interfaces, functional manager/functional manager interfaces, and sometimes even project manager/project manager interfaces.

Most important are the interfaces between the project managers and the various functional managers supporting the project. These relationships are almost inevitably adversary since they involve a constantly shifting balance of power between two managers on essentially the same reporting level.

The interface with top management is important because it represents the project manager's source of authority and responsibility. The project manager must not only have the real and unqualified support of top management, but must also have a clear and readily accessible communication link with them. The project manager must be able to get the "ear" of top management whenever necessary.

The interfaces between the various functional managers are important because they are the least visible to project managers who might not be immediately aware of trouble spots.

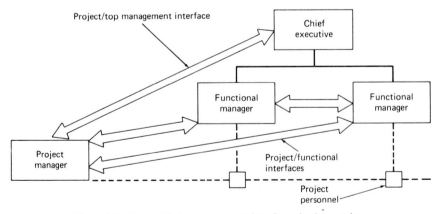

Figure 3-3. The multiple management interfaces in the matrix.

The Balance of Power

Having implemented project management, top management must recognize that they have placed a new player in the management game—the project manager. Problems are to be expected, particularly in a matrix organization where a new situation has been created with natural conflict or adversary roles between the project managers and the functional managers who support the projects. This managerial relationship can best be described as a balance of power between the two managers involved as illustrated by Figure 3-4. This relationship has also been described as a balance of interest and a sharing of power (6). But this does not imply that the shared power is ever truly balanced, because in reality the balance of power is a dynamic, constantly changing condition that cannot be static even if so desired.

There is no way to assure a balance of power at every managerial interface. Theoretically, it should be possible to divide the authority and responsibility more or less equally between the project and functional managers, which implies a very clear balance of power between the two managers. This is not only very difficult, but it doesn't happen very often. Various authors have attempted to clearly delineate the authority and responsibilities of both project and functional management so as to assure a balance of power (3). Certainly such a delineation can indicate where

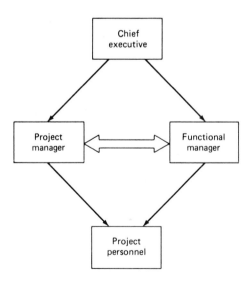

Figure 3-4. The balanced matrix.

major responsibilities lie, but cannot guarantee a balance of power. In fact, there are many reasons why it is almost impossible to have a true balance of power between functional and project management. Not the least of these reasons is the fact that a matrix consists of people, and all people—including managers—are different from each other. Managers have differing personalities and differing management styles. Some management styles depend on the persuasive abilities of the manager, while others depend on or tend to fall back on strong support from top management.

Since projects, programs, or products are usually the most important of all of a company's activities, project managers are very important persons. They are the persons who put the company in a position where it can lose money or make a profit. Therefore, in terms of the balance of power, it would seem that projects would always have the scale of power tipped in their direction, particularly with the firm support of top management. Not necessarily so! In fact, not usually so, at least in a matrix organization. In a pure project organization, there is no question as to who holds the power. But in a matrix organization the functional managers have powerful forces on their side. The functional manager is normally perceived by project personnel to be the real boss. This is inevitable since functional management is part of the management ladder in the hierarchy which goes directly up to the president of the company, and it is therefore perceived to be "permanent" by the employees. After all, the functional organization represents the "home base" to which project personnel expect to return after the completion of the project.

Very strong top management support for the project manager is necessary to get the matrix to work, and even very strong support will not guarantee project success. However, the matrix will not work without it. Project managers must get the job done by any means at their disposal even though they may not be perceived as the real boss.

The Project/Functional Interface

The secret of the successfully functioning matrix can thus be seen to be not just a pure balance of power, but more a function of the interface or interface relationships between the project and individual functional managers. Every project decision and action must be negotiated across this interface. This interface is a natural conflict situation since many of the goals and objectives of project and functional management are so very different. Depending on the personality and dedication of the respective managers, this interface relationship can be one of smooth-working cooperation or bitter conflict. A domineering personality or power play usually is not the answer. The overpowering manager may win the local skirmish, but usually manages sooner or later to alienate everyone working on the project. Cooperation and negotiation are the keys to successful decision making across the project/functional interface. Arbitrary and one-sided decisions by either the project or functional manager can only lead to or intensify the potential for conflict. Unfortunately for project managers, they can accomplish little by themselves, they must depend on the cooperation and support of the functional manager. The old definition of successful management—"getting things done by working through others"—is essential for successful project management in the matrix organization.

The most important interface that the project manager has in a matrix organization is with the functional managers. The conventional matrix two-boss model does not adequately emphasize this most important relationship. Obviously, neither the project manager nor the functional manager can simply sit in his or her office and give orders. The two managers must be communicating with each other on at least a daily basis, and usually more often. The organizational model shown in Figure 3-4 shows the managerial relationship as a double-ended arrow indicating that the relationship is a two-way street. Consultation, cooperation, and constant support are necessary on the part of both the project and functional managers. This is a very important relationship, key to the success of any matrix organization, and one which must be carefully nurtured and actively promoted by both project and functional management.

Strong Versus Weak Matrices

Achieving an equal balance of power between project and functional management may be a desirable goal; certainly it should be a way of minimizing potential power struggles and possible conflicts. There is no certain way to assure that there is an "equal" balance of power, and it is probably seldom really achieved. However, it can be approached by assuming that the project managers have the full support of top management and that they report at a high enough level in the management hierarchy. In fact top management can, whenever desirable, tilt the scales of power in either direction.

In many situations it may not be desirable to have an equal balance of power. For instance, a project may be so important to the company, or the budget and schedule so tight that top management feels that the project manager must be in a very strong position. Or perhaps the project managers feel that they must tilt the organizational balance of power in their favor to obtain better project performance. On the other hand, top management may feel that functional management needs more backing. In either case, the balance of power can be tilted in either direction by changing any one or any combination of the following three factors:

1. The Administrative Relationship—The levels at which the project and involved functional managers report, and the backing which they receive from top management.
2. The Physical Relationship—The physical distances between the various people involved in the project.
3. The Time Spent on the Project—The amount of time spent on the project by the respective managers.

These three factors can be used to describe whether the matrix is strong or weak. The strong matrix is one in which the balance of power is definitely on the side of project management. This can be shown by the model in Figure 3-5. A weak matrix has been described by project managers as one in which the balance of power tilts decisively in the direction of line or functional management.

The managerial alternatives have been described as a continuum ranging from pure project to functional as shown in Figure 3-6 (7). The matrix falls in the middle of the continuum, and can range from very weak to very strong depending on the relative balance of power.

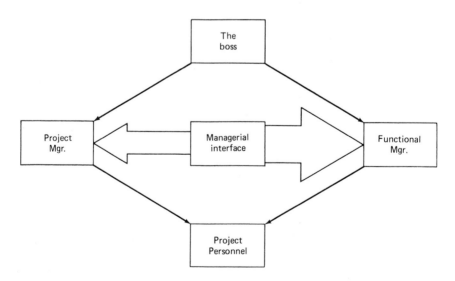

Figure 3-5. The balance of power in a strong matrix.

THE INTEGRATION PROCESS

As previously indicated, project integration doesn't just happen, it must be made to happen. It is more than just fitting components together; the system has to function as a whole. The integration process consists of all of the specific actions that project managers must initiate to ensure that their projects are integrated. Integration cannot be an afterthought, and it does not consist only of actions that can be accomplished after the subsystems have been completed. Therefore, the critical actions leading to integration must take place very early in the life cycle of the project, particularly during the implementation phase, to ensure that integration takes place. In "pure" project organizations there is no question as to who initiates these actions, project managers run their own empires. In matrix organizations, however, project managers encounter particular difficulties and problems in carrying out their integrative functions.

THE CRITICAL ACTIONS OF INTEGRATION

The integration process is difficult to separate from general good management practice; however, there are a number of critical actions which are uniquely important to the job of project management. These actions must be initiated and continually monitored by project managers if project integration is to occur. The project manager is the single point of integrative responsibility, and is the only person who can initiate these actions. These critical actions are of two types: (a) those which are essentially just

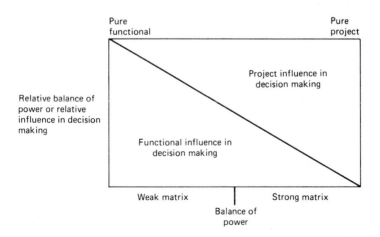

Figure 3-6. The balance of power in weak and strong matrices.

good project management practice and which must extend over the entire life of the project, and (b) specific one-time actions which must be taken by some member of management (usually the project manager or a member of top management) to ensure that the project is integrated. The most important of these actions are as follows (22):

1. Getting started on the right foot.
2. Planning for project integration.
3. Developing an integrated Work Breakdown Structure, schedule, and budget.
4. Developing integrated project control.
5. Managing conflict.
6. Removing roadblocks.
7. Setting priorities.
8. Facilitating project transfer.
9. Establishing communication links.

Getting Started on the Right Foot

To achieve successful project integration, it is of course very important that the project get started on the right foot. There are a number of specific things that must be done, both by top management and by the project manager (22). The secret of project success is dependent on making these critical actions very early in the project life cycle. For the most part these actions are inseparable from the normal actions that must be taken to implement any successful project; however, they must be made during the project implementation phase. If the right decisions are made at this time, the project can be expected to run smoothly and the integration process will proceed as planned.

The most important decisions and resulting actions are those taken by top management, and many of these actions must be taken well before the project is actually started. Not all of these actions are directly concerned with the integration function, but they are all necessary for the successful implementation of project management. The most critical of the actions which must be taken by top management are the following:

1. Completely selling the project management concept to the entire organization.
2. Choosing the type or form of project organization to be utilized.
3. Issuing a project charter to completely delineate all project and functional authority and responsibilities.
4. Choosing the project manager or project managers.

5. Choosing the right functional managers to participate in the project and/or matrix organization.
6. Supplying adequate resources to the project organization such as finances, equipment, personnel, computer support, etc.
7. Continuing strong support for the project and for the project manager.

The above list of actions is more or less in the order that the actions must be taken, and most of them must be taken prior to the actual implementation of the project.

After top management has successfully implemented project management and has given it full support, the action passes to the newly appointed project managers. There are a number of specific actions that the project managers must now initiate to start their projects on the road to success, and to ensure project integration. The project manager is the single point of integrative responsibility, and is the only person who can initiate and monitor these actions. The most critical of these actions are as follows:

1. Issuance of the Project Implementation Plan.
2. Creation of the project Work Breakdown Structure (WBS).
3. Development of the project organization.
4. Issuance of the Project Procedures Guide.
5. Issuance of a Project Material Procurement Forecast.
6. Issuance of Work Authorizations.

These actions are more or less sequential, although they are strongly interrelated and must be worked on at the same time. The most important consideration is that documentation implementing the above actions be issued as early in the project life cycle as possible. Much of this effort should have been accomplished prior to the initiation of the project, such as during proposal preparation. Even so, a great deal of effort is required during the "front end" of a project to accomplish these actions, and to ensure that project integration takes place.

Planning for Project Integration

Integration doesn't just happen—it must be planned. The project manager must develop a detailed planning document that can be used to get the project initiated, and to assure that all project participants understand their roles and responsibilities in the project organization.

The project manager is the only person in the key position of having an overview of the entire project system, preferably from its inception, and therefore can best foresee potential interface or other integration problems. After identifying these key interfaces, the project manager can keep a close surveillance on them to catch and correct any integration problems when they first occur. Particularly important in the project plan is a clear delineation of the project requirements for reporting, hardware delivery, completion of tests, facility construction, and other important milestones.

An important part of the project plan should be the integration plan. This plan is a subset of the project plan and may even be a separate document if a single department or even a separate contractor is responsible for system or project integration. In any case, the integration plan should define and identify all interface events, interrelationships between tasks and hardware subsystems, and potential interface problems. The integration plan should then analyze the interrelationships between tasks and the scheduled sequence of events in the project.

Project managers must continually review and update both the administration and technical portions of their project plans to provide for changes in scope and direction of their projects. They must assure that budget and resource requirements are continually reviewed and revised so that project resources are utilized in the most effective manner to produce an integrated system.

The most complete and well integrated project plan is worthless if no one uses it. Only the project manager can ensure that all task managers are aware of their roles and responsibilities in the attainment of project success. But continuous follow-up by the project manager is necessary to assure adherence to the project plan, and awareness of any necessary revision.

Developing an Integrated Work Breakdown Structure, Schedule, and Budget

Solving the project manager's problems starts with the fact that every project must be broken down into subdivisions or tasks which are capable of accomplishment. Creating this Work Breakdown Structure (WBS) is the most difficult part of preparing a project plan because the project manager must ensure that all of the tasks fit together in a manner that will result in the development of an integrated workable system. The WBS can be considered to be the "heart" of the project integration effort. Too often a WBS is prepared by breaking up the project along easily differentiated organizational lines with very little thought as to how the final system fits together. However, the WBS is the system "organization chart" which schematically portrays the products (hardware, software, services, and other work tasks) that completely define the system (4). Therefore, it is best to prepare the WBS by breaking down the project first into subsystems and then into components and finally into tasks that can readily be accomplished. These lower-level tasks or "work packages" can be most effectively estimated and carried out if they are within single organizational units.

This process of breaking down a project into tasks or work packages, that is, creating a WBS, is just the first step. The WBS must then be carefully integrated with the schedule and budget if the project is to succeed. Each work package must have an integrated cost, scheduled start, and scheduled completion point. The WBS serves as the project framework for preparing detailed project plans, network schedules, detailed costing, and job responsibilities. A realistic WBS assures that project integration can truly be achieved.

Developing Integrated Project Control

The most prolific project planning is useless if project control is ineffective. Whatever type of planning and control technique is used, all the important interfaces and interface events must be identified. Interface events such as hardware or facility completions will be important project milestones. The project network plan must be based on the interface events in order to facilitate analysis of the entire project on an integrated basis. Resource allocation and reporting periods can then be coordinated with interface events, and schedules and budgets can be designed on an integrated basis.

Managing Conflict

Project managers have been described as conflict managers (10). This does not mean that they should constantly be fire fighters; however, they cannot avoid this role in resolving conflicts, particularly when the conflict involves project resources such as project personnel. Conflicts are very likely to occur in the temporary project environment where the project manager is often the new player who has not had time to develop good working relationships with project team members or with supporting functional managers. The conflict potential is also increased by the great differences between project and functional goals and objectives, and by the unavoidable competition between projects for resources.

It is inevitable that problems occur at organizational and subsystem interfaces. These problems may or may not result in actual open conflict between individuals or organizations. A common situation is personal conflict between the two managers involved at an interface. Conflict situations result primarily from the concerned groups or managers losing sight of the overall project goals or having differing interpretations of how to get the job accomplished. Project managers must continually be on the lookout for real and potential conflict situations and resolve them immediately if they expect to have an integrated project.

Removing Roadblocks

Roadblocks are inevitable whenever there are separate organizational units which must support project efforts, particularly if the projects are matrixed. Roadblocks are inevitable in such a complex organization, and are the inevitable result of conflict situations. Resolving the conflict will eliminate many roadblocks, but there are always other roadblocks set up intentionally or unintentionally by managers and other personnel not directly involved with the project. These roadblocks may be the result of conflicting needs for resources and personnel, or conflicting priorities for the use of facilities and equipment. Administrative roadblocks often occur because managers outside the project do not understand or sympathize with the project urgency. Such roadblocks are difficult to deal with, and the project manager may be forced to go to top management to get a satisfactory resolution.

Setting Priorities

In order to resolve or prevent conflict situations, the project manager is continually faced with the problem of setting priorities. There are two types of priorities that are of major concern to project managers:

1. The overall company or organizational priorities which relate project needs to the needs of other projects within the organization, and to overall organizational needs.
2. The priorities within projects for the utilization of personnel, equipment, and facilities.

The first type of priority may be beyond the control of project managers, but it is a problem with which they must be continually concerned. Pity the poor project manager who is so busy getting the job done that he or she forgets to cement a working and personal relationship with members of top management. The result may be a low project priority that dooms the project to failure. The second type of priority is within the project organization and therefore completely within the control of the project manager. These priority problems must be handled on a day-to-day basis, but in a manner that will promote the integration of the project system.

Facilitating Project Transfer

Project transfer is the movement of a project through the company organizations from the conceptual phase to final delivery to the customer. Project transfer doesn't just happen, it must be carefully planned and provided for in the scheduling and budgeting of the project. The project manager has the responsibility of ensuring that project transfer takes place without wasteful effort and on schedule. The steps in a typical project transfer are shown in Figure 3-7.

If the product or system is to be delivered to the customer on schedule, it must move from block to block as indicated in Figure 3-7, which involves crossing a number of organizational interfaces. This transfer process must be expedited or even forced by the project manager if it is to be completed on schedule. The basic problem is that of making certain that the project is transferred quickly, without organizational conflict, without unnecessary redesign or rework, and without loss of relevant technology or other information. Experience has shown that the best method of ensuring effective project transfer is to utilize people who can move with the project across organizational interfaces. The project manager has two alternatives to facilitate project transfer: (a) the designation of suitable qualified personnel who can move forward with the project, that is, change their role as indicated by the left to right dashed arrows in Figure 3-7, (b) the utilization of personnel who can move backward in the organization and serve as consultants or active working members of the project team. When the project moves forward they serve as transfer agents in moving the project forward in the organization (22). Various possible personnel transfers are shown by the right to left solid arrows in Figure 3-

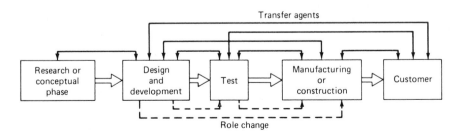

Figure 3-7. Project transfer.

7. Great importance must be placed on having customer, manufacturing, and/or construction representatives take part in the design phase of the project.

Establishing Communication Links

The last of the integration actions, that of constantly maintaining communication links, is perhaps the most difficult and troublesome because it involves the necessity for considerable "people" skills on the part of project managers. Most project managers find that they spend at least half of their time talking to people—getting information, delegating, clarifying directives, and resolving conflicts and misunderstandings. Much of this time is involved with project managers' critical responsibilities for maintaining all communication links within and outside their projects in order to ensure project integration. Internal communication links must be maintained between each subdivision of the project, and the project managers must make sure that all project team members talk with each other. In addition, the project manager is personally responsible for maintaining communication linkages outside of the project. Many of the external communication links can be personally expedited by the project manager, and in most cases the communication consists of written documents.

Communication linkages internal to the project, however, must function continuously, with or without documentation, and whether the project manager is personally involved or not. These internal communication linkages are most important to the health of the project since they involve the technical integration of the subsystems of the product or project. However, there are usually very real barriers to effective communications across any two such subsystem interfaces. In order to assure that problems don't accumulate and build up at these interfaces, the project manager must act as a transfer agent or a communications expediter. The model shown in Figure 3-8 illustrates the interface problem.

The project manager must serve as the bridge to make sure that the communication barriers do not occur. Communication barriers can be caused by a variety of circumstances and occurrences which the project manager must watch for. A communication barrier may or may not result in actual conflict depending upon the individuals involved, but the possibility always exists.

The project manager is the one person always in a position to expedite communication linkages. He or she can be considered to be a transfer agent who expedites the completion of the communication link by personally transferring information and project requirements across the interface. Considering the number of interfaces in a complex, multidisciplinary

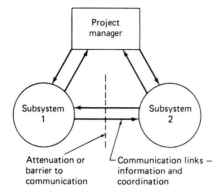

Figure 3-8. The project manager as communications expediter.

matrix-organized project, this process becomes a major effort for the project manager. The only saving grace is that many of these interfaces will be trouble free, and communication problems will not all occur at the same time.

Communication barriers may be caused by a variety of circumstances and occurrences. Some of the causes of communication barriers are as follows (19, 21):

1. Differing perceptions as to the goals and objectives of the overall company or organizational system can cause problems. In addition, a lack of understanding of project objectives is one of the most frequent and troublesome causes of misunderstanding. It can be directly attributed to insufficient action on the part of the project manager, since he or she has the major responsibility for defining project objectives. Even when these objectives are clearly stated by the project manager, they may be perceived differently by various project team members.

2. Differing perceptions of the scope and goals of the individual subsystem organizations can likewise restrict communications. Again it is the responsibility of the project managers to clarify these problems, at least as to how they impact their projects.

3. Competition for facilities, equipment, materials, manpower, and other resources can not only clog communication routes but can also lead to conflict.

4. Personal antagonisms or actual personality conflicts between managers and/or other personnel will block communication flow. There may also be antagonism toward project managers by line managers who perceive them as a threat to their authority or their empire.

5. Resistance to change or the NIH (not invented here) attitude may also detrimentally affect communication links between organizational units.

As indicated in Figure 3-9, the project manager has four important communication links: (a) upward to top management, (b)downward to the people working on the project, (c) outward to line managers and other projects at the same managerial level, and (d) outward to the customer or client. The project manager has a major responsibility for maintaining communications with the chief executives in the organization who must be provided with timely, up-to-date progress reports on the technical and financial status of the project. Similar reports must be provided to the client or customer, particularly if the customer is outside of the company, such as a governmental agency.

The other important communication link is with the people working on the project. The project manager must keep them informed by means of project directives and personal communications. In addition, there is a continual stream of reports from the discipline/line-organization managers and specialists who are working on the project.

Many of these reports concern project and administrative details and can be evaluated by administrators and assistant project managers. How-

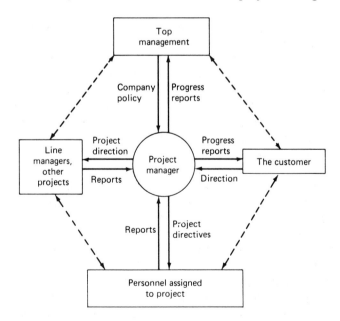

Figure 3-9. The project manager's communication links.

ever, the ultimate decision as to the worth of a report, and as to whether it should be included in progress reports to the customer and/or top management, is in the hands of the project manager. His or her communicative skills, therefore, must include the ability to accurately and rapidly evaluate, condense, and act on information from many sources.

Attenuation in these communication links at the organizational interfaces must be minimized. This means that project managers must have an open line to top management. Conversely, they cannot have too many line managers interpreting their instructions and project objectives to the people working on the project. Without open communication links, project managers will surely fail. There are also a number of important communication links outside the immediate scope of the project. The four most important such links are shown by the dashed arrows in Figure 3-9. For instance, the customer will at times talk directly to top management without going through the project manager. Project managers have to recognize the existence and the necessity for these sometimes bothersome communication links; and rather than fight them, they should endeavor to make use of them.

CONCLUSIONS

Project integration consists of ensuring that the pieces of the project come together as a "whole" at the right time and that the project functions as an integrated unit according to plan. In other words, the project must be treated as a system. Project managers carry out their job of project integration in spite of project and system complexity, and of course their job is the most difficult in a matrix organization.

To accomplish the integration process, project managers must take a number of positive actions to ensure that integration takes place. The most important of these actions is that of maintaining communication links across the organizational interfaces and between all members of the project team. Project managers must be continually expediting communication links throughout their projects. Of almost equal importance is the need for the project manager to develop a Work Breakdown Structure which ensures project integration by providing a "framework" on which to build the total project. These integrative actions are every bit as important as the project manager's other principal function of acting as a catalyst to motivate the project team.

Project integration is just another way of saying interface management since it involves continually monitoring and controlling (i.e., managing) a large number of project interfaces. The number of interfaces can increase exponentially as the number of organizational units increases; and the life of a project manager in a matrix organization can become very complex indeed. Interfaces usually involve a balance of power between the two managers involved. This balance of power can be tilted in favor of either manager, depending on the desires of top management. Project managers must continually keep their eyes on the various managerial interfaces affecting their projects. They must take prompt action to ensure that power struggles don't degenerate into actual conflict. It takes very little foot dragging to sabotage even the best project. Integration doesn't just automatically occur. The project manager must put forth great effort to ensure that it happens.

REFERENCES

1. Archibald, Russell D. *Managing High-Technology Programs and Projects* (Wiley. New York, 1977), p. 66.
2. Ibid., p. 5.
3. Cleland, David I. and King, William R. *Systems Analysis and Project Management,* 2nd Ed. (McGraw-Hill. New York, 1975), p. 237.
4. Ibid., p. 343.
5. Davis, Stanley M. and Lawrence, Paul R. *Matrix.* (Addison-Wesley. Reading, Mass., 1977).
6. Davis, Stanley M. "Two Models of Organization: Unity of Command versus Balance of Power." *Sloan Management Review* (Fall, 1974), pp. 29–40.
7. Galbraith, Jay R. "Matrix Organization Design." *Business Horizons* (February, 1971), pp. 29–40.
8. Galbraith, Jay R. *Designing Complex Organizations* (Addison-Wesley. Reading, Mass., 1973).
9. Galbraith, Jay R. *Organization Design* (Addison-Wesley. Reading, Mass., 1977).
10. Kerzner, Harold. *Project Management: A Systems Approach to Planning, Scheduling and Controlling* (Van Nostrand Reinhold. New York, 1979), p. 247.
11. Koontz, Harold and O'Donnell, Cyril. *Principles of Management: An Analysis of Managerial Functions* (McGraw-Hill. New York, 1972), p. 46.
12. Ibid., p. 50.
13. Lawrence, Paul R. and Lorsch, Jay W. *Organization and Environment: Managing Differentiation and Integration* (Harvard University, Division of Research, Graduate School of Business Administration. Boston, 1967).
14. Lawrence, Paul R. and Lorsch, Jay W. "New Management Job: The Integrator." *Harvard Business Review* (November–December, 1967), pp. 142–151.
15. Lawrence, Paul R. and Lorsch, Jay W. *Developing Organizations: Diagnosis and Action* (Addison-Wesley. Reading, Mass., 1969).
16. Lorsch, Jay W. and Morse, John J. *Organizations and Their Members: A Contingency Approach* (Harper & Row. New York, 1974), pp. 79–80.
17. Morris, Peter W. G. "Managing Project Interfaces—Key Points for Project Success," Chapter 1 in *Project Management Handbook,* ed. Cleland, David L. and King, William R. (Van Nostrand Reinhold. New York, 1st Ed. 1983), pp. 3–36.
18. Sayles, Leonard R. "Matrix Management: The Structure with a Future." *Organizational Dynamics* (Autumn, 1976), pp. 2–17.

19. Stickney, Frank A. and Johnson, William R. "Communication: The Key to Integration." *1980 Proceedings of the Project Management Institute Annual Seminar/Symposium,* Phoenix, Ariz. (Project Management Institute. Drexel Hill, Pa., 1980), pp. I-A.1-13.
20. Stuckenbruck, Linn C. "Project Manager—The Systems Integrator." *Project Management Quarterly* (September, 1978), pp. 31–38.
21. Stuckenbruck, Linn C. "The Integration Function in the Matrix." *1979 Proceedings of the Project Management Institute Annual Seminar/Symposium,* Atlanta, Ga. (Project Management Institute. Drexel Hill, Pa., 1979), pp. 481–492.
22. Stuckenbruck, Linn C. *The Implementation of Project Management: The Professionals Handbook* (Addison-Wesley. Reading, Mass., 1981), Chapter 6.
23. Stuckenbruck, Linn C. "Interface Management—Or Making The Matrix Work," in *Matrix Management Systems Handbook,* ed. Cleland, David I. (Van Nostrand Reinhold. New York, 1984). pp. 330–343.

Section II
The Project Organization

This section emphasizes the organizational dimensions of project and matrix management.

Chapter 4 presents Russell D. Archibald's depiction of the project office and project team—integral elements of the organization for projects that warrant a full-time project manager. He presents detailed specifications of the duties of the various project participants.

In Chapter 5 Richard L. Patterson expands on the role of the assistant project manager in terms of sets of needs—those of the project, the client, the contractor, and the individual. While these are presented specifically in terms of structuring a role for the assistant project manager, they are more generally relevant to understanding project organizational needs. Various projects in which this role was made operational are described.

The project team is also discussed in terms of its behavioral dimensions in Chapters 30, 31, and 32 of Section VIII.

4. Organizing the Project Office and Project Team: Duties of Project Participants*

Russell D. Archibald†

The approach described in this chapter is based on typical major project situations involving the design, manufacture, assembly, and testing of complex hardware and software systems. This presumes the following conditions:

- The project (or program) warrants a full-time project manager.
- The project office is held to minimum size, with maximum use of functional contributors in existing departments.

This chapter summarizes the functions of the project office and the project team under these conditions, describes the duties of key persons involved in the project, and discusses their relationships.

The situation frequently occurs wherein one project manager is responsible for several projects, or, when multiple small projects exist, the general manager will retain the project manager responsibility himself. In still other situations, a manager of projects is appointed. In such multiproject cases, centralized project planning and control is usually desirable. The positions and duties described here are still required, but they may be organized differently.

---

* Adapted from Chapter 6, "Organizing the Project Office and Project Team," *Managing High Technology Programs and Projects,* by Russell D. Archibald (John Wiley & Sons, Inc., New York, 1976).
† Russell D. Archibald is President, Archibald Associates, Los Angeles, California, consultants in project management, international business development, and strategic growth management. Mr. Archibald has directed major domestic and international programs with the Bendix Corporation and ITT; has consulted on program management to numerous large and small companies in eleven countries, as well as the U.S. Air Force; and has written and lectured extensively on this subject over the past 26 years.

FUNCTIONS OF THE PROJECT OFFICE AND PROJECT TEAM

The project office supports the project manager in carrying out his responsibilities. Thus his basic charter, organizational relationship, and the nature of the project itself will influence the makeup of the project office. The presence or absence of other projects, and of a central project planning office, will also affect the organization of the project office.

The *project team* includes all functional contributors to the project, as well as the members of the project office. The general functions to be carried out during completion of the overall project by members of the project team are the following:

- Project and task management.
- Product design and development.
- Product manufacture.
- Purchasing and subcontracting.
- Product installation and test.

The relationships of these functions to the project manager are shown in the generalized project organization chart in Figure 4-1. Each of these functions is discussed in the following paragraphs.

Project and Task Management

The management functions are simply those necessary to enable the project manager to fulfill his basic responsibility: overall direction and coordination of the project through all its phases to achieve the desired results within established budget and schedule, at the project level. Management of each functional task is the responsibility of the appropriate functional manager or staff member.

Product Design and Development

The basic purpose of this general function is to produce adequate documentation (and often a prototype product or system) so that the product may be manufactured in the quantity required within the desired cost and schedule. These functions may be defined as

- Systems analysis, engineering, and integration.
- Product design.
- Product control (quality, cost, configuration).

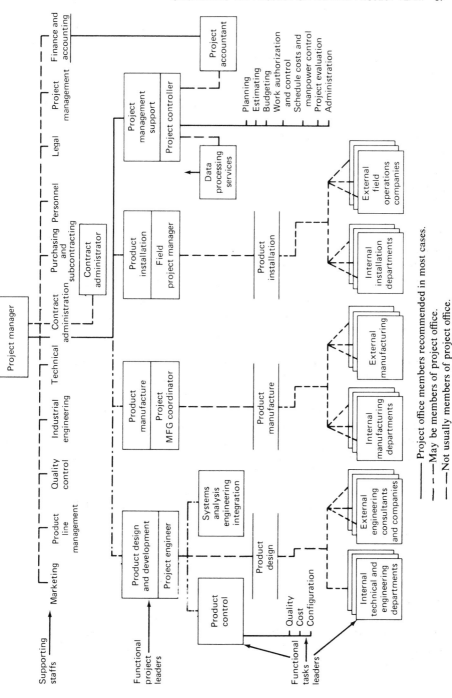

Figure 4-1. Generalized organization of the project team.

Systems analysis, engineering, and integration functions include system studies; functional analysis and functional design of the system or product; and coordination and integration of detailed designs, including functional and mechanical interfaces between major subsystems or components of the product.

Product design functions include the detailed engineering design and development functions needed to translate the functional systems design into specifications, drawings, and other documents which can be used to manufacture, assemble, install, and test the product. This may also include the manufacture and test of a prototype or first article system or product, using either model shop or factory facilities on a subcontract basis.

Product control functions include product quality control, using established staff specialists and procedures; product cost control, including value engineering practices; product configuration control, including design freeze practices (to establish the "base line" design), engineering change control practices, and documentation control practices.

It should be noted that the term "product" refers to *all* results of the project: hardware, software, documentation, training or other services, facilities, and so on.

The project office in a specific situation may perform none, a few, or all of these product design and development functions, depending on many factors. Generally a larger share of these functions will be assigned to the project office (together with adequate staff) when the product is new or unusual to the responsible unit, when the project is large and of long duration, or when there is little confidence that the work will be carried out efficiently and on schedule within established engineering departments. When several engineering departments, for example, from different product lines or different companies, are contributing to the product design and development, the functions of systems analysis, engineering and integration, and of product control, should be assigned to the project office.

Except in the situation described above, these functions should be performed by project team members within existing engineering departments, under the active coordination of the project manager.

Product Manufacture

This general function is to purchase materials and components, fabricate, assemble, test, and deliver the equipment required to complete the project. These functions are carried out by the established manufacturing departments within the project's parent company or by outside companies on a subcontract or purchase order basis.

The project manager, however, must coordinate and integrate the manufacturing functions with product design and development on one hand and field operations (if any) on the other. *The lack of proper integration between these areas is the most common cause of project failure.*

In order to achieve this integration, it is necessary to appoint a project manufacturing coordinator or equivalent who will, in effect, act as a project manager for product manufacture. He is a key project team member. He may be assigned full time to one major project, or he may be able to handle two or more projects at one time, if the projects are small.

It is recommended that the project manufacturing coordinator remain within the appropriate manufacturing department. When two or more divisions or companies perform a large part of the product manufacture, each must designate a project manufacturing coordinator, with one designated as the lead division for manufacture. If it is not possible to designate a lead division, then the coordination effort must be accomplished by the project office.

Purchasing and Subcontracting

This function is sometimes included with the product manufacture area, but it is normally important enough to warrant full functional responsibility.

A separate project purchasing and subcontracting coordinator with status equivalent to that of the manufacturing coordinator should be appointed to handle all purchasing and subcontracting matters for the project manager. This person should be a part of the purchasing department where he can maintain day-to-day contact with all persons carrying out the procurement functions.

Product Installation, Test, and Field Support

Many projects require field installation and test of the system or equipment, and some include continuing field support for a period of time. In these cases, a field project manager (or equivalent) is required.

When field operations are a part of the project, this phase is usually clearly recognized as being of a project nature and requiring one person to be in charge. This field project manager is almost always a member of an established installation department (or equivalent) if such a department exists within the responsible company. Since engineering and manufacturing operations frequently overlap the installation phase, the overall project manager's role continues to be of critical importance to success while field operations are in progress. However, in the relationship between the project manager and the field project manager, the project manager retains the overall responsibility for the coordination of the entire project. For projects involving major construction, a Field Project Manager will be required whose duties and responsibilities are equivalent to the project manager as outlined earlier.

Assignment of Persons to the Project Office

As a general rule, it is recommended that the number of persons assigned to a project office under the supervision of the project manager be kept as small as possible. This will emphasize the responsibility of each functional (line) department or staff for their contribution to the project and retain to the maximum degree the benefits of specialized functional departments. It will also increase flexibility of functional staffing of the project, avoid unnecessary payroll costs to the project, and minimize reassignment problems when particular tasks are completed. This will enable the project manager to devote maximum effort to the project itself, rather than to supervisory duties related to a large staff.

With adequate project planning and control procedures, a highly qualified project staff can maintain the desired control of the project. In the absence of adequate planning and control procedures to integrate the functional contributions, it is usually necessary to build up a larger staff with as many functional contributors as possible directly under the project manager in order to achieve control. Experience indicates that this is an expensive and frequently awkward approach, and it aggravates the relationships between the project manager and contributing functional managers.

The persons who should be assigned (transferred) permanently to the project office are those who

- Deal with the management aspects of the project.
- Are needed on a full-time basis for a period of at least six months.
- Must be in frequent close contact with the project manager or other members of the project office in the performance of their duties.
- Cannot otherwise be controlled effectively, because of organizational or geographic consideration.

Persons may be physically moved to the Project Office while retaining their permanent reporting relationships to a functional manager. This is a more frequent arrangement than officially transferring them out of the functional department to the project manager.

The recommended assignment location of each of the key people on the project team follows.

Project Manager.   The project manager is always considered the manager of the project office (which could be a one-man office).

Project Engineer.   The project engineer may be assigned to the project office in charge of product design and development where the product is new to the company or where several divisions are involved, as discussed earlier. Otherwise, he should always remain within the lead engineering department.

Contract Administrator.   The contract administrator should remain a member of the contract administration staff, except on very large programs extending over a considerable period of time. He may be located physically in the project office while remaining with his parent organization.

Project Controller.   The project controller should always be assigned to the project office, except where he is not needed full time or where a centralized planning and control function adequately serves the project manager.

Project Accountant.   The project accountant should remain a member of the accounting department, except on very large programs extending over a considerable period of time. Like the contract administrator, he may physically be located in the project office while remaining with his parent organization.

Manufacturing Coordinator.   The manufacturing coordinator should remain a member of the manufacturing organization, preferably on the staff of the manufacturing manager or within production control. When more than one division is to contribute substantially to product manufacture, it may be necessary to assign him to the project office to enable effective coordination of all contributors.

Purchasing and Subcontracting Coordinator.   This coordinator should remain a member of the purchasing department in most cases.

Field Project Manager. The field project manager should remain a member of the installation or field operations department, if one exists, except under unusual circumstances that would require him to be assigned to the project office.

Project Team Concept

Whether a person is assigned to the project office or remains in a functional department or staff, all persons holding identifiable responsibilities for direct contributions to the project are considered to be members of the project team. Creating awareness of membership in the project team is a primary task of the project manager, and development of a good project team spirit has proven to be a powerful means for accomplishing difficult objectives under tight time schedules.

The Project Organization Chart

Figure 4-2 shows a typical representation of a project team in the format of a classic organization chart. This type of representation can be confusing if not properly understood, but it can also be useful to identify the key project team members and show their relationships to each other and to the project manager *for project purposes*. This recognizes that such a chart does not imply permanent superior-subordinate relationships portrayed in the company organization charts.

PROJECT MANAGER DUTIES

The following description of project manager duties is presented as a guide for development of specific duties on a particular project. Some of

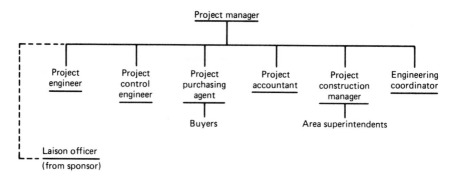

Figure 4-2. Typical construction project task force.

the duties listed may not be practical, feasible, or pertinent in certain cases, but wherever possible it is recommended that all items mentioned be included in the project manager's duties and responsibilities, with appropriate internal documentation and dissemination to all concerned managers.

General

- Rapidly and efficiently start up the project.
- Assure that all equipment, documents, and services are properly delivered to the customer for acceptance and use within the contractual schedule and costs.
- Convey to all concerned departments a full understanding of the customer requirements of the project.
- Participate with responsible managers in developing overall project objectives, strategies, budgets, and schedules.
- Assure preparation of plans for all necessary project tasks to satisfy customer and management requirements, with emphasis on interfaces between tasks.
- Assure that all project activities are properly and realistically scheduled, budgeted, provided for, monitored, and reported.
- Identify promptly all deficiencies and deviations from plan.
- Assure that actions are initiated to correct deficiencies and deviations, and monitor execution of such actions.
- Assure that payment is received in accordance with contractual terms.
- Maintain cognizance over all contacts with the customer and assure that proper staff members participate in such contacts.
- Arbitrate and resolve conflicts and differences between functional departments on specific project tasks or activities.
- Maintain day-to-day liaison with all functional contributors to provide communication required to assure realization of their commitments.
- Make or force required decisions at successively higher organizational levels to achieve project objectives.
- Maintain communications with higher management regarding problem areas and project status.

Customer Relations

In close cooperation with the customer relations or marketing department:

- Receive from the customer all necessary technical, cost, and scheduling information required for accomplishment of the project.
- Establish good working relationships with the customer on all levels: management, contracts, legal, accounts payable, system engineering, design engineering, field sites, and operations.
- Arrange and attend all meetings with customer (contractual, engineering, operations).
- Receive and answer all technical and operational questions from the customer, with appropriate assistance from functional departments.

Contract Administration

- Identify any potential areas of exposure in existing or potential contracts and initiate appropriate action to alert higher management and eliminate such exposure.
- Prepare and send, or approve prior to sending by others, all correspondence on contractual matters.
- Coordinate the activities of the project contract administrator in regard to project matters.
- Prepare and participate in contract negotiations.
- Identify all open contractual commitments.
- Advise engineering, manufacturing, and field operations of contractual commitments and variations allowed.
- Prepare historical or position papers on any contractual or technical aspect of the program, for use in contract negotiations or litigation.

Project Planning, Control, Reporting, Evaluation, and Direction

- Perform, or supervise the performance of, all project planning, controlling, reporting, evaluation, and direction functions.
- Conduct frequent, regular project evaluation and review meetings to identify current and future problems and initiate actions for their resolution.
- Prepare and submit weekly or monthly progress reports to higher management, and to the customer if required.
- Supervise the project controller and his staff.

Marketing

Maintain close liaison with Marketing and utilize customer contacts to acquire all possible marketing intelligence for future business.

Engineering

- Insure that Engineering fulfills its responsibilities for delivering, on schedule and within product cost estimates, drawings and specifications usable by manufacturing and field operations, meeting the customer specifications.
- In cooperation with the Engineering, Drafting, and Publications Departments define and establish schedules and budgets for all engineering and related tasks. After agreement release funding allowables and monitor progress on each task in relation to the overall project.
- Act as the interface with the customer for these departments (with their assistance as required).
- Assure the control of product quality, configuration, and cost.
- Approve technical publications prior to release to the customer.
- Coordinate engineering support related to the project for Manufacturing, Installation, Legal, and other departments.
- Participate (or delegate participation) as a voting member in the Engineering Change Control Board on matters affecting the project.

Manufacturing

- Insure that Manufacturing fulfills its responsibility for on-schedule delivery of all required equipment, meeting the engineering specifications within estimated manufacturing costs.
- Define contractual commitments to Production Control.
- Develop schedules to meet contractual commitments in the most economical fashion.
- Establish and release manufacturing and other resource and funding allowables.
- Approve and monitor production control schedules.
- Establish project priorities.
- Approve, prior to implementation, any product changes initiated by Manufacturing.
- Approve packing and shipping instructions based on type of transportation to be used and schedule for delivery.

Purchasing and Subcontracting

- Insure that Purchasing and Subcontracting fulfill their responsibilities to obtain delivery of materials, equipment, documents, and services on schedule and within estimated cost for the project.

- Approve make-or-buy decisions for the project.
- Define contractual commitments to Purchasing and Subcontracting.
- Establish and release procurement funding allowables.
- Approve and monitor major purchase orders and subcontracts.
- Specify planning, scheduling, and reporting requirements for major purchase orders and subcontracts.

Installation, Test, and Other Field Operations

- Insure that Installation and Field Operations fulfill their responsibilities for on-schedule delivery to the customer of materials, equipment, and documents within the cost estimates for the project.
- Define contractual commitments to Installation and Field Operations.
- In cooperation with Installation and Field Operations, define and establish schedules and budgets for all field work. After agreement, release funding allowables and monitor progress on each task in relation to the overall project.
- Coordinate all problems of performance and schedule with Engineering, Manufacturing, and Purchasing and Subcontracting.
- Except for customer contacts related to daily operating matters, act as the customer interface for Installation and Field Operations departments.

Financial

In addition to the financial project planning and control functions described:

- Assist in the collection of accounts receivable.
- Approve prices of all change orders and proposals to the customer.

Project Closeout

- Insure that all required steps are taken to present adequately all project deliverable items to the customer for acceptance and that project activities are closed out in an efficient and economical manner.
- Assure that the acceptance plan and schedule comply with the customer contractual requirements.
- Assist the Legal, Contract Administration, and Marketing or Commercial Departments in preparation of a closeout plan and required closeout data.

- Obtain and approve closeout plans from each involved functional department.
- Monitor closeout activities, including disposition of surplus materials.
- Notify Finance and functional departments of the completion of activities and of the project.
- Monitor payment from the customer until all collections have been made.

PROJECT ENGINEER DUTIES

General

The project engineer is responsible for the technical integrity of his project and for cost and schedule performance of all engineering phases of the project. Specifically, the responsibilities of the project engineer are the following:

- Insure that the customer performance requirements are fully understood and that the company is technically capable of meeting these requirements.
- Define these requirements to the smallest subsystem to the functional areas so that they can properly schedule, cost, and perform the work to be accomplished.
- Insure that the engineering tasks so defined are accomplished within the engineering schedules and allowables (manpower, materials, funds) of the contract.
- Provide technical direction as necessary to accomplish the project objectives.
- Conduct design review meetings at regular intervals to assure that all technical objectives will be achieved.
- Act as technical advisor to the project manager and other functional departments, as requested by the project manager.

In exercising the foregoing responsibilities, the project engineer is supported by the various engineering departments.

Proposal Preparation and Negotiation

During the proposal phase, the project engineer will do the following:

- Coordinate and plan the preparation of the technical proposal.
- Review and evaluate the statement of work and other technical data.

- Establish an engineering proposal team or teams.
- Within the bounds of the overall proposal schedule, establish the engineering proposal schedule.
- Reduce customer engineering requirements to tasks and subtasks.
- Define in writing the requirements necessary from Engineering to other functional areas, including preliminary specifications for make or buy, or subcontract items.
- Coordinate and/or prepare a schedule for all engineering functions, including handoff to and receipt from Manufacturing or Purchasing.
- Review and approve all Engineering subtask and task costs, schedules, and narrative inputs.
- Coordinate and/or prepare overall engineering cost.
- Participate in preliminary make-or-buy decisions.
- Participate in overall cost and schedule review.
- Participate, as required, in negotiation of contract.
- Bring problems between the project engineer and engineering functional managers to appropriate engineering directors for resolution.

Project Planning and Initiation

The project engineer is responsible for the preparation of plans and schedules for all engineering tasks within the overall project plan established by the project manager. In planning the engineering tasks, he will compare the engineering proposal against the received contract. Where the received contract requirements dictate a change in cost, schedule, or technical complexity for solution, he will obtain approval from the director of engineering and the project manager to make the necessary modifications in engineering estimates of the proposal. During this phase, the project engineer will:

- Update the proposal task and subtask descriptions to conform with the contract, and within the engineering allowables prepare additional tasks and subtasks as required to provide a complete engineering implementation plan for the project.
- Prepare a master engineering schedule in accordance with the contractual requirements.
- Prepare, or have prepared, detailed task and subtask definitions and specifications. Agree on allowables, major milestones, and evaluation points in tasks with the task leaders and their functional managers.
- Through the functional engineering managers, assign responsibility for task and subtask performance, and authorize the initiation of

work against identified commitments based on cost and milestone schedules, with approval of the project manager.

- Using contract specifications as the base line, prepare, or have prepared, specifications for subcontract items.
- Participate and provide support from appropriate engineering functions in final make-or-buy decisions and source selection.
- Prepare, or have prepared, hardware and system integration and acceptance test plan. Review the test plan with Quality Assurance and advise them as to the required participation of other departments.

Project Performance and Control

The project engineer is responsible for the engineering progress of the project and compliance with contract requirements, cost allowables, and schedule commitments. Within these limits, the project engineer, if necessary, may make design changes and task requirement changes in accordance with his concept and assume the responsibility for the change in concert with the functional engineering managers and with the knowledge of the project manager. No changes may be made that affect other functional departments without the knowledge of that department, documentation to the project manager, and the inclusion of the appropriate charge-back of any variance caused by change. He maintains day-to-day liaison with the project manager for two-way information exchange. Specific responsibilities of the project engineer are the following:

- Prepare and maintain a file of all project specifications related to the technical integrity and performance.
- Prepare and maintain updated records of the engineering expenditures and milestones and conduct regular reviews to insure engineering performance as required.
- Initiate and prepare new engineering costs-to-complete reports as required.
- Establish work priorities within the engineering function where conflict exists: arbitrate differences and interface problems within the engineering function, and request through functional managers changes in personnel assignments if deemed necessary.
- Plan and conduct design review meetings and design audits as required, and participate in technical reviews with customer.
- Prepare project status reports as required.
- With the project manager and other functional departments, partici-

pate in evaluation and formulation of alternate plans as required by schedule delays or customer change requests.

- Assure support to Purchasing and Subcontracting, Manufacturing, Field Operations, and support activities by providing liaison and technical assistance within allowables authorized by the project manager.
- Modify and reallocate tasks and subtasks, open and close cost accounts, and change allowable allocations within the limits of the approved engineering allowables, with the concurrence of the functional managers involved. Provide details to the project manager of all such actions prior to change.
- As requested by the project manager, support Legal and Contracts Administration by providing technical information.
- Review and approve technical aspects of reports for dissemination to the customer.
- Authorize within the approved allowables the procurement of material and/or services as required for the implementation of the engineering functional responsibility.
- Adjudicate technical problems and make technical decisions within scope of contractual requirements. Cost and schedule decisions affecting contractual requirements or interface with other functions are to be approved by the appropriate engineering function manager with the cognizance of the director of engineering (or his delegate) and the project manager.
- Approve all engineering designs released for procurement and/or fabrication for customer deliverable items.
- Bring problems arising between the project engineer and engineering functional managers to the engineering director for resolution.
- Bring problems arising between the project engineer and functions outside engineering to the project manager for resolution, with the cognizance of the director of engineering and the director of the other functions.

CONTRACT ADMINISTRATOR DUTIES

General

Contract administration is a specialized management function indispensable to effective management of those projects carried out under contract with customers. This function has many legal implications and serves to protect the company from unforeseen risks prior to contract approval and during execution of the project. Experience dictates that well-qualified, properly organized contract administration support to a project manager is vital to the continuing success of companies responsible for major sales contracts.

Contract administration is represented both on the project manager's team and on the general manager's staff. A director of contract administration has the authority to audit project contract files and to impose status reporting requirements that will disclose operational and contractual problems relating to specific projects. The director of contract administration is also available to provide expertise in the resolution of contract problems beyond the capability of the contract administrator assigned to a given project.

The project contract administrator is responsible for day-to-day administration of (a) the contract(s) that authorize performance of the project and (b) all subcontracts with outside firms for equipment, material, and services to fulfill project requirements.

Proposal Preparation

- When participation of an outside subcontractor is required, assure that firm quotations are obtained based on terms and conditions compatible with those imposed by the customer.
- Review with the Legal and Financial Department all of the legal and commercial terms and conditions imposed by the customer.
- Review the proposal prior to submittal to assure that all risks and potential exposures are fully recognized.

Contract Negotiation

- Lead all contract negotiations for the project manager.
- Record detailed minutes of the proceedings.
- Assure that all discussions or agreements reached during negotiations are confirmed in writing with the understanding that they will be incorporated into the contract during the contract definition phase.
- Assure that the negotiating limits established by the Proposal Review Board (or equivalent) are not exceeded.

Contract Definition

- Expedite the preparation, management review, and execution of the contract, as follows:
  —Clarify the contract format with the customer.
  —Establish the order of precedence of contract documents incorporated in reference.

—Set the date by which the contract will be available in final form for management review prior to execution.

—Participate with the project manager in final briefing of management on the contract terms and conditions prior to signature.

Project Planning Phase

- Establish channels of communication with the customer and define commitment authority of project manager, contract administrator, and others.
- Integrate contract requirements and milestones into the project plan and schedule; including both company and customer obligations.
- Establish procedures for submission of contract deliverables to customer.
- Establish mechanics for monthly contract status reports for the customer and management.

Project Execution Phase

- Monitor and follow up all contract and project activities to assure fulfillment of contractual obligations by both the company and the customer.
- Assure that all contract deliverables are transmitted to the customer and that all contractually required notifications are made.
- Record any instance where the customer has failed to fulfill his obligations and define the cost and schedule impact on the project of such failure.
- Identify and define changes in scope and customer-caused delays and force majeure, including:
  - —Early identification and notification to customer.
  - —Obtaining of customer's agreement that change of scope or customer-caused delay or force majeure case has actually occurred.
  - —In coordination with the project manager and the project team, preparation of a proposal that defines the scope of the change(s) and resulting price and/or schedule impact for submittal to the customer for eventual contract modification.
- Assist in negotiation and definition of contract change orders.
- Participate in project and contract status reviews and prepare required reports.
- Arrange with the customer to review the minutes of joint project review meetings to assure that they accurately reflect the proceedings.

- Assure that the customer is notified in writing of the completion of each contractual milestone and submission of each contract deliverable item, with a positive assertion that the obligation has been fulfilled.
- Where the customer insists on additional data or work before accepting completion of an item, monitor compliance with his requirement to clear such items as quickly as possible.

Project Closeout Phase

- At the point where all contractual obligations have been fulfilled, or where all but longer-term warranties or spare parts deliveries are complete, assure that this fact is clearly and quickly communicated in writing to the customer.
- Assure that all formal documentation related to customer acceptance as required by the contract is properly executed.
- Expedite completion of all actions by the company and the customer needed to complete the contract and claim final payment.
- Initiate formal request for final payment.
- Where possible, obtain certification from the customer acknowledging completion of all contractual obligations and releasing the company from further obligations, except those under the terms of guaranty or warranty, if any.

Project/Contract Record Retention

Prior to disbanding the project team, the project contract administrator is responsible for collecting and placing in suitable storage the following records, to satisfy legal and internal management requirements:

- The contract file, which consists of:
  Original request for proposal (RFP) and all modifications.
  All correspondence clarifying points in the RFP.
  Copy of company's proposal and all amendments thereto.
  Records of negotiations.
  Original signed copy of contract and all documents and specifications incorporated in the contract by reference.
  All contracts and modifications (supplemental agreements).
  A chronological file of all correspondence exchanged between the parties during the life of the program. This includes letters, telexes, records of telephone calls, and minutes of meetings.

Acceptance documentation.
Billings and payment vouchers.
Final releases.
- Financial records required to support postcontract audits, if required by contract or governing statutes.
- History of the project (chronology of all events—contractual and noncontractual).
- Historical cost and time records that can serve as standards for estimating future requirements.

PROJECT CONTROLLER DUTIES

The primary responsibility of the project manager is to plan and control his project. On some smaller or less complex projects, he may be able to perform all the planning and controlling functions himself. However, on most major projects, it will be necessary to provide at least one person on his staff who is well qualified in project planning and control and who can devote his full attention to these specialized project management needs. This person is the project controller. (A number of other equivalent job titles are in use for this position.) On very large or complex programs or projects, the project controller may require one or more persons to assist him in carrying out his duties and responsibilities.

If a centralized operations planning and control function exists in the company, that office may provide the needed planning and control services to the project manager. In that case the project controller would be a member of the Operations Planning and Control Office and would have available to him the specialists in that office. In other situations, the project controller may be transferred from Operations Planning and Control to the project office for the duration of the project.

The duties of the project controller are described in the following sections.

General

- Perform for the project manager the project planning, controlling, reporting, and evaluation functions as delegated to him, so that the project objectives are achieved within the schedule and cost limits.
- Assist the project manager to achieve clear visibility of all contract tasks so that they can be progressively measured and evaluated in sufficient time for corrective action to be taken.

Project Planning and Scheduling

- In cooperation with responsible managers, define the project systematically so that all tasks to be performed are identified and hierarchically related to each other, including work funded under contract or by the company, using the project breakdown structure or similar technique.
- Identify all elements of work (tasks or work packages) to be controlled for time, manpower, or cost, and identify the responsible and performing organizations and project leaders for each.
- Define an adequate number of key milestones for master planning and management reporting purposes.
- Prepare and maintain a graphic project master plan and schedule, based on the project breakdown structure, identifying all tasks or work packages to be controlled in the time dimension, and incorporating all defined milestones.
- Prepare more detailed graphic plans and schedules for each major element of the project.

Budgeting and Work Authorization

- Obtain from the responsible manager for each task or work package a task description, to include:
  Statement of work.
  Estimate of resources required (man days, computer hours, etc.).
  Estimate of labor, computer, and other costs (with assistance of the project accountant).
  Estimate of start date, and estimated total duration and duration between milestones.
- Prepare and maintain a task description file for the entire project.
- Summarize all task manpower and cost estimates, and coordinate needed revisions with responsible managers and the project manager to match the estimates with available and allocated funds for the project in total, for each major element, and for each task.
- Prepare and release, on approval of the project manager and the responsible functional manager, work authorization documents containing the statement of work, budgeted labor, and cost amounts; scheduled dates for start, completion, and intermediate milestones; and the assigned cost accounting number.
- Prepare and release, with approval of the project manager, revised work authorization documents when major changes are required or

have occurred, within the authorized funding limits and the approval authority of the project manager.

Work Schedules

- Assist each responsible manager or project leader in developing detailed plans and schedules for assigned tasks, reflecting the established milestone dates in the project master plan.
- Issue current schedules to all concerned showing start completion dates of tasks and occurrence dates of milestones.

Progress Monitoring and Evaluation

- Obtain weekly reports from all responsible managers and project leaders of:
  Activities started and completed.
  Milestones completed.
  Estimates of time required to complete activities or tasks under way.
  Changes in future plans.
  Actual or anticipated delays, additional costs, or other problems that may affect other tasks, the schedule, or project cost.
- Record reported progress on the project master plan and analyze the effect of progress in all tasks on the overall project schedule.
- Identify major deviations from schedule and determine, with the responsible managers and the project manager, appropriate action to recover delays or take advantage of early completion of tasks.
- Obtain monthly cost reports and compare to the estimates for each current task, with summaries for each level of the project breakdown structure and the total project.
- Through combined evaluation of schedule and cost progress compared to plan and budget, identify deviations that require management action and report these to the project manager.
- Participate in project review meetings, to present the overall project status and evaluate reports from managers and project leaders.
- Record the minutes of project review meetings and follow up for the project manager all resulting action assignments to assure completion of each.
- Advise the project manager of known or potential problems requiring his attention.
- Each month or quarter obtain from each responsible manager an estimate of time, manpower, and cost to complete for each incomplete task or work package; and prepare, in cooperation with the

project accountant, a revised projection of cost to complete the entire project.

Schedule and Cost Control

- When schedule or budget revisions are necessary, due to delay or changes in the scope of work, prepare, negotiate, and issue new project master plan and schedules and revised work authorization documents, with approval of the project manager, within the authorized funding limits and the approval authority of the project manager.
- In coordination with the project accountant, notify the Finance Department to close each cost account and reject further charges when work is reported complete on the related task.

Reporting

- Prepare for the project manager monthly progress reports to management and the customer.
- Provide cost-to-complete estimates and other pertinent information to the project accountant for use in preparing contract status reports.
- Prepare special reports as required by the project manager.

PROJECT ACCOUNTANT DUTIES

The basic function of the project accountant is to provide to the project manager the specialized financial and accounting assistance and information needed to forecast and control manpower and costs for the project. The project accountant duties are as follows:

- Establish the basic procedure for utilizing the company financial reporting and accounting system for project control purposes to assure that all costs are properly recorded and reported.
- Assist the project controller in developing the project breakdown structure to identify the tasks or project elements that will be controlled for manpower and cost.
- Establish account numbers for the project and assign a separate number to each task or work element to be controlled.
- Prepare estimates of cost, based on manpower and other estimates provided by the controller, for all tasks in the project when required to prepare revised estimates to complete the project.
- Obtain, analyze, and interpret labor and cost accounting reports, and

provide the project manager, project controller, and other managers in the project with appropriate reports to enable each to exercise needed control.

- Assure that the information being recorded and reported by the various functional and project departments is valid, properly charged, and accurate, and that established policies and procedures are being followed for the project.
- Identify current and future deviation from budget of manpower or funds, or other financial problems, and in coordination with the project controller notify the project manager of such problems.
- Prepare, in coordination with the project manager and the project controller, sales contract performance reports as required by division or company procedures on a monthly basis for internal management purposes, and for submission to any higher headquarters.

MANUFACTURING COORDINATOR DUTIES

General

The general duties and responsibilities of the manufacturing coordinator (sometimes called the project leader—manufacturing) are to plan, implement, monitor, and coordinate the manufacturing aspects of his assigned project (or projects, where it is feasible for him to coordinate more than one contract).

Specific Duties

- Review all engineering releases before acceptance by manufacturing to insure they are complete and manufacturable (clean releases), and that all changes are documented by a formal written engineering change request.
- Participate in the development of project master schedules during proposal, negotiation, and execution phases, with particular emphasis on determination of requirements for engineering releases, critical parts lists, equipment requirements, and so on, to insure meeting delivery requirements.
- Monitor all costs related to assigned projects to assure adherence to manufacturing costs and cost schedules, analyze variances and recommend corrective action, collect needed information and prepare manufacturing cost to complete.
- Develop or direct the development of detailed schedules for assigned projects, coordinating the participation of manufacturing and product

support engineering, material planning, fabrication, purchasing, material stores, assembly, test, quality control, packing and shipping, in order to insure completion of master project schedule within budget limits; provide information and schedules to different functional groups in order for action to be initiated.

- Approve all shipping authorizations for assigned projects.
- Provide liaison between the project manager and Manufacturing; diligently monitor manufacturing portions of assigned projects and answer directly for manufacturing performance against schedules; prepare status reports and provide information needed to prepare costs to complete as required.
- Take action within area of responsibility and make recommendations for corrective action in manufacturing areas to overcome schedule slippages; obtain approval from the project manager for incurring additional manufacturing costs.
- Coordinate requests for clarifications of the impact of contract change proposals on manufacturing effort.
- Participate in the preparation and approval of special operating procedures.
- Review and approve for manufacturing all engineering releases and engineering change notices affecting assigned projects, and participate in Change Control Board activity.
- Represent project manager on all Make/Buy Committee actions.

FIELD PROJECT MANAGER DUTIES

General

The field project manager (or equivalent) has overall responsibility for constructing required facilities and installing, testing, and maintaining for the specified time period, and handing over to the customer, all installed equipment and related documentation as specified by the contract. This includes direct supervision of all company and subcontractor field personnel, through their respective managers or supervisors.

Specific Duties

- Participate in the development of project master schedules during proposal, negotiation, and execution phases, with particular emphasis on determination of equipment delivery schedules and manpower and special test equipment needs.

- Monitor all field operations costs for the project to assure adherence to contract allowables. Analyze variances and recommend corrective actions. Collect needed information and prepare field operations cost to complete.
- Develop or direct the development of detailed schedules for all field operations; coordinate the equipment delivery schedules from Manufacturing and subcontractors with field receiving, inspection, installation, testing, and customer acceptance procedures, with due regard for transportation and import/export requirements, to insure completion of the master project schedule within budget limits; provide information and schedules to different functional groups or departments in order for action to be initiated.
- Provide liaison between the project manager and Installation and Field Operations; diligently monitor field operations portion of the project and answer for performance against schedules; prepare status reports.
- Take action and make recommendations for corrective action in field operations and other areas to overcome schedule slippages; obtain approval of the project manager for incurring additional installation costs.
- Coordinate requests for clarifications of the impact of contract change proposals on field operations.

5. Developing the Role of the Assistant Project Manager by Assessing the Needs of Project Clients

Richard L. Patterson*

INTRODUCTION

In the many discussions and papers on the subject of project management and related management concepts, techniques, and procedures there appears to be a dearth of information on the role of the Assistant Project Manager.

The reasons for this condition are not necessarily clear nor are they really germane to our discussion—but isn't it about time we took a closer look at this fellow? Shouldn't we delve into questions like who needs him and why? What function does the Assistant Project Manager perform? Where does he fit into the organization? And finally, what is his personal stake in his role?

Three basic principles evolve almost immediately during any analysis of the role of the Assistant Project Manager, namely:

- The role must provide for the accomplishment of substantial and productive functions within the scope of the total project.
- The role must fulfill certain basic needs of both the Client and the Contractor.
- The role should provide a meaningful challenge to the holder and at the same time encourage his personal growth and development.

---

* Mr. Patterson spent nine years as a project manager for Bechtel Power Corporation. During this time he managed the design, procurement, and construction of two multi-unit, coal-fired power generating stations, each costing over $500 million. These assignments gave him first-hand experience at effectively utilizing assistant project managers. He is a registered Civil Engineer and a member of the ASCE and the Project Management Institute.

SPECIFIC NEEDS OF THE PROJECT

A Project Manager is primarily concerned with the successful completion of his project. It is from the real-life world of the project itself that the specific needs for an Assistant Project Manager arise and from which his basic role is ultimately defined.

Essentially most of our larger engineering and construction projects today, and especially those in the power generation field, challenge the Project Manager's span of control at their very outset. Some of the more significant factors which strain this span include the following:

- The extreme physical size of many of today's projects.
- The large capital costs and lengthy schedules of the projects.
- The significant financial exposure of the Client during the project cycle.
- The range and complexities of the technologies involved.
- Special services required of the Contractor in addition to his normal offerings and demonstrated capabilities.
- Geographic spread of the basic project and the major subcontractors' efforts.
- Special procurement considerations such as
  —Client/Contractor legal relationships and divisions in procurement responsibilities or activities.
  —Extensive supplier/subcontractor qualification, inspection, expediting, or test requirements.
  —Extensive commercial evaluations and negotiations to obtain satisfactory escalation provisions.
  —International as well as national procurement activities with attendant financial, legal, or administrative considerations.
- The tremendous impact of regulatory agencies and their proliferation at national, state, and local levels.
- The increasing public interest and the scrutiny of intervenors into more and more elements of a project.
- Construction and construction-related activities including such factors as
  —Labor relations and union matters.
  —Site logistics and support.
  —Housing and associated socioeconomic considerations.
  —Insurance.

These typical and basic strains on project management generally prevail throughout the average power project life cycle and obviously require the continuing attention of the Contractor's and the Client's management.

But it is also important to note that most large and long-term projects go through several major changes in emphasis and many shifts in the tenor of their operations during their life cycles.

For example, in the early stages of a power project we may be concerned with such factors as site selection, housing requirements, fuel transport, major long-lead hardware procurement, environmental reports, criteria development, and basic estimates and schedules associated with the conceptual design. As the final design is developed, the project emphasis shifts to detailed engineering demands with particular attention devoted to engineering calculations, drawings, and the preparation of detailed specifications. Subsequently, project concern will center upon the qualification of vendors and subcontractors, the preparation of bid packages, bid evaluations, and material availability, while the design, costs, and schedules undergo continuing and strengthening refinements. In the meantime, field mobilization must be planned and the site prepared. Then, with the pouring of the first major concrete, the activity in the field increases very rapidly. Now special attention must be focused on the timely delivery of hardware and materials, and getting the necessary engineering drawings to the field to ensure orderly and effective progression in a total construction effort that may involve several thousand workers. As construction advances, the project emphasis again shifts; this time to the installation and checkout of equipment, the resolution of equipment problems, and the progressive start-up of the plant.

These typical project patterns are not exempt from the unexpected or unusual problems which also serve to change management plans and expectations. Further, it should be emphasized that with each changing project pattern there is usually both a qualitative and quantitative impact upon project management. The special skills, technology, or professional requirements change with each new pattern. Similarly, the intensity of project management attention and devotion to certain project areas must shift with each change in the project pattern.

Naturally, both the Contractor and the Client desire that the Project Manager bring to the project the widest (and deepest) possible personal exposure and professional experience in all facets of the job. However, it is a rare individual who can fulfill all the demands of today's major projects.

In such cases the capabilities and experience of an Assistant Project Manager can be used to complement and supplement those of the Project Manager in one or more areas of concern and during one or more major time frames of the project. Proper matching of skills and background coupled with timely assignment can greatly strengthen the Contractor's project management and the true span of control.

GENERAL NEEDS OF THE CLIENT

The Client desires that the needs of the project be satisfied as discussed in the previous section. He also has some very specific needs of his own.

The Client has a concern in the day-to-day availability of the Project Manager. In the Project Manager's absence, the Client invariably requires assurance that adequate management attention is being given to the project operations and that a designated and capable individual—within management—is available to respond to his needs.

Similarly, the Client has an overriding interest in the continuity of his project and generally looks with favor on the presence of a designated assistant in the Contractor's organization who can eventually (and smoothly) move into the Project Manager's shoes, if and when required. Some Clients may actively participate in the actual selection of this assistant by establishing certain qualifications or criteria for the role, or by other means.

The very fact that the Client has brought a Contractor on board is presumptive of his needs. Normally the statement of work and related contract documents will identify these needs adequately. However, it is not always possible to fully define certain key concerns or overriding needs, especially in regard to personnel qualifications, staffing, and organization.

While the Client may have no direct interest in the personal growth or development of each individual within the Contractor's organization, he does have a general and continuing concern for the overall strength and depth of the Contractor's project team.

In this respect, it is not uncommon for the Client to view the Contractor's organization as an extension of his very own. In this context then, the Client frequently demonstrates a strong advocacy for furthering the growth and development of certain of the Contractor's people in parallel with his own in-house plans. Specifically, the establishment and development of the role of Contractor's Assistant Project Manager usually fits very nicely into the Client's personnel plans and policies.

GENERAL NEEDS OF THE CONTRACTOR

The Contractor's senior management, as well as many others within and without the Contractor's organization, will normally view the Project Manager as the primary contact (and expert) on his assigned job. And rightly so!

It naturally follows that the Project Manager is frequently sought out or solicited for reports, reviews, audits, special information or documents, and similar efforts by his own management. In addition, he is frequently called upon to head up meetings or conferences or to participate to a greater or lesser degree in related activities sponsored by others, both within and without his own organization. Obviously, he must be particularly concerned with those key management plans and operations which interface directly with his assignment.

Progressive companies will provide opportunities for deserving Project Managers to participate in executive management training courses and seminars to prepare them for positions of greater responsibility.

These demands upon the Project Manager's time make him less available to his own project organization which must deal with a multitude of questions on a day-to-day basis. Under such circumstances the assignment of an Assistant Project Manager to fill in for the Project Manager in his absence can ensure timely monitoring of operations, lend mature judgment and guidance to project personnel, provide for appropriate approvals (signature) where required, and do much to alleviate any work delays or encumbrances which might otherwise be brought about by the Project Manager's absence.

On many key projects the Contractor may have a further and naturally selfish need for the presence of an Assistant Project Manager. On long-term projects it is especially prudent for management to plan for the ultimate replacement of the Project Manager as the latter may move on to further challenges. The assignment of an Assistant Project Manager on a timely basis then becomes the Contractor's primary tool for achieving project continuity. Subsequently, an efficient transition or change in project management, with no unsettling Client or project team disturbances, can be made when required.

The successful Contractor is also alert to foster the personal growth and professional development of his own people. It is usually the more talented and motivated employees who actively seek out the promotional routes to management and who must be reassured, at timely intervals, by appropriate assignments of increasing responsibility and growth potential.

The role of an Assistant Project Manager, if properly structured, on a selected project can provide excellent training for the development of future Project Managers and at the same time maintain the dedication and motivation of the individual employee by providing him with meaningful challenges and opportunities. We stress the fact that the role must be properly structured, and for the benefit of all—the Contractor, the Client, the Project, and the Individual.

THE NEEDS OF THE INDIVIDUAL

Senior engineering and construction personnel on their way toward a management career will be attracted to the role of Assistant Project Manager if the position will

- Provide challenging work assignments.
- Utilize their professional skills, talents, and experience.
- Call for (tangible) productive work to achieve recognizable goals.
- Permit their professional development and growth.

A stimulating work environment must be afforded the Assistant Project Manager. His care and feeding, particularly if the role represents his first assignment with "manager" in the title, is of particular concern and may markedly affect project operations.

From the individual's standpoint—and ideally—all the foregoing factors should be equally represented in the assigned role. Regrettably, not all projects necessarily present such a balanced offering. However, it is extremely fortunate that most of today's large projects do offer a wide variety of experience to the young managerial candidate. By ensuring that the Assistant Project Manager is given adequate exposure to diverse elements of the project to enhance his growth and development, the Contractor's management can frequently compensate for occasional shortcomings in other specific areas of concern to the individual.

STRUCTURING THE ROLE

Structuring the role of an Assistant Project Manager on a specific project may turn out to be a challenging task. The interplay among the management, personal, and project variables and trade-offs must be carefully evaluated.

The individual candidates for the role will normally have clear-cut concepts of their personal requirements. However, as we pointed out earlier, it is a rare situation or project which will completely satisfy the personal needs of every candidate for the role or neatly supplement or complement the personal capabilities of the Project Manager.

While the general needs of the Contractor and the Client loom large and important, the specific needs of the project become the more compelling and should invariably establish the basic structure of the Assistant Project Manager's role.

However, within the total project needs there will usually be several marked variations in the relative priorities assigned to the various requirements. Moreover, there may be a wide disparity between disciplinary or functional needs on the project which cannot be easily reconciled or encompassed by the placement of any one individual. Finally, not all requirements can be neatly compartmentalized or effectively segmented from many other portions of the project to provide a nicely fenced-in area for the role of the Assistant Project Manager.

The timing of the assignment of the Assistant Project Manager is influenced primarily by the requirements of the project, which vary with time.

For the most part, the project scope and schedule can serve to identify the need dates for special assistance or added attention to certain project activities or events. In the case of very large and complex projects it may be desirable to staff the position coincident with the assignment of the Project Manager. On smaller or less complex projects, and especially those on a low burner in their early phases, it will usually be more prudent and cost effective to delay the assignment. In either case a project learning curve for the Assistant Project Manager should be considered so that when he is required to perform as Project Manager, he will have had time to assimilate the necessary project background and experience to enable him to perform satisfactorily.

While we have so far discussed the role of the Assistant Project Manager as that of a single individual, it should now be apparent that on certain demanding and complex projects two or more Assistant Project Managers may very well be required.

Throughout our discussion we have also consistently used the title "Assistant Project Manager." However, there is no mandatory requirement for this usage. Other titles appropriately matched to the Contractor's and Client's job classification and organizational concepts would also be suitable. Examples might include

- Deputy Project Manager.
- Associate Project Manager.

INTERPRETING THE ROLE

When the basic structure and background needs of the role of the Assistant Project Manager have been reconciled, his position can be implemented and integrated into the project organization.

Essentially there are three elementary organizational arrangements which should be considered, as shown in Figure 5-1. In the first case, the Assistant Project Manager is placed in a staff position relative to the Project Manager. This position is indicative of a more confined or segmented role and connotes a less than full-time backup for the Project Manager. This arrangement is most beneficial when an experienced staff person is assigned to the project to concentrate his expertise on specific

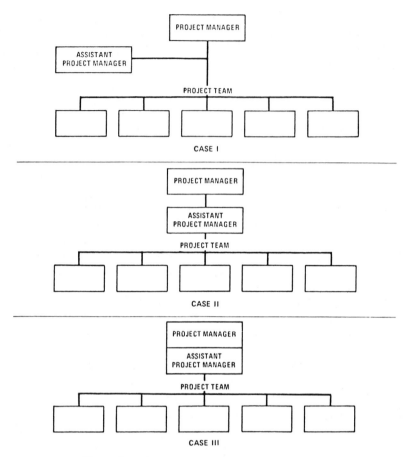

Figure 5-1. Elementary organizational arrangements.

problems. It provides only a minimum opportunity for training the Assistant Project Manager to take over the role of a Project Manager.

In the second case, the Assistant Project Manager is placed in a separate box directly below the Project Manager and with all line functions passing through his office. This organization is more indicative of a strong and rigid role for the Assistant Project Manager; it encompasses all project functions and full-time backup for the Project Manager. However, because of its rigidity this organizational approach may not necessarily increase the Project Manager's span of control and could tend to make the position of Assistant Project Manager a bottleneck.

In the third case, the Assistant Project Manager is placed in the same box with the Project Manager and directly beneath him. This arrangement reflects full-time backup for the Project Manager and a stronger measure of togetherness. The opportunity for increasing the Project Manager's span of control is greater through a sharing of the many duties. At the same time, the Assistant Project Manager may give special attention to certain functional, disciplinary, or other aspects of the project.

There are obvious merits in each approach and there can be several variations of these organizational concepts. In any case, the overriding concern of management should be to design or select the organizational arrangement which will respond best to the project needs and contribute most to project and Contractor/Client Team performance.

Some variations in the role of the Assistant Project Manager can be illustrated by a brief description and discussion of their actual employment in the engineering and construction of three current power generating projects.

ARIZONA NUCLEAR POWER PROJECT (ANPP)

This project for Arizona Public Service (and six other participating utilities) consists of three 1270-MW nuclear units (Palo Verde 1, 2, and 3) sited in south-central Arizona about 55 miles from Phoenix.

A unique feature of the project will be the use of reclaimed sewerage water from the City of Phoenix and six adjoining cities, which will be transported to the site by a large pipeline, to meet the extensive project cooling water makeup requirements.

A simplified version of the basic organization chart is shown in Figure 5-2. The water reclamation and pipeline effort is being handled by another

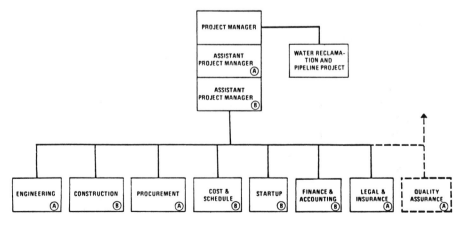

Figure 5-2. Simplified basic organization chart, Arizona Nuclear Power Project.

division of the company under the supervision of a separate Project Manager. This Project Manager reports to the ANPP Project Manager for coordination with the Prime Contract and its supporting documents and for coordination of his efforts on other contractual matters, budgets, procedures, procurement, and field support.

The scope, complexity, cost, and schedule of the total project merit the full-time attention of two Assistant Project Managers. The two were used differently in various stages of the project.

Final Design and Construction Phase.   In this arrangement, Assistant Project Manager A, with a strong background in engineering and project field engineering, directs his primary attention to

- Engineering.
- Procurement.
- Legal and Insurance.
- Quality Assurance.

Assistant Project Manager B, with extensive experience in cost engineering, subcontract management, and planning and scheduling, including home office and field efforts, concentrates his attention on construction, start-up, finance, accounting and cost, and schedule matters.

Both Assistant Project Managers are exposed to the entire range of project operations.

Construction Completion, Plant Start-up, and Contract Closeout.   Currently during this phase and in this arrangement, Assistant Project Manager A (with a background in engineering, business development, and office management) directs his primary attention to closeout efforts on the original Engineering-Procurement-Construction Contract which involves the supervision of Construction, Engineering, and Procurement departments.

Assistant Project Manager B, with extensive experience in start-up, concentrates his attention on completion of engineering, procurement, and construction leading to fuel load of Unit 3 and providing personnel to ANPP to support operation of Units 1 and 2.

SAN ONOFRE UNITS 2 AND 3

This project for Southern California Edison and San Diego Gas and Electric consists of two 1100-MW nuclear units sited on the coast of California about 60 miles south of Los Angeles. The project has been exposed to

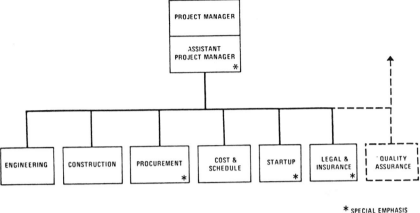

Figure 5-3. Simplified basic organization chart, San Onofre units 2 and 3.

numerous major criteria changes due to the many new regulatory guides issued by the NRC since its inception, and was exposed to extensive public scrutiny by various intervenors and the California Coastal Commission in its early design and licensing stages.

While the project site and Client and Contractor headquarters are within reasonable commuting distances of each other, there are a few significant geographical spreads in the project—for example, the turbine generators are furnished by English Electric.

A simplified version of the basic organization chart is shown in Figure 5-3. There is one very experienced Assistant Project Manager on this project who functions throughout the complete spectrum of the project, but is used extensively on procurement, start-up, and legal and insurance matters. The Assistant Project Manager has also recently been engaged in extensive restructuring/renegotiating of certain major subcontracts with companies experiencing serious financial and production difficulties which posed major problems to the project.

The Assistant Project Manager has a strong background in estimating, cost and schedule control, finance and accounting matters, and engineering administration. Nonetheless, he participates fully in all phases of the project and is a full backup for the Project Manager.

In the later stages of the project a Senior Project Manager was brought in to provide added management support during critical construction completion and start-up activities. The Senior Project Manager is in a direct line position over the Project Manager and Assistant Project Manager. With the original management team intact to direct the day-to-day operation of the project, the Senior Project Manager has the freedom to concentrate his efforts on specific problem areas and make key company, client, and supplier contacts as necessary.

This type of an arrangement shows how the project management concept and organization can be kept flexible to respond to the specific needs of the project.

CORONADO UNITS 1 AND 2

This project for Salt River Project consists of two 350-MW coal-fired units sited in eastern Arizona. Coal sources located along an existing main line railroad are being used. There was a separate design and construction management contract for a 43-mile railroad to handle unit trains of coal from the main line to the site. The railroad effort was designed and the construction managed by another division of the company which had the contract for the power plant.

A simplified version of the basic organization chart is shown in Figure 5-4.

In this situation the primary Project Manager functions as a manager of projects. At one time he had responsibility for three projects.

The primary long-term project is the design, procurement, and construction of the Coronado Generating Station. During the early stages of Coronado, construction and start-up work were being completed on the three 700-MW coal-fired units of the Navajo Project for the same client. A separate Assistant Project Manager for the completion of Navajo worked under the general guidance of the Coronado Project Manager to provide central contact and consistency of approach with the client.

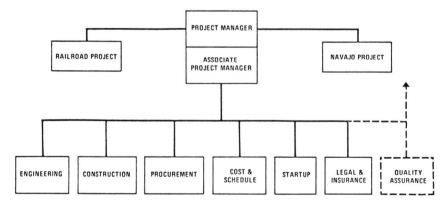

Figure 5-4. Simplified basic organization chart, Coronado units 1 and 2.

ENGINEERING

KEEP CURRENT ON ALL STATUS AND PROGRESS

PROVIDE CONTINUOUS MONITORING TO ENSURE THAT THE DESIGN IS CONSISTENT WITH

COST REDUCTION GOALS

REVIEW MAJOR STUDIES AND BID EVALUATIONS

REVIEW AND CONTINUOUS ENGINEERING AUDIT OF PAST JOB PROBLEMS

ATTEND DESIGN MEETINGS AND ASSIST IN CLIENT PROJECT ENGINEERING RELATIONS

CONSTRUCTION

KEEP CURRENT ON ALL STATUS AND PROGRESS INCLUDING HOUSING FOR CONSTRUCTION

PERSONNEL

PROCUREMENT

REVIEW AND COORDINATE INSPECTION, EXPEDITING AND EQUIPMENT DELIVERIES

PARTICIPATE IN AND CONDUCT BIDDER REVIEW OR PRE-AWARD CONFERENCES AS REQUIRED

COST AND SCHEDULE

CONDUCT INITIAL REVIEW FOR PROJECT MANAGEMENT APPROVAL:

TRENDS

CHANGE NOTIFICATIONS

PROJECT FINANCIAL STATUS REPORT

REVIEW, COORDINATE AND MONITOR FOR FULL IMPLEMENTATION:

COST AND SCHEDULE PROGRAMS (EMPHASIS ON ENG & H.O. COST CONTROL AND

ENGINEERING PROGRESS REPORTING)

SCHEDULE PREPARATION

CONTINUOUSLY MONITOR THE TREND PROGRAM FOR IMPLEMENTATION AND IDENTIFICATION

OF COST TRENDS AND COST REDUCTION ITEMS

COORDINATE IMPLEMENTATION OF SUGGESTED COST REDUCTION AND

EFFICIENCY MEASURES

INSURE THAT NON-REIMBURSABLE COSTS ARE BUDGETED AND CONTROLLED

COST AND SCHEDULE (Continued)

PREPARE CURRENT COMMENTS FOR PROJECT FINANCIAL STATUS REPORT

COORDINATE PREPARATION OF PFSR AND FORECASTS

CLIENT COMMENTS ON BILLINGS

STARTUP

KEEP CURRENT ON ALL STATUS

QUALITY ASSURANCE

REVIEW AND COORDINATE

LABOR RELATIONS AND SAFETY

REVIEW AND COORDINATE PREPARATION OF AFFIRMATIVE ACTION PROGRAM

INSURANCE

REVIEW AND COORDINATE

ADMINISTRATION AND CORRESPONDENCE

COMMUNICATION WITH CLIENT AS REQUIRED

REVIEW AND COORDINATE PREPARATION AND FULL IMPLEMENTATION:

EXTERNAL PROCEDURES

INTERNAL PROCEDURES

PREPARE MINUTES OF PROJECT REVIEW MEETINGS

PREPARE MINUTES OF EXECUTIVE STAFF MEETINGS

PREPARE MONTHLY REPORT

PREPARE WEEKLY REPORT TO MANAGEMENT

COORDINATE AND IMPLEMENT CONTRACT CHANGES INCLUDING NECESSARY COST ESTIMATES

PROJECT TEAM SPACE ARRANGEMENTS

USE OF COMPUTER IN FIELD OFFICE

PUBLISH ACTION ITEMS REPORT

Figure 5-5. Associate Project Manager routine duties.

The other division of the company assigned a Project Manager to direct the design, procurement, and construction management of the railroad spur. This Project Manager also worked under the general guidance of the Coronado Project Manager in order to maintain consistency in client relations and project procedures, and also to obtain close coordination between the field activities.

The Project Manager on the Coronado Project is assisted by an Associate Project Manager who is thoroughly integrated into the basic project. The Associate Project Manager has previous management experience and a strong background in project engineering. In day-to-day operations he concentrates upon the technical engineering interface with the Client and engineering-construction interfaces. The latter effort helps to achieve proper understanding and effective operations between these two major components of the project. Typical routine duties assigned the Associate Project Manager are listed in Figure 5-5.

SUMMARY

While we may have overlooked the role of the Assistant Project Manager in our formal discussions in the past, it is readily apparent that he can be a key man in the organization and can do much to improve the total management and performance of the project team.

The role of the Assistant Project Manager may vary considerably from project to project. There does not appear to be a universal approach which can satisfy all projects. Some of the major considerations in defining the role include the following:

- Special needs of the project.
- Client needs.
- Contractor needs.
- Capabilities and availability of the Project Manager.
- Capabilities and interests of the Assistant Project Manager.
- Geographic spread of activities.
- Various contractual arrangements and their implications.

Notwithstanding the many differences in the three examples we have cited, two very consistent factors stand out:

- All the Project Managers encourage the Assistant Project Manager to actively participate in all facets of the project.

- The experience and capabilities of the Assistant (Associate) Project Managers are being effectively concentrated on those areas of their expertise, while being exposed to the total project.

In the final analysis, the key requirement for the role of the Assistant Project Manager is to provide flexibility on the part of Contractor's management and the Client in best meeting the needs of all.

Section III
Organizational Strategy and Project Management

Project management is a tool for executing overall organizational strategy. Therefore it is inadequate to view project management only within the confines of the project. It must be considered within the context of the overall organization and *its* strategy.

In Chapter 6, William R. King describes the interrelationships of the various elements of business strategy. He demonstrates a method that can be used to ensure that the projects embarked on by an organization are those that are most compatible with its overall mission, strategy, and goals.

William E. Souder's Chapter 7 deals with techniques for evaluating and selecting projects. Project selection is the mechanism by which the organization ensures that it selects the "right," or the "best," projects for funding. A wide range of techniques are reviewed, each of which addresses a different objective and set of measures that may be applied. (The "strategic program evaluation" approach of Chapter 6 is another technique that may be used.)

In Chapter 8, the "owner's" role in strategically managing projects is delineated in specific terms that are as disparate as "resources" and "styles." This chapter integrates the many different dimensions that are necessarily brought into alignment if a project is to effectively contribute to the accomplishment of the organization's mission.

6. The Role of Projects in the Implementation of Business Strategy

William R. King*

There is a good deal of anecdotal evidence concerning business strategies that have failed because they were not implemented or because they were inappropriately implemented. Since projects and programs are the vehicles through which strategy is implemented, such failures strike at the heart of the value of project management to the organization.

In an audit of the existing and planned programs in the central research laboratory of a major diversified firm, the author found

- Programs and projects that could not be associated with any business or corporate objective or strategy.
- Programs and projects which apparently fell outside the stated mission of the corporation or the charter of the laboratory.
- Projects whose funding levels could not reasonably be justified in terms of the expected benefits to be produced.

Such observations have so frequently emanated from less formal analyses in other companies as to suggest the existence of a faulty linkage between corporate plans and strategy and the programs and projects through which they should be implemented.

* William R. King is University Professor in the Katz Graduate School of Business at the University of Pittsburgh. He is the author of more than a dozen books and 150 technical papers that have appeared in the leading journals in the fields of management science, information systems, and strategic planning. Among his major honors are the McKinsey Award (jointly with D. I. Cleland) for the "outstanding contribution to management literature" represented by their book *Systems Analysis and Project Management,* the IIE Book-of-the-Year Award for the first edition of this book, and designation as a fellow of the Decision Sciences Institute. Further biographical information is available in *Who's Who in the World* and *Who's Who in America.*

THE CHOICE ELEMENTS OF CORPORATE STRATEGY

Because of the semantics jungle which exists in the area of business policy and strategy, it is necessary to rather precisely define the terms to be used. The *choice elements of corporate strategy*—those choices that must be explicitly or implicitly made in the corporate strategic planning process—are the *Organization's:*

Mission—the "business" that the organization is in.

Objectives—desired future positions on roles for the organization.

Strategy—the *general direction* in which the objectives are to be pursued.

Goals—specific targets to be sought at specified points in time.

Programs/Projects—resource-consuming sets of activities through which strategies are implemented and goals are pursued.

Resource Allocations—allocations of funds, manpower, etc., to various units, objectives, strategies, programs, and projects.

These informal definitions are meant to provide a common framework for communication rather than to define the "correct" terminology. Various firms may use different terminology, but none can escape the need to make choices of each variety. (These strategic choice elements are treated in more detail elsewhere.*)

Most organizations conduct planning processes which are aimed at explicitly choosing all or some of these strategic choice elements. However, many firms fail to deal with all of the choice elements in the detail and specificity which each deserves.

Often, for instance, missions are dealt with implicitly, as in the case of the firm that responds to the mission concept by stating their mission to be: "We make widgets." Such a product-oriented view of the organization's business ignores new market opportunities and, perhaps, the firm's generic strengths. It is these opportunities and strengths which form the most likely areas for future success. Thus, it is these opportunities and strengths, rather than the current product line, which should define the mission.

Strategies are almost always explicitly chosen by firms, but often strategies are thought of in output, rather than input, terms. In such instances, strategies may be described in terms of expected sales and profits rather

---

* See William R. King and David I. Cleland, *Strategic Planning and Policy,* New York, Van Nostrand Reinhold, 1978, Chapters 3 and 6–9, from which portions of this material are adapted with the permission of the publisher.

than in terms of strategic directions such as product redesign, new products, or new markets.

Thus, the elements of strategic choice are inescapable in the sense that the avoidance of an explicit choice about any of the elements means that it is chosen implicitly. However, many firms make poor or inappropriate choices, both explicitly and implicitly, because they do not have a clear awareness of the relationships among the strategic choice elements and their innate interdependence.

RELATIONSHIPS AMONG THE STRATEGIC CHOICE ELEMENTS

One of the most important conditions for the effective implementation of plans has to do with the relationships among the strategic choice elements. If these relationships are well defined and carefully analyzed and conceived, the plan is likely to be implemented. If they are not, the plan is likely to be a voluminous document that requires substantial time and energy to prepare, but which is filed on the shelf until the next planning cycle commences. Indeed, many plans are so treated precisely because they do not carefully spell out the relationships among various strategic choice elements and therefore do not provide the appropriate information that is necessary to guide the many decisions which must be made to implement the plan and to develop and manage the projects and programs which are the operational essence of the plan.

Figure 6-1 shows the elements of strategic choice in the form of a triangle which illustrates that the mission and objectives are the highest-level elements. They are supported by the other elements—the strategies, goals, programs, and projects. The strategic resource allocations underlie each of these elements.

Figure 6-1. Relationship of strategic choice elements.

Figure 6-2 shows an illustration of these concepts in terms of a business firm. The mission chosen is that of "supplying system components to a worldwide nonresidential air conditioning market." Note that while this mission statement superficially appears to be product-oriented, it identifies the nature of the product (system components), and the market (worldwide nonresidential air conditioning) quite specifically. By exclusion, it guides managers in avoiding proposals for overall systems and strategies that would be directed toward residential markets. However, it does identify the world as the company's territory and (in an elaboration not shown here) defines air conditioning to include "air heating, cooling, cleaning, humidity control, and movement."

Supporting the base of the triangle are strategies, goals, and programs. The firm's strategies are stated in terms of a three-phase approach. First, the company will concentrate on achieving its objectives through existing

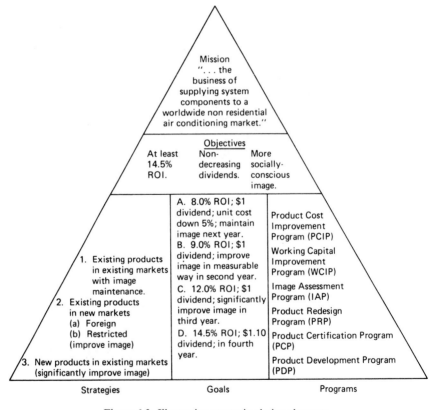

Figure 6-2. Illustrative strategic choice elements.

products and markets while maintaining its existing image. Then, it will give attention to new markets for existing products, foreign and restricted, while improving the company's image. "Restricted" markets may be thought of as those that require product-safety certification before the product can be sold in that market. Finally, it will focus on new products in existing markets while *significantly* improving its image.

Clearly, this is a staged strategy; one that focuses attention first on one thing and then on another. This staging does not imply that the first strategy element is carried through completely before the second is begun; it merely means that the first element is given primary and earliest attention, then the second and third in turn. In effect, the first element of the strategy has its implementation *begun* first. This will be made more clear in terms of goals and programs.

At the right base of the triangle, a number of the firm's programs are identified. Each of these programs is made up of a variety of projects or activities. Each program serves as a focus for various activities having a common goal. For instance, in the case of the Product Cost Improvement Program, the associated projects and activities might be as follows:

- Quality Control Project.
- Production Planning Improvement Project.
- Production Control System Development Project.
- Plant Layout Redesign Project.
- Employee Relations Project.

All of these projects and activities are focused toward the *single* goal of product cost improvement.

In the case of the Working Capital Improvement Program, the various projects and activities might include a "terms and conditions" study aimed at revising the terms and conditions under which goods are sold, an inventory reduction project, etc. Each of the other programs would have a similar collection of projects and activities focused on some single well-defined goal.

The goals are listed in the middle-lower portion of the triangle in Figure 6-2. Each goal is stated in specific and timely terms related to the staged strategy and the various programs. These goals reflect the desire to attain 8.0% ROI (a step along the way to the 14.5% objective) next year, along with a $1 dividend (the current level), a unit cost improvement of 5%, while maintaining image. For subsequent years, the goals reflect a climb to 14.5% ROI, a steady and then increasing dividend, and an increasing and measurable image consistent with the staged strategy that places image improvements later in the staged sequence. This is also consistent with the program structure, which includes an "Image Assessment Program," a program designed to develop methods and measures for quantitatively assessing the company's image.

Figure 6-3 shows the same elements as does Figure 6-2, with each being indicated by number, letter, or acronym. For instance, the block labeled 1 in Figure 6-3 represents the first stage of the strategy in Figure 6-2, the letter A represents next year's goal, etc.

The arrows in Figure 6-3 represent *some* illustrative relationships among the various objectives, programs, strategy elements, and goals. For instance, the arrows a,b, and c reflect direct relationships between specific timely goals and broad timeless objectives:

    a. A, next year's goals primarily relate to the objective of nondecreasing dividends.
    b. B, the second year's goals relate to the "more socially conscious image" objective.
    c. D, the quantitative ROI figure is incorporated as a goal in the fourth year.

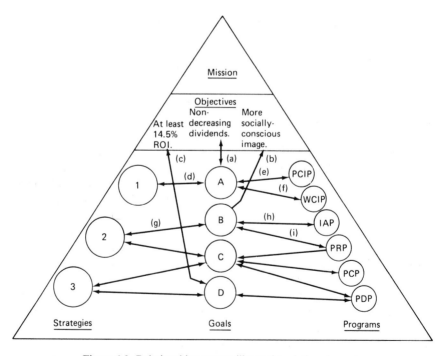

Figure 6-3. Relationships among illustrative choice elements.

Of course, each year's goals relate implicitly or explicitly to all objectives. However, these relationships are some of the most direct and obvious.

Similarly, arrow d in Figure 6-3 relates the first year's goals to the first element of the overall strategy in that these goals for next year are to be attained primarily through the strategy element involving "existing products in existing markets." However, arrows e and f also show that the Product Cost Improvement Program (PCIP) and the Working Capital Improvement Program (WCIP) are also expected to contribute to the achievement of next year's goals.

The second year's goals will begin to reflect the impact of the second strategy element (existing products in new markets) as indicated by arrow g in Figure 6-3. The effect of the Product Redesign Program (PRP) is also expected to contribute to the achievement of these goals (arrow i) as is the Image Assessment Program (IAP) expected to provide an ability to measure image by that time. The other arrows in Figure 6-3 depict other rather direct relationships whose interpretation is left to the reader.

From this figure, relationships among the various strategic decision elements can be seen:

1. Goals are specific steps along the way to the accomplishment of broad objectives.
2. Goals are established to reflect the expected outputs from strategies.
3. Goals are directly achieved through programs.
4. Strategies are implemented by programs.

Thus, the picture shown in Figure 6-3 is that of an interrelated set of strategic factors that demonstrate *what* the company wishes to accomplish in the long run, *how* it will do this in a sequenced and sensible way, and *what performance levels* it wishes to achieve at various points along the way.

STRATEGIC PROGRAM EVALUATION

Figures 6-1 to 6-3 make it clear that the various elements of strategic choice are mutually supportive. However, there remains the question of how this high degree of interdependence can be effectively attained.

Certainly, an understanding of the logical relationships that are depicted in these figures should itself lead to better subjective choices in the planning process. However, while subjective judgment can be appropriately applied at the higher levels of strategic choice because these elements are tractable, it is an inadequate basis for choice at the lower levels of program/project selection and funding.

In other words, no formal techniques are needed in choosing among alternative missions and objectives because these choices must inherently be made on a primitive basis of the personal values and goals of management and other stakeholders. At this level, there are only a few viable options from which choices must be made.

At the level of programs, projects, and resource allocations, quite the opposite is the case. There are many contenders and combinations of contenders to be considered. Thus, some formal approach may be useful. Indeed, such an approach is not only practically useful, but it forms the integrating factor in the array of strategic choice elements.

The integrating factor is a strategic program evaluation approach *which directly utilizes the results of the higher-level strategic choices to evaluate alternative programs, projects, and funding levels.* "Project selection" approaches are well known and widely used in industry for the selection of engineering projects, R&D projects, and new product development projects. However, if program/project evaluation is to be the key link in unifying the array of organizational strategic choice elements, the evaluation framework must itself be an integral element of the strategic plan.

Thus, potential projects and programs must be "filtered" through the application of strategic criteria that are based on the higher-level choices that have previously been made—the organization's mission, objectives, and strategies. The output of this filtering process is a set of rank-ordered project and program opportunities that can serve as a basis for the allocation of resources.

Other important criteria must come into play in implementing this evaluation process. These criteria are those that are *implicit* in a good specification of the organization's mission, objectives, and strategy. However, they must be *specifically addressed* if program and projects are to truly reflect corporate strategy. These criteria are as follows:

1. Does the opportunity take advantage of a *strength* that the company possesses?
2. Correspondingly, does it avoid a dependence on something that is a *weakness* of the firm?
3. Does it offer the opportunity to attain a *comparative advantage* over competitors?
4. Does it contribute to the *internal consistency* of the existing projects and programs?
5. Does it address a *mission-related opportunity* that is presented by the evolving market environment?
6. Is the level of *risk* acceptable?
7. Is it consistent with the established *policy guidelines?*

A Strategic Program Evaluation Illustration

A strategic program/project evaluation framework based on these criteria is shown as Table 6-1. In the leftmost column of the table is a set of evaluation criteria that relates to the example in Figures 6-2 and 6-3. The body of the table shows how a proposed new program to begin manufacturing of system components in Europe might be evaluated.

The "criteria weights" in the second column of the table reflect their relative importance and serve to permit the evaluation of complex project characteristics within a simple framework. A base weight of 20 is used here for the major criteria related to mission, objectives, strategy, and goals. Weights of 10 are applied to the other criteria.

Within each major category, the 20 "points" are judgmentally distributed to reflect the relative importance of subelements or some other characteristic of the criterion. For instance, the three stages of strategy and the four subgoals are weighted to ensure that earlier stages and goals are treated to be more important than later ones. This implicitly reflects the *time value of money* without requiring a complex discounting calculation.

The first criterion in Table 6-1 is the "fit with mission." The proposal is evaluated to be consistent with both the "product" and "market" elements of the mission and is thereby rated to be "very good," as shown by the 1.0 entries in the upper left.

In terms of "consistency with objectives," the proposal is rated to have a 20% chance of being "very good" in contributing to the ROI element of the objectives (see Figure 6-2), a 60% chance of being "good," and a 20% chance of being only "fair," as indicated by the likelihoods entered into the third row of the table. The proposed project is rated more poorly with respect to the "dividends" and "image" elements.

The proposal is also evaluated in terms of its expected contribution to each of the three stages of the strategy as outlined in Figure 6-2. In this case, the proposed project is believed to be one which would principally contribute to stage 2 of the strategy. (Note that only certain assessments may be made in this case since the stages are mutually exclusive and exhaustive.)

The proposal is similarly evaluated with respect to the other criteria.

The overall evaluation is obtained as a weighted score that represents the sum of products of the likelihoods (probabilities) as the 8, 6, 4, 2, 0 arbitrary level weights that are displayed at the top of the table. For instance, the "consistency with objectives—ROI" expected level weight is calculated as

$$0.2(8) + 0.6(6) + 0.2(4) = 6.0$$

Table 6-1. An Example of Strategic Program Evaluation.

PROGRAM PROJECT EVALUATION CRITERIA		CRITERIA WEIGHTS	VERY GOOD (8)	GOOD (6)	FAIR (4)	POOR (2)	VERY POOR (0)	EXPECTED LEVEL SCORE	WEIGHTED SCORE
Fit with mission	Product	10	1.0					8.0	80
	Market	10	1.0					8.0	80
Consistency with objectives	ROI	10	0.2	0.6	0.2			6.0	60
	Dividends	5		0.2	0.6	0.2		4.0	20
	Image	5			0.8	0.2		3.6	18
Consistency with strategy	Stage 1	10					1.0	0	0
	Stage 2	7	1.0					8.0	56
	Stage 3	3					1.0	0	0
Contribution to goals	Goal A	8					1.0	0	0
	Goal B	6	0.8	0.2				7.6	45.6
	Goal C	4		0.8	0.2			5.6	22.4
	Goal D	2					1.0	0	0
Corporate *strength* base		10				0.8	0.2	1.6	16
Corporate *weakness* avoidance		10				0.2	0.8	0.4	4
Comparative advantage level		10	0.7	0.3				7.4	74
Internal consistency level		10	1.0					8.0	80
Mission-related opportunity		10	1.0					8.0	80
Risk level acceptability		10				0.7	0.3	1.4	14
Policy guideline consistency		10			1.0			4.0	40
Total score									690

This is then multiplied by the criterion weight of 10 to obtain a weighted score of 60. The weighted scores are then summed to obtain an overall evaluation of 690.

Of course, this number in isolation is meaningless. However, when various programs and projects are evaluated in terms of the same criteria, their overall scores provide a reasonable basis for developing a ranking of projects that reflects their consistency with strategy. Such a ranking can be the basis for resource allocation since the top-ranked program is presumed to be the most worthy, the second-ranked is the next most worthy, etc.

SUMMARY

The strategic program evaluation framework that is developed and demonstrated here provides the integrating factor that is necessary if strategic plans are to be effectively implemented. The critical element of the evaluation approach is its use of criteria which ensure that programs will be integrated with the mission, objectives, strategy, and goals of the organization as well as criteria that reflect critical elements of strategy such as business strengths, weaknesses, comparative advantages, internal consistency, opportunities, and policies.

7. Selecting Projects That Maximize Profits**

William E. Souder*

INTRODUCTION

Project selection is one of the most important decisions managers make. No matter how well it is managed, a poorly chosen project can never be a winner. If a better project could have been selected, then a real opportunity has been forgone and real profits have been lost.

Most organizations will never see these lost profits. This is especially true if the project is well managed, achieves its target dates, and does not overrun its budget. Any thoughts about lost opportunities will be obscured by the euphoria that accompanies a job well done. However, the passing of time will dramatically distinguish those organizations that select the best projects. They will survive.

Thus, it is vitally important to the long-term future of every organization to select only the very best projects. Inferior projects must be identified and screened out as early as possible in the decision-making processes.

This chapter presents the state of the art in project selection techniques. All of these techniques are relatively inexpensive to use, compared with the benefits they provide.

** Selected portions of the material herein originally appeared in WM E. Souder, "A System for using R&D Project Evaluation Methods," *Research Management* Vol 21, No 5, September 1978, pp. 29–37, by permission.

* William E. Souder is Professor of Industrial Engineering and Engineering Management, and Director of the Technology Management Studies Institute, Department of Industrial Engineering, University of Pittsburgh, Pittsburgh, Pennsylvania 15261.

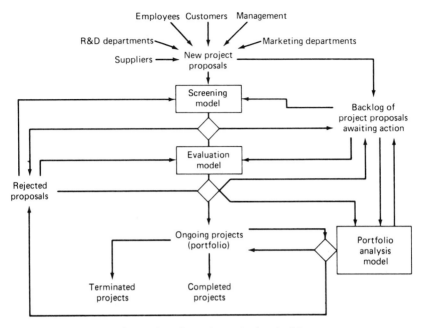

Figure 7-1. Illustration of a project selection decision process.

PROJECT SELECTION

Figure 7-1 depicts the range of project selection activities that normally occurs continuously in most organizations. Screening models provide useful preliminary information for distinguishing candidate projects, on the basis of a few prominent criteria. Evaluation models provide a more rigorous and comprehensive analysis of candidates which survive the screening model. Portfolio models can be used to determine an optimum budget allocation among those projects which survive the evaluation model.

Projects that survive these models may be backlogged to await the release of critical manpower or other resources. Backlogged projects will normally be retrieved at some later point in time; rejected projects will not. However, new information or changed circumstances may suddenly make a previously rejected project more attractive, or may cause a previously backlogged project to be rejected.

Thus, project selection processes are very dynamic. As time passes, screening, evaluation, and portfolio decisions may be repeated many times in response to changing information states, changes in the available

Table 7-1. Example of a Profile Model

CRITERIA OR REQUIREMENTS	EXTENT TO WHICH PROJECTS X AND Y MEET THE CRITERIA		
	High	Medium	Low
Reliability	X		Y
Maintainability	Y	X	
Safety		X	Y
Cost-Effectiveness	X	Y	
Durability	X		Y

X = project X's score   Y = project Y's score

resources and funds, changes in project achievements, or the arrival of new project proposals.

SCREENING MODELS

Profile Models

An example of a profile model is shown in Table 7-1. Note that the ratings are qualitative in nature. No numerical assessments are made. Rather, the project proposals are compared on the basis of a subjective evaluation of their attributes. These evaluations could be done by one individual or by group consensus. Alternatively, the profiles developed by several informed individuals could be compared (1, 2).

Profile models are simple and easy to use. They display the project characteristics and ratings in such a way that they are easily communicated and readily visualized. For instance, in Table 7-1 it is apparent at a glance that project X is generally a high performer, superior to project Y on all the criteria but one.

On the other hand, a profile model does not tell us anything about the trade-offs among the criteria. For example, the profile model in Table 7-1 does not tell us if the high performances of project X on reliability, cost-effectiveness, and durability compensate for its medium performances on maintainability and safety. Thus, there is no way to get a single overall score or rating for each project.

Checklists

Table 7-2 shows an example of a checklist. This type of model assumes that the decision maker can distinguish between several finite levels of the

Table 7-2. Example of a Checklist

CRITERIA OR REQUIREMENTS	TOTAL SCORE	CRITERION SCORES[a]				
		-2	-1	0	$+1$	$+2$
Project X	+5					
Reliability						✓
Maintainability					✓	
Safety					✓	
Cost-Effectiveness					✓	
Durability					✓	
Project Y	−2					
Reliability			✓			
Maintainability						✓
Safety				✓		
Cost-Effectiveness					✓	
Durability				✓		
Project Z	+5					
Reliability						✓
Maintainability						✓
Safety				✓		
Cost-Effectiveness					✓	
Durability					✓	

[a]*Scoring Scale:*
  +2 = Best possible performance
  +1 = Above average performance
   0 = Average performance
  −1 = Below average performance
  −2 = Worst possible performance

criteria or requirements (3, 4). Each candidate proposal or project is then subjectively evaluated by the decision maker and assigned a criterion score on each requirement. The criterion score is ascertained from a predesignated scoring scale that translates subjective evaluations into numerical scores. A total score is obtained for each project by summing its criterion scores. In general, for a checklist model

$$T_j = \sum_i s_{ij} \qquad (1)$$

Here, T_j is the total score for the jth project and s_{ij} is the score for project j on the ith requirement or criterion.

Checklist models improve on profile models by providing both a graphic profile of check marks and an overall total score for each candidate project. An analysis of target achievements and a comparison of several candidate projects is facilitated by the total scores. For instance, a total score of +2 or greater may be specified as a cut-off point for acceptable proposals. Projects could be priority classified by specifying total score ranges, for example, $T_j > +3$ is a high-priority project, $+1 \le T_j \le +3$ is a medium-priority project, etc.

Scoring Models

It is a short step from checklist models to scoring models. In a scoring model, each of $j = 1, \ldots, n$ candidate projects are scored on each of $i = 1, \ldots, m$ performance requirements or criteria. The criterion scores for each project are then combined with their respective criterion importance weights w_i to achieve a total score T_j for each project. Projects may then be ranked according to their T_j values.

For example, a simple additive scoring model would be

$$T_j = \sum_i w_i s_{ij} \qquad (2)$$

where s_{ij} is the score for project j on the ith criterion, and w_i is the criterion weight. This model is illustrated in Table 7-3.

The influence of the weights becomes apparent if one compares the results for the Weighted Scores in Table 7-3 with the results for the Total Scores in Table 7-2. The Criterion Scores in Table 7-3 contain the same information as the Criterion Scores in Table 7-2. The difference is simply a scale transformation; each Criterion Score in Table 7-3 is +3 larger than its counterpart in Table 7-2. The Weighted Scores in Table 7-3 show that projects X and Z do indeed differ. The checklist model (Table 7-2) did not show any difference between the Total Scores for these two projects. Scoring models are more accurate because they take the trade-offs between the criteria into account, as defined by the criterion weights (2, 4, 5).

Frontier Models

Figure 7-2 illustrates the outputs from a frontier model for seven different projects. The projects are plotted in such a way as to show their relative risks and returns. "Risk" expresses the project's chances of failure. This may be measured as $1 - p$, where p is the project's probability of success. Or it may be measured in terms of the likelihood that the project will *not* achieve some desired level of output, profit, etc. "Return" expresses the project's anticipated profits, sales, or some other measure of value which the decision maker wishes to use.

Table 7-3. Example of an Additive Scoring Model

CRITERION, i	CRITERION WEIGHT, w_i	$\times$	CRITERION SCORE,* s_{ij}	$=$	WEIGHTED SCORE
Project X:					
Reliability	4		5		20
Maintainability	2		3		6
Safety	3		3		9
Cost-Effectiveness	5		5		25
Durability	1		4		4
				$T_1 =$	64
Project Y:					
Reliability	4		1		4
Maintainability	2		5		10
Safety	3		2		6
Cost-Effectiveness	5		3		15
Durability	1		2		2
				$T_2 =$	37
Project Z:					
Reliability	4		5		20
Maintainability	2		5		10
Safety	3		2		6
Cost-Effectiveness	5		4		20
Durability	1		4		4
				$T_3 =$	60

*Scale: 5 = Excellent, . . . , Poor = 1

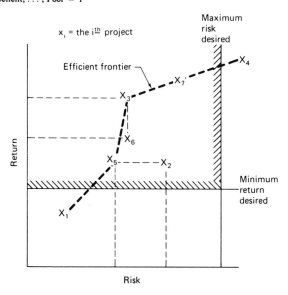

Figure 7-2. Illustration of a frontier model.

The efficient frontier in Figure 7-2 tracks the path of the most efficient return/risk ratios. For example, project 5 (denoted as X_5 in Figure 7-2) is more return/risk efficient than project 2 (denoted as X_2). Project 5 has the same return as project 2, but it has a lower risk level. Similarly, project 3 is more return/risk efficient than project 6 because of its higher return at the same risk level as project 6. The maximum desired risk and the minimum desired return levels established by the organization are also depicted in Figure 7-2. Acceptable projects must fall in the region formed by these boundaries. Thus, Figure 7-2 shows that a decision maker should accept projects 3, 5, and 7 and reject the others.

Frontier models are often very useful for examining returnrisk trade-offs within the organizational objectives. For instance, Figure 7-2 shows that the high-risk and high-return project 4 is ruled out by its high risk level. Yet its incremental return/risk ratio is the same as the acceptable projects 3 and 7. (All of these projects lie on the same line.) Thus, the decision maker may want to make an exception and retain project 4 for further study and analyses.

Frontier models may be used to indicate the need for greater diversification in idea generation and project proposals (3, 5). For example, Figure 7-2 shows that the acceptable projects are primarily of the medium- to high-risk variety. Whether or not the portfolio ought to be more diversified must be resolved on the basis of the organization's goals and objectives. A frontier model can only point out trends and situations for further analysis (3, 6, 7).

Using Screening Models

Screening models are very useful for weeding out those projects which are the least desirable. Since screening models are quick and inexpensive to use, they can economize on the total evaluation efforts by reducing the number of projects to be further evaluated. Because they require a relatively small amount of input data, they can be used where the projects are not well understood or where a minimum of data are available.

However, screening models don't provide much depth of information. And they usually are not sensitive to many of the finer distinctions between the projects. Rather, screening models are like a coarse sieve that provides a partial separation but permits some undesirables to pass through. Thus, screening models can be very useful for some applications. But the decision maker should not expect them to provide a comprehensive or complete analysis.

EVALUATION MODELS

Economic Index Models

An index model is simply a ratio between two variables, and the index is their quotient. Changing the values of the variables changes the value of the quotient, or the index.

An example of a commonly used index model is the return on investment (ROI) index model

$$\text{ROI Index} = \frac{\sum_i R_i/(1 + r)^i}{\sum_i I_i/(1 + r)^i} \tag{3}$$

where R_i is the net dollar returns expected from the project in the ith year, I_i is the investment expected to be made in the ith year, and r is an interest rate. The numerator of equation 3 is the present worth of all future revenues generated by the project, and the denominator is the present worth cost of all future investments.

Some other examples of index models are shown in Table 7-4. Ansoff's model uses both dollar values and index numbers as input data. The index numbers T and B are judgments. Olsen's index is a variation on Ansoff's index that uses all dollar input data. Viller's index is a kind of return on investment model, discounted by the compound likelihood of the project's success. Disman's index looks at the expected earnings over and above the cost to complete the project (2, 5).

Table 7-4. Examples of Index Models

Ansoff's Index

Project Figure of Merit $= \dfrac{rdp(T + B)E}{\text{Total Investment}}$

Olsen's Index

Project Value Index $= \dfrac{rdp\, SP\, n}{\text{Project Cost}}$

Viller's Index

Project Index $= rdp \left(\dfrac{E - R}{\text{Total Investment}} \right)$

Disman's Index

Project Return $= rp(E - R)$

Key: r = the probability of research success, d = the probability of development success, p = the probability of market success, T and B are respective indexes of technical and business merit, E = the present worth of all future earnings from the project, S = annual sales volume in units, P = unit profit, n = number of years of product life, R = present worth cost of research and development activities to complete the project

The single-number index or score that is produced by an index model can be used to rate and rank candidate projects. An example of the use of an index model is shown in Table 7-5. The index model is

$$V = \frac{P \times R}{C} \tag{4}$$

where V is the index. Four projects are evaluated using this model, and their relative rankings on the index V are shown in the last column of Table 7-5. Two projects, project 4 and project 5, are tied for first place in the rankings.

These hypothetical results point up some of the weaknesses of index models. One such weakness is the implicit trade-offs that often occur. For example, in computing the V index, project 5's lower cost compensates for its lower probability of success. This is why project 5 is as good as project 4 on the V index. However, any decision maker who wishes to avoid high risks would never rank project 5 as high as project 4. Note that project 5 has a risk of failure of $1 - P_5 = 1 - .4 = .6$. In fact, instead of ranking it first, the risk-averse decision maker might completely eliminate project 5 from any consideration at all. Thus, the index model in Table 7-5 may be completely inappropriate for some decision makers. It could lead them to make completely wrong decisions relative to their objectives.

This example shows that all index models should be carefully examined for their internal trade-offs. Unless the trade-offs are representative of those the decision maker would actually be willing to make, the model is inappropriate.

Another weakness of many index models is the sensitivity of the index to changes in some of their parameters. As an illustration, let us examine what happens to the V index as one goes from project 4 to project 1 in Table 7-5. The return increases by 50% (from $80,000 to $120,000). The

Table 7-5. Example of the Use of an Index Model

	RETURN (R)	COST (C)	PROBABILITY OF SUCCESS (P)	$V = \dfrac{P \times R}{C}$	RANKING
Project 4	$ 80,000	$2,000	.7	28	1st tie
Project 5	70,000	1,000	.4	28	1st
Project 1	120,000	2,000	.2	12	2nd
Project 3	10,000	1,000	.7	7	3rd
Project 2	10,000	1,000	.3	3	4th

risk goes from $1 - P_4 = .3$ to $1 - P_1 = .8$, for a 167% increase. Yet the V index falls by only 57%: from $V_4 = 28$ to $V_1 = 12$. Thus, these analyses show that this index model is relatively insensitive to risks. In fact, this is a biased model; it is biased toward obscuring risks.

Still another weakness of index models lies in their inability to consider multiple objectives. Because of this, an index model may be inappropriate. For example, suppose that the decision maker also wishes to diversify the portfolio, in addition to achieving high V values. Then, the decision maker might accept project 3 (Table 7-5) because it is a relatively inexpensive way (low-cost project) to get a high-probability project. Having some high-probability projects in the portfolio may be important. This may be especially true if the high-cost and high-risk project 1 is included in the portfolio. Yet the index model ranked project 3 next to last, because it could not incorporate this other objective for diversification into its analyses.

Of course, no index model can include everything. Index models are appealing because of their simplicity and ease of use. That is, they are attractive because they don't include everything. But the decision maker should be wary; index models can be deceptively appealing. Before placing great faith in the outputs from an index model, the decision maker should make sure that the model is unbiased and appropriate.

Risk Analysis Models

A risk analysis model provides a complete picture of the distribution of outcomes for each alternative project. An illustration of a risk analysis approach to the comparison of two candidate projects is shown in Figure 7-3. Project 1 has a most likely lifetime profit of $100 million, and project 2 has a most likely lifetime profit of $150 million. However, there is only a .4 probability that project 2 will in fact achieve the $150 million level. There is a .8 probability that project 1 will achieve the $100 million level. Project 2 provides an opportunity to achieve a larger profit than project 1. But it also carries some downside risk relative to project 1. In fact, there is a .3 probability that project 2 will yield lower profits than project 1, as shown in Figure 7-3. Given these data, a risk averter would be inclined to select project 1. Project 1 has a high chance of achieving a moderate profit, with very little chance of anything less or greater. A gambler would be more inclined to select project 2, which has a small chance at a larger profit. Thus, the risk analysis approach makes the risk-averter and gambler strategies more visible, thereby permitting a decision maker to consciously select decisions consistent with one of these chosen strategies.

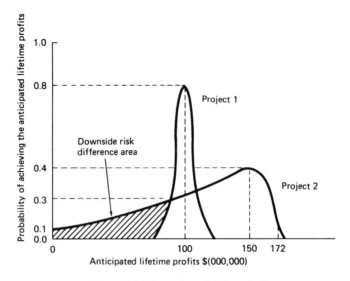

Figure 7-3. Illustration of risk analysis.

A picture like Figure 7-3 is usually not difficult to construct from a relatively small amount of data. Common methods for developing performance distributions for risk analysis include curve-fitting techniques, Monte Carlo simulation methods and modeling techniques (2, 8).

Value-Contribution Models

An example of a value-contribution (V-C) model is given in Table 7-6. Value-contribution models permit the decision maker to examine the degree of contribution which a project makes to the organization's hierarchy of goals.

To develop a V-C model, first list the organizational goals as a nested hierarchy. For instance, as shown in Table 7-6, there are two supergoals: short-range and long-range. Within each of these two supergoals, there are several subgoals. Within the short-range supergoal, the organization desires to achieve new product dominance and a profitability target, and to reduce their present environmental impacts. Within the long-range supergoal, the organization desires to maintain their technological state-of-art and market share.

The second step in developing a V-C model is value-weighting the goals. In the model illustrated in Table 7-6, the long-range and short-range supergoals are respectively value-weighted as $V = 60$ and $V = 40$. Note

Table 7-6. Value-Contribution Model*

PROJECT COSTS $ (000)	SHORT RANGE ORGANIZATIONAL GOALS (V = 60)			LONG RANGE ORGANIZATIONAL GOALS (V = 40)		TOTAL VALUE-CONTRIBUTION SCORE
	ACHIEVE NEW PRODUCT DOMINANCE (V = 30)	ACHIEVE THE PROFITABILITY TARGET (V = 20)	REDUCE ENVIRONMENTAL IMPACTS (V = 10)	MAINTAIN THE TECHNOLOGICAL STATE-OF-ART (V = 25)	MAINTAIN MARKET SHARE (V = 15)	
			SCORES			
Project A	$100	30	20	5	15	5	75
Project B	200	15	10	10	20	10	65
Project C	150	25	10	5	15	10	65

Normalized Value-Contribution:

Project A: $75 \div \$100,000 = \$75.0 \times 10^{-5}$
Project B: $65 \div \$200,000 = \$32.5 \times 10^{-5}$
Project C: $65 \div \$150,000 = \$43.3 \times 10^{-5}$

Rankings: Project A   1st
Project C   2nd
Project B   3rd

*V = the goal value-weight

that these values must sum to 100. That is, the value-weights are determined by allocating a total of 100 points among the supergoals according to their relative importance. In Table 7-6, the value-weights indicate that the short-range supergoal is one and one-half times as important as the long-range supergoal. Within each supergoal, the total points are similarly spread among the subgoals, in such a way as to indicate their relative importance. The complete set of value-weights thus indicates the level of value contribution which a project could make. For instance, a perfect project would score 30 on "Achieve New Product Dominance." Thus, a project with a perfect contribution to all the goals would have a total value contribution score of 100 points.

The actual scaling and scoring of the candidate projects within a V-C model can be done individually or by consensus. Value-weights and scoring scales can be constructed using value assessment methods or scoring model techniques (2, 3).

In the illustration in Table 7-6, project A is short-range oriented, project B is more long-range oriented, and project C is about evenly oriented to both the long and the short range. Project A has perfect scores on the new product dominance and profitability subgoals. It has less-than-perfect scores on the other goals. But because project A is more oriented toward the short range, it contributes more towards these higher-valued subgoals. Thus, it has the highest overall total value-contribution (last column of Table 7-6). Since the total costs of the projects vary, the total value-contribution scores must be normalized by dividing them by their respective project costs. These resulting normalized value-contribution scores may then be used to rank the candidates, as shown in the lower half of Table 7-6.

V-C models permit the decision maker to think in terms of the goal-orientedness of the candidate projects, and the levels of goal achievements. V-C models may also be useful when the decision maker is trying to assemble a balanced portfolio of several projects. For instance, the results in Table 7-6 show that projects A and B together provide the maximum contributions to the short-range subgoals, and they jointly make major contributions to the long-range subgoals.

Using Evaluation Models

Evaluation models are useful when the decision maker feels a need to have a more detailed and in-depth analysis than screening models can provide. Evaluation models permit the decision maker to make much finer discriminations between the candidate projects. On the other hand, evaluation models generally require a much greater volume and detail of data than screening models. Some evaluation models require finite numbers for life-cycle sales volumes, probabilities of success, and other parameters that may be very difficult to estimate.

In spite of the difficulties in applying them, evaluation models clearly have a place. There are times when it is difficult to make a decision without the kind of data and information that go into an evaluation model. Thus, by using the model as a guideline, the decision maker will be urged to more carefully search out and analyze the proper information. In many cases, using an evaluation model with only approximate data and rough estimates can be revealing and helpful to the decision maker.

PORTFOLIO MODELS

The Portfolio Problem

Table 7-7 illustrates the use of a portfolio model. The objective is to determine the best allocation of the available funds among the three alternative candidate projects. Projects A, B, and C each have four alternative funding levels: $0, $100,000, $200,000, and $300,000. The expected profits from the projects vary with these funding levels, as shown in Table 7-7. The higher funding levels result in improved products, which yield higher expected profits.

Several alternative allocations of the available $300,000 are possible. For instance, the funds can all be allocated to project C, for an expected profit return of $350 million. In this case, the other two projects would be zeroed out—no money would be spent on them. The available funds could also be spread evenly across the three projects. This would yield an expected profit return of $100 million + $120 million + $10 million = $230

Table 7-7. Illustration of a Portfolio Model

AVAILABLE FUNDS = $300,000			
ALTERNATIVE FUNDING LEVELS FOR EACH PROJECT	EXPECTED PROFITS ($M)		
	PROJECT A	PROJECT B	PROJECT C
$ 0	$ 0	$ 0	$ 0
100,000	100	120	10
200,000	250	285	215
300,000	310	335	350
Optimum Portfolio	*Expected Profits*		
Project A $100,000	$100M		
Project B 200,000	285M		
$300,000	$385M		

million. This is inferior to the above alternative of funding only project C at its upper limit. Continued searching will show that the optimum allocation is to fund project A at its $100,000 level, to fund project B at its $200,000 level, and to zero out project C. This portfolio yields the largest possible total expected profits, as shown in Table 7-7. There is no other allocation of the available funds that will achieve higher total expected profits.

It should be clear from this illustration that there are occasions when it may be more fruitful to purposely fund some projects at their lowest levels (project A) or to completely reject other projects (project C), in order to marshal funds for more productive uses (project B). The simple problem shown in Table 7-7 can be readily solved by enumerating and comparing all the alternative allocations. But when there are many candidate projects or alternative funding levels, operations research techniques and mathematical programming models are often used. These models have the advantage that various constraints may be included to insure that the portfolio is balanced for risk, or that exploratory research projects will not be disadvantaged in competing with other projects.

Mathematical Programming Methods for Portfolio Problems

In a portfolio model, candidate projects are implicitly prioritized by the amount of funds allocated to them. The general format of all such models is

$$\max \sum_j v_j(x_j) \qquad (5)$$

$$\text{subject to } \sum_j x_j \leq B \qquad (6)$$

where x_j is a project expenditure, B is the total budget for $j = 1, \ldots, n$ candidates (projects) for funding, and the value function, $v_j(x_j)$, can be nonlinear, linear, or single-valued. In the single-valued case (one value of v_j and one cost x_j for each jth project), the portfolio model is an index model with v_j as the prioritizing index.

A variety of "values" may be used in equation 5 above. Many portfolio models use expected values, so that equation 5 becomes

$$\max \sum_j v_j p_j(x_j) \qquad (7)$$

where $p_j(x_j)$ is the probability of achieving v_j. Other portfolio models use a total score, for example, a T_j "value" from a scoring model. In addition to equation 6, a typical constraint is

$$b_j^- \le x_j \le b_j^+ \qquad (8)$$

where b_j^- and b_j^+ are lower and upper project expenditure bounds. Also, portfolio models have been developed for multiple time periods, for example,

$$\max \sum_{ij} v_{ij}(x_{ij}) \qquad (9)$$

$$\text{subject to } \sum_{ij} x_{ij} \le B \qquad (10)$$

where $i = 1, \ldots , m$ time periods.

Literally hundreds of portfolio models have been proposed in the literature. Several literature reviews are available which summarize and evaluate these models (5, 9, 10, 11, 12).

GROUP AND ORGANIZATIONAL MODELS

Need for Structured Group Processes

Project selection decisions that are performed in organizational and group settings are often deeply infuenced by many human emotions, desires, and departmental loyalties. Many different parties normally become involved in the project selection decision-making process, either as suppliers of decision data and information, as champions of projects, as influencers, or as decision makers. Unless a spirit of trust and openness is felt by these parties, it is not likely that essential information will be completely and openly exchanged. Each involved party must come to appreciate the interpersonal needs of the other participants, and the larger missions of the organization vis-αa-vis their own wants. In order to achieve a total organizational consensus and commitment to a final decision, those involved must fully comprehend the nature of the proposed projects. This means that they must have a depth of factual knowledge. It also means that the parties must have a complete awareness of their own feelings, since much of the decision data are highly personal. Many decision settings fail because the participants' feelings are not crystallized and they have not fully exchanged their feelings. Thus, there is a need for a technique that bridges these behavioral gaps which are peculiar to organizational and group decision-making settings. A structured decision-making approach called the QS/NI process has been found to meet this need (2, 3).

The QS/NI Process

Though complex psychometric phenomena underly it (1, 2, 3), the mechanics of the Q-sorting (QS) method are relatively simple, as outlined in Table 7-8. Using this procedure, each participant sequentially sorts the projects into five priority categories.

Each individual who "Q-sorts" a set of candidate projects does so according to his own perceptions and understandings of their relative value. The result is a kind of prioritizing of the candidate projects, according to their perceived value (1, 2).

The nominal-interacting (NI) decision process begins with a "nominal" period in which each individual in the group silently and anonymously Q-

Table 7-8. The Q-Sorting Method

STEPS	RESULTS AT EACH STEP
1. For each participant in the exercise, assemble a deck of cards, with the name and description of one project on each card.	Original deck
2. Instruct each participant to divide the deck into two piles, one representing a high priority, the other a low priority level. (The piles need not be equal).	High level / Low level
3. Instruct each participant to select cards from each pile to form a third pile representing the medium priority level.	High level / Medium level / Low level
4. Instruct each participant to select cards from the high level pile to yield another pile representing the very high level of priority; select cards from the low level pile representing the very low level of priority.	Medium level; V. high level / High level / Low level / V. low level
5. Finally, instruct each participant to survey the selections and shift any cards that seem out of place until the classifications are satisfactory.	

sorts the candidate projects. These results are then tabulated in a tally chart and displayed to the entire group. The tally chart focuses on the group consensus process and the agreement-disagreement statistics, without revealing who voted for what.

The group is then given an "interacting" period in which they discuss the results in the tally chart. During this period, they may share and exchange data and rationales, they may challenge each other, etc. To help guide the group in their accommodation patterns, group process measures may be taken and periodically fed back to the group. These measures generally indicate whether the group is becoming more or less cohesive and suggest what they can do to improve their team potency. It is left up to the group to decide whether or not to take these potency-improving actions (2, 13, 14).

This QS/NI sequence of an individual Q-sort in a nominal setting followed by a group discussion or interacting period can be repeated for several rounds. Experience shows that two or three rounds are needed to stimulate complete information exchange, but more than four rounds dissipates the participants. The first nominal Q-sort period permits individuals to document their own thoughts and value judgments. The subsequent first interacting period confronts the group with a diversity of opinions to be resolved. The second nominal Q-sort period permits each individual to privately restructure his or her thoughts. The second interacting period provides an opportunity to refine opinions and work toward consensus. A third nominal Q-sort period provides the environment for closure and consensus. A consensus will usually emerge as the members adopt ideas and opinions from each other, acquire more information and interpersonal understandings, or become influenced by the enthusiasm of the group. The tally chart itself is consensus-inducing for those members who identify with the group effort (1, 2, 13, 14).

Table 7-9 presents an illustration of the tally charts for two rounds of the QS/NI process, for a twenty-person group, voting on seven projects. The arrows trace the changes in the individual Q-sorts from the first to the second nominal period. Note that the degree of consensus actually declined during this part of the exercise for project G. In this case, the discussion revealed a heretofore hidden lack of information and a fundamental lack of comprehension of this project by some of the subjects. This proposal was returned to the submitter for additional work, followed by resubmittal. A consensus was reached on this resubmitted project at the end of a third round of the QS/NI process. As shown in Table 7-9, the other projects rapidly converged to a strong consensus. Note the high incidence of "block voting" or coalition voting among these data, in

Table 7-9. Illustration of Results from the QS-NI Process

Projects		A	B	C	D	E	F	G
Categories	Very high priority	(=)	—	≢	(≡)	=	(≡)	(≡) (≡)
	High priority	(≢)	(≡)	≢	(≡)	(≡)	(≡) (—)	(≡)
	Intermediate priority	=	≢	≢	(≡)	≢	≢ = (—)	(≡) =
	Low priority	≡	(≡)	(≡)	≡	(≡)	(—)	(=)
	Very low priority	(≢)	(≡)		≡	(≡)		
1st round	K.S. test [a] D =	.10	.15	.25	.10	.05	.15	.40
	p =	>.20	>.20	<.15	>.20	>.20	>.20	<.05
	Consensus? [b]	No	No	T	No	No	No	T
2nd round	K.S. test [a] D =	.40	.60	.40	.65	.40	.35	.25
	p =	<.05	<.01	<.05	<.01	<.05	<.05	<.15
	Consensus? [b]	Yes	Yes	Yes	Yes	Yes	Yes	No

[a] Kolmogorov-Smirnov one-sample test of significance. The null hypothesis is that the cumulative observed distribution of votes (for that project) is not different from the cumulative rectangular distribution. D is the largest absolute difference between the observed and rectangular distributions for any category, divided by N. See: Sidney Siegel, *Nonparametric Statistics* (McGraw-Hill: New York, 1965), pp. 47–52.

[b] Group consensus for a single category exists where it contains 50% more votes than any other category and $p \leq .10$ in the K.S. test ($p \leq .10$ can exist for bimodally distributed votes). T indicates a tendency for consensus, in that two adjacent categories contain $\geq 2/3$ of the votes.

which small clusters of three to five persons are voting alike and changing their votes in a like manner. This is a common phenomenon in QS/NI exercises. The QS/NI process usually reveals a great deal about group interaction patterns and interpersonal power play strategies. Coalitions and advocate and adversary positions are usually made very visible by the QS/NI process (13, 14).

INTEGRATED SYSTEMS

Challenged by the need to explicitly take organizational and group processes into account, project selection model builders have taken two approaches: behavioral decision aids (BDA) and decentralized hierarchical modeling (DHM). In the BDA (behavioral decision aid) approach, group process techniques are overlain on classical and/or portfolio models to make them more organizationally effective. Note that Q-sorting is a BDA. So is the NI process. Overlaying project selection models with group processes in this way changes the entire philosophy of their use. Without a BDA, project selection models are inherently viewed as *means* to decide on the *best* projects. With a BDA, the models become *aids* to intergroup *communication and interpersonal interaction*. Decisions about the best projects become obvious once all the parties have complete information and their biases and fears have been dissipated. BDAs are vehicles for achieving this.

In the DHM (decentralized hierarchical modeling) approach, the parties to the decision dialogue via computer terminals until a consensus portfolio is arrived at. As illustrated in Figure 7-4, the process is initiated by top management sending budgetary guidelines to the divisional managers.

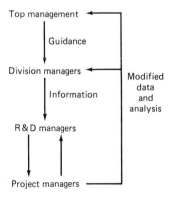

Figure 7-4. A DHM process.

Divisional managers react to these guidelines, modify them to fit their perceived circumstances, suggest prioritized program areas, and send all this information to the R&D managers. The R&D managers and the project management staff then confer to develop a proposed portfolio that fits the guidelines, and to calculate the value of their proposed portfolio vis-à-vis the given guidelines and goals. Cost-benefit calculations and project selection models are often used here. These results are sent back up by the hierarchy, with comments and analyses solicited at each stage. Top management reviews all this information and sends modified guidelines back down the hierarchy for another iteration. This process may be recycled several times, until all the parties come to consensus. The computer programs perform all the calculations, permitting all the information to be recalled in various formats (15, 17).

Because this process is carried out on a network of computer terminals, the number of face-to-face meetings is minimized and productivity increases. The process combines the features of electronic mail and interactive decision making, while still leaving the participants free to think and react in the privacy of their own offices. The process is a natural one: it follows the flow of most organizational budgeting exercises. Because it minimizes the number of face-to-face meetings, there are indications that this process avoids the social pressures and bandwagon effects that so often characterize face-to-face meetings. The DHM process appears to foster a more open and complete exchange of information, resulting in the selection of more effective projects and the enthusiastic support of these programs.

BDA and DHM systems elevate project selection models to their proper role as real decision aids. Integrated BDA/DHMs allow project selection models to be used as a *laboratory* for testing policies, sharing opinions, asking "what if" questions, and stimulating interdepartmental interactions throughout the *entire organization*.

SUMMARY

The selection of the best projects is a very important decision problem for project managers. Today's projects entail very large commitments which have the potential to become enormous regrets if an inferior project is selected.

Techniques, models, and integrated systems are available to aid in project screening, evaluation, and selection decision making. As Table 7-10 shows, the choice of one over another will depend on the nature of the projects being assessed and the decision problem at hand (1, 2, 3, 5, 15, 16, 17).

Table 7-10. Guide to Applying Project Selection Models.
X = This model or process is appropriate here.

	CHECK-LISTS	PRO-FILES	SCORING	FRONTIER	INDEX	RISK ANALYSIS	VALUE-CONTRI-BUTION	PORT-FOLIO	QS-NI	BCA/DHM SYSTEMS
Exploratory	X	X	X						X	X
Applied				X	X	X			X	X
Development						X	X	X	X	X
Type of Decision										
Problem:										
Screening	X	X	X	X	X				X	X
Prioritizing					X	X	X	X	X	X
Resource Allocation							X	X		X

REFERENCES

1. Souder, W. E. "Field Studies with a Q-Sort/Nominal Group Process for Selecting R&D Projects." *Research Policy, Vol. 5*(4) (1975), pp. 172–188.
2. Souder, W. E. *Management Decision Methods for Managers of Engineering and Research* (Van Nostrand Reinhold. New York, 1980), pp. 27–36, 64–73, 137–162.
3. Souder, W. E. "A System for Using R&D Project Evaluation Methods." *Research Management, Vol. 21*(5) (1978), pp. 29–37.
4. Moore, J. R. and Baker, N. R. "An Analytical Approach to Scoring Model Design: Application to Research and Development Project Selection." *IEEE Transactions on Engineering Management,* Vol. EM-16(3) (1969), pp. 90–98.
5. Souder, W. E. "Project Selection, Planning and Control," in *Handbook of Operations Research: Models and Applications,* ed.   Moder, J. J. and Elmaghraby, S. E. (Van Nostrand Reinhold. New York, 1970), pp. 301–344.
6. Markowitz, H. *Portfolio Selection* (Wiley. New York, 1960).
7. Sharpe, W. F. "A Simplified Model for Portfolio Analysis." *Management Science,* Vol. 9(1) (1963), pp. 277–293.
8. Hertz, D. B. "Risk Analysis in Capital Investment."*Harvard Business Review,* Vol. 42(1) (1964), pp. 95–106.
9. Dean, B. V. *Project Evaluation: Methods and Procedures* (American Management Association. New York, 1970).
10. Baker, N. R. and Freeland, J. "Recent Advances in R&D Benefit Measurement and Project Selection Methods." *Management Science,* Vol. 21(10) (1975), pp. 1164–1175.
11. Souder, W. E. "Analytical Effectiveness of Mathematical Programming Models for Project Selection." *Management Science.* Vol. 19(8) (1973), pp. 907–923.
12. Souder, W. E. "Utility and Perceived Acceptability of R&D Project Selection Models." *Management Science,* Vol. 19(12) (1973), pp. 1384–1894.
13. Souder, W. E. "Effectiveness of Nominal and Interacting Group Decision Processes for Integrating R&D and Marketing." *Management Science,* Vol. 23(6) (1977), pp. 595–605.
14. Souder, W. E. "Achieving Organizational Consensus with Respect to R&D Project Selection Criteria." *Management Science,* Vol. 21(6) (1975), pp. 669–691.
15. Souder, W. E. and Mandakovic, Tomislav. "R&D Project Selection Models: The Dawn of a New Era." *Research Management,* Vol. 24(4) (July–August, 1986), pp. 36–41.
16. Souder, W. E. *Managing New Product Innovations* (D.C. Heath/Lexington Books. Lexington, Mass., 1987).
17. Souder, W. E. *Project Selection and Economic Appraisal* (Van Nostrand Reinhold. New York, 1983).

BIBLIOGRAPHY

Ansoff, H. I. "Evaluation of Applied Research in a Business Firm." in *Technical Planning on the Corporate Level,* J. R. Bright ed. Harvard University Press, Cambridge, Mass., 1962.
Augood, Derek. "A Review of R&D Evaluation Methods." *IEEE Transactions on Engineering Management, EM-20,*(4):114–120 (1973).
Baker, N. R. and Freeland, J. "Recent Advances in R&D Benefit Measurement and Project Selection Methods." *Management Science, 21*(10):1164–1175 (1975).
Cetron, M. J. and Roepcke, L. H. "The Selection of R&D Program Content." *IEEE Transactions on Engineering Management, EM-14:*4–13 (December, 1967).

Clarke, T. C. "Decision Making in Technologically Based Organizations: A Literature Survey of Present Practice." *IEEE Transactions on Engineering Management, EM-21*(1):9–23 (1974).

Dean, B. V. and Sengupta, S. S. "On a Method for Determining Corporate Research and Development Budgets." In *Management Science Models and Techniques,* C. W. Churchman and M. Verhulst, eds. Pergamon Press, New York, 1960, pp. 210–225.

Gear, A. E., Lockett, A. G., and Pearson, A. W. "Analysis of Some Portfolio Selection Models for R&D." *IEEE Transactions on Engineering Management, EM-18*(2):66–76 (1971).

Gee, R. E. "A Survey of Current Project Selection Practices." *Research Management, 14*(5):38–45 (September, 1971).

Harris, J. S. "New Product Profile Chart." *Chemical and Engineering News, 39*(16):110–118 (April 17, 1961).

Hart, A. "Evaluation of Research and Development Projects." *Chemistry and Industry,* No. 13:549–554 (March 27, 1965).

Hess, S. W. "A Dynamic Programming Approach to R&D Budgeting and Project Selection." *IRE Transactions on Engineering Management, EM-9*:170–179 (December, 1962).

Merrifield, Bruce. "Industrial Project Selection and Management." *Industrial Marketing Management, 7*(5):324–331 (1978).

Murdick, R. G. and Karger, D. W. "The Shoestring Approach to Rating New Products." *Machine Design,* January 25, 1973:86–89.

Rosen, E. M. and Souder, Wm. E. "A Method for Allocating R&D Expenditures." *IEEE Transactions on Engineering Management, EM-12*:87–93 (September, 1965).

Rubenstein, A. H. "Studies of Project Selection in Industry." In *Operations Research in Research and Development,* B. V. Dean, ed. Wiley, New York, 1963, pp. 189–205.

Souder, Wm. E. "R&D Project Selection: A Budgetary Approach." *Transactions CCDA*:25–43 (Spring, 1966).

———. "Planning R&D Expenditures with the Aid of a Computer." *Budgeting, XIV*:25–32 (March, 1966).

———. "Solving Budgeting Problems with O.R." *Budgeting, XIV*:9–11 (July/August 1967).

———. "Selecting and Staffing R&D Projects Via Op Research." *Chemical Engineering Progress, 63*:27 + (November, 1967) (reprinted in *Readings in Operations Research,* W. C. House, Auebach, 1970).

———. "Experiences with an R&D Project Control Model." *IEEE Transactions on Engineering Management, EM-15*:39–49 (March, 1968).

———. "Suitability and Validity of Project Selection Models." Ph.D. Dissertation, St. Louis University, St. Louis, Missouri (August, 1970).

———. "R²: Some Results from Studies of the Research Management Process." *Proceedings AMIF*:121–130 (March, 1971).

———. "A Comparative Analysis of Risky Investment Planning Algorithms." *AIIE Transactions, 4*(1):56–62 (March, 1972).

———. "A Scoring Methodology for Assessing the Suitability of Management Science Models." *Management Science, 18*(10):526–543 (June, 1972).

———. "An R&D Planning and Control Servosystem: A Case Study." *R&D Management, 3*(1):5–12 (October, 1972).

———. "Effectiveness of Mathematical Programming Models for Project Selection: A Computational Evaluation." *Management Science, 19*(8):907–923 (April, 1973).

———. "Acceptability and Utility of Project Selection Models in Development R&D." *Management Science, 19*(12):1384–1394 (August, 1973).

———. "Autonomy, Gratification and R&D Outputs: A Small Sample Field Study." *Management Science, 20*(8):1147–1156 (April, 1974).

————. "Achieving Organizational Consensus with Respect to R&D Project Selection Criteria." *Management Science, 21*(6):669–681 (February, 1975).

————. "Experimental Test of a Q-Sort Procedure for Prioritizing R&D Projects." *IEEE Transactions on Engineering Management, EM-21*(4):159–164 (November, 1974).

————. "Field Studies with a Q-Sort/Nominal Group Process for Selecting R&D Projects." *Research Policy, 5*(4):172–188 (April, 1975).

————. "Effectiveness of Nominal and Interacting Group Decision Processes for Integrating R&D and Marketing." *Management Science, 23*(6):595–605 (February, 1977).

————. "A System for Using R&D Project Evaluation Models in Organizations." *Research Management, 21*(5):29–37 (September, 1978).

————. "An Appraisal of Eight R&D Project Evaluation Methods" to appear in *Corporate Strategy and Product Innovation,* 2nd ed. R. Rothbert, ed. Macmillan, New York, 1985.

————. *Management Decision Methods.* Van Nostrand Reinhold, New York, 1980.

————.*Project Selection and Economic Appraisal.* Van Nostrand Reinhold, New York, 1983.

————. *Managing New Product Innovations.* D.C. Heath/Lexington Books, Lexington, Mass., 1987.

————. and Mandakovic, Tomislav. "R&D Project Selection: The Dawn of a New Era." *Research Management, 24*(4):36–41 (July–August 1986).

Sullivan, C. I. "CPI Looks at R&D Project Evaluation." *Industrial and Engineering Chemistry, 53*(9):42A-46A (September, 1961).

Villers, Raymond. *Research and Development: Planning and Control,* Financial Executives Research Institute, Inc., 1964, pp. 30–38.

Watters, L. D. "Research and Development Project Selection: Interdependence and Multiperiod Probabilistic Budget Constraints." Ph.D. Dissertation, Arizona State University, Tempe, Arizona (1967).

8. Project Owner Strategic Management of Projects*

David I. Cleland†
William R. King‡

The purpose of this chapter is to prescribe a general approach for project owners to use in strategically managing capital projects.

PROJECT OWNER RESPONSIBILITY

Recent attention to the quality of project management in key energy-producing industries has raised a significant question: What are the responsibilities of the project owner for the management of capital projects, the building blocks of organizational strategy? For in determining "prudent and reasonable" management in these industries, much of the focus

---

* Portions of this chapter have been adapted from D. I. Cleland, "Project Owners: Beware," *Project Management Journal,* December 1986, pp. 83–93, and D. I. Cleland, "Pyramiding Project Management Productivity," paper presented at Project Management Institute Seminar/Symposium, Houston, Texas, October 1983.

† David I. Cleland is currently Professor of Engineering Management in the Industrial Engineering Department at the University of Pittsburgh. He is the author/editor of 15 books and has published many articles appearing in leading national and internationally distributed technological, business management, and educational periodicals. Dr. Cleland has had extensive experience in management consultation, lecturing, seminars, and research. He is the recipient of the "Distinguished Contribution to Project Management" award given by the Project Management Institute in 1983, and in May 1984, received the 1983 Institute of Industrial Engineers (IIE)-Joint Publishers Book-of-the-Year Award for the *Project Management Handbook* (with W. R. King). In 1987 Dr. Cleland was elected a Fellow of the Project Management Institute.

‡ William R. King is University Professor in the Katz Graduate School of Business at the University of Pittsburgh. He is the author of more than a dozen books and 150 technical papers that have appeared in the leading journals in the fields of management science, information systems, and strategic planning. Among his major honors are the McKinsey Award (jointly with D. I. Cleland) for the "outstanding contribution to management literature" represented by their book *Systems Analysis and Project Management,* the IIE Book-of-the-Year Award for the first edition of this book, and designation as a fellow of the Decision Sciences Institute. Further biographical information is available in *Who's Who in the World* and *Who's Who in America.*

must be on the issue of the project management role of the owners to adequately plan and control the use of resources on the project.

All too often senior managers who "own" a project fail to recognize the key role that a project plays in the design and implementation of strategy. Such failure leads the project owner to neglect the proactive management of projects in their strategic management of the enterprise. These failures can be costly. Concern about the adequacy of corporate management's performance in project management is evident in the following sampling of recent situations:

- *Forbes* magazine claims that the failure of the U.S. nuclear power program ranks as the largest managerial disaster in business (1).
- $1.2 billion of LILCO's increased costs for the Shoreham project were recommended for exclusion from the rate base as having been imprudently incurred (2).
- The State of Alaska alleged before the Federal Energy Regulatory Commission that $1.6 billion in imprudent management costs were associated with the design, engineering, and construction of the $8 billion Trans-Alaska Pipeline System. A settlement on this case was reached on February 13, 1986. The agreement provides that (a) the rate base will be reduced by $450 million in recognition of the State's allegations of imprudent management; (b) the oil companies will pay $35 million for the State's legal expenses in the proceedings; (c) the owners will refund about $750 million for excessive tariffs between 1981 and 1984; (d) the tariffs will be reduced immediately from about $6.20 per barrel to about $5.00; (e) tariffs will continue to decline throughout the term of the agreement based on an established formula; and (f) the terms of the settlement will apply even if the Federal Energy Regulatory Commission or Congress at some point decides to deregulate oil pipelines (3).
- The State of Missouri Public Service Commission found that the design of the Union Electric Company's Callaway nuclear plant was not sufficiently complete when construction began and that the problem continued throughout the project causing inefficiencies and delays (4).
- In a study of quality in the design and construction of nuclear power plants, it was found that the root cause for initial quality-detached problems was a failure of the utility to implement a management system that ensured adequate control over all aspects of the project (5).

In addition to the above examples, there are many critical comments of a more general nature such as Davis's remark that capital expenditure overruns and poor performance are symptoms of a widespread problem affecting pioneer projects (6), and Bates's statement that owners have paid inadequate attention to the soaring construction costs and the reasons for them (7). Even the Department of Defense has come under sharp criticism for the excessive costs of equipment for defense projects.

As a result of such widespread criticism, many owners in the utility industry have responded by building up personnel and developing better management systems. Such involvement has enabled the owners to obtain closer control over projects and reduce the risk they have assumed (8). But owners' recognition of the strategic responsibility they have for a project should begin at an earlier time: when a capital project is selected for funding. It is at this time that the project should be recognized as a basic building block in strategic management of the enterprise.

A project owner is expected to take charge, to provide the leadership required to see that the right things are done on the project. Owner responsibility starts before the project becomes a reality—during the formative stage where a "vision" is developed which lays on the requirement for a project development to support the organizational strategy. More specifically, the senior managers of the project owner organization have a responsibility to

- Justify and establish the project as a building block of organizational strategy.
- Communicate the need for and manner by which the project will be managed.
- Position the resources around the project through an organizational form capable of managing the project as an integrated entity.
- Maintain a perspective on the project while strategically managing the organization.
- Provide a management and organizational system capable of providing effective strategic planning and management.
- Use a *project management system* as a model for project strategy and management philosophy.
- Use proven, contemporary project management theory and practice in planning, organizing, leading, and controlling the use of project resources.

Archibald posits that strategically managing a company requires the following (9):

- A *vision* of the future of the organization at the top level.
- *Consensus and commitment* within the power structure of the organization on the mission and future direction of the organization.

- *Documentation* of the key objectives and strategies to be employed in fulfilling the mission and moving toward the future direction.
- *Implementation* or execution of specific programs and projects to carry out the stated strategies and reach the desired objectives.

Once a project owner recognizes the key role that projects play in affecting the enterprise strategy, then adequate leadership and management systems will be provided to ensure the proactive and effective management of all enterprise projects, both large and small. Adequate leadership starts by the project owners recognizing their strategic management responsibility.

OWNER STRATEGIC MANAGEMENT

Strategic management is concerned with the design of the organizational *mission, objectives,* and *goals* and the implementation *strategy* whereby enterprise purposes are attained.

A strategy is a series of prescriptions that provide the means, through the allocation of resources, for accomplishing organizational goals, objectives, and mission. In addition to allocating and committing resources for the future, a strategy also provides the general direction for the organization to pursue in reaching desired purposes. A strategy stipulates *what* resources are required, *why* they are required, *when* they are required, *where* they are needed, and *how* they will be used to accomplish ends. Resource allocations include anticipated expenditures for people, fixed assets, equipment, material, supplies, working capital, information, and management systems.

Strategy is the planned means for taking an organization from its present state to a desired future state. The purpose of a strategy is to provide the means to create something that does not currently exist. More specifically, the nature of strategy can be described thusly:

- It focuses on the organization as an entity.
- It emphasizes the key responsibility of the senior executive of the organization as a strategist to develop a sense of direction for the organization's future.
- It relates the organization's sense of direction in terms of identity, character, and purpose expounded in mission, objectives, and goals.
- It encourages the development of a consistent plan of action to execute the allocation of resources to gain strategic response to a changing competitive and environmental future.
- It provides for a balanced view of short-range and long-range organizational purposes.

- It integrates organizational policies, procedures, *programs, projects,* and action plans into a balanced approach to prepare for the future.

Programs and projects play a pivotal role as building blocks in attaining organizational purposes.

A program is (a) a related series of activities that continue over a broad period of time (normally years) and that are designed to accomplish broad goals or increase knowledge; (b) a related series of projects performed over time to accomplish a greater task or achieve a goal or objective; (c) a set of tasks, performed over time, which accomplish a specific purpose.

A project is a combination of human and nonhuman resources pulled together to accomplish a specified purpose in support of organizational strategies. Projects usually take the form of interrelated tasks performed by various organizations. A project has a well-defined objective, a target schedule, and a target cost (or budget). The attainment of a project objective is a tangible contribution to an organizational mission. *If a project overruns its cost and schedule, or fails to accomplish its technical performance objective, the implementation of an organizational strategy will be impaired.*

Effective strategic management means that organizational missions, objectives, goals, and strategies have been defined; an organizational design has been selected; and functional supporting plans, policies, systems, and procedures have been developed in response to changing environmental conditions and enterprise resources.

A PROJECT MANAGEMENT MODEL

A key part of the strategic management of an enterprise is the philosophical approach to the management of projects. Figure 8-1 provides a model of an effective approach. This model derived from but different than that provided by King in Chapter 6 (10).

Organizational Mission

At the apex of our triangular model is the organization's mission, the culminating strategic point of all organizational activity. An organization's mission is the most general strategic choice that must be made by its managers. An organization's mission tells what it is, why it exists, and the unique contribution it can make. The organization's mission answers the basic question: "What business are we in?"

The mission of an organization should provide the driving force to design suitable implementation strategies. Unfortunately many project organizations do have a concept of their mission, but fail to develop a comprehensive strategy for the consumption of resources to accomplish that mission. They fail to "work" the organization down through the successive levels of the model depicted in Figure 8-1.

Project Objectives

While the mission is the common thread that binds together the resources and activities of an organization, a *project objective* designates the future positions or destinations that it wishes to reach in its "projects" business. Project objectives are the end result of managing the financial, schedule, and technical performance work packages of the project in consonance with the project plan. The accomplishment of project objectives contributes directly to the mission of the organization. This contribution can be measured. The proper selection and management of project objectives are essential steps in the strategic management of the organization. Such objectives are the building blocks of the project management organization's mission. Project objectives are supported by project goals.

Project Goals

The distinctive features of project goals are their specificity and measurements on time-based points that the project team intends to meet in pursuit of its project objectives. For instance, in the management of a project, the completion of a work package in the project work breakdown structure means that progress has been made toward the objective of delivering the project on time, within budget, and in satisfaction of its operational objectives.

Mission, objectives, and goals are the triad of organizational direction. But this triad is not enough. The execution of organizational resources in support of this triad is contained in the project strategies.

Project Strategy

A project strategy is the design of the means to accomplish results. An expressed project strategy is a project plan which provides general direction on how resources will be used to attain project goals and objectives. A project plan should cover the following: (a) project scope; (b) objectives such as technical, profit, other; (c) technical and management approach; (d) deliverables; (e) end item specifications; (f) schedules; (g) resources; (h) contributions; (i) finances; (j) risk areas such as subcontractor default, technical breakthroughs, etc. (11).

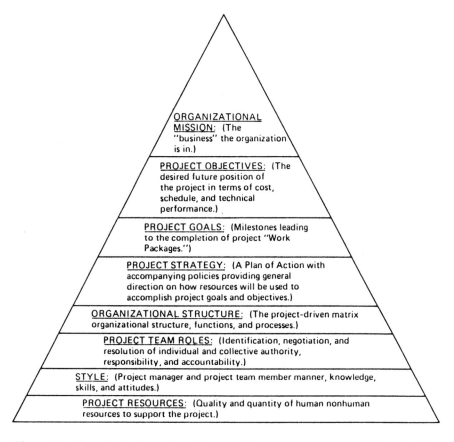

Figure 8-1. Elements in the project-driven matrix management system. (From Harold Kerzner and Daivd I. Cleland, *Project/Matrix Management Policy and Strategy*, Van Nostrand Reinhold, New York, 1985, p. 220.)

The nature of the project plan will vary depending on the project. The test of an adequate plan is its usefulness as a standard to judge project progress.

Organizational Structure

The organizational structure is the manner by which the resources are aligned into departments based on principles of functional, product, process, geographic, or customer bases. Introduction of project management provides the opportunity to realign the organization structure on some form of the matrix organization. The organization structure becomes a project-driven matrix, a complex organization design which requires a specific delineation of project team roles.

Project Team Roles

The structure of an organization defines the major territories that are assigned to each manager. Within each territory—production, finance, marketing, and so forth—specific roles require identification and negotiation, particularly in terms of the interaction of individuals with peers, subordinates, and supervisors. These role interrelationships come to focus through work packages and are held together by accepted authority, responsibility, and accountability of the project management team. Work packages are major work elements at the hierarchical levels of the work breakdown structure within the organization or within a project. They are used to identify and control work flows in the organization and have the following characteristics:

1. A work package represents a discrete unit of work at the appropriate level of the work breakdown structure (WBS) where work is assigned.
2. Each work package is clearly distinguished from all other work packages.
3. The primary responsibility of completing the work package on schedule and within budget can always be assigned to a member of the project team and never to more than one organizational unit.
4. A work package can be integrated with other work packages at the same level of the WBS to support the work packages at a higher level of the WBS.

Work packages are level-dependent, becoming increasingly more general at each higher level of the WBS and increasingly more specific at each lower level. A general manager would be expected to have primary responsibility to set project objectives, whereas a contract manager would be expected to take the lead in corporate maintenance agreements for a profit center manager to use in supporting equipment that has been delivered to a customer. An individual is designated as having primary responsibility for each work package. Others who have collateral responsibility involving the work package are also designated. When these collective roles have been designated, there remains no place to hide in the organization. If the work package is not completed on time or does not meet the performance standards, someone can readily be identified and held responsible and accountable for that work. Responsibility, authority, and accountability—the triad of personal performance in organized life—is not left to doubt when individual and collective roles have been adequately defined. This definition can be carried out through the process of Linear Responsibility Charting (LRC) (12).

Project team roles are affected by the management style that is followed in the organization.

Management Style

The style of the managers and professionals associated with the project is an important influence on project success or failure. Style depends on an individual's knowledge, skills, and attitudes, manifesting itself primarily in the individual's interpersonal relationships and management philosophies. The management styles of senior managers are echoed down through the organizational structure to the project team. Style is dependent on individual and collective knowledge, skills, and attitudes expressed in the cultural ambience of the project team.

Project Resources

Ultimately, the quality of the project end product and the schedule and cost to develop that product is dependent on the quality and quantity of the resources available and being applied to the project. The project owners have a key responsibility to provide the necessary resources to support the project as well as to maintain ongoing surveillance over the use of those resources.

Management Strategies

A strategy is a series of prescriptions that provide the means and set the general direction for accomplishing organizational goals, objectives, and mission. These prescriptions stipulate

- What resource allocations are required?
- Why?
- When?
- Where?
- How?

These allocations include anticipated expenditures for fixed assets, equipment, working capital, people, information, and management systems. In general, strategies include the following:

- Programs/program plans.
- Projects/project plans.
- Operational plans.
- Contingency plans.
- Policies
- Procedures
- Organizational design.
- General prescribed courses of action.
- Prescriptions for resource utilization.
- Strategic performance standards.

Projects are an essential building block in an enterprise strategy. Projects require active management to fulfill their role in moving the organization from its present position to a desired future position at some predetermined point in time. The project owner is a key member of the project team. Only the owner can determine the strategic fit of a project in the organization's strategy and establish the priorities and performance standards for the management of the project. Project owners have the ultimate obligation to see that certain responsibilities are accomplished to support both organizational and project ends. These responsibilities are embodied in the *strategic planning and management* role of the owners, in the *project management system* used to manage the project, as well as in the quality of support provided by the functional specialists working on the project. These responsibilities include

- Development and implementation both of adequate strategic plans for the enterprise and of project plans to support the project's technical performance objective, schedules, costs, and execution strategies.
- Development of an organizational design which delegates appropriate authority, responsibility, and accountability to the managers and professionals working on the project.
- Regular ongoing surveillance by responsible managers and professionals to monitor the use of resources on the project and the appropriate reallocation of resources as required to keep the project objectives on time and within budget.
- Design and use of policies, procedures, roles, and guidelines to facilitate the management of the project.
- Provision of knowledgeable and skillful people to work on the project.
- Development of the necessary information systems to support managers and professionals working on the project.

- Facilitation of an organizational culture that fosters, recognizes, and rewards prudent and reasonable project management.
- Rewarding of people for productive and quality results on the project.
- Selection of periodic internal and external audits to determine the efficacy of project management and to verify project status.
- Surveillance and ongoing communication with project "stakeholders" to ascertain and influence their perceptions of the project.
- Ensuring of the use of a contemporaneous body of knowledge and skill in the management of the project.
- Setting of the tone for leader and follower style within the culture of the corporation in the design and execution of projects.
- Replanning, recycling, and redesigning, as necessary, of the management systems used in the management of the project.

OWNERS' MANAGEMENT SYSTEM

Owners require a management system which enables them to play a proactive role in planning, organizing, and controlling resources used to support enterprise purposes. The starting point for an owner's management system is a clear statement of the enterprise's mission, that is, the "business" that the enterprise pursues. One utility company's mission is stated in the following way:

> Manage and direct the nuclear activities of the GPU System to provide the required high level of protection for the health and safety of the public and the employees. Consistent with the above, generate electricity from the GPU nuclear stations in a reliable and efficient manner in conformance with all applicable laws, regulations, licenses, and other requirements and the directions and interests of the owners.(13)

Once the mission of the enterprise is established through the operation of a *strategic planning system,* planning can be extended to select and develop organizational *objectives, goals,* and *strategies.* Projects are planned for and implemented through a *project management system* composed of the following subsystems:

- A *matrix-oriented organization subsystem* used in the management of the project.
- A *project management information subsystem,* which contains the intelligence essential to the effective planning, organization, and control of the project.

- The *planning subsystem,* which involves the development of project technical performance objectives, goals, schedules, costs, and strategies.
- The *project control subsystem,* which selects performance standards for the project schedule, budget, and technical performance objectives, and uses information feedback to compare actual progress with planned progress.
- The *cultural subsystem,* which concerns the perceptions, attitudes, and leader and follower style of the people working on the project.
- The *human subsystem,* which involves communications, negotiations, motivation, leadership, and the behavior patterns of the people working on the project.

Many of the above subsystems use techniques such as PERT, CPM, and related resource allocation methodologies.

Figure 8-2 depicts this project management system with all its subsystems. The utility owners who are responsible and accountable for the effective management of the project work through their board of directors and senior management with the project manager, functional managers, and functional specialists.

In the case of the Shoreham Project, the responsibility and accountability of the senior executives of the project owner's organization was made clear by the administrative law judges who concluded that

. . . Lilco (Long Island Lighting Company) failed to develop a project plan adequate to oversee S&W management of the project. . . . To identify roles and responsibilities, to develop accurate and timely reporting systems which would enable it to monitor, measure and control costs and scheduling, to adequately staff monitoring groups or to adequately prepare for its critical owner oversight role.

We conclude that, throughout Shoreham's construction, Lilco failed to staff adequately its prime area of responsibility as owner of the plant—cost and schedule control.

Lilco's measurement and reporting systems continually and repeatedly failed to accurately depict cost and schedule status at Shoreham. Lilco managers were unable to use Lilco's measurement systems to gain an accurate picture of what was happening on site and complained that Lilco's reporting systems were confused and cluttered.(2)

The law judges left no doubt as to the overall responsibility of the Lilco Board of Directors for the Shoreham Project:

We conclude that the limited information presented to the Board was inadequate for it to determine project status on the reasonableness of key management decision or to provide requisite guidance and direction to Lilco management.(2)

On the more positive side, there should be no doubt by project owners that effective planning and control contribute to the success of a project. For example, project success at Fluor Utah, Inc., is related to the quality of planning and control.

Figure 8-2. The project management system. (Adapted from D. I. Cleland, "Defining a Project Management System," *Project Management Quarterly*, December 1977).

During the early 1960s, after hundreds of projects had been completed at Fluor Utah, Inc., it became apparent that many projects successfully achieved their basic project objectives, while some failed to achieve budget, schedule, and performance objectives originally established.

The history of many of these projects was carefully reviewed to identify conditions and events common to successful projects, vis-à-vis those conditions and events that occurred frequently on less successful projects.

Common identifiable elements on most successful projects were the quality and depth of early planning by the project management group. Another major reason for the project success was the bolstering of the execution of a plan by strong management control over identifiable phases of the project (14).

In a study of the underlying causes of major quality-related problems in the construction of some nuclear power plants, the Nuclear Regulatory Commission concluded that the root cause was the failure or inability of some utility managements to implement a management system that ensured adequate control over all aspects of the project (5).

An important part of owner responsibility is the design of a suitable organizational approach to manage the project.

ORGANIZATIONAL DESIGN

An effective organizational design should take into consideration the roles (authority, responsibility, and accountability) of executives at the following organizational levels:

The Board of Directors for the exercise of trusteeship in the husbanding of corporate assets used in capital projects.

The CEO and Staff functioning as a "plural executive" for strategic and operating responsibility for the corporate entity through the optimal use of resources to achieve corporate mission, objective, and goals and to finish capital projects on time and within budget.

A *Senior Executive* who functions in the capacity of a "Manager of Projects" for directing individual project managers' activities; proposing, planning, and facilitating the implementation of project management plans, policies, procedures, techniques, and methodologies; and evaluating and controlling project progress.

The Project Manager who has residual responsibility and accountability for project results on time and within budget.

Functional Managers who provide specialized resources to support project needs.

Work Package Managers who are responsible for project work package budgets, schedules, and technical performance objectives.

Project Professionals working on the project who, depending on the nature of the matrix organization, report to both the functional manager and the project manager.

Appropriate policy documentation should exist which portrays in specific terms the organizational structure and the fixing of authority, responsibility, and accountability of managers at each organizational level.

The impact of an inadequate organizational design for the Shoreham Project was noted by the administrative law judges who said, "A major planning and management defect was confusion over roles and responsibilities"(2). They went on to say, "Lilco's organizational arrangement left lines of authority and responsibility blurred and unclear from the start"(2, p. 77).

A McKinsey & Company survey of twelve multibillion-dollar projects built during the last two decades emphasizes the necessity for an organizational plan to define the organizational structure for the project and to ensure the allocation of specific responsibilities within the structure. This survey states that the formal, written organizational plan should be prepared at the front end of the project to obtain mutual agreement from all parties and to make certain that all required responsibilities will be addressed. The survey concludes that an owner group's inability to let go of project management, even when it recognized significant gaps in its own ability to manage, was usually "rewarded" with significant difficulties and problems in completing the project (15).

A RAND Corporation study of "new technology" process plant construction finds that the most prominently mentioned management-related reason for increased costs is "diffuse decision-making responsibility for a project." The study concludes that the "general wisdom for construction projects" dictates that "one person needs to be given broad authority for all routine project decisions and a reasonable scope for fairly important decisions on schedules, allocation of monies, and all but major modifications." The study finds that it is "standard industry practice to appoint a project manager—in the case of a pioneer plant project, a project manager of long experience—who is responsible for the undertaking from shortly after the time that the project emerges from development until an operating plant is on-line"(16).

An adequate organizational design helps to facilitate adequate owner surveillance of a project.

OWNER ONGOING SURVEILLANCE

Ongoing surveillance of the project in order to ensure the results and control the application of organizational resources is essential to successful project management. Measurement of project results requires the development of certain standards, information feedback, and methods for comparing project plans with project results. It also requires ongoing exercise of "hindsight" in the initiation of corrective action to realign resources in order to accomplish the project objective and goals. Project owners are responsible for ensuring that regular, ongoing assessment of a project's progress is carried out to determine the status of that project. The following concepts and philosophies are essential elements for the assessment of project results:

1. The objective is to develop measurements of project trends and results through information arising out of the management of the project work breakdown structure.
2. Performance measurements are always to be tempered by the judgment of the managers and professionals doing the measurement.
3. The use of common measurement factors arises out of the status of project work packages consistent with the organizational decentralization of the project.
4. Measurements should be kept to a minimum relevant to each work package in the project work breakdown structure.
5. Measurements of work packages must be integrated into measurement of the project as a whole.
6. Measurements should be developed that are applicable to both current project results and future projections to project completion.
7. Measurement should be conducted around previously planned key result areas.

The *key result areas* of the project are those areas which are of sufficient basic importance to act as "direction indicators" of the project. To illustrate, these areas include

- Technical performance objectives.
- Cost objectives.
- Schedule objectives.
- Strategic synergistic fit with organizational product strategies.
- Potential financial return.
- Productive use of resources.
- Competitiveness.

The strategic plans of the enterprise should define these key result areas to provide performance standards for the ongoing evaluation of the project, and to seek answers to such questions as the following:

- What is going right on the project?
- What is going wrong?
- What problems are emerging?
- What opportunities are emerging?
- Where is the project with respect to schedule, cost, and technical performance objectives?
- Does the project continue to have a strategic fit with the enterprise's mission?
- Is there anything that should be done that is not being done?
- Is there any reallocation of corporate resources required to support the project needs?
- What explains the difference between planning and actual project progress?
- What replanning and reorganizing of corporate resources are required to support the project?

If owner senior managers are not actively involved and do not have sufficient knowledge to ask these questions and seek answers to them, then they are not getting the feedback they need on project progress in order to be prudent and reasonable in their management of the project. An independent audit of the project conducted on a periodic basis will also help the project owners to get the informed and intelligent answers they need.

PROJECT MANAGEMENT AUDIT

Once the decision is made to conduct an audit, an audit team should be formed and provided with the authority and resources to carry out the audit. All key functional and general managers should be committed to help facilitate the audit by making people and information available to the audit team. An organizational policy document should exist which outlines, as a minimum, the *purpose, scope, policy, responsibilities, and procedures* for the audit. If such a policy document exists, the culture of the organization will better support an audit philosophy. The project, functional, and general managers, expecting to be audited, will be encouraged to do a better job. There is considerable support in the project management literature for an independent project audit. For example, Chilstrom states:

Management audit of projects provides top management a means of independent appraisal in determining the effectiveness of the organization to successfully accomplish a project. This has become more important in recent years where most projects have matrix management requiring the functional organizations to meet the needs of many projects. Project success requires a capable project team that has responsive support from functional areas, and it is management's task to allocate needed resources and achieve the integration of all elements. In addition, the project team will directly benefit from the results of the audit, since findings and recommended actions will concentrate on both internal and external factors that are preventing the achievement of the project goals and plans.(17)

In noting the success of a large nuclear plant construction project, the project manager credited an ongoing critique as a significant contributor to the success of the project. Many times during the life of this project, independent groups were brought in to review it in order to help ensure that significant problems were not being overlooked (18).

In commenting on the role of independent reviews, Cabano notes:

. . . We believe the evidence to be conclusive that although project responsibilities and objectives can be met using only traditional project management techniques, programmatic adoption of "Independent Project Reviews" (IPR) as described herein can add measurably to the confidence, visibility, coordination, communications and overall synchronization of a project and substantially enhances its success potential.(19)

In a study of over 50 process industry large-to mega- scale projects, Cabano found that the use of an independent project review (audit) can measurably enhance the success potential of a project. In the project histories reviewed, teams of experts were used to help resolve major problems judged sufficient to jeopardize the stability and progress of the project. The study concludes that judicious project audit process can help to or provide early warning of problems, give more time for the development of remedial strategy, and even prevent major problems. The study suggests, however, that a review of this kind should not replace effective full-time surveillance by responsible individuals but should be used to supplement the existing management system (19).

How often should an audit be conducted considering that a thorough audit takes time and money? Generally, audits should be carried out at key points in the life cycle of a project, and at times in those phases of the life cycle that represent "go/no go" trigger points such as preliminary design, final engineering design, start of construction, start of licensing, start-up, and operation.

The conduct of independent audits by utility management was an established practice in the early to mid-1970s. For example, in 1975 the legislature of the state of North Carolina enacted a law to initiate a full and complete management audit of any public utility company (PUC) once every five years. Similar actions have been taken by PUCs in Missouri, Pennsylvania, New York, Oregon, Arizona, and Connecticut. *"It* [management auditing] *is an emerging trend of great significance* to regulators, consumers, and regulated alike"(20).

The organizational policy document is one instance of how the owners can work to gain the support of the culture of the organization for an audit philosophy. On a broader scale, the owner's attitudes and approach to the project set the cultural ambience in which the entire project is managed.

THE CULTURAL AMBIENCE

Culture is a set of refined behaviors that people strive toward in their society. It includes the whole complex of a society—knowledge, beliefs, art, ethics, morals, law, custom, and other habits and attitudes acquired by the individual as a member of society. Anthropologists have used the concept of culture in describing primitive societies. Modern-day sociologists have borrowed this anthropological usage to describe a way of life of a people.

The term "culture" is used to describe the synergistic set of shared ideas and demonstrated beliefs that are associated with a way of life in an organization using project management in the execution of its corporate strategy. An organization's culture reflects the composite management style of its executives, a style that has much to do with the organization's ability to adapt to such a change as the use of project management in corporate strategy. Arnold and Capella remind us that achieving the right kind of corporate culture is critical and that businesses are human institutions (21). Culture is that integrated pattern of human behavior that includes thought, attitudes, values, action, artifacts; it is the way things are done in organization.

An organization's culture consists of shared agreements, explicit or implicit, among organizational members as to what is important in behavior and attitudes expressed in values, beliefs, standards, and social and management practices. The culture that is developed and becomes characteristic of an organization affects strategic planning and implementation, project management, and all else.

It is possible to identify common cultural features that positively and negatively influence the practice of management and the conduct of technical affairs in an organization. Such cultural features develop out of and are influenced by

- The management leadership-and-follower style practiced by key managers and professionals.
- The example set by leaders of the organization.
- The attitudes displayed and communicated by key managers in their management of the organization.
- Manager and professional competencies.
- Assumptions held by key managers and professionals.
- Organizational plans, policies, procedures, rules, and strategies.
- The political, legal, social, technological, and economic systems with which the members of an organization interface.
- The perceived and/or actual characteristics of the organization.
- Quality and quantity of the resources (human and nonhuman) consumed in the pursuit of the organization's mission, objectives, goals, and strategies.
- The knowledge, skills, and experience of members of the organization.
- Communication patterns.
- Formal and informal roles.

Insight into the effect of a key executive's attitude was cited in a report to the Congress on Quality Assurance in the nuclear power plant industry:

One chief executive termed his utility's first planned nuclear plant as "just another tea kettle," i.e., just an alternative way to generate steam (this was before major quality problems arose at his project).(5)

The failure of some licensees (owners) to "treat quality assurance as a management tool, rather than as a paperwork exercise (5, p.3-11) affected the outcome of the project. Policies can affect the cultural ambience of an organization. For example:

. . . A characteristic of the projects that had not experienced quality problems was a constructive working relationship with and understanding of the NRC. For example, Florida Power and Light established a special office in Bethesda staffed by engineers to facilitate exchange of information with the NRC during the St. Lucie 2 licensing process. Also, senior management of Arizona Power Service has established the following *policies* concerning the NRC:

Don't treat NRC as an adversary; NRC is not here to bother us— they see many more plants than the licensee sees; inform NRC of what we (APS) are doing and keep everything up front; and nuclear safety is more important than schedule.(5, p. 3-21)

Attitudes of key managers play an important role in successfully completing a nuclear power plant. A management commitment to quality and a management view that NRC requirements are not the ultimate goals for performance carry great weight. For example:

> Of the projects studied there tended to be a direct correlation between the project's success and the utility's view of NRC requirements: more successful utilities tended to view NRC requirements as minimum levels of performance, not maximum, and they strove to establish and meet increasingly higher, self-imposed goals. This attitude covered all aspects of the project, including quality and quality assurance.(5, p. 3-19)

Manager/professional experience affects competence and this in turn affects the culture. A common thread running through four projects studied in a report to Congress was a lack of prior nuclear experience of some members of the project team, that is, owner utility, architect-engineer, construction manager, and construction. In three of the four cases this lack of experience was a major contributor to the quality-related problems that developed on these projects. Owner's inexperience is important because in at least three of the four cases the owner underestimated the complexity and difficulty of the nuclear project and treated it much as it would have another fossil project. The effect of inexperience was significant:

> . . . Generally, the utilities' lack of experience in and understanding of nuclear construction manifested itself in some subset of the following characteristics:

> 1. inadequate staffing for the project, in numbers, in qualifications, and in applicable nuclear experience
> 2. selection of contractors who may have been used successfully in building fossil plants but who had very limited applicable nuclear construction experience
> 3. over-reliance on these same contractors in managing the project and evaluating its status and progress
> 4. use of contracts that emphasized cost and schedule to the detriment of quality
> 5. lack of management commitment to and understanding of how to achieve quality
> 6. lack of management support for the quality program

7. oversight of the project from corporate headquarters with only a minimal utility presence at the construction site
8. lack of appreciation of ASME codes and other nuclear-related standards
9. diffusion of project responsibility and diluted project accountability
10. failure to delegate authority commensurate with responsibility
11. misunderstanding of the NRC, its practices, its authority, and its role in nuclear safety
12. tendency to view NRC requirements as performance goals, not lower thresholds of performance
13. inability to recognize that recurring problems in the quality of construction were merely symptoms of much deeper, underlying programmatic deficiencies in the project, including project management.(5, pp. 3-8, 3-9)

In some cases a poorly functioning QA Program had its roots in management's lack of appreciation or support for the quality function. Part of this lack of appreciation was attributed to management's unawareness of vital construction quality information which was known to the quality assurance staff. The existence of many organizational levels through which information flowed was "severely attenuated" when it reached senior management (5, p. 3-12).

The critical ambience of an organization using project management is subtle yet very real. In the project-driven organization the attitudes, values, beliefs, and management systems tend to become more participative and democratic. Owners can affect that culture to support successful project management.

SUMMARY

The owner cannot abdicate responsibility for the project to others, even experienced A&E firms, project management contractors, or constructors. Successful project management depends on a commitment by the owner to use contemporaneous project management theory and practice in designing and using appropriate management systems to proactively manage the project. Prudent owners must maintain close surveillance over project progress and remain in close touch with all project participants to glean their input into the status of the project. This means that an owner must be an active and knowledgeable participant on the project team. The owner's most critical commitments are that the project will be assertively managed, and that all project participants are provided strategic leadership for completion of the project on time and within budget so that enterprise strategy is enhanced.

Project owners who seek to recover investments through rate adjustments should find the use of the project management concepts depicted in this chapter useful to demonstrate their prudent and reasonable management of capital projects.

Project owners who seek to recover investments through rate adjustments should find the project management concepts described in this chapter useful to demonstrate their prudent and reasonable management of capital projects.

REFERENCES

1. "Nuclear Follies." *Forbes,* February 11, 1986.
2. Recommended Decision by Administrative Law Judges Wm. C. Levey and Thomas R. Matias on Case 27563, Long Island Lighting Company—Shoreham Prudence Investigation, State of New York Public Service Commission, March 11, 1985.
3. Rogovin, Huge & Lenzner, Law Offices, 1730 Rhode Island Avenue, N.W. Washington, D.C., 20036, Ltr., February 13, 1986.
4. Case No. ER-85-160 & EO-85-17, Determination of In-Service Criteria for the Union Electric Company's Callaway Nuclear Plant and Callaway Rate Base and Authority to file Tariffs Increasing Rates for Electric Service to Customers in Missouri, before the State of Missouri Public Service Commission, March 29, 1985.
5. U. S. Nuclear Regulatory Commission (NUREG-1055). *Improving Quality and the Assurance of Quality in the Design and Construction of Nuclear Power Plants* (Washington, D.C., 20555, May 1984).
6. Davis, David. "New Projects: Beware of False Economies." *Harvard Business Review* (March-April, 1985).
7. Bates, G. Stan. "Construction Industry Cost Effectiveness Project National CICE Activities—Update" *1983 Proceedings of the Project Management Institute* (October, 1983), p. V-D-2.
8. Theodore Barry & Associates. *A Survey of Organizational and Contractual Trends in Power Plant Construction, March, 1979.*
9. Archibald, Russell D. "Implementing Business Strategies through Projects," in *Strategic Planning and Management Handbook,* 2nd Ed., ed. King, W. R. and Cleland, D. I. (Van Nostrand Reinhold. New York, 1986).
10. Paraphrased from Kerzner, Harold and Cleland, David I. *Project/Matrix Management Policy and Strategy* (Van Nostrand Reinhold. New York, 1985), pp. 219–224.
11. Paraphrased from Archibald, Russell D. *Managing High-Technology Programs and Projects* (Wiley. New York, 1976).
12. See Chapter 16 of this handbook.
13. Clark, Philip R. "Looking Beyond the Lessons: A Utility Manager's Perspective." *Nuclear News* (April 1984), p. 64.
14. Duke, Robert, Wholsen, H. Frederick and Mitchell, Douglas R. "Project Management at Fluor Utah, Inc.," in *The State-of-the-Art of Project Management 1976–1977* (The Northern California Chapter of the Project Management Institute. San Francisco, 1977), pp. 28–37.

15. Anderson, J. *Organizing for Large Project Management—The Client's Needs* (McKinsey & Company. October, 1978).
16. Rand Corporation. *A Review of Cost Estimation in New Technologies: Implications for Energy Process Plants.* (July, 1978).
17. Chilstrom, Kenneth O. "Project Management Audits," in *Project Management Handbook,* ed. Cleland, D. I. and King, W. R. (Van Nostrand Reinhold. New York, 1983), p. 465.
18. Derrickson, W. B. "St. Lucie Unit 2—A Nuclear Plant Built on Schedule." *1983 Proceedings of the Project Management Institute (October, 1983), pp. V-E-1–V-E-14.*
19. Cabano, Louis J. "Independent Project Reviews." *Project Management Institute Seminar/Symposium* (October, 1984), p. 8.
20. Alden, Raymond M. "Utility Management Audits from a Managerial Viewpoint." *Public Utilities Fortnightly* (October 7, 1976) (emphasis added).
21. Arnold, Danny R. and Capella, Louis M. "Corporate Culture and the Marketing Concept: A Diagnostic Instrument for Utilities." *Public Utilities Fortnightly* (October 17, 1985), pp. 32–38.

Section IV
Life-Cycle Management

One of the important reasons for the efficacy of project management is the changing mix of resources that is demanded over the life cycle of a project.

In Chapter 9, William R. King and David I. Cleland portray the project life cycle as an important rationale for project management. They present various life-cycle concepts and show how the life cycle places demands on organizations that require a "new" form of management—the project management approach.

In Chapter 10, John R. Adams and Stephen E. Barndt review a set of organizational variables in terms of their impact on projects in various stages of the life cycle. They present a series of propositions that are based on their assessments of the results of studies of more than 20 R&D projects. These propositions allow one to predict the behavior of projects throughout their life cycle.

In Chapter 11, Herbert F. Spires considers an important, and often neglected, phase of the project life cycle—divestment. The phasing out of a project may be either a "natural" part of the life cycle or it may be extraordinary. In either case, phase-down creates unique problems that are associated with no other phases and with few other endeavors in life.

William R. King and Ananth Srinivasan integrate the life-cycle notions of this section with the strategic project context of Section III by demonstrating, in Chapter 12, how the traditional systems development life cycle has evolved into a broader life cycle for the systems of the organization. Although this chapter focuses on the important information systems domain, this integration is taking place for technology life cycles, sales life cycles, and other systems cycles as well.

9. Life-Cycle Management*

William R. King†
David I. Cleland‡

"Life cycle management" is a term that describes project management in terms of one of the most salient project characteristics—the life cycle. The life cycle of a project is an important factor in determining the need for, and value of, a project management approach.

BASIC LIFE-CYCLE CONCEPTS

There are a variety of life-cycle concepts that are in common use. These life cycles serve to illustrate the need for life cycle management.

Sales Life Cycles

Perhaps the best known life cycle is the sales life cycle. A product moves through various phases of sales life cycle after it has been placed on the

---

* Portions of this chapter have been paraphrased from *Systems Analysis and Project Management*, 2nd Edition, (McGraw-Hill Book Company, New York, 1975), by David I. Cleland and William R. King.

† William R. King is University Professor in the Katz Graduate School of Business at the University of Pittsburgh. He is the author of more than a dozen books and 150 technical papers that have appeared in the leading journals in the fields of management science, information systems, and strategic planning. Among his major honors are the McKinsey Award (jointly with D. I. Cleland) for the "outstanding contribution to management literature" represented by their book *Systems Analysis and Project Management,* the IIE Book-of-the-Year Award for the first edition of this book, and designation as a fellow of the Decision Sciences Institute. Further biographical information is available in *Who's Who in the World* and *Who's Who in America.*

‡ David I. Cleland is currently Professor of Engineering Management in the Industrial Engineering Department at the University of Pittsburgh. He is the author/editor of 15 books and has published many articles appearing in leading national and internationally distributed technological, business management, and educational periodicals. Dr. Cleland has had extensive experience in management consultation, lecturing, seminars, and research. He is the recipient of the "Distinguished Contribution to Project Management" award given by the Project Management Institute in 1983, and in May 1984, received the 1983 Institute of Industrial Engineers (IIE)-Joint Publishers Book-of-the-Year Award for the *Project Management Handbook* (with W. R. King). In 1987 Dr. Cleland was elected a fellow of the Project Management Institute.

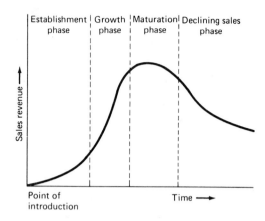

Figure 9-1. Product sales life cycle.

market. One of the authors* has referred to these life-cycle phases as *establishment, growth, maturation,* and *declining sales* phases. Figure 9-1 shows these phases in terms of the sales revenue generated by the product during its period of slow establishment in the marketplace, followed by a period of rapid sales increase, a peaking, and a long, gradual decline. Virtually every product displays these dynamic characteristics, although some may have a sales life cycle which is so long or short that the various phases are not readily distinguishable. For example, a faddish product such as "super balls" or "hula hoops" will have a very high-peaked sales curve with a rapid decline. Many such products will have a long, slow decline after an initially rapid decline from the peak. With other products, the maturation phase is very long and the declining sales phase very gradual. But the general life-cycle concept is virtually unavoidable for a successful product. Without product improvements, competition will eventually lure away customers, and consumers' attitudes, habits, and needs will change as time passes.

Of course, the sales portion of the life cycle of a product is really only one aspect of its entire life. Indeed, only products which are marketing successes ever get to experience the sales life cycle of Figure 9-1.

Systems Development Life Cycle

All products—sales successes or otherwise—begin as a gleam in the eye of someone and undergo many different phases of development before

---

* William R. King, *Quantitative Analysis for Marketing Management* (McGraw-Hill. New York, 1967), p. 113.

being marketed and subjected to the sales life-cycle considerations of Figure 9-1. For instance, the U.S. Department of Defense (DOD) and the National Aeronautics and Space Administration (NASA) have extensively defined and detailed phases which should be encountered with hardware systems development. Their system development life-cycle concept recognizes a natural order of thought and action which is pervasive in the development of many kinds of systems—be they commercial products, space exploration systems, or management systems.

New products, services, or roles for the organization have their genesis in ideas evolving within the organization. Typically, such "systems" ideas go through a distinct life cycle, that is, a natural and pervasive order of thought and action. In each phase of this cycle, different levels and varieties of specific thought and action are required within the organization to assess the efficacy of the system. The "phases" of this cycle serve to illustrate the systems development life-cycle concept and its importance.

The Conceptual Phase. The germ of the idea for a system may evolve from other research, from current organizational problems, or from the observation of organizational interfaces. The conceptual phase is one in which the idea is conceived and given preliminary evaluation.

During the conceptual phase, the environment is examined, forecasts are prepared, objectives and alternatives are evaluated, and the first examination of the performance, cost, and time aspects of the system's development is performed. It is also during this phase that basic strategy, organization, and resource requirements are conceived. The fundamental purpose of the conceptual phase is to conduct a "white paper" study of the requirements in order to provide a basis for further detailed evaluation. Table 9-1 shows the details of these efforts.

There will typically be a high mortality rate of potential systems during the conceptual phase of the life cycle. Rightly so, since the study process conducted during this phase should identify projects that have high risk and are technically, environmentally, or economically infeasible or impractical.

The Definition Phase. The fundamental purpose of the definition phase is to determine, as soon as possible and as accurately as possible, cost, schedule, performance, and resource requirements and whether all elements, projects, and subsystems will fit together economically and technically.

The definition phase simply tells in more detail what it is we want to do, when we want to do it, how we will accomplish it, and what it will cost. The definition phase allows the organization to fully conceive and define

Table 9-1. Conceptual Phase.

1. Determine existing needs or potential deficiencies of existing systems.
2. Establish system concepts which provide initial strategic guidance to overcome existing or potential deficiencies.
3. Determine initial technical, environmental, and economic feasibility and practicability of the system.
4. Examine alternative ways of accomplishing the system objectives.
5. Provide initial answers to the questions:
   a What will the system cost?
   b When will the system be available?
   c What will the system do?
   d How will the system be integrated into existing systems?
6. Identify the human and nonhuman resources required to support the system.
7. Select initial system designs which will satisfy the system objectives.
8. Determine initial system interfaces.
9. Establish a project organization.

the system before it starts to physically put the system into its environment. Simply stated, the definition phase dictates that one stop and take time to look around to see if this is what one really wants before the resources are committed to putting the system into operation and production. If the idea has survived the end of the conceptual phase, a conditional approval for further study and development is given. The definition phase provides the opportunity to review and confirm the decision to continue development, create a prototype system, and make a production or installation decision.

Decisions that are made during and at the end of the definition phase might very well be decisions to cancel further work on the system and redirect organizational resources elsewhere. The elements of this phase are described in Table 9-2.

Table 9-2. Definition Phase.

1. Firm identification of the human and nonhuman resources required.
2. Preparation of final system performance requirements.
3. Preparation of detailed plans required to support the system.
4. Determination of realistic cost, schedule, and performance requirements.
5. Identification of those areas of the system where high risk and uncertainty exist, and delineation of plans for further exploration of these areas.
6. Definition of intersystem and intrasystem interfaces.
7. Determination of necessary support subsystems.
8. Identification and initial preparation of the documentation required to support the system, such as policies, procedures, job descriptions, budget and funding papers, letters, memoranda, etc.

Production or Acquisition Phase. The purpose of the production or acquisition phase is to acquire and test the system elements and the total system itself using the standards developed during the preceding phases. The acquisition process involves such things as the actual setting up of the system, the fabrication of hardware, the allocation of authority and responsibility, the construction of facilities, and the finalization of supporting documentation. Table 9-3 details this phase.

The Operational Phase. The fundamental role of the manager of a system during the operational phase is to provide the resource support required to accomplish system objectives. This phase indicates the system has been proven economical, feasible, and practicable and will be used to accomplish the desired ends of the system. In this phase the manager's functions change somewhat. He is less concerned with planning and organizing and more concerned with controlling the system's operation along the predetermined lines of performance. His responsibilities for planning and organization are not entirely neglected—there are always elements of these functions remaining—but he places more emphasis on motivating the human element of the system and controlling the utilization of resources of the total system. It is during this phase that the system may lose its identity per se and be assimilated into the institutional framework of the organization.

If the system in question is a product to be marketed, the operational stage begins the sales life cycle portion of the overall cycle, for it is in this phase that marketing of the product is conducted. Table 9-4 shows the important elements of this phase.

The Divestment Phase. The divestment phase is the one in which the organization "gets out of the business" which it began with the concep-

Table 9-3. Production Phase.

1. Updating of detailed plans conceived and defined during the preceding phases.
2. Identification and management of the resources required to facilitate the production processes such as inventory, supplies, labor, funds, etc.
3. Verification of system production specifications.
4. Beginning of production, construction, and installation.
5. Final preparation and dissemination of policy and procedural documents.
6. Performance of final testing to determine adequacy of the system to do the things it is intended to do.
7. Development of technical manuals and affiliated documentation describing how the system is intended to operate.
8. Development of plans to support the system during its operational phase.

Table 9-4. Operational Phase.

1. Use of the system results by the intended user or customer.
2. Actual integration of the project's product or service into existing organizational systems.
3. Evaluation of the technical, social and economic sufficiency of the project to meet actual operating conditions.
4. Provision of feedback to organizational planners concerned with developing new projects and systems.
5. Evaluation of the adequacy of supporting systems.

tual phase. Every system—be it a product system, a weapons system, a management system, or whatever—has a finite lifetime. Too often this goes unrecognized, with the result that outdated and unprofitable products are retained, inefficient management systems are used, or inadequate equipment and facilities are "put up with." Only by the specific and continuous consideration of the divestment possibilities can the organization realistically hope to avoid these contingencies. Table 9-5 relates to the divestment phase.

Taken together, Tables 9-1 through 9-5 provide a detailed outline of the overall systems development life cycle. Of course, the terminology used in these tables is not applicable to every system which might be under development, since the terminology generally applied to the development of consumer product systems is often different from that applied to weapons systems. Both, in turn, are different from that used in the development of a financial system for a business firm. However, whatever the terminology used, the concepts are applicable to all such systems.

Table 9-5. Divestment Phase.

1. System phasedown.
2. Development of plans transferring responsibility to supporting organizations.
3. Divestment or transfer of resources to other systems.
4. Development of "lessons learned from system" for inclusion in qualitative-quantitative data base to include:
   a Assessment of image by the customer
   b Major problems encountered and their solution
   c Technological advances
   d Advancements in knowledge relative to department strategic objectives
   e New or improved management techniques
   f Recommendations for future research and development
   g Recommendations for the management of future programs, including interfaces with associate contractors
   h Other major lessons learned during the course of the system.

For instance, Curling* has identified several phases of a major Canadian weapons acquisition program comprised of a series of decisions organized around the complete system life-cycle objective. These phases are *Conception, Definition, Acquisition, Service,* and finally, *Disposal.* Within these phases Curling identifies the following elements:

a. Policy Planning and Project Initiation.
b. Project Definition.
c. Full-Scale Project Development.
d. Project Systems Integration.
e. Project Test and Evaluation.
f. Project Production.**

Pandia describes a project as typically consisting of yet other phases:

- Identification
- Formulation
- Evaluation
- Detailed Planning
- Design and Engineering
- Procurement
- Construction/Execution
- Completion
- Post-completion activities***

LIFE-CYCLE MANAGEMENT

Life-cycle management refers to the management of systems, products, or projects throughout their life cycle. In the context of the sales life cycle, life-cycle management is usually called "product management." In the development life cycle, it is usually called "project management." In all cases, life-cycle management is needed because the *life cycle reflects very different management requirements at its various stages.*

The traditional hierarchical organization is not designed to cope with the constantly changing management requirements dictated by life cy-

---

* David H. Curling, "A Personal Perspective of Acquisition (Equipment) Project Management," *1985 PMI Proceedings,* Vol. 2, Denver, pp. 1–12.
** Ibid., p. 3.
*** Rajeev M. Pandia, "Excellence in Integration of Project Phases," *1985 PMI Proceedings,* Vol. 2, Denver, pp. 1–2.

cles. It is established to effectively direct and control a much less dynamic milieu.

Variability of Input and Output Measures for Various Stages of the Life Cycle

The dynamism that is inherent in the life cycle is made apparent when one considers the variability in the measures that may be used to appropriately describe the inputs to, and outputs from, a system as it goes through its life cycle.

Such measures vary widely. For instance, in developing a new product, one might characterize the various phases of the project life cycle in terms of the proportional composition of the work force assigned to the activity. In the beginning, research personnel predominate; subsequently, their role diminishes and engineers come to the forefront; finally, marketing and sales personnel become most important.

Basic life-cycle concepts hold for all projects and systems. Thus an organizational system develops and matures according to a cycle which is much like that of a product. The measures used to define various phases of an organization's life cycle might focus on its product orientation, for example, defense versus nondefense, its personnel composition, for example, scientists versus nonscientists, its per-share earnings, etc. For a management information system, the life cycle might be characterized by the expenditure level during the developmental phase together with the performance characteristics of the system after it becomes operational.

A hardware system displays no sales performance after it is in use, but it does display definite phases of operation. For example, Figure 9-2 shows a typical failure rate curve for the components making up a com-

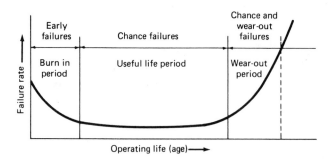

Figure 9-2. Component failure rate in a system as a function of age.

plex system. As the system is first put into operation, the failure rate is rather high because of "burn in" failures of weak components. After this period is passed, a relatively constant failure rate is experienced for a long duration; then, as wear-outs begin to occur, the component failure rate rises dramatically.

Perhaps a comparison of Figures 9-1 and 9-2 best illustrates the pervasiveness of life-cycle concepts and the importance of assessing the life cycle properly. Figure 9-1 represents a sales life cycle for a product. The most appropriate measure to be applied to this product's sales life cycle is "sales rate." Figure 9-2 shows the operating life cycle of a hardware system—for instance, a military weapons system. The concept is the same as that of Figure 9-1, but the appropriate measurement is different. In Figure 9-2 the "failure rate" is deemed to be the most important assessable aspect of the life cycle for the purpose for which the measurement will be used.

Life-Cycle Management Dimensions

The variability of the various input and output measures and the fact that different measures may be more appropriate at one stage of the life cycle than at another suggest that project management must focus on certain *critical generic project dimensions*. These dimensions are *cost, time and performance*.

Cost refers to the resources being expended. One would want to assess cost sometimes in terms of an expenditure rate (e.g., dollars per month) and sometimes in terms of total cumulative expenditures (or both).

Time refers to the timeliness of progress in terms of a schedule which has been set up. Answers to such questions as: "Is the project on schedule?" and "How many days must be made up?" reflect this dimension of progress.

The third dimension of project progress is *performance:* that is, how is the project meeting its objectives or specifications? For example, in a product development project, performance would be assessed by the degree to which the product meets the specifications or goal set for it. Typically, products are developed by a series of improvements which successively approach a desired goal, for example, soap powder with the same cleaning properties but less sudsiness. In the case of an airplane, certain requirements as to speed, range, altitude capability, etc., are set and the degree to which a particular design in a series of successive refinements meets these requirements is an assessment of the performance dimension of the aircraft design project.

Managing Over the Life Cycle

Since the mix of resources (inputs) and outputs associated with a project varies through the life cycle, the implication is strong that the appropriate techniques and strategies of management also vary during the various phases. Indeed, the need for management flexibility across the life cycle is one of the primary reasons that the traditional hierarchical organization is inadequate in dealing with project-intensive management situations.

The specific implications to project management are presented elsewhere in this volume. Table 9-6 shows a broad set of management strategies, developed by Fox,* that are associated with a five-stage life cycle:

1. Precommercialization.
2. Introduction.
3. Growth.
4. Maturity.
5. Decline.

The first stage of Fox's life cycle may be roughly thought of as the development life cycle that has itself previously been treated in terms of a number of stages. The remaining four stages represent the sales life cycle.

Table 9-6 clearly indicates the extreme variability in management strategy and outlook that is necessitated by the dynamics of the life cycle. The prospect of such flexibility being developed in the context of a traditional hierarchical organization, designed primarily to ensure efficiency and control, is remote. Therefore, the implications of life cycles to both the need for, and practice of, project management are straightforward.

Overall Organization Management Implications

An organization can be characterized at any instant in a given time by a "stream of projects" that place demands on its resources. The combined effect of all the "projects" facing an organization at any given time determines the overall status of the organization at that time.

The projects facing a given organization at a given time typically are diverse in nature—some products are in various stages of their sales life cycles, other products are in various stages of development, management subsystems are undergoing development, organizational subsystems are

---

* Harold W. Fox, "A Framework for Functional Coordination," *Atlanta Economic Review*, Vol. 23, No. 6 (1973), pp. 10–11. Used with permission.

Table 9-6. Fox's Hypotheses About Appropriate Business Strategies over the Product Life Cycle

	FUNCTIONAL FOCUS	R&D	PRODUCTION	MARKETING	PHYSICAL DISTRIBUTION
Precommercialization	Coordination of R&D and other functions	Reliability tests Release blueprints	Production design Process planning Purchasing dept. lines up vendors & subcontractors	Test marketing Detailed marketing plan	Plan shipping schedules, mixed carloads Rent warehouse space, trucks
Introduction	Engineering: debugging in R&D production, and field	Technical corrections (Engineering changes)	Subcontracting Centralize pilot plants; test various processes; develop standards.	Induce trial; fill pipelines; sales agents or commissioned salesmen; publicity	Plan a logistics system
Growth	Production	Start successor product	Centralize production Phase out subcontractors Expedite vendors ouput; long runs	Channel commitment Brand emphasis Salaried sales force Reduce price if necessary	Expedite deliveries Shift to owned facilities
Maturity	Marketing and logistics	Develop minor variants Reduce costs thru value analysis Originate major adaptations to start new cycle	Many short runs Decentralize Import parts, low-priced models Routinization Cost reduction	Short-term promotions Salaried salesmen Cooperative advertising Forward integration	Reduce costs and raise customer service level Control finished goods inventory

Table 9-6. Fox's Hypotheses About Appropriate Business Strategies over the Product Life Cycle (continued)

	FUNCTIONAL FOCUS	R&D	PRODUCTION	MARKETING	PHYSICAL DISTRIBUTION
				Routine marketing research; panels, audits	
Decline	Finance	Withdraw all R&D from initial version	Revert to subcontracting; simplify production line Careful inventory control; buy foreign or competitive goods; stock spare parts	Revert to commission basis; withdraw most promotional support Raise price Selective distribution Careful phase-out, considering entire channel	Reduce inventory and services

	PERSONNEL	FINANCE	MANAGEMENT ACCOUNTING	OTHER	CUSTOMERS	COMPETITION
Precommercialization	Recruit for new activities Negotiate operational changes with unions	LC plan for cash flows, profits, investments, planning; full costs, revenues Determine optimum lengths of LC stages thru present-value method	Final legal clearances (regulatory hurdles, patents) Appoint LC coordinator		Panels & other test respondents	Neglects opportunity or is working on similar idea

Stage						
Introduction	Staff and train middle management Stock options for executives	Accounting deficit; high net cash outflow Authorize large production facilities	Help develop production & distribution standards Prepare sales aids like sales management portfolio		Innovators and some early adopters	(Monopoly) Disparagement of innovation Legal & extra-legal interference
Growth	Add suitable personnel for plant Many gievances Heavy overtime	Very high profits, net cash outflow still rising Sell equities	Short-term analyses based on return per scarce resource		Early adopters & early majority	(Oligopoly): A few imitate, improve, or cut prices
Maturity	Transfers, advancements; incentives for efficiency, safety, and so on Suggestion system	Declining profit rate but increasing net cash inflow	Analyze differential costs revenue Spearhead cost reduction, value analysis, and efficiency drives	Pressure for resale price maintenance Price cuts bring price wars; possible price collusion	Early adopters, early & late majority, some laggards; first discontinued by late majority	(Monopoly) competition First shakeout, yet many rivals
Decline	Find new slots Encourage early retirement	Administer system, retrenchment Sell unneeded equipment Export the machinery	Analyze escapable costs Pinpoint remaining outlays	Accurate sales forecast very important	Mainly laggards	(Oligopoly) After 2nd shakeout, only few rivals

in transition, major decision problems such as merger and plant location decisions have been "projectized" for study and solution, etc.

Moreover, at any given time each of these projects will typically be in a different phase of its life cycle. For instance, one product may be in the conceptual phase undergoing feasibility study, another may be in the definition phase, some are being produced, and some are being phased out in favor of oncoming models.

The typical situation with products which are in the sales portion of their overall life cycle is shown in Figure 9-3, as projected through 1995 for the sales levels of three products, A, B, and C. Product B is expected to begin sales in 1988 and to be entering the declining sales phase of its cycle after 1991. Product A is already in the midst of a long declining sales phase. Product C is in development and will not be marketed until 1990. At any moment in time, each is in a different state. In 1991, for example, A is in a continuing decline, B is beginning a rather rapid decline, and C is just expanding rapidly.

Whatever measure is chosen to represent the activity level or state of completion of each of the projects in the stream facing an organization—be they products, product-oriented projects, management system-development projects, or decision-oriented projects—the aggregate of all of the projects facing the organization represents a stream of projects which it must pursue. Although the same measures (e.g., revenues, resources employed, percent completed, etc.) will not normally be applicable to all projects, the idea of a stream of projects—each at a different phase of its life cycle—is applicable to assessing the state of any dynamic organization.

The overall management implications of the stream of projects are clear from Figure 9-3. Top managers must plan in terms of the project stream.

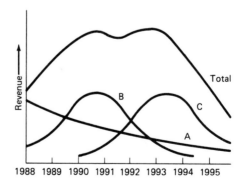

Figure 9-3. Life cycles for several products.

Since overall results are the sum of the results produced by the various projects, this planning must not only be in terms of long-run goals, but also in terms of the various steps along the way.

Most organizations do not wish to have their overall results appear to be erratic, so they must be concerned with the "sum" of the project stream at various points in time. A number of projects, each of which is pursuing a future goal quite well, might in sum not appear to be performing well at some points before they have reached their respective goals. In each case, for instance, although the progress of each may be adequate, each may still be in a phase of its life cycle where it is consuming resources more than it is producing results.

Thus, the problems associated with the overall management of an organization that is involved in a stream of projects are influenced by life cycles just as are the problems associated with managing individual projects.

10. Behavioral Implications of the Project Life Cycle*

John R. Adams†
Stephen E. Barndt‡

INTRODUCTION

During the last several decades, the technology needed to design and develop major new products has become increasingly diverse and complex. The increasing diversity arises from the need to integrate an ever-widening variety of professional and technical specialties into new product design. The increasing complexity results from the rapid rate at which knowledge has grown in each major technical specialty contributing to the product. This growth has spawned a large number of professional sub-areas as specialists strive to remain current in ever-narrowing technical fields. The increasing technical sophistication of major new products is widely recognized. What is not well known, however, is that the increasing diversity and complexity have caused extensive innovation in man-

---

* Portions of the material presented in this chapter were published earlier in "Organizational Life Cycle Implications for Major R & D Projects," *Project Management Quarterly,* Vol. IX, No. 4 (December 1978), pp. 32–39.

† Dr. John R. Adams holds the Ph.D. in Business Administration from Syracuse University. He is currently an Associate Professor of Organization and Management at Western Carolina University, Cullowhee, North Carolina and Director of their Master of Project Management Degree Program. Dr. Adams has published a number of articles on various aspects of project management, risk and uncertainty analyses, weapon systems acquisition, and logistics management in nationally distributed journals, and is a frequent speaker at national professional and at Department of Defense symposia. His experience includes management of major weapon systems acquisition programs and supervision of a major Air Force research laboratory.

‡ Stephen E. Barndt is A Professor of Management at the School of Business Administration, Pacific Lutheran University, Washington. Dr. Barndt, who earned his Ph.D. degree from The Ohio State University, has directed research into the behavioral aspects of project management and has published articles on that subject, among others. In addition, he has co-authored texts on project management and operations management. Dr. Barndt's project management experience includes performing as an assistant program manager and as an R&D project administrator.

agement systems for developing those products, resulting in the application of project management techniques to most major, advanced-technology, nonrepetitive efforts aimed at designing and developing new products or services.

The form of management known as project management was designed to ". . . provide sustained, intensified, and integrated management of the complex ventures" (1) and to pull together a combination of human and nonhuman resources into ". . . a temporary organization to achieve a specified purpose" (2). A project organization is established for a limited period of time to accomplish a well defined and specified set of objectives—to bring a new idea for a product through its conceptual and developmental phases to the point where the new product is available for use. When these carefully defined objectives are accomplished, the project is completed and the project organization is terminated. Thus a project has a clear, finite, and well-defined life cycle, a fact which has long been used to differentiate "projects" from the more traditional, long-term "functional" organization.

The field of management, as applied to complex organizations, has been the beneficiary of a growing body of knowledge. In particular, a great deal of research has been conducted in recent years to define organizational variables and evaluate their effect on the ongoing, functional organization. Little of this general material has reached the project management literature, however, and little specific research has been conducted to identify the specific organizational factors crucial to the project management field. This is not too surprising, since the modern concept of a project cutting across corporate, industry, and governmental boundaries to develop advanced-technology products is not much more than two decades old. A number of detailed topics relevant to project organizations, such as selecting an appropriate project manager (3), developing an effective, cross-functional, network-based management information system (4), and improving productivity in project management (5), have recently been more or less intensively investigated; and research efforts on such specialized project management topics continue. Little has been done, however, to understand the broader implications of the project life cycle. In particular, no comprehensive study exists which investigates how the project life cycle may influence and change the anticipated results of the organizational variables traditionally used to analyze functional organizations.

This chapter reviews a set of accepted organization theory variables for their potential impact on projects across the project life cycle. It then integrates the results of several independently conducted but mutually supporting cross-sectional studies involving over 20 major research and development (R&D) projects. The studies were designed specifically to analyze the impact of accepted organization theory variables over the life cycle of major R&D projects. The purpose is to suggest a set of propositions which will allow the practitioner and theoretician to predict the behavior of projects through their life cycles in terms of accepted organization theory variables. The results should improve our ability to plan for and manage the unique organizational problems likely to be experienced on projects because the project life cycle exists.

RESEARCH PROGRAMS AND PROJECTS

The concept of advanced-technology research and development projects has resulted from the need to develop ever-larger and more complex products for military, space, and commercial applications. The production and marketing strategies for such products frequently fail to fit within the constraints of a purely functional organization structure. The largest of these projects, for example the manned moon landing program, involves efforts which are simply too large for any single organization to deal with. These programs are typically sponsored and funded by a government organization such as the National Aeronautics and Space Administration (NASA), the Department of Transportation (DOT), the Department of Energy (DOE), or one of the Department of Defense agencies (the Army, Navy, or Air Force). The government agency provides the funds and overall managerial coordination. Private corporations, on the other hand, act as contractors or subcontractors, and each develops its own individual project which is responsible for achieving some portion of the overall program's goals. For example, when a new aircraft is being developed, there may be one major company responsible for designing the airframe, another for producing the engine, and a third for the avionics system, while still another develops the maintenance and support subsystems for the overall program. Similarly, in large privately sponsored projects such as developing new commercial aircraft, oceangoing ships, or offshore resource locating and extracting platforms, one firm might typically perform as the "prime," or integrating, contractor. Specific hardware and other development tasks are then performed on a contract basis by other firms or other divisions of the same firm. Each contributing organization thus supports its own major project whose output must contribute to the overall program objectives, while the sponsoring agency concentrates on coordinating the activities of the contributing organizations to meet overall schedule, budget, and performance objectives. In this situation the term "program" refers to the overall effort to achieve the end objective, a new aircraft or a "man on the moon," while the term "project" refers to an individual organization's activities leading to accomplishing its specialized goals in support of the program. The basic theory of the life cycle applies to both projects and programs, with the program milestones reflecting major accomplishments in one or more of the supporting projects.

THE PROJECT LIFE CYCLE

Special-purpose project organizations are molded around the specific goal or task to be accomplished. The essence of project management lies in planning and controlling one-time efforts, thus encompassing the managerial aspects of both projects and programs. The project organization exists only to solve some specified problem, generally one in which the "parent" or sponsoring organization has little or no prior experience. This description summarizes most current major developmental efforts, and therefore explains the dependence of such efforts on the concepts of project management. Both projects and programs draw from the same management theory base. The term "project management" is thus used in this chapter to apply to the management of both "projects" and "programs."

In current major project management efforts, the sponsor usually needs to develop some new product or system within critical predetermined (a) performance specifications, (b) time constraints, and (c) budget limitations. These, then, define the project's goal. Once the goal is satisfied, the project loses its purpose for existing and is dissolved. This is why the project organization exhibits a predictable life cycle: it is frequently said to be "born" when the sponsoring organization accepts responsibility for the problem and decides to accomplish the goal through project management; it "grows" and expands through the planning and initial execution phases as larger increments of money, personnel, production facilities, managerial time, and other such resources are devoted to the effort; it declines as the goal nears completion and resources that are no longer required are reassigned to other work efforts; and it "dies" when responsibility for the new product or system is turned over to the ongoing functional organization—the ultimate "customer" of the entire project. The project organization itself exists primarily to focus the undivided attention of key management and technical specialists on the task of resolving the specified problem across the life span of that problem's existence (6).

As a project proceeds through its life cycle it passes through an identifiable sequence of phases, distinguished from each other by the type of tasks characteristic of each phase and frequently by formal decision points at which it is determined if the project has been sufficiently suc-

Table 10-1. Managerial actions by project phase.

PHASE I CONCEPTUAL	PHASE II PLANNING	PHASE III EXECUTION	PHASE IV TERMINATION
Determine that a project is needed.	Define the project organization approach.	Perform the work of the project, (i.e., design, construction, production, site activation, testing, delivery, etc.)	Assist in transfer of project product.
Establish goals.	Define project targets.		
Estimate the resources the organization is willing to commit.	Prepare schedule for execution phase.		Transfer human and nonhuman resources to other organizations.
	Define and allocate tasks and resources.		
"Sell" the organization on the need for a project organization.	Build the project team.		Transfer or complete commitments
Make key personnel appointments.			Terminate project
			Reward personnel

cessful in the earlier phases to continue on into the next (7). Different authors identify from three to six separate phases, and there is no agreement on terminology. Nevertheless, general agreement does exist to indicate that each project phase involves different management considerations and presents different tasks to be performed (8). It should be noted that this involves two distinctly different views of the project. Table 10-1 identifies four project phases and specifies the general actions that must be taken by the sponsoring organization's management, and later by the senior project management, during each phase. Figure 10-1, on the other hand, identifies the same life-cycle phases but defines them in terms of the type of tasks that must be accomplished in that phase to prepare for transition into the next. In modern, major, high-technology research and development programs, the transition points between phases may be marked by formal program reviews held by the highest level of management in the sponsoring organization. These reviews are designed to authorize the resource expenditures necessary for the project to proceed into the next phase. It thus appears reasonable to classify projects according to the phase of the life cycle they are engaged in at the time of study, and to analyze major organizational variables as they affect the projects in the various life-cycle phases.

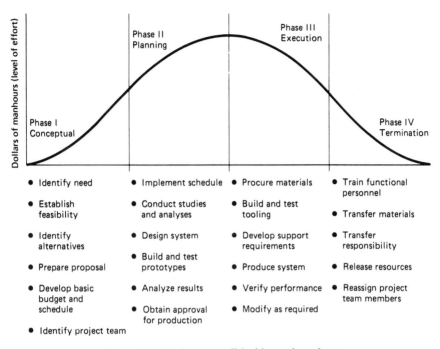

Figure 10-1. Tasks accomplished by project phase.

RELATIVE ORGANIZATIONAL VARIABLES

A large number of variables have been investigated over the years for their effect on the ongoing, traditional type of organization. The variables discussed below were analyzed for their relevance to project management because of their wide acceptance as important variables in analyzing organizations and because a research-based body of knowledge has developed concerning each one. All of these varaibles—organizational climate, conflict, satisfaction, size, and structure (level of bureaucracy)—are free to change as a project progresses through its life cycle. In addition, the project-peculiar variable "phase of project life cycle," discussed previously, requires further elaboration as it relates to the more universally applicable variables.

Organizational Climate

Organizational climate is a description of the organization as a whole (9). Litwin and Stringer defined organizational climate as ". . . a set of measurable properties of the work environment perceived directly or indirectly by the people who live and work in this environment and assumed to influence their motivation and behavior'' (10). These authors went on to suggest that both satisfaction and performance are affected by climate. Hellriegel and Slocum in their review of the literature cited several studies that clearly indicated a relationship between job satisfaction and organizational climate (11). However, the nature of the relationship between climate and performance is less clear. Although Likert (12) and Marrow, Bowers, and Seashore (13) found a more positive climate to be associated with higher productivity, Hellriegel and Slocum (11) cited both support and nonsupport for this finding and concluded there was no consistent relationship. The linkage, if any exists, may be indirect. Other variables may intervene between climate and performance. In addition to job satisfaction, intervening variables of particular interest may include conflict sources, conflict intensity, and conflict resolution modes. Climate may influence individuals to perceive more or less satisfaction with their work and to consequently be motivated more or less to perform to their capability. With respect to conflict, differing sources and intensities of conflict may result from or influence the climate. The combination of climate and conflict sources may in essence dictate or at least constrain the appropriateness of conflict resolution techniques. Use of these techniques may in turn influence climate and satisfaction.

Conflict

The essence of project management is that it is interfunctional and is frequently in conflict with "normal" organization structure and procedures, leading to a natural conflict system (14). The ability of the project manager to foster useful conflict, or to convert disruptive to useful conflict, can often determine his degree of success in achieving the project's goals (15). Thus one of the project manager's key functions is to maintain, in the face of conflicting objectives, a reasonable degree of harmony among the many organizational elements contributing to the project. Research conducted by Evan is important in confirming that differences in conflict do exist between the traditional functional organization and the project organization (16). Since both size and formalization of project organizations may vary over the life cycle, it would appear logical to investigate the changes in conflict that could also develop. Thamhain and Wilemon have done so for a variety of small, industrial projects. They found that the mean intensity of conflict from all sources, the pattern of conflict arising from various specified sources, and the conflict resolution modes used by project managers all vary systematically over the project life cycle (17). The purpose of one study (18) reported later in this chapter was to extend the Thamhain and Wilemon findings to determine their relevance to the major R&D project environment.

Job Satisfaction

Payne et al. described job satisfaction as an individual's affective response to his job (9). Although long a subject of research, the relationship of job satisfaction to performance is by no means settled. The preponderance of evidence indicates that the ties between job satisfaction and productivity or other measures of performance are weak or inconclusive (19). However, even the weak indicators of such a relationship should not be put aside lightly (20). In addition, there is conceptual appeal that such a link ought to exist in many situations.

Organization Size

Size has been shown to have a strong effect on perceived organizational climate in several manufacturing organizations. Payne and Mansfield, using a modified Business Organization Climate Index, reported a relatively strong positive relationship between size and most climate scales (21). Particularly noteworthy were the reported strong relationships between size and readiness to innovate, task orientation, job challenge, and scientific and technical orientation. All of these are climate dimensions that could be expected in many project organizations. Size may also be related to climate and other behavioral variables indirectly through its influence on the nature of the organization. Research has generally shown the existence of a positive relationship between size and organizational formalization (22). Increased size may dictate more links in the scalar chain, requiring greater formalization of communication and reporting systems. Increased size may also permit economies through greater functional specialization. As a consequence, the larger project organization may tend to be more functionally structured or mechanistic in nature.

Level of Bureaucracy

The level of bureaucracy may be defined as a continuum ranging from a mechanistic to an organic organizational structue. A mechanistic structure refers to an organization with communication directed primarily downward, high formalization of rules and procedures, adherence to the chain of command, low intergroup cooperation, and infrequent task feedback. An organic structure is characterized by high intergroup cooperation, frequent task feedback, open communication channels, low formalization of rules and procedures, and a lack of adherence to the chain of command. The latter characteristics describe the usual conception of a project organization. However, in large projects, particularly those related to major advanced-technology research and development programs, managers such as those producing program control documentation or running a project's information system may work in an environment differing little from that of the mechanistic organization where authority generally matches responsibility. A pure project manager, on the other hand, operating in an organic environment, may have responsibilities that far outreach his formal authority to marshal and direct the needed resources (15). Major project organizations may thus display a mixture of organic and mechanistic characteristics which could vary over the life cycle and have a major influence on the effectiveness of managerial actions.

Phase of Life Cycle

As a project progresses from the conceptual phase through the termination phase, the relative degree of uncertainty associated with the determination and performance of tasks decreases and the extent to which routine is applied to task accomplishment increases as shown in Figure 10-2. Studies of other types of organizations have shown a general tendency for organizations with either task routineness or reduced environmental un-

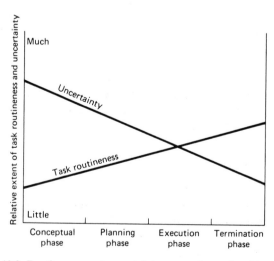

Figure 10-2. Routineness and uncertainty across the project life cycle.

certainty to become structurally more formalized and centralized (22). If the same relationship holds true in project organizations, and without the additional influence of organization size, the expectation would be that formalization (or level of bureaucracy) would increase as the project progresses. Further, since the major actions and activities change among the various phases, with differing pressures and problems arising, it should be expected that organizational climate, conflict sources, and conflict intensity would vary.

Based on the support from the literature cited above, and on several years of the authors' personal observation and research experience, Figure 10-3 was developed to demonstrate the relationships predicted to exist among the variables. As implied in the figure, size, degree of formalization (level of bureaucracy), organizational climate, and conflict source and intensity are at least partly a function of the peculiar problems and tasks that differentiate the various life-cycle phases. Organizational climate is also probably influenced by the degree of formalization of structure (level of bureaucracy), the general size of the organization itself, and the sources and intensities of conflict. Conversely, the intensity of conflict can be expected to increase as the organizational climate becomes less favorable. The degree of formalization of structure is expected to be a determinant of the sources of conflict as well as its intensity. The modes for resolving conflict should depend on the sources of those conflicts, their intensities, and the favorableness of the organizational climate. Job or work satisfaction is expected to be influenced by the overall organizational climate, the sources of conflict, the intensity of conflict, and the

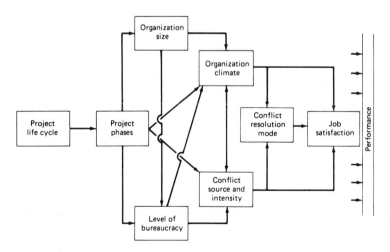

Figure 10-3. Predicted relationships among the organizational variables studied.

methods employed to resolve those conflicts. In general, the appropriateness of structure for task accomplishment; the extent and sources of conflict; the appropriateness, effectiveness, and acceptability of the methods employed in conflict resolution; the degree of favorableness or organizational climate; and the extent to which team members are satisfied with their work and work situation may all be expected to impact relative project performance.

PROJECT-SPECIFIC STUDIES

The authors have conducted or directed a number of studies designed to analyze the impacts of these traditionally accepted organizational variables over the several life-cycle phases of major R&D projects in terms of three phases distinguishable from each other by the type of tasks being performed, as well as by clearly defined, formal project reviews resulting in authorization for the project to proceed into the next phase. In several cases it is possible to logically divide the third phase into a third and fourth phase, two separate phases based on the type of tasks being performed. The separate research efforts culminated in the four notable reports summarized in Table 10-2. All data were obtained from the same organizational environment, although at different times. The sources of data were program offices of the United States Air Force charged with managing the research and development activities associated with acquiring new aircraft weapon systems. The responsibilities of these offices included conceptual studies, concept validation, hardware demonstration, prototype development, test article development and fabrication, test and evaluation, production, modification, and initial support activities. Program offices ranged in size from very small, approximately five individuals, to an office of more than two hundred.

Most data analyzed in the study was generated through use of questionnaires. Standard instruments, modified as necessary, were used to measure satisfaction, organizational climate, source of conflict, conflict intensity, and method of conflict resolution. Measures of organizational climate were obtained through use of the short-form version of the Likert Profile of Organizational Characteristics (12). The summed score of all questionnaire items may be considered an indicator of the individual's perception of the general style or system of management prevalent in the organization. The average of the scores for all project team personnel sampled in an organization or group of organizations was considered to represent the climate relative to that of other organizations and relative to an ideal climate of openness, support, trust, and participation. Job satisfaction was measured by use of the satisfaction scales from the Job Diag-

Table 10-2. Research Data.

SOURCE	SAMPLE	DATA COLLECTION	PERTINENT FINDINGS
Lempke and Mann (26)	142 program managers (95% response) randomly drawn from 13 program offices representing three phases of project life cycle.	Questionnaire, personally distributed, yielded data on organizational nature of tasks, phase of life cycle, and size of organization.	Organizations are most project oriented in early phase of project life, least project oriented in middle phase of project life. Organizations are smallest in early phase, largest in middle phase.
Barndt, Larsen, and Ruppert (24) and Haddox and Long(25)	185 program managers (80% response) randomly drawn from 13 program offices representing three phases of project life cycle.	Questionnaire, mailed to subject, yielded data on organizational climate, satisfaction, organizational size, and phase of life cycle.	1. Significant differences in organizational climate exist among phases. 2. Significant differences in organizational climate exist among program offices of different sizes. Organizational climate is correlated with satisfaction.
Eschman and Lee(18)	136 program managers (68% response) randomly drawn from 20 program offices representing four phases of project life cycle.	Questionnaire, personally distributed, yielded data on sources of conflict, intensity of conflict, method of conflict resolution, and phase of life cycle.	Conflict intensity changed across program life cycle, Air Force program managers perceived less intensity of conflict than civilian project managers, and Air Force and civilian project managers agreed on conflict resolution modes across life cycle phase.

1. Findings of the Barndt, Larsen, and Ruppert study.
2. Findings of the Haddox and Long study.

nostic Survey short form (23). The seven scales indicated in Table 10-3 provide separate measures of the individual's affective reactions or feelings obtained from actually performing at his job. Sources of conflict, conflict intensity, and method of conflict resolution were measured using a questionnaire developed by Thamhain and Wilemon (17) modified to fit the Air Force program environment. The questionnaire includes the seven potential conflict sources and five conflict-handling modes identified in Table 10-3, essentially measuring the frequency of occurrence of each. Finally, the level of bureaucracy was measured with a number of specifically designed questions.

The synthesis presented in this chapter involved extracting values of the major variables from the various studies and matching them with phases of the project life cycle. Analysis was necessarily restricted to identifying and demonstrating differences across life-cycle phases. No attempt is made to support the existence of cause-and-effect relationships.

BEHAVIORAL CHARACTERISTICS OF PROJECTS BY PHASE

The combination of study results supports the existence of marked similarities in the organizational environments of major R&D projects within the identified life-cycle phases. They also document several significant differences in the organizational environments characteristic of the separate phases. These similarities and differences are summarized in Table 10-3. Those studies which did not distinguish the execution phase from the termination phase drew most of their data for this portion of the life cycle from projects involved in tasks more descriptive of the execution phase, so it is assumed that the data presented for phases III (execution) and IV (termination) combined more nearly represent projects in phase III of the life cycle.

Phase I

Data from projects in the conceptual phase consistently indicate that the teams are small and use a relatively organic type of structure. The overall climate is rated low in the System 4 or participative management portion of Likert's scale. Conflict intensity is highest in this phase. Manpower resources is the most noteworthy source of this conflict, with the next four sources listed grouped closely behind as generators of conflict. While confrontation (in a problem-solving mode) is the favored means of conflict resolution, smoothing and compromise are also well-used techniques. The highest levels of satisfaction are found in this phase for six of the seven measures. Thus the organizational environment of Phase I is indicative of small participative work groups, with the members working together under considerable conflict and with a relatively informal set of work rules. They resolve their differences in a generally collegial manner with apparent concern for the feelings of others, and they derive considerable satisfaction from the work.

These findings are consistent with the theory of the life cycle and with observations of projects in action. This phase is basically concerned with preplanning activities, deciding that a project is required, and establishing the overall objectives and goals. These activities take place either before or during the identification of key personnel for assignment to the project. Thus there are only a few people knowledgeable of the project, and they must work together as a small, cooperative team to identify the work that needs to be performed. This is a truly innovative portion of the project effort, and it is generally accepted that conflict and innovation are necessary partners (15).

Phase II

Data from projects in the planning phase indicate a substantial increase in project organization size, a multiple of five to eight relative to the sizes encountered in Phase I. The type of structure is generally organic but with significant mechanistic characteristics, while the climate is rated midrange in a System 3, or consultative, type of organization. Conflict intensity is lower than in Phase I. Program priorities is the predominant conflict source, with the next four listed sources grouped closely together but in a clearly subordinate position. Confrontation and compromise are the preferred conflict resolution modes, while smoothing has decreased and forcing has increased in importance relative to Phase I. Internal work motivation rates high in this phase but is not supported by the other job satisfaction measures, indicating that overall satisfaction is not high in relative terms. The organizational environment of Phase II can be characterized as a relatively large work group organized along semiorganic lines with mechanistic tendencies—a consultative system. The members work together under considerable conflict which arises predominantly from project-oriented priorities, schedules, and technical issues. Differences are resolved in a generally collegial manner, but job satisfaction is not particularly high.

Here is where the project gets planned in detail, where budgets are defined and priorities are established. The work breakdown structure is developed to break the project effort into its individual tasks, while the planning and control networks are designed for imposing project priorities. The work group is expanding rapidly, so many relative strangers must work together. Simultaneously, the group is breaking into subunits to accomplish different aspects of the task, and these subgroups must immediately compete with others for priorities and resources. There

Table 10-3. Structural and Behavioral Characteristics of Phases.

VARIABLE	PHASE I CONCEPTUAL	PHASE II PLANNING	PHASE III EXECUTION	PHASE IV TERMINATION
SIZE (average number of managerial and technical personnel)	15 (range 11 to 18)	114 (range 49 to 169)	102 (range 42 to 207)	38 (range 30 to 46)
LEVEL OF BUREAUCRACY (average score between pure mechanistic, 1.0, and organistic, 7.0)	5.26	4.70	5.21	
ORGANIZATIONAL CLIMATE (average score, scale 0–720)	550.6-low system 4 (participative)	439.9-mid system 3 (consultative)	485.3-high system 3 (consultative)	
CONFLICT INTENSITY (on scale 0.0 to 3.0)	.704	.672	.621	.443
CONFLICT SOURCES (rank order of sources by intensity of conflict)	1. manpower resources 2. program priorities 3. technical issues 4. schedules 5. admin matters 6. cost objectives 7. personalities	1. program priorities 2. manpower resources 3. technical issues 4. schedules 5. admin matters 6. cost objectives 7. personalities NOTE: Numbers 2 and 3 tied.	1. program priorities 2. technical issues 3. admin matters 4. manpower resources 5. schedules 6. cost objectives 7. personalities	1. program priorities 2. admin matters 3. schedules 4. technical issues 5. manpower resources 6. cost objectives 7. personalities

CONFLICT RESOLUTION MODES (rank order, most to least used)	1. confrontation 2. smoothing 3. compromise 4. withdrawal 5. forcing	1. confrontation 2. compromise 3. smoothing 4. forcing 5. withdrawal	1. confrontation 2. compromise 3. forcing 4. smoothing 5. withdrawal	1. confrontation 2. compromise 3. smoothing 4. withdrawal 5. forcing
SATISFACTION (average score for general satisfaction, internal work motivation, pay satisfaction, security satisfaction, social satisfaction, supervisory satisfaction, growth satisfaction on a scale of 0–7)	Gen Sat - 5.83 IWM - 5.86 Pay Sat - 5.84 Sec Sat - 5.75 Soc Sat - 5.86 Sup Sat - 5.75 Growth Sat - 5.63	Gen Sat - 5.35 IWM - 5.98 Pay Sat - 5.50 Sec Sat - 5.30 Soc Sat - 5.41 Sup Sat - 5.70 Growth Sat - 5.10	Gen Sat - 5.29 IWM - 5.88 Pay Sat - 5.58 Sec Sat - 5.32 Soc Sat - 5.60 Sup Sat - 5.61 Growth Sat - 5.33	

should be little surprise that conflict is high in this phase. Further, since this is only the planning and design phase, many of the participants must recognize that they will not be available several years in the future to see the results of their work. Thus commitment to the project may be difficult to obtain, and consequently job satisfaction may also be difficult to generate and sustain.

Phase III

Data from projects in the execution phase indicate that project sizes are generally comparable to but reflect a wider range than those in Phase II. The type of organization is organic with some mechanistic tendencies, while the climate is rated near the high area of System 3, a consultative but near-participative type of organization. Conflict intensity is lower than in Phases I or II, but is still relatively high. Program priorities, technical issues, and administrative procedures are closely grouped as principal sources of conflict, clearly dominating the remaining sources. While confrontation and compromise remain the preferred conflict resolution modes, forcing is also an important technique in this phase. In general, job satisfaction in Phase III appears to be relatively low. It should be remembered in interpreting these data that the level of bureaucracy, organizational climate, and the satisfaction values were generated from data sources somewhat contaminated with Phase IV-type work tasks. The organizational environment of Phase III can be characterized as a relatively large work group organized along semiorganic lines with some mechanistic overtones. The members work together under a conflict situation arising from priorities and technical issues combined with the administrative procedures necessary to resolve them. Use of power and authority to resolve differences (forcing) is increased in Phase III, while job satisfaction is reduced.

The use of power and authority to resolve differences has long been associated with a relatively low level of job satisfaction. In this phase the job must actually be accomplished. Project personnel are "under the gun" to meet the schedules, budget limits, and performance criteria that earlier planners built into the project as goals. Any mistakes made in earlier projections show up here and must be resolved, along with all technical problems that have developed. Pressures to achieve the goals are intense. Conflict would be expected to be high in this situation. Job satisfaction may be reduced as the current participants see themselves responsible for resolving situations created by the errors and optimism of earlier project personnel.

Phase IV

The data from projects in the termination phase indicate a marked, significant reduction in project size from those in Phases II and III. Conflict
intensity is relatively low in this phase, with program priorities, administrative procedures, and schedules being dominant contributions. Confrontation, compromise, and smoothing are the preferred conflict resolution modes. Although not complete, these data indicate some significant
differences in the organizational environment of Phase IV relative to
Phases II and III. The environment can be characterized as medium-sized
groups working under relatively low conflict intensities. In terminating
their projects, the participants find that the principal conflicts are generated from project priorities and schedules, with the needed administrative
procedures taking on increased significance. Differences are resolved in
the collegial mode as was done in the earliest project phases.

This phase represents the end of the project. Those few personnel who
remain are involved in turning the completed product over to someone
else. Further, they are likely to be preoccupied with finding themselves
new jobs, since the ones they currently hold are in the process of being
eliminated. At this point, individuals are likely to experience less pressure
and to perceive less need to quickly resolve conflicts through forcing. The
task is essentially complete, and no amount of effort at this point is likely
to change the results. In this situation, low levels of conflict are to be
expected.

Reviewing the Life Cycle

Comparing the findings for each specific project life-cycle phase relative
to each other reveals some interesting relationships. In the most general
terms, the life-cycle theory is supported, with marked differences occurring in the organizational environments of projects from different phases.
More specific analysis indicates that project size clearly is quite different
across the phases. The planning and execution phases having by far the
largest project teams, the conceptual phase the smallest, the termination
phase has intermediate-sized project teams. The level of bureaucracy
parallels this pattern, with the greater bureaucracy corresponding to the
greater size, as would be expected. The level of bureaucracy measure
demonstrates statistically significant differences between the planning
phases and the conceptual and execution phases at above 95% level of
confidence. Organizational climate also changes markedly across phases,
with the early and later phases having projects more representative of

System 4, while the middle phases are more System 3-oriented. Statistical tests of the organizational climate scale indicated that all scores were significantly different from each other at the 95% level of confidence (24). Conflict intensity decreases consistently across the phases. The differences between alternate phases are statistically significant above the 95% confidence level, but those between adjacent phases are not (18). Thus there would appear to be a slowly declining trend in conflict intensity across life-cycle phases. Both the sources of conflict and the resolution modes change across phases in a manner consistent with the changes in size, level of bureaucracy, and organizational climate. Finally, job satisfaction in general seems to be highest for the smallest, most organic organizations and lower for those organizations most mechanistic in nature.

GENERALIZATIONS

The data referred to in this chapter were drawn from a variety of research efforts using different samples collected at different times over a two-year period. As such, the findings are not directly relatable to one another, and in some cases the observed differences are not statistically significant or cannot be tested for significance. Despite these methodological shortcomings, the synthesis, by noting important differences between projects in different phases, has served to strengthen the belief that there may be extensive variability in internal organizational environments over the life cycle of major projects. The fact that these findings are supported in the available literature as well as by the logic of careful observation lends credence to these documented results. The findings clearly indicate several differences between the projects representing various phases, and suggest others. Based on these differences several very tentative conclusions concerning the internal environments of projects over their life cycle were reached and are presented in the form of the following propositions:

- Individual project organizations tend to be relatively small in the early and late phases of their life cycle, and much larger in their middle phases. This may be a function of the different types of tasks being performed in each specific phase.
- Project organizations tend to be more mechanistic in nature and exhibit less favorable organizational climates in their middle phases than in either the early or late phases of the life cycle. The most favorable organizational climate and the most organic type of organization is found in the initial phase of the project life cycle. This may

be related to the size of the work groups found in the individual phases and to the resulting differences in organization structure.

- As the project progresses in its life cycle, the overall intensity of conflict decreases. Administrative matters and program priorities become relatively more important as sources of conflict, while manpower resources become less important sources of conflict. Cost objectives and individual personalities are relatively unimportant sources of conflict across the life cycle, although the conflicts they generate may be among the most difficult to resolve.
- As conflict resolution modes, smoothing decreases while compromise and forcing increase in relative use over most of the project life cycle. This trend reverses itself in the termination phase of the life cycle. This pattern of changes in conflict resolution modes may be associated with the changes in level of bureaucracy, size, and organizational climate which occur over the life cycle.
- Project organization size is negatively related to the extent of organic (project) orientation in the work group, perceived organizational climate, and the team member's job satisfaction.
- The perceived organizational climate in project organizations is positively related to the extent of organic (project) orientation in the work group and to the perceived job satisfaction of the team members.
- The smaller the project, the more closely it reflects the characteristics classically recognized as representing project teams—participative, dynamic, and collegial team efforts. Larger efforts clearly display the characteristics of more bureaucratic organizations.

The above relationships suggest that major changes may occur in the organizational and behavioral environments of the single project as it progresses through the phases of its life cycle. Such changes could have numerous implications for managers of project managers and for the project managers themselves.

Manager of Project Managers

One major implication of the project life cycle for the manager of project managers is that the idea of choosing a single project manager to see the project completely through its life cycle may need to be discarded, at least for the major, advanced-technology projects discussed here. Rather, it may be much more appropriate at the major project phase points to select a new project manager who is familiar with the types of tasks to be performed during the succeeding phase, and who may be best suited to the project environment anticipated to exist during that phase.

While his ideas are by no means universally accepted, Fiedler has shown that the relationship-motivated leader needs to achieve the best performance where tasks are unstructured, leader-member relations are either very good or very poor, and member behavior is influenced by the leader either by direct chain-of-command or through example, esteem, and expertise (27). The implication for the large research project is that a relationship-motivated project manager would achieve the best results in the conceptual or planning phases of the project, where the conditions closely match those specified by Fiedler's work. On the other hand, when tasks are better structured, the leader-member relations are relatively good, and the leader (because of a weak formal structure) can rely only to a limited extent on the direct and formal chain of command to effectively accomplish objectives, a task-motivated leader tends to obtain the best results (27). This set of conditions roughly parallels the situation in the execution and termination phases where organization climate is relatively favorable, tasks are relatively well structured, and the project manager has a less than mechanistic type of organization. Here, then, the best results might be expected form a task-oriented project manager. In addition, differences in the primary sources of conflict between the early and late phases, that is, manpower resources and program priorities respectively, further indicate the possibility that different managerial traits and different background experience and preparation may be called for in the project manager during different phases of the project life cycle.

Project Managers

During the early stages of the project, the characteristics of small size, varied tasks, a high degree of uncertainty, and the less formally structured organization appear to foster the more favorable organizational climates and higher levels of job satisfaction. The project manager is thus able to take advantage of the task commitment, the challenge, and the informality of the organic type of organization. Primary managerial functions of the project manager at this time should be to act as a communicator and facilitator, and to provide the various team members with information. The intent is to encourage participation and a team commitment to confronting and resolving conflicts. The goal should be for all team members to cooperate in accomplishing the project's goals, rather than to win an individual's point at the expense of the project.

In the later stages of the project, the project team diminishes from very large during the execution phase to very small toward the end of the termination phase. Here the project manager experiences a moderately formalized structure, perhaps as a legacy from the planning phase where rapid growth, high conflict intensities, and a great deal of environmental turbulence foster formalization in the effort to "get control of the situation." The degree of formalization in the latter phases can also be at least partly attributed to the routine nature of the tasks during the execution phase, and to the increased importance of technical issues as a source of conflict. A lower level of satisfaction is also experienced during this period, probably due to the higher levels of routine in the work itself, the lack of glory involved in "finishing the job," and personal concerns over future employment. Organizational climate, however, remains relatively formal despite these negative influences. In these later phases, the project manager should carry out the same managerial functions necessary early in the project and, in addition, should devote attention to reducing structural formalization as the project diminishes. This must be done with great care, however, to avoid undue shuffling of personnel or the appearance of demoting professionals unnecessarily. Reducing structure, it should be noted, is not an easy task. The project manager must counteract and overcome the "natural" bureaucratic tendencies of organizations to establish formalized sets of rules and procedures for almost every activity that can remotely be considered repetitive, and by this time the project has had several years to establish such procedures. This may well explain the well-known difficulty, expressed in many texts, in terminating or closing down a project (28).

The planning phase is characterized by a more formalized mechanistic-type structure and by large size, yet it also demonstrates high levels of uncertainty and conflict. This presents particularly challenging behavioral problems to the project manager. First, the tendency to overstructure the organization must be avoided to prevent hampering the cooperation and participative problem solving so necessary to successful projects. Second, the project manager must respond to the strong demands for establishing effective communication links. A dynamic project situation requires that project personnel generate and transmit information quickly in the face of new developments, establishing and encouraging relatively informal channels. Third, in order to facilitate a team approach to confronting and solving conflicts, the project manager needs to develop an identification with the project effort among the participants, to visibly use confrontation techniques himself, and to reward others for using these techniques. This implies a high degree of visibility and personal leadership.

CONCLUSION

In concluding this discussion of the project life cycle's behavioral implications for project managers and the managers of project managers, the authors offer these key suggestions:

- The project team size should be kept as small as possible, consistent with being able to accomplish the tasks. This requires a conscious and continuing effort, as there is a tendency to resolve problems by building a larger organization. The rationale may be to provide visibility in the parent organization, to make sure there are sufficient people to be "on top" of the situation, or simply to increase the project's power base. In any event, the increased number of people complicates communications and severely compounds the problems of effectively managing the project.

- Increased formalization of the project's structure (e.g., specialized groups, formal reports, chain of command, specified procedures) should be avoided whenever possible. The project manager should recognize and exercise the art of trading off the advantages of specialization and its resulting efficiency with the disadvantages of unfavorable organizational climate and poor job satisfaction. These disadvantages may be indicated by reduced identification with the project and a lack of initiative on the part of project team members, a situation which can be very costly to the project manager.

- Team members should be encouraged to work jointly to resolve conflicts in a manner that is best for the project as a whole, rather than for any one team member. This involves leadership by example, and places the greatest demands on the project manager. The project manager must establish open communication channels, take time out to listen, create challenging tasks, and praise good performance. This also means good management! The project manager should be prepared to spend a large share of the available time in leadership and communication tasks. If too little time is left for tracking technical, schedule, and budget issues, then the preferred solution would be to secure the services of a competent assistant manager to deal with such detail.

REFERENCES

1. Butler, A. G., Jr. "Project Management: A Study in Organizational Conflict." *Academy of Management Journal*, Vol. 16 (March, 1973), pp. 84–101.
2. Cleland, David I. and King, William R. *Systems Analysis and Project Management*, 3rd ed. (McGraw-Hill. New York, 1983).
3. Adams, J. R. and Barndt, S. E. "A Contingency Model for Project Manager Selection," in *Realities of Project Management*. Proceedings of the 9th Annual Project Management Institute Symposium, Chicago, 1977, pp. 435–442.
4. Woodworth, B. M. and Willie, C. T. "A Time Constrained Approach to Resource Leveling in Multiproject Scheduling." *Project Management Quarterly*, Vol. 7 (June, 1976), pp. 26–33.

5. Cleland, David I. *Pyramiding Project Management Productivity*, Vol. 15 (June, 1984), pp. 88–95.
6. Cable, Dwayne and Adams, John R. *Organizing for Project Management (Project Management Institute. Drexel Hill, Pa., 1982).*
7. Archibald, Russell D. *Managing High-Technology Programs and Projects* (Wiley. New York, 1976).
8. Roman, Daniel D. *Research and Development Management: The Economics and Administration of Technology* (Appleton-Century-Crofts. New York, 1968).
9. Payne, R. L., Fineman, S. and Wall, T. D. "Organizational Climate and Job Satisfaction: A Conceptual Synthesis." *Organizational Behavior and Human Performance,* Vol. 16 (1976), pp. 45–62.
10. Litwin, George H. and Stringer, Robert A., Jr. *Motivation and Organizational Climate* (Harvard University. Boston, 1968).
11. Hellriegel, D. and Slocum, J. W., Jr. "Organizational Climate: Measures, Research and Contingencies." *Academy of Management Journal,* Vol. 17 (June, 1974), pp. 255–280.
12. Likert, Rensis. *The Human Organization: Its Management and Value* (McGraw-Hill. New York, 1967).
13. Marrow, A., Bowers, D. and Seashore, S. *Management by Participation* (Harper & Row. New York, 1967).
14. Kirchof, N. S. and Adams, John R. *Conflict Management for Project Managers* (Project Management Institute. Drexel Hill, Pa., 1982).
15. Kerzner, Harold. *Project Management: A Systems Approach to Planning, Scheduling, and Controlling* (Van Nostrand Reinhold. New York, 1984), pp. 343–385.
16. Evan, William M. "Conflict and Performance in R & D Organizations: Some Preliminary Findings." *Industrial Management Review,* Vol. 7 (Fall, 1965), pp. 37–46.
17. Thamhain, Hans J. and Wilemon, David L. "Conflict Management in Project-Oriented Work Environments." *Sloan Management Review,* Vol. 16 (Spring, 1975), pp. 31–50.
18. Eschmann, Karl J. and Lee, Jerry S. H. "Conflict in Civilian and Air Force Program/Project Organizations: A Comparative Study." Unpublished master's thesis, School of Systems and Logistics, Air Force Institute of Technology (AU), Wright-Patterson AFB, Ohio (1977).
19. For example, see Vroom, H. Victor. *Work and Motivation* (Wiley. New York, 1964).
20. Organ, D. W. "A Reappraisal and Reinterpretation of the Satisfaction-causes-performance Hypothesis." *The Academy of Management Review,* Vol. 2 (January, 1977), pp. 46–53.
21. Payne, R. L. and Mansfield, R. "Relationships of Perceptions of Organizational Climate to Organizational Structure, Context, and Hierarchical Position." *Administrative Science Quarterly,* Vol. 18 (December, 1973), pp. 515–516.
22. Ford, Jeffrey D. and Slocum, John W., Jr. "Size, Technology, Environment, and the Structure of Organizations." *Academy of Management Review,* Vol. 2 (October, 1977), pp. 561–575. Also see Hendrick, Hal W., "Organizational Design," in *Handbook of Human Factors,* ed. Gavriel Salvendy (Wiley. New York, 1987) pp. 470–495.
23. Hackman, R. J. and Oldham, G. R. "The Job Diagnostic Survey: An Instrument for the Diagnosis of Jobs and the Evaluation of Job Redesign Projects." Technical Report No. 4., Department of Administrative Sciences, Yale University (1974).
24. Brandt, S. E., Larsen, J. C. and Ruppert, P. J. "Organizational Climate Changes in the Project Life Cycle." *Research Management,* Vol. 20 (September, 1977), pp. 33–36.
25. Haddox, Donald L. and Long, Neal A. "A Study of Relationships Among Selected Organizational Variables in System Program Offices During the Weapon System Acqui-

sition Process." Unpublished master's thesis, School of Systems and Logistics, Air Force Institute of Technology, Wright-Patterson AFB, Ohio (1976).

26. Lempke, Roger P. and Mann, Greg A. "The Effects of Tenure and Task Organization on Air Force Program Managers' Role Stress." Unpublished master's thesis, School of Systems and Logistics, Air Force Institute of Technology, Wright-Patterson AFB, Ohio (1976).

27. Fiedler, Fred E. and Chemers, Martin M. *Leadership and Effective Management* (Scott, Foresman. Glenview, Ill., 1974).

28. Kerzner, Harold. *Project Managers for Executives* (Van Nostrand Reinhold. New York, 1982), pp. 320–370.

11. Phasing Out the Project

Herbert F. Spirer*
David H. Hamburger†

It is much harder to finish a project than to start it. Start-up is a time of excitement: the team is being formed and resources allocated; the client/customer‡ is enthusiastic; and planning efforts are supported by the natural high spirits and optimism that go with beginning a new enterprise. But the finish of a project is a time of decline. Both the client/customer and the project personnel look to new ventures, the plans which brought the project to this point are now outdated, and the entrepreneurial spirit which motivated and involved the project personnel has been replaced by

---

* Herbert F. Spirer is Professor of Information Management in the School of Business Administration of the University of Connecticut at Stamford. Holding degrees in engineering physics from Cornell University and in operations research from New York University he was an engineer, project manager, and engineering manager prior to joining the faculty of the University. His home study courses in project management for engineering, software development, construction, and engineering department management and quality control have been adopted by over twenty engineering and professional societies. He has been a frequent lecturer and seminar leader on project management and consults to many corporations and financial institutions on project management and its integration with strategic planning. He has given papers on project management at meetings of the Decision Sciences Institute and the Project Management Institute.
† David H. Hamburger, PE, MBA, MME, a principle with David Hamburger, Management Consultant, Inc., has over thirty years of diverse experience as a management consultant, operations manager, project manager, engineer, and educator. He has acquired a broad range of practical experience in both line and project management functions with AMF and Dorr-Oliver Corp.—successfully executing projects in the military, industrial, municipal, and international sectors of the economy. As a management consultant and educator he has shared this experience nationally with numerous universities, federal and municipal government agencies, and industrial firms; providing consulting services and conducting seminars on project management, technical management, financial management, and cost estimating and control. He is also an Adjunct Professor in the MBA program of the School of Business Administration of the University of Connecticut at Stamford. He has written a home study course on cost estimating and a project management text and seminar workbook. In addition, several of his papers on project management have been published in various technical journals and presented to various professional societies.
‡ The term "client/customer" refers to the internal or external customer (or "user") who contracts for the project and wants achievement of its goals.

a sense of dullness as the staff deals with a seemingly endless set of details. But successful and complete closure is important: the success of future projects can be affected by the way in which the project is phased out; many contracts allow the client/customer to withhold a disproportionate share of the payments due until items such as spare parts lists and procurement drawings are delivered. How project personnel are phased out affects their performance in future projects, and proper closure can provide input to the postperformance audit as well as the basis for rational estimates and sources of extensions into new products and projects.

WHY IS THE PROJECT BEING TERMINATED?

The *natural* termination of a project occurs when the project's stated goals have been met. But it may not yet be time to celebrate.

- The project staff may have successfully completed acceptance testing in the manufacturing environment for a microprocessor-based pharmaceutical product test system in time to support market entry, and matched changes in scope by time and cost allocations, and had no cost overruns. But the project is unfinished. The operator's manual is a copy of an edited manuscript, the parts list does not include standard designations for all parts, engineering drawings have not been updated, several required forms have not been completed, and so forth. These are the details which the closure team must complete.

Some projects end less successfully. This *unnatural* termination occurs when some constraint has been violated, when performance is inadequate, or when the project's goals are no longer relevant or desired. The most frequent causes for unnatural termination are time and money.

- Although soil borings indicated that the foundations were solid, the partially erected structure has shifted and the cost of correcting the situation exceeds available resources.
- The project to develop a particular experiment for a space vehicle will not be completed until two weeks after the scheduled launch date. Since this spacecraft has a narrow window of time for meeting its planetary target, a project which is two minutes late is valueless.

Even when the reason for terminating a project is beyond the control of project personnel (government funds are cut, the price of fossil fuels doubles or halves, the client goes bankrupt), there must be a closure process, both to clean up the loose ends and to meet the contractual requirements of phaseout.

THE PROJECT MUST BE TERMINATED EFFICIENTLY

The participants, both client and project personnel, may overlook the importance of efficient project phaseout as they lose interest in the project or actively seek new assignments or, fearing that they will be out of a job when the project ends, "drag their feet." But failure to terminate the project efficiently can mean the difference between financial success or failure, a happy client and the potential for additional work or an unhappy client who will look elsewhere for future services, or an organization that benefits from its technical and administrative achievements or one that must start over each time a new project is initiated. The person managing the phaseout effort must understand the significance of these points and motivate the team accordingly.

When a project is completed late or inefficiently, the organization's "bottom line" can be seriously affected. The project's cost can increase if the termination process is stretched out, the staff is not reduced in an orderly manner, or the client withholds payment awaiting contractual compliance (meeting specifications, satisfying objectives, furnishing the specified deliverables, etc.). In addition, if the client, dissatisfied with the closeout effort, becomes uncooperative and refuses to negotiate back-charges, penalties, or liquidated damages claims, or the validity, scope, and cost of changes, project costs rise. When termination is dragged out, the organization's posture in closing out its open purchase orders and subcontracts is affected. And as time passes and the right people and information are no longer available, costs will continue to accumulate.

In the phaseout effort, project personnel must always remember that a satisfied client is final proof of project success. Client satisfaction depends as much on supporting documentation, training, field assistance, spare parts, and other services as on the major deliverables, because without these support functions the major deliverables might be misused or abused. If the client is dissatisfied, goodwill diminishes and the supplier's reputation deteriorates with consequent loss of future business and a possible increase in warranty claims.

The client's profitability can be affected if the client does not receive the operating instructions or information required to comply with government regulations in a timely fashion. Added operating costs, lost revenue, fines, and the cost of correcting a noncompliance situation are among the factors which can reduce the client's profitability.

Warranty service, an element of a contract with an external client, is important to both the client and supplier, and mishandling during project closeout can create problems for both organizations. A warranty start date, which is established by the project termination manager and accepted by the client, is needed to limit the supplier's postproject financial liability. If the appropriate project data (drawings, vendor documentation, specifications, manuals, contract terms, relevant correspondence) are transferred to the organizational entity responsible for warranty management, performance will be more effective and long-term client relations will be enhanced.

The lessons learned in executing a project are also proof of project success, and effective transfer of this information from the project team to the functional departments is a major responsibility of the termination project manager. The manager must transfer the technical data before the project team is dispersed, taking with them the knowledge and techniques they developed during the course of the project. It is also important to add the actual project financial performance data to the organization's estimating data base. Proper cataloging and storage of the project files is essential in case of warranty claims, orders for replacement parts, similar future contracts, or litigation.

All of this means that, while the phaseout process may not seem as exciting as start-up, it is as essential for project success and client satisfaction.

THE TERMINATION OF A PROJECT IS A PROJECT

Since managing a project's termination is as important as managing its start-up, many organizations assign a specific management team to attend to phaseout details. And the task of termination fits the classical definition of a project as a one-time unique goal with specific resource constraints (3, p. 4; 1, p. xi).* Research (4) has shown that conflict increases on projects when project objectives are unclear to the project personnel.

When management sights the end of a project, the project manager must determine the "profile" of project management tools and techniques to be used to bring this subproject to successful completion. As noted, closure has special problems and needs which determine plans, schedules, and personnel use.

Just as the tools should be tailored to the special characteristics of phaseout, so must the choice of project manager for this phase. The project manager and team which deal successfully with start-up and completion of major goals may not be ideally suited for the special problems, both technical and emotional, which accompany phaseout. A project manager who understands these problems and is temperamentally compatible with project closure must be chosen. Choosing the phaseout team

---

* Numbered references are given at the end of this chapter.

and transferring project authority to it is an important mission for management.

PEOPLE COUNT—IN PROJECT TERMINATION

We divide our concerns about project phaseout into emotional ("affective") and intellectual ("cognitive") parts which management must deal with when a project is being terminated. Figure 11-1, a structured tree

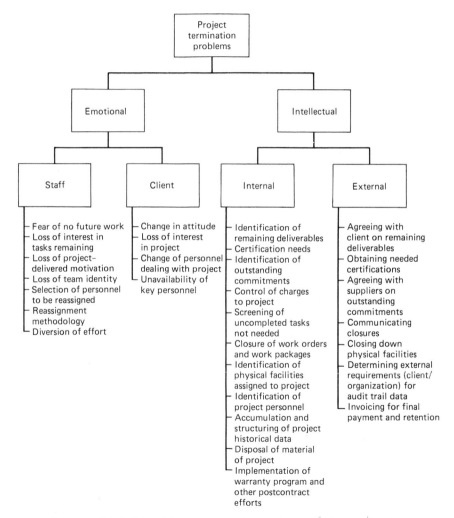

Figure 11-1. Work breakdown structure for problems of project termination.

diagram analogous to a work breakdown structure, illustrates both the general and detailed nature of phaseout issues. This figure shows that emotional issues have to do primarily with *spirit* and intellectual issues primarily with *detail*. Combining spirit with attention to detail accounts for many of the phaseout problems faced by the project management staff.

The following emotional issues concern the project staff, both those reporting directly to the project manager and those with matrix relationships:

- *Fear of no future work.* That the project is ending is no mystery to anyone. What is less clear is whether there is more work out there for the project staff. Even when there are other projects needing support, many members of the team may fear for their continued employment. This may result in a "philosophy of incompletion," and "foot-dragging" is often encountered as no one wants the project to end. Design documents take remarkably long to retrieve, instructions are repeatedly misunderstood or not acted upon, tools disappear or are not available, and tasks are stopped dead when the slightest impediment occurs. The staff seems to be working in slow motion.
- *Loss of interest in tasks remaining.* Start-up involves challenging tasks: problems to be solved, new methods to be applied, resources to be allocated. The end of a project involves familiar and often tedious tasks: completion of documents, refinement of known techniques and products, and the withdrawal of resources. The "fun" has gone out of these tasks. As a result, technical people lose interest, and many project personnel spend more time—often successfully—looking for new assignments on new or ongoing projects with more interesting tasks than they spend on completion of their current project. The result can be poor performance on the essential phaseout tasks.
- *Loss of project-derived motivation.* The concept of a project-derived mission, shared among the project team members, is recognized as one of the advantages of a project structure (2). As the project staff is reduced and activities focus on details that do not seem to relate directly to the project's goals, motivation diminishes and the sense of teamwork is lost.
- *Loss of team identity.* During phaseout new personnel with different skills are brought on board (e.g., technical writers for the operator's manuals, contract administrators) and long-term members of the team are assigned elsewhere. The perception of the project team as an ongoing group diminishes. The "team" is less interested in doing the tasks and meeting the deadlines.

- *The effect of personnel reassignment.* In almost all projects, termination is accompanied by a reduction in personnel needs. A key issue for the project manager is whom to reassign and whom to keep. The project manager rarely has the luxury of making this decision solely on the basis of project need. The needs of the organization must be balanced against those of the project, and project members may be resentful about the decisions made about their future.
- *Reassignment methodology.* Reassigning personnel must be carefully staged. Will there be a project reassignment office? Are personnel to be reassigned on an *ad hoc* basis, or will there be single or multiple mass transfers? If reassignment is not carried out consistent with the needs of termination, both reassignment and the ongoing phaseout activities can be adversely affected. Other managers may make "raids" on the staff, saying that "this project is running down anyway." Project team members may seek new projects while charging time to the project and neglecting their assigned tasks. Inept reassignments can destroy morale and any spirit of teamwork on the remaining tasks.
- *Diversion of effort.* When a project is running down, other tasks have a way of seeming much more important than those concerned with phaseout. Priorities change and it becomes harder to convince the client that project personnel are actually working towards a satisfactory finish.

Clients are also affected by the transition to termination, and the project manager must deal with this as well.

- *Changes in attitude.* The "steam" has gone out of the project and the client now worries about the problems of past performance on future success. Even where performance of the major deliverables has been satisfactory, the customer recalls when compromises were made, milestones missed—memory of the petty difficulties takes over.
- *Loss of interest.* As the staff loses interest, so does the customer. The excitement, the new challenges and, not unimportantly, the opportunity to allocate resources generously, shifts to new projects elsewhere. The client is involved in new projects, focusing on these instead of the almost finished job. Many clients regard the phaseout process as a nuisance, cluttered with detail and dull decision making.
- *Change of personnel on the project.* In both technical and managerial areas, the "first team" withdraws. The lead designers and managers move to new projects; the best inspectors, contract administrators, technicians, and project officers are moved elsewhere, and the client must now deal with a new team concerned with inspection and docu-

mentation. The customer, comfortable with the old team, must make new, and short-lived, relationships.

- *Unavailability of client's key personnel.* Personnel at the client location whose specialized skills are important to those technical tasks which remain may be unavailable because of reassignment (and perhaps, geographical changes). The customer's engineer who knows the source of specifications for exotic materials may be assigned to another project and does not return phone calls; the contract administrator who can give definitive interpretations of contractual boilerplate has gone elsewhere. Locating these people and making them available takes time and costs money, as does "making do" without them.

RESOLUTION OF THE EMOTIONAL ISSUES

Most of the emotional problems caused by termination are similar for both client and project staff since they arise from the same causes. But the project manager must deal with clients and project staff differently.

The project manager has authority over the project staff and internal issues and can exercise influence and power to resolve problems. But the manager has no authority, minimal influence, and little power over the client/customer. The project manager does have two client-motivating factors: to "get the project off the books" with the minimum difficulty and administrative problems and to make sure that documentation, spare parts, and similar support functions do not become problems.

Within the performing organization, the project manager has all the managerial and leadership tools that were available for the start-up and middle phases; these tools can be modified for phaseout. Using these tools effectively will help ensure that future projects function smoothly.

The project manager must recognize, first and foremost, that a guaranteed paycheck is a primary concern of most employees. No matter how spirited the staff, how committed the organization to long-term employment for all employees, or how large the backlog of project work, the project manager can never assume that all employees are unconcerned about future work. Even in organizations where there has never—in decades—been a layoff or reduction in work, at the end of a project many employees worry about the future. And where there has been a history of layoffs at the end of projects, employee concern is guaranteed. Even if there is no overt concern about future employment, the project manager should discuss the prospects for future work for the project staff. Conversely, if there is no future work, the project manager should "level" with the staff and then take special measures to ensure that staff morale is reinforced so the job at hand can be successfully completed.

Honesty is the best policy, and the project manager who is honest with his staff about future prospects will gain a great deal of support for project closeout work. The project manager should tell the staff as a group and individually the nature of the backlogged work and the pattern of reassignment. Open sessions where the manager meets with the staff and fields questions about future prospects are an effective management tool. The session should be scheduled when the project termination phase is defined (see below) and repeated when the manager senses rising concern about these issues. Indications are: failures to close out individual tasks and to follow agreed-upon instructions ("I don't remember you asking for that"), absences and tardiness, disappearances at work and slow performance. The project manager, sensing employee fears, should be positive, not punitive or authoritarian. These fears, whether stemming from a rational base or not, are genuine, and the project leader must deal with them.

A second major task is to offset the loss of interest in tasks, project-derived motivation, and team identity. The following specific management tools have been found helpful:

- *Define the project termination as a project.* Make it clear that closeout has its own project identity. Some project managers give the closeout its own project name. "Start-up" meetings for the beginning of termination help establish the concept that there *is* a well-defined goal to be met—closing out the job properly.
- *Provide a team identity.* A project name provides a base for the team. If the team is large or separated geographically, a closeout newsletter can give a feeling of identity. Some organizations issue T-shirts, caps, and other identifying insignia. In some cases, where the organization didn't support these modest outlays, project managers have been known to pay for them because the cost was small compared with the long-term benefits the manager got from the increased motivation and successful completion of the project.
- *Bring the team together frequently.* As closeout requires different skills, the staff changes and there is a tendency to allow the new staff to operate loosely as individuals rather than as members of a team with a common goal. To offset this, and to improve communications, the manager should schedule regular get-togethers. These are not "meetings." A meeting implies a lengthy sit-down session. Such sessions have their place in closeout, but not as a tool to maintain team spirit and improve motivation. These are stand-up sessions, limited in length (for psychological reasons), which give the project manager the opportunity to introduce new members, announce reassignments, talk about new work following phaseout, and deal with

problems and schedules—all within a team framework. Weekly or even daily stand-up meetings, limited to ten minutes, can become so much a part of project identity that a chance omission results in a flood of inquiries.

- *Get out to the project staff.* It is not always possible to bring the entire staff together on a regular basis. Some projects are geographically dispersed, or job requirements may prevent full attendance. The project manager offsets this limitation by getting out of the office and meeting on an individual basis with the staff. This presence provides a sense of identity with the team and the project office as well as a communications link.

Reassignment presents special problems. The method for selecting which project members are to be retained and which reassigned, and how reassigned personnel are oriented to their new assignments, affects phaseout. During phaseout, you need to retain those people with the greatest flexibility, the most independence, the best sense for detail, and the highest level of skill. Flexibility and skill are needed because of the variety tasks that arise during phaseout. Independence is essential as teamwork and close supervision are lessened, and a feel for detail helps assure that no pieces are left hanging.

The method of reassignment should reassure personnel of their future with the organization. And it must also be consistent with keeping a highly motivated work force. Below are some guidelines for the project manager facing this task.

- *Make each reassignment decision a conscious, deliberate choice.* Think through each reassignment decision, weighing the factors in each case. Don't make blanket decisions ("drop all electrical engineers"); they will come back to haunt you.
- *Hold the right personnel.* It's natural to want the best people for the job remaining. But closeout personnel need different qualities from those who began the project. Careful choices are essential.
- *Carry out reassignments openly.* Make sure that the project staff knows the reassignment plans; if the staff finds out from some other source, it creates resentment and it is easier for misunderstandings to occur.
- *Play an active role in reassignment.* The project manager should play an active role and not wait for the "mechanics" of reassignment to happen. Is the Human Resources Department playing an active role? The manager should get to them early and offer support. And other key people in the organization should be contacted.

Communication is important. As the team reduces in size and perceived importance, the project manager must work with both individual staff members and functional managers to ensure that everyone knows the importance—both to them and the organization—of an orderly and complete closeout.

The project manager is responsible, within the parameters of his job assignment, for staff morale. But this manager has neither authority nor the capacity to reward the client. The client's interest and support can be maintained, however, through an appeal to the mutual benefits of a quick and well-managed closeout. The project manager can assure client cooperation at all levels by stressing the following benefits:

- *Personal and organizational credit for closure.* Both the individuals and their organization gain credit when there are no loose ends and a project is "wiped off the books" in an orderly manner.
- *Availability of future support for the project's deliverables.* Proper termination means that spare parts will be available in future years, manuals are complete and drawings up-to-date. If the client is assured that these phaseout items will be delivered, relations between client and supplier will remain at a high level.
- *Identification of warranty obligations and the start/completion dates.* Advising the client of warranty support will aid postcloseout planning.
- *Effective and equitable closeout negotiations.* If both parties are well prepared and willing to compromise, the project closeout will be easier to achieve and this, in the long run, will serve both client and supplier.

INTELLECTUAL PROBLEMS OF PROJECT TERMINATION

The concern for *detail* is dominant among the intellectual issues. The intellectual branch of the work breakdown in Figure 11-1 illustrates the myriad of details involved in closeout, separated into two categories: internal and external. Internal issues are those concerned with the project itself and its staff:

- *Identification of remaining deliverables.* The contract, or other governing document, specifies deliverables such as tooling, test procedures, spare parts, spare parts lists, drawings, manuals, fixtures, shipping containers, restoration of modified facilities to original form, etc. To identify what is still undone, the project manager must match *delivered* items against contractual deliverables. If this is not done, contract administrators, auditors, or other client representatives may find undelivered items at a time when the costs of completion will be higher.

- *Certification needs.* Certificates of conformance with environmental or regulatory standards may be a part of the contract requirements (or implicit, such as UL approval). Some test procedures require multiple certifications, and the project manager must know of these requirements.
- *Identification of outstanding commitments.* It can happen in any project, especially those of large scope and lengthy time: project closeout is almost finished and a vendor delivers a surprise carload of components which are not needed. The best of commitment records can be incomplete, cancellations can be mishandled and never identified, or a genuine mistake can be made. Less dramatic, but just as difficult to resolve, is the commitment which is properly recorded, still outstanding—but no longer needed. The manager must resolve these difficulties or relations with vendors will deteriorate.
- *Control of charges to the project.* By the closeout phase, the project's charge accounts are common knowledge to an army of employees. Deliberately or inadvertently, they may charge to the project although not working on it.
- *Screening of incompleted tasks not needed.* Not all tasks being worked on may be needed. These "tag ends" can persist to the very end of the project.
- *Closure of work orders and work packages.* Once these uncompleted and unnecessary tasks have been identified, their formal authorizations must be ended. In addition, tasks which have been completed but are still carried on the records as open to charges must be identified and closed.
- *Identification of physical facilities assigned to the project.* During the course of the project, physical facilities—buildings, warehouses, typewriters, test equipment, machine tools, cars, trucks, etc.—may have been assigned to the project. The project manager is responsible for their care, and after they are no longer needed they should be redirected to projects where they can provide additional benefits to offset their cost and prevent possible continued charges to the completed project.
- *Identification of project personnel.* The manager of compensation for a major company reports that the first thing he does when entering a new facility is to ask the line manager for a list of personnel, which he then compares with a physical census of employees in the operation. The two lists rarely agree. While it is possible that some team mem-

bers may be working in remote locations and others carrying out tasks which require no supervision, it is important that the labor charges be correct—the lists should agree as closely as possible.

- *Accumulation and structuring of project historical data.* A project history puts technical and managerial achievements on record, making them available to others in the organization, is a guide to the management of future projects, is the basis for improved cost estimates for future projects and audits, can provide support in postproject disputes, and gives credit where credit is due.
- *Disposal of project material.* A project accumulates quantities of expendables, raw materials, components, partially finished assemblies, rejected units, files, catalogs, etc. The project team must dispose of these, for use in other projects if possible, or for scrap if this is impossible.
- *Implementation of the warranty program and other postcontract efforts.* Permanent functional groups, not the project team, are responsible for executing the warranty program and other postcontract activities such as in-service training, system and operating staff performance appraisal, periodic inspections, operator retraining, etc. But the project team is responsible for an orderly transfer of these functions at project termination. The responsible groups must be informed of their specific obligations and all relevant project data (contracts, drawings, purchase orders, manuals, client communications, etc.) must be transferred. Information about the client and the working relationships is also relevant. The client should be advised of these new contacts for each postcontract task. Both formal introductions and informal get-togethers can reinforce the new relationships.

External issues are those concerned with the client, vendors, subcontractors, and any other project-related entities not within the purview of the organization.

- *Agreeing with client on remaining deliverables.* Contractual statements may need interpretation. Project management knows what are the deliverable items and the specific requirements to be imposed on the remaining deliverables as well as which contractual items are no longer needed. There may be negotiations about the exact nature of the deliverables, as well as possible deletions and the trade-offs of additions against the deletions. If the specifications cannot be satisfied, financial settlement may be necessary. Every such modification or clarification is a potential change of scope and must be treated (via contract office, sales, etc.) and documented (change orders, change of scope, contract modification, letter of agreement, etc.).

- *Obtaining needed certifications.* Each certification has the potential of being a project in its own right. The deliverables—the specific documents or models required—must be identified and assembled. Finding the appropriate path for gaining certification can be a demanding task.
- *Agreeing with suppliers on outstanding commitments.* As with internal factors, some modification or cancellation of outstanding commitments is likely during phaseout. If costs are to be kept to a minimum and vendors kept satisfied, negotiations will be necessary.
- *Communicating closures.* The project manager must ensure that the closure of work orders and packages is fully understood and then carried out. Shrinking the project reduces staff contact and, to assure that work has been stopped and closeout requirements met (such as accumulation of charges, test results, delivery of fixtures, etc.), the project manager must make a conscious effort to communicate with the staff.
- *Closing down physical facilities.* Closing down the facilities often calls for a concentrated effort. Retrieving capital equipment which has been lent and operating equipment which has been installed can be difficult, even if the contract is considered watertight. For example, in certain space projects where equipment and facilities were maintained in other countries, closure was hampered by governments refusing to allow removal of the goods—a form of hostage for which a ransom had to be paid.
- *Determining external requirements for audit trail data.* Different clients/customers have different requirements for record retention for use in postproject audits. These may not be available as part of the contract. Often they must be determined through references given in the contract, or by specific agreement with the client.
- *Invoicing for final payment and retention.* The final invoice is *the* final item in project termination, signifying completion of the contract work. The resulting cash flow has a direct impact on the cost of financing the project; expediting this milestone should be the principal concern of the project manager and staff. In addition, reduction of any retention (payments withheld by a client to protect against nonperformance) should be addressed at periodic intervals throughout the termination phase as the risks perceived by the client diminish.

RESOLUTION OF THE INTELLECTUAL PROBLEMS

To deal with these problems, the project manager needs an array of analytical tools—mostly graphical—and a special set of personal skills. First we present the analytical tools for termination:

- *Tree diagrams.* Tree diagrams are hierarchical models which are useful in organizing project entities when discussing termination with the project staff, other departments, and the client. Figure 11-1 is a tree diagram which may be useful to some project managers in organizing and communicating the closeout tasks. Figure 11-2 is another tree diagram—similar to the work breakdown structure—for organizing elements of work in a project termination. The tree must fit the particular project, and this example is actually a fragment of a particular project, used here to illustrate the tree's use. Tree diagrams may be used to track deliverables remaining. If there was a work breakdown structure for the start of the project, the delivered items are crossed off; the remaining deliverables are now easily defined. In the absence of such a work breakdown structure, the project manager can create one from the contractual documents and cross off delivered items. Similarly, tree diagrams can be used to track outstanding work orders. Using the first level of the tree to represent the performing departments, closed work orders can be crossed off.
- *Matrices.* Matrix models are useful when two or three entities must be related. For example, in determination of certification needs and

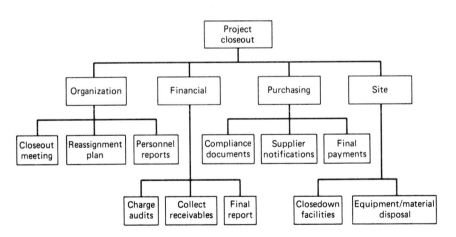

Figure 11-2. Tree diagram for a project termination.

managing the completion of certification, the two entities may be *product* and *governing specification*. Figure 11-3 shows how a matrix model may be used to collect information concerning the relationship between these two entities. Once created, in the process of collecting and organizing the information, the matrix becomes a reference for everyone working on the job and a means of communication. Checking the relationships for accuracy is quite easy with a model such as Figure 11-3. A typical three-entry case occurs in dealing with outside commitments, as shown in Figure 11-4. Here, the status of the commitment, as well as the vendor, is of interest; status is signified by the code letter in the box corresponding to the intersection of vendor and commitment. Matrix models for three entities are used to show responsibilities of differing levels. Figure 11-5 is used for assigning the levels of different individuals in meeting the records of the project. Here, the nature of responsibility and input function is shown by a code letter at the intersection points. The need for this type of matrix model is greatest when project personnel are shifting, when departmental boundaries are crossed, when it is important not to miss any details, etc., as occurs in project termination. The use of matrix models is limited only by the manager's imagination.

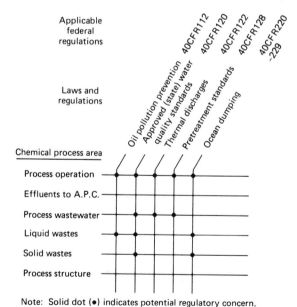

Note: Solid dot (•) indicates potential regulatory concern.

Figure 11-3. Matrix model for product versus governing specification (a portion).

	Amtel	Matarol	Pilog	State semi	Macropolis
Z80 chips	N	D			C
8080 chips	C		C		I
96K RAM	I		C		N
48K RAM	D			N	D
4K ROM	D		C		I
EPROMs	N		C		D

Note:
D, to take delivery.
N, in negotiation.
I, awaiting information.
C, closed.
Blank indicates no commitment,
past or present.

Figure 11-4. Matrix model for relationship among commitment, vendor, and status.

	Vice president operations	Quality assurance manager	Director of projects	Project manager	Task engineer	Automatic equip. manager
Quality assurance manual	A	P				
QA procedure index	A	P				
QA audit schedule			P/E	R		
Drawings auto equipment	A				P	R
Drawings calibration blocks				A	P	
Spare parts specifications			A	R	P	
Calculation notebooks			A	R	P	P

Note:
P — Prepare
A — Approve
R — Review
E — Execute

Figure 11-5. Matrix model for assignment of responsibility for records in project termination.

- *Lists*. Lists are the project manager's primary planning and control tool. This is a direct result of the termination process where *every* item must be accounted for. There can be no tasks left outstanding. By screening documents and talking with those concerned (internal and external to the project), the manager can produce listings of tasks to be done. At higher levels, these listings can be converted to trees (to provide structure and graphic communication) and matrices (where there is interaction). Where task interdependence is important, a network plan (CPM or PERT) may be prepared, but for the short term of project termination, as well as for weeky and daily supervision, the manager can work from lists. For this, checklists are convenient for showing what has been left undone. Figure 11-6 shows part of a checklist.

It is not unusual for the project manager to have a file or notebook of such checklists, one for each area of activity.* To provide a good audit trail, the dates when each task is completed should be marked on the checklist. Computers can be used to maintain such lists using data base management programs of modest size and cost, providing continually available listings which are free from recurring costs and the difficulties of dealing with a centralized information system. A "punchlist" is often used by the client to formally detail the contractual deficiencies which must be corrected before the scope of supply is accepted.

The personal attributes needed by the project manager responsible for phaseout include the following:

- *Knowledge of financial systems and accounting*. The concerns of the project manager are primarily managerial, especially in those financial areas of cost and accounting. The manager must understand cost accounting principles and systems, going beyond the organization's system to encompass the vendor's accounting system since this may be essential to getting agreement on outstanding commitments. Control of changes similarly calls for understanding of cost accounting.
- *Technical knowledge of the project*. The project manager must understand the design work even if he or she is not capable of actually carrying it out. To specify deliverables, screen tasks for need, close down facilities, and safely dispose of equipment and material, the project manager must know what is going on technically; managerial skills alone are not enough.

---

* An example of a checklist for project closeout appears in Russell D. Archibald, *Managing High-Technology Programs and Projects* (Wiley, New York, 1976), Appendix C.

FINANCIAL	Responsible person/dept	Due date	Remarks
Close work orders			
Close task accounts			
Audit charges			
Close payables			
Collect receivables			
Terminate commitments			
Prepare final cost summary			

DOCUMENTATION

Spare parts list			
Design drawings			
Procurement specs			
Equipment specs			
Test procedures			
Parts lists			
Maintenance manuals			

Figure 11-6. Section of checklist for project termination.

- *Negotiating skills.* Both internally and externally, negotiation plays a large part in closure. Project termination is about rapidly removing obstacles at the best cost—and if the manager has no negotiating skills, minor (and major) obstacles could result in delays and added cost. Without negotiating skills, the manager will have trouble assisting personnel with reassignment, disposing of project material, getting agreement on deliverables and commitments, obtaining certifications, closing down physical facilities, and determining audit requirements. There are many successful *styles* of negotiation, and the project manager only needs to master one.
- *A sense of urgency concerning details.* There are many times during the start-up and middle phases when the best strategy is to focus on the "big picture" and bypass the details. But termination is about the trees, not the forest—details are what it's about. Some managers are good in dealing with the forest, others with the trees, and a rare few are good at both.

THE END IS THE BEGINNING

A complete project termination is necessary for maximum goodwill and minimum cost. Because both project personnel and purpose are highly result-oriented, it is common to have the major items delivered on time and in working order but the project's end delayed for months and even years. The willingness and ability to bring the job to a satisfactory close are essential to the success of project organizations. A timely, complete closeout of a project shows good management and sets the stage for further relationships between the client/customer and the project organization.

The project manager's last task is to seek opportunities for either extensions of the project or new business. By seeking such opportunities and documenting them, the project manager ensures that the end of one project is the beginning of others.

REFERENCES

1. Lock, Dennis. *Project Management* (Gower Press. Epping, 1979).
2. Middleton, C. J. "How to Set Up a Project Organization." *Harvard Business Review Reprints Series,* No. 67208.
3. Mulvaney, John. *Analysis Bar Charting* (Management Planning and Control Systems. Washington, 1977).
4. Thamhain, Hans J. and Wilemon, David L. "Diagnosing Conflict Determinants in Project Management." *IEEE Transactions on Management,* Vol. EM-22 (1) (February 1975).

12. The Evolution of the Systems Development Life Cycle: An Information Systems Perspective

William R. King*
Ananth Srinivasan†

Rapidly changing technology is becoming increasingly important to successful organizational strategy. Whether the technology be that which is developed in laboratories as the basis for new products or the computer technology that must be integrated into a modern manufacturing system, overall business results are increasingly sensitive to the effective integration of technology into strategy.

Nowhere is this change more apparent than in the information systems area, in which the information systems development life cycle (ISDLC) has been a fundamental management tool. A variety of changes have been occurring in the ISDLC that have led organizations to develop a better ability to manage information as a resource and to integrate information systems into their "organizational behavior."

Despite recent concern that the modern "end-user computing" environment may represent the death-knell of the ISDLC, it appears that there is, and will continue to be, a major role for systems development life cycle (SDLC) notions as guiding frameworks for information systems (IS)

* William R. King is University Professor in the Katz Graduate School of Business at the University of Pittsburgh. He is the author of more than a dozen books and 150 technical papers that have appeared in the leading journals in the fields of management science, information systems, and strategic planning. Among his major honors are the McKinsey Award (jointly with D. I. Cleland) for the "outstanding contribution to management literature" represented by their book *Systems Analysis and Project Management*, the IIE Book-of-the-Year Award for the first edition of this book, and designation as a fellow of the Decision Sciences Institute. Further biographical information is available in *Who's Who in the World* and *Who's Who in America*.
† Ananth Srinivasan is Associate Professor at Case Western Reserve University's Weatherhead School of Management. He received his Ph.D. at the University of Pittsburgh and has served as Associate Editor of the *MIS Quarterly*. His research has been published in the *MIS Quarterly, Communications of the ACM*, and the *Academy of Management* Journal, among other journals.

development. Of course, the modern SDLC has evolved to become more expansive and more robust than the "traditional" SDLC (11).

Here, we discuss this evolving role of the systems development life-cycle concept in the context of computer-based information support. The concept itself has been changing and expanding, partly in response to reported failures of information systems projects to live up to popular expectations. More importantly, the recognition of information as a corporate resource (37) and its integral role in organizational decision making has also led to this evolving role of the life-cycle concept. The implied rigidity of the traditional definitions of the SDLC concept, coupled with rapidly changing organizational environments, have caused some to express the need for flexibility to be built into the system development process (1). This would allow for the modification of the traditional life-cycle definitions to suit the contingencies faced by specific organizations in given situations.

This chapter focuses on these modifications by elaborating on classic life-cycle notions and discussing "new" phases that precede and follow those that were traditionally defined. We also discuss prototyping as a system development methodology, primarily to contrast it with the life-cycle concept. There has been considerable interest in prototyping as an "alternative" to the SDLC. Here, we show that it is complementary, rather than antithetical, to the modern version of the SDLC.

THE SYSTEMS DEVELOPMENT LIFE CYCLE

The systems development life cycle (SDLC) is one of the fundamental concepts of the field of complex systems. The general notion of life cycles is widely used in management, engineering and elsewhere. For instance, the product life cycle is a fundamental marketing concept (17), and the organizational life cycle has been studied extensively (36).

The systems development life cycle traces its roots to those concepts and techniques that were developed in the weapons systems development context. There, the complexity of the systems under development dictated a need for management concepts and ideas that could aid in the management of great complexity (27).

The SDLC idea was quickly recognized to have a natural applicability in the development of complex computer systems. Thus, it became one of the fundamental concepts that provides a framework for much of the thinking, practice, and research in the area. It is difficult to conceive of an area of information systems practice and research that does not either deal directly with the systems development life cycle or in some fashion take account of the relevant stage or stages of the life cycle.

THE IMPORTANCE OF THE SDLC

Most people who are first introduced to the SDLC concept see it as a natural, logical, and intuitively appealing description of the complex systems development process. Because it has such descriptive appeal, it is easy to ignore or forget its significant implications.

The notion of applying an ever-changing mix of resources—people, money, and skills—to a large-scale effort in an organized fashion is rather new. It is largely in the past few decades that this has been routinely and pervasively practiced in highly technical and complex contexts. Previously, organizations were more static and operated over time with basically the same set of resources. If the nature of the task facing the organization changed, it adapted or it did not survive. Changes in the nature or amount of organization resources were largely accomplished on a reactive basis to accommodate to uncontrollable changes in the environment or in the task. The idea that such adaptation should be expected, anticipated, and planned for is the innovation that is represented by the SDLC.

While the SDLC may be viewed as descriptive of what *does* happen in order to efficiently and effectively accomplish large-scale system development efforts, it has vast normative implications. The SDLCs that were developed in the weapon systems context by the U.S. Air Force and NASA prescribed a set of activities that were to be conducted in each phase of the life cycle as well as a set of outputs to be produced as a consequence of the activities in each phase (10) and Chapter 12.

The normative information SDLC may be thought of as providing the framework for the specification of the management actions and practices that are necessary to successfully address complexity and to administer constantly changing requirements for resources.

The pragmatic organizational implications of the life cycle reflect the fact that quite distinct and different varieties of resources, amounts of resources, and varieties of expertise are required at various stages in the life cycle (17).

In the IS context, the need to apply and manage different varieties and amounts of resources and different varieties of skills in clear (28). For example, while analytic expertise may predominate in the systems design stage, interpersonal and organizational expertise is most important at the point at which the finished model or system is being placed into routine usage (61), and while the total level of effort may be small in the early conceptual states, it is necessarily much larger and more diverse in the detailed design and programming phases.

Various authors have prescribed the specific managerial inputs, outputs and actions for the various stages of the ISDLC (8, 11). Here, we review these only as it is necessary to focus on the important evolving changes that have taken place in the conceptualization and application of the ISDLC.

THE EVOLUTION OF THE ISDLC

The ISDLC description that best suits the objective of demonstrating the evolution that has taken place is that of Davis (11). He defines three broad phases, described as follows:

> *Definition*—". . . the process which defines the requirements for a feasible cost/effective system."
> *Physical Design*—the translation of requirements into ". . . a physical system of forms, procedures, programs, etc., by systems design, computer programming and procedure development."
> *Implementation*—the phase in which the ". . . resulting system is tested and put into operation" (11).

This "classic" information systems development life cycle, as described by Davis (11), is represented in the center portion of Figure 12-1 in terms of the "definition," "physical design," and "implementation" phases. Although many more detailed descriptions of the classic ISDLC have been developed and used (8) this three-phase description is adequate to provide a basis for describing evolving life-cycle concepts and applications.

This "classic ISDLC" has undergone significant evolutionary change in recent years. In part, this reflects a response to the relative lack of success that has been achieved in meeting some of the early optimistic goals and forecasts for the computer support of management (49, 63).

However, more importantly, it reflects an evolving appreciation of the significant role of information as a resource and of computerized information systems as an integral part of the organization.

In its entirety, Figure 12-1 shows the expanded systems development life cycle that has evolved over the past several decades. The evolution of the ISDLC has been of three basic varieties:

1. *Extensions* of the "classic ISDLC," as shown in the middle of Figure 12-1, to include stages that precede and succeed those of the classic cycle.
2. Greater concern with information as a resource and with the information *function* in the organization rather than merely with specific systems development *projects*.

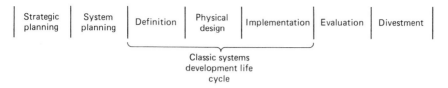

Figure 12-1. Expanded systems development life cycle.

3. A *blurring of the clear distinctions* that once existed among the phases.

Life-Cycle Extensions

Figure 12-1 shows how the traditional life cycle has been "extended" through the addition of both prior and post phases. These additions have had the purpose of viewing information more as a resource and less as merely a service. The result has been a recognition of the need to better integrate information systems into the organization. For the first time in the computer age, this integration promises to make such systems an integral part of the management process. If this does indeed continue to occur, the old view of computers as a technical oddity operated by specialists to provide a specific service to the "real" organization will change to a view of computers as an integral element of day-to-day organizational management.

These extensions of the classic life cycle are described in Figure 12-1 in terms of two "prior" phases—labeled "Strategic planning" and "Systems planning"—and two "post" phases—labeled "Evaluation" and "Divestment." (The next major section of this chapter discusses each of these phases.)

Functional Orientation

Many diverse computer systems and applications have been developed in most organizations in recent decades. This has led to a recognition that concern must be given to this *organizational function,* rather than merely to a series of distinct development projects.

If this were not done, redundant systems and applications would undoubtedly be developed by various managers and departments. Similarly, without such a functional orientation, the organization would be likely to proceed haphazardly with its system development efforts.

Distinctions Among the Life-Cycle Phases

A value of, and rationale for, the ISDLC concept has been the need for different mixes of skills and resource levels during each of the phases. For instance, in the definition phase, there is generally less of a need for technical computer skills (e.g., programmers) and more need for systems analysts who can assess decision problems and information requirements (10). In the physical design phase, these relative needs shift.

The evolving view of the ISDLC has served to blur these traditional distinctions. For instance, the definitional phase of the traditional life cycle has changed in terms of the recognition of the need for inclusion of "implementation" *criteria* into the general systems design phase. Thus, considerations from a later phase in the life cycle enter into an earlier one (61). This tends to blur the conceptual distinction between the two phases as well as to alter the required mix of resources in each phase. This is so because if implementation criteria are to be developed in the definitional stage, some of the skills and resources that are usually thought of a being required primarily in the later implementation phase come to be required in the earlier definitional phase.

One such "resource," for instance, is "user involvement"—the role played, and time spent, by prospective systems users in the design process. In the early days of the computer era, user involvement was generally limited to the implementation phase, together with having users be consulted about information needs early in the definitional phase (15). Now, "user involvement" has spread to every phase of the process; even to the physical design phase, which has always been the "technical heart" of the ISDLC that was solely reserved for those with technical expertise.

This involvement of users in physical design reflects both the influence of the implementation phase and the latter evaluation phase on the earlier phases (45). This blurring of the distinctions among the phases does not mean that the ISDLC is outmoded. Rather, it is now understood to be more complex and multidimensional than it was previously thought to be.

THE PHASES OF THE EXPANDED ISDLC

The classic ISDLC, as represented by the middle three phases in Figure 12-1, forms the core of the expanded version of the life cycle. The beginning point of the expanded cycle is a phase—the "strategic planning" phase—that is an extension of the classic cycle as well as a reflection of the need for a more functionally oriented approach.

The Strategic Planning Phase

The purpose of this phase is to ensure the integration of management decision support systems into the organization. In this phase, the organization's purposes are used as a basis for deciding on a role to be played by information and selecting a mission or charter for the IS function.

King (39) has prescribed a process of "strategic planning for information systems" that relates various organizational "stakeholders" (5), their objectives and goals, the organization's mission, objectives, and strategies, and other salient characteristics to an "information systems strategy set." The information systems strategy set is the *product* of a planning process in that it is derived from the organization's "strategy set." This transformation is achieved by specifying a desired role for information, an IS mission and set of information *systems* objectives that are congruent with the overall organization's *business* strategy and objectives as well as with strategic organizational attributes (such as its degree of decentralization). This ensures that conflicts between the information system function and other elements of the organization are kept at a minimum.

This process is depicted in Figure 12-2 in terms of the translation of an "Organizational strategy set" into a "IS strategy set." This approach, developed by King (39) in the MIS context and adopted by IBM (25), produces the specification of a chosen role for such systems in the organization, a strategy for their development, and general objectives and constraints under which the strategy will be implemented.

Detailed discussion of the process shown in Figure 12-2 is given by King (39, 42). The process is executed by explicitly deriving each element of the IS strategy set from the collection of elements in the organizational

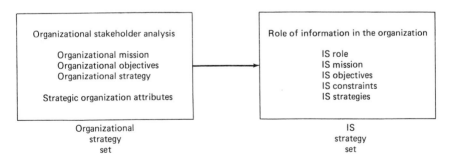

Figure 12-2. The process of strategic planning for information systems.

strategy set (as well, in some cases, as from other elements of the IS strategy set).

This is best demonstrated by an illustration adapted from King (39, 42) that relates primarily to the development of informational support for the strategic level of management. Suppose that a firm has selected, through its organizational strategic planning process, a number of *business* objectives and strategies as shown in Table 12-1. Further, suppose that a number of strategic organizational attributes have also been identified by system planners as being potentially relevant to the various kinds of strategic information systems that the organization might develop. These illustrative objectives, strategies, and attributes constitute the organizational strategy set, each element of which is identified in Table 12-1 by appropriate subscripted letter designations.

Table 12-2 shows elements of an illustrative "IS strategy set" that is derived from the organizational strategy set of Table 12-1. It specifies a role for information and IS in the organization that is chosen on the basis of providing the greatest level of support for the fulfillment of the business mission, objectives, etc., as specified in Table 12-1. More specifically, it addresses the specific mission of "strategic information systems."

The IS strategy set also entails a set of strategic information system

Table 12-1. Illustrative Organizational Strategy Set.

ORGANIZATIONAL OBJECTIVES		ORGANIZATIONAL STRATEGIES		STRATEGIC ORGANIZATIONAL ATTRIBUTES	
O_1:	To increase earnings by 10% per year	S_1:	Diversification into new businesses	A_1:	Management is highly sophisticated
O_2:	To improve cash flow	S_2:	Improvements in credit practices	A_2:	Poor recent performance has fostered a recognition of the need for change
O_3:	To maintain a high level of customer good will	S_3:	Product redesign	A_3:	Most managers are experienced users of computer services
O_4:	To be perceived as socially responsible	S_4:	Improvement in productivity	A_4:	There is a high degree of decentralization of management authority
O_5:	To produce high-quality, safe products			A_5:	Business is highly sensitive to the business cycle
O_6:	To eliminate vulnerability to the business cycle				

Table 12-2. IS Strategy Set.

Role of Information in Organization
Information is to be viewed as a resource that is used and managed in a fashion similar to other organizational resources. The organization's information systems will therefore no longer be merely a service; rather they will directly support all levels of management as well as be considered as providing a resource that is to be exploited to its maximum potential.

Strategic Information Systems Mission
To permit the efficient and effective assessment of alternative business strategies in terms of organization's mission and objectives using the best of available data to complement managerial judgment.

Strategic Information Systems Objectives
SO_1:   To permit the prediction and assessment of the potential performance of prospective new products based on historical data and the proposed characteristics of the products.

SO_2:   To facilitate the effective identification and assessment of potential acquisition candidates.

SO_3:   To provide a capability for the continuous monitoring of overall performance and the degree to which organizational objectives are being achieved.

Strategic Information Systems Constraints
SC_1:   The availability of funds for systems development may be significantly reduced in periods of business downturns.

SC_2:   The overall strategic decision support system must provide the capability for managers at corporate, business unit, and divisional level to obtain and *use* performance data at the relevant organizational level.

Strategic Information Systems Strategies
SS_1:   Design systems on modular basis. Design so that benefits may be directly derived from each module as it is completed.

SS_2:   Develop "performance and objectives data base" and related subsystems initially.

objectives. Each of these objectives is directly related to, and derived from, elements of the organizational strategy set. For instance, the second systems objective—that of facilitating the identification and assessment acquisition candidates—is directly based on three of the organization's business objectives (O_1, O_2, and O_6 from Table 12-1), one of its strategies (S_1 in Table 12-1), and one strategic organizational attribute (A_2 in Table 12-1).

Table 12-2 also shows a strategic constraint (SC_1) under which IS development must occur. Because of a strategic attribute of the business (A_5 in Table 12-1), the availability of funds may be reduced in periods of business downturn. This, in turn, leads to a systems development strategy that directs that strategic systems be developed on a modular basis so that if funds are cut off, benefits will be derived from those modules that are already developed.

This organizational process, called "strategic planning for IS," is a precursor to the "systems planning" phase that is more commonly discussed in the literature and that is sometimes itself referred to as "strategic planning for IS." For instance, Ein-Dor and Segev (16) essentially view the two phases as a single one in that some elements of both the "strategic planning" and "systems planning" phases in Figure 12-1 are dealt with under the rubric of "strategic planning for IS." However much question there may be about terminology, though, there is no question that the consideration of the strategic elements of the organization, which have long been recognized to be essential to the fullest realization of IS potential (48), are now being made operational (25).

The Systems Planning Phase

The "beginning" of the classic information systems development life cycle is usually described in terms of the identification of a need or the preparation of a preliminary proposal for a single new system. This is usually taken to be the first activity performed in the "definition" phase of the classic life cycle. The recognition of the limitations of this as a starting point in the life cycle reflects the need for *planned integration* of the various systems that are directed toward accomplishing the objectives of management.

Many organizations develop "successful" systems to perform a wide variety of functions without due regard for their integration. King and Cleland (10), for example, describe bank systems for checking, savings, loans, etc., that were not sufficiently well integrated to routinely provide management with a list of customers that reflected which bank services were being used and which were not used by each customer. Separate systems adequately performed their specific transaction-processing functions, but the data produced could not be readily integrated in a fashion that would facilitate more active management (such as through focused promotion of specific services to those who were already customers for other services).

The need for hardware and software compatibility is another important aspect of systems integration. Many companies are now experiencing the same incompatibilities in the new technologies of "office automation" as they experienced some years ago with computers. Two units of a firm may each purchase or lease an item of equipment and successfully put it to use only to subsequently discover that the technical incompatibility of the hardware, software, or both, prevents them from integrating the two systems. Thus, if consolidation of the same function in the two organizational units is desired by higher-level management, the systems hinder, rather than facilitate, the organization's integration of its information systems (35).

The "systems planning" phase of Figure 12-1 is directed toward the resolution of such difficulties. In this organizational planning phase, conducted prior to the commencement of specific information systems development projects, the proposed system is viewed in the context of other organizational systems. Viewed in a somewhat more proactive way, the systems planning phase is that in which the *need for* a new system or the *possibility of* new systems should be identified.

The systems planning phase is therefore the operationalization of the idea of planning for the wide variety of individual systems that may comprise the organization's overall information system. In terms of the modern concept of "information resource management," this may entail such diverse entities as electronic mail, automated offices, and telecommunications, as well as the more traditional MIS and EDP systems (7).

Sometimes the phase described here as "systems planning" is, in fact, inappropriately termed "strategic planning for MIS" (e.g., Head (24)) because it *takes into account* some of environmental factors that make up *one* of the dimensions that is an inherent element of strategic planning (43). However, as described in McLean and Soden (53), the starting point for this variety of planning is most often the IS mission or charter and environmental factors are considered to be constraints, or in McLean and Soden's terms ". . . opportunities and risks to be considered" (53, p. 24).

The Definition Phase

The initial, or "definition," phase of the classical systems development life cycle begins with the "IS strategy set" as it applies to the particular system to be developed. Often, when the previous stages are not, in fact, carried out, this stage was prescribed to begin with a survey of user requirements (23). Now, "user involvement" is believed to be an essential and integral part of this phase. The potential system users are not merely passive respondents to a survey, but active participants in developing the general systems design (58, 59).

The other subphases of the "system definition" phase are well recognized (11). The output of the phase should be a "general design" for a specific IS to be subsequently translated into greater physical detail (40). The general design is understood to be a road map for the development of the detailed design.

However, in recent years the definitional phase has been enriched and broadened by the addition of criteria related to the later implementation phase. Much of the early literature of IS development treated "implementation" as a technical objective—for example, the testing of the system under operating conditions (21).

When systems were found to "fail," or to go unused, or not to meet usage criteria because of nontechnical considerations, the idea of implementation was broadened to include organizational and behavioral dimensions. Prescriptions to resolve this difficulty ranged from simple ideas of "selling" the system, to more sophisticated ones involving the systems designer acting as an agent of change (66), to improved training of the system's users so that they would be better able to appreciate the benefits of computerization (55). In all instances, this early view of implementation required *changes on the part of the system users.*

The evolving view of implementation sees this later stage in the life cycle as the source for a set of *goals* that are to be attended to in *each of the prior phases of the life cycle.* Schultz and Slevin (61) have prescribed "technical validity" and "organizational validity" as parallel goals to be sought in developing a model of a decision, or a system. King (41) has discussed the inherent trade-offs that will often be necessary if systems are to have a high likelihood of being accepted and used for the purpose intended by the intended users.

The traditional relegation of implementation *issues* to the implementation *phase* suggested that the process was one of developing the "optimal" (technical) system, and *then,* of having the designer consider what must be done to get the design accepted by the user. This "after-thought" view of implementation issues serves to implicitly relegate them to a low level of relative importance as well as to explicitly restrict the feasible range of implementation alternatives.

The modern view is to deal with implementation issues as early as possible in the life cycle and to continue to raise them throughout. The underlying premise of this broader concept of system optimality is simple: that it is better to develop a good system that is used for the needed purpose than to develop one which is theoretically optimal but which is not implemented.

While this criterion, or guiding principle, is more philosophical than operational, Cleland and King (10) have provided a specific IS system design process based on the criterion. Others (50, 54) have studied and prescribed other approaches to achieving greater concern for implementation in the definition phase.

Ginzberg (19) deals with this issue in terms of trying to predict systems failures at an early stage in the development cycle. By assessing users' expectations about the system in the definition stage, the management of system development projects is more easily facilitated, thereby increasing the probability of a successful system. The results obtained in his study seem to indicate that it is important for systems designers and managers to know how realistic user expectations about the system are at the definition stage of the ISDLC. In this manner, critical implementation issues are dealt with very early in the life cycle of the system. This "broader" view of implementation is also the central notion of the view of system implementation in terms of an organizational change process (47).

The Physical Design Phase

While the techniques of physical design have evolved as havehardware and software, perhaps the most significant evolution in this phase has been in terms of user involvement and of multistage design.

In the user involvement dimension, this highly technical phase was previously viewed as the sole province of the analyst. However, the analyst is now viewed more as a catalyst who translates the user's functional and logical designs into physical reality (51). The "political" dimensions of the physical design process are also of concern since desired changes in the system may place users and designers in conflict (33) or create conflicts among user groups who have different sets of needs (18, 46).

These complicating factors, together with the inherent imprecision in the trade-offs among technical and implementation-oriented criteria which must be applied in this phase, have led to an emerging multistage view of the physical design phase.

Such trade-offs require a continuing process of adjustment and readjustment because many of the factors are so imprecise. In effect, tentative design parameters of the system must be evaluated on various bases of both a technical and organizational nature *before* they are made permanent. This means that the evolving systems design must be evaluated on a continuing basis. Thus, the evaluation phase of the life cycle, formerly thought of as being one of the latter stages, becomes a part of the physical design stage.

King and Rodriguez (45) have presented a methodology for such an ongoing evaluation process. In applying this methodology in a DSS context, Dutta and King (14) found that certain design features of an evolving DSS were viewed to be overly complex by the intended users. This led to technical changes in the systems design while it was still in the prototype stage.

Such a view of the physical design phase requires that it be multistage

in some sense. This may be operationalized as modular design (40), prototyping* (31), or in some other way. However, the continuing assessment
of the systems in both technical and organizational terms requires that
proposed system characteristics be identified and subjected to scrutiny.
Whether this is done in the form of "experiments" with users on a prototype system (45) or in some other fashion, the ongoing reconfiguration of
the system in response to those assessments must be made feasible. This
can only be achieved through a multistage view of the physical design
phase.

Sprague (64) has described this process as it applies to decision support
systems as a "collapsing" of the traditional life-cycle phases into a single
phase that is iteratively applied. Keen (31) has similarly shown how "prototyping" can be used as a basis for assessing and predicting the value of
decision support systems.

The Implementation Phase

Implementation of management science and MIS was one of the "hot
topics" of the 1970s. The papers presented at the first implementation
conference in Pittsburgh (61) reflect the dominant view of implementation
that was then held. Although some authors were proposing notions of an
"adaptive approach" to systems implementation, the empirical perspective afforded to the concept of implementation centered around "putting
the model or system into use." Traditional approaches to implementation
in the MIS area also reflect this stress on systems use. Davis (11) represents the classical view of MIS implementation where he defines the
implementation stage as that which begins after the development efforts
have been accomplished and the system has commenced operation. This
view of implementation was perhaps best captured by the framework of
Anderson and Hoffman (4) who viewed the implementation effort as comprising three distinct phases: installation (which was traditionally the systems analyst's view of implementation); implementation, which encompasses the process of using the system (which was traditionally the user's
view of implementation); and the integration of the model with its results
into management behavior.

Contrary to this classical view of implementation, some researchers
were proposing a new view of the implementation process based on a
theory of organizational change. This "broader" perspective on implementation was deemed appropriate in light of the narrowness in the (now)

---

* Since prototyping is seen by some to be an "alternative" to the ISDLC, we shall deal with
it in more detail in a subsequent section.

classical definitions. Specifically, it was argued that by neglecting to consider implementation issues in the earlier phases of the life cycle, a major portion of the causes of user satisfaction or dissatisfaction was being ignored.

This significant evolution in thinking is based on substantial evidence concerning the implementation failures that have occurred (51). Much of the study and research devoted to implementation has focused on "organizational change" (20, 32, 70), the role of the user (15, 44, 67), user characteristics (9, 69), and organizational characteristics (18) that may be taken into account in the system design.

Alter (3) extensively summarizes the many factors that have been identified as resulting in increased risk of implementation failure. Schultz and Slevin (61) and Doktor, Schultz, and Slevin (13) have provided compendiums of the evolving thinking in the area.

With respect to the elements of the implementation phase itself, as distinct from the integration of implementation concerns and criteria into other phases of the life cycle, various approaches have been taken. For instance, Gremillion (22) has broadly focused on the training and integration aspects of the implementation phase.

The Evaluation Phase

While even the most traditional view of the information systems life cycle involved some evaluation component (usually as an element of the implementation phase), it was generally *post hoc* and relatively insignificant. Much of the evaluation of earlier periods can be characterized as post mortems of system failures (12, 51, 52).

A popular approach to evaluation involved using the extent of system usage as a surrogate for system success. The argument proposed in favor of this approach was that in cases where use of the system was nonmandatory, increased system usage is brought about because the user believes that such use has improved his performance. The inability of researchers to clearly establish this link between system use and decision performance led to different conceptualizations of the system evaluation phase, although some studies have indeed shown a positive correlation between "perceived system worth" and system usage (60).

Expanded life-cycle thinking integrates the evaluative phase into the prior stages of the life cycle just as it does with the implementation phase (15). Moreover, it extends the dimensions of the system to be evaluated well beyond technical considerations and the degree of usage to the domain of perceived values and beyond. For instance, King and Rodriguez (45) have assessed a Decision Support System (DSS) in terms of attitudes, values, information usage behavior, and decision impact. Ginzberg (19) also uses both behavioral (usage) and attitudinal measures. Keen and Scott-Morton (34) discuss a wider variety of evaluation criteria that may be considered for DSSs. Keen (31) discusses a "value analysis" approach that emphasizes the qualitative benefits that are derived from such systems.

The evaluation phase must also account for the changes and enhancements that will inevitably be proposed after a system is put into operation. Any such changes or enhancements demand that evaluations be made, for if the costs and benefits of proposed changes are not evaluated, resources may be consumed that could otherwise be put to better use.

The Divestment Phase

The "last" stage of the life cycle is divestment. The formalization of this phase recognizes that "everything must end" and that the phaseout of a system should not represent failure. This variety of thinking has been applied to products and to entire businesses during the past decade. As the strategic planning and systems planning phases of the expanded systems development life cycle have been developed, the use of this sort of thinking in business has naturally led to its application in the systems context.

Despite the fact that the divestment phase for a system cannot generally be viewed as even potentially "profitable," as can the same phase of a business or product life cycle, the idea is rather new that the declining effectiveness and productivity of a system is inevitable, although not uncontrollable, and that it should therefore be planned for (10, 40).

Thus, when a system is perceived in this fashion, it can be viewed as an asset to be "milked" via judicious and limited planned investments rather than as one to either be "saved" through large incremental investment or "junked" and replaced by a costly alternative system.

The inclusion of this viewpoint into the earlier "systems planning" phase can lead to the extension of the "natural" life of some systems through cost-effective enhancements, the evolution of some systems into others that are of significantly greater power and effectiveness, and the eventual planned joint phaseout and phasein of systems that are directed toward the same objectives.

Prototyping

One outcome from the need for a modified and evolutionary concept of system development has been the advocacy of prototyping as a development methodology. An excellent review of the literature on this subject may be found in Jenkins and Lauer (26). As Naumann and Jenkins (56) point out, a number of phrases have been used in the literature to essentially connote the prototyping approach in software development. Among the phrases are "heuristic development," "infological simulation," and "middle-out design."

Prototyping has long been used in manufacturing design as a means to work toward a final product by the production of intermediate (and hence imperfect and incomplete) versions that would be evaluated and modified over several iterations. Inherent in the prototyping approach is the idea of iterative design in system development. The application of the concept to information system development is primarily a reflection of the availability of new technology (and consequent enhanced development tools), the premise that information systems can be developed and used by senior executives, and the emergence of applications designed for relatively small user groups.

There have been some claims that prototyping is an alternative to the SDLC methodology, and studies have been performed to compare the viability of the two approaches. Alavi (2) reported that in an experimental study that compared the two approaches, the prototyping approach received a more favorable overall evaluation than did the SDLC approach to system development. Further, reduced conflict was reported between users and designers involved in the prototyping approach and a more adequate level of user participation was reported in the process that used prototyping. These results appear to indicate that prototyping is a "better" approach to system development compared to the ISDLC approach. It is our position that this conclusion is not necessarily valid.

The study mentioned above assumes that the two approaches are mutually exclusive of each other and, further, that either one may be used as the system development methodology in the context of developing an application system. This is not valid. There are clearly some applications where prototyping, when used as the *dominant* method of development, may work very well (see Keen's (30) discussion about adaptive design). Similarly, there exist large, complex applications for which the ISDLC approach has to be used in order to manage and control the intricacies that are involved. Prototyping could clearly be used here in the overall life-cycle context to deal with well-defined subproblems but certainly not as a replacement of it. This is especially true of applications development for the federal government, the aerospace industry, and other applications that tend to be of considerable size. Ironically, the results of Alavi's study also show that the ISDLC process was easier from a management control point of view compared to the prototyping process.

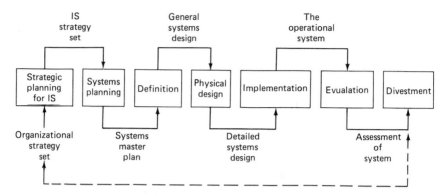

Figure 12-3. Input-output description of expanded information systems development life cycle.

In this chapter, our view of the expanded ISDLC notion incorporates the *spirit* of prototyping. Our concept of the modified life cycle takes into account the flexibility concern described earlier by providing for iterations in the process (see Figure 12-3). While we do not claim that this is the ideal process for *all* applications, it would certainly be well suited for large applications that are fairly complex and include a substantial user base.

SUMMARY

The evolving phases of the systems development life cycle in an organization are portrayed in Figure 12-3 in terms of their inputs and outputs. The output of each phase can be seen to be the input to the subsequent phase.

The "organizational strategy set" is the output of the organization's strategic *business* planning. It is, in turn, the input that begins the initial "strategic planning for information systems" phase of the systems life cycle. The strategic planning phase converts this into an "IS strategy set" that gives details of the role to be played by information and information systems in the organization, developmental strategies for systems, etc.

The "systems planning" phase converts the systems strategy set into a systems master plan. The master plan describes the objectives, roles, and time frames for the development of the various systems that comprise the organization's overall decision support function.

In the definitional phase for a particular system, a "general design" for the system, which fulfills that system's role and objectives as reflected in the master plan, is developed. This is then converted into a detailed design in the "physical design" phase.

The "implementation" phase involves the conversion of the design into reality and into the organization's behavior. The "evaluation" phase produces a formal assessment of how well the system is meeting the goals established earlier and whether it is playing the organizational role that was established for it. The last phase is the "divestment" phase, in which the system is converted or phased out in accordance with the organization's master plan.

The dotted line linking the first and last phases of the expanded cycle reflects the integration of assessments made in the latter stages with planning in the earlier ones. In effect, the class life cycle has been expanded into an ongoing organizational process in which new systems are being developed to play new roles as well as to replace outdated ones that are being phased out.

The evolution of the classic ISDLC into this expanded version has had the effect of converting information and computer systems into a resource that is "managed"—planned for, evaluated, divested, etc.—in much the same way as are the organization's other resources. The impact of this has been an increase in the level of integration of computer information systems into organizations. While this is probably an inevitable development in the long run, the timeliness and manner in which it is being accomplished will undoubtedly have a great influence on managerial productivity and on managerial effectiveness.

REFERENCES

1. Ahituv, Neumann N., S., and Hadass, M. "A Flexible Approach to Information System Development." *MIS Quarterly,* Vol. 8(2) (June, 1984), pp. 69–78.
2. Alavi, M. "An Assessment of the Prototyping Approach to Information Systems Development." *Communications of the ACM,* Vol. 27(6) (June, 1984), pp. 556–563.
3. Alter, S. *Decision Support Systems: Current Practice and Continuing Challenges* (Addison-Wesley. Reading, Mass., 1980).
4. Anderson, J. C. and Hoffman, T. R. "A Perspective on the Implementation of Management Science." *Academy of Management Review,* Vol. 3(3) (1978), pp. 563–571.
5. Ansoff, I. *Corporate Strategy* (McGraw-Hill. New York, 1965).
6. Anthony, R. N. *Planning and Control Systems: A Framework for Analysis.* Division of Research, Harvard Graduate School of Business Administration, 1965.
7. Bell, D. "Communications Technology: for Better or for Worse." *Harvard Business Review* (May–June, 1979).
8. Benjamin, R. *Control of the Information Systems Development Cycle* (Wiley. New York, 1971).
9. Carlson, E. D., Grace, B. F. and Sutton, J. A. "Case Studies of End User Requirements for Interactive Problem Solving Systems." *MIS Quarterly,* Vol. 1(1) (1977), pp. 51–63.
10. Cleland, D. I. and King, W. R. *Systems Analysis and Project Management,* 2nd Ed. (McGraw-Hill. New York, 1975).

11. Davis, G. B. *Management Information Systems: Conceptual Foundations, Structure, and Development* (McGraw-Hill. New York, 1974).
12. Diebold, J. "Bad Decisions on Computer Use." *Harvard Business Review* (January–February, 1969).
13. Doktor, R., Schultz, R. L. and Slevin, D. P. (eds.). *Implementation of Management Science* (TIMS Studies in Management Science, North Holland, 1979).
14. Dutta, B. K. and King, W. R. "A Competitive Scenario Modeling System." *Management Science,* Vol. 26(3) (March, 1980), pp. 261–273.
15. Edstrom, A. "User Influence and Success of MIS Projects: A Contingency Approach." *Human Relations,* Vol. 30(7) (1977), pp. 589–607.
16. Ein-Dor, P. and Segev, E. "Strategic Planning for MIS." *Management Science,* Vol. 24(15) (1978), pp. 1631–1641.
17. Fox, H. W. "A Framework for Functional Coordination." *Atlanta Economic Review,* Vol. 23(6), (1973).
18. Ghymn, K. I. and King, W. R. "Design of a Strategic Planning MIS." *OMEGA,* Vol. 4(5) (1976), pp. 595–607.
19. Ginzberg, M. J. "Early Diagnosis of MIS Implementation Failure: Promising Results and Unanswered Questions." *Management Science,* Vol. 27(4) (1981), pp. 459–478.
20. Ginzbergr, M. J. "A Process Approach to Management Science Implementation." Unpublished Ph.D. dissertation, M.I.T., 1975.
21. Gregory, R. H. and Van Horn, R. L. *Automatic Data-Processing Systems,* 2nd Ed. (Wadsworth. Belmont, Calif., 1969).
22. Gremillion, L. L. "Managing the Implementation of Standardized Computer Bases Systems." *MIS Quarterly,* Vol. 4(4)(December, 1980), pp. 51–59.
23. Hall, T. P. "Systems Life Cycle Model." *Journal of Systems Management,* Vol. 31(4) (April, 1980).
24. Head, R. V. "Strategic Planning for Information Systems." *Infosystems* (October, 1978), pp. 46–54.
25. IBM. *Business Systems Planning: Information Systems Planning Guide,* 1981.
26. Jenkins, A. M. and Lauer, T. W. "An Annotated Bibliography on Prototyping." Unpublished Discussion Paper #228, Indiana University, Division of Research, School of Business, 1983.
27. Johnson, R. A., Kast, F. and Rosenzweig, J. E. *The Theory and Management of Systems* (McGraw-Hill. New York, 1967).
28. Kaiser, K. and King, W. R. "The Manager-Analyst Interface in Systems Development." *MIS Quarterly,* Vol. 6(1) (1982).
29. Keen, P. G. W. "Decision Support Systems: Translating Analytical Techniques into Useful Tools." *Sloan Management Review* (Spring 1980a), pp. 33–44.
30. Keen, P. G. W. "Adaptive Design for Decision Support Systems." *Database,* Vol. 12(1), (Fall, 1980b), pp. 15–25.
31. Keen, P. G. W. "Value Analysis: Justifying Decision Support Systems." *MIS Quarterly* (1981a), pp. 1–66.
32. Keen, P. G. W. "Information Systems and Organizational Change." *Communications of the ACM,* Vol. 24(1) (1981b), pp. 24–33.
33. Keen, P. G. W. and Gerson, E. M. "The Politics of Software Engineering." *Datamation* (November, 1977), pp. 80–86.
34. Keen, P. G. W. and Soctt-Morton, M. S. *Decision Support Systems: An Organizational Perspective* (Addison-Wesley. Reading, Mass., 1978).
35. Ketron, R. W. "Four Roads to Office Automation." *Datamation* (November, 1930).
36. Kimberly, J. H. and Miles, R. H. *The Organizational Life Cycle* (Jossey-Bass. San Francisco, 1980).

37. King, W. R. "Exploiting Information as a Strategic Business Resource." *International Journal on Policy and Information,* Vol. 8(1) (June, 1984), pp. 1–8.
38. King, W. R. and Zmud, R. W. "Managing Information Systems: Policy Planning, Strategic Planning, and Operational Planning," in *Proceedings of the Second International Conference on Information Systems,* ed. Ross, C. A. (Cambridge, Mass., 1981), pp. 299–308.
39. King, W. R. "Strategic Planning for MIS." *MIS Quarterly,* Vol. 2(1) (1978), pp. 27–37.
40. King, W. R. *Marketing Management Information Systems* (Petrocelli/Charter. New York, 1977).
41. King W. R. "Methodological Optimality in Operations Research." *OMEGA,* Vol. 4(1) (1976), pp. 9–12.
42. King, W. R. "Integrating Computerized Planning Systems into the Organization." *Managerial Planning* (1982).
43. King, W. R. and Cleland, D. I. *Strategic Planning and Policy* (Van Nostrand Reinhold. New York, 1978).
44. King, W. R. and Cleland, D. I. "Manager-Analyst Teamwork in Management Information Systems." *Business Horizons* (April, 1971), pp. 59–68.
45. King, W. R. and Rodriguez, J. I. "Evaluating Management Information Systems." *MIS Quarterly* (September, 1978), pp. 43–51.
46. Kling, R. "The Organizational Context of User-Centered Software Designs." *MIS Quarterly* (December, 1977), pp. 41–52.
47. Kolb, D. A. and Frohman, A. L. "An Organization Development Approach to Consulting." *Sloan Management Review,* Vol. 12(1) (1970), pp. 51–65.
48. Kreibel, C. H. "The Strategic Dimension of Computer Systems Planning." *Long Range Planning,* Vol. 1(1) (1968), pp. 7–12.
49. Leavitt, H. J. and Whisler, T. L. "Management in the 1980s." *Harvard Business Review* (November–December, 1958).
50. Lucas, H. "Empirical Evidence for a Descriptive Model of Implementation." *MIS Quarterly* (June, 1978), pp. 27–41.
51. Lucas, H. *Why Information Systems Fail* (Columbia University Press. New York, 1975).
52. McKinsey and Co. "Unlocking the Computer's Profit Potential." *Computers and Automation* (April, 1969).
53. McLean, E. R. and Soden, J. V. (eds.). *Strategic Planning for MIS* (Wiley. New York, 1977).
54. Mintzberg, H. "Impediments to the Use of Management Information." (National Association of Accountants. New York, 1975).
55. Murdick, R. G. and Ross, J. E. "Management Information Systems: Training for Businessmen." *Journal of Systems Management* (October, 1969).
56. Naumann, J. D. and Jenkins, A. M. "Prototyping: The New Paradigm for Systems Development." *MIS Quarterly,* Vol. 6(3) (September, 1982), pp. 28–44.
57. Norton, D. P. "Information System Centralization: The Issues," in *Information Systems Administration,* ed. McFarlan, F. W., Nolan, R. and Norton, D. (Holt, Rinehart and Winston. New York, 1973), Chapter 12.
58. Powers, R. F. and Dickson, G. W. "MIS Project Management: Myths, Opinions, and Reality." *California Management Review,* Vol. 15(3) (Spring, 1973), pp. 147–156.
59. Reisman, A. and de Kluyver, C. A. "Strategies for Implementing Systems Studies," in *Implementing OR/MS,* ed. Schultz, R. L. and Slevin, D. P. (North Holland. 1975), pp. 291–309.
60. Robey, D. "User Attitudes and MIS Use." *Academy of Management Journal, Vol. 22(3) (1979), pp. 527–538.*

61. Schultz, R. L. and Slevin, D. P. "Implementation and Organizational Validity: An Empirical Investigation," in *Implementing OR/MS,* ed. Schultz, R. L. and Slevin, D. P. (North Holland. 1975), pp. 153–182.
62. Shultz, G. and Whisler, T. (eds.). *Management, Organization and the Computer* (Free Press. New York, 1960).
63. Simon, H. A. *Administrative Behavior* (Macmillan. New York, 1947).
64. Sprague, R. H. "A Framework for the Development of Decision Support Systems." *MIS Quarterly* (December, 1980), pp. 1–26.
65. Sprague, Ralph H. and Olson, Ronald L. "The Financial Planning System at Louisiana National Bank." *MIS Quarterly,* Vol. 3(3) (1979), pp. 35–46.
66. Stern, H. "Human Relations and Information Systems." *Interfaces,* Vol. 1(2) (February, 1971).
67. Swanson, E. B. "Management Information Systems: Appreciation and Involvement." *Management Science,* Vol. 21(2) (October, 1974), pp. 178–188.
68. Welsch, Gemma M. "Successful Implementation of Decision Support Systems Pre-installation Factors, Service Characteristics, and the Role of the Information Transfer Specialist." Ph.D. Dissertation, Northwestern University, 1980.
69. Zmud, R. W. "Individual Differences and MIS success: A Review of the Empirical Literature." *Management Science,* Vol. 25(10) (1979), pp. 966–979.
70. Zmud, R. W. and Cox, J. F. "The Implementation Process: A Change Approach." *MIS Quarterly,* Vol. 3(2) (1979), pp. 35–43.

BIBLIOGRAPHY

Churchman, C. W. *The Design of Inquiring Systems* (Basic Books, New York, 1971).
Gallagher, C. A. "Perceptions of the Value of an MIS," *Academy of Management Journal,* Vol. 17 (1), 46–55 (1974).
King, W. R. and Cleland, D. I. *Strategic Planning and Policy* (Van Nostrand Reinhold, New York, 1978).
Lientz, B. P., Swanson, E. B., and Tompkins, G. E. "Characteristics of Application Software Maintenance," *Communications of the ACM,* Vol. 21 (6), (1978).
Maish, A. M. "A User's Behavior Toward His MIS," *MIS Quarterly,* Vol. 3 (1), (1979).
Robey, D. and Zeller, R. L. "Factors Affecting the Success and Failure of an Information System for Production Quality," *Interfaces,* Vol. 8, (2), 70–75 (1978).
Schewe, C. D., "The Management Information's Systems User: An Exploratory Behavioral Analysis," *Academy of Management Journal,* Vol. 19 (4), 577–590 (1976).

Section V
Project Planning

This section provides "tools" that can be used in planning a project. It focuses on the various perspectives of the "owners," bidders, managers, and other project stakeholders.

In Chapter 13, David I. Cleland describes the process by which the impact of the various project stakeholders can be taken into account in developing the project plan.

Chapter 14 focuses on the work breakdown structure (WBS)—one of the most basic project planning tools. There, Gary D. Lavold discusses its use in various phases of the planning process as well as its role in project control.

The best-known tools of project planning—network plans—are reviewed by Joseph J. Moder in Chapter 15. Network plans, useful in both project planning and control, vary from the simple to the complex, with varying data requirements and ease of use. Moder reviews a wide range of these techniques from which the most appropriate one may be selected.

In Chapter 16, the linear responsibility chart (LRC)—a powerful tool of organizational planning—is discussed by David I. Cleland and William R. King. The LRC is shown to have a variety of uses in the organization as well as in the project.

In Chapter 17, Harold Kerzner discusses the pricing dimension of project planning. Pricing requires that a work breakdown structure (Chapter 14) first be developed. Then, it can be "priced out." Kerzner relates pricing to the WBS as well as to other planning tools—the linear responsibility chart (Chapter 16) and network plans (Chapter 15).

Contract development, treated in Chapter 18 by M. William Emmons, represents the transition from project planning to project implementation. Mr. Emmons presents contract development as the keystone that provides support to the overall project management process.

The view of a project from the standpoint of the bidder is treated by Hans J. Thamhain in Chapter 19—"Developing Winning Proposals."

13. Project Stakeholder Management*

David I. Cleland†

The management of a project's "stakeholders" means that the project is explicitly described in terms of the individuals and institutions who share a stake or an interest in the project. Thus, the project team members, subcontractors, suppliers, and customers are invariably relevant. The impact of project decisions on all of them must be considered in any rational approach to the management of a project. But management must also consider others who have an interest in the project and by definition are also stakeholders. These stakeholders are outside the authority of the project manager and often present serious management problems and challenges.

Because project stakeholder management (PSM) assumes that success depends on taking into account the potential impact of project decisions on *all* stakeholders during the entire life of the project, management faces a major challenge. For in addition to identifying and assessing the impact of project decisions on stakeholders who are subject to the authority of the management, they must consider how the achievements of the project's goals and objectives will affect or be affected by stakeholders outside their authority. Project stakeholders, often called *intervenors* in the nuclear power plant construction industry, can have a marked influence on a project. At one nuclear power plant numerous bomb threats over the

---

* Portions of this chapter have been paraphrased from David I. Cleland, "Project Stakeholder Management," *Project Management Journal,* September 1986, pp. 36–44. Used by permission.

† David I. Cleland is currently Professor of Engineering Management in the Industrial Engineering Department at the University of Pittsburgh. He is the author/editor of 15 books and has published many articles appearing in leading national and internationally distributed technological, business management, and educational periodicals. Dr. Cleland has had extensive experience in management consultation, lecturing, seminars, and research. He is the recipient of the "Distinguished Contribution to Project Management" award given by the Project Management Institute in 1983, and in May 1984, received the 1983 Institute of Industrial Engineers (IIE)-Joint Publishers Book-of-the-Year Award for the *Project Management Handbook* (with W. R. King). In 1987 Dr. Cleland was elected a Fellow of the Project Management Institute.

life of the project impacted construction schedules, shut down work on select areas, frustrated managers and professionals, and forced more intensive security provisions to include physical searches of people, equipment, and vehicles. Further impact on the project came about in the form of antinuclear blockades and demonstrations which impacted productivity. In the fall of 1981, the Abalone Alliance, an antinuclear organization, planned, organized, and attempted a blockade of the plant. The plant operating crew, management staff, draftsmen and national guard and law enforcement personnel had to be housed and fed at the plant. Total costs associated with such intervenor action cannot be calculated; schedule delays, inefficient work activity, and absenteeism occurred because of the physical threat factors.

Stakeholder management is an important part of the strategic management of organizations. There is abundant literature in the management field that establishes the need to analyze the enterprise's environment and its stakeholders as part of the strategic management of the enterprise. See, for example, F. J. Aguilar (1), W. R. Dill (2), H. Mintzberg (3), and Weiner and Brown (4).

Political, economic, social, legal, technological, and competitive "systems" affect an enterprise's ability to survive and grow in its environment. A project is also impacted by its "systems" environment. Project managers need to identify and interact with key institutions and individuals in the project's "systems" environment. For example, see Radosevich and Taylor (5), Burnett and Youker (6). An important part of the analysis of the project's "systems" environment is an organized process for identifying and managing the probable stakeholders in that environment. This management process is necessary in order to determine how the probable stakeholders are likely to react to project decisions, what influence their reaction will carry, and how the stakeholders might interact with each other and the project's managers and professionals to affect the chances for success of a proposed project strategy. Cleland and King (7), Rothschild (8), King and Cleland (9), Freeman (10), and Mendelow (11) have presented strategies for dealing with stakeholders in the corporate context. This chapter will suggest a strategy for the assessment of the influence of outside or external project stakeholders and a technique for the management of such stakeholders.

OUTSIDE STAKEHOLDER IMPACT

Effective management cannot be carried out without considering the probable influence that key *outside* stakeholders may have on the project.

Some recent project management experiences highlight the role of these stakeholders:

- In the investigation of the management prudence of the Long Island Lighting Company (LILCO) Shoreham Project, the County of Suffolk, the New York State Consumer Protection Board, and the Long Island Citizens in Action (intervenors) argued that the project suffered from pervasive mismanagement throughout its history. The record, in the view of these intervenors, established that approximately $1.9 billion of Shoreham's cost was expended unnecessarily "as a result of LILCO's mismanagement, imprudence or gross inefficiency" (12).
- One reason that the Supersonic Transport program failed in the United States was that the managers had a narrow view of the essential players and generally dismissed the key and novel role of the environmentalists until it was too late (13).
- Some stakeholders can provide effective insight into strategic issues facing an industry. For example, in the nuclear power generation industry, the Advanced Reactor Development Subpanel of the Energy Research Advisory Board's Civilian Nuclear Power Panel submitted a report in January 1986 on the status of Advanced Reactor Development Program in the United States. This comprehensive statement reported on the three key areas on this program: (a) problem justification and current realities, (b) program redirection, and (c) Advanced reactor program recommendations. In the recommendations of this report, clear direction was given for future reactor development leading to more economical and fuel-efficient reactors. Such recommendations help to develop future strategies for other stakeholders, such as electric utilities and their suppliers, the Department of Energy, state public utility commissions, etc. More importantly, the proceedings of the Advanced Reactor Development Subpanel provide a forum for an exchange of viewpoints about nuclear power among stakeholders, some of whom may be viewed as adverse by other stakeholders. For example, the Union of Concerned Scientists, a prominent antinuclear group that represents intervenors in proceedings before the Nuclear Regulatory Commission (NRC) has been critical of a "cozy relationship" between government regulatory officials and utility officials (14).
- Public utility commissions (PUCs) are key and formidable stakeholders in the design, engineering, construction, and operation of nuclear power generating plants. In the past two years, state PUCs have

disallowed the recovery of billions of dollars in electrical rate setting. Some utilities have been penalized for imprudent spending on nuclear plants; others have been told that their plants were not needed. For example, the Pennsylvania State Public Utility Commission ruled that the Pennsylvania Power and Light Company's newly opened 945-MW $2 billion Susquehanna Unit 2 nuclear plant would provide too much generating capacity for the utility's customers. The utility was only allowed to recover taxes, depreciation, and other operating costs. The Missouri Public Service Commission recently disqualified Union Electric Company from charging ratepayers for $384 million of the $3 billion spent on the new Callaway nuclear plant in central Missouri. The commission cited high labor expenses, improper scheduling of engineering, and "inefficient, imprudent, unreasonable, or unexplained costs" during four years of delay (15).

- Diverse stakeholders, or intervenors, are taking active roles in rate-setting case hearings. For example, when the Union Electric Company of St. Louis, Missouri, instituted proceedings for authority to file tariffs increasing rates for electric service, the following parties were granted permission to intervene in the proceedings: "twenty-five cities, the State of Missouri, the Jefferson City school district, the Electric Ratepayers Protection Project, the Missouri Coalition for Environment, the Missouri Public Interest Research Group, Laclede Gas Company, Missouri Limestone Producers, Dundee Cement Company, LP Gas Association, Missouri Retailers Association, the Metropolitan St. Louis Sewer District, and the following industrial intervenors: American Can Company, Anheuser Busch, Inc., Chrysler Corporation, Ford Motor Company, General Motors Corporation, Mallinckrout, Inc., McDonnell Douglas Corporation, Monsanto Company, National Can Corporation, Nooter Corporation, PPG Industries, Inc., Pea Ridge Iron Ore Company, River Cement Company, and St. Joe Minerals Corporation (Monsanto et al.)." (16).

MANAGEMENT RESPONSES

- Care was taken during the design and construction of the Hackensack Meadowlands sports complex to develop cooperation among each of the groups concerned with environmental impact, transportation, development, and construction.
- On the James Bay project, special effort was made to stay sensitive to social, economic, and ecological pressures (17).
- James Webb and his colleagues at NASA were adept at stakeholder

management during the Apollo program. NASA gained the support not only of the aerospace industry and related constituencies but also of the educational community, the basic sciences, and the weather forecaster profession (18).

● Obviously, in addition to special groups, the general public, often synonymous with the consumers or customers, is an important stakeholder group. At the Niagara Mohawk Power Corporation in Syracuse, New York, plans for achieving public acceptance of the atom as a source of electric power began long before the company had any specific plans for constructing its own nuclear plant. Niagara Mohawk began to inform the public of progress in using the atom for electric power generation soon after the Atomic Energy Act was signed in 1954. A full-scale successful public relations program was carried out before and continued after the initiation of the project (19). A study of quality problems in the Nuclear Power Plant Construction Industry provides insight into stakeholder management.

Action taken by two electric utilities to facilitate an effective relationship with the NRC stakeholder included the following:
—Florida Power & Light established a special office near the NRC headquarters to facilitate exchange of information during the licensing process.
—Senior management of Arizona Public Service established the following policy concerning NRC:

Don't treat NRC as an adversary; NRC is not here to bother us—they see many more plants than the licensee sees; inform NRC of what we (APS) are doing and keep everything up front; and nuclear safety is more important than schedule. (20)

Attitudes of key managers play an important role in successfully dealing with key stakeholders. In the nuclear power generation industry, management commitment to quality and a management view that NRC requirements are not the ultimate goals for performance carry great weight. For example:

Of the projects studied there tended to be a direct correlation between the project's success and the utility's view of NRC requirements: more successful utilities tended to view NRC requirements as minimum levels of performance, not maximum, and they strove to establish and meet increasingly higher, self-imposed goals. This attitude covered all aspects of the project, including quality and quality assurance. (21)

PSM Justification

The principal justification for adopting a PSM perspective springs from the enormous influence that key external stakeholders can exert. Thus it can be argued that the extent to which the project achieves its goals and objective is influenced by the strategies pursued by key stakeholders. Stakeholder management leading to stakeholder cooperation enhances project objective achievement, while stakeholder neglect hinders it.

In working with project managers in the development of project strategy which encompass a PSM philosophy, a number of basic premises can serve as guides for the development of a PSM approach:

- PSM is essential for ensuring success in managing projects.
- A formal approach is required for performing a PSM process:
  —Projects extending over multiyear life cycles are subject to so much change that informal means of PSM are inadequate.
  —Reliance on informal or hit-or-miss methods for obtaining PSM information is ineffective for managing the issues that can come out of projects.
- PSM should provide the project team with adequate intelligence for the selection of realistic options in the management of project stakeholders.
- Information on project stakeholders can be gained from a variety of sources, some of which might superficially seem to be unprofitable.

Objective of PSM

PSM is designed to encourage the use of proactive project management for curtailing stakeholder activities that might adversely affect the project and for facilitating the project team's ability to take advantage of opportunities to encourage stakeholder support of project purposes. These objectives can be achieved only by integrating stakeholder perspectives into the project's formulation processes and developing a PSM strategy. The project manager is then in a better position to influence the actions of the stakeholders on project outcome.

Failing to recognize or cooperate with adverse stakeholders may well hinder a successful project outcome. Indeed, strong and vociferous adverse stakeholders can force their particular interest on the project manager at some time, perhaps at a time least convenient to the project. PSM is thus a necessity, allowing the project manager to set the timetable so that he can maintain better control. A proactive PSM process is designed to help the project team develop the best possible strategies.

PSM Process

This process consists of the execution of the management functions of planning, organizing, motivating, directing, and controlling the resources used to cope with external stakeholders' strategies. These functions are interlocked and repetitive; the emergence of new stakeholders will require the reinitiation of these functions at any time during the life cycle of the project. This management process is continuous, adaptable to new stakeholder threats and promises, and changing strategies of existing stakeholders. Putting the notion of stakeholder management on a project life-cycle basis emphasizes the need to be aware of stakeholder influence at any time.

The management process for the stakeholders consists of the phases depicted in Figure 13-1 and discussed below.

Identification of Stakeholders

The identification of stakeholders must go beyond the internal stakeholders. Internal stakeholders must of course bᴗ taken into account in the development of project strategies. Their influence is usually supportive of project strategies since they are an integral part of the project team. A prudent project manager would ensure that these internal stakeholders play an important and supportive role in the design and development of project strategies. Such a supportive role is usually forthcoming since the project manager has some degree of authority and influence over these individuals. External stakeholders may not be supportive.

External stakeholders are not usually subject to the legal authority of the project manager; consequently, such stakeholders provide a formidable challenge to manage. A generic set of external stakeholders would include the following:

- Prime contractor.
- Subcontractors.
- Competitors.
- Suppliers.
- Financial institutions.
- Governmental agencies, commissions; judicial, legislative and executive branches.
- The general public represented through consumer, environmental, social, political, and other "intervenor" groups.
- Affected local community.

Figure 13-1. Project stakeholder management process.

Figure 13-2 depicts a typical network of project stakeholders, both internal and external.

Care must be taken to identify all of the potential stakeholders, even those whose stake may seem irrelevant at the time. Freeman points out that a historical analysis of an organization's interface with its environment is useful in identifying potential stakeholders (10). The development of a list of the "strategic issues" that currently face and have faced the parent organization and the industry over the past several years can be useful in identifying stakeholders who have been involved in these issues.

PROJECT STRATEGIC ISSUES

A strategic issue is a condition or pressure, either internal or external, to a project that will have a significant effect on, for example, the financing, design, engineering, construction, licensing, and/or operation of a nuclear power generating plant (22). Strategic issue management is found in the

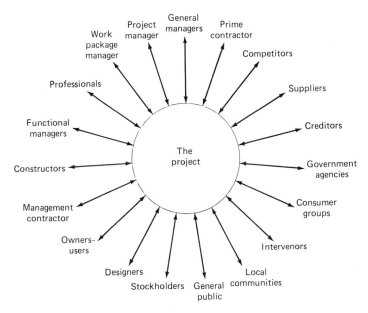

Figure 13-2. Project stakeholder network.

field of strategic planning and management (23). In project management the notion of strategic issue management is not as pervasive. Yet a project that has as long a life cycle as a nuclear power generating plant will probably be impacted during its life cycle by many issues that are truly strategic by nature. For example, both a project team and a project owner need to be aware of the following typical strategic issues that will have a significant effect on the outcome of a nuclear power generating plant project.*

● *Licensability*
    —Unless a plant can be licensed in the United States, it has little value to the utility industry since all of their plants must meet the federal codes and standards as well as the nuclear regulatory guides for the particular concept. Many of these codes, standards, and guides are not applicable to a concept if it has not been previously licensed. The first-of-a-kind of a particular concept through

---

* These strategic issues were developed during a research project by David I. Cleland and Dundar F. Kocaoglu: The Design of a Strategic Management System for Reactor Systems, Development and Technology, DOE, with the assistance of A. N. Tardiff and C. E. Klotz of the Argonne National Laboratory.

the process becomes precedent setting. As such, it will receive a commensurate amount of attention from the Nuclear Regulatory Commission (NRC) staff, so much so that joint groups will be set up with representation from the Department of Energy (DOE) and the NRC, and a bevy of consultant experts to answer the thousands of questions posed by the NRC staff and to draft appropriate revisions to the existing federal codes, regulations, and guides for future applicability to the new concept.

This strategic issue can take years to resolve when one includes the judicial and state and local hearing processes that a nuclear plant must face. The lack of firm and predictable policy emanating from the NRC at the present time adds to the risk and uncertainty involved in the management of this strategic issue. Such risks and uncertainties are reflected in the increased costs and schedules for the project. The NRC, which licenses the plant, and state and local governments who conduct hearings to ascertain the proper allocation of costs for the utility's rate base are key stakeholders.

- *Passive Safety*
—Passive safety, as it relates to a nuclear power plant, refers to the plant's ability to take advantage of inherent, natural characteristics to move itself into a safe condition without the need to activate an automatic auxiliary safety system or to impose a set of predetermined operator procedures to do the same.

For example, all of the commercial reactors being built and operated in the United States today require the activation, within a prescribed time period, of an auxiliary system, automatically or by an operator, to shut down.

If one allows the system to operate without adding reactivity (similar to adding coal to a fire) and assuming the cooling systems remain effective (the pumps operate, the valves open and close on cue, the heat exchangers transfer heat, etc.) the reactor will eventually shut itself down. The difficulty comes when the operating plant cannot remove reactivity from the reactor (like removing coal from the fire) and/or maintain the effectiveness of the cooling systems.

Passive safety is the dominant strategic issue facing the nuclear power generating industry today. The nuclear accidents at Three Mile Island and Chernobyl have intensified the search for a nuclear power plant that promises passive safety. Nuclear vendors and utility companies are key stakeholders keenly interested in passive safety. Indeed, all of us are stakeholders wanting economical and safe power generating capacity in the modern world.

- *Power Costs*
  —The components of the power costs are capital costs, operations and maintenance (O&M), and fuel costs. For a typical nuclear power plant, the capital cost component is four times the O&M cost, which is approximately equal to the fuel cost. Hence, it is evident that capital cost is the most significant component, and it is discussed in more detail below.
  —One of the significant factors leading to the current hiatus in orders for nuclear power plants is that these systems are extremely capital intensive and have relatively low fuel costs. Coal and oil fire plants are the opposite, that is, they have a relatively low capital cost component while their fuel costs are extremely high.
  —Construction times for many of the recent U.S. nuclear plants have exceeded ten years. The licensing and judicial processes in the United States have accounted for much of the delay, but other factors, such as utility management, have also taken their toll. Whatever the reasons, the delays have an extraordinary impact on the resultant capital investment in these plants even before they have produced one kilowatt-hour of electricity. It is not uncommon to experience the interest paid on the capital to build the plant to be greater than 50% of the capital investment in the plant. As a result, there has been an inordinate increase in the capital cost component such that nuclear power has lost its competitive power cost edge over its closest competitor, coal. Five approaches might be pursued to alleviate this problem:
    Reform the licensing process.
    Design the plants to be constructed quickly on-site.
    Build smaller plants.
    Supply turnkey plants with guarantees.
    Simplify the plants and reduce the amount of material used.
  —Utilities, nuclear reactor manufacturers, A&E firms, plant constructors, and state regulatory commissions are the principal stakeholders concerned about the power costs strategic issue.

- Reliability of Generating System
  —The reliability of a nuclear power plant must be extremely high, particularly as it relates to the safety systems and components. There are reliability differences from one concept to another, for example, one might have fewer moving parts, fewer systems, fewer components, fewer things to go wrong. Generally, a plant that has been designed, developed, tested, fabricated, constructed, operated, and maintained under a stringent quality assur-

ance (QA) umbrella will be more reliable than one that has not. Concepts that maximize factory vs. on-site fabricated and assembled systems tend to be more reliable since QA can be more easily applied at the factory. Gravity and natural circulation-dependent systems tend to be more reliable than forced circulation systems. The importance of these and more reliable approaches to a nuclear power plant cannot be overemphasized, particularly in view of Three Mile Island, Chernobyl, and public attitudes toward nuclear power. Utilities are the principal stakeholders here.

- *Nuclear Fuel Reprocessing*
  —Commercial nuclear fuel reprocessing in the United States is virtually nonexistent. Instead the U.S. government has agreed to accept for a price the spent fuel for U.S. reactors for long-term storage. Europe and Japan, however, have viable programs to recover for future use the nuclear fissionable fuel from spent fuel assemblies. Any concepts, such as breeder, which require reprocessing technology must carry the burden of developing this technology as well as the nuclear proliferation stigma attached to it. Thus any future nuclear plant ordered by authority in the U.S. may require the arrival of a liquid metal reactor technology which provides for the use of reprocessed fuel. The time frame for such fuel-reprocessing capability is circa 2040 by best current estimates. Utilities and reactor manufacturers are the principal stakeholders.

- *Waste Management*
  —Public reaction (e.g., to shipments of nuclear wastes) is becoming increasingly severe. Hence, minimum waste streams and movement of such wastes outside the plant boundaries is advisable. Poor management and cost overruns aside, one of the biggest issues for the nuclear power industry is the 1500 metric tons of lethal atomic waste that it produces each year. The waste disposal program conceived and managed by the U.S. government and the nuclear power industry to store radioactive fuel safely is troublesome (24). Utilities, states (where storage sites are located), and the general public are vested stakeholders in this strategic issue.

- *Capital Investment*
  —Closely akin to the strategic issue of power costs is the financial exposure and risks that investors of nuclear power plants have experienced over the last several years. For support of nuclear power to be resumed by the Wall Street financial houses, it is important that the current conditions change along the lines noted in the discussion of the power costs issue, that is,

Reform the licensing process.

Design the plants to be constructed quickly on-site.

Build smaller plants.

Supply turnkey plants with guarantees.

Simplify the plants and reduce the amount of material used.

—Investment agencies are the principal stakeholders along with the state public utility groups that must rule on the acceptability of a capital investment cost into the utility's rate base.

- *Public Perception*
  —Table 13-1 summarizes this strategic issue quite clearly. The experts rank nuclear power twentieth in the list of high-risk items, whereas the others rank it first or close to first. Note that X-rays and nonnuclear electric power fall into the same dilemma. When the United States converted from DC to AC in the early 1920s, the same problem arose. Some extensive, innovative technical and management approaches must be successfully implemented to turn the rankings around.
  —The public perception of nuclear power and its associated risks aggravated by the nuclear accidents at Three Mile Island and Chernobyl has made this strategic issue more acute.
- *Advocacy*
  —Not many government interest research programs can proceed through the government bureaucracy without a strong advocate with the ability to establish and maintain a substantial support base for the program. The support must be broad and include, as is the case with the research in an advanced reactor development program, key individuals within the Department of Energy, White House, Office of Management and Budget, Congress and staff offices, the nuclear community (the stakeholders), the science community (NSF, NAS, certain universities), Wall Street, and others. With such backing the "public" generally supports the program by definition. An effective advocate(s) is an essential ingredient. Military aircraft and the aircraft carrier had Billy Mitchell; the nuclear submarine fleet had Hyman Rickover; the space program had Werner von Braun—the list of successful efforts led by able champions is long. Thus a reactor manufacturer who contemplates obtaining government funds to be added to corporate monies for the development of research in advanced nuclear reactors would be a vitally interested stakeholder to determine what advocacy existed for such research both in the government and in the corporation itself.

Table 13-1. Risk: A Matter of Perception.
Four Groups Rank What's Dangerous and What's Not[a,b]

	EXPERTS	LEAGUE OF WOMEN VOTERS	COLLEGE STUDENTS	CIVIC CLUB MEMBERS
Motor vehicles	1	2	5	3
Smoking	2	4	3	4
Alcoholic beverages	3	6	7	5
Handguns	4	3	2	1
Surgery	5	10	11	9
Motorcycles	6	5	6	2
X-rays	7	22	17	24
Pesticides	8	9	4	15
Electric power (nonnuclear)	9	18	19	19
Swimming	10	19	30	17
Contraceptives	11	20	9	22
General (private) aviation	12	7	15	11
Large construction	13	12	14	13
Food preservatives	14	25	12	28
Bicycles	15	16	24	14
Commercial aviation	16	17	16	18
Police work	17	8	8	7
Fire fighting	18	11	10	6
Railroads	19	24	23	20
Nuclear power	20	1	1	8
Food coloring	21	26	20	30
Home appliances	22	29	27	27
Hunting	23	13	18	10
Prescription antibiotics	24	28	21	26
Vaccinations	25	30	29	29
Spray cans	26	14	13	23
High school and college football	27	23	26	21
Power mowers	28	27	28	25
Mountain climbing	29	15	22	12
Skiing	30	21	25	16

[a] People were asked to "consider the risk of dying as a consequence of this activity or technology."

[b]*Source:* Decision Research; Eugene, Oregon (*Washington Post,* May 21, 1986).

- *Environment*
  —From an environmental viewpoint, the nuclear advocates had essentially convinced the general public that nuclear power plants were essentially environmentally benign—until the press convinced the public otherwise after the Three Mile Island incident. The Chernobyl incident reinforced this conviction. Certainly the environmental impact of the Chernobyl accident on its surrounding area appears to be serious.
  —Recovering from the image of Chernobyl will be no easy task. Much work must be done to assure that such an incident cannot occur in the United States, and this fact must be convincingly transmitted to the potential owners of nuclear power plants, the administration, the Congress, and above all the general public itself. The most environmentally benign and inherently safe nuclear plant should go a long way in settling this issue. Unfortunately, such a plant may be decades away. Environmental groups such as the Sierra Club see themselves as key stakeholders concerned about this strategic issue.
- *Safeguards*
  —One must keep fissionable material out of unauthorized hands— the objective of the nuclear safeguards activity. A nuclear plant security system that does this better than another should have an edge. For example, if throughout the fuel cycle of a particular plant the fissionable fuel avoids a plant configuration that can be used as source material for a weapon, then one could say that it is "nonproliferation proof."
  —Then the next consideration is, "Which plant configuration minimizes the exposure of the weapons-grade nuclear material during its fuel cycle operations?" A fuel cycle concept which keeps the fuel in the reactor vessel or at least on site-during its lifetime may have some significant safeguard advantages.
  —Nuclear power is an emotional issue aggravated by the recent accidents at Three Mile Island and Cernobyl. Before these accidents the public had a false sense of security; a continuing lack of education about radiation produced a fear of the unknown. Many stakeholders exist whose mission in whole or in part is directed to reshape public and legislative opinion about nuclear power. A nuclear power plant project team needs to be aware of all these potential stakeholders; there are many. For example, a partial list would include
    Advanced Reactor Development Subpanel of the Energy
    Research Advisory Board's Civilian Nuclear Power Panel

U.S. Committee for Energy Awareness
Institute of Nuclear Power Operations
Edison Electric Institute
American Public Power Association
Electric utilities
State public utility commissions
National Rural Electric Cooperative Association
Nuclear Regulatory Commission
American Nuclear Insurers
Mutual Atomic Energy Liability Underwriters
Oak Ridge Associated Universities
American Nuclear Energy Council
Atomic Industrial Forum (Nuclear)
Committee on Radioactive Waste Management (Nuclear)
Educational Foundation for Nuclear Science
Fusion Energy Foundation
Institute of Nuclear Materials Management
International Atomic Energy Agency
Nuclear Energy Women
Nuclear Records Management Association
Universities Research Association
Americans for Nuclear Energy
Citizens Energy Council
Clamshell Alliance
Coalition for Non-Nuclear World
Committee for Nuclear Responsibility
Concerned Citizens for the Nuclear Breeder
Environmental Coalition on Nuclear Power
League Against Nuclear Dangers
Mobilization for Survival
Musicians United for Safe Energy
National Campaign for Radioactive Waste Safety
Natural Guard Fund
Nuclear Information and Resource Service
Safe Energy Communications Council (Nuclear)
Sierra Club Radioactive Waste
Supporters of Silkwood (Nuclear)
Task Force Against Nuclear Power
Union of Concerned Scientists
Western Interstate Energy Board
World Information Service on Energy

Committee to Bridge the Gap
Constructors/A&E firms
Project management contractors
Reactor vendors

Although a historical perspective can give insight into a project's probable stakeholders, the project team should be alerted to strategic issues in the competitive and environmental systems that can change the project's future.

For example, one key strategic issue facing the U.S. nuclear power industry is to foster public acceptance of nuclear power. Recognizing this, the industry has launched a major public relations campaign to improve its image. The U.S. Committee for Energy Awareness (CEA) launched a $20 million media campaign in July 1983 to facilitate public acceptance as well as understanding that leads to agreement and support (25).

Identification of the relevant external stakeholders can be accomplished through the interaction of the project team. Through discussion and compilation of a list of some of the strategic issues facing the project, the less obvious stakeholders can be discovered. Once a list of the stakeholders has been developed, that list should become an integral part of the project plan and be reviewed along with other elements of the plan during the project's life cycle to determine if the stakeholders' perceptions or views of the project have changed. To do so will require information on the stakeholders.

GATHERING INFORMATION

To systematize the development of the stakeholder information means that questions such as the following need to be considered:

- What needs to be known about the stakeholder?
- Where and how can the information be obtained?
- Who will have responsibility for the gathering, analysis, and interpretation of the information?
- How and to whom will the information be distributed?
- Who has responsibility for the use of the information in the decision context of the project?
- How can the information be protected from "leakage" or misuse?

Some of the information collected on the project's external stakeholders may include sensitive material. One cannot conclude that all such stakeholders will operate in an ethical fashion. Consequently, all information collected should be assumed to be sensitive until proven otherwise and protected accordingly. This suggests the need for an associated security system patterned after a company's business intelligence system. Such a system would include a classification system for some information on a "need-to-know" basis while some would be available to all interested parties.

The following precautions should be considered in planning for a PSM information system:

- One individual responsible for security.
- Internal checks and balances.
- Document classification and control such as periodic inventory, constant record of whereabouts, and prompt return.
- Locked files and desks.
- Supervised shredding or burning of documents no longer useful.
- Confidential envelopes for internal transmission of confidential documents.
- Strict security of offices containing sensitive information (26).

Information on the stakeholders is available from a wide variety of sources. When such information is obtained, the highest standards of ethical conduct should be followed. The potential sources of stakeholder information and the uses to which such information can be put are so numerous that it would not be practical to list all sources and uses here. The following sources are representative and can be augmented according to a particular project's needs:

- Project team members.
- Key managers.
- Business periodicals such as the *Wall Street Journal, Fortune, Business Week, Forbes,* and others.
- Business reference services—*Barrons, Moody's Industrial Manual,* the *Value Line Investment Survey,* etc.
- Professional associations.
- Customers/users.
- Suppliers.
- Trade associations.
- Local press.
- Trade press.
- Annual corporate reports.

- Articles, papers presented at professional meetings.
- Public meetings.
- Government sources (27).

Once the information has been collected, it must be analyzed and interpreted by the substantive experts. The project manager should draw on the company's professional personnel for help in doing this analysis. Once the analysis has been completed, the specific target of the stakeholders' mission can be determined.

Identification of Mission

Once the stakeholders have been identified and information gathered about them, analysis is carried out to determine the nature of their mission or stake. This stake may be a key building block in the stakeholder's strategy. For example, the Nuclear Regulatory Commission manages the licensing of nuclear power plants to promote the safe and peaceful commercial use of the atom. A useful technique to better understand the nature of the *external* stakeholder's claim in the project is to categorize the stake as *supportive* or *adverse* to the project. It is in the best interest of the project manager to keep the supportive stakeholders well informed of the project's status. Care has to be taken in dealing with the potentially adversary stakeholders. Information for these stakeholders should be handled on a ''need-to-know'' basis because such information can be used against the project. This information should be treated as confidential. However, communication channels with these stakeholders should be kept open, for this is critical to getting the project point of view across. Adversary stakeholders will find ways to get information on the project from other sources which can be erroneous or incomplete, giving the opportunity for misunderstanding and further adversary behavior.

Once the stakeholders' mission is understood, then their strengths and weaknesses should be evaluated.

Stakeholders' Strengths and Weaknesses

An assessment of stakeholders' strengths and weaknesses is a prerequisite to understanding their strategies. Such analysis is found in nearly all prescriptions for a strategic planning process (28). This process consists of the development of a summary of the most important strengths on which the stakeholders base their strategy and the most significant weaknesses they will probably avoid in pursuing their interests on the project.

Identifiying five or six strengths and weaknesses of a stakeholder should provide a sufficient data base on which to reach a judgment about the efficacy of a stakeholder's strategy.

An adversary stakeholder's strength may be based on such factors as

- The availability and effective use of resources.
- Political alliances.
- Public support.
- Quality of strategies.
- Dedication of members.

Accordingly, an adversary's weaknesses may emanate from

- Lack of political support.
- Disorganization.
- Lack of coherent strategy.
- Uncommitted, scattered membership.
- Unproductive use of resources.

Once these factors have been developed, they can be tested by answering questions for each proposed project strategy for coping with the stakeholders:

- Does this strategy adequately cope with a strength of the stakeholder?
- Does this strategy take advantage of an adversary stakeholder's weakness?
- What is the relative contribution of a particular stakeholder's strength in countering the project strategy?
- Does the adversary stakeholder's weakness detract from the successful implementation of the stakeholder's strategy? If so, can the project manager develop a counter strategy that will benefit the project?

For a proposed strategy to be successful, it should be built on a philosophy which recognizes the value of going through a specific strengths-weaknesses analysis and developing the project strategy to facilitate the project's success. This can be done, however, only if there is a full understanding of the stakeholder's strategy.

Identification of Stakeholder Strategy

A stakeholder strategy is a series of prescriptions that provide the means and set the general direction for accomplishing stakeholder goals, objectives, and mission. These prescriptions stipulate

- What resource allocations are required.
- Why they are required.
- When they are required.
- Where they will be required.
- How they will be used

These resource allocations include plans for using resources, policies, and procedures to be employed, and tactics used to accomplish the stakeholder's end purposes. Once the stakeholder's strategy is understood, then the stakeholder's probable behavior can be predicted.

Prediction of Expected Stakeholder Behavior

Based on an understanding of external stakeholder strategy, the project team can then proceed to predict stakeholder behavior in implementing strategy. How will the stakeholder use his resources to affect the project? Will an intervenor stakeholder picket the construction site or attempt to use the courts to delay or stop the project? Will a petition be circulated to stop further construction? Will an attempt be made to influence future legislation? These are the kinds of questions that, when properly asked and answered, provide a basis for the project team to develop specific countervailing strategies to deal with adversary stakeholder influence. In some cases a stakeholder will provide help to another stakeholder. For example, a group of dedicated nuclear advocates formed an industry association to assure the nuclear operating safety that the Nuclear Regulatory Commission was not able to provide. This association, the Institute of Nuclear Power Operations (INPO), is dedicated to improving the safety of nuclear plants. INPO has over 400 employees, an operating budget of $400 million, and sufficient clout to bring its 55 utility members into line. INPO sets safety standards and goals, evaluates plant safety, and provides troubleshooting assistance to its sponsors.

Currently INPO is overseeing the training of plant operators and supervisors. In its role as a stakeholder of nuclear power, INPO works closely with the Nuclear Regulatory Commission. If INPO finds areas for improvement in a utility's operation, it is the utility that alerts the Nuclear Regulatory Commission (29).

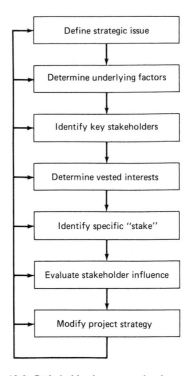

Figure 13-3. Stakeholder impact evaluation process.

The prediction of stakeholder behavior can be facilitated by the project team taking the lead in analyzing the probable impact of the stakeholder on a project. A step-by-step approach for analyzing such impact on a project would consist of the following, depicted in Figure 13-3 and described below (30):

- Identify and define each potential strategic issue in sufficient detail to ascertain its relevance for the project.
- Determine the several key factors which underlie each issue and the forces that have caused that issue to emerge. These forces can usually be categorized into *political, social, economic, technological, competitive, or legal forces.*
- Then identify the key stakeholders that have, or might feel that they have, a vested interest in the project. Remember that one strategic issue may have several different stakeholders who share a vested interest in that issue. Stakeholders usually perceive a vested interest in a strategic issue because of the following:

—*Mission Relevancy.* The issue is directly related to the mission of the group. For example, members of the Sierra Club see the potential adverse effect of a nuclear power plant project on the environment which club members vow to project.

—*Economic Interest.* The stakeholders have an economic interest in the strategic issue. A crafts union would be vitally interested in the wage rates paid at a project construction site.

—*Legal Right.* A stakeholder has a legal right in the issue such as is the case of the Nuclear Regulatory Commission's involvement in the licensing process for the operation of a nuclear generating plant.

—*Political Support.* Stakeholders see the issue as one in which they feel the need to maintain a political constituency. A state legislator would be concerned about the transportation of nuclear wastes from a power plant to a repository site within the state, or the transportation of wastes across the state.

—*Health and Safety.* The issue is related to the personal health and safety of the group. Project construction site workers are vitally interested (or should be) in the working conditions at the site.

—*Life Style.* The issue is related to the life style or values enjoyed by a group. Sportsman groups are interested in the potential pollution of industrial waste in the waterways.

—*Opportunism.* Opportunists see the issue as one around which they can rally, such as a protest meeting at a nuclear power plan construction plant.

—*Competitive Survival.* The issue is linked to the reason for existence of a group of stakeholders. For example, members of the investment community see clearly the financial risks of nuclear plant construction today, considering the uncertainty in the licensing of a nuclear power plant.

Once the stakeholders have been identified, clarify the specific stake held by each stakeholder, then reach a judgment on how much potential influence the stakeholder has on the project and its outcome. Table 13-2 can be used to summarize such interests. Development of this table should be done by the project team, who are in the best position to identify the probable impact of a stakeholder's vested interest. By perusing such a table a general manager can get a summary picture of which stakeholders should be "managed" by the project team. Stakeholders whose interest scores high on the table should be carefully studied and their strategies and actions tracked to see what potential effect such actions will have on the project's outcome. Once such potential effect is

Table 13-2. Summary of Stakeholders' Interest

STAKEHOLDER INTEREST	STAKEHOLDERS										
	1	2	3	4	5	6	7	8	9	10	11
Mission relevance											
Economic interest											
Legal right											
Political support											
Health and safety											
Life style											
Opportunistic competitive survival											

Vested Interest:
  High - H
  Low - L
  Medium - M

determined, then the project strategy should be adjusted through resource reallocation, replanning, or reprogramming to accommodate or counter the stakeholder's actions through a stakeholder management strategy.

Project Audit

An independent audit of the project conducted on a periodic basis will also help the project tream to get the informed and intelligent answers they need on strategic issues and stakeholder interests. Both internal and external audits performed by third parties to analyze the project's strengths, weaknesses, problems, and opportunities can shed light on how well the stakeholders are being managed. There is a symbiotic relationship between the project and its stakeholders. The project cannot exist without its stakeholders; conversely, the stakeholders rely to some extent on the project for their existence.

Implementation of Stakeholder Management Strategy

The final step in managing either the supportive or adverse project stakeholders is to develop implementation strategies for dealing with them. An organizational policy which stipulates that stakeholders will be actively managed is an important first step of such implementation strategies. Once this important step has been taken, then additional policies, action plans, procedures, and the suitable allocation of supporting resources can be established to make stakeholder management an ongoing activity. Once implementation strategies are operational, then the project team has to take a proactive posture in doing the following:

- Insure that the key managers and professionals fully appreciate the potential impact that both supportive and adverse stakeholders can have on the project outcome.
- Manage the project review meetings so that stakeholder assessment is an integral part of determining the project status.
- Maintain contact with key external stakeholders to improve chances of determining stakeholder perception of the project, and their probable strategies.
- Insure an explicit evaluation of probable stakeholder response to major project decisions.
- Provide an ongoing, up-to-date status report on stakeholder status to key managers and professionals for use in developing and implementing project strategy.
- Provide a suitable security system to protect sensitive project information that might be used by adverse stakeholders to the detriment of the project.

SUMMARY

The specification of a project stakeholder management process helps to assure the timely and credible information about the capabilities and options open to each stakeholder. Once these options have been identified, the project team is in a position to predict stakeholder behavior and the effect such behavior might have on the project's outcome. Then the project team can develop its own strategies to best "manage" the stakeholders.

Attitudes play an important role in the management of a project. A positive attitude which accepts that proactive management of stakeholders can reduce the chances of the project team being surprised and unprepared for adverse stakeholder action will be a meaningful contribution to project success. The alternative is for the stakeholder to "manage" the project with the risk of an outcome detrimental to the project's best interests.

An example of project stakeholders and the "stake" such organizations have was drawn from the nuclear power plant industry, an industry that has had managerial problems and challenges on a monumental scale. In addition, an approach was suggested for analyzing the impact of stakeholders on a project.

REFERENCES

1. Aguilar, F. J. *Scanning the Business Environment* (Macmillan. New York, 1967).
2. Dill, W. R. "Environment as an Influence on Managerial Autonomy." *Administrative Science Quarterly* (March, 1958), pp. 409–443.
3. Mintzberg, H. *The Structure of Organizations* (Prentice-Hall. Englewood Cliffs, N.J., 1979).
4. Weiner, E. and Brown, A. "Stakeholder Analysis for Effective Issues Management" *Planning Review* (May, 1986), pp. 27–31.
5. Radosevich, R. and Taylor, C. *Management of the Project Environment.* U.S. Department of Agriculture.
6. Burnett, N. R. and Youker, R. EDI Training Materials, copyright (copyright) 1980 by the International Bank for Reconstruction and Development.
7. Cleland, David I. and King, William R. *Systems Analysis and Project Management,* 3rd Ed. (McGraw-Hill. New York, 1983).
8. Rothschild, W. E. *Putting It All Together: A Guide to Strategic Thinking.* (AMACOM. 1976).
9. King, William R. and Cleland, David I. *Strategic Planning and Policy* (Van Nostrand Reinhold. New York, 1978).
10. Freeman, R. E. *Strategic Management—A Stakeholder Approach* (Pitman. Boston, 1984).
11. Mendelow, Aubrey. "Stakeholder Analysis for Strategic Planning and Implementation," in *Strategic Planning and Management Handbook* (Van Nostrand Reinhold. New York, 1986).
12. *Case 27563, Long Island Lighting Company—Shoreham Prudence Investigation,* State of New York Public Service Commission, Recommended Decision by Administrative Law Judges Wm. C. Levy and Thomas R. Matias, March 13, 1985, p. 57.
13. Horwitch, Mel. "The Convergence Factor for Successful Large-Scale Programs: The American Synfuels Experience as a Case in Point," in *Matrix Management Systems Handbook,* ed. Cleland, David I. (Van Nostrand Reinhold. New York, 1984).
14. Reported in *The Phoenix Gazette,* June 27, 1984, p. PV-12.
15. Glasgall, William. "The Utilities' Pleas Are Falling on Deaf Ears." *Business Week* (June 17, 1985), p. 113.
16. *Cases No. ER-85-160 & ED 85-17,* State of Missouri Public Service Commission, Jefferson City, March 29, 1985.
17. See Behr, Peter G. "James Bay Design and Construction Management." *ASCE Engineering Issues, Journal of Professional Activities* (April, 1978).
18. Ginsburg, E., Kuhn, J. W. and Schnee, J. *Economic Impact of Large Public Programs: The Nash Experience* (Salt Lake City. Olympus Publishing Company, 1976).
19. See Albright, Donald C. "What to Do Before the Atom Comes to Town." *Public Relations Journal* (July, 1965), pp. 16–20.
20. NUREG 1055, *Improving Quality and the Assurance of Quality in the Design and Construction of Nuclear Power Plants, A Report to Congress,* Division of Quality Assurance, Safeguards, and Inspection Programs, Office of Inspection and Enforcement, U.S. Regulatory Commission, Washington, D.C. 20555, May, 1984.

21. See Reference 20 above.
22. Definition paraphrased from Brown, J. K. "This Business of Issues: Coping with the Company's Environments." *The Conference Board Report,* No. 758, 1979.
23. King, William D. "Environmental Analysis and Forecasting: The Importance of Strategic Issues." *Journal of Business Strategy* (Winter, 1981), p. 74.
24. See Janet Novack. "Billion Dollar Shaft." *Forbes* (August 25, 1986), pp. 113–116.
25. See Reference 14 above.
26. Paraphrased from King, W. R. and Cleland, D. I. *Strategic Planning and Policy* (Van Nostrand Reinhold. New York, 1978).
27. Gathering stakeholder information is similar to gathering information on competitors. For a detailed discussion of how this can be done, see Chapter 11 in King, W. R. and Cleland, D. I. *Strategic Planning and Policy* (Van Nostrand Reinhold. New York, 1978), pp. 246–270.
28. See Reference 8 above.
29. For more on the role of INPO, see Cook, James. "INPO's Race Against Time," *Forbes* (February 24, 1986), pp. 54–55.
30. Paraphrased from Weiner, Edith and Brown, Arnold. "Stakeholder Analysis for Effective Issues Management." *Planning Review* (May, 1986), pp. 27–31.

14. Developing and Using the Work Breakdown Structure

Garry D. Lavold*

INTRODUCTION

During the last two decades the emergence of projects with diverse ownership, long time spans, integral government involvement, and requirements for large quantities of diverse resources has put new strains on project management capabilities and project communication systems. The widespread usage of the personal computer (PC) has added another dimension for the requirement of an effective means of system integration utilizing a common communication language. This chapter proposes that a properly designed and implemented work breakdown structure (WBS), with associated coding structure and dictionary, forms an effective basis for project control systems, policies, and procedures for all projects. The WBS helps in organizing and planning all phases of a project.

Project management requires effective, precise information throughout all phases of the project and between all personnel involved with the project. A well-designed WBS provides the basis for the design of these project control information systems (either PC or mainframe based). The common WBS with PCs at different locations allows for easy data coordination. The definition of the WBS as supplied by the Department of Energy in its Performance Measurement Systems guidelines is as follows:

Work Breakdown Structure. A product-oriented family tree division of hardware, software, services, and other work tasks which organizes,

---

* Mr. Garry Lavold holds a Bachelor of Sciences in Chemical Engineering and a Master of Business Administration from the University of Alberta. As an engineer with Gulf Oil from 1969 to 1974 he was involved in all phases of construction and start-up of an 80,000-BPD grass roots refinery. From 1974 Mr. Lavold has worked with NOVA, an Alberta Corporation, including two years as manager of project control for the prebuild of the Alaska Highway Gas Pipeline Project. At the present he is President of Novacorp Pressure Transport with responsibility for all company operations.

defines, and graphically displays the product to be produced, as well as the work to be accomplished to achieve the specified product.*

The "product to be produced" is the completion of a project within a specified time frame and budget while conforming to constraints of public interest groups and governments. Having the WBS as a discipline applied to the project ensures that all participants, both owners and contractors, are fully aware of the work required to complete the project. This utilization of the WBS as the foundation on which all estimates, schedules, and project outlines are developed ensures that the WBS will become the central medium through which all groups communicate information with one another.

Essential to the management of the project is the establishment of the WBS early in the project life. This will enable all participants to implement effective information channels at the beginning of the project life cycle. Utilizing the WBS as an information basis with outside groups, such as governmental agencies, will simplify the regulatory process in that all communication regarding the project will be via a common basis, thereby enabling both industry and government personnel to communicate on a common basis of understanding.

This chapter presents an overview of the environment within which the WBS should operate, the essential elements and concepts to be included during the design of the WBS, and one example of a WBS currently being used on a pipeline project.

COMMUNICATION—USERS OF THE WBS

In the environment of large projects consisting of large cash expenditures, multiple owners, many contractors, and in most cases, government involvement with complex technological facilities, the requirement for information integration and communication is an order of magnitude greater than encountered in the past. These large projects deal with millions of dollars over a multiyear span; this means that as the projects proceed, the environment within which the project was conceived is quite often very different from the environment in which the project is completed. The requirement of government involvement, regulations, and monitoring necessitates that all groups have a common information basis despite changing environments. The WBS coding philosophy and methodology can also

---

* "mini-PMS Guide," Performance Measurement System Guidelines, Attachment 1 (Department of Energy. Washington, D.C. 1977), pp. A1–4.

be applied to small projects with each project using a common WBS on a PC-based system.

This chapter proposes that for all projects, the WBS should become the common information basis, the common language, and the device whereby diverse users can communicate back and forth from the very inception of the project to its final completion. These users include owners, project management personnel, contractors, designers, and government agencies. The integration of the users and their information is illustrated in Figure 14-1.

The left side of Figure 14-1 illustrates the functional groups (prime users), either in the owner's organization, contractor's organization, or a mixture thereof, that must perform the work required to design and construct the project. These users are responsible for the work and exchange information with each other, using the WBS as a common basis of understanding. A properly designed WBS will enable these functional groups to have a precise communication linkage by which all the data illustrated as "input data" can be gathered and distributed. Normally required key input data also are illustrated as follows:

- Budgets—which represent the expected yearly cash flows.
- Estimates—which provide the cost of the project on a facility basis.
- Productivities—the expected production rates to be achieved by design groups, drafting groups, and the construction crews.

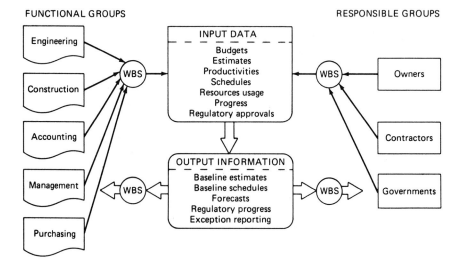

Figure 14-1. Work breakdown structure information integration.

- Schedules—the expected timing and sequence of all the activities necessary to complete the project.
- Resource usage—the expected quantities of manpower, equipment, and consumables required over the life of the project.

All the preceding information is prepared, using the WBS to define all the required elements. This use of the WBS enables all of the elements to be correlated on a common basis. The interrelating of cost, schedule, and productivity on a consistent basis is essential for accurate progress measurement and project control. Having all information collected on a common basis ensures that all work to be done is comparable to a well-defined baseline.

All input data would be collected from the functional groups, using the WBS to define all the elements. Shown in the middle section of Figure 14-1 is the "output information." The data from all the groups are consolidated to provide overall project budgets, schedules, and estimates. This provides a baseline estimate and schedule for the construction of the project, using the WBS; and as the project proceeds, forecasts against these baselines are made utilizing the WBS. The regulatory progress and exception reporting are also done, utilizing WBS as the common basis and the device by which all progress reporting and forecasting are done. Thus, the WBS is an integral part of all project reporting and project planning.

The original groups who prepare the outline and the concept of the project define it to a stage from which the WBS can be prepared. Thus, the first phase is the complete definition of a project and its associated WBS. The WBS works as an effective tool in organizing the work into logical groupings.

The next phase is to report against the baseline, and finally, to prepare a reconciliation against the estimate to measure overall performance on the project. The use of a common coding, a common structure, and a common language, from the start of the project life to the finish, enables problems and their solutions to be readily definable by the common WBS.

The right side of Figure 14-1 illustrates the responsible groups—the people who require the project, who are involved in building the project, or who are involved in approving the project. The owners, the contractors, and, on the larger projects, the government agency must be communicated with. This communication or information flow will use the WBS at a summary level, whereas the functional groups on the left side communicate normally at a detailed level of the WBS. The output information from the consolidated baseline format at a summary level of WBS will be utilized by the owners and the contractors for preparing the proposals to shareholders and/or for submissions to the government. Later, this WBS breakdown will be used in preparing the original bid documents and, as the progress proceeds, in preparing the progress to date and forecast to completion reports.

Thus, as can be seen, the WBS should be used from the start to the finish of the project for planning, tracking, and reconciliation. It is the device by which the users such as owners, contractors, and the government can organize information among themselves and with the people who are performing the work required to complete the project successfully.

SYSTEM INTEGRATION—USING THE WBS

The user community, as described in the preceding section, communicates with each other using a common language defined by the WBS. To give the users the information they require involves support from project control systems and accounting systems. Typical project control systems include scheduling, progress and performance measurement, manpower, equipment, material tracking, cost monitoring, and forecasting systems. Project accounting systems usually include ledgers such as accounts receivable, accounts payable, capital assets, and a project cost ledger. Each one of these systems in both accounting and project control may be independent, automated, or manual, although for most large projects, these systems would be automated. Or, for smaller projects on different sites, the common WBS would be used to report to a central control center. When all the systems above are grouped as project control and/or accounting, systems information transfer between the respective systems can be analyzed.

As the explanation proceeds describing the project control and project accounting information transfer, it must be realized that this transfer would be applied to all other subsystems as well. By highlighting the two overall systems, the principles, ideas and concepts will be explained on an overall basis.

Figure 14-2 illustrates the project accounting and project control systems which both collect data using the WBS. These systems receive data on the common basis of the dictionary and code structure directly associated with the WBS. The project control systems, whether manual or automated, always serve the purpose of collecting, as precisely as possible, timely information which is current and which can be used for management reporting and forecasting. The project control system's key function is to warn management early of any impending problems which, with management's decisions, can be solved or at least have their impact re-

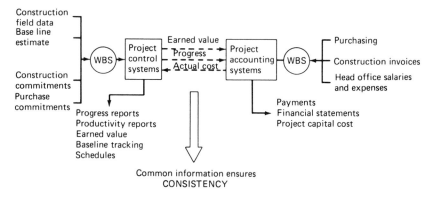

Figure 14-2. Work breakdown structure system integration.

duced. These systems do not have precise cost information but supply vital current key information to manage the project. All information is collected, sorted, and reported via the WBS code structure. The project control systems, either central or PC-based, use this code for all aspects of monitoring cost, schedule, and productivity, and future planning.

The use of the WBS code for entering all information into the project control systems ensures that all progress data collected are comparable to a baseline. Use of actual progress and resource data compared to the baseline allows forecasts of anticipated problems to be analyzed. These results from the systems can be used for control in a meaningful manner through the use of WBS, since all references to the information are made via a uniform and consistent referencing method. Thus the WBS forms an integral part of the control process.

The project accounting systems, which by design are precise but not normally as timely as the project control systems, collect the official or auditable information for cost and resource usage on the project. The resource usage or cost is collected via invoices from contractors, time sheets, personnel working on the project, and expenses of the personnel doing the work. This information is collected by the WBS, with payments being recorded for the WBS elements. Having the project accounting system able to verify the actual costs that were spent, against the estimate and against the budget, by common means allows the actual cost of the progress to date to be tracked precisely against the estimate of cost as well as against the forecasted cost to complete. The more this common tie (i.e., WBS), between the accounting and the project control systems is used, the better it is for the management of the project since it is possible to analyze results, not system discrepancies. With all information collected on a common basis, the WBS ensures that the engineer, the accountant, and management are all referring to the same information with the same meaning.

One of the problems typically present in many projects is that the accounting and project control systems are not using identical coding. Utilizing the WBS in conjunction with the existing accounting coding, or using it uniquely for the project without having to adapt to the existing accounting code, can ensure that as the project proceeds, estimates can be verified and sound projections can be made. This is essential to proper management of the project because it ensures that explanations of cost or schedule problems will be made on a organized basis. The key to providing proper explanations is the disciplined usage, by every person involved in both systems, of the WBS, which is a dictionary of definitions and a fixed coding structure that is unique for all project activities. The precision of this type of reporting ensures that, as the project proceeds, every individual involved is well aware of the project problems, their proposed solutions, the cost estimate, and the actual cost of these problems or their solutions.

The method of integration using the WBS as described above, between the project accounting and the project control systems, is also applicable to the purchasing system, which may feed either project control or project accounting, and any other systems that are utilized within the project. Each system, whether manual or automated, should include the WBS as part of its system definition. It is a discipline and an information organizer be present which should in all applicable systems to ensure that the required common linkages are available.

WBS—RESPONSIBILITY RELATIONSHIP

The WBS provides an information organizer between both the users and the systems. This was previously illustrated in Figures 14-1 and 14-2. Communication utilizing the WBS is on a facility basis or a contract basis. The WBS defines the project in a structured format via the facilities and the items required to build the facilities, or the contracts required to complete construction of the facilities. The WBS structure should reflect as accurately as possible on paper the physical project to be completed. Utilizing the WBS in this format requires that the management structure or organization responsibility centers (which are responsible for the various components of the project) be defined separately. The relationship between the management structure and the WBS is illustrated in Figure 14-3.

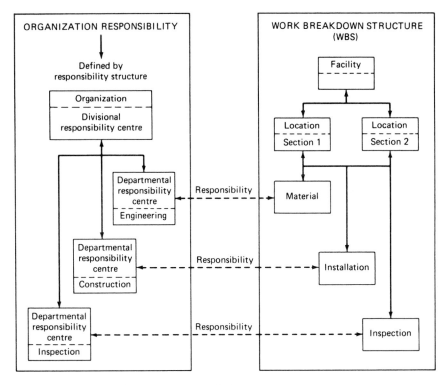

Figure 14-3. Responsibility/WBS relationship.

The right side of Figure 14-3 illustrates the WBS or the project tree which defines the project. On the left is the organizational responsibility as defined by a responsibility structure. The overlay of this organizational responsibility on the WBS creates the management matrix. This management matrix is designed specifically to allow for the case of the large project where there may be many organizations involved in the project. Usually, the basic facility definition does not change through time, whereas organizational responsibilities will change as the project progresses through the project life cycle. The WBS will be designed to provide the total precise project definition on a facility basis, with the major responsibility assignments being overlayed as required to allow assignment of responsibility centers for managing parts of the project, without upsetting the project records, the information exchanges, and systems required to manage the project.

The concept of using the management matrix is essential to effective management of projects where costs, schedules, and resource usage need to be tracked from project inception through to its completion, which can be several years later. The common fixed basis is the WBS which will not change with organizational responsibility, but can only be revised with a scope change in the project definition. At that time the WBS is normally added to with the basic structure and definitions of the WBS remaining. The WBS provides stability to the information for the cost control and accounting systems as well as to the personnel involved with the project for the life of the project. As the organization responsibility assignments change, the management responsibilities for the various segments of the project will change; but by having the WBS tied to the facilities, this changing organizational responsibility will not interfere with cost, schedule, and progress reporting. The key to this will be that the information from the WBS data base will be provided to different people at different times, but the base information remains the same and is collected on that basis.

The consistency in tracking information through the use of the WBS allows for consistent reporting to governments, senior management, owners, contractors, and other participants. This is a key factor in project control. It is therefore important in designing the WBS not to build the organization-responsibility structure as part of the WBS, because if the organization structure is built into the WBS, the end result, due to rapidly changing definitions, will be a nonuseful project control tool. Therefore, the WBS should be designed, structured, and coded to the project being performed, regardless of the organization managing it.

The organization structure should be considered in light of how the project is to be managed on an overall basis. Next must be considered the design and development of a WBS, as a key project control tool to be used between the groups responsible for the project and systems utilized to measure project progress.

WBS DEVELOPMENT

Overview

When the project plan is developed, the WBS must be defined with regard to all the elements that are required to make it a working entity. The base elements are

1. Structure.
2. Code.
3. Reporting.

Before integrating these elements, one must first look at each one separately, then their relationship to each other.

In the design of the project WBS, the "management philosophy" must be considered. The WBS can be a facility-oriented tree or a contract-oriented tree representing the hierarchical components of the project to be managed. The approach to the design of the WBS and its development will depend upon the management philosophy adopted. If it is contract-oriented, it must be related to the entity to be built.

WBS Structure

The structure of the WBS must be such that each level is significant and meaningful, both from a data collection and an overall reporting point of view. This means that every level of the structure developed has significance and relates to a facility contract actually being built or managed within the project, and can be used to generate a required or meaningful report.

The overall design of the structure of the WBS is the key to an effective working system. Therefore, it must be studied very carefully from an input and output of information point of view. Since the WBS serves as a common information exchange language, it is the language, the code, and the structure by which all information on the project is gathered, and it is also the device by which all information of the project is disseminated. Therefore, the structure will be built in a hierarchical manner, or as a tree, such that the bottom level will represent the detailed information and will be large in scope. The base level of the WBS structure is the lowest level of information required to manage the project. This is the lowest level of information at which a user can foresee a need to communicate or monitor. It is the lowest level that the line managers and the construction personnel will require to manage the project.

The next level up the structure will be narrower and will supply information to another level of users. These upper levels will supply significant information for management—significant from the point of view of providing information that is meaningful to various levels of management. This significance ensures that not too many levels are built into the structure. The structure must be designed so that it is meaningful and hierarchical. Twenty levels are too many to manage effectively. Four, five, up to six generally appears to be an adequate number of levels in a large project. In some cases, two sets of the five levels may be used—a base set of five for the detailed collection of data rolling up to a contract level or a major facility level; and five as a superstructure or overlay which ties together the larger components of the facility or the larger contracts. This would allow up to a total of ten levels, but with two distinct purposes. This double-level structure of the WBS works very well and does not restrict the WBS development.

As each level of the structure is designed, consideration must be made as to how information will flow upward to the next level. This transition from one level to another should happen in a natural manner. It should not be forced so that it is difficult or, as the information flows upward, becomes meaningless. As a new structure is being designed, it should be based on the most likely case and should have some flexibility for additions, although this flexibility for additions will come mainly from the coding once the structure has been set. A simple example of such a structure would have the facilities of the top level followed by the items to build the facility at the lower levels.

When a WBS is designed, provisions should be made so that when the structure is translated into code, the coding is meaningful to the user. This means that the user can identify the WBS as a facility tree of physical assets which he can recognize when he goes out in the field. It is of paramount importance that the usage of the WBS be designed in such a way that it becomes THE project language. Thus, in a project, items that the user understands and sees as a major physical unity become elements of the WBS.

The structure is the essential base around which the coding is built and the reporting capabilities of the WBS determined. Thus the structure design is key to an effective WBS.

Code Design

The design of the coding is the key to establishing the WBS as the device to be used by the accounting and project control systems. An effective, meaningful code will assist the user and will complement the structure design described above. Whether the user be the field accountant, the field clerk, or senior management, the code should have common meaning to all. The top level of the code could be relevant major subsystems such as pipeline, compressor stations, and meter stations, or the process plant, buildings, and off-sites. It would be a level above this which would represent the project. The code is the ingredient which the user and the functional groups building the project must work with on a daily basis. In designing the code, one must give consideration to the information collected and the methods used to collect it. The user, who analyzes the raw data collected and puts the proper code on it so that the information can be entered into the applicable recording system via the WBS code, must understand the code.

The code design is directly related to the structure development. Each level of the structure represents a segment of the code. The code design is the assimilation of a group of digits to represent a physical facility to be built. At the top level the project does not need to be coded; at the next level the key facilities to be built are coded utilizing the first digit of the code. If the number of key facilities to be managed is nine or less, the code will typically be a one-digit code, assuming only numerics are used for coding. If alphas and numerics are used, then the level can have 35 different items. The next level below the facility in the structure represents the key items or key contracts to be utilized in building the facility. This level will typically be a two-digit code which gives the flexibility to define 99, or, if alphas are used, more than 99 different items. In the designing of the code, the level above always determines the meaning of the level below. An example of this is illustrated in Figure 14-4, which shows a WBS utilized for pipeline construction.

Figure 14-4 illustrates the code which can be used in a four-level WBS. The top level, "Pipeline Construction," is one digit (2), the next level, "Mainline Location," is three digits (212). These three digits represent

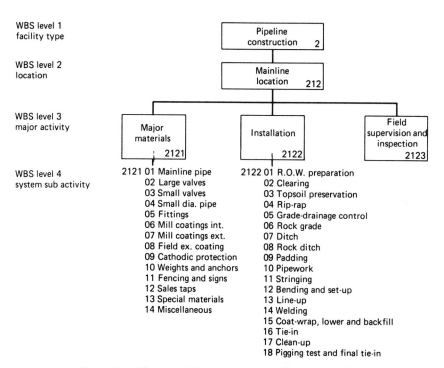

Figure 14-4. Work breakdown structure pipeline construction.

the type of facility to be built and its physical location. The next two levels, shown as 3 and 4, provide a breakdown of all the items required to build the facility. Note that each level of the code hierarchy is dependent on the levels above to determine the complete definition of a given level. This allows elements in level 4 to vary according to the type of facility to be built as defined in levels 1, 2, or 3. If at all possible, at a specific level, identical coding should reference similar information. This will facilitate a more understandable code. This ability for lower levels of the WBS to have different meanings depending on the upper levels allows for more project scope to be accommodated without adding unnecessary digits to the code. Although the code is developed in a hierarchical manner, it is desirable within the structure for the code at a given level to be the same in as many places as possible across the project. The code illustrated in Figure 14-4 always uses the same level 3 code of _ _ _ 1 for Materials, _ _ _ 2 for Installation, and _ _ _3 for Inspection for all facilities on the project. This provides the capability for material, installation and/or inspection costs, schedules, or productivity information to be produced.

When the code is designed, the users must be considered. The users are the people who must code all the information that is to be utilized by the systems. Development of the code should occur in such a way that the user can understand its meaning and significance. Many companies have used alpha characters to give this meaning in a simple form. For example, they may code M for manpower, E for equipment, and C for consumables.

Integration of the code and the structure is such that every level of the structure has a specific number of digits of code assigned to it. This is where the structure hierarchy becomes important in the code design. If the structure has 20 levels, this necessitates that the coding have a minimum of 20 digits, which is too long; thus a compact structure which gives compact coding will supply a system that the people will use. It is paramount in the design of the code and the structure that usage and simplicity be kept clearly in mind. The "nice-to-have" information should be of secondary importance in the design, ensuring that essential information can be retrieved from a simple effective structure and related coding.

Reporting Considerations

In the designing of the WBS, all levels of reporting should be looked at from senior management, or overall project management, down to the lowest level of the person recording the information and the project engineer who wants to know in detail exactly what is happening on this project. The WBS should be designed so that all reports generated from the WBS are automatic without requiring extravagant report-writing methods to extract the information collected. The reports required should be looked at and checked to see that both the WBS and the reports are meaningful and representative of what is really required. Once this has been determined, the WBS design should reflect the reports that will be produced for the various levels of management who are involved in the project. Thus, a level in the structure often becomes a level in the reporting hierarchy to the various project management personnel. When the structure, the reporting, and the usage considerations are incorporated into the coding, the first part of the code supplies the management report, and as the code expands it supplies the detailed project reports.

The consideration of the reporting requirements in the WBS design also helps to define the exact reports that will be available to management as the project proceeds. In going through this design phase, management will be able to review the reports they expect to see from the appropriate project management people, and on the detail level, the personnel doing the estimates and the schedules of the baseline work will be able to review exactly the level of detail they will see later for verifying their estimates. On the output side of the WBS, the structure and code design will be influenced by the requirements of the different groups responsible for different areas of management. This is not to be confused with the responsibility overlay matrix.

As the reports are designed, the prime requirement is to generate the applicable management information required on a facility basis and not the responsibility information required for functional or organizational responsibility reporting. It must be kept clear in the designing of the reports that they are not the departmental or functional reports but the progress reports for the progress to date for the completion or construction of a particular facility. It must be clearly stated to the users that the WBS only applies to facility-related reports.

Coordination of Structure, Code, and Report Requirements in WBS Design

The preparation of the WBS requires the integration of the structure, code, and reporting requirements. Initially, the scope of the project is outlined through a pictorial representation of the WBS which should be prepared. This illustration, note Figure 14-4 for example, should be circulated without coding to the user community at both the worker level and the management level.

At this formative stage, it is important that much forward looking or insight into the project be considered. The structure should be simple, clear and have meaning, and then this should be linked to the code after the structure has been finalized. The coding should then be prepared. Sample reports using the WBS should be drawn up and circulated for review. These reports should be generated using test data and the proposed code.

The design of the structure, the code, and the reports should contain as much input as possible from the groups that will be using it, given whatever time, cost, or system constraints which are applied to the particular project. In many cases existing systems such as accounting, or existing policies and procedures within the company, may dictate the shape of the WBS. These constraints must be worked around, and an effort should be made to make the WBS as close as possible to the "ideal" required. These constraints should not be the primary determinants of the structure but must be considered in the design. These stumbling blocks and the hurdles must be overcome because this project control tool (WBS) is an absolute necessity in any project with multiple owners, many contractors, and/or government intervention.

When the WBS is completed, it must be presented and explained to all the users. It should be in book form, which can be readily updated. The first section in the book should illustrate the WBS structure with pictorial drawings, the next section should illustrate the code, either pictorially or graphically, and the final section should be a dictionary of definitions defining the content of each WBS element. These definitions are necessary in projects, ensuring that when a term is used, it is used as the project means it to be used, not with historical meanings which vary from group to group. A careful documentation of the meaning in the dictionary of each WBS element with regard to cost, schedule, and resource requirements for the activity ensures that all users will gather and supply information with common meaning to personnel involved with the project. The WBS manual containing coding, definitions, and explanations for usage is the last key step in the development of the WBS. A supplement to the manual may contain samples of the report formats to be utilized by the groups and illustrations as to how these tie into the WBS.

Upon completion of the manual, it should then be the responsibility of the project manager's staff to explain it to all users and personnel involved in the project. They should explain why it is necessary, and when and what it is required for. The why is to ensure that all information collected, reported, and forecast against has common meaning, regardless of the information source. It should be explained for usage in all communications (the what) on budgets, estimates, schedules, productivities, performance, and items associated with management of the project and should be done with reference to the applicable WBS element. This reference should be used and maintained from the very first day (the when) the project is clearly defined to the final reconciliation of the project. WBS should be used by the engineers, project control, and accounting. The WBS is used everywhere that information on the project's progress is collected.

EXAMPLES OF A WBS

Background

The previous section described the required elements for the preparation of the WBS as the foundation for establishing project control. The characteristics to be considered in WBS development and usage are

1. Management philosophy.
2. User groups.
3. System integration.
4. WBS—Responsibility Relationship.
5. WBS Components:
   - structure
   - code
   - reporting

The development process described was used for the preparation of a WBS for the Canadian section of the Alaska Highway Gas Pipeline Project (AHGPP).

Figure 14-5 illustrates the overall project, which starts from Prudhoe Bay through Alaska down through the Yukon, British Columbia, Alberta, and Saskatchewan. Thus the project covered a large geographical area. Overall, as can be seen by the map, there were many companies and governments involved. The lines from Caroline to Monchy, Saskatchewan, and from Caroline to Kingsgate, British Columbia were begun in late 1980 and completed two years later. This prebuild project of about $1 billion Canadian was completed successfully under budget and ahead of schedule. The WBS as described was used in the manner and for all the applications mentioned.

Management Philosophy

The management philosophy for the project required a WBS designed on a facility basis.

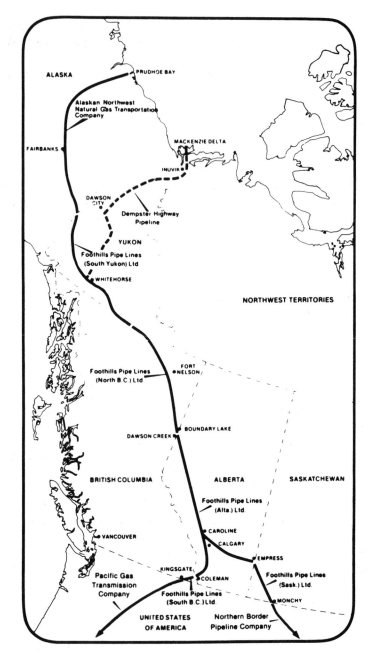

Figure 14-5. The Alaska Highway Gase Pipeline Project.

User Groups

The planned Canadian line was over 2000 miles with pipe sizes varying from 36 to 56 inches in diameter. Along this section of the route were approximately 21 compressor stations each with over 25,000 horsepower. The user community for this project, as shown in Figure 14-1, had functional groups which were part of four companies, with the responsible groups including two owner companies, government agencies, and contractors. This diverse owner community with the multifunctional centers required a very precise WBS to ensure effective project information flow.

Systems Integration

The functional groups in all six Canadian companies used the WBS as part of their budgeting, estimating, accounting, and scheduling systems utilizing both manual and automated systems. All information collected by these systems was summarized using the WBS and then forwarded to management on a common basis using both manual and automated interfaces. The prebuild project clearly illustrated the effective integration of systems, as the WBS was utilized by all required systems.

WBS Development

The WBS was developed to meet the needs of all the users described previously. A segment illustrating the WBS structure developed is shown as Figure 14-4. This illustrates the different levels of the structure with their applicable coding. As can be seen from Figure 14-4, the first level is facility, the second location, the third prime activity, and the fourth describes subactivity. For each of these levels, there are specific reports. The top level—facility type—supplies cost, productivity, and schedule information on a facility basis, which is a top management report. To provide additional detail, the reports for each specific facility was generated for cost, schedule, productivity, manpower, and equipment usage for each level of the WBS shown. The final two levels of activity— the prime activity and subactivity—enable the designer, the cost engineer, and the scheduler to monitor specific items required to build a particular facility. These levels represent the engineering technical level which is required for the detailed management of the project. As can be seen in Figure 14-4, the hierarchical rollup is natural in that each level rolls to the next level in a meaningful fashion.

The code is shown in Figure 14-4 and is graphically illustrated in 14-6. On the left of Figure 14-6 is a map of Alberta showing the facilities to be

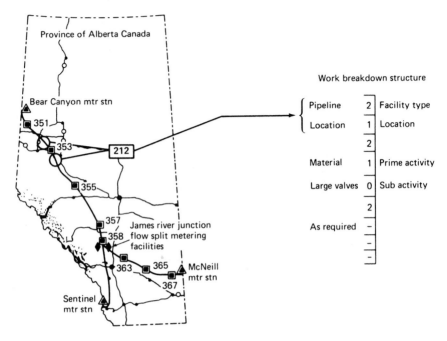

Figure 14-6. Work breakdown structure pipeline construction.

constructed. The section highlighted is a section of pipeline to be built at the particular location shown. Code 2 is always pipeline, with 212 being pipeline at location 12. Also in the drawing are locations 363, etc., which are compression facilities at designated locations. This figure illustrates a portion of the code and its meaning. This type of illustration is very useful in training staff in the usage of WBS.

An example of the usage of this coding is presented in Figure 14-7. This is the standard commitment report on a WBS basis for a particular location. The left side of the figure is the WBS code (six digits in this case). The capability of nine digits is allowed to supply future flexibility as the project proceeds. If more information is needed in a particular area, then the WBS can expand to receive the information without redesigning the code or structure, while maintaining the flow of information in a hierarchical manner. The first three digits identify the facility type and its location, as shown in Figure 14-6. Then come the materials as the next digit, which is represented by a "1." The materials code for the items required for pipeline are next. The authorized dollars illustrated are for the items authorized for purchase for the particular location. As the project pro-

WBS Code	WBS Description	Current authorized	Incurred cost this period	to date	Committed cost this period	to date	Estimate to complete	Estimated final total
212100	Unallocated							
212101	Mainline pipe	37,505						
212102	Large valves	420						
212103	Small valves	21						
212104	Small diameter pipe	2						
212105	Fittings	47						
212106	Mill coating internal	329						
212107	Mill coating external							
212108	Field coating external	460						
212109	Cathodic protection							
212110	Weights and anchor	785						
212111	Fencing and signs							
212112	Sales taps	54						
212113	Special materials – coating							
212114	Miscellaneous	88						
	Sub-total materials	39,711						

ceeds, the incurred costs will be recorded as well as committed costs. In addition, estimates to complete will be done so that an estimated final total cost can be determined for this part of the project. The report shown in Figure 14-7 is only one of many which can be generated within the WBS framework. This example of the pipeline project illustrates a WBS which is utilized in the multicompany environment for a large project where the WBS is a key project control tool. Thus, as illustrated, a properly designed WBS is the basis for effective project control tools.

CONCLUSIONS

It appears that for now and the foreseeable future, projects with long time spans from the conceptual stage to operation, large capital expenditures, complex ownership, and government involvement will become more common.

In this complex environment, or with many small projects, it is absolutely essential to have a precisely defined methodology for the WBS with which all involved personnel can exchange information, plan the project, and organize reporting. With the usage of personal computers, many smaller projects at different locations can be managed using the same WBS to give overall control on a common reporting basis.

This chapter has outlined the reasons why a properly designed WBS becomes the essential tool for effective project management in a project environment. It has illustrated the components and requirements to prepare the required WBS. The prime reasons the WBS should be used are the following:

1. Developing the WBS early in the project life cycle provides a method for clear definition of the project scope, and the process of WBS development helps all participants to clearly understand the project during the initial stages.
2. The use of the WBS code for monitoring and forecasting of all cost, schedule, and productivity information ensures that project management personnel will have a baseline to which comparison can be made. When a common definition for all information on the project is established, effective and logical management decisions can be made.
3. With multiple participants and changing personnel, it is essential that all terms used mean the same to all participants. This consistency of definition is established through the development and use of the WBS with associated code and dictionary.

4. The WBS becomes the basis from which all information flow between information systems can be established, and upon which all facility-type reporting is available.

Thus a properly designed and developed WBS, with its structure, code, and dictionary, supplies the common base for project management by having cost, schedule, and productivity information all using WBS definitions forming the foundation of quality project control for any project.

15. Network Techniques in Project Management

Joseph J. Moder*

Project management involves the coordination of group activity wherein the manager plans, organizes, staffs, directs, and controls, to achieve an objective with constraints on time, cost, and performance of the end product. This chapter will deal primarily with the planning and control functions, and to some extent the organization of resources. *Planning* is the process of preparing for the commitment of resources in the most economical fashion. *Controlling* is the process of making events conform to schedules by coordinating the action of all parts of the organization according to the plan established for attaining the objective.

It can also be said that project management is a blend of art and science: the art of getting things done through and with people in formally organized groups; and the science of handling large amounts of data to plan and control so that project duration and cost are balanced, and excessive and disruptive demands on scare resources are avoided. This chapter will deal with the science of project planning and control that is based on a network representation of the project plan, also referred to as critical path methods.

It is appropriate at this point to elaborate on the term *project*. Projects may, on the one hand, involve routine procedures that are performed repetitively, such as the monthly closing of accounting books. In this case, critical path methods are useful for *detailed* analysis and optimization of the operating plan. Usually, however, these methods are applied to

* Joseph J. Moder is Professor in the Department of Management Science at the University of Miami, Coral Gables, Florida. He received his B.S. degree from Washington University, his Ph.D. from Northwestern University, and he did Post Doctoral work in Statistics and Operations Research at Iowa State University and Stanford University. He was a Visiting Professor of Engineering Production at the University of Birmingham, England. His research interests include applied statistics and project management methodology. He has published numerous articles and several books in these fields, and has conducted short courses and research projects in these areas.

one-time efforts; notably construction work of all kinds; maintenance operations; moving, modifying, or setting up a new factory or facility of some sort; etc. Critical path methods are applicable to projects which encompass an extremely wide range of resource requirements and duration times.

In project management, although similar work may have been done previously, it is not usually being repeated in the identical manner on a production basis. Consequently, in order to accomplish the project tasks efficiently, the project manager must plan and schedule largely on the basis of his experience with similar projects, applying his judgment to the particular conditions of the project at hand. During the course of the project he must continually replan and reschedule because of unexpected progress, delays, or technical conditions. Critical path methods are designed to facilitate this mode of operation.

HISTORY OF THE EARLY DEVELOPMENT OF CRITICAL PATH METHODS

Until the advent of critical path methods, there was no generally accepted formal procedure to aid in the management of projects. Each manager had his own scheme which often involved the use of bar charts originally developed by Henry Gantt around 1900. Although the bar chart is still a useful tool in production management, it is inadequate as a means of describing the complex interrelationships among project activities associated with contemporary project management.

This inadequacy was overcome by the significant contribution of Karol Adamiecki in 1931 (1).* He developed a methodology in a form that he called a Harmony graph. This is essentially a bar chart, rotated 90 degrees, with a vertical time scale, a column (movable strip) for each activity in the project, and a very clever means of showing the interrelationship among project activities. This work was evidently completely overlooked by others in this field. It was not until 1957–1958 that a more formal and general approach toward a discipline of project management occurred. At this time several techniques were developed concurrently, but independently. The technique called Critical Path Method (CPM) was developed in connection with a very large project undertaken at Du Pont Corporation by Kelley and Walker (6). The objective there was to determine the optimum (minimum total cost) duration for a project whose activity durations were primarily deterministic variables.

---

* Numbered references are given at the end of this chapter.

A similar development occurred in Great Britain where the problems of overhauling an electricity generating plant were being studied (7). The principal feature of their technique was the determination of what they called the "longest irreducible sequence of events."

A somewhat different approach to the problem, called Project Evaluation and Review Technique (PERT), was developed in conjunction with the Polaris weapons system by Malcolm and others (8). The objective there was to develop an improved method of planning, scheduling, and controlling an extremely large, complicated development program in which many of the activities being conducted were at or beyond the state of the art, and hence the actual activity duration times were primarily random variables with considerable variance.

DEVELOPMENT OF THE NETWORK PLAN CONCEPT

Although all of the above developments were conducted independently, they are essentially all based upon the important concept of a *network* representation of the project plan. The network diagram is essentially an òutgrowth of the bar chart which was developed by Gantt in the context of a World War I military requirement. The bar chart, which is primarily designed to control the time element of a program, is depicted in Figure 15-1(a). Here, the bar chart lists the major activities comprising a hypothetical project, their scheduled start and finish times, and their current status. The steps followed in preparing a bar chart are as follows:

1. Analyze the project and specify the basic approach to be used.
2. Break the project down into a reasonable number of activities to be scheduled.
3. Estimate the time required to perform each activity.
4. Place the activities in sequence of time, taking into account the requirements that certain activities must be performed sequentially while others can be performed simultaneously.
5. If a completion date is specified, the diagram is adjusted until this constraint is satisfied.

The primary advantage of the bar chart is that the plan, schedule, and progress of the project can all be portrayed graphically together. Figure 15-1 shows the five-activity plan and 15-week schedule, and current status (end of third week) indicates, for example, that activity B is slightly behind schedule. In spite of this important advantage, bar charts have not been too successful on one-time-through projects with a high engineering content, or projects of large scope. The reasons for this include the fact that the simplicity of the bar chart precludes showing sufficient detail to

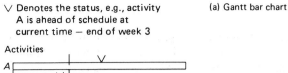

∨ Denotes the status, e.g., activity
A is ahead of schedule at
current time — end of week 3

(a) Gantt bar chart

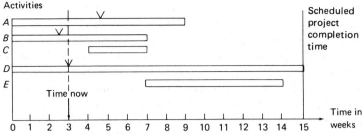

(b) Project network

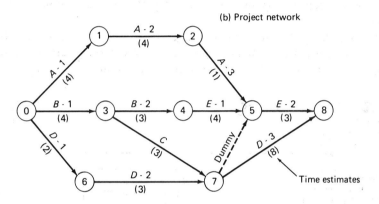

(c) Time-scaled network

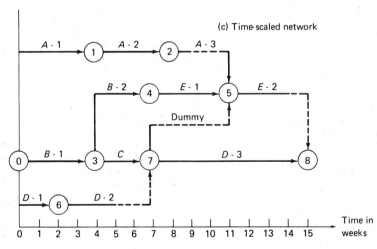

Figure 15-1(a),(b),(c). Comparison of bar chart, project network, and time-scaled network. (From *Project Management with CPM, PERT and Precedence Diagramming*, 3rd Ed., J. J. Moder, C. R. Phillips and E. W. Davis, © 1983 by Litton Educational Publishing, Inc. Reprinted by permission of Van Nostrand Reinhold Co.)

enable timely detection of schedule slippages on activities with relatively long duration times. Also, the bar chart does not show explicitly the dependency relationships among the activities. Hence, it is very difficult to impute the effects on project completion of progress delays in individual activities. Finally, the bar chart is awkward to set up and maintain for large projects, and it has a tendency to quickly become outdated and lose its usefulness. With these disadvantages in mind, along with certain events of the mid-fifties such as the emergence of large technical programs, large digital computers, general systems theory, etc., the stage was set for the development of a network-based project management methodology. Something like the critical path method literally had to emerge.

Before taking up the logic of networking, it will be useful to preview the scope of critical path methods as the basis of a dynamic network-based planning, scheduling, and control procedure, as shown in Figure 15-2.

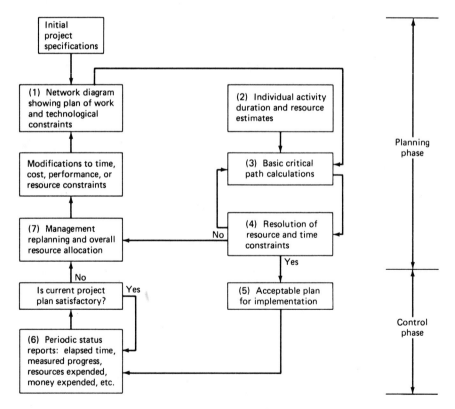

Figure 15-2. Dynamic network-based planning and control procedure.

Step 1, which is the representation of the basic project plan in the form of a network, will be treated in the next section. Steps 2 and 3 will then be considered to estimate the duration of the project plan and determine its critical path. Considered next are the techniques which comprise Step 4; they are designed to modify the initial project plan to satisfy time and resource constraints placed on the project. Finally, the control phase of project management, Step 6, will be considered.

THE LOGIC OF NETWORKS AS MODELS FOR PROJECT PLANS

The first step in drawing a project network is to list all jobs (activities) that have to be performed to complete the project, and to put these jobs in proper technological sequence in the form of a network or arrow diagram. An aid to this process is to organize the project activities in the form of a hierarchical (tree) structure called a work breakdown structure. Such a diagram is shown in Figure 15-3, with the work broken down vertically. In addition, you can break down the organization that is to be used to carry out the project as shown horizontally at the bottom of Figure 15-3. When hierarchical codes are assigned to each of these breakdowns, it is then easy to produce specialized reports by selecting only those activities having the desired codes. For example, an organizational breakdown report could be produced to cover all Engineering activities, or Engineering-Design. Similarly, a work breakdown report could be produced to cover all Engine, or Engine-Compressor activities.

Each job in the project is indicated by an arrow, with nodes, called events, placed at each end of the arrows. Events represent points in time and are said to occur when all activities leading into the event are completed. In Figure 15-4, for example, when the two activities "select operators" and "prepare training material" are completed, the event numbered 10 is said to occur. It should be pointed out that the two predecessor activities of Event 10 need not be completed at the same time; however, when they are both completed, Event 10 occurs, and only then may the activity "train operators" begin. Similarly, when this activity is completed, Event 15 occurs, and the successor activities "test process A" and "test process B" each *may* then begin. It is important to note that the ordering of these activities is based on the "technology" of the resources being utilized.

Activities require the expenditure of time and resources to complete; eight time units and three instructors in the above example. The length of the arrow is not important, but its direction relative to other activities and events indicates the *technological constraints* on the order in which the activities making up the project may be performed.

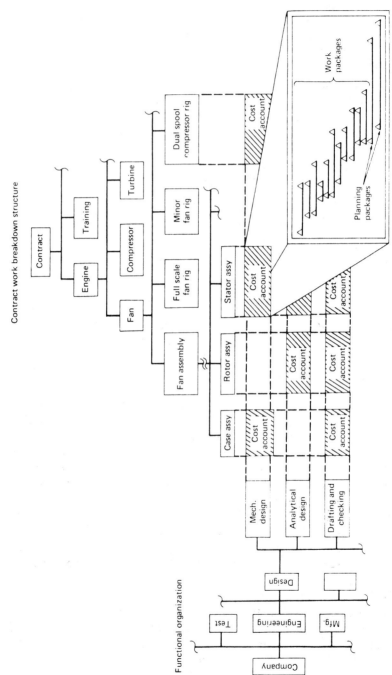

Figure 15-3. Interrelationship between work breakdown structure and functional organization. (From *Project Management with CPM, PERT and Precedence Diagramming*, 3rd Ed., J. J. Moder, C. R. Phillips, and E. W. Davis, © 1983 by Litton Educational Publishing, Inc. Reprinted by permission of Van Nostrand Reinhold Co.)

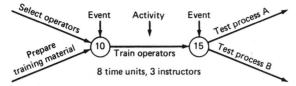

Figure 15-4. An example arrow diagram activity.

There is also a need for what is called a *dummy* activity, which requires neither time nor resources to complete. Activity 7-5 in the middle of Figure 15-1 is an example of such an activity. Its sole purpose is to show precedence relationships, that is, that activities C and D-2 must (technologically) precede activity E-2.

The project network is then constructed by starting with the initial project event which has no predecessor activities and occurs at the start of the project. From this event, activities are added to the network using the basic logic described above. This process is continued until all activities have been included in the network, the last of which merge into the project end event which has no successor activities. In carrying out this task the novice must be extremely careful to avoid the common error of ordering the activities arbitrarily according to some preconceived idea of the sequence that the activities will probably take when the project is carried out. If this error is made, the subsequent scheduling and control procedures will be unworkable. However, if the network is faithfully drawn according to technological constraints, it will be a unique project model which only changes when fundamental changes in the plan are made. It will also present maximum flexibility in subsequent scheduling of the activities to satisfy resource constraints.

The preparation of the project network presents an excellent opportunity to try out, or simulate on paper, various ways of carrying out the project, thus avoiding costly and time-consuming mistakes which might be made "in the field" during the actual conduct of the project. It also presents an opportunity to solicit inputs from project team members to gain their wisdom and their future cooperation and allegiance. At the conclusion of the planning operation, the final network presents a permanent record giving a clear expression of the way in which the project is to be carried out so that all parties involved in the project can see their involvement and responsibilities.

The Time Element

After the planning or networking, the *average duration* of each job is estimated, based upon the job specifications and a consideration of the resources to be employed in carrying out the job. The best estimates will usually be obtained from the person(s) who will supervise the work or who has had such experience.

These time estimates are placed beside the appropriate arrows. If we were then to sum the durations of the jobs along all possible paths from the beginning to the end of the project, the longest one is called the critical path, and its length is the expected duration of the project. Any delay in the start or completion of the jobs along this path will delay completion of the whole project. The rest of the jobs are "floaters" which have a limited amount of leeway (slack) for completion without affecting the target date for the completion of the project.

These concepts are illustrated at the bottom of Figure 15-1 where the network activities have been plotted to scale on a time axis. This diagram shows the critical path quite clearly. It consists of activities B-1, C, and D-3, and has an overall duration of 15 weeks. The slack along the other network paths is shown by the dashed portion of the network arrows. For example, the path D-1 and D-2 has 2 weeks of slack, that is, 7 weeks are available to carry out these two jobs which are expected to require only 5 weeks to complete.

The above time-scaled network can be considered as a graphical solution to what is called the *basic scheduling computations*. This is not an operational procedure; it was used here primarily for illustrative purposes.

The objective of the scheduling computations is to determine the critical path(s) and its duration, and to determine the amount of slack on the remaining paths. It turns out that this can best be accomplished by computing the earliest start and finish, and latest start and finish times for each project activity.

BASIC SCHEDULING COMPUTATIONS

A programmable algorithm for the basic scheduling computations is given by equations 1 through 7 below, in terms of the following nomenclature.

D_{ij} estimate of the mean duration time for activity i-j
E_i earliest occurrence time for event i
L_i latest allowable occurrence time for event i
ES_{ij} earliest start time for activity i-j
EF_{ij} earliest finish time for activity i-j
LS_{ij} latest allowable start time for activity i-j
LF_{ij} latest allowable finish time for activity i-j

S_{ij} total slack (or float) time for activity i-j
FS_{ij} free slack (or float) time for activity i-j
T_s schedule time for the completion of a project or the occurrence of certain key events in a project

Earliest and Latest Event Times

Assume that the events were numbered (or renumbered by a simple algorithm) so that the initial event is 1, the terminal event is t, and all other events (i-j) are numbered so that $i < j$. Now let $E_1 = 0$ by assumption, then

$$E_j = \max_i (E_i + D_{ij}) \qquad 2 \leq j \leq t \qquad (1)$$

E_t = (expected) project duration, and
$L_t = E_t$ or T_s, the scheduled project completion time. Then,

$$L_i = \min_j (L_j - D_{ij}) \qquad 1 \leq i \leq t - 1 \qquad (2)$$

Earliest and Latest Activity Start and Finish Times and Slack

$$ES_{ij} = E_i \qquad \text{all } ij \qquad (3)$$
$$EF_{ij} = E_i + D_{ij} \qquad \text{all } ij \qquad (4)$$
$$LF_{ij} = L_j \qquad \text{all } ij \qquad (5)$$
$$LS_{ij} = L_j - D_{ij} \qquad \text{all } ij \qquad (6)$$
$$S_{ij} = L_j - EF_{ij} \qquad \text{all } ij \qquad (7)$$

The above equations embody two basic sets of calculations. First, the *forward pass calculations* are carried out to determine the earliest occurrence time for each event j (E_j), and the earliest start and finish times for each activity i-j (ES_{ij} and EF_{ij}). These calculations are based on the assumption that each activity is conducted as *early* as possible, that is, they are started as soon as their predecessor event occurs. Since these calculations are initiated by equating the initial project event to time zero ($E_1 \equiv 0$), the earliest time computed for the project terminal event (E_t) gives the expected project duration.

The second set of calculations, called the *backward pass calculations,* are carried out to determine the latest (allowable) occurrence times for each event i (L_i), and the latest (allowable) start and finish times for each activity i-j (LS_{ij} and LF_{ij}). These calculations begin with the project end event by equating its latest allowable occurrence time to the scheduled project duration, if one is specified ($L_t \equiv T_s$), or by arbitrarily equating it to $E_t(L_t \equiv E_t)$ if no duration is specified. This is referred to as the "zero-slack" convention. These calculations then proceed by working backwards through the network, always assuming that each activity is conducted as *late* as possible.

To facilitate these hand calculations, *all times will be assumed to be "end-of" times.* Thus, the initial project activities, that is, those without predecessors, that follow the *initial* network event, will have an early start time of zero, which corresponds to the scheduled calendar date for the project start. A start time of zero means at the *end of* day zero, which is the same as the *start of* day one. On the other hand, computer runs give outputs transformed to calendar dates; but they also follow a different convention.

Computer Date Convention: Activity start times denote the *beginning of* the day (or other time period) corresponding to the given activity start date, while finish times denote the *end of* the day (or other time period) corresponding to the given finish date of the activity.

Again, to simplify the hand calculations, all times will be assumed to be *end-of* times. Hence for an activity start time of t, it means at the *end of* working day t, which is the same as the beginning of working day $t + 1$.

Role of Hand Computation Procedure

The misuse of computers is not uncommon in the application of critical path methods. This occurs notably in making the above scheduling computations during the initial development of an acceptable project plan; an operation previously described as Steps 3 and 4 in Figure 15-2. At this stage it is important that the momentum of a project planning session must not be broken by the requirement for a computer run, and furthermore, it is more economical to perform these computations once by hand, regardless of the size of the network.

For this purpose a set of special networking symbols is useful to avoid making arithmetic errors. The key to these symbols is given in Figure 15-5, and their application is given in Figure 15-6, where the network employed is essentially the same as that used in Figure 15-1.

The start of the project at time zero is noted by setting $E_0 = 0$ in Figure 15-6. Then, equation 4 gives the early finish time for activity 0-1 as $EF_{01} = E_0 + D_{01} = 0 + 2 = 2$. Since event 1 has but one predecessor, activity 0-1, its early occurrence time is given by $E_1 = EF_{01} = 2$. The application of equation 1 occurs at all "merge" events (5, 7 and 8). For example, at event 5 the early event time $E_5 = 11$ is computed as follows:

$$E_5 = \max_{i=2,4} (E_2 + D_{25} = 6 + 1 = 7; E_4 + D_{45} = 7 + 4 = 11) = 11$$

Reading earliest expected and latest allowable activity start
and finish times and float from the special symbols

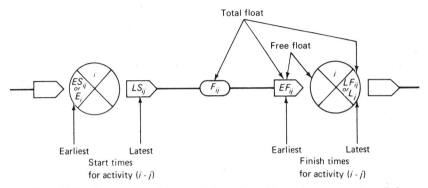

Figure 15-5a. Key to use and interpretation of special activity and event symbols.

Forward pass

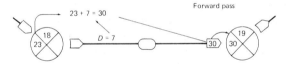

Begin with zero for the earliest start time for the initial project event and compute earliest finish times for all succeeding activities. For a typical activity, place its earliest start time (say, 23 days from project start) in the left quadrant of the event symbol. Then add its duration (7) to the earliest start time to obtain its earliest finish time (30). Write 30 in the arrow head.

Where activities merge, insert in the left quadrant of the event symbol the largest of the earliest finish times written in the arrowheads of the merging activities.

Backward pass

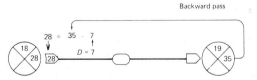

Place the scheduled completion time for the final event in the right quadrant of the project terminal event symbol. For other events, insert instead the latest allowable event occurrence time. For a typical activity, subtract its duration (7) from the latest completion time (35) to obtain the latest allowable activity start time (28). Write 28 in the arrow tail.

Where two or more activities "burst" from an event, insert in the right quadrant of the event symbol the smallest of the latest allowable activity start times.

Figure 15-5b. Steps in scheduling computations using special activity and event symbols. (From *Project Management with CPM, PERT and Precedence Diagramming*, 3rd Ed., J. J. Moder, C. R. Phillips and E. W. Davis, © 1983 by Litton Educational Publishing, Inc. Reprinted by permission of Van Nostrand Reinhold Co.)

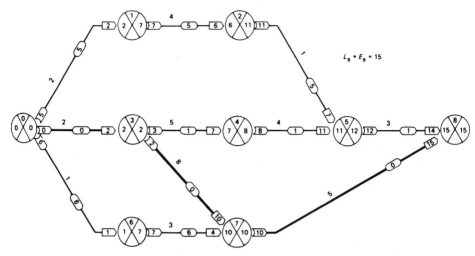

Figure 15-6. Illustrative network employing the special activity and event symbols showing completed computations. (From *Project Management with CPM, PERT, and Precedence Diagramming,* 3rd Ed., J. J. Moder, C. R. Phillips and E. W. Davis, © 1983 by Litton Educational Publishing, Inc. Reprinted by permission of Van Nostrand Reinhold Co.)

The backward pass is initiated by using the zero-slack convention, that is, letting $L_8 = E_8 = 15$. Working backwards from here, the latest start time for activity 5-8 is obtained from equation 6 as $LS_{58} = L_8 - D_{58} = 15 - 3 = 12$. Since event 5 has but one successor, activity 5-8, its latest occurrence time is given by $L_5 = LS_{58} = 12$. The application of equation 2 occurs at all "burst" events (0 and 3). For example, at event 3 the latest event time $L_3 = 2$ is computed as follows:

$$L_3 = \min_{j=4,7}, (L_4 - D_{34} = 8 - 5 = 3, L_7 - D_{37} = 10 - 8 = 2) = 2$$

The Critical Path and Slack Paths

Among the many types of slack defined in the literature, two are of most value and are discussed here: they are called total activity slack, or simply total slack, and activity-free slack, or simply free slack. They are also referred to as total float and free float, with the same definitions.

Total Activity Slack. *Definition:* Total activity slack is equal to the difference between the earliest and latest allowable start or finish times for the activity in question. Thus, for activity *i-j*, the total slack is given by

$$S_{ij} = LS_{ij} - ES_{ij} \quad \text{or} \quad LF_{ij} - EF_{ij}$$

Activity-Free Slack. Merge point activities, which are the last activities on slack paths, have what is called activity-free slack.

Definition: Activity-free slack is equal to the earliest occurrence time of the activity's successor event, minus the earliest finish time of the activity in question. Thus, for activity *i-j*, the free slack is given by

$$FS_{ij} = E_j - EF_{ij} \quad \text{or} \quad ES_{jk} - EF_{ij}$$

Critical Path Identification. *Definition:* The critical path is the path with the least total slack.

We will point out later that whenever scheduled times are permitted on intermediate network events, the critical path will not always be the longest path through the network. However, the above definition of the critical path always applies. For this reason, a computer run should be made before introducing intermediate scheduled times so that the longest path through the network can be determined by the computer.

If the "zero-slack" convention of letting $L_t = E_t$ for the terminal network event is followed, then the critical path will have zero slack. This situation is illustrated in Figure 15-6, where $L_8 = E_8 = 15$. However, if the latest allowable time for the terminal event is set by T_s, an arbitrary scheduled duration time for the completion of the project, then the slack on the critical path will be positive, zero, or negative, depending on whether $T_s > E_t$, $T_s = E_t$, or $T_s < E_t$, respectively. The last situation indicates, of course, that the completion of the project is expected to be late, that is, completion after the scheduled time, T_s. This is generally an unsatisfactory situation, and replanning (Steps 3 and 4 in Figure 15-2) would be required.

To carry out this replanning, it is quite helpful to be able to determine the critical path and its duration with a minimum of hand computation. This can be accomplished from the *forward pass computations alone.* Referring to Figure 15-6, start with the end event, 8, which must be on the critical path. Now trace backwards through the network along the path(s) with $EF_{ij} = E_j$. In this case we proceed to event 7 because $EF_{78} = E_8 = 15$, while $EF_{58} = 14 \neq E_8$. In like manner we proceed backwards to event 3 and then to the initial event zero. Thus the critical path is 0-3-7-8, with a duration of 15 time units, determined from the *forward pass computations alone.*

If the backward pass computations are also completed, then total slack and free slack can also be computed. For example, path 0-1-2-5 has a total slack of 5. This is the amount of time by which the actual completion time of this path can be delayed without causing the duration of the overall project to exceed its scheduled completion time. When the critical path has zero slack, as in this example, then the total slack is equal to the amount of time that the activity completion time can be delayed without affecting the earliest start time of any activity or the earliest occurrence time of any event *on the critical path*. For example, activity 0-1 has a total slack of 5 and a free slack of 0. If its completion time is delayed up to 5 time units, it will affect the early start times of the remaining activities on this slack path; however, it will not affect any event on the critical path (event 8 in this case). On the other hand, activity 2-5 has a total slack of 5 and a free slack of 4. Its completion can be delayed up to 5 time units without affecting the critical path (event 8), and it can be delayed up to 4 (free slack) without affecting *any* other event or activity in the network.

Multiple Initial and Terminal Events, and Scheduled Dates

In most projects there will be any number of key events, called milestones, which denote the *start* or *finish* of an activity or group of activities. These milestones may be required to conform to arbitrary scheduled dates, and thus they may override the usual forward and backward calculations. These schedule constraints may be one of three different types:

NET: *N*ot *E*arlier *T*han a specified date.

NLT: *N*ot *L*ater *T*han a specified date (this is the usual type of schedule).

ON: Exactly *ON* a specified date.

Conventions: A NET schedule affects the *early* time of an activity start or finish and hence it is considered in making the *forward* pass calculations. Similarly, a NLT schedule affects the *latest* time of an activity start or finish and hence it is considered in making the *backward* pass calculations. Finally an ON schedule affects both the *early* and *late* times and hence it is used in both the *forward* and *backward* pass calculations, and becomes both the early and late time for the activity in question.

These schedule times apply to all network events, including the initial and terminal network events. To illustrate the effect of a scheduled time for an intermediate network event, consider event 5 in Figure 15-6, with the schedule constraints shown in Table 15-1.

The four cases in Table 15-1 marked as no effect involve scheduled times that are less restrictive than the existing forward or backward pass calculations. For example, a NET = 10 on event 5 has no effect because activity 4-5 already has an early finish time of 11 ($EF_{45} = 11$) which is later or more constraining than NET = 10. Hence, $E_5 = 11$ remains unchanged by the imposition of this schedule constraint. This same result would also hold for any NET time less than 10. However, NET = 12 (or more) would

Table 15-1. Effects of Various Schedule Constraints on the
Intermediate Event 5 in Figure 15-6.

TYPE OF CONSTRAINT	SCHEDULE TIME	EFFECT ON FORWARD AND BACKWARD PASS CALCULATIONS
NET	10 or less	None
NET	12 (or more)	$E_5 = 12$ (or more) instead of 11
NLT	13 or more	None
NLT	11 (or less)	$L_5 = 11$ (or less) instead of 12
ON	11	None on forward pass
ON	11	$L_5 = 11$ (on backward pass) instead of 12
ON	12	$E_5 = 12$ (on forward pass) instead of 11
ON	12	None on backward pass
ON	10	$E_5 = 10$ (on forward pass) instead of 11
ON	10	$L_5 = 10$ (on backward pass) instead of 12

affect the forward pass calculations because it is more constraining (later) than the early finish times of activities 2-5 and 4-5, that is, $EF_{25} = 7$ and $EF_{45} = 11$.

Table 15-1 indicates how these schedule constraints may or may not change the early/late times computed in the forward and backward pass calculations. If a NLT schedule of 10 was placed on event 5, then the latest time for this event would become $L_5 = 10$, and the critical path would become 0-3-4-5, since it would have the *least slack* of -1 time units ($LF_{45} - EF_{45} = 10 - 11 = -1$). Note also that this path does not go completely through the network. The longest path through the network would continue to be 0-3-7-8.

Another network complication is the occurrence of multiple initial and/ or terminal events. For example, suppose there are several projects, each with their own networks, that are competing for a common set of resources. Since a number of algorithms require single initial and terminal events, a procedure is needed to combine these projects into one network with a single initial and terminal event. This can be accomplished by the use of dummy initial and terminal events to which each project connects with dummy activities. Duration times are assigned to the latter to impute the correct project start time relative to the early start time assigned to the initial dummy event, and the correct finish time relative to the late finish time assigned to the terminal dummy event.

TIME-COST TRADE-OFF PROCEDURES

The determination of the critical path and its duration was described above. This constitutes Step 3 in Figure 15-2. Moving on to Step 4, if the earliest occurrence time for the network terminal event exceeds the scheduled project duration, then some modification of the network may be required to achieve an acceptable plan.

These modifications might take the form of a major change in the network structure. For example, changing the assumption that one set of concrete forms is available to the availability of two sets may result in a considerable change in the network and reduction in the project duration.

A different procedure that is frequently employed to handle this problem is referred to as time-cost trade-off. Referring to Figure 15-6, we might ask the question, how can we most economically reduce the duration of this project from its current level of 15 time units, say weeks, to 14 weeks? To accomplish this, the critical path, that is, 0-3, 3-7, 7-8, must be reduced by 1 week. The decision in this case would be to buy a week of time on that activity (or those activities) where it is available at the lowest additional (marginal) cost. If this turns out to be activity 3-7 or 7-8, then the resulting project will have two critical paths, each of 14 weeks duration, that is, 0-3, 3-4, 4-5, 5-8, and 0-3, 3-7, 7-8. Thus further reductions in this project duration will be more complicated because both paths must now be considered. One must also constantly consider buying back time previously bought on certain activities. This problem very rapidly reaches the point where a computer is required to obtain an optimal solution.

The Critical Path Method (CPM)

The CPM procedure, developed by Kelley and Walker (6) to handle this problem, arises when we ask for the project schedule which minimizes *total project costs*. This is equivalent to the project activity schedule that just balances the marginal value of time saved (in completing the project a time unit early) against the marginal cost of saving it. The total project cost is made up of the indirect costs, determined by the accounting department considering normal overhead costs and the "value" of the time saved, plus the *minimum* direct project costs, determined as follows by the CPM procedure.

The CPM computational algorithm is based on an assumed linear cost versus time relationship for each activity. With this input, this problem can be formulated as a linear programming problem to minimize the total project *direct* costs, subject to constraints dictated by the activity time-cost curves, and the network logic.

Although this is an elegant algorithm, it is rarely applied today, primarily because of the unrealistic basic assumption of the unlimited availability of resources. Nevertheless, it is an important concept that is frequently applied in the simple manner illustrated at the beginning of this section.

The important consideration of limited resources is treated in the next section.

SCHEDULING ACTIVITIES TO SATISFY TIME AND RESOURCE CONSTRAINTS

To illustrate how Figure 15-6 can be used to solve resource allocation problems, suppose that activities 1-2, 3-4, and 5-8 require the continuous use of a special piece of equipment during their performance. Can this requirement be met without causing a delay in the completion of this project?

With the aid of Figure 15-6, it is very easy to see that the answer to this question is yes, if the following schedule is used. The reasoning proceeds as follows. First, activities 1-2 and 3-4 must precede 5-8, so the first question is which of these two activities should be scheduled first. Reference to Figure 15-6 indicates that both have an early start time of 2, and since the floats are 5 and 1 for activities 1-2 and 3-4, respectively, the activity ordering of 1-2, 3-4, and 5-8 follows.

One can, of course, ask more involved questions dealing with the leveling of the demand for various personnel skills. From a computer standpoint, these questions are the most important ones involved in the use of critical path methods.

A Heuristic Resource Scheduling Procedure

Resource allocation problems in general can be categorized as the determination of the scheduled times for project activities which do one of the following:

1. Level the resource requirements in time, subject to the constraint that the project duration will not be increased.
2. Minimize the project duration subject to constraints on the limited availabilities of resources.
3. Minimize the total cost of the resources and the penalties due to project delay—the long-range planning problem.

The combinatorial nature of this problem has prevented it from yielding to the optimal solution techniques of mathematical programming. Because of this lack of success with optimization procedures, major attention has been devoted to developing heuristic procedures which produce "good" feasible solutions. The procedures described below are an example of such heuristic procedures known as the "least slack first rule," or its equivalent name, the "minimum late start time rule." Collectively, they are essentially schemes for assigning priorities to the activities that are used in making the activity sequencing decisions required for the resolution of resource conflicts.

Serial Versus Parallel Scheduling Procedures

A popular scheduling procedure to solve the first and second problems defined above consists of scheduling activities one day at a time, working from the first to the last day of the project. Each day, the activities that are ready to start (all predecessors complete) are ordered in a list with least slack first. Then, working through this list, as many activities as possible are scheduled (resource availability permitting). At the end of each day, the resources available are updated, as well as the early start and finish times of all delayed activities. This process is then repeated until the entire project has been scheduled. This procedure is known as *parallel scheduling*.

Another approach, known as *serial scheduling,* ranks all activities in the project only once at the start, using some heuristic such as *least slack first*. The activities are then scheduled one at a time (serially), as soon as all of their predecessors are *scheduled* (not necessarily completed), and they are considered for scheduling in the order in which they appear in the list. This procedure tends to schedule activities serially along network paths, whereas the approach described above tends to schedule activities in parallel along different paths.

An example of these two methods of scheduling is shown in Figures 15-7 and 15-8; it utilizes the network previously shown in Figure 15-6. Two resources are considered, A and B; however, the method could handle any number of resources. The schedule shown in Figure 15-7 is based on unlimited resources and shows all activities at their early start/finish times. Note that a maximum of 14 units of resource A and 8 units of resource B are required. Now consider the limited resource case where only 9 units of A and 6 units of B are available. If we apply the serial and parallel procedures described above, the order in which the activities are actually scheduled, along with their scheduled start/finish times are shown in Table 15-2, and the corresponding bar chart in Figure 15-8.

In this example, the two methods resulted in the same activity schedules as shown in Table 15-2. This will not, of course, always be the case. However, the order in which the activities were scheduled is quite different for these two methods. The activities are grouped in Table 15-2 by paths. The first three activities (0-3, 3-7, and 7-8) have zero slack and form

Activity	A	B	D	ES	S	LS	1	2	3	4	5	6	7	8	9	10	11	12	13	14	15
0–1	3	—	2	1	5	6	x 3A	x 3A													
1–2	—	2	4	3	5	8			x 2B	x 2B	x 2B	x 2B									
0–3	6	—	2	1	0	1	x 6A	x 6A													
3–4	—	2	5	3	1	4			x 2B	x 2B	x 2B	x 2B	x 2B								
2–5	4	—	1	7	5	12							x 4A								
4–5	2	—	4	8	1	9								x 2A	x 2A	x 2A	x 2A				
0–6	3	—	1	1	6	7	x 3A														
3–7	4	4	8	3	0	3			4A 4B	4A 4B	4A 4B	4A 4B	4A 4B	4A 4B	4A 4B	4A 4B					
6–7	5	—	3	2	6	8			x 5A	x 5A	x 5A										
5–8	—	5	3	12	1	13												x 5B	x 5B	x 5B	
7–8	2	—	5	11	0	11											x 2A	x 2A	x 2A	x 2A	x 2A
Level of resource A assigned							12	14	9	9	4	4	8	6	6	6	4	2	2	2	2
Level of resource B assigned									8	8	8	8	6	4	4	4		5	5	5	

Figure 15-7. Resource loading with all activities scheduled at their early start times. (From *Project Management with CPM and PERT,* 2nd Ed., J. J. Moder and C. R. Phillips, © 1970 by Litton Educational Publishing, Inc. Reprinted by permission of Van Nostrand Reinhold Co.)

the critical path. Note how the *serial* method tends to schedule the activities sequentially along each path, whereas the *parallel* method moves back and forth among all four of the paths in this network.

EVALUATION OF SEVERAL SCHEDULING HEURISTICS

Two categories of heuristics that have been found most effective are those incorporating some measure of time, such as activity slack or duration, and those incorporating some measure of resource usage. Davis (4) has

Activity	Resource Req. A	B	D	ES	S	LS
0-1	3	—	2	1	5	6
1-2	—	2	4	3	5	8
0-3	6	—	2	1	0	1
3-4	—	2	5	3	1	4
2-5	4	—	1	7	5	12
4-5	2	—	4	8	1	9
0-6	3	—	1	1	6	7
3-7	4	4	8	3	0	3
6-7	5	5	3	2	6	8
5-8	—	5	3	12	1	13
7-8	2	—	5	11	0	11
Level of resource A assigned (trigger level = 9)						8, 6, 4, 2
Level of resource B assigned (trigger level = 6)						6, 4, 2

Figure 15-8. Resource loading with limited resources (9 units of A and 6 units of B) using either serial or parallel scheduling. (From *Project Management with CPM and PERT*, 2nd Ed., J. J. Moder and C. R. Phillips, © 1970 by Litton Educational Publishing, Inc. Reprinted by permission of Van Nostrand Reinhold Co.)

Table 15-2. Comparison of Serial Versus Parallel Scheduling for the
Illustrative Network Shown in Figure 15-6.

		TYPE OF SCHEDULING			
		PARALLEL		SERIAL	
ACTIVITY	INITIAL FLOAT	ORDER OF SCHEDULING	SCHEDULE[a]	ORDER OF SCHEDULING	SCHEDULE[a]
0-3	0	1	1-2	1	1-2
3-7	0	3	3-10	2	3-10
7-8	0	9	11-15	11	11-15
3-4	1	4	3-7	3	3-7
4-5	1	8	8-11	4	8-11
5-8	1	11	13-15	8	13-15
0-1	5	2	1-2	5	1-2
1-2	5	7	8-11	6	8-11
2-5	5	10	12	7	12
0-6	6	5	3	9	3
6-7	6	6	4-6	10	4-6

[a] A schedule of 3-7 for activity 3-4 means the activity is scheduled to be performed on the 3rd through the 7th days, including the 3rd day. Hence, the sta t time is at the *beginning of* while the finish time is at the *end of* the working day indicated.

made an extensive comparison of eight heuristics on some 83 network problems for which the optimal solutions were obtained using his bounded enumeration procedure. The rules tested included:

1. *Minimum Late Start Time* (LST)—order by increasing LST.
2. *Minimum Late Finish Time* (LFT)—order by increasing LFT.
3. *Resource Scheduling Method*—order by increasing d_{ij}, where d_{ij} = increase in project duration resulting when activity j follows i; = $\max[0; (E_i - L_j)]$, where E_i and L_j denote the early finish time of activity i and the late start time of activity j, respectively. The above activity comparison is made on a pairwise basis among all activities in the eligible activity set.
4. *Shortest Imminent Operation*—order by increasing activity duration.
5. *Greatest Resource Demand*—order by decreasing total resource demand.
6. *Greatest Resource Utilization*—priority given to that combination of activities which results in maximum resource utilization in each scheduling interval; a rule which requires the use of zero–one integer programming to implement.

7. *Most Jobs Possible*—similar to Rule 6, except the number of active jobs is maximized.
8. *Select Jobs Randomly*—order the eligible activities by a random process.

The first four rules above were studied because they are very popular in the open literature on scheduling. The next three rules were included because they have been reported to be used in some of the many computer programs available for project scheduling on a commercial basis. The detailed workings of these programs have been kept secret. The last rule was included as a benchmark of human performance—presumably an experienced scheduler can outperform this rule.

The primary evaluation made in this study was based on the average percentage increase in project duration over the optimal schedule. On this basis the first three rules, having percentages of 5.6, 6.7, and 6.8, respectively, were considerably better than Rule 8, based on random selection, which had a percentage of 11.4. Also, Rules 5, 6, and 7, having percentages of 13.1, 13.1, and 16.0, respectively, gave poorer schedules than Rule 8.

While average performance is a reasonable guide in selecting scheduling rules, it should be pointed out that it is the nature of heuristics that no one rule will always give the best schedule. For this reason, one can argue that if the problem warrants a near optimal schedule, then several different heuristics should be applied. It also suggests that an important research area is to relate heuristic rule performance with simple parameters that describe the network and its resource constraints.

A Realistic Scheduling Procedure

Although the above heuristic scheduling procedure is oversimplified for most practical applications, it has three important properties. First, it can handle any number of resources. Second, it can handle any number of projects as long as their scheduled start and finish times are given. Finally, the procedure can be used as the basis for a more generally applicable scheduling procedure, such as that developed by Wiest (11). Some of its features are as follows:

1. Variable crew sizes are permissible.
2. Splitting or interrupting an activity is permissible.
3. Assignment of unused resources is incorporated.

The application of Wiest's procedure to solve Problem 2 cited in the section entitled A Heuristic Resource Scheduling Procedure is obvious. It can also be used to solve the long-range planning problem, 3 above, by evaluating the total cost of alternative levels of available resources and the penalties associated with delays in the completion of certain projects.

PROBABILISTIC CONSIDERATIONS IN NETWORKING

There are two probabilistic aspects of critical path methods that are of some importance. The first involves those projects in which special milestone events occur, such as the end of test or evaluation activities. The special nature of these events is that they may have several *possible* successor activities, but only one will be selected and the others will be ignored. This situation is referred to as probabilistic branching. For example, in a space vehicle project, an evaluation activity may result in the choice of a solid or a liquid fuel engine, but not both. Also, as a result of a "failure" in some test, such projects may require recycling to an earlier network event, forming a closed loop. Neither of these situations is permissible according to the network logic assumed above.

The occurrence of these situations can be handled by drawing the network in general rather than specific terms. For example, the network plan for the above situation would be drawn up without reference to whether the engine was liquid or solid fuel. Also, the loop situation would be handled by omitting the loop and including its time effect in other network activities. Where more refined planning is required, a special simulation language called GERT (Graphical Evaluation and Review Technique) has been developed by Pritsker (10) which permits the above situations to be built into the network.

The second stochastic aspect of critical path methods deals with the fact that the actual duration of a project activity is usually a (hypothetical) random variable rather than a deterministic constant. Up to now, the effects of the variance in activity performance times on the procedures we have discussed have either been assumed to be negligible or have been neglected. The initial consideration of this problem led to the development of PERT, as cited in the opening section.

The PERT Statistical Approach to Project Management

One of the chief concerns in the development of PERT was meeting the schedules placed on key milestone events, where considerable uncertainty in actual activity performance times existed. Because of this emphasis on events, which is a long-standing United States government practice in controlling projects by monitoring milestones, the activity labels were placed inside the event symbols. This convention, however, has no effect on the network logic described above, and thus represents a minor difference from the networking procedures described above. A major difference in procedures arises, however, from the efforts to estimate, from the project plan, the probability that the milestone schedules would be met.

The approach to this problem, which is frequently taken in developments of this type, was to collect input information on the basic elements of the system, and from it synthesize their effects on system performance. In this case the input information consisted of a measure of the uncertainty in activity duration times, and from this the uncertainty in meeting schedules was computed.

PERT Three Time Estimates

In the PERT approach, the actual activity performance time, t, is assumed to have a hypothetical probability distribution with mean, t_e, and variance, σ_t^2. It is referred to as hypothetical because its parameters must be estimated before any actual observations are made. When the activity is finally completed, the actual time can be regarded as the first (and last) sample from this hypothetical distribution. Estimates of t_e and σ_t^2 must therefore be based on someone's judgment, which in turn is based on a "sampling" of prior work experience.

The PERT activity input data is in the form of three time estimates, called a, m, and b. They denote the optimistic, most likely, and pessimistic estimates of t, respectively. Statistically, these are the zero percentile, the mode, and the 100 percentile of the hypothetical probability distribution.

A rule of thumb in statistics is that the standard deviation can be estimated roughly as ⅙ of the range of the distribution. This follows from the fact that at least 89% of any distribution lies within three standard deviations from the mean, and for the normal distribution this percentage is more than 99.7%. Thus the estimate of the variance is given by

$$\text{variance of } t \equiv \sigma_t^2 = [(b - a)/6]^2 \tag{8}$$

While the above formula is a part of the original PERT procedure, the author prefers to define a and b as the 5 and 95 percentiles, which in turn calls for replacing the divisor 6 in equation 8 by 3.2.

To derive an estimate of the mean requires an assumption about the shape of the probability distribution of t. In the development of PERT, it was assumed that a plausible (and mathematically convenient) distribution for t is the Beta distribution whose standard deviation was ⅙ of its range. For this distribution, equation 9 gives a linear approximation to the true (cubic) relationship between the mean, t_e, and the mode, m:

$$\text{mean of } t \equiv t_e = (a + 4m + b)/6 \qquad (9)$$

PERT Probability Calculation

At this point the scheduling computations described in the section entitled Basic Scheduling Computations can be carried out using only the mean values computed from equation 9 for each activity. The PERT procedure then considers the activities on the critical path(s) through the network, and ignores all others; a rather strong simplifying assumption. If there are several critical paths, then the one with the largest variance is chosen to represent the network. Assuming the actual activity performance times for these activities to be *independent random variables* with means, t_{ei}, and variances, σ_{ti}^2, the statistical properties of the "project" duration follow directly from the central limit theorem. Assuming the critical path consists of N activities, and denoting the sum of their actual durations by T, this can be written as follows:

$$T = \sum_{i=1}^{N} t_i$$

$$\text{mean of } t \equiv T_e = \sum_{i=1}^{N} t_{ei} \qquad (10)$$

$$\text{variance of } T \equiv \sigma_T^2 = \sum_{i=1}^{N} \sigma_{ti}^2 \qquad (11)$$

shape of distribution of T: Normal

probability of meeting schedule T_s

$$= P\{T \leq T_s\} = P\left\{Z \leq \frac{T_s - T_e}{\sigma_T}\right\} \qquad (12)$$

where Z has a normal distribution with zero mean and unit variance, so that the last probability is read from the standard table of the cumulative normal distribution. By varying T_s over a range of times of interest, one can obtain a graph giving the cumulative probability of meeting the project schedule for alternative scheduled completion times.

The basic assumption that the t_i's above are independent random variables must be emphasized. Since a project manager will normally expedite a project when it falls behind schedule, the independence is violated. Hence the interpretation of the probability given by equation 12 is *the probability that the project will meet the schedule without having to be expedited.* This, of course, is very useful for planning purposes since it is computed at the outset of the project. If the calculated probability is low, say <0.75, then the project manager can anticipate the need to expedite the project and can exercise convenient or inexpensive options early in the project.

The simplifying assumption made above, that is, basing the probability computation on the critical path and ignoring all others, warrants further discussion. It is possible for a subcritical path, with a relatively high variance, to have a lower probability of meeting a schedule than the "longer" critical path. A more bothersome point is that the effect of this assumption at every network merge event is to introduce a negative bias in the estimated earliest expected time for the event. While these effects can assume practical significance, it is surprising to the author how accurate the PERT estimates are in most cases.

There are ways of estimating when the above assumption will cause a significant error. The most appropriate solution, where the refinement is called for, is to use simulation. The GERT language cited earlier is very easy to use for this purpose. The output of the simulation includes, among other things, the probability that each activity will be on the actual critical path through the network. This notion replaces the idea of a fixed critical path and slack on the remaining paths. An alternative practical solution is to use a method called PNET (12). It involves a relatively simple procedure of determining a *set* of (assumed) statistically independent paths that "represent" the project network. The probability of meeting a scheduled date is then approximated by the product of the separate probabilities that each path in the *set* will meet the schedule. This method works surprisingly well.

Applications of PERT

PERT is much like the CPM time-cost trade-off algorithm in that it is seldom used. However, the reasons are different. It is the author's opinion that most project managers either have not learned to use PERT probabilities effectively, or they have no confidence in them. This is unfortunate because there are legitimate situations where PERT probabilities can be a useful tool, and there are also some basic advantages in the three time estimate system.

Several studies have shown that when the variance of t is high, the mean activity duration time can be estimated more accurately using the three time estimate PERT procedure, than the one time estimate system which is now used quite widely. Also, a project manager's attention should be drawn to the high-variance activities as potential problem areas in the conduct of the project.

NETWORK TIME AND COST CONTROL PROCEDURES

Having completed the presentation of planning and scheduling techniques, the attention now turns to project control as depicted by Step 6 in the dynamic project management procedure outlined in Figure 15-2. To periodically assess how well the plan is working, actual progress information regarding time and cost performance of activities is entered into the system, and the network is updated.

Network Time Updating

Updating a network to reflect current status is similar to the problem introduced in the section entitled Multiple Initial and Terminal Events, and Scheduled Dates, in that a project under way is equivalent to a project with multiple start events. After a project has begun, varying portions of each path from the initial project event to the end event will have been completed. By establishing the status on each of these paths from progress information, the routine forward pass scheduling computations can then be made. No change in the backward pass computation procedure is necessary, since progress on a project does not affect the network terminal event(s), unless the scheduled completion date is revised.

Additional updating information is required if changes in the project plan are made which require revisions in the network or in the activity duration time estimates. Also, if an activity has not started, but its predecessor event has occurred since the last network update, then a scheduled start time or some "built-in" assumption about its start time must be entered into the system.

An update may indicate that the critical path has shifted, or more important, that the slack on the critical path has become negative. In this case, replanning will be in order to bring the project back onto schedule.

To illustrate this updating procedure, consider the network presented in Figure 15-9, which indicates an expected project duration of 15 days. Suppose we have just completed the fifth work day on this project, and the progress is as reported in Table 15-3.

The actual activity start and finish times given in Table 15-3 have been written above the arrow tails and heads, respectively, in Figure 15-9. Events that have already occurred have been cross-hatched, and activi-

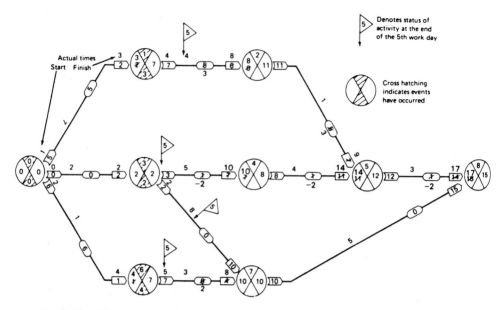

Figure 15-9. Illustrative network showing time status of project. (From *Project Management with CPM, PERT and Precedence Diagramming*, 3rd Ed., J. J. Moder, C. R. Phillips, and E. W. Davis, © 1983 by Litton Educational Publishing, Inc. Reprinted by permission of Van Nostrand Reinhold Co.)
* Moder, J. J., C. R. Phillips and E. W. Davis *Project Management with CPM, PERT and Precedence Diagramming*, 3rd Ed., (Van Nostrand Reinhold, New York, 1983), p. 92.

Table 15-3. Status of Project Activities at the End of the Fifth Working Day

ACTIVITY	STARTED	FINISHED
0–1	1	3
1–2	4	—
0–3	0	2
3–7	2	—
0–6	2	4
3–4	5	—
6–7	5	—

NOTE: all times given are at the *end* of the stated working day.

ties that are in progress have been so noted by a flag marked 5 to denote that the time of the update is the end of the fifth working day.

Having an actual, or assumed, start time for the "lead" activities on each path in the network, the forward pass calculations are then carried out in the usual manner. The original times are crossed out, with the new updated times written nearby. These calculations indicate that the critical path has shifted to activities 3-4-5-8, with a slack of minus two days. Assuming we were scheduled to complete the project in 15 days, the current status indicates we are now two days behind schedule.

Computerized network updating essentially follows the above procedure. However, with computerization, additional flexibility and convenience are offered. Most programs will allow any *one* or *two* of the following items as inputs for each activity in progress during the last reporting period.

Actual Activity Start Time.
Actual Activity Finish Time.
Duration Completed.
Percentage of Duration Completed.
Duration Remaining.

One other input is the "data date", that is, the date up to which the above progress is being reported. The computer will then compute appropriate values for the remaining three or four items listed above that are not given as inputs. Also, after all activity inputs are complete, it will compute updated early/late start/finish times for each activity in the project.

Network Cost Control

Network cost control considers means of controlling the dollar expenditure as the project progresses in time and accomplishment. While network-based expenditure status reports may take many forms, they are primarily directed at the following basic questions.

1. What are the actual project costs to date?
2. How do the actual costs to date compare with planned costs to date?
3. What are the project accomplishments to date?
4. How do the actual costs of specific accomplishments compare with the planned costs of these same accomplishments?
5. By how much may the project be expected to overrun or underrun the total planned cost?
6. How do the above questions apply to various subdivisions and levels of interest within the project?

The major problem in the development of systems to answer these questions is the conflict between traditional functionally oriented accounting and a system based upon network activities. One solution to this problem is the use of groups of activities, called "work packages," in the coding of cost accounts. For example, in the construction industry a work package is often taken as a separate bid item. This, however, still does not solve all of the problems of allocating overhead and sharing various joint costs.

When used as an accounting base, network activities lend themselves to major increases in the amount of detail available to and required of the manager. This is both the promise and the inherent hazard of such systems, and it is one of the primary tasks of the system designer to achieve the level of detail that provides the greatest return on the investment in the system.

Network cost control employs an "enumerative cost model" in which activity costs are assumed to occur linearly in time. Thus, if the project budget is apportioned among the activities, cumulative cost versus time curves can be computed based on the earliest and latest allowable activity times. These two curves will bound the curve based upon the scheduled times for each activity. The latter is then taken as the plan or target against which progress is measured. Such a curve is shown as the middle curve in Figure 15-10, and is marked "Budgeted cost and work value." Using the nomenclature shown below, two important control variances can be defined.

$$T_{Now} = \text{Time of Update or Time Now}$$
$$T_S = \text{Scheduled Project Completion Time}$$
$$T_F = \text{Forecasted Project Completion Time}$$
$$ACWP = \text{Actual Cost of Work in Place at } T_{Now}$$
$$BCWS = \text{Budgeted Cost of Work Scheduled for Completion at } T_{Now}$$
$$BCWP = \text{Budgeted Cost of Work in Place at } T_{Now}$$

$$\text{Cost Variance at } T_{Now} = \left(\frac{BCWP - ACWP}{BCWP}\right) 100\% \qquad (13)$$

$$\text{Schedule Variance at } T_{Now} = \left(\frac{BCWP - BCWS}{BCWP}\right) 100\% \qquad (14)$$

The cost variance given in equation 13 is computed at each update time. It gives the total percent project cost over (under) run up to time T_{Now}, and is used to aid in forecasting the eventual total project cost.

The schedule variance given in equation 14 is used to compare planned

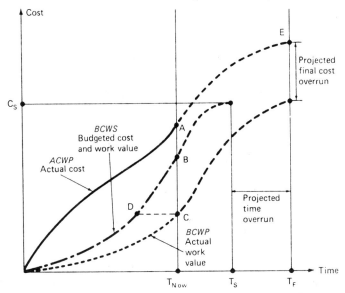

Figure 15-10. Project cost vs. time curve to illustrate cost and cash flow variances.

versus actual budgeted expenditure *rates* to aid the evaluation of *time* status. For example, a zero cost variance and a negative schedule variance would indicate project cost is currently on budget, but resources are not being applied to the project at the planned rate. This in turn may indicate that manpower limitations may not allow making this up in the future, and hence completion of the project may be delayed. The two variances in equations 13 and 14 are defined so that positive percentages are desirable (under budget and ahead of schedule) and negative percentages are undesirable (over budget and behind schedule).

To illustrate these concepts, consider the following oversimplified setting which involves only one activity rather than an entire network.

Project Plan:	Construct foundations for 40 identical tract homes in one continuous period.
Schedule Plan:	Construct 10 foundations per week.
Cost Plan:	Cost (budget) per each home is $2000, for a total project cost of $80,000.
Progress Report:	At the end of one week 8 foundations have been completed at a total (actual) cost of $18,000.
Questions:	Where does this project stand with respect to cost and budget? If the current trend continues, what will be the total project cost and duration?

From T_{Now} = 1 week, and the Schedule and Cost plans, *BCWS* is computed to be $20,000.

$$\text{BCWS} = 10 \text{ foundations} \times \left(\frac{\$2000}{\text{foundation}}\right) = \$20,000.$$

From the Progress report we determine that $ACWP$ = $18,000 and $BCWP$ = $16,000.

$$\text{BCWP} = 8 \text{ foundations in place} \times \left(\frac{\$2000}{\text{foundation}}\right) = \$16,000.$$

Thus, the Cost and Schedule variances at T_{Now} = 1 week are as follows:

$$\text{Cost Variance} = \left(\frac{\$16,000 - \$18,000}{\$16,000}\right) 100\% = -12.5\%$$

$$\text{Schedule Variance} = \left(\frac{\$16,000 - \$20,000}{\$16,000}\right) 100\% = -25\%$$

Thus, the project is 12.5% over budget and 25% behind schedule. If this trend continues throughout the project, the following will result:

Estimated Total Project Cost = $80,000 × 1.125 = $90,000.
Estimated Project Duration = 4 weeks × 1.25 = 5 weeks.

Progress Control Signals

Another approach to the cost control problem is to use absolute dollar value variances as given by equations 15 and 16.

$$\text{Cost Variance} = BCWP - ACWP \tag{15}$$
$$\text{Schedule Variance} = BCWP - BCWS \tag{16}$$

Referring to Figure 15-10, the Cost Variance is the distance between points C and A, which in this case indicates a large negative difference or cost overrun. Similarly, the Schedule Variance is the distance between points C and B, which is also a large negative difference denoting behind schedule. The months behind could be approximated by the time difference for points C minus D.

Equations 15 and 16 are defined so that positive values are good (under budget and ahead of schedule) whereas negative values are undesirable (over budget and behind schedule). A powerful set of control signals, suggested by Brown (2), can be developed by combining this information with the project float on the critical path. The latter can be positive (ahead of schedule), or negative (behind schedule); it could also be expressed as a percentage by dividing the float by the expected project duration. Consider the following nomenclature for these signals.

C+ Positive Cost Variance (Under Budget)
C− Negative Cost Variance (Over Budget)
S+ Positive Schedule Variance (Ahead of Schedule)
S− Negative Schedule Variance (Behind Schedule)
F+ Positive Float on the critical path (Ahead of Schedule)
F− Negative Float on the critical path (Behind Schedule)

These three signals expressed in percentages (equations 13 and 14) or dollars (equations 15 and 16) are issued at each project update. They can be used to give very useful information about the status of the project. Recall that C± deals with cost management, whereas F± deals with schedule management of the critical path, and S± deals with schedule management of the entire project, not just the critical path activities.

For example, (C+, S+, F+) would indicate that project performance is good from all angles, whereas the opposite signal, (C−, S−, F−), might be explained by possible labor problems, budgets and schedules too tight, or just poor overall management. A mixed signal like (C+, S+, F−) might indicate a well-managed project (C+ and S+) that needs a recovery plan for the critical path (F−). Similarly (C+, S−, F+) might indicate a well-managed (C+ and F+) but understaffed project (S−).

Each of the major computer firms, plus a number of other corporations, have developed cost control computer packages of varying complexity. They may include the following:

1. Separate progress report outputs for three or more levels of indenture in the organization, for example, a program manager report, subproject manager reports, and finally task manager reports under each subproject.
2. Elaborate computer-printed graphical type outputs of resource requirements versus time; actual and planned expenditures versus time; bar chart type outputs showing activity early start, late finish, and scheduled times; etc.
3. Data base reports for cost estimating, labor standards, etc.
4. All too infrequently, a resource-leveling subroutine.

OTHER NETWORKING SCHEMES

The activity-on-arrow networking logic presented above was the system utilized in the development of PERT and CPM, and is still used today. However, it is not the easiest for the novice to learn. For this reason, another scheme, called activity-on-node, has gained considerable popularity.

The Activity-on-Node Networking Scheme

The activity-on-node system is merely the reversal of the other, that is, the nodes represent the activities and the arrows become the connectors to denote the precedence relationships. Neither of these networking schemes, however, can cope with the problem of rapidly escalating numbers of activities when two or more jobs follow each other with a lag. Since this situation occurs quite frequently, particularly in construction work, the networking scheme called precedence diagramming is gaining considerable attention.

Precedence Diagramming

An extension to the original activity-on-node concept called precedence diagramming appeared around 1964 in the User's Manual for an IBM 1440 computer program (5). Extensive development of this procedure has since been conducted by K. C. Crandall (3). This procedure extends the PERT/CPM network logic from a single type of dependency to include three other types, illustrated in Figure 15-11. It is based on the following nomenclature.

SS_{ij} denotes a start-to-start constraint, and is equal to the minimum number of time units that must be complete on the preceding activity (i) prior to the start of the successor (j).

FF_{ij} denotes a finish-to-finish constraint, and is equal to the minimum number of time units that must remain to be completed on the successor (j) after the completion of the predecessor (i).

FS_{ij} denotes a finish-to-start constraint, and is equal to the minimum number of time units that must transpire from the completion of the predecessor (i) prior to the start of the seccessor (j). (Note, this is the sole logic constraint used in PERT/CPM, with $FS_{ij} = 0$.)

SF_{ij} denotes a start-to-finish constraint, and is equal to the minimum number of time units that must transpire from the start of the predecessor (i) to the completion of the successor (j).

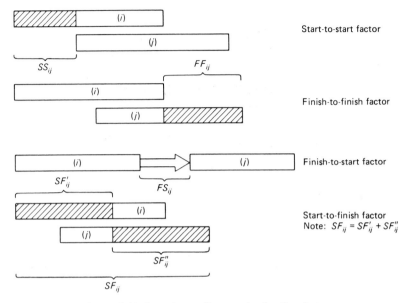

Figure 15-11. Precedence diagramming lead/lag factors.

The above constraint logic will be applied in the next section to illustrate the powerful features of precedence diagramming. It will also point up an anomaly that can occur that needs explanation. Before this is done, however, a simple example will be presented to illustrate the use of arrow versus node versus precedence diagrams.

Comparison of Arrow, Node, and Precedence Diagrams

Consider a simple project consisting of digging and forming a foundation as shown in Figure 15-12. Each task is estimated to take three days, one day each for sections A, B, and C. Also, assume that for technical reasons, the three sections must be carried out in the order A, then B, and then C.

A strictly sequential arrow diagram plan is shown in part (a) of Figure 15-12; it would require six days to execute. To save time, suppose Forming A is started on the second day rather than the fourth day as assumed in part (a). This plan would require only four days, and is shown in part (b), again in the form of an arrow diagram. Notice that a dummy activity, 3-4, and a total of seven activities are required to diagram this project plan. An identical plan is shown in part (c) in the form of a node diagram. Note here that all arrows merely denote precedence relationships; they are all $FS0$

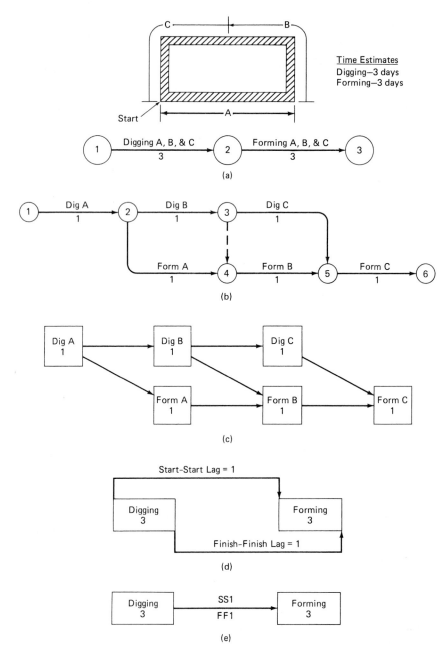

Figure 15-12. Comparison of arrow, node, and precedence network diagrams for a simple project.

constraints, the only type allowed in arrow or node diagrams. The node diagram is preferred by most users because it eliminates the need for the subtle dummy shown as activity 3-4 in part (b). Although the node diagram in part (c) is easier to draw than the arrow diagram, it still requires that Digging and Forming each be broken down into three parts. This proliferation of activities can be avoided by using precedence diagramming as shown in part (d), or the alternative form in part (e).

Because node diagrams eliminate the need for the subtle dummy, and are generally considered easier to draw, they have rapidly replaced the arrow diagram in most microcomputer project management software packages. Similarly, because precedence diagramming avoids the need to break an activity into several pieces when it is conducted concurrently with other activities as shown in Figure 15-12(b), (c), (d), and (e), this form of networking is being used in all of the better project management software packages. It should be noted that precedence diagramming restricted to *FS0* constraints becomes a node diagram, and hence it can be used to describe a node or precedence diagram.

While the forward and backward pass computations for precedence diagrams are quite complex, it is essentially the same for arrow and node diagrams. This is illustrated in Figure 15-13, which is the node form of the arrow diagram previously presented in Figure 15-6. The early/late start/ finish times are presented in a compact form in node diagrams, around the node symbol.

Precedence Diagram Anomalies

Consider a construction subcontract consisting of *Framing* walls, placing *Electrical* conduits, and *Finishing* walls, with the duration of each task estimated to be 10 days, using standard size crews. If the plan is to perform each of these tasks sequentially, the equivalent arrow diagram in Figure 15-14(a) shows that a project duration of 30 days will result.

To reduce this time, these tasks could be carried out concurrently with a convenient lag of, say, two days between the start and finish of each activity. This plan is shown in Figure 15-14(b), in precedence diagram notation. The equivalent arrow diagram shown in Figure 15-14(c) indicates a 14-day project schedule. One important advantage of Figure 15-14(b) over 15-14(c) is that each trade is represented by a single activity instead of two or three subactivities. Also note how the $SS = 2$ and $FF = 2$ lags of Figure 15-14(b) are built into the equivalent arrow diagram in Figure 15-14(c). For example, the first two days of the Electrical task in Figure 15-14(c) must be separated from the remainder of this task to show that two days of Electrical work must be completed prior to the *start* of

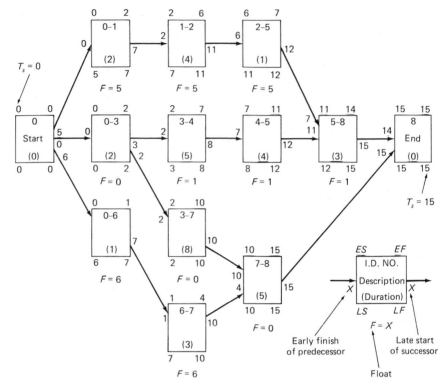

Figure 15-13. Node diagram equivalent to Figure 15-6, showing the forward and backward pass calculations and float.

the Finishing task. Similarly, the last two days of Electrical work must be separated from the remainder of this task to show that Framing must *finish* two days before Electrical is finished. Thus, the 10-day Electrical task must be broken up into three subactivities of two, six, and two days duration, respectively.

So far, precedence diagramming is easy to follow and is parsimonious with activities. But let us see what happens if the durations of the three tasks in this project are unbalanced by changing from 10, 10, 10, to 10, 5, and 15 days, respectively. These changes are incorporated in Figures 15-14(d) and 15-14(e), along with appropriate new lag times. Note that $SS = 2$ was chosen between Framing and Electrical to insure that a full day's work is ready for Electrical before this task is allowed to start. Similarly, $FF = 3$ was chosen between Electrical and Finishing because the last day of Electrical work will require three days of Finishing work to complete the project. The other lags of one day each were chosen as minimal or

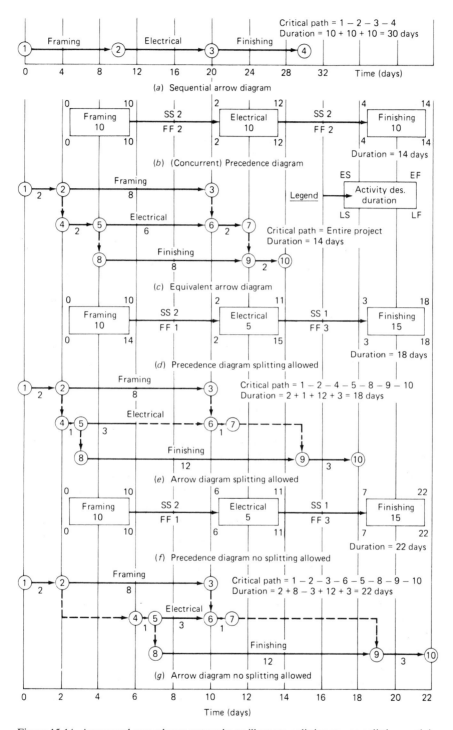

Figure 15-14. Arrow and precedence networks to illustrate splitting vs. no splitting; activities are shown at their early start times. (From *Project Management with CPM, PERT and Precedence Diagramming*, 3rd Ed., J. J. Moder, C. R. Phillips, and E. W. Davis, © 1983 by Litton Educational Publishing, Inc. Reprinted by permission of Van Nostrand Reinhold Co.)

convenience values needed in each case. These lags define the activity breakdown shown in Figure 15-14(e) where we see that the critical path is the *start* of Framing (1-2), then the *start* of Electrical (4-5), and finally the *totality* of Finishing (8-9-10). This is also shown in the precedence diagram, Figure 15-14(d), where $ES = LS = 0$ for the *start* of Framing, $ES = LS = 2$ for the *start* of Electrical, and finally $ES = LS = 3$ *and* $EF = LF = 18$ for the totality of Finishing. Since the precedence diagram shows each of these tasks in their totality, $EF \neq LF$ even though $ES = LS$ for the Framing and Electrical tasks. For Framing in Figure 15-14(d), $LF - EF = 14 - 10 = 4$ days of float, which corresponds to the 4 days of float depicted by activity 7-9 in Figure 15-14(e). Similarly, for Electrical in Figure 15-14(d), $LF - EF = 15 - 11 = 4$ days of float, which is also depicted by activity 7-9 in Figure 15-14(e). The middle Electrical activity (5-6) in Figure 15-14(e) *appears* to have an additional path float of four days, or a total of eight days. This attribute is not shown at all in Figure 15-14(d) because it depicts only the beginning and end points of each activity, but not intermediate subactivities such as 5-6. Closer examination will show, however, that any delay in the start of activity 5-6 exceeding three days would cause the Finishing crew to run out of work, and hence the critical path would be delayed. This problem is shared by both arrow and precedence diagrams, and the user should understand this. It does not, however, present a real problem in the applications since the job foreman generally has no difficulty in the day-to-day management of this type of interrelationship among concurrent activities. It is generally felt that it is not worthwhile to further complicate the networking and the computational scheme to show all interdependencies among activity segments, since these tasks can be routinely managed in the field.

A very important difference between Figures 15-14(c) and (e), other than the four-day difference in the project durations, lies in the Electrical task which is represented by three subactivities in both diagrams. In Figure 15-14(c) these three subactivities are expected to be conducted without interruption. However, in Figure 15-14(e) this is not possible. Here, the last day of the Electrical task (6-7) must follow a four-day interruption because of the combination effect of constraint $SS = 1$ depicted by activity 5-8, and constraint $FF = 1$ depicted by activity 3-6. This forced interruption will henceforth be referred to as *splitting* of the Electrical task.

If necessary, *splitting* can be avoided in several ways. First, the duration of the Electrical task could be increased from five to nine days. But this is frequently not desirable in projects such as maintenance or construction because it would decrease productivity. The second way to avoid *splitting* would be to delay the start of the Electrical task for four days, as shown in Figure 15-14(g), where it is assumed that activity splitting is not allowed. At first, it may seem that there is no difference between these two alternatives, but this is not so. Reflection on Figure 15-14(g) shows that delaying the start of the Electrical task to avoid *splitting* will delay the start of the Finish work, and hence the completion of the project is delayed by four days. But increasing the duration of the Electrical task will not have this effect. Actually, we have described an anomalous situation where an *increase* of four days in the duration of an activity on the critical path (starting four days earlier and thus running four days longer), will *decrease* the duration of the project by four days, from 22 to 18. If you are used to dealing with basic arrow diagram logic ($FS = 0$ logic only), this anomaly will take some getting used to. It results from the fact that the critical path in Figure 15-14(g) goes "backwards" through activity 5-6, and thus *subtracts* from the total duration of this path. As a result, the project duration *decreases* while the duration of an activity on the critical path is *increased*. This anomalous situation occurs whenever the critical path *enters* the *completion* of an activity through a *finish* type of constraint (*FF* or *SF*), goes backwards through the activity, and leaves through a *start* type of constraint (*SS* or *SF*).

The precedence diagram in Figure 15-14(f) shows that the entire project is critical, since $ES = LS$ and $EF = LF$ for each task. While it appears that the Electrical task has float in Figure 15-14(g), this is not true since *splitting* is not allowed. No-splitting is a constraint not explicitly incorporated in the arrow diagram logic.

Critical Path Characteristics

Wiest (13) describes the anomalous behavior of activity 5-6 in Figure 15-14(g) picturesquely by stating that this activity is *reverse* critical. Similarly, in Figure 15-14(d) and (e) both Framing and Electrical are called *neutral* critical. They are critical because their $LS = ES$, but they are called *neutral* because their $LF > EF$, and the project duration is independent of the task duration. A task is *neutral* critical when a pair of start time constraints result in the critical path entering and exiting from the starting point of the task, or a pair of finish time constraints enter and exit from the finish point of a task. These situations could also be referred to as *start* or *finish* critical. In Figure 15-14(d) and (e), the Framing and Electrical tasks are both *start* critical, while Finishing is *normal* or *increase* critical. That is, a delay in the completion of the Finishing task will have a *normal* effect on the project duration, causing it to *increase*. Wiest

(13) suggests that precedence diagram computer outputs would be more useful if they identified the way in which tasks are critical. The author suggests that the following nomenclature be considered for this purpose:

IC— denotes an activity that is critical to an *In*crease in its duration.

DC— denotes an activity that is critical to a *De*crease in its duration.

BC— denotes an activity that is *Bi*critical, both to an *In*crease or *De*crease in its duration.

SC— denotes an activity that is critical to its *St*art Time.

FC— denotes an activity that is critical to its *Fi*nish Time.

MIC— denotes an activity whose *M*iddle portion is critical to an *In*crease in its duration.

MDC— denotes an activity whose *M*iddle portion is critical to a *De*crease in its duration.

MBC— denotes an activity whose *M*iddle portion is *Bi*critical to both an *In*crease or *De*crease in its duration.

NC— denotes an activity that is *N*oncritical.

To conclude this discussion, it should be noted that the critical path always starts with a job (or a job start), it ends with a job (or a job finish), and in between it consists of an alternating sequence of jobs and precedence arrows. Although the critical path may pass through a job in any one of the many ways listed above, it *always moves forward* through precedence constraint arrows. Hence, any *increase* in the lead-lag times associated with *SS, SF, FF,* or *FS* constraints on the critical path will always result in a corresponding *increase* in the project duration.

Following the suggestion of stating the nature of the criticality of activities on the critical path, for Figure 15-14(d) this would consist of the following alternating activities and precedence constraints: Framing (*Start Critical—SC*); *SS*2; Electrical (*Start Critical—SC*); *SS*1; Finishing (*Increase Critical—IC*). Similarly, for Figure 15-14(f) it would be: Framing (*IC*); *FF*1; Electrical (*DC*); *SS*1; Finishing (*IC*). It should be noted here that Electrical is labeled decrease critical (*DC*), which puts the manager on notice that any *decrease* in the duration of this activity will increase the duration of the project. As stated above, it is *decrease* critical because its predecessor constraint is a *finish* type (*FF*1), and its successor constraint is a *start* type (*SS*1).

Computational Procedures

Obviously the forward and backward pass computational problem becomes more complex with precedence diagramming, and it calls for establishment of somewhat arbitrary ground rules which were unnecessary with the unique nature of basic arrow diagram logic. In the computational procedures to follow, we will assume that the specified activity durations are fixed, for example, because of the productivity argument cited above. This assumption can be relaxed, of course, by varying the activity durations of interest, and repeating the calculations. Regarding task splitting, three basic cases will be treated.

Case 1: Activity splitting *is not* allowed on any activities, such as shown in Figure 15-14(g).

Case 2: Activity splitting *is* allowed on all activities, such as shown in Figure 15-14(e).

Case 3: Combination of 1 and 2; activity splitting is permitted only on designated activities.

Figures 15-14(g) and (e) represent Cases 1 and 2, respectively. The effect of not allowing splitting (of the Electrical task) is a four-day increase in the project duration. Here, the choice must be made between the (extra) cost of splitting the Electrical task, and the cost of a four-day increase in project duration. Case 3 is provided to allow the project manager to take the possible time (project duration) advantage concomitant with splitting on those activities where it can be tolerated, and to avoid splitting on those activities where it cannot be accommodated.

The computational procedure for Case 1 is reasonably simple and will be described below. The procedure for Case 2 is considerably more complex; it is given in Reference 8. The computational procedure for Case 3 merely amounts to the application of the Case 1 *or* the Case 2 procedure to each activity in turn, depending on whether the activity is designated as one where splitting *is not* allowed, or *is* allowed, respectively.

Computational Assumptions

The computational procedure for Case 1—No Splitting Allowed, is analogous to the arrow diagram procedure described above. In making the forward pass calculations, one must consider *all* constraints leading into the activity (j) in question, that is, the start time constraints (SS_{ij} and FS_{ij}) *as well as* the finish time constraints (SF_{ij} and FF_{ij}). For *each* constraint, the early start time for activity (j) is computed, and the maximum (latest) of these times then becomes the early start time (ES_j) for activity (j). Because some project activities may only have finish time constraints, it would be possible for the above procedure to lead to a negative ES_j time, or a time earlier than the specified project start time. For example, referring to Figure 15-15, we see that activity D has no *start* time constraint. If the duration of activity D was 22 (instead of 12), then its early start time would be $EF - D = ES$, or $19 - 22 = -3$ (instead of 7). This would be an erroneous negative value. To prevent the occurrence of this error, an additional time, called the INITIAL TIME, is introduced. It is usually set equal to zero, or else to an arbitrarily specified (nonzero) project scheduled start time, and it overrides the start times computed above if they are all negative, or less (earlier) than the specified project start time.

The backward pass computations follow a similar procedure to find the late finish times for each activity, working backwards along *each* constraint leaving the activity (i) in question. In this case, an additional time, called TERMINAL TIME, is required to prevent the occurrence of a late finish time (LF_i) *exceeding* the project duration, or the scheduled project completion time. As usual, the project duration is taken as the maximum (latest) of the early finish times computed for each activity in the forward

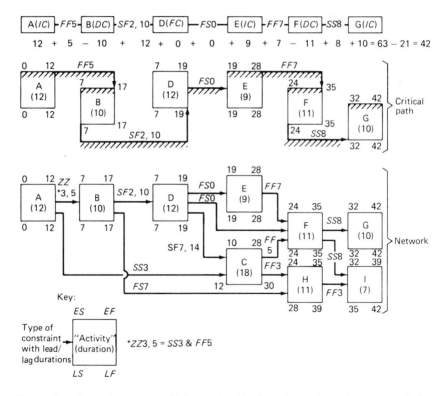

Figure 15-15. Example network with forward and backward pass times shown—no splitting allowed.

pass computations. For example, this is equal to 42 units in Figure 15-15, which is the largest of all activity early finish times.

The computational procedure given below has the same requirement that prevailed for arrow diagram computations. It requires that the activities be topologically ordered. That is, activities are arranged so that successors to any activity will *always* be found below it in the ordered list. The two-step computational procedure is then applied to each activity, working the list from the top down. When the computations are performed by hand on a network, this ordering is accomplished automatically by working one path after another, each time going as far as possible. Again, this is the same procedure required to process an arrow diagram.

Forward Pass Computations—No Splitting Allowed

The following two steps are applied to each project activity, in topological sequence. The term called INITIAL TIME is set equal to zero, or to an arbitrarily specified project scheduled start time.

STEP 1: Compute ES_j, the early start time of the activity (j) in question. It is the maximum (latest) of the set of start times which includes the INITIAL TIME, and one start time computed from *each* constraint going to the activity (j) from predecessor activities indexed by (i).

$$ES_j = \underset{\text{all } i}{\text{MAX}} \begin{cases} \text{INITIAL TIME} \\ EF_i + FS_{ij} \\ ES_i + SS_{ij} \\ EF_i + FF_{ij} - D_j \\ ES_i + SF_{ij} - D_j \end{cases}$$

STEP 2: $EF_j = ES_j + D_j$

Backward Pass Computations—No Splitting Allowed

The following two steps are applied to each project activity in the reverse order of the forward pass computations. The term called TERMINAL TIME is set equal to the project duration, or to an arbitrarily specified project scheduled completion time.

STEP 1: Compute LF_i, the late finish time of the activity (i) in question. It is the minimum (earliest) of the set of finish times which includes the TERMINAL TIME, and one finish time computed from *each* constraint going from activity (i), to successor activities indexed by (j).

$$LF_i = \underset{\text{all } j}{\text{MIN}} \begin{cases} \text{TERMINAL TIME} \\ LS_j + FS_{ij} \\ LF_j + FF_{ij} \\ LS_j + SS_{ij} + D_i \\ LF_j + SF_{ij} + D_i \end{cases}$$

STEP 2: $LS_i = LF_i - D_i$

Example Problem

To illustrate the application of the above algorithm, a small network consisting of nine activities with a variety of constraints, is shown in Figure 15-15. The forward pass calculations are as follows, based on the assumption that the project starts at time zero, that is, INITIAL TIME = 0.

Activity A
$ES_A = \{\text{INITIAL TIME} = 0\} = 0$
$EF_A = ES_A + D_A = 0 + 12 = 12$

Activity B
$$ES_B = \underset{A}{\text{MAX}} \begin{cases} \text{INITIAL TIME} = 0 \\ ES_A + SS_{AB} = 0 + 3 = 3 \\ EF_A + FF_{AB} - D_B = 12 + 5 - 10 = 7 \end{cases} = 7$$
$EF_B = ES_B + D_B = 7 + 10 = 17$

Activity D
$$ES_D = \underset{B}{\text{MAX}} \begin{cases} \text{INITIAL TIME} = 0 \\ ES_B + SF_{BD} - D_D = 7 + (2 + 10) - 12 = 7 \end{cases} = 7$$
$EF_D = ES_D + D_D = 7 + 12 = 19$

Activity C
$$ES_C = \underset{A,D}{\text{MAX}} \begin{cases} \text{INITIAL TIME} = 0 \\ ES_A + SS_{AC} = 0 + 3 = 3 \\ ES_D + SF_{DC} - D_C = 7 + (7 + 14) - 18 = 10 \end{cases} = 0$$
$EF_C = ES_C + D_C = 10 + 18 = 28$
ETC.

The backward pass calculations are as follows, wherein the TERMINAL TIME is set equal to the project duration, determined from the forward pass calculations to be 42, that is, the *EF* time for the last critical path activity, G.

Activity G

$LF_G = \{\text{TERMINAL TIME} = 42\} = 42$

$LS_G = LF_G - D_G = 42 - 10 = 32$

Activity I

$LF_I = \{\text{TERMINAL TIME} = 42\} = 42$

$LS_I = LF_I = 42 - 7 = 35$

Activity H

$LF_H = \underset{I}{\text{MIN}} \left\{ \begin{array}{l} \text{TERMINAL TIME} = 42 \\ LF_I - FF_{HI} = 42 - 3 = 39 \end{array} \right\} = 39$

$LS_H = LF_H - D_H = 39 - 11 = 28$

Activity F

$LF_F = \underset{G,I}{\text{MIN}} \left\{ \begin{array}{l} \text{TERMINAL TIME} = 42 \\ LS_G - SS_{FG} + D_F = 32 - 8 + 11 = 35 \\ LS_I - SS_{FI} + D_F = 35 - 8 + 11 = 38 \end{array} \right\} = 35$

$LS_F = LF_F - D_F = 35 - 11 = 24$

ETC.

From the computational results shown in Figure 15-15, the critical path consists of activities A − B − D − E − F − G. The nature of the criticality of each activity is indicated at the top of Figure 15-15, along with the critical constraints between each pair of activities. Activities A, E, and G are *increase* (normal) critical, activities B and F *decrease* critical (noted by the reverse direction cross hatching), and activity D is only *finish* time critical. The duration of the critical path, 42, is also noted, with the net contributions of the activity durations being $(12 - 10 + 0 + 9 - 11 + 10) = 10$ and the contributions of the constraints being $(5 + 12 + 0 + 7 + 8) = 32$, for a total of 42 time units. The early/late start/finish times for each activity have the conventional interpretations. For example, for the critical activity E, both the early and late start/finish times are 19 and 28; the activity has no slack. But for activity H, the early start/finish times are 24 and 35, while the late start/finish times are 28 and 39. In this case, the activity has four units of activity slack or free slack, because the completion of activity H can be delayed up to four units without affecting the slack on its successor activity I.

CONCLUDING REMARKS

Critical path methods represent a modern tool to aid the project manager. But they are only models of the dynamic real world interplay of money, people, materials, and machines, directed in time to accomplish a stated goal. Starting with the simple logic of the deterministic arrow diagram, they can be embellished to capture the stochastic elements of the problem, the random duration of the activity times by PERT, and the random nature of the network by GERT. More recently, precedence diagramming has been added to this array of models to depict more closely how many projects are actually conducted, without the proliferation of project activities. Finally, the role of the computer looms large when sophisticated resource allocation or general management information systems development questions are asked; or, when large projects extending over a long period require frequent updating, possibly for several levels of management, to control both time and cost. Network techniques form the vehicle for the conduct of these important management developments.

There are literally hundreds of project management microcomputer software packages on the market today.* As mentioned above, PERT probabilities and CPM time-cost trade-off techniques are not often used today. For this reason, they have only been incorporated in a very few specialized packages. Except for these procedures, programs costing less than $1000 can be found to carry out all of the *basic* procedures outlined in this chapter, including the drawing of bar charts, project networks (not time-scaled), tracking costs and resources, and in some cases allowing the use of precedence diagramming. In addition to these capabilities, programs costing between $1000 and $2000 can be found to carry out *all* of the procedures (not just the basics) outlined in this chapter, including multiproject limited-resource scheduling or resource leveling, earned-value cost analysis, and the production of a wide array of reports that can be customized by the user. Programs costing more than $2000 only provide a few additional features such as plotting time-scaled networks, the flexibility of allowing any type of networking (arrow, node, or precedence), and almost unlimited network size. Microcomputer project management software packages are usually quite "friendly," so even the "small" user can afford to adopt them. Their use will go a long way to advancing the application of the planning and control procedures outlined in this chapter.

---

* Computer software for project management is discussed in Chapter 28.

REFERENCES

1. Adamiecki, Karol. "Harmonygraph." *Przeglad Organizacji* (Polish Journal of Organizational Review) (1931).
2. Brown, John W. "Evaluation of Projects Using Critical Path Analysis and Earned Value in Combination." *Project Management Journal* (August, 1985), pp. 59–63.
3. Crandall, Keith C. "Project Planning with Precedence Lead/Lag Factors." *Project Mngt. Quarterly,* Vol. 6(3) (1973), pp. 18–27.
4. Davis, E. W. and Patterson, J. H. "A Comparison of Heuristic and Optimum Solutions in Resource Constrained Project Scheduling." *Manage. Sci.* (1974).
5. IBM. *Project Management System, Application Description Manual* (H20-0210) (IBM. 1968).
6. Kelley, J. F. "Critical Path Planning and Scheduling: Mathematical Basis." *Oper. Res.,* Vol. 9(3) (1961), pp. 296–320. Kelley, J. and Walker, M. "Critical-path Planning and Scheduling" in *Proceedings of the Eastern Joint Computer Conference,* 1959.
7. Lockyer, K. G. *An Introduction to Critical Path Analysis,* 3rd Ed. (Pitman. London, 1969), p. 3.
8. Malcolm, D. G., Roseboom, J. H., Clark, C. E. and Fazar, W. "Applications of a Technique for R and D Program Evaluation (PERT)." *Oper. Res.,* Vol. 7(5) (1959), pp. 646–669.
9. Moder, J. J., Phillips, C. R. and Davis, E. W. *Project Management with CPM, PERT and Precedence Diagramming,* 3rd Ed. (Van Nostrand Reinhold. New York, 1983).
10. Pritsker, A. B. and Burgess, R. R. *The GERT Simulation Programs.* Department of Industrial Engineering. Virginia Polytechnic Institute, 1970. Pritsker, A. B., et al. "GERT: Graphical Evaluation and Review Techniques, Part I. Fundamentals—Part II. Probabilistic and Industrial Engineering Applications." *J. Ind. Eng.,* Vols. 17(5) and 17(6) (1966).
11. Wiest, J. D. "A Heuristic Model for Scheduling Large Projects with Limited Resources." *Manage. Sci.,* Vol. 13(6) (February, 1967), pp. B359–B377.
12. Ang, A. H-S, Abdelnour, J. and Chaker, A. A. "Analysis of Activity Networks Under Uncertainty." *J. of the Eng. Mech. Div.* (Proc. of Am. Soc. Civil Eng.), Vol. 101(EM4) (August, 1975), pp. 373–387.
13. Wiest, Jerry D. "Precedence Diagramming Methods: Some Unusual Characteristics and Their Implications for Project Managers." *Journal of Operations Management,* Vol. 1(3) (February, 1981), pp. 121–130.

16. Linear Responsibility Charts in Project Management*

David I. Cleland†
William R. King‡

The organizational model which is commonly called the *organization chart* is much derided in the literature and in the day-to-day discussions among organizational participants. However, organizational charts can be of great help in both the planning and implementation phases of project management.

In this chapter we shall explore a systems-oriented version of the traditional chart. Initially, we shall do this in the context of a chart which will be helpful to managers in aligning the project organization, that is, the implementation function. We shall then present an adaptation of the concept of the systems-oriented chart which has proved to be useful in the planning phase of a project.

* Portions of this chapter have been paraphrased from *Systems Analysis and Project Management*, 3rd Ed., by David I. Cleland and William R. King (McGraw-Hill, New York, 1983 with the permission of the publisher).

† David I. Cleland is currently Professor of Engineering Management in the Industrial Engineering Department at the University of Pittsburgh. He is the author/editor of 15 books and has published many articles appearing in leading national and internationally distributed technological, business management, and educational periodicals. Dr. Cleland has had extensive experience in management consultation, lecturing, seminars, and research. He is the recipient of the "Distinguished Contribution to Project Management" award given by the Project Management Institute in 1983, and in May 1984, received the 1983 Institute of Industrial Engineers (IIE)-Joint Publishers Book-of-the-Year Award for the *Project Management Handbook* (with W. R. King). In 1987 Dr. Cleland was elected a Fellow of the Project Management Institute.

‡ William R. King is University Professor in the Katz Graduate School of Business at the University of Pittsburgh. He is the author of more than a dozen books and 150 technical papers that have appeared in the leading journals in the fields of management science, information systems, and strategic planning. Among his major honors are the McKinsey Award (jointly with D. I. Cleland) for the "outstanding contribution to management literature" represented by his book *Systems Analysis and Project Management*, the IIE award for the first edition of this book, and designation as a fellow of the Decision Sciences Institute. Further biographical information is available in *Who's Who in the World* and *Who's Who in America*.

THE TRADITIONAL ORGANIZATIONAL CHART

The traditional organizational chart is of the pyramidal variety; it represents, or models, the organization as it is *supposed* to exist at a given point in time.

At best, such a chart is an oversimplification of the organization and its underlying concepts which may be used as an aid in grasping the concept of the organization. Management literature indicates various feelings about the value of the chart as an organization tool. For example, Cyert and March say: (1)

Traditionally, organizations are described by organization charts. An organization chart specifies the authority or reportorial structure of the system. Although it is subject to frequent private jokes, considerable scorn on the part of sophisticated observers, and dubious championing by archaic organizational architects, the organization chart communicates some of the most important attributes of the system. It usually errs by not reflecting the nuances of relationships within the organization: it usually deals poorly with informal control and informal authority, usually underestimates the significance of personality variables in molding the actual system, and usually exaggerates the isomorphism between the authority system and the communication system. Nevertheless, the organization chart still provides a lot of information conveniently—partly because the organization usually has come to consider relationships in terms of the dimensions of the chart.

Jasinski is critical of the traditional, pyramidal organizational chart because it fails to display the nonvertical relations between the participants in the organization. He says: (2)

Necessary as these horizontal and diagonal relations may be to the smooth functioning of the technology or work flow, they are seldom defined or charted formally. Nonetheless, wherever or whenever modern technology does operate effectively, these relations do exist, if only on a nonformal basis.

LINEAR RESPONSIBILITY CHARTS (LRCs)

The linear responsibility chart (LRC) goes beyond the simple display of formal lines of communication, gradations of organizational level, departmentation, and line-staff relationships. In addition to the simple display, the LRC reveals the task-job position couplings that are of an advisory, informational, technical, and specialty nature.

The LRC has been called the "linear organization chart," the "linear chart," and the "functional chart." None of these names adequately describes the device. The LRC (or the table or grid, as Janger calls it) (3) shows who participates, and to what degree, when an activity is performed or a decision made. It shows the extent or type of authority exercised by each executive in performing an activity in which two or more executives have overlapping authority and responsibility. It clarifies the authority relationships that arise when executives share common work. The need for a device to clarify the authority relationships is evident from the relative unity of the traditional pyramidal chart, which (1) is merely a simple portrayal of overall functional and authority models and (2) must be combined with detailed position descriptions and organizational manuals to delineate authority relationships and work-performance duties.

The typical pyramidal organizational chart is not adequate as a tool of organizational analysis since it does not display systems interfaces. It is because of this inadequacy that a technology of position descriptions and organizational manuals has come into being. As organizations have grown larger and larger, personnel interrelationships have increased in complexity, and job descriptions and organizational manuals have grown more detailed. Typical organizational manuals and position descriptions have become so verbose that an organizational analysis can be lost in semantics. An article in *Business Week* reflected on the problem of adequate organizational tools in this manner: (4)

> The usual way to supplement it [the pyramid organization chart] is by recourse to a voluminous organizational manual prescribing the proper relationships and responsibilities. But the manuals—cumbersome and often outdated—rarely earn much attention.

Position descriptions do serve the purpose of describing a single position, but an executive is also concerned with how the people under his jurisdiction relate to one another. On many occasions, executives are confronted with the task of examining and explaining relationships. Project management, corporate staff organization, concepts of product planning, the development of a corporate plan—all these lead to highly complex working relationships. A dynamic organization is often—even continually—redefining large numbers of positions and establishing new responsibility and authority patterns.

Structure and Philosophy of the LRC

Typically, the LRC shows these characteristics:

1. Core information from conventional organizational charts and associated manuals displayed in a matrix format. (5)
2. A series of position titles along the top of the table (columns).
3. A listing of responsibilities, authorities, activities, functions, and projects down the side of the chart (rows).
4. An array of symbols indicating degree or extent of authority and explaining the relationship between the columns and the lines.

Such an arrangement shows in one horizontal line all persons involved in a function and the extent and nature of their involvement. Furthermore, the one vertical line shows all functions that a person is responsible for and the nature of his responsibility. A vertical line represents an individual's job description; a horizontal line shows the breakout of a function or task by job position.

One potential value of such a chart is the analysis required to create it, that is, the necessary abstracting and cross-referencing from position descriptions and related documentation manuals. The LRC in Figure 16-1 illustrates the authority interrelationships of a series of positions composing a definable unit. This chart conveys the same message by extensive organizational manuals, position descriptions, memorandums of agreement, policy letters, etc. It shows at a glance not only the individuals' responsibilities for certain functions but, what may be even more valuable, the way a given position relates to other positions within the organization.

But why not use the more conventional procedure of position analysis and position description for this sort of thing? There are two primary advantages to this mode of presentation. First, position descriptions and position guides are better at laying down responsibilities and authority patterns than at *portraying relationships*. Second, this type of charting depicts the work of top management as an *integrated system* rather than as a series of individual positions. The chart makes it easy to compare the responsibilities of related executives; in the coordination of budgets, for example, six individuals share the responsibility, ranging from "must be consulted" to "may be consulted" and "must be notified." The filled-in chart provides a quick picture of all the positions involved in the performance of a particular function.

	Board	President	Vice-president marketing-advertising	Vice-president engineering and R&D	Director of manufacturing	Vice-president finance	Secretary-treasurer	Vice-president foreign operations
Establish basic policies and objectives	2	1	3	3	3	3	3	3
Direct operations, control and planning functions	2	1	4	4	4	4	4	4
Fix relationships between central office and operating divisions	2	1	3	3	3	3	3	3
Control expansion — merger — acquisition plans	2	1	3	3	3	3	3	3
Administer merger — acquisition operations		2	1	3	3	3	3	3
Establish marketing policies and procedures		2	1		4			4
Coordinate sales forecasts and projections	5	2	1		5			3
Coordinate advertising plans	5	5	1					4
Coordinate engineering, research and development	5	2	3	1	4	4		4
Coordinate new product programs		2	3	1	4	3		4
Administer research and development center		3		1				
Establish accounting policies and procedures		2				1		
Administer financing, borrowing, equity	2	2				1	3	
Coordinate budgets	5	2	3	4	1	3		
Administer legal and tax matters		2				1		
Utilization of manufacturing facilities		3					1	
Coordinate training and safety programs		2	1				1	
Coordinate and administer capital expenditures	2	2	4	4	3	1	3	
Administer insurance plans and stockholder relations		2			4		1	
Coordinate foreign and export operations		2	4	4				1

Code
1 Actual responsibility   4 May be consulted
2 General supervision   5 Must be notified
3 Must be consulted

Figure 16-1. Authority interrelationships in a unit. (From Allen R. Janger, "Charting Authority Relationships," *The Conference Board Record* (December, 1964).

In the words of Allen R. Janger, concerning the chart of Figure 16-1: (6)

The top line . . . shows that the *president* is responsible for establishing basic policies and objectives. He works under the general supervision of his *board of directors,* and with the consultation of his corporate staff. Responsibility for coordinating engineering, research and development . . . is parceled out in a bit more complicated fashion. The *vice president, engineering, research, and development* carries the actual responsibility. He operates under the general supervision of the *president,* but must carry on close consultations with the *vice president, marketing and advertising* and the *director of manufacturing.* Consultation with the *vice president, finance* on R&D matters is not mandatory but may be required. It is also understood that the *board of directors* will be informed of significant developments.

By reading down the chart it is possible to summarize rapidly a position's salient responsibilities. As depicted, the *president* has actual responsibility for establishing basic policies and objectives, direction of operating control and planning functions, fixing relationships between the corporate headquarters and the product divisions, and control of expansion, merger, and acquisition plans. Other top management functions are the direct responsibilities of other corporate executives, although the president generally exercises supervision over them. He must at least be consulted on the administration of the R&D center and the utilization of manufacturing facilities. The *vice president, marketing and advertising* need only notify him about advertising plans.

Staff-line and project-functional relationships pose some of the more challenging problems of project management, particularly in light of the desirability of the deliberate conflict between the functional managers and the project manager. The deliberate conflict must be planned so that respective prerogatives are recognized and protected. The use of a chart similar to that shown in Figure 16-2 can do much to define and postulate the functional-project relationships, as well as the staff-line, staff-staff interfaces in the project environment.

The chart shown in Figure 16-2 is different from the chart for top management shown in Figure 16-1 in that the starting point is different. Figure 16-2 emphasizes the purchasing function and its subfunctions. The essence of the analysis is the determination of the sphere of each executive's authority in each of the key purchasing activities and of the extent of that authority. When these facts are ascertained, the relevant positions are listed at the top of the chart, and the appropriate symbols are added.

The chart shows the roles of the various executives in manufacturing-related purchasing activities.

Figure 16-1 does more than clarify authority relationships; it can double as a collection of position guides. Its perspective is adequate to permit it to be used as an organizational chart of the top management of the organization. Figure 16-2, on the other hand, cannot serve as an organizational chart since it is not possible to get an overall picture of a position or a unit and its responsibilities from the chart. Figure 16-2 shows only the purchasing activities related to manufacturing; the nonpurchasing activities of the positions, which could be significant, are not shown.

Limitations of LRCs

Charts such as those shown in Figures 16-1 and 16-2 are not a panacea for all organizational difficulties. The LRC is a pictorial representation, and it is subject to the characteristic limitations and shortcomings of pyramidal organizational charts. The LRC does reveal the functional breakout of the work to be done and the interrelationships between the functions and job positions; however, *it does not show how people act and interact.*

It is doubtful that any contemporary management theorists would deny that organizational effectiveness is as dependent on the informal organization of human actions and relations as it is on the structured, formal organization. The LRC, as we have so far discussed it, is limited to showing the man-job relationships that constitute the formal organization; it does not purport to reveal the infinite number of variations in human relations arising out of the informal organization. The LRC technique simply extends the scope of charting formal organizations wherever they are located in the hierarchical order. Thus, a note of caution is in order about the LRC. But, as Karger and Murdick have implied, we still must give it a vote of confidence. (7)

> Obviously, the LRC chart has weaknesses, of which one of the larger ones is that it is a mechanical aid. Just because it says something is a fact does not make it true. It is very difficult to discover, except generally, exactly what occurs in a company—and with whom. The chart tries to express in specific terms relationships that cannot always be delineated so clearly; moreover, the degree to which it can be done depends on the specific situation. This is the difference between the formal and informal organizations mentioned. Despite this, the Linear Responsibility Chart is one of the best devices for organization analysis known to the authors.

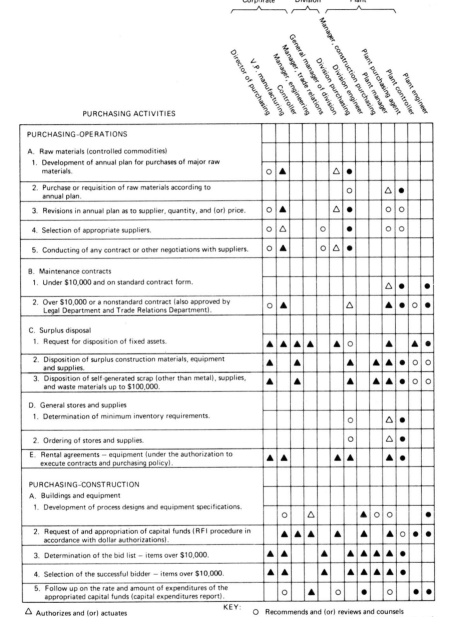

Figure 16-2. Functional authority relationships. (*From Allen R. Janger,* "Charting Authority Relationships," *The Conference Board Record* (December, 1964).

The LRC In Input-Output Terms

The LRC can be visualized as an input-output device. For example, if the job positions of the managing subsystem are considered to be the inputs, task accomplishments the outputs, and matrix symbols the specific task-to-job relationships, then the overall LRC can be looked upon as a diagram of the managing subsystem from a systems viewpoint (Figure 16-3 diagrammatically illustrates this idea).

If two additional steps are added to this charting scheme, the systems viewpoint can be made more explicit. First, if systems terminology is used to structure the LRC matrix symbols and if the personnel affected are indoctrinated in the philosophy of an LRC, then many of the facets of the informal organization (8) can be formalized and assimilated along with the formal organization into the managing-subsystem structure. The second step is to use the *systems symbols* from one row (one task) of the LRC to draw a schematic diagram, as indicated by the symbols of that row; this would show the interrelationships or intercouplings between the persons involved in accomplishing a task (see Figure 16-4).

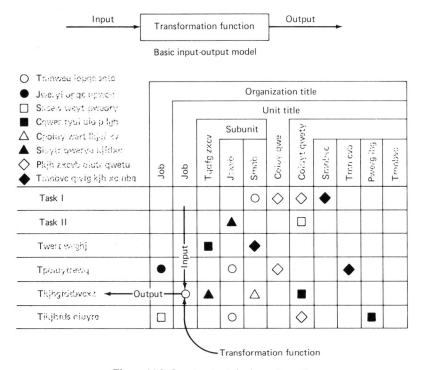

Figure 16-3. Input-output-device schematic.

Task/Job Relationships Symbol titles

- ○ Work is done
- ● Direct supervision
- □ General supervision
- ■ Intertask integration
- △ Occasional intertask integration
- ▲ Intertask coordination
- ◇ Occasional intertask coordination
- ◆ Output notification mandatory

Task/Job Relationships	Division manager	Branch manager	Test activity integrator	Test facility manager	Test data planner	Test and documents coordinator	Branch manager	Section supervisor (Data A&A)	Instrumentation engineer	Section supervisor (Elec. mach.)	Test equipment engineer	Test article engineer	Section supervisor (Electronic)	Electrical systems engineer	R.F. systems engineer	Cmd and C+I systems engineer	Test equipment engineer
Major functional area: test program activities																	
Approve test-program changes	○	▲					▲	◇									
Define test objectives	●	○					■	▲		▲			▲				
Determine test requirements	□	●	○	▲	▲	▲	■	◇		◇			◇				
Evaluate test-program progress	●	○	▲	◇			▲										
Make test-program policy decisions	○	▲					▲										
Write test-program responsibility doctrine	□	●	○				■			◇			◇				
Major functional area: integration of test-support act																	
Chair-test working group	□	●	○				■			◇			◇				
Prepare milestone-test schedules		●	○				■	◆		◆			◆				
Write test directive		●	○	▲	▲	▲	△			◇			◇				
Write detailed test procedures			◇	◇	◆	◆	□	■	△	●	■	○	●	○	○	○	■
Coordinate test preparations			△	■	◇		●	○	▲	○	▲	▲	○	▲	▲	▲	▲
Verify test-article configuration			◆	■		▲		■				○		○	○	○	
Major functional area: all systems test																	
Certify test readiness	●	■	△	△			○	▲		▲			▲				
Perform test-director function	○	▲	▲	◇			■										
Perform test-conductor function	●						○	■		■			■				
Analyze test data				▲	◇		■	■		●	○	○	●	○	○	○	○
Resolve test anomalies	□			◇			●	▲	▲	○	▲	■	○	■	■	■	▲
Prepare test report	□	■	◇	◇	◆		●	○		○			○				

Figure 16-4. Systems LRC for equipment test division.

The organization's work-subsystem chart could yield another advantage if the titles for the tasks and activities of the LRC were used. If this were done, the managing-subsystem schematic could also be used for diagrammatically integrating the work subsystem and the managing subsystem. A third step would be to superimpose a string of managing-subsystem schematics on the *total* work-subsystem chart to give an overall analytical view of how the organization operates; this would show the stream of interpersonal relations that serve to control, change, and otherwise facilitate the accomplishment of the tasks essential to the realization of the organizational goals.

The Systematized LRC

A systematized LRC could be structured to serve as the basis for drawing a managing-subsystem schematic diagram by following the three steps.

Arrangement and Form of Inputs: Job Positions.   The job positions involved in the analysis are listed across the top of the LRC matrix. As can be seen from the sample in Figure 16-4, these job positions are arranged in such a manner that the line structure around them indicates the administrative ordering of the job positions. This method of showing job positions provides a means of integrating the pyramidal organization chart into the LRC. This can be seen by comparing the top portion of the LRC in Figure 16-4 with the corresponding traditional organizational chart in Figure 16-5. The chart should show only the jobs being analyzed. If the analysis concerns only the executives and engineers of an organizational unit, for example, nothing will be gained by including jobs such as those of secretaries, clerks, and draftsmen, even though they are vital parts of the organizational effort. The LRC, like any other chart, must be brief and simple to be effective.

Listing Outputs: Tasks and Activities.   The tasks and activities related to the job positions are listed on the left side of the matrix. These tasks and activities should be listed in groupings and subgroupings that would facilitate the analysis and enhance the perspective view of the chart. If the tasks are extracted from the organization's work-subsystem chart, this scheme would enable the work subsystem to be integrated into the managing subsystem. Whether this method or some other is chosen, it is very important that complete, accurate, and agreed-upon descriptions of the tasks be selected. The relative ease of accomplishing the analysis and the subsequent usefulness of the LRC will depend strongly on the adequacy of the task statements.

Description and Definition of Matrix Symbols: Task-Job Relationships. There are a number of ways in which a person (a job position) can be related to a task. For example, he may be the person who takes some direct action concerning the task, he may be the person's supervisor, or

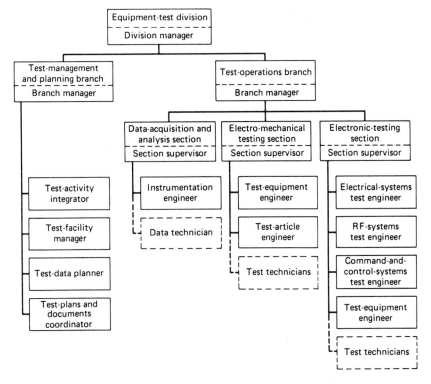

Figure 16-5. Organizational chart for equipment test division.

perhaps he is an advisor on how to do the work. Perhaps he advises as to what needs to be done from a standpoint of intertask sequencing, for example, as a production scheduler. He may even be someone in the system who only needs to be notified that an operation on the task has been completed. In each case, there exists what may be called a *task-job relationship* (TJR).

From a systems viewpoint, each TJR can be visualized as falling into one of three major categories: (1) transfer function, (2) control loop, or (3) input-output stream. The LRC shown in Figure 16-4 for the equipment test division of an electrical equipment company uses the eight TJRs defined below. The first three of these are usually found in papers and articles about the LRC; the other five have been retitled and changed so as to be more meaningful for a systems treatment.

Transfer Function: Work Is Done/TJR (WID/TJR). The WID/TJR is the transfer-function aspect of the managing-subsystem model. It is the actual juncture of the managing and the work subsystems. The given inputs of information, matter, and energy (i/m/e) are transformed into predetermined outputs of i/m/e in accordance with the program of instructions (policies, rules, procedures) furnished to the person for this job position.

Control Loop: "Direct Supervision/TJR (DS/TJR). The DS/TJR constitutes the prime operational control element in the WID/TJR control loop. The person in the DS job position is considered to be the administrative supervisor of the person in the WID job position. The DS/TJR evaluates the quantity, quality, and timeliness of the WID/TJR outputs through the use of policy guidance information, program directives, procedures, WID input-output comparisons, schedules, and other managerial feedback, measurement, and control devices. The omission of this TJR from a row (task) indicates that the WID/TJR is of such a routine, stable nature that frequent contact with the DS/TJR is not normally required in operation of the transfer function.

General Supervision/TJR (GS/TJR). The GS/TJR is a second-order operational-control element and a first-order or prime source of policy guidance for the WID/TJR. The person in the GS job position is the administrative supervisor of the person in the DS job position. The primary role of the GS/TJR is to furnish the DS and WID job positions with a framework of policies and guidance of a scope that permits as much *closed-loop* decision-making flexibility as possible in attainment of the desired WID/TJR outputs. The exclusion of the GS/TJR from a given WID/TJR control loop indicates that WID actions are seldom taken that involve questions of conformance to, or exceptions from, existing GS policy.

Intertask Integration/TJR (II/TJR). The II/TJR is placed in the WID/TJR control loop to indicate the need for consideration of functional compatibility between this WID/TJR and other WID/TJRs. The extent of the involvement of the II/TJR in the control loop is the extent to which the transfer functions of the tasks concerned are interlocked or functionally interdependent. The person in the II job position does not have an administrative role in the WID/TJR control loop.

Occasional Intertask Integration/TJR (OII/TJR). The OII/TJR is similar in concept and definition to the II/TJR, discussed above. The principal difference is the specialty nature of this TJR as opposed to the general or routine nature of the II/TJR. The omission of this TJR and (or) the II/TJR from a control loop indicates that the WID/TJR is, as a rule, functionally independent of, and hence decoupled from, other transfer functions in the work subsystem.

Input-Output Stream: Intertask Coordination/TJR (IC/TJR). The IC/TJR is an information *input* to the WID/TJR and hence does not appear in the control loop; it has nothing to do with the "shape" or "how" of the transfer function. Intertask sequencing, schedule compatibility, quantities, qualities, and other matters of a "what" and "when" nature are indicated by the use of the IC/TJR.

Occasional Intertask Coordination/TJR (OIC/TJR). The OIC/TJR is similar to the IC/TJR, discussed above, except that its use indicates only specialized instances of coordination instead of being a routine input.

Output Notification Mandatory/TJR (ONM/TJR). The ONM/TJR is placed in the *output* of the WID/TJR transfer function when it is essential or critical that the ONM job position receive some specialized, exact, or timely information concerning the WID/TJR outputs. The concept of this TJR is one of passive transmission of information only and is not coordinative.

The LRC format, as discussed to this point, consists of job positions administratively ordered, tasks and activities grouped in some meaningful way, and TJRs defined along the lines of systems terminology. The subsequent analytical process involves the findings and determinations that lead to inserting the TJRs in the boxes of the LRC matrix. If a TJR symbol does not appear in a box, the analyst has concluded that the job position is not intercoupled with the WID job position of the task.

The completed analysis is then a systematized LRC model of the managing subsystem. This model displays the following characteristics of, and information about, an organizational unit:

The pyramidal organizational chart is incorporated into the top of the matrix through the use of lines to partition the job positions administratively.

The tasks and activities of the work subsystem are listed according to some functional flow plan.

The TJR symbols in the LRC matrix show the types of intercouplings between the person who offsets the work subsystem—the WID job position—and other persons with an interest in the task.

The TJRs also serve to show how the managing and work subsystems are integrated.

The overall model yields a perspective view of how the *static* formal organization is combined with the *passive* work subsystem to become a *dynamic* functioning entity that maintains a continuous balance with its environment while transforming its information-matter-energy inputs into the outputs that satisfy the ever-changing goals and objectives of the organization.

System Model Schematic Diagrams

One additional diagram can be constructed that will further illustrate the systems nature of the managing subsystem. If a WID/TJR and its associated task title are combined in one rectangle, and if the remaining TJRs are then intercoupled with that WID/TJR, and if each is enclosed in separate rectangles arranged about, and interconnected with, the WID in accordance with their respective TJRs, the resulting schematic diagram will convey a systems concept of the interpersonal relations involved in accomplishing a given task. Figure 16-6 shows the arrangement of TJRs in a system model schematic format. Figure 16-7 is a system model schematic of the task "Write detailed test procedures," which appears in Figure 16-4. If all tasks of the organization's work subsystems are properly analyzed and charted and if the system model schematic for each task is shown with its respective tasks and interconnections with the other schematics, the results should give an overall portrayal of the organization's integrated work subsystem and managing subsystem, such as is shown by the sketch in Figure 16-8.

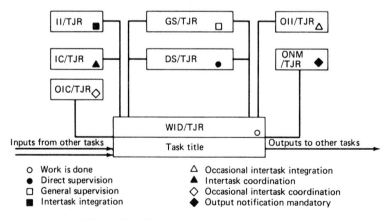

Figure 16-6. System model schematic format.

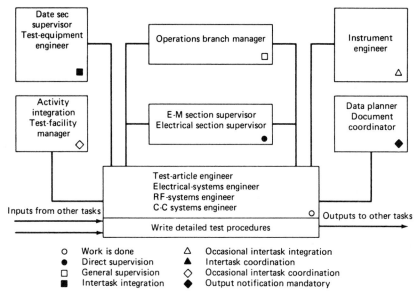

Figure 16-7. System model schematic of the task, "Write detailed test procedures."

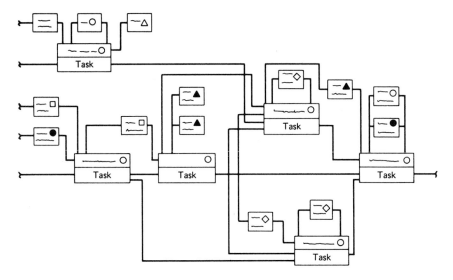

Figure 16-8. Integration of an organization's work and managing subsystems.

THE LRC IN PLANNING

While the primary focus of the LRC has been descrptive, it may also be used in a prescriptive mode to aid in the systems design aspect of planning. This approach has been developed by the authors within the context of a Department of Justice study in the Buffalo, New York, Police Department. (9)

The approach utilizes both a descriptive and normative LRC-like model of the organization as the basis for developing a "consensus" model through negotiation.

Figure 16-9 depicts a descriptive chart which characterizes one aspect of policy planning—policy formulation.

The entries in the chart represent a number of organizational characteristics with regard to the planning decision area:

1. Authority and responsibility relationships.
2. Initiation characteristics.
3. Input-output characteristics.

The codes used to describe these characteristics for internal units are

I—Initiation
E—Execution
A—Approval
C—Consultation
S—Supervision

Subscripts on these coded symbols describe with whom the relationship exists. For instance, the simplified macrolevel chart of Figure 16-9 shows on the first row that the analysis of routine complaints (E) is handled at the police captain level under the supervision of an inspector (S) with the police commissioner having approval authority (A). In performing this function, the captain has the consultation of uniformed patrolmen (C_7 where the subscript 7 indicates with whom the consultation takes place). Another consultation takes place when the deputy commissioner consults with the commissioner (C_4) at the approval stage.

Various informational linkages with interfacing environmental organizations are also depicted in these charts. Figure 16-9 shows only one such linkage—that involving "other city departments" who both provide input (i) to and receive output (o) from the mayor (2) in his approval role.

The model of Figure 16-9 is a descriptive one in that it depicts authorities, responsibilities, initiations, inputs, and outputs *as they actually occur in the organization.*

	1	2	3	4	5	6	7	8	9	10	11	12
	City council	Mayor	Comptroller commissioner budget director	Police commissioner	Deputy commissioner	Inspector	Captain	Uniformed patrolman	Police administrator	Other city departments	Boards and agencies	Federal government
Routine complaints				A	C_4	S	E	C_7				
Observation of field practices				A	S	E						
Crime analysis												
Court decisions												
Analysis of social problems												
New legislation				A	S	E						
Issue clarification definition				A	S	E						
Selection of alternatives				A	E	C_5						
Obtaining relevant facts												
Analysis of facts												
Review		A		E						$2^{1.0}$		
Formulation				E	C							
Articulation				A	S_4	S	E					
Training for implementation					A	S	E					
Execution and control				A	S	E	C_4					

Figure 16-9. Model of existing policy-making process.

A descriptive model of the organizational and environmental system such as that provided by Figure 16-9 and other associated charts is a useful "road map" for guiding information analysis. It provides insights into "who does what," the interactions among organizational units and between internal and external units, the general nature of information required, the direction of information flow, and the manner in which information requirements are generated.

However, the use of a model of this variety alone as a basis for system design would represent an abrogation of the information analyst's proper role. Instead of creating a system to serve an existing organizational system, he should attempt to restructure the decision-making process so that the system may be oriented toward the support of a more nearly "optimal" process.

To do this, the analyst must call on the best of the knowledge and theory of management to construct a normative model of the organization. For instance, a police department which is not already using a program budget structure should be aided in developing one. A *normative* for the same "policy formulation" area to which the descriptive model of Figure 16-9 applies may be developed. Most organizations will not find it desirable to directly adopt such a prescriptive model. However, an "open minded" organization will usually find some elements of the model which it wishes to adopt.

The development of a consensus model hinges on an objective comparison of a descriptive model, such as that of Figure 16-9, with a normative model. This comparison and evaluation must be done by managers, with the aid and advice of analysts.

One possible medium for this process, which has been used successfully by the authors, is that of a "participative executive development program." The program involved the system participants as "students" and the analysts as "teachers." The normative model was developed and discussed in lecture-discussion sessions. After it had been communicated fully, workshops were used to facilitate the detailed evaluation and comparison of the descriptive and normative models. Recommendations emanating from the workshops were reviewed by top management, and those which were approved were incorporated into a consensus model of the system.

SUMMARY

This chapter demonstrates the values and limitations of traditional organizational charts and introduces a variety of charts—all based on the *linear responsibility chart* (LRC)—which can aid in both the planning and implementing phases of management.

REFERENCES

(1) Richard M. Cyert and James G. March, *A Behavioral Theory of the Firm* (Prentice-Hall, Englewood Cliffs, N.J., 1963), p. 289.
(2) Frank J. Jasinski, "Adapting Organization to New Technology," *Harvard Business Review* (January–February, 1959), p. 80.

(3) Allen R. Janger, "Charting Authority Relationships," *The Conference Board Record* (December, 1964).

(4) "Manning the Executive Setup," *Business Week* (April 6, 1957), p. 187.

(5) For example, one writer proclaimed: "On one pocket-size chart it shows the facts buried in all the dusty organizational manuals—plus a lot more."

(6) Allen R. Janger, "Charting Authority Relationships," *The Conference Board Record* (December, 1964).

(7) Delmar W. Karger and Robert G. Murdick, *Managing Engineering and Research* (The Industrial Press, New York, 1963), p. 89.

(8) The informal organization is not what the name implies, i.e., a casual, loosely structured community of people who have similar interests. The informal organization can be most demanding on its members. Its standards of performance and loyalty and its authority patterns can be anything but loose. It can be the most powerful of alliances existing between people having vested interests.

(9) See William R. King and David I. Cleland, "The Design of Management Information Systems: An Information Analysis Approach," *Management Science,* Vol. 22(3) (November, 1975), pp. 286–297.

17. Pricing Out the Work

Harold Kerzner*

The first integration of the functional unit into the project environment occurs during the pricing process. The total program costs obtained by pricing out the activities over the scheduled period of performance provides management with a fundamental tool for managing the project. During the pricing activities, the functional units have the option to consult program management for possible changes to work requirements as well as for further clarification.

Activities are priced out through the lowest pricing units of the company. It is the responsibility of these pricing units, whether they be sections, departments, or divisions, to provide accurate and meaningful cost data. Under ideal conditions, the work required (i.e., man-hours) to complete a given task can be based upon historical standards. Unfortunately for many industries, projects and programs are so diversified that realistic comparison between previous activities may not be possible. The costing information obtained from each pricing unit, whether or not it is based upon historical standards, should be regarded only as an estimate. How can a company predict the salary structure three years from now? What will be the cost of raw materials two years from now? Will the business base (and therefore the overhead rates) change over the period of performance? The final response to these questions shows that costing out performance is explicitly related to an environment which cannot be predicted with any high degree of certainty.

Project management is an attempt to obtain the best utilization of resources within time, cost, and performance. Logical project estimating

* Dr. Harold Kerzner is Professor of Systems Management and Director of The Project/ Systems Management Research Institute at Baldwin-Wallace College. Dr. Kerzner has published over 35 engineering and buisness papers and ten texts: *Project Management: A Systems Approach to Planning, Scheduling and Controlling; Project Management for Executives; Project Management for Bankers; Cases and Situations in Project/Systems Management; Operations Research; Proposal Preparation and Management; Project Management Operating Guidelines; Project/Matrix Management Policy and Strategy; A Project Management Dictionary of Terms; Engineering Team Management.*

techniques are available. The following thirteen steps provide a logical sequence in order to obtain better resource estimates. These steps may vary from company to company.

STEP 1: PROVIDE A COMPLETE DEFINITION OF THE WORK REQUIREMENTS

Effective planning and implementation of projects cannot be accomplished without a complete definition of the requirements. For projects internal to the organization, the project manager works with the project sponsor and user (whether they be executives, functional managers, or simply employees) in order for the work to be completely defined. For these types of in-house projects, the project manager can wear multiple hats as project manager, proposal manager, and even project engineer on the same project.

For projects funded externally to the organization, the proposal manager (assisted by the project manager and possibly the contract administrator) must work with the customer to make sure that all of the work is completely defined and that there is no misinterpretation over the requirements. In many cases, the customer simply has an idea and needs assistance in establishing the requirements. The customer may hire an outside agency for assistance. If the activity is sole-source or perhaps part of an unsolicited effort, then the contractor may be asked to work with the customer in defining the requirements even before any soliciting is attempted.

A complete definition of project requirements must include

- Scope (or statement) of work.
- Specifications.
- Schedules (gross or summary).

The scope of work or statement of work (SOW) is a narrative description of all the work required to perform the project. The statement of work identifies the goals and objectives which are to be achieved. If a funding constraint exists, such as "this is a not-to-exceed effort of $250,000," this information might also appear in the SOW.

If the customer supplies a well-written statement of work, then the project and proposal managers will supply this SOW to the functional managers for dollar and man-hour estimates. Unless the customer maintains a staff of employees to provide a continuous stream of RFP/RFQs,*

---

* RFP (Request for Proposal); RFQ (Request for Quote).

the customers must ask potential bidders to assist them in the preparation of the SOW. As an example, Alpha Company wishes to build a multimillion-dollar chemical plant. Since Alpha does not erect such facilities on a regular basis, Alpha would send out inquiries instead of a formal RFP. These inquiries are used not only to identify potential bidders, but also to identify to potential bidders that they will have to develop an accurate SOW as part of the proposal process. This process may appear as a feasibility study. This is quite common especially on large dollar-value projects where contractors are willing to risk the additional time, cost, and effort as part of the bidding process. If the proposal is a sole-source effort, then the contractor may pass this cost on to the customer as part of the contract.

The statement of work is vital to proposal pricing and should not be taken lightly. All involved functional managers should be given the opportunity to review the SOW during the pricing process. Functional managers are the true technical experts in the company and best qualified to identify high-risk areas and prevent anything from "falling through the crack." Misinterpretations of the statement of work can lead to severe cost overruns and schedule slippages.

The statement of work might be lumped together with the contractual data as part of the terms and conditions. The proposal manager may then have to separate out the SOW data from the RFP. This is vital for the pricing effort.

This process is essential because misinterpretation of the statement of work can cause severe cost overruns. As an example, consider the following two situations:

- Acme Corporation won a Navy contract in which the Government RFP stated that "this unit must be tested in water." Acme built a large pool behind their manufacturing plant. Unfortunately, the Navy's interpretation was the Atlantic Ocean. The difference was $1 million.
- Ajax Corporation won a contract to ship sponges across the United States using aerated boxcars. The project manager leased boxcars that had doors on the top surface. The doors were left open during shipping. The train got caught in several days of torrential rainstorms and the boxcars eventually exploded, spreading sponges across the countryside. The customer wanted boxcars aerated from below.

The amount of money and time spent in rewording the technical data in the SOW for pricing is minimal compared to cost of misinterpretation.

The second major item in the definition of the requirements is the identification of the specifications, if applicable. Specifications form the basis from which man-hours, equipment, and materials are priced out. The specifications must be identified such that the customer will understand the basis for the man-hour, equipment, and materials estimates. Small changes in a specification can cause large cost overruns.

Another reason for identifying the specifications is to make sure that there will be no surprises for the customer downstream. The specifications should be the current revision. It is not uncommon for a customer to hire outside agencies to evaluate the technical proposal and to make sure that the proper specifications are being used.

Specifications are in fact standards for pricing out a proposal. If specifications either do not yet exist or are not necessary, then work standards should be included in the proposal. The work standards can also appear in the cost volume of the proposal. Labor justification backup sheets may or may not be included in the proposal, depending upon RFP/RFQ requirements.

For R&D proposals, standards may not exist and the pricing team may have to use educated guesses based upon the estimated degree of difficulty, such as:

- Task 02-15-10 is estimated to be 25% more difficult than a similar task accomplished on the Alpha Project, which required 300 man-hours. Hours needed for Task 02-15-10 are therefore 375.
- Task 03-07-02 is estimated at 450 hours. This is 20% more than the standard because of the additional reporting constraints imposed by the customer.

The standards mentioned here are usually the technical standards only.

The technical standards and specifications may be called out by the customer or, if this is a follow-on project, then the customer will expect the work to be performed within the estimate on the previous activity. If the standards or specifications will be different, then an explanation must be made or else the customer (and line managers) may feel that he has been taken for a ride. Customers have the tendency of expecting standards to be lowered on follow-on efforts because the employees are expected to be performing at an improved position on the learning curve.

The key parameter in explaining the differences in standards is the time period between the original cost estimate and the follow-on or similar cost estimate. The two most common reasons for having standards change are

- New technology requires added effort.
- Key employees with the necessary skills or expertise have either left the organization or are not available.

In either event, justifications of the changes or modifications must be made so that the new ground rules are understood by all pricing and reviewing personnel.

The third item in the identification of the requirements is the gross schedule. In summary, the gross schedule identifies the major milestones of the project and includes such items as:

Start date.
End date.
Other major milestone activities.
Data items and reports.

If possible, all gross schedules which are used for pricing guidelines should contain calendar start and end dates. Unfortunately, some projects do not have definable start and end dates and are simply identified by a time spread. Another common situation is where the end date is fixed and the pricing effort must identify the start date. This is a common occurrence because the customer may not have the expertise to accurately determine how long it will take to accomplish the effort.

Identifying major milestones can also be a tedious task for a customer. Major milestones include such activities as long-lead procurement, prototype testing, design review meetings, and any other critical decision points. The proposal manager must work closely with the customer or in-house sponsor either to verify the major milestones in the RFP or to identify additional milestones.

Major milestones are often grossly unrealistic. In-house executives of the customer and the contractor occasionally identify unrealistic end dates because either resources will be idle without the completion at this point in time, not enough money is available for a longer project, or management wants the effort completed earlier because it affects management's Christmas bonus.

All data items should be identified on the gross schedule. Data items include written contractual reports and can be extended to include handout material for customer design review meetings and technical interchange meetings. Data items are not free and should be priced out accordingly. There is nothing wrong with including in the pricing effort a separate contingency fund for "unscheduled or additional" interchange meetings.

STEP 2: ESTABLISH A LOGIC NETWORK WITH CHECKPOINTS

Once the work requirements are outlined, the project manager must define the logical steps necessary to accomplish the effort. The logic network (or arrow diagram as it is more commonly referred to) serves as the basis for the PERT/CPM diagrams and the Work Breakdown Structure.* The arrow diagram simply shows the logical sequence of events, generally at the level which the project manager wants to control the program. Each logic diagram activity should not be restricted to specific calendar dates at this point because line managers should price out the work, initially assuming

- Unlimited resources.
- No calendar constraints.

If this is not done during the initial stages of pricing, line managers may commit to unrealistic time, cost, and performance estimates. After implementation, the project manager may find it impossible to force the line manager to meet his original estimates.

STEP 3: DEVELOP THE WORK BREAKDOWN STRUCTURE

The simplest method for developing the work breakdown structure is to combine activities on the arrow diagram. If each activity on the arrow diagram is considered to be a task, then several tasks can be combined to form projects and the projects, when combined, will become the total program. The WBS may contain definable start and end dates in accordance with the gross schedule at this point in time, although they may have to be altered before the final WBS is firmly established. Most project managers prefer to work at the task level of the WBS (Level 3). The work is priced out at this level and costs are controlled at this level. Functional managers may have the option of structuring the work to additional levels for better estimating and control.

Often the arrow diagram and WBS are considered as part of the definition of the requirements, because the WBS is the requirement that costs be controlled at a specific level and detail.

STEP 4: PRICE OUT THE WORK BREAKDOWN STRUCTURE

The project manager's responsibility during pricing (and even during execution, for that matter) is to establish the project requirements which identify the "What," "When," and "Why" of the project. The functional managers now price out the activities by determining the "How," "Who," and "Where" of the project. The functional managers have the right to ask the project manager to change the WBS. After all, the func-

---

* See Chapter 14 for a detailed treatment of WBSs and Chapter 15 for a discussion of PERT/CPM and network plans.

tional managers are the true technical experts and may wish to control their efforts differently.

Once the Work Breakdown Structure and activity schedules are established, the program manager calls a meeting for all organizations which will be required to submit pricing information. It is imperative that all pricing or labor costing representatives be present for the first meeting. During this "kickoff" meeting, the Work Breakdown Structure is described in depth so that each pricing unit manager will know exactly what his responsibilities are during the program. The kickoff meeting also resolves the struggle-for-power positions of several functional managers whose responsibilities may be similar or overlap on certain activities. An example of this would be quality control activities. During the research and development phase of a program, research personnel may be permitted to perform their own quality control efforts, whereas during production activities, the quality control department or division would have overall responsibility. Unfortunately, one meeting is not sufficient to clarify all problems. Follow-up or status meetings are held, normally with only those parties concerned with the problems that have arisen. Some companies prefer to have all members attend the status meetings so that all personnel will be familiar with the total effort and the associated problems. The advantage of not having all program-related personnel attend is that time is of the essence when pricing out activities. Many functional divisions carry this policy one step further by having a divisional representative together with possibly key department managers or section supervisors as the only attendees to this initial kickoff meeting. The divisional representative then assumes all responsibility for assuring that all costing data be submitted on time. This may be beneficial in that the program office need only contact one individual in the division to learn of the activity status, but may become a bottleneck if the representative fails to maintain proper communication between the functional units and the program office or if the individual simply is unfamiliar with the pricing requirements of the Work Breakdown Structure.

During proposal activities, time may be extremely important. There are many situations where a Request for Proposal (RFP) requires that all responders submit their bids no later than a specific date, say 30 days. Under a proposal environment, the activities of the program office, as well as those of the functional unit, are under a schedule set forth by the proposal manager. The proposal manager's schedule has very little, if any, flexibility and is normally under tight time constraints in order that the proposal may be typed, edited, and published prior to date of submittal. In this case, the RFP will indirectly define how much time the pricing units have to identify and justify labor costs.

The justification of the labor costs may take longer than the original cost estimates, especially if historical standards are not available. Many proposals often require that comprehensive labor justifications be submitted. Other proposals, especially those which request almost immediate response, may permit vendors to submit labor justification at a later date.

In the final analysis, it is the responsibility of the lowest pricing unit supervisor to maintain adequate standards, if possible, so that almost immediate response can be given to a pricing request from a program office.

The functional units supply their input to the program office in the form of man-hours. The input may be accompanied by labor justifications, if required. The man-hours are submitted for each task, assuming that the task is the lowest pricing element, and are time-phased per month. The man-hours per month per task are converted to dollars after multiplication by the appropriate labor rates. The labor rates are generally known with certainty over a 12-month period but from there on are only estimates. How can a company predict salary structures five years hence? If the company underestimates the salary structure, increased costs and decreased profits will occur. If the salary structure is overestimated, the company may not bé competitive. If the project is government funded, then the salary structure becomes an item under contract negotiations.

The development of the labor rates to be used in the projection are based upon historical costs in business base hours and dollars for either the most recent month or quarter. Average hourly rates are determined for each labor unit by direct effort within the operations at the department level. The rates are only averages, and include both the highest-paid employees and lowest-paid employees together with the department manager and the clerical support.* These base rates are then escalated as a percentage factor based upon past experience, budget as approved by management, and the local outlook and similar industries. If the company has a predominant aerospace or defense industry business base, then these salaries are negotiated with local government agencies prior to submittal for proposals.

The labor hours submitted by the functional units are quite often overestimated for fear that management will "massage" and reduce the labor hours while attempting to maintain the same scope of effort. Many times management is forced to reduce man-hours either because of insufficient

---

* Problems can occur if the salaries of the people assigned to the program exceed the department averages. Also, in many companies department managers are included in the overhead rate structure, not direct labor, and therefore their salaries are not included as part of the department average.

funding or just to remain competitive in the environment. The reduction of man-hours often causes heated discussions between the functional and program managers. Program managers tend to think in the best interests of the program, while functional managers lean toward maintaining their present staff.

The most common solution to this conflict rests with the program manager. If the program manager selects members for the program team who are knowledgeable in man-hour standards for each of the departments, then an atmosphere of trust can develop between the program office and the functional department such that man-hours can be reduced in a manner which represents the best interests of the company. This is one of the reasons why program team members are often promoted from within the functional ranks.

The ability to estimate program costs involves more than just labor dollars and labor hours. Overhead dollars can be one of the biggest headaches in controlling program costs and must be estimated along with labor hours and dollars. Although most programs have an assistant program manager for cost whose responsibilities include monthly overhead rate analysis, the program manager can drastically increase the success of his program by insisting that each program team member understand overhead rates. For example, if overhead rates apply only to the first forty hours of work, then, depending on the overhead rate, program dollars can be saved by performing work on overtime where the increased salary is at a lower burden.

The salary structure, overhead structure, and labor hours fulfill three of four major input requirements. The fourth major input is the cost for materials and support. Six subtopics are included under materials/support: materials, purchased parts, subcontracts, freight, travel, and other. Freight and travel can be handled in one of two ways, both normally dependent on the size of the program. For small dollar-volume programs, estimates are made for travel and freight. For large dollar-volume programs, travel is normally expressed as between three and five percent of all costs for material, purchased parts, and subcontracts. The category labeled other support costs may include such topics as computer hours or special consultants.

The material costs are very time-consuming, more so than the labor hours. Material costs are submitted via a bill of materials which includes all vendors from whom purchases will be made, project costs throughout the program, scrap factors, and shelf lifetime for those products which may be perishable.

Information on labor is usually supplied to the project office in the form of man-hours/department/task/month. This provides a great degree of flexibility in analyzing total program costs and risks, and is well worth the added effort. Costs can be itemized per month, task, or even department. Computers, with forward pricing information, will convert the man-hours to dollars. Raw materials are always priced out as dollars per month with the computer providing the forward pricing information for escalation factors.

STEP 5: REVIEW WBS COSTS WITH EACH FUNCTIONAL MANAGER

Once the input is received from each functional manager, the project team integrates all of the costs to ensure that all of the work is properly accounted for, without redundancy. An important aspect of this review is the time-phased manpower estimates. It is here where the project manager brings up the subject of limited rather than unlimited resources and asks the line managers to assess the various risks in their estimates.

As part of the review period, the project manager must ask the following questions:

- Was sufficient time allowed for estimating?
- Were the estimates based upon history or standards, or are they "best guesses"?
- Will the estimates require a continuous shifting of personnel in and out of the project?
- Will there be personnel available who have the necessary skills?

Obviously, the answers to these questions can lead into a repricing activity.

STEP 6: DECIDE UPON THE BASIC COURSE OF ACTION

After the review with the functional managers, the project manager must decide upon the basic course of action or the base case. This is the ideal path that the project manager wishes to follow. Obviously, the decision will be based upon the risks on the project and the projected trade-offs which may have to be made downstream on time, cost, and performance.

The base case may include a high degree of risk if it is deemed necessary to satisfy contractual requirements. This base case approach and accompanying costs should be reviewed with the customer and upper-level management. There is no point in developing finalized, detailed PERT/CPM schedules and the program plan unless there is agreement on the base case.

STEP 7: ESTABLISH REASONABLE COSTS FOR EACH WBS ELEMENT

Since the project will be controlled through the WBS, the project manager must define, with reasonable accuracy and confidence, his target costs for each WBS element, usually at Level 3. Once the project is initiated, these costs will become the basis for the project targets. The problem here is that the costs were based upon unlimited resources. Limited resources may require overtime, or perhaps the work will have to be performed during higher cost escalation periods. These factors must be accounted for.

STEP 8: REVIEW THE BASE CASE COSTS WITH UPPER-LEVEL MANAGEMENT

Once the base case is formulated, the pricing team member, together with the other program office team members, perform perturbation analyses in order to answer any questions that may come up during the final management review. The perturbation analysis is designed as a systems approach to problem solving, where alternatives are developed in order to respond to any questions that management may wish to consider during the final review.

The base case, together with the perturbation analysis costs, are then reviewed with upper-level management in order to formulate a company position for the program as well as to take a hard look at the allocation of resources required for the program. The company position may be to cut costs, authorize work, or submit a bid. If the program is competitive, corporate approval may be required if the company's chief executive officer has a ceiling on the dollar bids he can authorize to go out of house.

If labor costs must be cut, the program manager must negotiate with the functional managers as to the size and method for the cost reductions. Otherwise, this step may simply entail the authorization for the functional managers to begin the activities or to develop detailed plans.

STEP 9: NEGOTIATE WITH FUNCTIONAL MANAGERS FOR QUALIFIED PERSONNEL

Once the base case costs are established, the project manager must begin the tedious effort of converting all estimates to actual calendar dates and time frames based upon limited resources. Detailed schedules cannot be established without some degree of knowledge as to exactly which employees will be assigned to key activities. Highly qualified individuals may be able to accomplish the work in less time and may be able to assume added responsibilities.

Good project managers do not always negotiate for the best available resources because either the costs will be too great with those higher-paid individuals or the project priority does not justify the need for such individuals.

Accurate, detailed schedules cannot be developed without some degree of knowledge as to who will be available for the key project positions. Even on competitive bidding efforts, customers require that the resumes of the key individuals be included as part of the proposal.

STEP 10: DEVELOP THE LINEAR RESPONSIBILITY CHART

Once the key employees are assigned to the activities, the project manager works with the functional managers in assigning project responsibilities. The project responsibilities may be assigned in accordance with assumed authority, age, experience on related efforts, maturity, and interpersonal skills.

The linear responsibility chart, if properly developed and used, is an invaluable tool not only in administering the project, but also in estimating the costs.* The linear responsibility chart permits the project manager the luxury of assigning additional work to qualified personnel, of course upon approval of the functional managers. This additional work may be assigned to lower-salaried individuals so that the final costs can come close to the departmental averages, assuming that the work was priced out in this fashion.

The linear responsibility chart development has a direct bearing upon how the costs are priced out and controlled. There are three methods for pricing out and controlling costs.

- Work is priced out at the department average and all work is charged to the project at the department average salary, regardless of who performed the work.
- Work is priced out at the department average but all work performed is billed back to the project at the actual salary of those employees who are to do the work.
- The work is priced out at the salary of those employees who will perform the work and the costs are billed back the same way.

---

* See Chapter 16 for detailed treatment of the linear responsibility chart.

Each of these methods has its advantages and disadvantages as well as a serious impact on the assignment of responsibilities.

STEP 11: DEVELOP THE FINAL DETAILED AND PERT/CPM SCHEDULES

Work standards are generally based upon the average employee. The assignment of above or below average employees can then cause the schedules to be shifted left or right. These detailed schedules are now based upon limited resources and provide the basis for accurate cost estimating. If at all possible, "fat" and slack time should be left in the schedules so as to provide some degree of protection for the line managers. Fat and slack should be removed only as a last resort to lower costs, such as in the case of wanting to remain competitive or on buy-ins.

It should be obvious at this point that project pricing is an iterative process based upon optimization of time, cost, and performance together. After the detailed schedules are developed, the entire pricing process may have to be reaccomplished. Fortunately, the majority of the original estimates are usually salvageable and require only cosmetic modifications unless the customer provides major changes to specifications or quantity revisions because initial cost estimates were grossly unacceptable.

STEP 12: ESTABLISH PRICING COST SUMMARY REPORTS

Although the pricing of a project is an iterative process, the project manager must still burden himself at each iteration point by developing cost summary reports so that key project decisions can be made during the planning. There are at least two times when detailed pricing summaries are needed: in preparation for the pricing review meeting with management and at pricing termination. At all other times it is possible that "simple cosmetic surgery" can be performed on previous cost summaries, such as perturbations in escalation factors and procurement cost of raw materials. The list identified below shows the typical pricing reports.

- A detailed cost breakdown for each WBS element. If the work is priced out at the task level, then there should be a cost summary sheet for each task, as well as rollup sheets for each project and the total program.
- A total program manpower curve for each department. These manpower curves show how each department has contracted with the project office to supply functional resources. If the departmental manpower curves contain several "peaks and valleys," then the project manager may have to alter some of his schedules so as to obtain

some degree of manpower smoothing. Functional managers always prefer manpower-smoothed resource allocations.

- A monthly equivalent manpower cost summary. This table normally shows the fully burdened cost for the average departmental employee carried out over the entire period of project performance. If project costs have to be reduced, the project manager performs a parametric study between this table and the manpower curve tables.
- A yearly cost distribution table. This table is broken down by WBS element and shows the yearly (or quarterly) costs that will be required. This table, in essence, is a project cash flow summary per activity.
- A functional cost and hour summary. This table provides top management with an overall description of how many hours and dollars will be spent by each major functional unit, or division. Top management would use this as part of the forward planning process to make sure that there are sufficient resources available for all projects. This also includes indirect hours and dollars.
- A monthly labor hour and dollar expenditure forecast. This table can be combined with the yearly cost distribution, except that it is broken down by month, not activity or department. In addition, this table normally includes manpower termination liability information for premature cancellation of the project by outside customers.
- A raw material and expenditure forecast. This shows the cash flow for raw materials based upon vendor lead times, payment schedules, commitments, and termination liability.
- Total program termination liability per month. This table shows the customer the monthly costs for the entire program. This is the customer's cash flow, not the contractor's. The difference is that each monthly cost contains the termination liability for man-hours and dollars, on labor and raw materials. This table is actually the monthly costs attributed to premature project termination.

These tables are used both by project managers and upper-level executives. The project managers utilize these tables as the basis for project cost control. Top level management utilizes these tables selecting, approving, and prioritizing projects, as shown in Figure 17-1.

STEP 13: DOCUMENT THE RESULTS INTO A PROGRAM PLAN

The final step in cost estimating is to document all of the results into a project plan. The cost information will also be the basis for the cost volume of the proposal. The logical sequence of events leading up to the

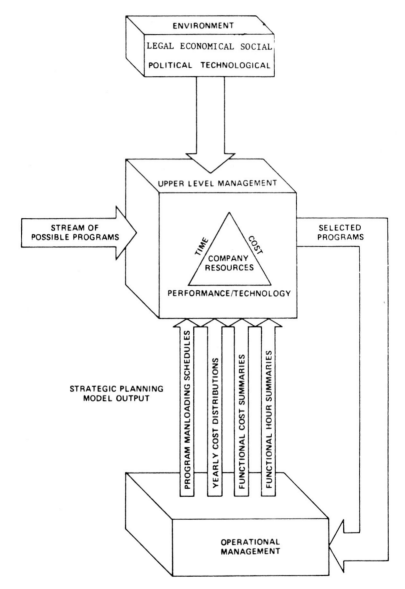

Figure 17-1. Systems approach to resource control. (From Harold Kerzner, *Project Man-agement: A Systems Approach to Planning, Scheduling and Controlling*, Second Edition (Van Nostrand Reinhold, New York, 1984, p. 681).

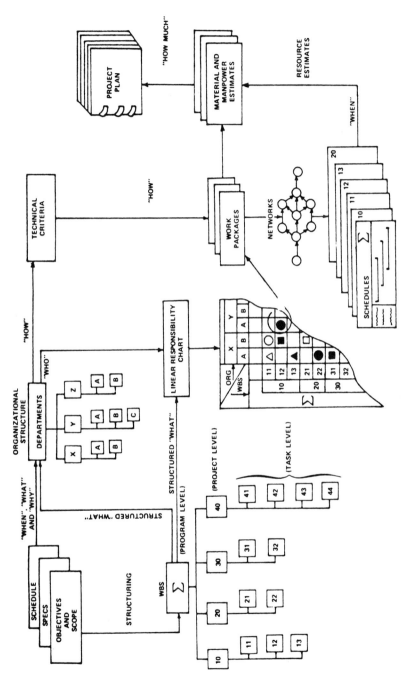

Figure 17-2. Project planning. (From Harold Kerzner, *Project Management for Executives* Second Edition (Van Nostrand Reinhold, New York, 1985, p. 585).

program plan can be summarized as in Figure 17-2. Pricing is an iterative process, at best. The exact pricing procedure will, of course, differ for projects external to the organization as opposed to internal.

Regardless of whether you are managing a large or small project, cost estimating must be accomplished in a realistic, logical manner in order to avoid continuous panics. The best approach, by far, is to try to avoid the pressures of last-minute estimating, and to maintain reasonable updated standards for future estimating. Remember, project costs and budgets are only estimates based upon the standards and expertise of the function managers.

18. Contracts Development—Keystone in Project Management

M. William Emmons*

A keystone is placed at the crown of an arch to provide integrity to the structure and to capitalize on the strength of each individual component. Contracts development as the keystone in project management provides the support to and brings together those activities which have been accomplished and those activities which are to oe accomplished. The keystone concept is that the precontracting activities have been accomplished by the owner and the post-activities will be accomplished by the contractor; contracts development is an activity which requires a mutual accomplishment—the best efforts of both owner and contractor. Figure 18-1 depicts the project phases and activities performed in each phase.

INTRODUCTION

Owner and Contractor Objectives

Contracts development presents challenges to contractor and owner. The interaction is based on long-term and short-term objectives of each. In the short term, the more narrow view, the contractor is competing for the project to build its work load; the owner wants to find the best contractor to accomplish the execution successfully.

---

* M. William Emmons retired from Exxon Corporation in July, 1986, after 34 years in project management related assignments. During his last 11 years with Exxon, Mr. Emmons headed the contracting function of Exxon Chemical Company, assisting world wide affiliates in selecting contractors and negotiating contracts for a full range of petrochemical and associated facilities. Mr. Emmons is currently Principal Associate Contract Management with Pathfinder, Inc., of Cherry Hill, New Jersey, a professional consulting firm assisting owners, contractors, financial institutions, legal institutions, and insurance firms with a comprehensive scope of organizational, venture, and project management services.

Figure 18-1. Project phases.

The longer-term objectives are more complex but also tend to become incorporated into short-term objectives. The contractor's objectives include:

- Winning a sufficient number of contracts to maintain a viable and growing organization.
- Being awarded contracts which add to its library of technology and skills.
- Providing a reasonable financial return to its owners, investors, and employees.

The owner's longer-term objectives include:

- Completing projects within anticipated/estimated cost—to meet its criteria for return on invested funds.
- Completing on or before scheduled completion—to meet its commitment to customers.
- Providing quality plants/facilities—to meet its operation/maintenance criteria and ability to produce quality products.
- Constructing facilities safely, and providing facilities which will operate safely—to meet its commitment to provide a safe and healthy environment for its employees and for the community.

With these objectives firmly in place, the owner and contractor each approach project management in general, and contracts development in particular, from its own perspective. The owner's and contractor's parallel approaches are diagrammed in Figure 18-2.

The Art and Science of It

Defining "art" as a skill in performance acquired by experience, study, or observation, and "science" as knowledge attained through study or practice, contracting has elements of both. Both skill and knowledge are applied: the skill of understanding persons and organizations—how they act and react in specific circumstances—and of being able to synthesize scenarios to plan for reasonable and successful discussions and negotiations. The application of knowledge requires a disciplined gathering, analysis, and implementation strategy in order that each project experience provides a vernier adjustment to contracting tools—documents, procedures, and evaluation mechanisms.

Business and Technical Linked

The design and construction of projects is, on the surface, a technical exercise. To build safely and accurately, and to provide a project/facility which will operate as planned and provide a safe and healthy environment for those who use it requires specialized technical knowledge and skill. But the other side of the coin is to do it economically. To provide such a project/facility within the budgeted funding and to operate within the cost parameters established requires specialized business knowledge and skill. Project management and contracts development need a combination of technical and business knowledge and skill to assure a successful venture.

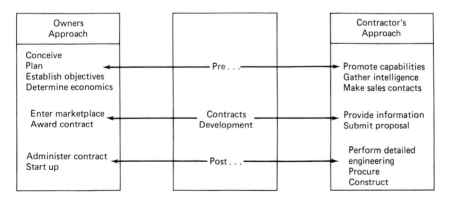

Figure 18-2. Approaches—project/contracts development.

Human Traits Emphasis

Sensitivity, trust, integrity, and openness are active words in contracts development, as they should be in all relationships. To find the best solution, to provide the best in service to company and individuals, and to achieve professional stature are the goals. Human traits are part of the recipe; we should, as the old song says, "accentuate the positive and eliminate the negative" in our encounters.

CONTRACTING PRINCIPLES

The basic principles which guide contracting are those which will provide for a successful venture, and will provide to owner and contractor the benefits each expect for their involvement. Only the most basic principles are cited here, since each company, whether contractor or owner, must establish its own set of principles and communicate these to its own employees and to its clients and customers.

Competitive Bidding

The first principle is competitive bidding. There is little argument that competitive bidding, that is, awarding contracts based on the solicitation and review of proposals from several contractors, improves the industry. The owner benefits from the pressures of the marketplace in terms of economic design, procurement of equipment and materials, subcontracting, and optimized cost in general. The contractor benefits in terms of sharpening the skills and creativity of its employees, discovering techniques and methods to improve productivity, and lowering costs and increasing profits in general. However, inherent within competitive bidding as a principle is the recognition that contracting without competition may be required under certain circumstances. Such negotiated contracting is achieved by soliciting a proposal from a single selected contractor and negotiating mutually agreed terms and conditions. This is not counter to competitive bidding, it only indicates a limitation to competitive bidding. Two prime circumstances which dictate negotiation versus competition are (1) when there is a single source of technology, thus limiting the owner's choice of contractor, and (2) when the "best" contractor is already identified as the result of current work at site, duplication of facilities, or recent bidding experience. A corollary principle related to negotiated contracts is that the terms and conditions proposed by the contractor and sought by the owner should reflect the current marketplace; neither side should seek an unwarranted advantage.

Single Responsibility

The second principle is related to the term "single responsibility." In such a circumstance the owner awards a single contract to a single contractor for all work (engineering, procurement, construction) on all facilities included in the project. Lines of communication, responsibilities, liabilities, and accountabilities are clearer, and control systems related to cost, schedule quality, and safety have the best chance to be successfully applied. However, in this less-than-simple world, a split of the work is often required to take advantage of the best available skills, technology, capabilities, and knowledge in the marketplace. Figure 18-3 indicates such vertical and horizontal splits. Alternative X is a horizontal split, alternative Y vertical, and alternative Z a mix.

Fairness and Ethics

A very important principle to be cited here is that fair and ethical practices be established and followed by all parties and persons. It is important to create a mutual sense of trust within and between the parties. Without such trust a partnership cannot be successful, a contractual relationship will be strained, and the success of the venture may be in jeopardy. Beyond the moral obligations, fair and ethical practice makes good business sense. Written communications to document all discussions between the parties, equal treatment of all contractors by the owner, and strict sealed bid procedures all contribute to creating the desired atmosphere of trust.

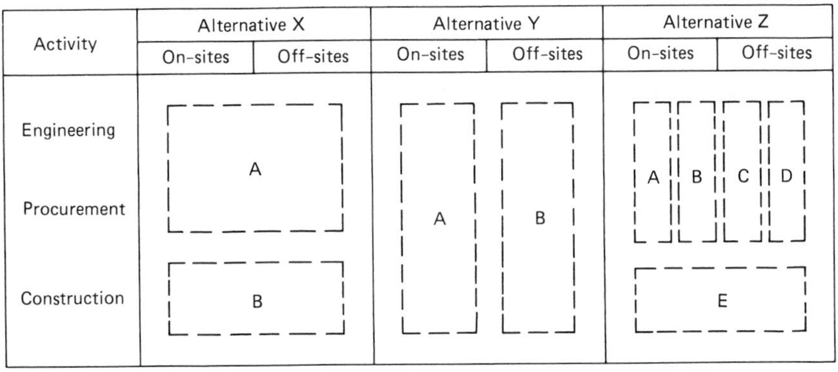

Activity	Alternative X		Alternative Y		Alternative Z	
	On-sites	Off-sites	On-sites	Off-sites	On-sites	Off-sites
Engineering	A		A	B	A B	C D
Procurement						
Construction	B				E	

Figure 18-3. Project execution alternatives. (*Note:* A, B, C, D, and E indicate separate contractors.)

Management's Right To Know

A final principle may seem obvious but often is forgotten: management has the right to know. The group responsible for contracts development needs to make an intentional effort to keep management advised of progress, at times when approvals are required, of course, but also when key activities have been achieved. It is too easy to perform the tasks as planned, achieve anticipated results, and expect to move on. But such progress should be reported. This principle provides for "no surprises," and allows communication between management and the contracting group.

SEQUENCE OF CONTRACTING ACTIVITIES

As in all undertakings, contracting follows a set sequence of activities. And each step builds on the previous step and provides the basis for the next step. Figure 18-4 sets forth the sequence of contracting activities. The elapsed time has not been shown in Figure 18-4 since each contracting effort will require a different time frame depending on type of contract, owner's requirements related to reviews and approvals, complexity of projects including number of plants, technology, grass roots versus revamp, location of facilities and contractors' offices, etc. In general, a minimum of three months should be allowed for a reimbursable cost con-

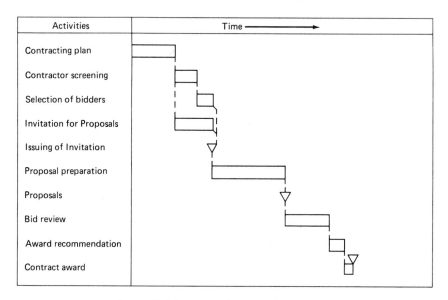

Figure 18-4. Sequence of contracting activities.

tracting exercise, and five months for lump sum. (Lump sum requires more extensive prequalification of bidders, and more time for contractors to prepare their bids.) It is important that the contracting effort start early to allow sufficient time for decisions to be made on appropriate data and study, to avoid hurried decisions and potential mistakes. And (this is very important) even if the contracting time is condensed due to market pressures, business confidentiality, or other reason, each step shown should be taken, even briefly, to assure that the best contractor is selected and an acceptable contract is developed to provide a solid basis for a successful project.

CONTRACTING PLAN

The architect develops the plans before the cathedral is built. So it is with contracting. The development of the contracting plan is an essential ingredient to successful contracts development. Without a plan, there is no direction/guide for the participants. A poorly conceived plan will result in false starts, mistakes, and frustrations to both owner and contractors. It is not only the contracting effort that is affected, but the whole of project execution: cost, schedule, quality, and safety.

The Planning

The contracting planning consists of (1) the gathering of all data and information related to the project which will have, or has the potential to have, an impact on the contracting effort; (2) a thorough analysis of such data and information including the effect on cost, schedule, quality, and safety aspects of the project; (3) the structuring of the potential alternative contracting strategies/approaches including qualifying and quantifying the advantages and disadvantages of each; and (4) selecting the best contracting strategy and viable alternatives.

Information and Data Gathering.   The information and data required will cover (1) facilities (type of units, technology, size, cost); (2) location factors (existing versus new, construction mode, potential conflicts if working within an operating plant, e.g., hot work permits, emergency situations); (3) scope of services required from contractor (engineering, procurement, construction); (4) key project dates (availability of basic design specifications, turnaround/shutdown timing, completion date); (5) project and appropriation approval requirements and timing; (6) financing considerations (source, amounts, restraints, contractor involvement); (7) contracting marketplace (capacity, work load, technology, applicable experience); and (8) status of vendor and subcontractor marketplace.

Analysis and Strategy.   All information and data are analyzed, checking the interactions among all elements, and then developing various contracting alternatives, each of which is considered applicable to the project and is judged capable of bringing the project to a successful conclusion.

After determining the advantages and disadvantages of each potential alternative, it is necessary to quantify the differences in order to select that alternative which best meets the owner's objectives—cost, schedule, quality, and safety. Viable retreat strategies also need to be identified in the event the chosen alternative cannot be achieved.

The Contracting Plan

The results of the contracting planning are documented for presentation to, and review and approval by, the appropriate management; this document is the Contracting Plan. Included in the Contracting Plan will be the following sections:

- Executive Summary
- Purpose of Plan
- Project Background and Factors
- Contracting Principles and Policies
- Analysis of Contracting Alternatives
- Recommended Contracting Strategy
- Viable Retreat Strategies
- Detailed Schedule of Contracting Activities
- Preliminary Schedule for Project Execution
- Potential Concerns/Problems and Resolutions
- Contracting Procedures
- Contractors to Be Screened
- Draft of Screening Telex/Letter
- Decisions and Approvals Required

The Contracting Plan, after management approval, will guide the contracting effort. However, it will be subject to review at various times, for example, after screening, to verify or change the strategy. Changes may require the Plan to be revised and reissued.

CONTRACTOR SCREENING

For most projects, the number of contractors who can perform the work, or claim such capability and experience, is large. The process of contractor screening is to start with the total known population; select those who appear to have the capability and experience required (the "long list"); contact that group to gather up-to-date information on their capacity, experience, capability, and other items; and select a limited number to submit bids (the "short list"). This process has a number of advantages: (1) by considering the total population and developing the "long list" the owner is more sure that all contractors with applicable capability are considered, and contractors are assured that efforts made to keep owners aware of their company's capabilities will be productive; (2) contacting the "long list" to gather up-to-date information assures that recent/current changes in offices, experience, projects, etc., are part of the basis for selecting bidders; and (3) limiting the number of bidders provides each contractor a fair chance in a competitive atmosphere, and conserves the owner's resources required for bid review.

The screening process is in itself an application of the fairness principle stated as one contracting principle. All potential bidders receive the same information, and the capability, experience, and interest of each is considered in selecting the bidding slate.

The Screening Telex/Letter

The initial contact with the potential contractors is through the sending of a screening telex or letter. The use of a written document is an absolute necessity. The use of a written document ensures that all contractors receive the same information, thus avoiding misunderstandings or incomplete data which are likely to occur as a result of telephone calls and personal conversations. And it also ensures the uniformity of replies from the contractors, thus allowing for an easier and surer analysis and selection of the bidding slate. The written reply from the contractor will be an organizational response, not individual, and the owner can accept the reply as the contractor's management decision without a need for further time-consuming discussions.

The screening telex/letter is essentially in two parts. The first part provides information to the contractors regarding the facilities, contracting strategy, and key contracting-related dates. The second part requests information from the contractors related to their capability to accomplish the project. The information provided to the contractors includes the following:

- Description of facilities—nonproprietary/nonconfidential information on technical basis, capacity, product slate, special materials or features, etc.
- Proposed contracting basis and timing—type of contract, scope of

contractor's services, dates established for release of invitation for proposals, receipt of proposals, and contract award.

- Key project dates—availability of basic design specification, start of detailed engineering, start of field construction, and mechanical completion.
- Other significant factors.

The information requested from the contractors includes:

- Willingness to submit a proposal—on the contracting basis described.
- Engineering office—location, number of personnel, and current/projected work load.
- Tentative project execution plans—organization, application of experience, construction mode, and location of primary activities.
- Corporate and office experience—facilities, technology, engineering for location/country, and construction at location.
- Other significant information.

Analysis of Contractors' Replies

The replies to the screening telex/letter will be consistent and will lend themselves to a direct line-by-line comparison and evaluation. The objective of the analysis is to identify the "short list" of contractors who are judged to be able to accomplish the project, meeting all the owner's objectives, and are judged able to submit competitive proposals in the current marketplace. The analysis normally consists of two steps: first are "musts," items with which the contractor must conform to be considered as a potential bidder; second are "wants," items which define the work required to complete the project but which need to be evaluated in order to determine the comparative levels of capabilities of the contractors.

The "musts" list should be relatively short, including (1) willingness to submit a proposal in conformance with the established basis; (2) sufficient personnel, both in skills and number, to perform the work; (3) financial stability to assure completion of work; (4) no conflict related to technology; and (5) ability to perform work at the location, including meeting any licensing, permit, or registration requirements. There may be others but the list should be kept short. The result of this step will be simply, yes, the contractor can be considered as a bidder, or no, it cannot.

The second step is to evaluate the "wants" list for each contractor which passed the "musts." The owner, for this exercise, must establish a list of items which are important to and required for the execution of the project, weighting each one as to its impact and importance. The items normally comprise the data and information requested from the contractors in the screening telex/letter including office capacity and work load, experience, and tentative execution plans. These are weighted based on the specific requirements of the project. For example, technology experience would be weighted high if a project included some highly sophisticated technology; or, in a location which had a long history of labor relation problems, knowledge and experience in construction at the location would receive a higher weighting.

Each contractor is rated for each item on the "wants" list. The scale is established by the owner depending on the degree of sophistication wanted and/or the relative/comparative differences anticipated in the contractors' performances. (A scale could be: 1 = "above average," 2 = "average," 3 = "below average"; or 1 = "oustanding" . . . 3 = "above average" . . . 5 = "average" . . . 7 = "below average" . . . 10 = "unacceptable.")

Selection of Bidders

The selection process is now prepared. The rating given to each contractor for each item on the "wants" list is multiplied by the weighting for that item to establish the component for each line item. The sum of the components for each contractor will identify those contractors which best meet the objectives of the owner for the specific project. Sometimes the result of the analysis will confirm the judgments previously made by the owner, but often there will be surprises. In either case, the process is successful.

But the final selection of the four or five contractors for the "short list" is not complete. Beware of the "numbers game." The sum of the components will identify the best group, possibly six to eight, with small differences in the totals. Subjective factors, factors not able to be included in the "wants" list, should be considered in the final selection. However, this final step should be for the purpose of confirming the rating-times-weighting results or making changes based on real issues; it is not the time to revert to a "my-favorite-contractor" syndrome.

After the selection of the bidding slate has been approved, the selected bidders are contacted to reconfirm their willingness to bid. Only then can the Invitation for Proposals be issued.

INVITATION FOR PROPOSALS

Since the owner has planned the venture, in the planning has established certain policies and principles which will guide its implementation, and has established economic goals, the owner must communicate these and all other aspects of contracts development and project execution to all the bidders in a consistent manner. That is the purpose of the Invitation for Proposals. The Invitation for Proposals is a set of documents, each with its own purpose, which provides a complete basis for the preparation and submission of proposals by contractors, and contains the base documents which will make up the contract to be signed by the parties at contract award. The Invitation for Proposals consists of:

- Transmittal Letter.
- Information to Bidders.
- Proposal Form.
- Agreement Form.
- Job Specification.

All the above documents are issued to all bidders; at contract award, after appropriate modifications as a result of agreements between the owner and the selected contractor, the Agreement and the Job Specification constitute the Contract for the project.

Transmittal Letter

The Transmittal Letter is an essential part of the Invitation. It is sent jointly to all bidders; thus each will know its competition, and if the selection of the bidding slate has been done well, the degree of competition will increase immediately. The letter sets forth only the key items, for example, describes the content of the Invitation package, indicates that the Invitation documents are to be returned to owner at award, states date and time the proposals are to be submitted, and includes other critical, significant items.

Information To Bidders

If each bidder were left on its own to prepare a response to a solicitation for a proposal, the comparison by the owner would at best be chaotic. The Information to Bidders (and the Proposal Form) are developed to avoid that situation by ensuring the consistency and comparability of all proposals. The Information to Bidders is a memorandum which describes in detail the ground rules and procedures which each contractor must follow in the preparation and submission of its proposal. It references the other documents in the Invitation package and establishes the content of the contractor's proposal, including, in certain cases, specifying the format required in submitting information and/or data. The Information to Bidders will contain as a minimum the following:

- Location and brief description of facilities.
- Type of contract (lump sum, reimbursable cost, etc.), contracting mode (competitive, negotiated), scope of services (engineering, procurement, construction).
- Content of Invitation for Proposals.
- Anticipated schedule for issuing owner-prepared specifications to contractor.
- Owner's contact(s) during bidding (name, address, telephone, etc.).
- Requirements regarding exceptions to and comments on Agreement Form.
- Requirements regarding exceptions and alternatives to Job Specification.
- Requirements and content of the technical proposal to be submitted by the contractor.
- Requirements and content of the project execution proposal to be submitted by the contractor.
- Instructions to the contractor regarding the submission of its proposal (number of copies, date and time, name, address, notifications, etc.).

Other significant items will be included which clarify the owner's policies (conflict of interest, business ethics, written documentation); emphasize owner's intent or requirements (safety, merit versus union shop, signing of contract at award, audit, etc.); or direct the contractor's attention to portions of other documents in the Invitation package (confidentiality of owner's information, risk management and insurance policy, use of Proposal Form, content of Job Specification, etc.). When the Information to Bidders is prepared, it should be remembered that the contractor's proposal can only be as good as the instructions provided. Well-developed instructions will make the contractor's work of preparation more efficient and effective, and the selection of the successful contractor for award easier.

Proposal Form

The Proposal Form is prepared to serve as the base document used by the contractor in submitting its proposal. It is developed in parallel with the Agreement Form so that for every piece of information and data required to complete the Agreement Form and prepare it for signature is requested from the bidders. Attachment forms, request for special attachments, etc., are all included as part of the Proposal Form. A representative listing of such items requested includes the following:

- Mechanical completion date.
- List of subcontracted services or work.
- Names of key project personnel.
- Insurance coverages and deductibles.
- Lump sum prices.
- Rates for reimbursable cost contracts, including payroll burdens, departmental overheads, etc.
- Reimbursable cost fixed fees.
- Rates for computer, reproduction, and construction tools.
- Salary and wage charts.
- Estimated scope of engineering and construction management services.
- Employee policies for travel, relocation, etc.
- Exceptions and comments on Agreement Form.
- Exceptions and alternatives to Job Specification.

Thus, the Proposal Form becomes the base document in the contractor's proposal; extra copies of the Proposal Form are sent with the Invitation package and the contractor is required to fill in the form (no changes or alterations allowed), have it signed by an officer, and submit it to the owner (each contractor fills in the required number, each is signed).

Agreement Form

The Agreement Form is a draft prepared by the owner which contains the terms and conditions which it proposes as the basis of the contractual agreement between the parties. Said terms and conditions will govern the rights, duties, obligations, responsibilities, and liabilities of the owner and contractor during the execution of the project. It is either (1) a legal document which is administered by the project teams (owner's and contractor's) during project execution, or (2) an administrative document to guide the actions of the parties during execution, which must be in conformance with law, or (3) both. In any case, it is very important that this document, after it is modified during the bidding and bid review by mutual consent of the owner and contractor, becomes part of the day-to-day tools of the project teams; it eases problems and avoids conflicts.

The owner, in preparing the document, should assess and distribute risk in accordance with the ability of each party to control or provide for in some way. The contractor, in preparing its proposal, should plan execution procedures to control its risk, provide for potential liabilities through insurance and/or risk contingencies in its quotes, and offer exceptions only when it cannot control or provide for otherwise. It is of course necessary to achieve an acceptable contractual basis for a contract to be awarded. And this must be done prior to contract award so that the contractor and owner have no extraneous issues to resolve which will interfere with the execution of the project.

The owner should have standard documents, developed with input from and approval of its law, tax, financial, risk management, and other staff functions, to use as the base document for all contracts. This will assure more efficient contracting, consistency of approach to contractors, and easier responses by a contractor from project to project.

Job Specification

The Job Specification is a compilation of various individual documents, which when taken as a whole define (1) the administrative and procedural requirements for performing all work and services under the contract ("coordination procedure"); (2) the standards to be achieved related to operability, safety, and quality of materials and equipment, and the facilities as a whole (general and specific "standards and practices"); and (3) description of the facilities to be engineered and constructed ("design specifications").

The Job Specification will be a dynamic, evolving document. The type of contract will determine the scope of the Job Specification included in the Invitation for Proposals. For lump sum contracting, the entire Job Specification is required; for reimbursable cost, only the "coordination procedure" is required. Thus, for reimbursable cost contracting much of the Job Specification is issued to the contractor over a period of time during the early phases of project execution. Changes to the Job Specification can only be authorized by the owner, and in each event, if there is a resulting impact on the contractor's cost, schedule, and lump sum price or reimbursable cost fee, a change order is issued by the owner to adjust the respective item.

The contractor will offer exceptions and alternatives to the Job Specification as part of its proposal; these will be resolved during bid review and appropriate modifications will be made in the various documents. At contract award the Contract will consist of the Agreement and the Job Specification; the Agreement will be the precedent document.

CONTRACTORS' PROPOSALS

The Invitation for Proposals is issued to the bidders and each contractor begins the preparation of its proposal. The key to the work of preparing a proposal, and to submitting a proposal which will be viewed favorably by the owner, is a thorough knowledge of the content of the Invitation for Proposals documents. The proposal preparation team should spend sufficient time to become familiar with all aspects of the documents. Questions should be asked of the owner to clarify any item not fully understood (assumption of meanings must be avoided). Visits to the site should normally be made to gain firsthand understanding of potential problems and possible solutions. Often the owner will require such visits, usually a combined visit by all bidders to assure consistency in information given to all bidders. The contractor should assign a leader to its proposal effort, preferably the person to be proposed as its project manager, and enlist other full-time and part-time personnel as appropriate.

The contractor's proposal must address the needs of the specific project. Standard "boilerplate" will not give the owner a satisfactory impression that the contractor understands the project requirements or the scope of work. Alternative execution schemes should be developed and evaluated. These alternatives would address the following items: project organization, key personnel, and staffing; conventional versus computer-assisted engineering and drafting; alternative sources of equipment and materials; subcontracting versus direct hire construction; type of control systems; etc. Evaluation of alternatives provides the basis from which the contractor can choose the proper ingredients which will provide the owner with the lowest-cost facility consistent with the quality and safety parameters and within the desired completion schedule.

Although the owner's Job Specification may seem specific and even appear inflexible, an owner is normally willing to consider unique concepts and innovative ideas which will enhance the project without compromising plant safety and operability. And such concepts and ideas often give the contractor a competitive edge.

The contractor's proposal will consist of three separate proposals:

- Commercial Proposal.
- Project Execution Proposal.
- Technical Proposal.

Commercial Proposal

The Commercial Proposal will consist of the Proposal Form, with all blanks filled in as required and including all attachments, tables, and information requested. This section of the contractor's proposal contains all business terms (lump sum prices, reimbursable cost fees, fixed rates, estimates of services, etc.), plus proposed exceptions, comments, and alternatives to the Agreement Form and Job Specification. It is the most sensitive section of the proposal. Therefore, the Commercial Proposal must always be kept separate from other sections and sealed in special envelopes when the proposal is delivered to the owner. This "sealed bid" procedure enables the owner to maintain the security of the information. The content of the Commercial Proposal is limited to members of the bid review team who have a need to know; no one outside the team has access to the information.

Project Execution Proposal

The content of the Project Execution Proposal will be that defined in the Information to Bidders; it will contain the following material:

- Corporate organization charts including reporting and financial responsibilities to parent organizations.
- Experience on similar projects and in performing engineering and/or construction work at the location.
- Project execution plans which detail how the work on the project will be accomplished including the coordination and management within the engineering office, between offices, and between engineering and field construction.
- Project organization chart showing lines of authority and communications, and job description of each key position, names of proposed key personnel (with resumes and references).
- Work load charts showing total technical personnel and the number of engineering and construction management persons available for assignment to this project.
- Preliminary work schedule reflecting as much detail as is available to the contractor during the preparation of its proposal.
- Detailed explanation of how the contractor plans to perform each function of project execution, namely: engineering, procurement, subcontracting, cost control and estimating, planning and scheduling, expediting, inspection, material control, field construction, and construction management.

- An explanation of contractor's safety practices and how they will be implemented on this project.

Technical Proposal

The content of the Technical Proposal will vary more than any other portion, from very detailed to none required. If the proposal encompasses the provision of the technology, then of course the contractor must provide sufficient information for the owner to make a comparison of proposals and a decision. However, when a competitive proposal is submitted, the technology should be presented in two packages. One will contain nonproprietary/nonconfidential information only; this is submitted to the owner as part of the base proposal, and will be opened and evaluated as part of the initial phase of the bid review. The second package will contain proprietary/confidential information; this will be completed at the same time as the base proposal, sealed for security, and either submitted to owner for holding or held by contractor or a third party until it is needed. If the contractor's proposal remains in contention after the initial review, a confidentiality agreement can be signed and the owner can inspect the second package. This procedure relieves both the owner and contractor of the unnecessary exposure of proprietary information.

Lump sum proposals will contain certain technical details on equipment and materials to be incorporated into the project. This provides the owner a basis for evaluating the facilities to be designed by the contractor to assure itself that the plant will meet the requirements of the Job Specification.

Reimbursable cost proposals for projects which have no technology or process design component normally do not require a Technical Proposal.

BID REVIEW

Bid Review—General

Proposals are submitted by contractors to the person designated by the owner, at the location and time stipulated. Their work for the moment is completed; they must now wait for a response. The owner initiates the bid review phase of contracting. It is often said that contracting planning is the most important step in contracting, and it may be. However, if the owner does not properly plan and implement a thorough and effective bid review, the whole process can be "blown," and the objective of selecting the best contractor, in terms of cost, schedule, quality, and safety, may not be achieved. Bid review is the most difficult step in contracting. It requires a sensitive balancing of facts versus judgments, of objective versus subjective reasoning, of work tasks versus cost, of time versus contract price, of risks versus opportunities. Lump sum and reimbursable cost bid reviews differ considerably. Although the basic procedures apply to all bid reviews, each bid review will be different and the procedures for each effort must be tailored.

Bid Review Practices

The bid review is a complex effort and will follow certain basic practices:

- Bid review planning.
- Dedicated bid review team.
- Sequential review.
- Reviews within bid review.
- Owner-contractor interactions.
- Contract signed at award.

Bid Review Planning. Continuing, progressive planning is required throughout the contracts development. Planning for the bid review ensures that it will be an efficient, effective exercise. The plan developed will require all parties involved to "buy in" and will be the only guide and basis during the actual bid review. Of course events may require some adjustments, but, since the adjustment will be made from a written plan, it will be quicker and easier, and better understood by the participants.

The planning should address all related project and contracting factors including the expected content of the contractors' proposals, bid review objectives, the bid review team's indication of time and activities for each, and a detailed explanation of activities from bid opening to contract award. A typical table of contents of an actual Bid Review Procedure Plan is as follows:

Table of Contents

Project Background
Contracting Background
    Strategy
    Screening
    Bidders
Invitation for Proposals
Contractors' Proposals
Bid Review—General
    Location

Objectives
Sequence
Award
Bid Review Team and Responsibilities
Bid Review—Specifics
  Bid Opening
  Documentation/Internal Communications
  Communications with Bidders
  Initial Review/Selecting Contenders
  Visits to Contractors' Offices
  Evaluation of Key Personnel
  Selection of Contractor for Award
Contract Award
  Award Recommendation
  Contract Award/Signing

In addition to the body of the document, attachments providing relevant details where necessary to further explain the project, and forms which will be used during the bid review are included.

Dedicated Bid Review Team.   Qualified personnel to review the various portions of the contractors' proposals must be selected, relieved of their normal duties during the bid review period, and fully informed of the project and contracting matters. A thorough review/discussion of the Bid Review Procedure Plan with the bid review team prior to receiving proposals is a prime requirement. A typical bid review team organization is shown in Figure 18-5.

Sequential Review.   The bid review will follow the steps set out in the Bid Review Procedure Plan. There is a basic two-step sequence normally followed. The first step occurs after opening and registering all proposals. All parts of each proposal are read completely, all data and information are tabulated to check for completeness and consistency, all necessary calculations are made (for all items not quoted as fixed prices) in order to compare business terms, and the technical, project execution, contractual and other items are evaluated. With this accomplished, the contractors who offer the most complete proposals, submit competitive business terms, provide technical bases conforming to the specifications in the Invitation for Proposals, and offer satisfactory project execution plans and procedures will be identified as contenders for award. The obverse is that the contractors who submit high business terms, and whose technical

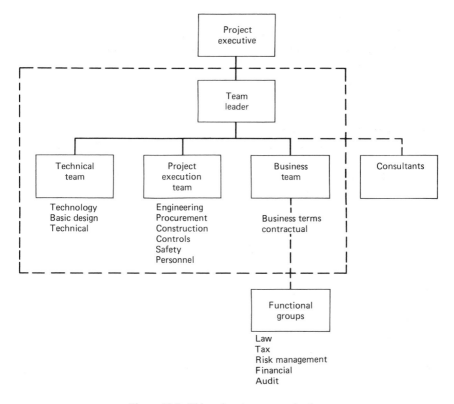

Figure 18-5. Bid review team organization.

and/or project execution plans and procedures are judged to be no stronger than the other contractors, will be dropped from contention.

The second step is then to make a thorough review of the proposals of all contractors remaining in contention. This is the time-consuming portion of the bid review. Whereas the initial step may take up to four days, this step normally takes up to four weeks—even longer in some cases.

Reviews Within Bid Review.   Figure 18-5 (bid review team organization) provides the clue to the reviews-within-bid review concept. If the project/ contracting requires technical input, then there will be three separate reviews: technical, project execution, and business. Each is conducted as a closed review, limited to those persons assigned to that area of the review. No person on an individual team will provide details of the evaluation and appraisal of their part of the review to any person on the other teams. Only the bid review team leader will have access to the entire procedures and actions. This procedure ensures an objective approach for the entire review, and helps maintain security of the proposals' content.

At the conclusion of the detailed review, the three teams share their conclusions and the melding of comparisons and evaluations leads to the selection of the contractor for contract award.

Owner-Contractor Interactions.   There will be extensive interactions between owner and contractor during this period. Formal, written documentation will be the rule. The normal mode is owner-question/contractor-answer. It should be kept in mind that the owner's effort is aimed at clarifying and understanding the proposals, and trying to "upgrade" each proposal to its best possible position. Many times the owner's questions may be a way of making suggestions to strengthen the proposal. The contractor's effort is aimed at providing all necessary information, answering questions promptly, and watching for opportunities to offer technical and/or project execution alternatives which will enhance its proposal.

The bid review requires fair and impartial treatment of all proposals and all contractors. Personnel of owner and contractors must remain vigilant to assure that they are acting in the best interests of both parties. The actual advantage should be with the contractor who makes the best proposal—and only that. Contacts should always be at a business level during bid review; to vary from that can only lead to questions of propriety and perceived or actual conflicts. Being concerned for business ethics is the primary guide in owner-contractor interactions.

Contract Signed at Award.   An important strategy/practice is that all reviews, activities, discussions, and evaluations must be completed before contract award. This includes, most importantly, the resolving of all exceptions, alternatives, and comments to the Contract documents, allowing for the signing of the Contract at contract award. This allows the work to begin immediately after contract award, and the contractor's and owner's project teams can give their undivided attention to the project. In addition, it is simple logic that to know what you have agreed to do before you do it will result in better relationships.

Lump Sum Bid Review

The objective of a lump sum bid review is to determine which contractor offers the lowest lump sum price and provides a proposal which conforms to all technical, project execution, and contractual requirements. Normally the lowest lump sum price, after bid review, determines the successful contractor. However, such factors as plant operating costs (related to equipment selection and/or technology), extraneous owner's cost for travel or relocation costs, etc., or other items may influence the final decision if the quoted lump sum prices are close.

Figure 18-6 charts a typical lump sum bid review. Since lump sum prices are quoted, relatively little work is required in the review of business terms. The major effort is in the review of the technical proposals. Specialists in process technology and design, process equipment, materials, machinery, control systems, electrical, safety and fire protection, and environmental will review the technical proposals to ensure that the plant and facilities being proposed fully conform to the requirements of the Job Specification. Contractors will offer exceptions and alternatives which will provide a more economical plant and a more competitive proposal. These must be evaluated and accepted or rejected (usually with a corresponding adjustment to the quoted lump sum price).

The review of the project execution proposal focuses on the proposed execution plan, key project personnel, and the contractor's procedures and techniques to provide assurances that the contractor can deliver a plant as put forward in its proposal.

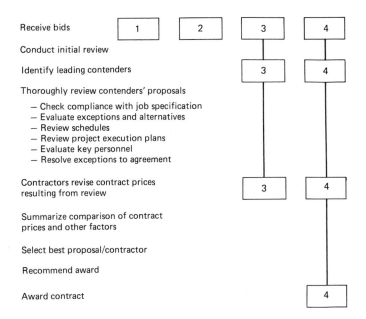

Figure 18-6. Lump sum bid review.

In order to be able to sign the contract at the time of contract award, participants must resolve all exceptions to the Agreement Form during bid review.

After all portions of the proposals have been reviewed, all exceptions, alternatives, questions, and comments have been resolved, and the bid review team is satisfied that all elements are acceptable and in conformance with the Invitation for Proposals, then the selection of the contractor for award can be made.

Reimbursable Cost Bid Review

The objective of a reimbursable cost bid review is to determine which contractor offers the best combination of business terms, technical expertise, and project execution capability. The review is more difficult than a lump sum bid review since a firm total price is not quoted and the bid review team must evaluate the contractors' expertise and capability and quantify the differences to determine which contractor will be able to meet all the owner's technical and project execution requirements and complete the project at the lowest overall cost. This exercise requires experienced personnel with the ability to make objective and subjective evaluations and judgments and translate these into concrete impacts on project cost and project schedules.

Figure 18-7 charts a typical reimbursable cost bid review. The reimbursable cost bid review will consist of a detailed review of all portions of contractors' proposals—commercial, technical, and project execution.

Commercial Proposal.   The commercial proposal includes business terms and contractual considerations. Business terms consist of fee, salaries and wages, payroll burdens, departmental overheads, and fixed rates for computer, reproduction, and other services.

Fee is normally quoted as a fixed amount covering all services performed by the contractor. It consists of the contractor's general corporate overhead and all profit. The contractor also may quote certain cost factors related to changes and an allowance for adjustment to the fee over the life of the project for such changes.

An estimate is made of the total cost of each contractor's engineering, procurement, and construction management services, using the contractor's business terms included in the proposal and the owner's estimate of the hours to be expended. An allowance to cover changes is added.

After all calculations are completed, checked, and tested for reasonableness, a summary of the results is prepared. Figure 18-8 shows a typical summary of business terms. The comparison of the business terms

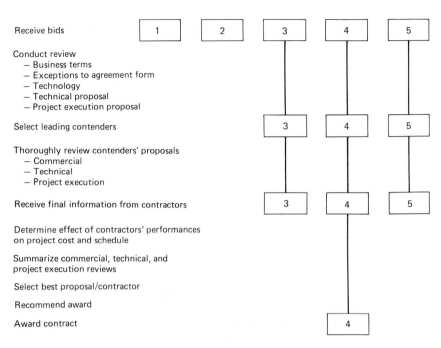

Figure 18-7. Reimbursable cost bid review.

	Contractors			
	A	B	C	D
<u>Fees</u>	XXX	XXX	XXX	XXX
Engineering and procurement				
Salaries and wages	XXX	XXX	XXX	XXX
Payroll burdens	XXX	XXX	XXX	XXX
Departmental overheads	XXX	XXX	XXX	XXX
Allowance for changes	XXX	XXX	XXX	XXX
Subtotal	XXX	XXX	XXX	XXX
Construction management				
Salaries and wages	XXX	XXX	XXX	XXX
Payroll burden	XXX	XXX	XXX	XXX
Expenses	XXX	XXX	XXX	XXX
Allowance for changes	XXX	XXX	XXX	XXX
Subtotal	XXX	XXX	XXX	XXX
Other services (as applicable)	XXX	XXX	XXX	XXX
Total estimated services	XXX	XXX	XXX	XXX
Differential Cost	Base	+	+	+

Figure 18-8. Summary of business terms.

is an important element in the bid review and determines the relative competitiveness of the bidders. However, it is not, as in a lump sum bid review, the primary selection criterion. Experience has shown that a contractor's performance capability can have sufficient impact on savings related to total project cost to offset higher business terms.

Project Execution Proposal.   The project execution proposal contains details on the plans, systems, techniques, and procedures which the contractor will follow in executing the project. These are grouped into four categories:

- Detailed Engineering.
- Procurement/Purchasing.
- Project Controls.
- Field Construction.

Each category is reviewed in detail with each contractor to confirm strengths and discover weaknesses. The objective is to encourage each contractor to modify its proposal in such ways as to capitalize on the strengths and eliminate the weaknesses to bring its project execution proposal up to its best possible position.

When the proposals are analyzed and upgraded, the following items/elements within each category are addressed:

- Detailed Engineering
  —Project organization
  —Office capacity
  —Availability and quality of personnel
  —Key project personnel
  —Project team effectiveness
  —Coordination of work functions
  —Quality of drawings and specifications
  —Standards, procedures, and techniques
  —Use of models and computers
  —Experience: facilities, owner, location
  —Familiarity with codes
- Procurement/Purchasing
  —Project organization
  —Availability and quality of personnel
  —Procedures and techniques
  —Forms and paper flow
  —Experience: facilities, owner, location

—Knowledge of marketplace
—Knowledge of vendors and subcontractors
—Interaction with engineering
—Familiarity with codes
- Project Controls
  —Project organization
  —Procedures and techniques
  —Forms and paper flow
  —Use of computers
  —Availability and quality of personnel
  —Forcasting procedures
  —Reporting systems: quality and timeliness
  —Progress measurement techniques
  —Interaction with engineering and field
- Field Construction
  —Project organization
  —Quality control procedures
  —Safety awareness and procedures
  —Reporting and communications
  —Availability and quality of personnel
  —Knowledge of local labor
  —Experience: facilities, owner, location

The technique for evaluating the project execution capability and translating the evaluation into a cost impact generally is as follows.

EVALUATING ITEMS/ELEMENTS WITHIN CATEGORIES. Each item/element is evaluated with a judgment as to whether it is a strength in the proposal which would have a positive impact on the project cost (i.e., lower the cost), or a weakness which would have a negative impact, or a neutral item having no impact on the cost. These evaluations/judgments are made based on the proposals, question and answer exchanges, review of contractor's past experience, reference checks, and visits to the contractor's office to discuss the project execution with the contractor's personnel (in particular those who will be working on the project) and review actual details on some of the contractor's current assignments. The visit to the contractor's office is the most important.

RATING CONTRACTOR IN EACH CATEGORY. The strength-weakness-neutral evaluations for the items/elements within each category can be weighted by the bid review team, based on the importance of each to the project objectives, and each category can be assigned a numerical rating. The rating will reflect the anticipated performance of the contractor measured against a standard of performance experienced by an "average" contractor on the owner's previous projects. (In a rating scale of 1 to 5, 3 would represent an "average" performance, with 1 representing an anticipated outstanding performance, and 5 representing an anticipated poor performance.)

CALCULATING IMPACT ON PROJECT COST. The performance of the contractor within each category, or a subcategory, will impact a certain portion of the project cost. For example, a contractor's performance in the category of purchasing/procurement will impact the cost of materials, equipment, and subcontracts. The bid review team can determine which areas are impacted within each category and from the owner's cost estimate assign the cost to that area. The team also needs to determine the variation in anticipated cost from an outstanding performance (a 1 rating in the above rating scale) and a poor performance (a 5 rating). (If the team decides that the variation will be ±10%, a 1 rating will reduce the cost area effect by the category by 10%, and a 5 rating will add 10%.)

The calculation of the cost impact for each category will be (i) the ratio of assigned rating versus "average" rating ("1" assigned 100% of savings, "2" assigned 50% of savings, "3" no impact, "4" assigned 50% of added cost, "5" assigned 100% of added cost) times (ii) the cost of area affected times (iii) the anticipated percentage variation. The algebraic sum of the calculated impacts for each category indicates the relative impact which each contractor's performance will have on the project cost and identifies the best execution contractor.

Technical Proposal. The review of the technical proposal is not as detailed as for a lump sum proposal unless the proposal includes the provision of technology. Otherwise the review is generally integrated into the project execution review.

Bid Review Summary

Upon completion of the three separate reviews—commercial, project execution, technical—the bid review team will combine the results and make the selection of the contractor to recommend for award.

AWARD RECOMMENDATION

After the bid review is completed, and after the best proposal/best contractor has been identified and selected, an Award Recommendation is prepared. The purpose of the Award Recommendation is twofold: (1) to present the conclusion to management for approval, and (2) to document the results of the bid review for the records. The Award Recommendation will consist of the following:

- Introduction/Purpose.
- Project Background.
- Contracting Background.
- Award Recommendation.
- Summary of Business Terms.
- Summary of Project Execution Proposals.
- Summary of Technical Proposals.
- Status of Contract Documents.
- Significant Issues and Resolutions.
- Summary of Bid Review.
- Steps to Contract Award.

CONTRACT AWARD

After approval by management, all open items, if any, are resolved with the selected contractor, the Contract documents are modified to reflect the owner-contractor agreements, and the Contract is awarded and signed.

CONCLUSION

The partnership created during the contracts development phase of a project, following well-established techniques and procedures, has a firm foundation. The project can be successful; the owner can meet its objectives; the contractor can meet its objectives. But success is not assured. The project is now in the hands of the contractor's and owner's project management teams. A continuing emphasis on partnership, a continuing basis of trust and mutual respect, and the application of fairness and reasonableness by both parties will allow the proper application of engineering and construction skills and knowledge for the successful completion of the work.

19. Developing Winning Proposals

Hans J. Thamhain*

MARKETING PROJECTS AND PRODUCTS

New contracts are the lifeblood for many project-oriented businesses. The techniques for winning these contracts follow established bid proposal practices which are highly specialized for each market segment. They often require intense and disciplined team efforts among all organizational functions, especially from operations and marketing. They also require significant customer involvement.

What Makes Project Marketing Different?

Projects are different from products in many respects. Marketing projects requires the ability to identify, pursue, and capture one-of-a-kind business opportunities. The process is characterized as follows:

1. *Systematic Effort.* A systematic effort is usually required to develop a new program lead into an actual contract. The program acquisition effort is often highly integrated with ongoing programs and involves key personnel from both the potential customer and the performing organization.
2. *Custom Design.* While traditional businesses provide standard products and services for a variety of applications and customers, projects are custom-designed items to fit specific requirements of a single customer community.
3. *Project Life Cycle.* Project-oriented businesses have a beginning and an end and are not self-perpetuating. Business must be generated on

* Hans J. Thamhain is Associate Professor of Management at Bentley College in Waltham, MA. He has held engineering and project management positions with GTE, General Electric, Westinghouse, and ITT. Dr. Thamhain is well known for his research and writings in project management which include 4 books and 60 journal articles. He also conducts seminars and consults in all phases of project management for industry and government.

a project-by-project basis rather than by creating demand for a standard product or service.

4. *Marketing Phase.* Long lead times often exist between project definition, start-up, and completion.

5. *Risks.* Risks are present, especially in the research, design, and production of programs. The program manager has not only to integrate the multidisciplinary tasks and program elements within budget and schedule constraints, but also to manage inventions and technology.

6. *Technical Capability to Perform.* This capability is critical to the successful pursuit and acquisition of a new project or program.

In addition to the above differences of project versus product businesses, there is another distinction that can be drawn on the basis of external versus internal opportunities. While the remainder of this chapter focuses on developing new business from external sources, the process and challenges are very similar for pursuing company-internal business such as a new product development. Competition over scarce resources and business alternatives, as well as sound business practices, make the budget approval for a new internal development often a very intricate, involved, and highly competitive process. A brief comparison of internally versus externally funded contrast acquisitions and executions is summarized in Table 19-1.

Selling a Project

In spite of the risks and problems, contract profits are usually very low on projects in comparison with those from commercial business practices. One may wonder why companies pursue project businesses. Clearly there are many reasons why projects and programs are good business.

1. Although immediate profits, as a percentage of sales, are usually small, the return on capital investment is often very attractive. Progress payment practices keep inventories and receivables to a minimum and enable companies to undertake programs many times larger in value than the assets of the total company.

2. Once a contract has been secured and is being managed properly, the program is of relatively low financial risk to the company. The company has little additional selling expenditure and has a predictable market over the life cycle of the program.

3. Program business must be viewed from a broader perspective than motivation for immediate profits. It provides an opportunity to de-

Table 19-1. Characteristics of Internal Versus External Contracts.

ITEM	COMPANY-INTERNAL DEVELOPMENT SUCH AS NEW PRODUCT DEVELOPMENT	COMPANY-EXTERNAL CONTRACT VIA BID PROPOSAL
New product idea	Evolutionary process driven either by market needs or technological capabilities. Often the process involves personnel involvement throughout the organization.	Opportunity-driven process based on single customer needs and requirements.
Product (or service design)	Standard product designed for a variety of applications and customers, company-funded development.	Custom-designed item to fit specific requirement. Customer-funded development.
Funding	Company-internal funding through budgeting process.	Customer funding via competitive bidding process.
Pricing	Competitive pricing, highly dynamic, strategically influenced.	Negotiated price, often based on actual cost.
Engineering kickoff	Design kickoff based on general management decision after careful study.	Design kickoff. Based on customer contract award after complex bidding process.
Role of engineering-marketing team	Strong engineering-marketing cooperation prior to product development. Predominately marketing "effort during product introduction and beyond."	Strong engineering-marketing team effort throughout preproposal and proposed phase—then effort shifts to engineering.

velop the company's technical capabilities and to build an experience base for future business growth.

4. Winning one program contract often provides attractive growth potential, such as (1) growth with the program via additions and changes; (2) follow-on work; (3) spare parts, maintenance, and training; and (4) the ability to compete effectively in the next program phase, such as nurturing a study program into a development and finally a production contract.

In summary, new business is the lifeblood of an organization. It is especially crucial in project-oriented businesses, which lack the ongoing nature of conventional markets.

PROPOSAL TYPES AND FORMATS

The majority of proposals that are prepared by companies are based on inquiries received from prospective clients. The inquiry stipulates the conditions under which the clients wish the work to be done. The responses we make to inquiries received from clients are termed "proposals," even though in many cases no commitment is proposed. Accordingly, proposals can be classified broadly in two major categories: *qualification proposals* and *commercial bid proposals*.

The *qualification proposal* generally gives information about company organization, qualifications, working procedures, or information for a specific area of technology. Qualification proposals make no offer to perform services and make no commitments of a general or technical nature. These are also called *informational proposals* if the contents relate to company organization, general qualifications, and procedures. They are sometimes called *white papers, technical presentations,* or *technical volumes* if technical and economic data are provided for a specific area of technology. A special form of the qualification proposal is the presentation.

The commercial bid proposal offers a definite commitment by the company to perform specific work or services, or to provide equipment in accordance with explicit terms of compensation. A commercial bid proposal may also contain the type of information usually found in qualification proposals.

Both qualification and commercial proposals may be presented to the client in various forms under a wide variety of titles, depending on the situation, for example, the client's requirements and the firm's willingness to commit its resources under the specific circumstances involved. The most common forms are:

- Letter proposals.
- Preliminary proposals.
- Detailed proposals.
- Presentations.

There are no sharp distinctions among these on the basis of content. Differentiation is mainly by the extent of the work required to prepare them. Included in the following paragraphs are definitions of these most common forms.

Letter proposals are either qualification or commercial proposals. They are brief enough to be issued in letter form rather than as bound volumes.

Preliminary proposals are either qualification or commercial proposals and are large enough to be issued as bound volumes. They may be paid technical and/or economic studies, bids to furnish services, or other offerings of this kind.

Detailed proposals are most often commercial bid proposals, generally including the preparation of a detailed estimate. They are the most complex and inclusive proposals. Because of the high cost of preparation and the high stakes involved in the commitments offered, organization and contents of the documents are defined and detailed to a much greater degree than other kinds of proposals.

Presentations are generally in the nature of oral qualification proposals. Selected personnel, specialized in various areas, describe their subjects verbally to client representatives in time periods varying from an hour to an entire day. To aid in the success of a presentation, audio-visual aids are encouraged. Many companies maintain a library of photographic slides developed just for this purpose.

DEFINING THE MARKET

Customers come in various forms and sizes. Particularly for large programs with multiple-user groups, customer communities can be very large, complex, and heterogeneous. Very large programs, such as military or aerospace undertakings, are often sponsored by thousands of key individuals representing the user community, procuring agencies, Congress, and interest groups. Selling to such a diversified heterogeneous customer is a true marketing challenge which requires a highly sohpisticated and disciplined approach.

The first step in a new business development effort is to define the market to be pursued. The market segment for a new program opportunity is normally in an area of relevant past experience, technical capability, and customer involvement. Good marketeers in the program business have to think as product line managers. They have to understand all dimensions of the business and be able to define and pursue market objectives consistent with the capabilities of their organizations.

Market Predictability

Program businesses operate in an opportunity-driven market. It is a mistaken belief, however, that these markets are unpredictable and unmanageable. Market planning and strategizing are important. New program opportunities develop over periods of time, sometimes years for larger programs. These developments must be properly tracked and cultivated to form the basis for management actions such as (1) bid decisions, (2) resource commitment, (3) technical readiness, and (4) effective customer liaison.

The strategy of winning new business is supported by systematic, disciplined approaches which are illustrated in Figure 19-1 and discussed in five basic steps:

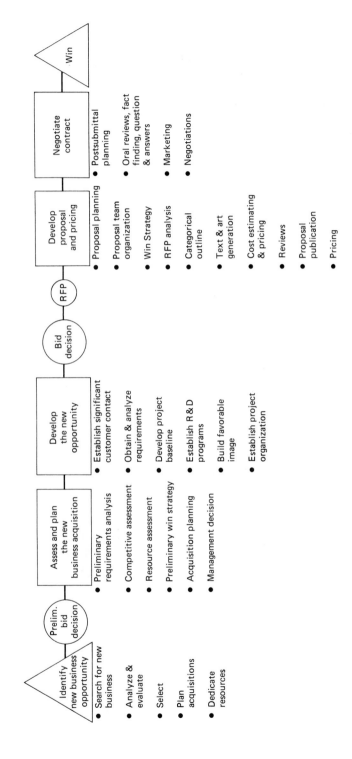

Figure 19-1. Major phases and milestones in a bid proposal life cycle.

1. Identifying new business opportunities.
2. Planning the business acquisition.
3. Developing the new contract opportunity.
4. Developing a winning proposal and pricing.
5. Negotiating and closing the contract.

IDENTIFYING NEW BUSINESS OPPORTUNITIES

Identifying a new program opportunity is a marketing job. During the initial stages one does not evaluate or pursue the opportunity—that comes later. Furthermore, identifying new opportunities should be an ongoing activity. It involves the scanning of the relevant market sector for new business. This function should be performed by all members of the project team in addition to marketing support groups. There are many sources for identifying new business leads such as customer meetings on ongoing programs, professional meetings and conventions, trade shows, trade journals, customer service, advertising of capabilities, and personal contacts.

All one can expect at this point is to learn of an established or potential customer requirement in one of the following categories:

- Follow-on to previous or current programs.
- Next phase of program.
- Additions or changes to ongoing programs.
- New programs in your established market sector or area of technological strength.
- New programs in related markets.
- Related programs, such as training, maintenance, or spares.

For most businesses, ongoing program activities are the best source of new opportunity leads. Not only are the lines of customer communication better than in a new market but, more importantly, the image as an experienced, reliable contractor hopefully has been established, giving a clear competitive advantage in any further business pursuit.

The target result of this analysis is an acquisition plan and a bid decision. Analyzing the new opportunity and preparing the acquisition plan is an interactive effort. Often many meetings are needed between the customer and the performing organization before a clear picture emerges of both customer requirements and contractor's capabilities. A major fringe benefit of proper customer contact is the potential for building confidence and credibility with the customers. It shows that your organization understands their requirements and has the capability to fulfill them. This is a necessary prerequisite for eventually negotiating the contract. The new business identification phase concludes with a formal analysis of the new project opportunity, which is summarized in the following section.

PLANNING THE BUSINESS ACQUISITION

The acquisition plan provides the basis for the formal bid decision and a detailed plan for the acquisition of the new business. The plan is an important management tool which provides *an assessment of the new program opportunity as a basis for appropriating resources for developing and bidding the new business.*

Typically the new business acquisition plan should include the following elements:

1. *Brief Description of New Business Opportunity.* A statement of the requirements, specifications, scope, schedule, budget, customer organization, and key decision makers.
2. *Why Should We Bid?* A perspective with regard to establishing business plans and desirable results, such as profits, markets, growth, and technology.
3. *Competitive Assessment.* A description of each competing firm with regard to their past activities in the subject area, including (a) related experiences, (b) current contracts, (c) customer interfaces, (d) specific strengths and weaknesses, and (e) potential baseline approach.
4. *Critical Win Factors.* A listing of specific factors important to winning the new program, including their rationales. (Example: low implementation risk and short schedule important to customer because of need for equipment in two years.)
5. *Ability to Write a Winning Proposal.* The specifics needed to prepare a winning proposal, including (a) availability of the right proposal personnel, (b) understanding of customer problems, (c) unique competitive advantage, (d) expected bid cost to be under customer budget, (e) special arrangements such as teaming or license model, (f) engineering readiness to write proposal, and (g) ability to price competitively.
6. *Win Strategy.* A chronological listing of critical milestones guiding the acquisition effort from its present position to winning the new program. It should show those activities critical for positioning yourself uniquely in the competitive field. This includes timing and responsible individuals for each milestone. For example, if low implementation risk and short schedules are important to the customer, the summary of the win strategy may state:

(a) Build credibility with the customer by introducing key personnel and discussing baseline prior to request for proposal, (b) stress related experiences on ABC program, (c) guarantee 100% dedicated personnel and list program personnel by name, (d) submit detailed schedule with measurable milestones and specific reviews, (e) submit XYZ module with proposal for evaluation.

7. *Capture Plan.* A detailed action plan in support of the win strategy and all business plans. This should integrate the critical win factors and specific action plan. All activities, such as timing, budgets, and responsible individuals identified, should have measurable milestones. The capture plan is a working document to map out and guide the overall acquisition effort. It is a living document which should be revised and refined as the acquisition effort progresses.
8. *Ability to Perform Under Contract.* This is often a separate document, but a summary should be included in the acquisition plan stating (a) technical requirements, (b) work force, (c) facilities, (d) teaming and subcontracting, and (e) program schedules.
9. *Problems and Risks.* A list of problems critical to the implementation of the capture plan, such as (a) risks to techniques, staffing, facilities, schedules, or procurement; (b) customer-originated risks; (c) licenses/patents/rights; and (d) contingency plan.
10. *Resource Plan.* A summary of the key personnel, support services, and other resources needed for capturing the new business. The bottom line of this plan is the total acquisition cost.

There are many ways to present the acquisition plan. However, an established format, which is accepted as a standard throughout the organization, has several advantages. It provides a unified standard format for quickly finding information during a review or analysis. Standard forms also serve as checklists. They force the planner not only to include information conveniently obtainable, but also to seek out the other data necessary for winning new business. Finally, a standard format provides a quick and easy assessment of the new opportunity for key decision makers.

The Bid Board

Few decisions are more fundamental to new business than the bid decision. Resources for the pursuit of new business come from operating profits. These resources are scarce and should be carefully controlled.

Bid boards serve as management gates for the release and control of these resources. The bid board is an expert panel, usually convened by the general manager, which analyzes the acquisition activities to determine their status and also to assess investment versus opportunity in acquiring new business. An acquisition plan provides the major framework for the meeting of such bid boards.

Major acquisitions require a series of bid board sessions, starting as early as 12 to 18 months prior to the request for proposal. Subsequent bid boards reaffirm the bid decision and update the acquisition plans. It is the responsibility of the proposal manager to gather and present pertinent information in a manner that provides the bid board with complete information for analysis and decision. A simple form, such as shown in Table 19-2, can help in organizing and summarizing the information needed. This requires significant preparation and customer contact. A team presentation is effective as all disciplines should be involved.

Table 19-2. Request for Approval of Bid Decision.

Date: _____

No: _____

1. Client _____
2. Project _____
3. Units and Capacities _____
4. Location _____
5. Scope of Work _____
6. Value of Project _____
7. Type of Contract _____
8. Type of Proposal _____
9. Proposal Cost _____
10. Due Date of Proposal _____
11. % Probability to Go Ahead _____
12. % Probability for Award to Company _____
13. Other Factors
    a. Time of Award (if long range) _____
    b. Financing (if financing involved) _____
    c. Source of Know-how (if other than company) _____
    d. Special Contract Conditions (if not company standard) _____
    e. Manpower Availability (if not readily available) _____
    f. Secrecy Conditions (if any) _____
    g. Competition (if known) _____
    h. Unusual factors (if any) _____

Management Review Committee

Approved By: _____   Date: _____

The Bid Decision

After the proposal inquiry is received and logged in, it should be screened as soon as possible to facilitate the bid/no-bid decision. Because most inquiries have a short response time, the sooner a decision can be made, the longer you have to prepare your proposal. As part of the screening process, it is important that the sales representative or proposal manager review the document thoroughly to determine its total value to the organization. It also allows the decision makers to determine if they have the capabilities required to bid on the job. The technical nature of the current marketplace is such that organizations must compete in specialized areas of an industry. Careful screening of the inquiry may also reveal that more information is needed to prepare a responsive proposal properly. A bid/ no-bid decision is usually made based upon a set of criteria judged to be important in selecting projects that contribute to an organization's continued growth and success. A typical set of criteria to be answered is shown in Table 19-3.

Once a decision is made not to bid on a project, the customer should be notified in writing. Some organizations respond with a form letter, but such a response could cause the customer to interpret this as lack of interest and could result in loss of future work. A specific letter for that inquiry should be prepared, explaining to the customer why your organization could not respond.

PHASES OF A TYPICAL CONTRACT DEVELOPMENT

We live in a competitive world. Winning new business requires significant homework in preparation for the bid proposal. Selling a new program is often unique and different from selling in other markets. It requires selling an organization's capability for a custom development—something that has not been done before. This is different from selling an off-the-shelf product that can be examined prior to contract. It requires establishing your credibility and building confidence in the customer's mind so that your organization is selected as the best candidate for the new program. Such a "can-do" image can be built in four phases.

First: Significant Customer Contact

Early customer liaison is vital in learning about the customer's requirements and needs. It is necessary to define the project baseline, the potential problem areas, and the risks involved.

Table 19-3. Checklist in Support of Bid Decision.

1. Does company have capabilities and resources to perform the work?
2. Can company phase in the work to meet client schedule?
3. What is company's technical position?
4. What is company's approach to project execution?
5. Is project of special importance to client?
6. Would doing project enhance our reputation?
7. What has been our past experience and contractual relationship with client?
8. What is company's commercial approach and price strategy?
9. What are client's future capital expenditures?
10. Who is the competition and do they have any special advantages?
11. Does client have preferred contractor and if so, why?
12. What is the probability of project going ahead?
13. Does project meet the immediate or long-range objectives of the company?
14. Other work prospects for company in next six months? one year?
15. Other special factors and considerations?

Establishing meaningful customer contact is no simple task. Today's structured customer organizations involve many key decision-making personnel, conflicting requirements and needs, and biases. There rarely is only one person responsible for signing off on a major procurement. Technical and marketing involvement at all levels is necessary to reach all decision-making parties in the customer community. Your new business acquisition plan will be the road map for your marketing efforts. The benefits of this customer contact are that you:

- Learn about the specific customer requirements.
- Obtain information for refining the baseline prior to proposal.
- Participate in customer problem solving.
- Build a favorable image as a competent, credible contractor.
- Check out your baseline approach and its acceptability to the customer.
- Develop rapport and a good working relationship with the customer.

Second: Prior Relevant Experience

Nothing is more convincing to an engineering customer than demonstrated prior performance in the same or a related area of the new program. It shows the customer that you have produced on a similar task. This reduces the perceived technical risks and associated budget and schedule uncertainties. Therefore it is of vital importance to demonstrate to the customer that your organization (1) understands their new requirements, and (2) has performed satisfactorily on similar programs. This image of an experienced contractor can be communicated in many ways:

- Field demonstration of working systems and equipment.
- Listing of previous or current customers, their equipment, and applications.
- Model demonstrations.
- Technical status presentations.
- Product promotional folders.
- Technical papers and articles.
- Trade show demonstrations and displays.
- Slide or video presentation of equipment in operation.
- Simulation of the system, equipment, or services.
- Specifications, photos, input/output simulations of the proposed equipment.
- Advertisements.

Demonstrating prior experience is integrated and interactive with the customer liaison activities. To be successful, particularly on larger programs, requires both leadership and discipline. Start with a well-defined customer contact plan as part of your overall acquisition plan. This requires well-planned involvement at all levels in order to make these contacts with relevant personnel in the customer community. One major benefit received from these intensive marketing efforts is that you create an image with the customer as an experienced, sound contractor. Second, you are learning more about the new program, its specific requirements, the risks involved, as well as the concerns and biases of the customer. This information will make it easier to respond effectively to a formal or informal request for proposal.

Third: Readiness to Perform

Once the basic requirements and specifications of the new program are known, it is often necessary to mount a substantial technical preproposal effort to advance the baseline design to a point that permits a clear definition of the new program. These efforts may be funded by the customer or borne by the contractor. Typical efforts include (1) feasibility studies, (2) system designs, (3) simulation, (4) design and testing of certain critical elements in the new equipment or the new process, (5) prototype models, or (6) any developments necessary to bid the new job within the desired scope of technical and financial risks.

Development prior to contract is expensive, has no guarantee of return, and precludes the company from pursuing other activities. Then why do organizations spend their resources for such development? It is often an absolutely necessary cost for winning new business. These early developments reduce the implementation risks to an acceptable level for both the customer and the contractor. Further, these developments might be necessary to catch up with a competitor or to convince the customer that certain alternative approaches are preferable.

Clearly, preproposal developments are costly. Therefore they should be thorough and well detailed and approved as part of the overall acquisition plan. The plans and specific results should be accurately communicated to the customer. This will help to build quality image for your firm while giving the potential contractor additional insight into the detailed program requirements. Finally, one should not overlook two sources of funding for these activities: (1) customer funding for these advanced programs prior to contract—often the customer is willing to fund contract-definition activities because it may reduce the risks and the uncertainties of contractual performance; (2) inclusion with other ongoing developments—the program manager might find that a similar effort is under way in a corporate research department or even within the customer's organization.

Fourth: Establishing the Organization

Another element of credibility is the contractor's organizational readiness to perform under contract. This includes facilities, key personnel, support groups, and management structure. Reliability in this area is particularly critical in winning a large program relative to your company size. Often a contractor goes out on a limb and establishes a new program organization to satisfy specific program or customer requirements. This may require major organizational changes.

Few companies go into reorganization lightly, especially prior to contract. However, in most cases it is possible to establish all the elements of the new program organization without physically moving people or facilities, and without erecting new buildings. What is needed is an organization plan exactly detailing the procedures to be followed as soon as the contract is awarded. Further, the new program organization can be defined on paper together with its proper charter and all structural and authority relationships. This should be sufficient for customer discussion and will give a head start once the contract is received. Usually it is not the moving of partitions, people, or facilities that takes time, but determining where to move them and how to establish the necessary working relationships.

As a checklist, the following organizational components should be defined clearly and discussed with the customer prior to a major new contract:

- Organizational structure.
- Charter.
- Policy-management guidelines.
- Job description.
- Authority and responsibility relationships.
- Type and number of offices and laboratories.
- Facilities listing.
- Floor plans.
- Staffing plan.
- Milestone schedule and budget for reorganization.

A company seldom needs to reorganize completely to accommodate a new program. It requires resources and risks for both the contractor and the customer. Most likely the customer and program requirements can be accommodated within the existing organization by redefining organizational relationships, authority, and responsibility structures without physically moving people and facilities. Matrix organizations in particular have the flexibility and capacity to handle large additional program business with only minor organizational changes.

Fifth: The Kickoff Meeting

Soon after the decision to bid has been made, a preliminary proposal kickoff meeting or proposal strategy planning meeting should be held. This meeting, chaired by the proposal manager, consists of the heads of the various contributing departments, the sales representative, and possibly senior management. Because there is a limited amount of time available for preparation of a proposal, it is mandatory that the proposal effort be planned in all aspects to make the most use of that time.

After the strategy meeting and development of a preliminary proposal plan, the proposal manager calls a kickoff meeting. This meeting is attended by all participants working on the proposal or their representatives. The proposal manager writes a kickoff memo or notice to inform the participating departments what is required to be discussed at the meeting regarding the proposal effort. The purpose of the kickoff meeting is to inform all participants of the proposal plan and objectives.

To ensure a good start, the following topics should be covered in every kickoff meeting:

- *Project scope.* The type of plant or unit, the client, the project location, the order of magnitude total installed cost (if known), the job or proposal number, and any other general identification are designated, as well as the proposal manager and other key personnel.
- *Commercial objectives.* The type of proposal required is discussed as well as the management philosophy to be incorporated into the proposal. The marketing representative can often effectively provide background information on the client's requirements, exceptions, and the competitive challenges.
- *Proposal staffing.* Three factors—the proposal schedule, man-hour budget, and the technical proposal requirements—determine which departments will participate and also set the specific proposal staffing requirements. Staffing should have been settled before the kickoff meeting.
- *Assignments of participants.* Work assignments with clear areas of responsibility will be made. Relationships between participating departments should be spelled out.
- *Proposal dates, schedules, and budget.* The key dates for issuance of proposal documents and completion of important portions of the work should be discussed and the participants advised of the available man-hour budget and deadlines.
- *Qualifications.* The proposal must be tailored to sell the client on your qualifications and capabilities. The desired strategy to accomplish this should be communicated to all involved.
- *Type of estimate.* Unless the type of estimate to be submitted with the proposal has already been decided, the proposal manager defines clearly the requirements and the type of information that must be generated by the participants in the proposal effort.
- *Final proposal contents.* Specific requirements for the contents should be brought to everyone's attention. The proposal manager develops and includes a tentative table of contents for the proposal documents under discussion. Definite assignments for preparation of the draft write-ups for each section of the proposal are also made.
- *Working information.* Copies or a summary of the inquiry documents are distributed before or during the kickoff together with any other information from the client that is to be used in preparing the proposal.

The kickoff meeting is the prefered device for starting the proposal work, especially for complex efforts. It is held shortly after work authorization has been received and sales objectives have been established. Production work on the proposal begins after the kickoff meeting.

The proposal manager sets the meeting time and place. Attendance is limited to those who actually contribute to the definition and initiation of the proposal effort, such as the following persons:

- Sales representatives responsible for the inquiry.
- Heads of departments and groups responsible for any of the proposal work.
- Key personnel from departments and groups responsible for any of the proposal work, if they have been selected.
- The general manager of operations and a member of the legal department responsible for proposal review, who are notified of the meeting so they may attend if they wish.

There are no strict rules for the agenda of a kickoff meeting because of the wide variations in the nature of the inquiries received and the proposals developed in reply to them. However, in general, the following topics should be covered in every kickoff meeting to ensure a good start:

1. Purpose. Type of proposal and estimate to be prepared.
2. Plan of approach. Explanation of methods to be used.
3. Action. Specific duties of individuals and groups.
4. Proposal schedule. Indication of key dates for internal submission of parts of the work.

In addition to covering the elements of the client's request and the proposal response to them, the kickoff meeting also serves to:

- Outline the marketing strategy behind the proposal.
- Establish management's interest in the project.
- Introduce team members to each other.
- Create interchange of ideas and suggestions early.
- Obtain overall agreement of work assignments and timing.
- Develop a winning attitude in the proposal effort.

The proposal manager is responsible for preparing the minutes of the kickoff meeting, which are issued no later than the second working day after the meeting.

DEVELOPING A WINNING PROPOSAL

Bid proposals are payoff vehicles. They are one of the final products of your marketing effort. Whether you are bidding on a service contract or an engineering development, a government contract or a commercial program, the process is the same and, in the end, you must submit a proposal.

Yet with all due respect to the importance of the bid proposal as a marketing tool, many senior managers point out that the proposal is only one part of the total marketing effort. The proposal is usually not the vehicle that sells your program—the proposal stage may be too late. The program concept and the soundness of its approach, the alternatives, your credibility, and so on, must be established during the face-to-face discussions with the customer. So why this fuss about writing a superior proposal? Because we still live in a competitive world. Your competition is working toward the same goal of winning this program. They, too, may have sold the customer on their approaches and capabilities. Hence among the top contenders, the field is probably very close. More importantly, beating most of the competition is not good enough. Like in a poker game, there is no second place. Therefore, while it is correct that the proposal is only part of the total marketing effort, it must be a superior proposal. Proposal development is a serious business in itself. Table 19-4 shows a topical outline for a typical major bid proposal which is broken into three volumes: technical, management, and cost, a common subdivision used in formal bidding practices.

Most people hate to work on proposals. Proposal development requires hard work and long hours, often in a constantly changing work environment. Proposals are multidisciplinary efforts of a special kind. But like any other multifunctional program, they require an orderly and disciplined effort which relies on many special tools to integrate the various activities of developing a high-scoring quality proposal. This is particularly true for large program proposals which require large capital commitments. Smaller proposals often can be managed with less formality. However, at a minimum, they should include the following tasks to ensure a quality bid proposal:

- Proposal team organization.
- Proposal schedule.
- Categorical outline with writing assignments and page allocation.
- Tone and emphasis/win strategy.
- RFP analysis.
- Technical baseline review.
- Draft writing.
- Reviews.
- Art/illustration development.
- Cost estimating.
- Proposal production.
- Final management review.

Table 19-4. Bid Proposal Content: Three Volumes.

The bid package consists of three basic parts or volumes with the following subtopics

1. TECHNICAL PROPOSAL	2. MANAGEMENT	3. COST PROPOSAL
Introduction and background to contractor's company	Process schedule	Price for services offered in proposal
Organization of contractor's company	Process description	Breakdown of price (materials, labor, etc.)
Schedule of professional personnel	Operating requirements	Escalations (lump sum contract)
Resume of key personnel or a resume summary	Plot plans and elevations	Amount for subcontract work
Project management policy or philosophy	Process flow diagrams	Amount of off-site facilities
Description of contractor's engineering department	Engineering flow diagrams	Taxes
Description of contractor's procurement department	Utilities flow diagrams	Royalty payment
Description of contractor's financial controls department	Heat and material balance	Alternative systems
Experience list of similar plants built	Equipment list	Optional equipment
Experience list of large complexes built	Equipment data sheets	Prior adjustments (labor, efficiency, etc.)
Experience list of all plants built by contractor	General facilities, such as piping, instrumentation, electrical, civil, construction, etc.	Schedule of payments
Experience list of using a client's process	Contractor's or client's specifications or standards	
Photographs of plants built by contractor	Services provided by contractor	
Draft contract	Services provided by client	
	Model and/or rendering of proposed plant	

For each activity or milestone the plan should define the responsible individual(s) and schedules.

Storyboarding Facilitates Group Writing

Most bid proposals are group writing efforts. Organizing, coordinating, and integrating these team efforts can add significantly to the complexities and difficulties of managing proposal developments. Especially for the larger engineering development bids, storyboarding is a technique that facilitates the group writing process by breaking down its complexities and integrating the proposal work incrementally.

How Does It Work?

Storyboarding is based on the idea of splitting up the proposal writing among the various contributors and then developing the text incrementally via a series of writing, editing, and review phases, typically in the following order and timing:

1.	Categorical Outline	Completion at Day 1
2.	Synopsis of Approach	Day 3
3.	Roundtable Review	Day 4
4.	Topical Outline	Day 5
5.	Storyboards	Day 10
6.	Storyboard Review	Day 11
7.	Storyboard Expansion	Day 22
8.	Staff Review	Day 24
9.	Editing	Day 28
10.	Printing and Delivery	Day 30

The number and type of phases indicated in the above listing, together with the timing, might be typical for a major bid proposal development with a 30-day response time. However, the above listing can also serve as a guide for larger or smaller proposals by scaling the effort up or down. For larger efforts more iterations are suggested among phases 5 and 9, while smaller efforts can be scaled down to seven phases, including only phases 4 through 10.

The actual timing of proposal developments should be scheduled like any other project. A bar graph schedule is sufficient and effective for most proposal efforts. Each phase is briefly described next.

Phase One: Categorical Outline

The first step in the storyboarding process is the development of a categorical outline. This is a listing of the major topics or chapters to be covered in the proposal. For larger proposals, the categorical outline might form the first two levels of the table of content, such as shown in Figure 19-2. The categorical outline should also show for each category (1) the responsible author, (2) a page estimate, and (3) references to related documents. The Categorical Outline can often be developed *before* the receipt of the RFP, and should be finalized at the time of proposal kickoff.

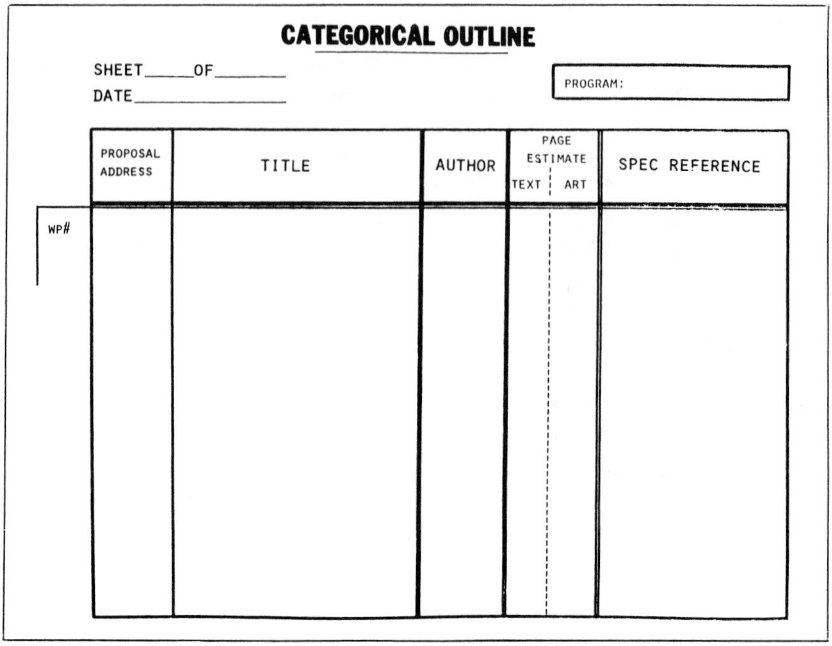
CATEGORICAL OUTLINE

SHEET_____OF_______

DATE_______________

PROGRAM:

PROPOSAL ADDRESS	TITLE	AUTHOR	PAGE ESTIMATE TEXT	ART	SPEC REFERENCE

WP#

Figure 19-2. Typical Categorical Outline form for a major proposal.

Phase Two: Synopsis of Approach

A synopsis of approach is developed for each categorical topic by each responsible author. The Synopsis is an outline of the approach which addresses three questions related to the specific topic:

1. What does the customer require?
2. How are we planning to respond?
3. Why is the approach sound and good?

The format of a typical Synopsis is shown in Figure 19-3. As an alternative, the proposal manager can prepare these forms and issue them as policy papers instead of having each author develop them.

In preparation for the review, the completed Synopsis forms and Categorical Outline can be posted on a wall, in sequential order. This method of display facilitates in a very effective way open group reviews and analysis.

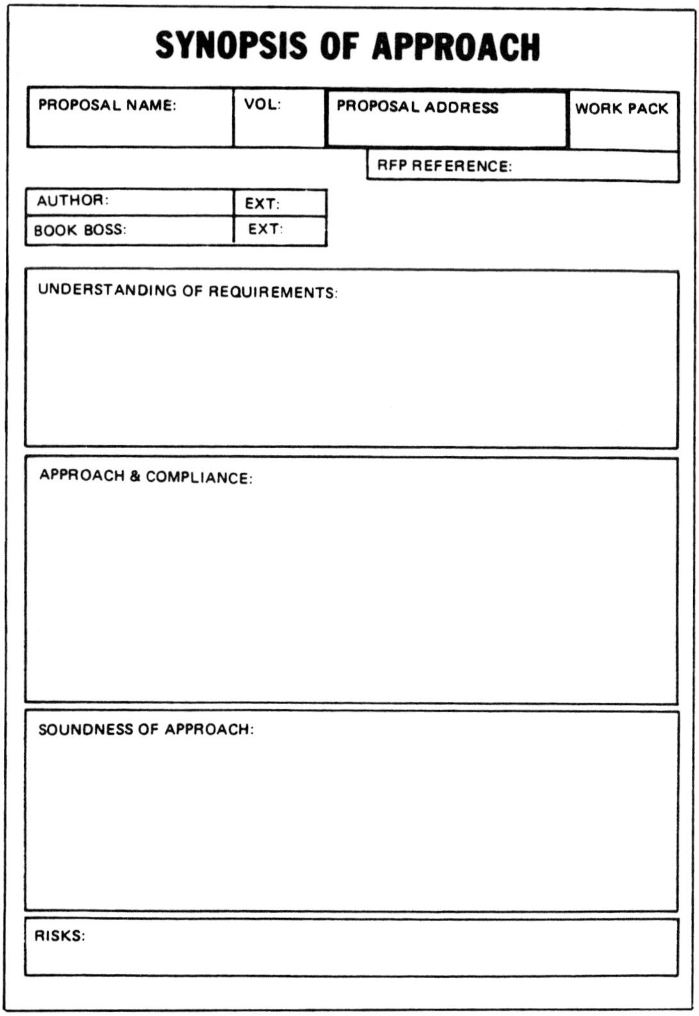

SYNOPSIS OF APPROACH

PROPOSAL NAME:	VOL:	PROPOSAL ADDRESS	WORK PACK

RFP REFERENCE:

AUTHOR:	EXT:
BOOK BOSS:	EXT:

UNDERSTANDING OF REQUIREMENTS:

APPROACH & COMPLIANCE:

SOUNDNESS OF APPROACH:

RISKS:

Figure 19-3. Typical Synopsis form which is used to expand each categorical topic from Figure 19-2.

Phase Three: Roundtable Review

During this phase, all Synopsis of Approach forms are analyzed, critiqued, augmented, and approved by the proposal team and its manager. It is the first time that, in summary form, the total proposal approach is continuously displayed. Besides the proposal team, technical resource managers, marketing managers, contract specialists, and upper management should participate in this review, which usually starts four days after the proposal kickoff.

Phase Four: Topical Outline

After the review and approval of the Synopsis forms, the Categorical Outline is expanded into the specific topics to be addressed in the proposal. This Topical Outline forms the Table of Content for the bid proposal. Similar to the Categorical Outline, each topic defines the responsible writer, page estimates, and document references. A form example is shown in Figure 19-4.

TOPICAL OUTLINE

SHEET_____OF_______

DATE______________

PROGRAM:

PROPOSAL ADDRESS	TITLE	AUTHOR	PAGE ESTIMATE TEXT	ART	SPEC REFERENCE

Figure 19-4. Topical Outline sample form, which explains the Categorical Outline of Figure 19-2.

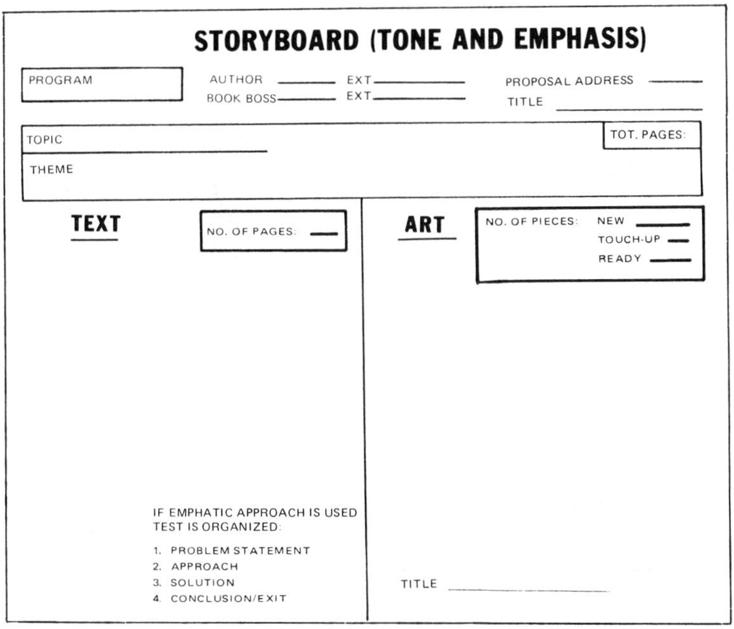

STORYBOARD (TONE AND EMPHASIS)

PROGRAM

AUTHOR ______ EXT ______

BOOK BOSS ______ EXT ______

PROPOSAL ADDRESS ______

TITLE ______

TOPIC

THEME

TOT. PAGES:

TEXT

NO. OF PAGES: ___

ART

NO. OF PIECES: NEW ___ TOUCH-UP ___ READY ___

IF EMPHATIC APPROACH IS USED TEST IS ORGANIZED:

1. PROBLEM STATEMENT
2. APPROACH
3. SOLUTION
4. CONCLUSION/EXIT

TITLE ______

Figure 19-5. Storyboard format.

Phase Five: Storyboard Preparation

The Storyboard preparation is straightforward. Typically, a one-page Storyboard is prepared for each topic by the assigned writer. As shown in Figure 19-5, it represents a detailed outline of the author's approach to the writeup for that particular topic. Often the Storyboard form is divided into three parts: (1) topic and theme section, (2) text outline on the left side of the form, and (3) summary of supporting art to be prepared on the right side of the form.

The Storyboard takes a first cut at the key aspects of each topic. The topic heading, theme (if any), problem statement, and exit or conclusion must be written out in full, just the way they might appear in the final text. Expression of these key sentences is important. They must be relevant, responsive, and comprehensive.

The composition of text and art is arranged on the Storyboard in this format for convenience only. As shown in Figure 19-6, the text format can be chosen either modular or nonmodular. For the modular concept the storyboard format is copied into the proposal layout, text left, illustrations right; while in nonmodular form the art becomes an integral part of

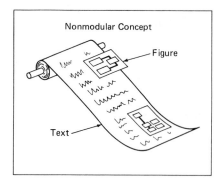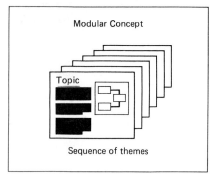

Figure 19-6. Nonmodular versus modular concept of text and art presentation.

the text. The final layout should, however, be of no concern to the authors at this point in the proposal development cycle.

Storyboards are one of the most important elements in the proposal development. They should be typed for clarity and easy comprehension during the review sessions.

Phase Six: Storyboard Review

The completed Storyboard forms are pasted on the walls of the review room in a logical sequence, hence presenting the total story as we want to tell it to the customer.

Storyboard Reviews should start within five working days after the Synopsis Reviews. The reviews are held in a special area and attended by the author, the proposal team, and key members of the functional organization. The Storyboard Review permits a dialogue to take place between the proposal team and its management and the author. All participants of each notice of the review is given by both the daily bulletin and microschedule.

The review permits the proposal team to insert, modify or correct any approach taken by an author. An additional output of the Storyboard Review is a final Proposal Outline. This Proposal Outline includes categorical headings, topics, and art log numbers, and provides the PMT with a proposal overview and serves as a control document. The Storyboard Review provides the team with the single most important opportunity to change direction or change approaches in the proposal preparation.

Similar to the Synopsis Review, Storyboarding is an interactive process. During the reviews, a copy of the latest Storyboard should always be on display in the control room.

Phase Seven: Final Text Generation by Expanding Storyboards

After Storyboard approval, each author prepares a Storyboard Expansion. It is the expansion of information on each topic into about a 500-word narrative. As part of the Storyboard Expansion, all authors should finalize their art work and give it to the publications specialist for processing. The completed Storyboard Expansions present the first draft of the final proposal. The material is given to the technical editor who will perform edit for clarity. Each responsible author must review and approve the final draft, which might cycle through the editing process several times.

This final text generation is the major activity in the proposal development process. All other prior activities are preparatory to this final writing assignment. If the preparations up to the Storyboard Review are done properly, writing the final text should be a logical and straightforward task without the hassles of conceptional clarification and worries about integration with other authors.

As a guideline, 10 working days out of a 30 working day RFP-response period may be a reasonable time for this final text generation. Because of its long duration, it is particularly important to set up specific milestones for measuring intermediate progress. The process of final text generation should be carefully controlled. The proposal specialist, if available, will play a key role in the integration, coordination, and controlling of this final text generation and its output.

The final text should be submitted incrementally to the publication department for editing, word processing or typing, and media storage for future retrieval.

Phase Eight: Staff Review—A Final Check

The final proposal review is conducted by the proposal team and its management group plus selected functional managers who will later provide the contractual services to the contract. In addition, a specialty review committee may be organized to check the final draft for feasibility, rationale, and responsiveness to the RFP. For a given chapter or work package, this Staff Review is accomplished in less than a day. The comments are reviewed by the original authors for incorporation.

Phase Nine: Final Edit

After these review comments are incorporated, the entire proposal is turned over to the publication department for final format editing, completion of art, word processing, and proofreading of the final reproducible copy. The proposal is then returned to the publication specialist or proposal specialist with all of the completed art for a final check. The authors are then given a final opportunity to look at the completed proposal. Any major flaws or technical errors that may have crept into the copy are corrected at that time.

Phase Ten: Printing and Delivery

The proposal is now ready for paste-up, printing, and delivery to the customer.

NEGOTIATING AND CLOSING THE CONTRACT

Sending off the bid proposal signals the start of the postsubmission phase. Regardless of the type of customer or the formalities involved, even for an oral proposal, the procurement will go through the following principal steps:

1. Bid proposals received.
2. Proposals evaluated.
3. Proposal results compared.
4. Alternatives assessed.
5. Clarifications and new information from bidders.
6. Negotiations.
7. Award.

While bidders usually have no influence on proposal evaluation or source selection process, they can certainly prepare properly for the upcoming opportunities of customer negotiations. Depending on the procurement, these opportunities for improving the competitive position come in the following forms:

Follow-up calls and visits.
Responding to customer requests for additional information.
Fact finding requested by customer.
Oral presentations.
Invitations to field visits.
Sending samples or prototypes.
Write paper.
Supportive advertising.
Contact via related contract work.

Plant or office visits.
Press releases.
Negotiations.

The bidder's objective on all postsubmission activities should be improving the competitive position. For starters, the bidder must assess the proposal relative to customer requirements and competing alternatives. In order to do this realistically the bidder needs customer contact. Any opportunity for customer contact should be utilized. Follow-up calls and visits are effective in less formal procurements, while fact finding and related contract work are often used by bidders in formal buying. These are just a few methods to open officially closed doors into the customer community.

Only through active customer contact is it possible to assess realistically the competitive situation and organize for improvement and winning negotiations. Table 19-5 provides a listing of steps for which the bidder should organize. Customer contact and interaction are often difficult to arrange, especially in more formal procurements, which may require innovative marketing approaches.

While the proposal evaluation period is being used by the customer to determine the best proposal, the bidder has the opportunity to improve his position in three principal areas: (1) clarification of proposed program scope and content, (2) image building as a sound, reliable contractor, and (3) counteracting advances made by competing bidders.

The proposal evaluation period is highly dynamic in terms of changing scores, particularly among the top contenders. The bidder who is well organized and prepared to interact with the customer community stands the best chance of being called first for negotiations, thus gaining a better basis for negotiating an equitable contract. Table 19-5 provides some guidelines for organizing and preparing for the postsubmission effort.

RECOMMENDATIONS TO MANAGEMENT

Winning a bid proposal depends on more than the pricing or right market position, or luck. Winning a piece of business depends on many factors which must be carefully developed during the preproposal period, articulated in the bid proposal, and fine-tuned during contract negotiations. Success is geared to hard work, which starts with a proper assessment of the bid opportunity and a formal bid decision. To be sure, a price-competitive bid can help in many situations. However, it may be interesting to note some research findings. A low price bid is advantageous toward winning only in contracts with low complexity, low technical risk, and

Table 19-5. Organizing the Postsubmission Effort.

1. *Reassess your proposal.* Study your proposal and reassess (1) strengths, (2) weaknesses, and (3) compliance with customer requirements.
2. *Plan action.* Develop an action plan listing all weak points of your proposal, potential for improvement, and actions toward improvement.
3. *Open communications.* Establish and maintain communications with the customer during the proposal evaluation period. Determine the various roles people play in the customer community during the evaluation.
4. *Find your score.* Try to determine how you scored with your proposal. Find out what the customer liked, disliked, and perceived as risks; credibility problems and standing against the competition. To determine your score realistically and objectively requires communications skills, sensitivity, and usually a great deal of prior customer contact. Determining your proposal score is an important prerequisite for being able to clarify specific items and to improve your competitive position.
5. *Seek interaction.* Seek out opportunities for interacting with the customer as early as possible. Such opportunities may be presenting additional information for clarifying or enhancing specific proposed items. The meeting or presentation should be requested by the customer. It is a great opportunity for the bidder to "sell" a proposal further. This includes clarifications, modifications, options, and image building.
6. *Prepare for formal meetings.* Be sure you are well prepared for meetings, fact-finding sessions, or presentations requested by the customer. This is your opportunity not only to clarify, but also to strengthen your proposal, show additional material, and introduce new personnel if needed.
7. *Reassess cost and price.* Cost and proposed effort are often fluid during the initial program phases. Many times the discussion of the proposal narrows down the real customer requirements. This provides an opportunity to reassess and adjust the bid price.
8. *Obtain start-work order.* It is often possible to obtain a start-work order before the program is formally under contract. This provides a limited mutual commitment and saves time.
9. *Stay on top until closure.* From the time of bid submission to obtaining the final contract, the bidder must keep abreast with all developments in the customer community which affect the proposal. Try to help the customer justifying the source selection and be responsive to customer requests for additional information and meetings. Frequent interaction with the customer is pervasive.
10. *Conduct formal negotiations.* Negotiation comes in many forms. Program contract negotiations mostly center on the technical performance, schedule, and cost. They should be conducted among the technical and managerial personnel of the contracting parties. If in addition to the technicalities the contract covers extensive legal provision, terms, and conditions, the bidder should seek the interpretation and advice of legal counsel.

high competition. In most other situations price is a factor toward winning only in the context of all competitive components such as the following:

- Compliance with customer requirements.
- Best-fitting solution to customer problem.

- Real demand.
- Relevant past experience.
- Credibility.
- Long-range commitment to business segment.
- Past performance on similar programs.
- Soundness of approach.
- Cost credibility.
- Competitive price.
- Delivery.
- After-sale support.
- Logistics.

The better you understand the customer, the better you will be able to communicate the strength of your product relative to the customer requirements.

Some specific recommendations are made to help business managers responsible for winning new contracts, and professionals who must support these bid proposal efforts, to better understand the complex interrelationship among organizational, technical, marketing, and behavioral components, and to perform their difficult role more effectively.

1. *Plan Ahead.* Develop a detailed business acquisition plan which includes a realistic assessment of the new opportunity and the specific milestones for getting through the various steps needed for bidding and negotiating the contract.
2. *Involve the Right People, Early.* In order to get a realistic assessment of the new opportunity against internal capabilities and external competition, form a committee of senior personnel early in the acquisition cycle. These people should represent the key functional areas of the company and be able to make a sound judgment on the readiness and chances of their company to compete for the new business effectively.
3. *Closeness to the Customer.* Especially for the larger contracts, it is important that the bidding firm has been closely involved with the customer prior to the RFP, and if possible, during the bid preparation. A company that has been closely involved with the customer in helping to define the requirements, in conducting feasibility studies with the customer, or in executing related contract work will not only understand the customer requirements better, but also have higher trust and credibility regarding their capacity to perform by comparison to a company that just submits a bid proposal.
4. *Select Your Bid Opportunities Carefully.* Bid opportunities are usu-

ally plentiful. Only qualified bidders who can submit a competitively attractive proposal have a chance of winning, submitting
"more" proposals does nothing to improve your win ratio. It only
drains your resources. Each bid opportunity should be carefully
assessed to determine whether you really have the ingredients to
win.

5. *Make Bid Decisions Incrementally.* A formal bid decision, especially for the larger proposals, requires considerable homework and
resources. By making these decisions in several steps, such as
initial, preliminary, and final, management can initially quickly
screen a large number of opportunities and narrow them down to a
shorter list without spending a lot of time and resources. Then the
available resources can be concentrated to analyze those opportunities which really seem to be most promising.

6. *Be Sure You Have the Resources to Go the Full Distance.* Many
bid proposal activities require large amounts of resources and time.
In addition, resources may be needed beyond the formal bidding
activities for customer meetings, site visits, and negotiations. Further, the customer may extend the bid submission deadline, which
will cost you more money as you continue to refine your proposal.
Serious consideration should be given at the very beginning of any
potential bid whether you truly have the resources and are willing
to commit them. Develop a detailed cost estimate for the entire
proposal effort.

7. *Obtain Commitment* from senior management to make the necessary resources available when needed. This includes personnel and
facilities.

8. *Do Your Homework.* Before any proposal writing starts, you
should have a clear picture of the strengths, weaknesses, and limitations of (1) the competing firms and (2) your company. In addition, you need to fully understand (3) the customer requirements,
constraints, such as budgets, and biases. This requires intense customer contact and market research.

9. *Organize the Proposal Effort* prior to the RFP. Run the proposal
development like any other project. You need a well-defined step-
by-step action plan, schedules, budgets, team organization, and
facilities. You also have to prepare for support services such as
editing and printing.

10. *Grow a Proposal Specialist.* The efficiency and effectiveness of the
proposal development can be greatly enhanced with a professional
proposal specialist. This is an internal consultant who can lead the
team through the proposal development process including providing the checks and balances via reviews and analysis.

11. *Know Your Competition.* Marketing intelligence comes in many forms. The marketeer who is in touch with the market knows his competition. Information can be gathered at trade shows, bidder's briefings, customer meetings, and professional conferences, and from the literature and via special market service firms.

12. *Develop a Win Strategy.* Define your niche or "unfair advantage" over your competition and build your win strategy around it. Only after intensive intelligence gathering from the competition and the customer and careful analysis of these market data against your strengths and weaknesses, can a meaningful win strategy be developed. Participation of key personnel from all functions of the organization is necessary to develop a meaningful and workable win strategy for your new contract acquisition.

13. *Develop the Proposal Text Incrementally.* Don't go from RFP to the first proposal draft in one step. *Use the Storyboard process.*

14. *Be fully compliant to the RFP.* Don't take exceptions to the customer requirements unless absolutely unavoidable. A formal RFP analysis listing the specific customer requirements helps to avoid unintended oversights and also helps in organizing your proposal.

15. *Demonstrate Understanding of Customer Requirements.* A summary of the requirements and brief discussions helps to instill confidence in the customer's mind that you understand the specific needs.

16. *Demonstrate Ability to Perform.* Past, related experiences will score the strongest points. But showing that your company performed on similar programs, that you have experienced personnel, and that you have done analytical homework against the requirements may rate very favorably with the customer too, especially when you have other advantages such as innovative solution, or favorable timing or pricing.

17. *Progress Reviews.* As part of the incremental proposal development, assure through reviews which check (1) compliance with customer requirements, (2) soundness of approach, (3) effective communication, and (4) proper integration of topics into one proposal.

18. *Red Team Reviews.* For "must-win" proposals it may be useful to set up a special review team that evaluates and scores the proposal, similar to the process used by the customer. Deficiencies which may otherwise remain hidden can often be identified and dealt with during the proposal development. Such a "red team review" can be conducted at various stages of the proposal development. It is important to budget enough time for revising the proposal after red team review.

19. *Use Editorial Support.* A competent editor should work side-by-side with the technical proposal writers. A good editor can take text at a rough draft stage and "finalize" it regarding logic, style, and grammar. However, the proper content has to come from the technical author. Therefore, for the process to work, text often cycles between the author and editor several times until both agree to it. The professional editor not only frees the technical writer for the crucial innovative technical proposal development, but also provides clarity and consistency to the proposal. Further, this procedure increases the total writing efficiency by a factor of 2. That is, using professional editors reduces the total proposal *writing* budget to one half of what it would cost otherwise.

20. *Price Competitively.* Pricing is a complex issue. However, for most proposals, a competitively priced bid has the winning edge. Knowing the customer's budget and some of the cost factors of the competition can help in fine-tuning the bidding price. Further, cost-plus proposals must have cost credibility, which is being built via a clearly articulated cost model and a description of its elements of cost. Pricing should start at the time of the bid decision.

21. *Prepare for Negotiations.* Immediately after proposal submission, work should start in preparation of customer inquiries and negotiations. Responses to customer inquiries, regarding clarifications on the original bid, can be used effectively to score additional technical points and build further credibility.

22. *Conduct Postmortem.* Regardless of the final outcome, a thorough review of the proposal effort should be held and the lessons learned be documented for the benefit of future proposals.

A FINAL NOTE

Winning new contract business is a highly competitive and costly undertaking. To be successful, it requires special management skills, tools, and techniques which range from identifying new bid opportunities to bid decisions and proposal developments.

Companies that win their share of new business usually have a well-disciplined process; they also have experienced personnel who can manage the intricate process and lead a multifunctional team toward writing a unified winning proposal. Their managements use good logic and judgment in deriving their bid decisions; they also make fewer fundamental mistakes during the acquisition process. These are the managers who position their companies uniquely in the competitive field by building a quality image with the customer and by submitting a responsive bid proposal that is competitively priced. These are the business managers who target specific opportunities and demonstrate a high win ratio.

CONTRACT INFORMATION SOURCES

HANDBOOKS AND REFERENCE BOOKS

Anatomy of a Win, by Jim M. Beveridge Associates, 8448 Wagner Creek Road, Talent, OR 97540. 1978.

Business Guide to Dealing with the Federal Government, Drake Publishers Inc., 381 Park Avenue South, New York, NY 10016. 1973.

Contract Planning and Organization, United Nations Publications, United Nations, LX2300, New York, NY 10017. 1974.

Grantmanship and Fundraising by Armand Lauffer, Sage Publication. 1984.

How to Create a Winning Proposal, by J. Ammon-Wexler and Catherine ap Carmel, Mercury Communications, 730 Mission Street, Santa Cruz, CA 95060. 1977.

Positioning to Win by Jim M. Beveridge and E. J. Velton, J. M. Chilton, 1982.

Selling to United States Government, United States Sm; 'l Business Administration, Washington, DC 20416. 1973.

Source Guide to Government Technology and Financial Assistance by Harry Greenwald et al, Prentice-Hall, 1982

Research and Development Directory, Government Data Publications, annually.

Technical Marketing to the Government, by Robert A. Rexroad, Dartness Corp., Chicago.

PERIODICALS AND NEWSPAPERS

Briefing Papers, Federal Publications, 1725 K Street, NW, Washington, DC 20006. Bimonthly.

Commerce Business Daily, U.S. Department of Commerce, Office of Field Services, U.S. Government Printing Office, Washington, DC 20402.

Forms of Business Agreement, Institute of Business Planning, IPB Plaza, Englewood Cliffs, NJ 07632. Monthly.

Government Contractor, Federal Publications, 1725 K Street NW, Washington, DC 20006. Biweekly.

Government Contracts Reports, Commerce Clearance House, 4025 West Peterson Avenue, Chicago, IL 60646. Weekly.

New Business Report (Monthly Newsletter) by Executive Communications, Inc., New York, NY.

NCMA Newsletter, National Contract Management Association, 675 East Wardlow Road, Long Beach, CA 90807. Monthly.

DIRECTORIES

Directory of Government Production Prime Contracts, Government Data Publication, Washington, DC. Annual.

Government Contracts Directory, Government Data Publications, 422 Washington Building, Washington, DC 20005. Annual.

Government Contracts Guide, Commerce Clearing House, 4025 West Peterson Avenue, Chicago, IL 60646.

Selling to NASA, U.S. Government Printing Office, Washington DC 20402.

Selling to Navy Prime Contractors, U.S. Government Printing Office, Washington DC 20402.

United States Government Purchasing and Sales Directory, U.S. Small Business Administration, U.S. Government Printing Office, Washington DC 20402. 1972.

ON-LINE DATA BASES

Defense Market Measurement System, Frost and Sullivan, 109 Fulton Street, New York, NY 10038.

Federal Register, Capitol Services, 511 Second St. NE, Washington, DC 20002.

U.S. Government Contract Awards, SCD Service, System Development Corp., 2500 Colorado Ave., Santa Monica, CA 90406.

ASSOCIATIONS AND SOCIETIES

Electronic Industries Association (EIA), 2001 Eye Street, NW, Washington, DC 20006.

National Contract Management Association, 6728 Old McLean Village Dr., McLean, VA 22101, (703) 442-0137.

National Council of Technical Service Industries, 1845 K Street, NW, Suite 1190, Washington, DC 20006.

BIBLIOGRAPHY

Behling, John H. *Guidelines for Preparing the Research Proposal,* U. Press of America, 1984.

Edelman, F. "Art and Science of Competitive Bidding." *Harvard Business Review, 43* (July–August 1965).

Frichtl, P. "Tactics for Tactics." *Industrial Distributor:* 9 (July, 1986).

Guyton, Robert, et al. *Prerequisits for Winning Government R&D Contracts,* Universal Technology Corporation, 1983.

Hanssman, F. and Rivett, B. H. P. *"Competitive Bidding." Operations Research Quarterly,* 10:49–55 (1959).

Kerzner, Harold and Loring, Roy J. *Proposal Preparation and Management Handbook,* Van Nostrand Reinhold, New York, 1982.

Holtz, Herman. *Government Contracts: Proposal-manship and Winning Strategies.* Plenum, New York, 1979.

Lehman, D. H. "A Technique for Lowering Risks During Contract Negotiations." *Transportation Engineering Managers, 33:*79–81 (May, 1986).

Merrifield, D. Bruce, *Strategic Analysis, Selection and Management of R&D Projects,* American Management Association, New York, 1977.

Newport, J. P., Jr. "Billion Dollar Bids in Sealed Envelopes." *Fortune:*42 (April, 1985).

Owens, Elizabeth, "Effective Proposals of the competitive Businessman," *Data Management, 25:*22 (January, 1987).

Park, W. R. *Construction Bidding for Profits.* Wiley, New York, 1979.

Porter-Roth, Bud. *Proposal Development—A Winning Approach.* PSI Research, 1986.

Public Management Institute Staff, *How to get Federal Contracts,* Public Management, 1980.

Robertson, J. "Government 11-th Hour Bid Cancellation Case No-Bids Team Efforts." *Electronic News, 30* (May 21, 1984).

Rugh and Manning, *Proposal Management Using the Modular Approach,* Peninsula Publication Company, 1982.

Simmonds, K. "Competitive Bidding—Deciding the Best Combination of Non-Price Features." *Operational Research Quarterly, 19:*5–15 (1968).

Steward, Rodney, D. and Steward, Ann L. *Proposal Preparation,* Wiley, New York, 1984.

Thamhain, H. J. "Marketing in Project-Oriented Business Environments." *Project Management Quarterly* (December, 1982).

Wantuck. "Bidding for Fair Play." *Nations Business, 73:*39–40 (September, 1985).

Whalen, Tim, Improved Proposal Writing Utility, Coherance, and Emphasis," *Bulletin of the Association for Business Communication,* Vol. 69 (December 1986).

Section VI
Project Implementation

This section focuses on a number of dimensions that are of particular importance in the successful implementation and execution of projects. As in all human endeavor, the best laid plans may come to naught if inadequate attention is paid to certain critical factors.

In Chapter 20, Jeffrey K. Pinto and Dennis P. Slevin identify the "critical success factors" for effective project management using data collected from project managers in various contexts. These factors may be taken as guides to the project manager as to whether he or she should focus attention in the various phases of the project life cycle.

John L. Heidenreich, in Chapter 21, addresses the critical quality dimension in the project management. Since quality considerations are becoming ever more important in industry, this factor warrants special attention as any project is implemented.

In Chapter 22, the legal standards for prudent and efficient project management, which must serve to guide the way in which the project is carried out, are outlined. In our litigious society, legal considerations, like quality concerns, stand out as warranting special attention in implementing a project.

20. Critical Success Factors in Effective Project Implementation*†

Jeffrey K. Pinto‡
Dennis P. Slevin**

INTRODUCTION

The process of project implementation, involving the successful development and introduction of projects in the organization, presents an ongoing
challenge for managers. The project implementation process is complex,
usually requiring simultaneous attention to a wide variety of human,
budgetary, and technical variables. As a result, the organizational project
manager is faced with a difficult job characterized by role overload, frenetic activity, fragmentation, and superficiality. Often the typical project

* Portions of this chapter were adapted from Dennis P. Slevin and Jeffrey K. Pinto,
Balancing Strategy and Tactics in Project Implementation', *Sloan Management Review,*
Fall, 1987, pp. 33–41, and Randall L. Schultz, Dennis P. Slevin, and Jeffrey K. Pinto,
'Strategy and Tactics in a Process Model of Project Implementation'', *Interfaces,* 16:3,
May-June, 1987, pp. 34–46.
** Dennis P. Slevin is an Associate Professor of Business Administration at the University
of Pittsburgh's Joseph M. Katz Graduate School of Business. He holds a B.A. in Mathematics from St. Vincent College, a B.S. in Physics from M.I.T., an M.S. in Industrial Administration from Carnegie-Mellon, and a Ph.D. from Stanford University. He has had extensive
experience as a line manager, including service as the CEO of four different companies,
which qualified him as a member of the Young Presidents' Organization. He presently
serves as a director of several corporations, and consults widely. He publishes in numerous
professional journals, and is co-editor of *Implementing Operations Research Management
Science; The Management of Organizational Design, Volumes I and II;* and *Producing
Useful Knowledge.* He has written the pragmatic *Executive Survival Manual* for practicing
managers.
‡ Jeffrey K. Pinto is Assistant Professor of Organization Theory at the College of Business
Administration, University of Cincinnati. He received his B.A. in History and B.S. in
Business from the University of Maryland, M.B.A. and Ph.D. from the University of Pitts-
burgh. He has published several papers in a variety of professional journals on such topics as
project management, implementation, instrument development, and research methodology.

manager has responsibility for successful project outcomes without suffi-cient power, budget, or people to handle all of the elements essential for project success. In addition, projects are often initiated in the context of a turbulent, unpredictable, and dynamic environment. Consequently, the project manager would be well served by more information about those specific factors critical to project success. The project manager requires the necessary tools to help him or her focus attention on important areas and set *differential priorities* across different project elements. If it can be demonstrated that a set of factors *under the project manager's control* can have a significant impact on project implementation success, the pro-ject manager will be better able to effectively deal with the many demands created by his job, channeling his energy more efficiently in attempting to successfully implement the project under development.

This chapter reports on a program of research that has developed the following tools and/or concepts for the practicing project manager.

- A set of ten empirically derived critical project implementation suc-cess factors.
- A diagnostic instrument—the Project Implementation Profile (PIP) for measuring the ten factors.
- A ten-factor model of the project implementation process.
- Measures of the key elements of project Strategy and Tactics.
- The effect of Strategy and Tactics on project implementation suc-cess.
- The impact of the project life cycle on the relative importance of the critical success factors.

In addition, we propose that as the project moves forward through its life cycle, the project manager must be able to effectively transition from strategic to tactical issues in order to better influence project success. Implications are suggested for practicing managers along with specific approaches to managing the strategy-tactics interface.

DEFINITIONS

Before attempting a discussion of the project implementation process, it is first important that some of the key concepts in this chapter be adequately defined, in an effort to remove some of the ambiguity from concepts which are often subject to a wide range of individual interpretations.

What Is a Project?

While almost everyone has had experience with projects in one form or another, developing a definition of what exactly a project is is often difficult. Any definition of a project must be general enough to include examples of the wide variety of organizational activities which managers consider to be "project functions." However, the definition should be narrow enough to include only those specific activities which researchers and practitioners can meaningfully describe as "project-oriented." Two of the many definitions of projects that have been offered may be considered as follows:

> A project is an organization of people dedicated to a specific purpose or objective. Projects generally involve large, expensive, unique, or high risk undertakings which have to be completed by a certain date, for a certain amount of money, within some expected level of performance. At a minimum, all projects need to have well defined objectives and sufficient resources to carry out all the required tasks. (24, p. 498)

The second definition is offered by Cleland and Kerzner (7), in their work *A Project Management Dictionary of Terms,* and includes the following characteristics:

> [A project is] A combination of human and nonhuman resources pulled together in a temporary organization to achieve a specified purpose. (7, p. 199)

A project, then, can be defined as possessing the following characteristics:

- A defined beginning and end (specified time to completion).
- A specific, preordained goal or set of goals.
- A series of complex or interrelated activities.
- A limited budget.

What Is Successful Project Implementation?

In addition to defining the concept of organizational projects, it is important, before attempting any discussion of the steps leading to a successful project, to describe just exactly what a "successful project" is. Project implementation success has been defined many ways to include a large variety of criteria. However, in its simplest terms, project success can be thought of as incorporating four basic facets. A project is generally considered to be successfully implemented if it

- Comes in on-schedule (time criterion).
- Comes in on-budget (monetary criterion).

- Achieves basically all the goals originally set for it (effectiveness criterion).
- Is accepted and used by the clients for whom the project is intended (client satisfaction criterion).

By its basic definition, a project comprises a defined time frame to completion, a limited budget, and a specified set of performance characteristics. Further, the project is usually targeted for use by some client, either internal or external to the organization and its project team. It seems reasonable, therefore, that any assessment of project implementation success should include these four measures.

The Project Life Cycle

One method that has been used with some regularity in order to help managers conceptualize the work and budgetary requirements of a project is to make use of the idea of the project life cycle. The concept of the life cycle is familiar to most modern managers. Life cycles are used to explain the rise and demise of organizations, phases in the sales life of a product, etc. In a similar fashion, managers often make use of the life-cycle concept as a valuable tool for better understanding the stages in a project and the likely materials requirements for the project through each distinct phase.

Figure 20-1 shows an example of a project life cycle. This representation of the project life cycle is based on the work of Adams and Barndt (1) and King and Cleland (10). As can be seen, the project's life cycle has been divided into four distinct stages, including:

1. *Conceptualization*—The initial project stage. At this stage a project is determined as being necessary. Preliminary goals and alternatives are specified, as well as the possible means to accomplish those goals.
2. *Planning*—This stage involves the establishment of a more formalized set of plans to accomplish the initially developed goals. Among planning activities are scheduling, budgeting, and the allocation of other specific tasks and resources.
3. *Execution*—The third stage involves the actual "work" of the project. Materials and resources are procured, the project is produced, and performance capabilities are verified.
4. *Termination*—Once the project is completed, there are several final activities that must be performed. These activities usually include the release of resources and transfer of the project to the clients and, if necessary, the reassignment of project team personnel.

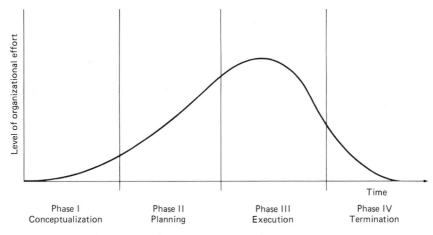

Figure 20-1. Stages in the project life cycle. (Based on Adams and Barndt; King and Cleland (10).)

As Figure 20-1 also shows, in addition to the development of four project stages, the life cycle specifies the level of organizational effort necessary to adequately perform the tasks associated with each project stage. Organizational effort can be measured using surrogates such as amount of man-hours, expenditures, assets deployed, or other measures of organizational resource utilization. As one would suspect, during the early Conceptualization and Planning stages, effort requirements are minimal, increasing rapidly during late Planning and project Execution, before diminishing again in the project's Termination. As a result, the concept of project life cycles can be quite useful to a manager, not only in terms of distinguishing among the stages in the project's life, but also through indicating likely resource requirements to be expected at each stage.

DEVELOPMENT OF THE TEN-FACTOR MODEL OF PROJECT IMPLEMENTATION

Project information was obtained from a group of over 50 managers who had some project involvement within the last two years. Participants were asked to consider a successful project with which they had been involved and then to put themselves in the position of a project manager charged with the responsibility of successful project implementation. They were then asked to indicate things that they could do that would substantially help implementation success. This procedure, sometimes called Project Echo, was developed by Alex Bavelas (4). Responses were then sorted into categories by two experts. Both experts sorted the responses into ten categories and interrater agreement based on percentage of responses similarly sorted across the total number was 0.50, or 119 out of 236. Eliminating duplications and miscellaneous responses, a total of 94 usable responses were classified across 10 factors. These 10 factors formed the basis for the conceptual model and the diagnostic instrument for measuring relative strength of each factor.

The first factor that was developed was related to the underlying purpose for the implementation and was classified *Project Mission*. Several authors have discussed the importance of clearly defining goals at the outset of the project. Morris (15) classified the initial stage of project management as consisting of a feasibility decision. Are the goals clear and can they succeed? Bardach's (3) six-step implementation process begins with instructions to state the plan and its objectives. For both these authors and the purposes of our study, Project Mission has been found to refer to the condition where the goals of the project are clear and understood, not only by the project team involved, but by the other departments in the organization. Underlying themes of responses classified into this factor include statements concerning clarification of goals as well as belief in the likelihood of project success.

The second factor discerned was that of *Top Management Support*. As noted by Schultz and Slevin (19), management support for projects, or indeed for any implementation, has long been considered of great importance in distinguishing between their ultimate success or failure. Beck (6) sees project management as not only dependent on top management for authority, direction, and support, but as ultimately the conduit for implementing top management's plans, or goals, for the organization. Further, Manley (14) shows that the degree of management support for a project will lead to significant variations in the clients' degree of ultimate acceptance or resistance to that project or product. For the purposes of our classification, the factor Top Management Support refers to both the nature and amount of support the project manager can expect from management both for himself as leader and for the project. Management's support of the project may involve aspects such as allocation of sufficient resources (financial, manpower, time, etc.) as well as the project manager's confidence in their support in the event of crises.

The third factor to be classified was that of *Project Schedule/Plans*. Project schedule refers to the importance of developing a detailed plan of the required stages of the implementation process. Ginzberg (8) has drawn parallels between the stages of the implementation process and the Lewin (12) model of Unfreezing-Moving-Freezing, viewing planning and scheduling as the first step in the "Moving" stage. Kolb and Frohman's (11) model of the consulting process views planning as a two-directional stage, not only as necessary to the forward-going change process, but as an additional link to subsequent evaluation and possible reentry into the system. Nutt (16) further emphasizes the importance of process planning, breaking down planning into four stages: formulation, conceptualization, detailing, and evaluation. As developed in our model, Project Schedule/ Plans refers to the degree to which time schedules, milestones, manpower, and equipment requirements are specified. Further, the schedule should include a satisfactory measurement system as a way of judging actual performance against budget and time allowances.

The fourth factor that was determined is labeled *Client Consultation*. The "client" is referred to here as anyone who will ultimately be making use of the result of the project, as either a customer outside the company or a department within the organization. The need for client consultation has been found to be increasingly important in attempting to successfully implement a project. Indeed, Manley (14) found that the degree to which clients are personally involved in the implementation process will cause great variation in their support for that project. Further, in the context of the consulting process, Kolb and Frohman (11) view client consultation as the first stage in a program to implement change. As this factor was derived for the model, Client Consultation expresses the necessity of taking into account the needs of the future clients, or users, of the project. It is, therefore, important to determine whether clients for the project have been identified. Once the project manager is aware of the major clients, he is better able to accurately determine if their needs are being met.

The fifth factor was concerned with *Personnel* issues, including recruitment, selection, and training. (See Table 20-1.) An important, but often overlooked, aspect of the implementation process concerns the nature of the personnel involved. In many situations, personnel for the project team are chosen with less-than-full regard for the skills necessary to actively contribute to implementation success. Some current writers on implementations are including the personnel variable in the equation for project team performance and project success. Hammond (9) has developed a contingency model of the implementation process which includes "people" as a situational variable whose knowledge, skills, goals, and personalities must be considered in assessing the environment of the organization. Only after such a diagnosis takes place can the project management team begin to set objectives and design the implementation approach. For the model, Personnel, as a factor, is concerned with developing a project team with the requisite skills to perform their function. Further, it is important to determine whether project management has built sufficient commitment toward project success on the part of team members.

The sixth factor to be discussed was labeled *Technical Tasks*. It is

Table 20-1. Factor Definitions.[a]

1. *Project Mission*—Initial clearly defined goals and general directions.
2. *Top Management Support*—Willingness of top management to provide the necessary resources and authority/power for project success.
3. *Project Schedule/Plan*—A detailed specification of the individual actions steps for project implementation.
4. *Client Consultation*—Communication, consultation, and active listening to all impacted parties.
5. *Personnel*—Recruitment, selection, and training of the necessary personnel for the project team.
6. *Technical Tasks*—Availability of the required technology and expertise to accomplish the specific technical action steps.
7. *Client Acceptance*—The act of "selling" the final project to its ultimate intended users.
8. *Monitoring and Feedback*—Timely provision of comprehensive control information at each stage in the implementation process.
9. *Communication*—The provision of an appropriate network and necessary data to all key actors in the project implementation.
10. *Troubleshooting*—Ability to handle unexpected crises and deviations from plan.

Source: Slevin and Pinto, (1986, pp. 57–58), From the article "The Project Implementation Profile: New Tool for Project Managers" which appeared in *Project Management Journal,* September, 1986.

important that the implementation be well managed by people who understand the project. In addition, there must exist adequate technology to support the project. Technical Tasks refers to the necessity of not only having the necessary personnel for the implementation team, but ensuring that they possess the necessary technical skills and have adequate technology to perform their tasks. Steven Alter (2), writing on implementation risk analysis, identifies two of the eight risk factors as being caused by technical incompatibility: the user's unfamiliarity with the systems or technology, and cost ineffectiveness.

In addition to Client Consultation at an earlier stage in the project implementation process, it remains of ultimate importance to determine whether the clients for whom the project has been initiated will accept it. *Client Acceptance* refers to the final stage in the implementation process, at which time the ultimate efficacy of the project is to be determined. Too often project managers make the mistake of believing that if they handle the other stages of the implementation process well, the client (either internal or external to the organization) will accept the resulting project. In fact, as several writers have shown, client acceptance is a stage in project implementation that must be managed like any other. As an implementation strategy, Lucas (13) discusses the importance of user participation in the early stages of system development as a way of improving the likelihood of later acceptance. Bean and Radnor (5) examine the use of "intermediaries" to act as a liaison between the designer, or implementation team, and the project's potential users as a method to aid in client acceptance.

The eighth factor to be considered is that of *Monitoring and Feedback*. Monitoring and Feedback refer to the project control processes by which at each stage of the project implementation, key personnel receive feedback on how the project is comparing to initial projections. Making allowances for adequate monitoring and feedback mechanisms gives the project manager the ability to anticipate problems, to oversee corrective measures, and to ensure that no deficiencies are overlooked. Schultz and Slevin (19) demonstrate the evolving nature of implementation and model-building paradigms to have reached the state including formal feedback channels between the model builder and the user. From a budgeting perspective, Souder et al. (23) emphasize the importance of constant monitoring and "fine-tuning" of the process of implementation. For the model, Monitoring and Feedback refers not only to project schedule and budget, but to monitoring performance of members of the project team.

The ninth factor was that of *Communication*. The need for adequate communication channels is extremely important in creating an atmosphere for successful project implementation. Communication is not only essential within the project team itself, but between the team and the rest of the organization as well as with the client. As the factor Communication has been developed for the model, it refers not only to feedback mechanisms, but the necessity of exchanging information with both clients and the rest of the organization concerning project goals, changes in policies and procedures, status reports, etc.

The tenth and final factor to emerge from classification of the model is *Trouble Shooting*. As the participants in the study often pointed out, problem areas exist in almost every implementation. Regardless of how carefully the project was initially planned, it is impossible to foresee every trouble area or problem that could possibly arise. As a result, it is important that the project manager make adequate initial arrangements for "troubleshooting" mechanisms to be included in the implementation plan. Such mechanisms make it easier not only to react to problems as they arise, but to foresee and possibly forestall potential trouble areas in the implementation process.

THE MODEL

As Figure 20-2 shows, a framework of project implementation has been developed for heuristic purposes, based on the ten factors discovered in our analysis. Some general characteristics of the model should be noted:

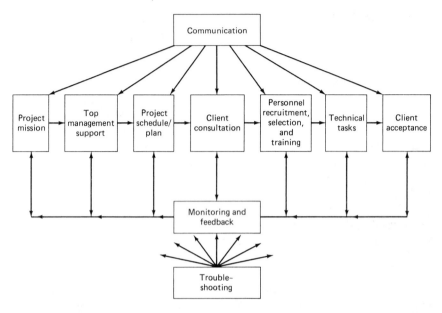

Figure 20-2. Ten key factors of the project implementation profile. (Copyright © 1984 Randall L. Schultz and Dennis P. Slevin. Used with permission.)

1. The factors appear to be both time sequenced and interdependent.

Conceptually, one could argue that the factors are sequenced to occur (or be considered) in a logical order instead of randomly or concurrently. To illustrate, consider that, according to the framework, it is first important to set the goals or define the mission and benefits of the project before seeking top management support. Furthermore, one could argue that unless consultation with the project's clients has occurred early in the process, chances of subsequent client acceptance and use, denoting successful implementation, will be negatively affected. Nonetheless, it is important to remember that in actual practice, considerable overlap and reversals can occur in the ordering of the various factors and the sequencing as suggested in the framework is not absolute.

2. The factors for a project implementation can be laid out on a critical path.

Related to the temporal aspect, the factors of project implementation can be laid out in a rough critical path, similar to the critical path methodology used to develop a new product or to determine the steps in an OR/ MS project. In addition to the set of seven factors along the critical path, ranging from Project Mission to Client Acceptance, other factors such as Communication and Monitoring and Feedback are hypothesized to necessarily occur simultaneously and in harmony with the other sequential factors. As several project managers have indicated to us over the course of this research, it is important that Communication always occur or that Troubleshooting be available throughout the implementation process. It should be noted, however, that the arrows in the model represent information flows and sequences, not necessarily causal or correlational relationships.

3. The model allows the manager to actively interact with and systematically monitor his project.

The sequence of a project implementation is an important consideration for any project manager. Not only are there a prescribed set of steps to be taken in the project implementation process, but because of the order of the steps to be taken, the manager is provided with a checklist for determining the status of the project at any given stage. This monitoring capacity enables the manager to determine where the project is in terms of its life cycle and how rapidly it is moving forward. Further, the manager has the ability to determine the chances for successful implementation given attention has been paid to the proper sequencing of steps and consideration of relevant critical success factors in the implementation process.

A 100-item instrument (10 items per factor) was developed and has been used to measure the relative level of each of these critical success factors (21). This instrument was further refined and reduced to a 50-item instrument (5 items per factor) and is a useful diagnostic tool for project implementation. This instrument has been included in its entirety along with percentile norms for over 400 projects as an implementation aid for project managers.

Table 20-2 demonstrates the results of a recent study in which the ten critical factors were assessed in terms of their overall contribution to project success (17). A data base of over 400 projects were sampled in an effort toward empirical verification of the importance of each of the ten initially developed critical success factors. As can be seen, each of the ten factors was found to be significantly related to project success. Further, the cumulative r-square value, representing total amount of the variance explained by the ten factors, was .615. In other words, over 61% of the causes of project implementation success can be explained by the ten critical success factors.

Table 20-2. Results of Multiple Regression on the
Ten Critical Success Factors.[a]

FACTOR	BETA	T-VALUE	SIG. T
Mission	.72	19.99	$p < .001$
Top Management Support	.32	10.60	$p < .001$
Schedule	.32	10.92	$p < .001$
Client Consultation	.39	11.86	$p < .001$
Personnel	.31	10.54	$p < .001$
Technical Tasks	.43	11.25	$p < .001$
Client Acceptance	.39	11.46	$p < .001$
Monitoring and Feedback	.29	10.89	$p < .001$
Communication	.32	10.38	$p < .001$
Troubleshooting	.35	11.15	$p < .001$

[a] Total regression equation $F = 47.8$, $p < .001$. Cumulative adjusted r-square = .615.

STRATEGY AND TACTICS

As one moves through the ten-factor model shown in Figure 20-1, it becomes clear that the general characteristics of the factors change. In fact, the factors can be grouped into meaningful patterns, or more general subdimensions. As Table 20-3 shows, the first three factors, (Mission, Top Management Support, and Schedule) are related to the early "planning" phase of the implementation process. The second dimension, composed of the other seven factors (Client Consultation, Personnel, etc.), may be seen as concerned with the actual process, or "action," of the implementation. These factors seem less planning in nature and more based on the operationalization of the project implementation process.

These "planning" versus "action" elements in the critical implementation success factors show significant parallels to the distinction between

Table 20-3. Strategic and Tactical Critical
Success Factors.

STRATEGY	TACTICS
Mission	Client Consultation
Top Management Support	Personnel
Schedule/Plans	Technical Tasks
	Client Acceptance
	Monitoring and Feedback
	Communication
	Troubleshooting

strategy and tactics in the strategic management field. Strategy is often viewed as the process of deciding on overall organizational objectives as well as planning on how to achieve those goals. Tactics are seen as the deployment of a wide variety of human, technical, and financial resources to achieve those strategic plans. Strategy, then, is concerned with the up-front planning, while tactics are specifically focused on how best to operationalize, or achieve, those plans.

It is important that managers understand the differences between strategic and tactical issues. Both are vital to project success, but differentially so as the project moves forward to completion. One method for clarifying the distinction raised between strategy and tactics is through the development of a taxonomy that demonstrates the diverse nature of the two functions. This taxonomy is especially useful if applied to the project management context because it has important implications for determining the relationship between strategy and tactics and the previously mentioned planning versus action aspects of the implementation process. Table 20-4 shows a sample of ten issues which have differing implications for project implementation when approached from either a strategic or a tactical viewpoint.

From a conceptual standpoint, the first three critical success factors are primarily "strategic" in nature, while the last seven are more "tactical." Using the model and the measurement instrument (See Appendix), it is possible to monitor the level of strategy (sum of percentile scores on the first three factors) and tactics (sum of percentile scores on the last seven factors) as the project moves forward in time. In addition to showing the Project Implementation Profile, Appendix 1 also exhibits the set of percentile scores for each of the critical success factors, based on a data base of 418 projects. The manager is able to assess scores on each of the ten factors for his specific project and compare those percentile scores with this previously gathered sample of projects.

STRATEGY-TACTICS INTERACTION

In addition to the above conceptualization regarding project implementation as a two-stage process, involving initial strategic actions and supporting tactical activities, there are further implications for project performance based on a consideration of strategic and tactical issues. Figure 20-3 shows the breakdown of strategy and tactics by high and low scores depending upon the level to which these issues were addressed in the project implementation. A high "score" on strategy would imply that the strategy is well developed and effective, as is the similar case with tactics. This value could be assessed either in a subjective or intuitive manner or

Table 20-4. Taxonomy of Strategic Versus Tactical Issues.[a]

	STRATEGY	TACTICS
1. *Level of Conduct*—Level within the organization at which project implementation activities and issues are performed or addressed.	Top management	Mid- to lower levels of management
2. *Subjective/Objective Assessment*—The activities concerned with assessing project goals or status.	Greater subjectivity used at strategic level	Less use of subjective values
3. *Nature of Problem*—The types of problems which arise and must be dealt with during the project implementation process.	Unstructured, one at a time	More structured and repetitive
4. *Information Needs*—The determination of the types and quantity of information that is required for the project.	Large amount of information needed, much that is external	Need for internally generated, specific information
5. *Time Horizons*—The scope or time frame of management's vision in implementing and evaluating the project.	Long-term, but it varies by the problem	Short-term and more constant
6. *Completeness*—The degree to which the scope of the entire organization is considered.	Covers the entire scope of the organization	Concerned only with the suborganizational unit involved
7. *Reference*—Involves the source, or frame of reference, of the activity to be considered.	The source of all planning in the organization is original	Done in pursuit of strategic plans
8. *Detail*—Concerned with how broad or specific problems are laid out and how generally they need to be addressed.	Broad and general	Narrow and problem specific
9. *Ease of Evaluation*—The ease of determining the efficiency and effectiveness of various activities involved in the implementation.	Difficult, because of generality	Easier, because of specificity
10. *Point of View*—The assessment of the focus or viewpoint of the various actors involved in the project implementation.	Corporate	Functional

"Taxonomy of Strategic vs. Tactical Issues", Source: Schultz, Slevin, and Pinto, (1987, p. 38) adapted originally from G. A. Steiner, *Top Management Planning,* MacMillan, NY, 1969.

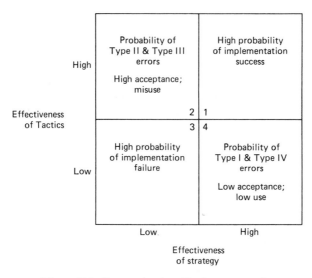

Figure 20-3. Strategy/tactics effectiveness matrix.

more systematically, through use of a project implementation assessment instrument. For example, it may be determined by the project manager that one or more factors within the strategic or tactical clusters is deficient, based on a data base of similar, successful projects. Such deficiencies could have serious implications for the resulting viability of the project under construction.

It may further be possible to speculate on some of the likely outcomes for projects being implemented, given the various combinations of strategic and tactical scores. Figure 20-3 demonstrates the four possible combinations of performance of strategic and tactical activities. It is important to note that the values ''high'' and ''low'' in Figure 20-3 are meant to imply strategic and tactical *quality,* that is, effectiveness of operations performed under the two clusters.

Four types of errors may occur in the implementation process. The first two error types were originally proposed in the context of the development of the field of statistics and statistical tests. The last two error types have been suggested as the result of research on implementation and other organizational change paradigms.

In an organizational setting, *Type I error* occurs when an action should have been taken and was not. To illustrate, consider a situation in which strategic actions have been adequately performed and suggest development and implementation of a project. Type I error will occur when little action is subsequently taken and the tactical activities are inadequate to the degree that the project is not developed.

Type II error, in the context of project implementation, is defined as taking an action when, in fact, none should be taken. In practical terms, Type II error would likely occur in a situation in which project strategy was ineffective, inaccurate, or poorly done. However, in spite of initial planning inadequacies, goals and schedules were operationalized during the tactical stage of the implementation.

Type III error may also be a consequence of low strategy effectiveness and high tactical quality. Type III error has been defined as solving the wrong problem, or "effectively" taking the wrong action. In this scenario, a problem has been identified, or a project is desired, but due to a badly performed strategic sequence, the wrong problem has been isolated and the subsequently implemented project has little value in that it does not address the intended target. Again, the implications for this error type are to develop and implement a project (tactics), often involving large expenditures of human and budgetary resources, for which inadequate or incorrect initial planning and problem recognition was done (strategy).

The final type of error that is likely to be seen in project implementation is *Type IV error*. Type IV error can be defined as taking an action which solves the right problem but the solution is not used by the organization. An example of Type IV error would occur following an effective strategy that has correctly identified the problem and proposed an effective, or "correct" solution; in this case, a project. Type IV error would result if, following the tactical operationalization, the project was not used by the clients for whom it was intended.

In addition to commenting on possible types of error which may be associated with each cell in Figure 20-3, it is important to understand some of the other aspects of likely outcomes for projects falling within each of the four cells.

Cell 1: High Strategy—High Tactics

Quadrant 1 shows the setting for those projects which have been rated highly effective in carrying out both strategy and tactics during the implementation process. Not surprisingly, we would expect that the majority of projects corresponding to this situation would be successfully implemented. In addition to high quality strategic activities (Mission, Top Management Support, Project Schedule) these projects have also been effectively operationalized. This operationalization has taken the form of a "high" rating on tactical issues (Client Consultation, Personnel, etc.). As stated, it would be reasonable to expect resulting projects to generally show a high frequency of implementation success.

Cell 3: Low Strategy—Low Tactics

The reciprocal of the first case is in the third quadrant and consists of a situation in which both strategic and tactical functions were inadequately performed. It would be expected that projects falling into this quadrant would have a high likelihood of implementation failure. Not only is initial strategy low, or poorly performed, but subsequent tactics are also ineffective.

Cell 4: High Strategy—Low Tactics

While the results of projects rated as high strategy—high tactics and low strategy—low tactics may be intuitively obvious, perhaps a more intriguing question concerns the likely outcomes of projects found in the "off-diagonal" of Figure 20-3, namely, high strategy—low tactics and low strategy—high tactics. It is interesting to speculate on the result of these "mixed" scenarios in attempting to assess project success. In fact, it has been found that project implementation efforts falling within these two cells often tend to exhibit characteristics of unique, but fairly consistent, patterns.

Cell 4 refers to the situation in which the project strategy was effectively performed but subsequent tactics were rated as ineffective. As can be seen from Figure 20-3, in addition to a high likelihood of Type I and Type IV errors, one would expect projects classified in this quadrant to exhibit a strong tendency toward "errors of inaction" such as low acceptance and low use by organization members or clients for whom the project was intended. Little is done in the way of effective tactical project implementation following initial competent strategic activities. Low acceptance and use are likely outcomes because tactical duties, including Client Consultation and "selling" of the final project, are poorly performed.

Cell 2: Low Strategy—High Tactics

The final cell represents the reverse of the previous case. In this alternative, project strategy is poorly conceived or initial planning is inadequately developed but tactical operationalization is effectively managed. One of the likely outcomes for projects classified into this cell is what are referred to as "errors of action." Because of poor strategy, a project may be initially developed and rushed into its implementation without clear ideas of its purpose. In fact, the project may not even be needed by the organization. However, tactical follow-up is well managed to the point where the inadequate or unnecessary project is implemented. This scenario represents a classic example of the "errors of action" in many areas of modern management. The mind-set is often one of "Go ahead and do it" rather than spending enough time early in the project's life to fully develop the strategy and assess whether or not the project is needed and how it should be approached.

STRATEGY AND TACTICS OVER TIME

Strategy and tactics are both essential for successful project implementation, but differently so at various stages in the project life cycle. Strategic issues are most important at the beginning of the project. Tactical issues become more important towards the end. This is not to say that there should not be a continuous interaction and testing between the strategic and tactical factors. Strategy is not static and often changes in the dynamic corporation, making continuous monitoring essential. Nevertheless, a successful project manager must be able to transition between strategic and tactical considerations as the project moves forward.

As Figure 20-4 shows, a recent study of over 400 projects has demonstrated that strategic issues become less important and tactical issues become more important to project success over the life of a project (17). The importance value shown in Figure 20-3 has been measured by regression beta weights showing the combined relationships between strategy, tactics, and project success over the four project life-cycle stages. During the early stages, conceptualization and planning, strategy is shown to be

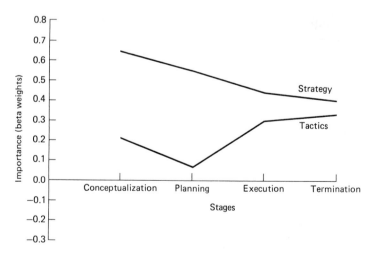

Figure 20-4. Changes in strategy and tactics across the project life cycle ($n = 418$).

of significantly greater importance to project success than are tactics. As the project moves toward the final termination stage, project strategy and tactics achieve almost equal importance. It appears that throughout the project, initial strategies and goals continue to "drive" the project tactics. In other words, strategy continues to influence and shape tactics. At no point does strategy become unimportant to project success, while tactics increase in efforts to operationalize strategic demands.

These changes in the importance of strategy and tactics to project success have important implications for the project manager. The successful manager must be versatile and able to adapt to these changing circumstances. A project manager who is a brilliant strategist but an ineffective tactician has a strong likelihood of committing errors of Type I and Type IV as the project moves downstream. In addition, these errors may occur after substantial resources have already been expended and commitment made for the project. In contrast, the project manager who is excellent at tactical execution but weak in strategic thinking has a probability of committing errors of Type II and Type III as shown in quadrant 2, Figure 20-3. These errors will more likely occur early in the process, but perhaps stay somewhat undiscovered because of the effectiveness of the manager's execution skills.

IMPLICATIONS FOR MANAGERS

Based on the demands facing project managers and the discussion of strategy and tactics which has been developed in this chapter, there are several conclusions which can be drawn relative to project critical success factors, along with practical implications for managers to help control the project implementation process.

1. Use a Multiple-Factor Model

Project management is a complex task in which the manager must attend to many variables. The more specific one can be with regard to the definition and monitoring of those variables, the more likely a successful outcome for the project will occur. Earlier in this chapter, we had listed a set of ten critical success factors which have been empirically shown to be strongly related to project success, as demonstrated by recent research. In addition to simply providing a list of factors for the project manager to consider, our research has also led to the development of a process framework of project implementation. Within this framework, the ten critical success factors are shown to contain a degree of sequentiality, in that the various factors become more critical to project success at different points in the project life cycle. As a result, it is important for the project manager to make use of a multiple-factor model, first to understand the variety of factors impacting on project success, and then to be aware of their relative importance across stages in the project implementation process.

2. Think Strategically Early in the Project Life Cycle

Another important implication in our discussion of project strategy and tactics is the breakdown of the ten critical factors into two distinct subdimensions, relating to the concepts of strategy and tactics. Further, it was shown that it is important to consider the "strategic" factors early in the project life cycle, during the Conceptualization and Planning stages when they become most important. As a result, it is necessary to accentuate the strategy factors (Mission, Top Management Support, and Schedule/Plans) during these early stages. It is argued that at this time, these factors are the most significant predictors of project success.

A practical suggestion for organizations implementing projects would be to bring the project manager and his team on board early in the project life cycle (preferably during the Conceptualization phase). Many managers make the mistake of not involving members of their project teams in early planning and conceptual meetings, perhaps under the assumption that the team members should only concern themselves with their specific jobs. In fact, it is very important at an early stage that both the project manager *and* the project team members "buy in" to the goals of the project and the means to achieve those goals. The more project team members are aware of these goals, the greater the likelihood of their taking active part in the monitoring and troubleshooting of the project and, consequently, the higher the quality of those activities for the project implementation.

3. Think More Tactically as the Project Moves Forward in Time

As Figure 20-4 shows, by the later "work" stages of execution and termination, strategy and tactics are of almost equal importance to project implementation success. Consequently, it is important that the project manager shift the emphasis in the project from "What do we want to do?" to "How do we want to do it?" The specific critical success factors associated with project tactics tend to reemphasize the importance of focusing on the "How" instead of the "What." Factors such as Personnel, Client Consultation, Communication, Monitoring, etc., are more concerned with attempts to better manage the specific action steps in the project implementation process. While we argue that it is important to bring the project team on board during the initial strategy phase in the project, it is equally important to manage their shift into a tactical, action mode in which their specific project team duties are performed to help the project toward completion.

4. Make Strategy and Tactics Work for You and Your Project Team

One of the points we have attempted to reinforce in this chapter is that either strong strategy or strong tactics by themselves will not ensure project success. When strategy is strong and tactics are weak, there is a great potential for creating strong, well-intended projects that never get off the ground. Cost and schedule overruns, along with general frustration, are often the side effects from projects which encounter such "errors of inaction." On the other hand, a project which starts off with a weak or poorly conceived strategy and receives strong subsequent tactical operationalization has the likelihood of being successfully implemented, but solves the wrong problem (Type III error). New York advertising agencies can tell horror stories of ad campaigns which were poorly conceived but still implemented, sometimes costing millions of dollars, and were subsequently assessed a disaster and scrubbed.

In addition to having project strategy and tactics working together, it is important to remember (again following the diagram in Figure 20-4) that initially conceived strategy should be used to "drive" tactics. Strategy and tactics are not independent of each other, but should be used together in sequence. Hence, strategy, which is developed in the earliest stages of the project, should be made known to all project team members during the entire implementation process. At no point do the strategic factors become unimportant to project success, but instead they must be continually assessed and reassessed over the life of the project. Using the example of a military scenario, tactics must be used in constant support of the overall strategy. Strategy contains the goals that were initially set and are of paramount importance to any operation.

5. Consciously Plan for and Manage Your Project Team's Transition from Strategy to Tactics

The project team leader needs to actively monitor his or her project through its life cycle. Important to the monitoring process is the attempt to accurately assess the position of the project in its life cycle at several different points throughout the implementation process. For the project manager, it is important to remember that the transition between strategy and tactics involves the inclusion of an additional set of critical success factors. Instead of concentrating on the set of three factors associated with project strategy, the project manager must also include the second set of factors, thus making use of all the ten factors relating to both strategy and tactics.

An important but often overlooked method to help the project leader manage the transition from strategy to tactics is to make efforts to continually communicate the changing status of the project to the other members of the project team. Communication reemphasizes the importance of a joint, team effort in implementing the project. Further, it reinforces the status of the project relative to its life cycle. The project team is kept aware of the specific stage in which the project resides as well as the degree of strategic versus tactical activities necessary to successfully sequence the project from its current stage to the next phase in its life cycle. Finally, communication helps the project manager keep track of the various activities performed by his or her project team, making it easier to verify that strategic vision is not lost in the later phases of tactical operationalization.

CONCLUSIONS

This chapter has attempted to better define the process of project implementation through exposing the manager to a set of empirically derived factors found to be critical to project success. A ten-factor model has been presented showing these key factors and their hypothesized interrelationships. In addition, a diagnostic instrument, the Project Implementation Profile, has been presented in its entirety as a potential tool for project management and control (See Appendix). It is suggested that the PIP be used on a regular basis as a monitor of these ten key behavioral factors. It was shown that these factors may be subdimensionalized to include those activities related to initial project strategy and subsequent tactical follow-up. These dimensions of strategy and tactics are useful for the project manager in that they prescribe a two-stage process to successful project implementation.

The ability to transition successfully between early strategy and later tactics is an important characteristic for project managers to possess. Figure 20-3 showed a 2-by-2 diagram of likely outcomes for projects when strategy and/or tactics were poorly performed. Figure 20-4 demonstrated the relative importance of strategy and tactics over four distinct stages in the project life cycle, showing that strategy is of great importance initially and decreases over the life cycle while tactics steadily increase in importance. Finally, some specific suggestions were presented for project managers, in an effort to help them better manage the transition which projects go through over their life cycle.

As was stated initially, the project management process represents a complex task. The project manager is continually assaulted with a wide variety of demands on his time and resources. Because of the dynamic nature of most projects, it is becoming increasingly difficult for the project manager to keep adequate control over every aspect in the project which requiresattention. This chapter has offered some suggestions to project managers who are intent on better understanding their project during its implementation process, but are at a loss as to how to go about attempting to more adequately ensure project success.

REFERENCES

1. Adams, J. R. and Barndt, S. E. "Behavioral Implications of the Project Life Cycle," in *Project Management Handbook,* ed. Cleland, D. I. and King, W. R. (Van Nostrand Reinhold. New York, 1983), pp. 222–244.
2. Alter, S. "Implementation Risk Analysis," in *The Implementation of Management Science,* ed. Doktor, R., Schultz, R. L. and Slevin, D. P. (North-Holland. New York, 1979), pp. 103–120.
3. Bardach, E. *The Implementation Game* (MIT Press. Cambridge, Mass., 1977).
4. Bavelas, A. "Project Echo: Use of Projective Techniques to Define Reality in Different Cultures." Personal communication, Stanford University, 1968.
5. Bean, A. S. and Radnor, M. "The Role of Intermediaries in the Implementation of Management Science," in *The Implementation of Management Science,* ed. Doktor, R., Schultz, R. L. and Slevin, D. P. (North-Holland. New York, 1979), pp. 121–138.
6. Beck, D. R. "Implementing Top Management Plans Through Project Management," in *Project Management Handbook,* ed. Cleland, D. I. and King, W. R. (Van Nostrand Reinhold. New York, 1983), pp. 166–184.
7. Cleland, D. I. and Kerzner, H. *A Project Management Dictionary of Terms* (Van Nostrand Reinhold. New York, 1985).
8. M. J. Ginzberg, "A Study of the Implementation Process," in *The Implementation of Management Science,* ed. Doktor, R., Schultz, R. L. and Slevin, D. P. (North-Holland. New York, 1979), pp. 85–102.
9. Hammond, J. S. III. "A Practitioner-Oriented Framework for Implementation," in *The Implementation of Management Science,* ed. Doktor, R., Schultz, R. L. and Slevin, D. P. (North-Holland. New York, 1979), pp. 35–62.
10. King, W. R. and Cleland, D. I. "Life Cycle Management," in *Project Management Handbook,* ed. Cleland, D. I. and King, W. R. (Van Nostrand Reinhold. New York, 1983), pp. 209–221.
11. Kolb, D. A. and Frohman, A. L. "An Organizational Development Approach to Consulting." *Sloan Management Review,* Vol. 12 (1970), pp. 51–65.
12. Lewin, K. "Group Decision and Social Change," in *Readings in Social Psychology,* ed. Newcomb and Hartley (Holt, Rinehart and Winston. New York, 1952), pp. 459–473.
13. Lucas H. C. Jr. "The Implementation of an Operations Research Model in the Brokerage Industry," in *The Implementation of Management Science,* ed. Doktor, R., Schultz, R. L. and Slevin, D. P. (North-Holland. New York, 1979), pp. 139–154.
14. Manley, J. H. "Implementation Attitudes: A Model and a Measurement Methodology," in *Implementing Operating Research and Management Science,* ed. Schultz, R. L. and Slevin, D. P. (Elsevier. New York, 1975), pp. 183–202.
15. Morris, P. W. G. "Managing Project Interfaces—Key Points for Project Success," in

Project Management Handbook, ed. Cleland, D. I. and King, W. R. (Van Nostrand Reinhold. New York, 1983), pp. 3–36.

16. Nutt, P. C. "Implementation Approaches for Project Planning." *Academy of Management Review,* Vol. 8 (1983), pp. 600–611.

17. Pinto, J. K. "Project Implementation: A Determination of Its Critical Success Factors, Moderators, and Their Relative Importance Across the Project Life Cycle." Unpublished doctoral dissertation, University of Pittsburgh, 1986.

18. Pinto, J. K. and Slevin, D. P. "Critical Factors in Successful Project Implementation." *IEEE Transactions on Engineering Management,* Vol. EM-34 (1987) pp. 22–27.

19. Schultz, R. L. and Slevin, D. P. "Implementation and Management Innovation," in *Implementing Operations Research and Management Science,* ed. Schultz, R. L. and Slevin, D. P. (Elsevier. New York, 1975), pp. 3–22.

20. Schultz, R. L., Slevin, D. P. and Pinto, J. K. "Strategy and Tactics in a Process Model of Project Implementation." *Interfaces,* Vol. 17, May–June, 1987 pp. 34–46.

21. Slevin, D. P. and Pinto, J. K. "The Project Implementation Profile: New Tool for Project Managers." *Project Management Journal,* Vol. 18 (1986), pp. 57–71.

22. Slevin, D. P. and Pinto, J. K. "Balancing Strategy and Tactics in Project Implementation." *Sloan Management Review,* Vol 29, No. 6, pp. 33–41.

23. Souder, W. E., Maher, P. M., Baker, N. R., Shumway, C. R. and Rubenstein, A. H. "An Organizational Intervention Approach to the Design and Implementation of R&D Project Selection Models," in *Implementing Operations Research and Management Science,* ed. Schultz, R. L. and Slevin, D. P. (Elsevier. New York, 1975), pp. 133–152.

24. Steiner, G. A. *Top Management Planning,* (MacMillian, New York, 1969).

25. Tuman, G. J. "Development and Implementation of Effective Project Management Information and Control Systems," in *Project Management Handbook,* ed. Cleland D. I. and King, W. R. (Van Nostrand Reinhold. New York, 1983), pp. 495–532.

PROJECT IMPLEMENTATION PROFILE

Project Name: _____

Project Manager: _____

Profile Completed By: _____

Date: _____

Briefly describe your project, giving its title and specific goals:

_____

_____

_____

_____

Think of the project implementation you have just named. Consider the statements on the following pages. Using the scale provided, please circle the number that indicated the *extent* to which you agree or disagree with the following statements as they relate to activities occurring in the project about which you are reporting.

PROJECT IMPLEMENTATION PROFILE

FACTOR 1 – PROJECT MISSION

	Strongly Disagree			Neutral			Strongly Agree
1. The goals of the project are in line with the general goals of the organization	1	2	3	4	5	6	7
2. The basic goals of the project are made clear to the project team	1	2	3	4	5	6	7
3. The results of the project will benefit the parent organization	1	2	3	4	5	6	7
4. I am enthusiastic about the chances for success of this project...................	1	2	3	4	5	6	7
5. I am aware of and can identify the beneficial consequences to the organization of the success of this project	1	2	3	4	5	6	7

Factor 1 – Project Mission Total	

FACTOR 2 – TOP MANAGEMENT SUPPORT

	Strongly Disagree			Neutral			Strongly Agree
1. Upper management is responsive to our requests for additional resources, if the need arises	1	2	3	4	5	6	7
2. Upper management shares responsibility with the project team for ensuring the project's success........................	1	2	3	4	5	6	7
3. I agree with upper management on the degree of my authority and responsibility for the project	1	2	3	4	5	6	7
4. Upper management will support me in a crisis	1	2	3	4	5	6	7
5. Upper management has granted us the necessary authority and will support our decisions concerning the project	1	2	3	4	5	6	7

Factor 2 – Top Management Support Total	

PROJECT IMPLEMENTATION PROFILE

FACTOR 3 — PROJECT SCHEDULE/PLAN

	Strongly Disagree			Neutral			Strongly Agree
1. We know which activities contain slack time or slack resources which can be utilized in other areas during emergencies ...	1	2	3	4	5	6	7
2. There is a detailed plan (including time schedules, milestones, manpower requirements, etc.) for the completion of the project.........................	1	2	3	4	5	6	7
3. There is a detailed budget for the project....	1	2	3	4	5	6	7
4. Key personnel needs (who, when) are specified in the project plan..............	1	2	3	4	5	6	7
5. There are contingency plans in case the project is off schedule or off budget........	1	2	3	4	5	6	7

Factor 3 — Project Schedule/Plan Total	

FACTOR 4 — CLIENT CONSULTATION

	Strongly Disagree			Neutral			Strongly Agree
1. The clients were given the opportunity to provide input early in the project development stage	1	2	3	4	5	6	7
2. The clients (intended users) are kept informed of the project's progress	1	2	3	4	5	6	7
3. The value of the project has been discussed with the eventual clients.........	1	2	3	4	5	6	7
4. The limitations of the project have been discussed with the clients (what the project is *not* designed to do)..........	1	2	3	4	5	6	7
5. The clients were told whether or not their input was assimilated into the project plan	1	2	3	4	5	6	7

Factor 4 — Client Consultation Total	

PROJECT IMPLEMENTATION PROFILE

FACTOR 5 — PERSONNEL

	Strongly Disagree		Neutral			Strongly Agree	

1. Project team personnel understand their role on the project team.................. 1 2 3 4 5 6 7

2. There is sufficient manpower to complete the project............................ 1 2 3 4 5 6 7

3. The personnel on the project team understand how their performance will be evaluated........................... 1 2 3 4 5 6 7

4. Job descriptions for team members have been written and distributed and are understood........................... 1 2 3 4 5 6 7

5. Adequate technical and/or managerial training (and time for training) is available for members of the project team 1 2 3 4 5 6 7

Factor 5 — Personnel Total	

FACTOR 6 — TECHNICAL TASKS

	Strongly Disagree		Neutral			Strongly Agree	

1. Specific project tasks are well managed 1 2 3 4 5 6 7

2. The project engineers and other technical people are competent.................... 1 2 3 4 5 6 7

3. The technology that is being used to support the project works well............. 1 2 3 4 5 6 7

4. The appropriate technology (equipment, training programs, etc.) has been selected for project success................ 1 2 3 4 5 6 7

5. The people implementing this project understand it 1 2 3 4 5 6 7

Factor 6 — Technical Tasks Total	

PROJECT IMPLEMENTATION PROFILE

FACTOR 7 – CLIENT ACCEPTANCE

	Strongly Disagree		Neutral			Strongly Agree
1. There is adequate documentation of the project to permit easy use by the clients (instructions, etc.).................	1	2	3	4	5	6	7
2. Potential clients have been contacted about the usefulness of the project...........	1	2	3	4	5	6	7
3. An adequate presentation of the project has been developed for clients..............	1	2	3	4	5	6	7
4. Clients know who to contact when problems or questions arise........................	1	2	3	4	5	6	7
5. Adequate advanced preparation has been done to determine how best to "sell" the project to clients........................	1	2	3	4	5	6	7

Factor 7 – Client Acceptance Total	

FACTOR 8 – MONITORING AND FEEDBACK

	Strongly Disagree		Neutral			Strongly Agree
1. All important aspects of the project are monitored, including measures that will provide a complete picture of the project's progress (adherence to budget and schedule, manpower and equipment utilization, team morale, etc.)............................	1	2	3	4	5	6	7
2. Regular meetings to monitor project progress and improve the feedback to the project team are conducted.............	1	2	3	4	5	6	7
3. Actual progress is regularly compared with the project schedule......................	1	2	3	4	5	6	7
4. The results of project reviews are regularly shared with all project personnel who have impact upon budget and schedule...........	1	2	3	4	5	6	7
5. When the budget or schedule requires revision, input is solicited from the project team...........................	1	2	3	4	5	6	7

Factor 8 – Monitoring and Feedback Total	

PROJECT IMPLEMENTATION PROFILE

FACTOR 9 — COMMUNICATION

	Strongly Disagree		Neutral			Strongly Agree	

1. The results (decisions made, information received and needed, etc.) of planning meetings are published and distributed to applicable personnel.................... 1 2 3 4 5 6 7

2. Individuals/groups supplying input have received feedback on the acceptance or rejection of their input................... 1 2 3 4 5 6 7

3. When the budget or schedule is revised, the changes *and* the reasons for the changes are communicated to all members of the project team................................ 1 2 3 4 5 6 7

4. The reasons for the changes to existing policies/procedures have been explained to members of the project team, other groups affected by the changes, and upper management.......................... 1 2 3 4 5 6 7

5. All groups affected by the project know how to make problems known to the project team .. 1 2 3 4 5 6 7

Factor 9 — Communication Total	

FACTOR 10 — TROUBLESHOOTING

	Strongly Disagree		Neutral			Strongly Agree	

1. The project leader is not hesitant to enlist the aid of personnel not involved in the project in the event of problems........ 1 2 3 4 5 6 7

2. "Brainstorming" sessions are held to determine where problems are most likely to occur.............................. 1 2 3 4 5 6 7

3. In case of project difficulties, project team members know exactly where to go for assistance............................. 1 2 3 4 5 6 7

4. I am confident that problems that arise can be solved completely 1 2 3 4 5 6 7

5. Immediate action is taken when problems come to the project team's attention 1 2 3 4 5 6 7

Factor 10 — Troubleshooting Total	

PROJECT IMPLEMENTATION PROFILE

PROJECT PERFORMANCE

	Strongly Disagree			Neutral			Strongly Agree
1. This project has/will come in on schedule	1	2	3	4	5	6	7
2. This project has/will come in on budget.......	1	2	3	4	5	6	7
3. The project that has been developed works, (or if still being developed, looks as if it will work)............................	1	2	3	4	5	6	7
4. The project will be/is used by its intended clients	1	2	3	4	5	6	7
5. This project has/will directly benefit the intended users: either through increasing efficiency or employee effectiveness	1	2	3	4	5	6	7
6. Given the problem for which it was developed, this project seems to do the best job of solving that problem, i.e., it was the best choice among the set of alternatives............................	1	2	3	4	5	6	7
7. Important clients, directly affected by this project, will make use of it	1	2	3	4	5	6	7
8. I am/was satisfied with the process by which this project is being/was completed	1	2	3	4	5	6	7
9. We are confident that nontechnical start-up problems will be minimal, because the project will be readily accepted by its intended users	1	2	3	4	5	6	7
10. Use of this project has led/will lead directly to improved or more effective decision making or performance for the clients.............................	1	2	3	4	5	6	7
11. This project will have a positive impact on those who make use of it...............	1	2	3	4	5	6	7
12. The results of this project represent a definite improvement in performance over the way clients used to perform these activities..............................	1	2	3	4	5	6	7

PROJECT PERFORMANCE TOTAL	

PROJECT IMPLEMENTATION PROFILE

Percentile Scores
How does your project score?

Now see how your project scored in comparison to a data base of 409 projects. If you are below the 50 percentile on any factor, you may wish to devote extra attention to that factor.

Percentile Score	Raw Score				
% of individuals Scoring Lower	**Factor 1** Project Mission	**Factor 2** Top Management Support	**Factor 3** Project Schedule/ Plan	**Factor 4** Client Consultation	**Factor 5** Personnel- Recruitment, Selection, Training
100%	35	35	35	35	35
90%	34	34	33	34	32
80%	33	32	31	33	30
70%	32	30	30	32	28
60%	31	28	28	31	27
50%	30	27	27	30	24
40%	29	25	26	29	22
30%	28	23	24	27	20
20%	26	20	21	25	18
10%	25	17	16	22	14
0%	7	6	5	7	5

510

PROJECT IMPLEMENTATION PROFILE

After you have compared your scores, you may plot them on the next page and mark any factors that need special effort.

Percentile Score			Raw Score			
% of Individuals Scoring Lower	Factor 6 Technical Tasks	Factor 7 Client Acceptance	Factor 8 Monitoring and Feedback	Factor 9 Communication	Factor 10 Trouble-shooting	Project Performance
100%	35	35	35	35	35	84
90%	34	34	34	34	33	79
80%	32	33	33	32	31	76
70%	30	32	31	30	29	73
60%	29	31	30	29	28	71
50%	28	30	28	28	26	69
40%	27	29	27	26	24	66
30%	26	27	24	24	23	63
20%	24	24	21	21	21	59
10%	21	20	17	16	17	53
0%	8	8	5	5	5	21

PROJECT IMPLEMENTATION PROFILE

Tracking Critical Success Factors Grid

Percentile Rankings

	0%	10%	20%	30%	40%	50%	60%	70%	80%	90%	100%
1. Project Mission											
2. Top Management Support											
3. Project Schedule											
4. Client Consultation											
5. Personnel											
6. Technical Tasks											
7. Client Acceptance											
8. Monitoring and Feedback											
9. Communication											
10. Troubleshooting											
Project Performance											

21. Quality Program Management in Project Management

John L. Heidenreich*

Completing a project on time and within cost loses importance if quality is not attained. The news media frequently report instances of inadequate quality that result in costly product recalls, construction condemnation before completion, rework and delays, accidents, and, on occasion, deaths. In addition to the adverse financial and safety effects, inadequate quality is detrimental to the image of an organization and can adversely affect future business potential. Project management includes managing for quality, as well as managing to complete a project on time and within cost.

Quality Program management is the element of project management that is designed to assure the attainment of quality. Its goal is to do the right things right the first time. It accomplishes its goal by utilizing basic elements of good management: planning, organization, implementation, feedback, and corrective action.

This chapter addresses management responsibilities and actions regarding Quality Program management in project management, including:

- Understanding quality.
- Establishing objectives, philosophy, and policies.
- Balancing schedule, cost, and quality.
- Quality Program planning.
- Organization.

* John L. Heidenreich has 13 years of hands-on experience in quality management and consulting. He has consulted for the U.S. Nuclear Regulatory Commission, the Chicago Operations Office of the U.S. Department of Energy, state and local government agencies, oil companies, utilities, contractors, manufacturers, and material manufacturers and suppliers. His management analysis of U.S. Nuclear Regulatory Commission programs was published in NUREG 1055. He has prepared Quality Program manuals and procedures, conducted seminars, and performed management evaluations and audits nationally and internationally. He holds a B.S. degree in Physics from Western Illinois University.

- Quality Program implementation.
- Feedback of quality-related information.
- Taking corrective action.

UNDERSTANDING QUALITY

Quality Achievement

What is quality? In construction and manufacturing industries, quality has generally become accepted to mean fitness for use or compliance with requirements. For an organization to prosper, fitness for use must be attained in an efficient and economical manner. Compliance to requirements must be preceded by the establishment of appropriate requirements. Quality doesn't just automatically happen. To achieve quality requires a clear definition of function, performance objectives, and design, environmental and service conditions; translation of those requirements into working documents, such as specifications, drawings, procedures, and instructions; identification of the working documents in construction and manufacturing process control documents; performance of quality-affecting activities in accordance with requirements of the working documents; and verification that the requirements have been met.

Top management and all project personnel must understand that attaining quality is the responsibility of top management and all project personnel performing quality-affecting activities, not just the Quality department. When an organization experiences financial problems, top management does not hold the Finance department solely responsible. Instead, it recognizes that the financial problems are not caused by the Finance department, but are the result of other problems within the organization. Quality problems are usually attributed to deficiencies or breakdowns in Quality Programs. Because Quality Programs are prepared by Quality departments, they are blamed and held accountable for the problems. However, the Quality department did not define function, performance objectives and design, environmental, and service conditions, did not translate those requirements into working documents, and did not manufacture, install, or construct the item. Marketing, usually with the assistance of engineering, is responsible for the clear definition of requirements to be met. Engineering is responsible for translating those requirements into specifications, drawings, procedures, and instructions. Purchasing, manufacturing, fabrication, installation, and construction are responsible for performing activities in accordance with the requirements of the working documents. Management of each function performing the above activities is responsible for assuring the activities are properly performed. Typically, the Quality department is responsible for establishing a Quality Program to control these activities and for verifying that the Quality Program is implemented and the requirements of specifications, drawings, procedures, and instructions identified on the process control documents are met. Quality problems are normally the result of breakdowns in the management and implementation of any of these activities. Quality problems can be minimized through the understanding of quality and the implementation of basic management practices.

Quality Program

A Quality Program is a systematic approach to planning and controlling quality during a project. It improves management by establishing consistent methods of operation for all quality-affecting activities and controls changes in those methods. It results in increased productivity and a reduction in overall project costs.

Management in many organizations views a Quality Program as an unnecessary expense and an impediment to productivity. In such organizations, Quality Programs either are not established or are not effective. In regulated industries that have Quality Program requirements, management in many organizations views a Quality Program as a necessary expense and evil, but an impediment to productivity. In such organizations, Quality Programs are established, but usually are not effective. Management that views a Quality Program as an effective management tool, discovers that quality improves through focusing attention on preventing errors, productivity improves and project costs decrease through the reduction in rework and schedule delays, and the costs for the Quality Program are offset by the resulting savings in costs.

Quality Program activities of establishing documented methods of control of quality-affecting activities, training personnel in the methods, implementing the methods, verifying implementation, measuring effectiveness, and identifying and correcting problems to prevent recurrence are simply good business practices. There is no contradiction between good controls for quality and good business.

OBJECTIVES, PHILOSOPHY, AND POLICIES

The top management of the organization responsible for a project is responsible for defining the objectives and philosophy of the organization. It is also responsible for establishing policies to assure clear understanding of those objectives and the philosophy by all managers. It is important to include quality in the objectives, philosophy, and policies in order to document top management's commitment to quality and its expectations that the entire organization considers the attainment of quality to be one of its primary goals. No one is basically opposed to quality, so top management often believes that its attainment is a naturally understood goal. Through its actions, top management establishes what is important. Failure to emphasize quality results in a perception by other management that quality is not as important as other goals, such as schedule and cost. This perception filters throughout the organization to the worker level, and quality may be sacrificed at the expense of schedule and cost. Top management inclusion of quality in its objectives, philosophy, and policies is an important initial step toward establishing an effective Quality Program and the attainment of quality.

BALANCING SCHEDULE, COST, AND QUALITY

For a project to be successful, top management must establish a meaningful balance between schedule, cost, and quality. Emphasis on schedule can result in a project completed on time that is over cost and has unacceptable quality. Emphasis on cost can result in a project within cost that is not completed on time and that has unacceptable quality. Emphasis on quality can result in a project with the desired quality that is not completed on time and is over cost. To establish the necessary balance between schedule, cost, and quality, top management of the organization responsible for a project must include the quality function with the other organizational functions in providing input during early project planning. To maintain the balance, top management must provide for project management integration of cost, schedule and quality planning, control and performance data throughout all phases of the project. The quality function must be included with the other organizational functions in providing feedback to top management concerning project problems and the effectiveness of the Quality Program. Top management must react promptly and effectively to cause changes in the Quality Program and project management as dictated by the feedback.

QUALITY PROGRAM PLANNING

Quality Program planning must be performed before the start of project activities and should involve all of the organizational elements responsible for project management. The early involvement of each organizational element permits integration of quality concepts into initial project management activities, such as the development of project plans, work breakdown structures, work packages, and cost accounts. It provides the opportune time to develop each organizational element's understanding of the importance of quality to the project. Through each organizational element's input, it also provides them with a sense of ownership of the Quality Program. The Quality Program does not just become a program invoked by top management which disregards the concerns of those to be held responsible for its implementation.

Most projects progress through several stages, such as conceptual, development, design, manufacture, construction, installation, operation, maintenance, and modification. The Quality Program should evolve with the project since the quality-affecting activities change as the project progresses through its stages. In addition, requirements, technology, and the working environment may change throughout the life of a project. Project personnel must accept this fact and react positively in response to such change.

The controls necessary for an organization are dependent upon the activities for which it is responsible. To be cost effective, the degree of control should be based upon the significance of activities in relation to their impact on safety, quality, cost, and schedule. Factors to consider include the consequences of malfunction or failure, complexity of the project organization and the work to be performed, accessibility for repair or replacement, degree to which compliance can be determined through inspection and tests, and quality history.

The initial step in planning is to identify the objectives to be achieved and all activities and items critical to achieving the objectives in accordance with requirements. This task can be accomplished through the project management activity of establishing project plans and work breakdown structures.

The second step is to analyze the significance of the activities and items by using various analysis techniques, such as Failure Mode and Effects Analysis and Design of Experiments. The use of these analysis techniques can be found in many publications. A brief description of these techniques follows.

Failure Mode and Effects Analysis

Failure Mode and Effects Analysis is conducted prior to production or construction activities to prevent the first problem from occurring. It involves identifying each possible failure mode of the item, system, or structure and its probability of occurrence; the effects of failure and severity of the effects; potential causes of failure; current controls intended to prevent the cause or detect the failure; and the likelihood of the failure being detected by existing controls; and then initiating action to eliminate the potential failure modes or reduce their occurrence.

Design of Experiments

Design of Experiments is also conducted prior to production or construction activities. It involves choosing certain factors for study, varying those factors in a controlled fashion, observing the effect of such action, and making a decision based upon the most favorable results.

The third step in planning is to establish control measures commensurate with the significance of the activities and items. This can be accomplished by classifying the activities and items into several groups based upon their significance and defining the measures of control to be applied to each group. Inspection and test plans should be prepared for each group or for specific activities and items, as applicable, which itemize inspection, surveillance, and test points in the sequence of events pertaining to the activities and items.

The fourth step is to integrate the control measures and inspection, surveillance, and test points into the overall management of the project. The control measures should be defined in a Quality Assurance Manual, and administrative and technical procedures. The inspection, surveillance, and test points should be incorporated into work package activities and administrative and technical procedures.

During Quality Program planning, consideration should be given to the need for special controls, processes, skills, and equipment, and to incorporate the appropriate features of the concepts of Quality Control, Quality Assurance, Statistical Process Control, Quality Improvement, Employee Participation Teams, and Quality Costs. Organizations have tended to utilize a specific concept as the solution to their quality problems. The results have often been disappointing. Each concept is but one aspect of a broader, comprehensive Quality Program. A description of each of these quality concepts follows.

Quality Control

Quality Control has become accepted as the measurement of the characteristics of an item or process to determine its conformance to specified requirements and the taking of action when nonconformance exists. Quality Control is commonly considered to be inspection, examination, and testing and is an important aspect of Quality Programs. Inspection, examination, and testing of every item and activity, although often necessary based upon the significance of an item or activity, is prohibitively expensive. The factors of monotony, fatigue, and human error result in unacceptable items still being accepted. Sampling plans have been developed based upon theories of probability to provide a more economical and efficient basis for Quality Control. Samples of items and activities are inspected, examined, or tested and the results dictate acceptance or rejection of the entire lot of items or activities. Different sampling plans are applied to different characteristics following classification of the characteristics based upon their significance to safety, quality, cost, and schedule. Sample plans recognize and provide that a small percentage of items and activities will still be unacceptable. The judicious use of Quality Control is a vital part of verification of quality. Its use is normally dictated by an evaluation of the costs of Quality Control versus the affects of finding problems late in the project. It is used at the initial stages of an activity or process to verify that the activity or process is producing satisfactory results, at various stages of activities or processes during their periods of performance to verify that the activity or process continues to produce satisfactory results, and for final acceptance of completed items and structures. However, inspections, examinations, and tests are conducted after work is performed and they identify problems after they occur. When experiencing quality problems, the initial reaction of management is often to increase the number of Quality Control personnel, believing that this will solve their problems. It won't solve their problems. It will result in increased verification of quality, but does not address the more important issue of preventing unsatisfactory quality.

Organizations that base their Quality Programs solely on Quality Control do not have cost-effective programs. Quality cannot be obtained effectively and economically solely by Quality Control.

Quality Assurance

Quality Assurance has become accepted to mean planned and systematic actions to provide confidence that specified requirements are met and that items, systems, and structures will perform satisfactorily in service. It will not improve quality when requirements are inadequately specified or design is inadequate. Quality Assurance concentrates on preventing problems in addition to identifying and correcting them. Quality Assurance includes both the functions of attaining quality and of verifying quality. It extends from the top executive to the workers and typically encompasses activities of marketing, engineering, procurement, production control, material control, manufacturing, fabrication, inspection, testing, handling, storage, shipping, receiving, erection, installation, operation, maintenance, repair, and modification. The nature and extent of actions is dependent upon the quality-affecting activities performed or contracted.

The documented description of the planned and systematic actions is the organization's Quality Assurance Program. It typically describes the activities and items to which it applies and the organizational structure, interfaces and interface responsibilities, functional responsibilities, levels of authority, lines of communication, and methods or systems of control for quality-affecting activities.

In the manufacturing and construction industries, the following activities generally are included in a Quality Assurance Program:

- Reviewing project objectives or incoming contracts or order documents to determine and define technical and quality requirements, to identify omissions and inadequate definition of requirements, and to identify and provide for any required controls, processes, equipment, and skills.

- Controlling design activities to assure that quality is designed into the product and to assure consideration of performance, reliability, maintainability, safety, producibility, standardization, interchangeability, and cost. This includes specifying design methods and design inputs; translating the inputs into design and technical documents; verifying design adequacy prior to release through design reviews, alternate calculations, or qualification tests; obtaining vendor and contractor assistance early in the design process; and controlling design interfaces, design changes, and as-constructed configurations. Design interfaces are the interfaces and controls between participating design organizations.

- Controlling procurement activities, which includes selection and qualification of vendors and contractors who have shown evidence of their capability of achieving quality; assuring that technical, quality, and Quality Program requirements are included or referenced in procurement documents; reviewing and approving vendor and contractor Quality Programs and administrative and technical procedures; assessing vendor and contractor performance against requirements; requiring corrective action for conditions adverse to quality; and requiring notification and approval of design, material, and Quality Program changes.

  Supplier and contractor performance to requirements is a key ingredient to achieving quality during the project. The value of purchased materials, items, and services is normally a major percentage of the overall project cost. Yet many organizations utilize price as the key factor in awarding contracts and purchase orders. They fail to realize that throughout all project phases, the least costly item or service is not always the one with the lowest initial price. Costs associated with the repair or rework of completed work and the replacement of items as a result of inadequate quality is more costly than savings realized through the lowest initial price. Vendor and contractor selection and continued use should be based upon a combination of cost, schedule, and quality considerations.

- Establishing documented instructions, procedures, specifications, and drawings which include or reference acceptance criteria, for performing quality-affecting activities.
- Controlling the preparation, review for adequacy, approval, issuance, and revision of documents specifying quality requirements and describing quality-affecting activities. This includes establishing measures for assuring the adequacy and control of supplier and contractor documents as well.
- Controlling purchased items and services, including evaluation of their adequacy. This is normally achieved through performing surveillances of supplier and contractor activities, performing inspection, and reviewing supplier and contractor furnished evidence of quality, such as test reports and documentation of statistical process control.
- Identifying and controlling material and items so that only accepted materials and items are used or installed.
- Controlling processes affecting quality through the use of process control documents which specify applicable instructions, procedures, specifications and drawings.
- Controlling inspections, examinations, and tests to verify conformance to specified requirements and to demonstrate that items will perform satisfactorily in service. This includes identification of status to assure that required inspections, examinations, and tests are performed.
- Controlling measuring and testing equipment to maintain its accuracy.
- Controlling handling, cleaning, preservation, storage, packaging, and shipping of items to prevent damage or loss.
- Controlling activities and items that do not conform to specified requirements.
- Identifying and promptly correcting conditions adverse to quality.
- Specifying, preparing, maintaining, and later dispositioning records that furnish evidence of quality. Records are considered a primary

means of providing objective evidence of Quality Program implementation and the attainment of quality.

- Performing audits to determine compliance with the Quality Program and its effectiveness.
- Performing trend analysis to identify repetitive conditions adverse to quality.

Quality Assurance, by being planned and systematic actions, is a management system and a key management tool for attaining quality.

Statistical Process Control

Statistical Process Control involves using statistical data to improve processes and prevent deficiencies. It consists of performing capability studies to determine variability in a process or equipment, identifying the causes of variability, changing the process to reduce the variability, and monitoring the results of the process change. It is used to improve consistency and to prevent nonconforming work, rather than to identify nonconformances and take action based upon inspection results. The result is improved quality and productivity and reduction in inspection, rework, scrap, and process costs. Statistical Process Control is based upon mathematical theories of probability and uses tools such as frequency distributions, histograms, control charts, and problem solving techniques. However, implementation of Statistical Process Control can be accomplished by most personnel with basic training in application of the techniques and without education and training in the mathematical theories. Control charts, with control limits tighter than tolerance requirements and based upon process capability, are used to plot and trend values of characteristics to determine when something is about to go wrong with a process. As points fall outside the control limits, the cause is determined and corrective action is taken. Establishing control charts for all characteristics is not cost effective. Therefore, control charts are established for the key characteristics, and other characteristics are subject to random inspections. Numerous computer programs exist for the analysis of Statistical Process Control data, and the principles of Statistical Process Control can be applied to problem solving in many areas of project activities.

Quality Improvement

Quality Improvement consists of actions that result in improved quality of activities, items and structures. It involves establishing and collecting measurement data, identifying problems or potential improvements, and taking action to improve performance or usability. The concept has been used to improve quality and productivity of personnel in all departments within an organization and to make error prevention an inherent part of each activity. It provides top management with a measure of effort and forces each organizational element to assess its performance and productivity and take action to improve it. Productivity is simply measured as a ratio of output to input and can be managed through measurement in nearly every activity. It is affected by facilities, equipment, materials, workers, methods, and management. It can be improved through analysis and redefinition of tasks, work flow and allocation of resources. It is not uncommon for the costs of errors, rework, and repeated operations of all departments within an organization to exceed 25% of the total sales of the organization. To be effective, improvement actions must have the support of top management. A common approach is to establish a council or committee consisting of various members from top management and the management of operational departments. The council or committee is responsible for organizing objectives, developing strategy and measurement methods, publicizing results, and providing employee recognition. Working groups established by the council or committee include a council or committee member to provide continuity and evidence of management involvement. Through the establishment of Employee Participation Teams, problems are solved at the lowest possible level. The improvement program is a continuous process throughout all phases of the project.

Employee Participation Teams

Employee Participation Teams, also called Quality Circles, are teams of employees formed to identify and solve problems. Their success requires creation of a participative environment and an understanding of small-group dynamics, decision-making processes, and structured problem-solving techniques, such as brainstorming, cause and effect analysis, pareto analysis, and data gathering and sampling. Pareto analysis involves listing problems by their level of importance and frequency of occurrence and concentrating initial actions on correcting the most significant problems and their causes. Employee Participation Teams are an effective tool to gain employee involvement in problem identification and solving and have resulted in increased motivation of employees to attain quality.

Quality Costs

Quality Costs are used to measure the effectiveness of Quality Programs and to control the efforts of all departments. They are based upon facts and are an effective management tool for budgeting, identifying major and costly problem areas, and allocating manpower. Their use involves determining quality-related costs and their trends and taking action to reduce the costs and improve quality. Quality Costs are an effective Quality Program management tool for presenting the need for and impact of a Quality Program to top project management.

Four categories are typically established for Quality Costs, with numerous elements in each category. The categories are prevention, costs associated with establishing and implementing a Quality Program; appraisal, costs associated with evaluating conformance to requirements; internal failure, costs associated with materials, products, and structures that fail to meet requirements and are scrapped or cause rework or repair activities during their completion; and external failures, costs associated with defective products and structures after their completion as identified by the user. The costs are normally identifiable by accounting through established accounting systems with the assistance of the Quality department. Quality Cost Reports are a financial document which should be issued to top management by accounting on a monthly or quarterly basis. The basic concept is that investments in prevention and appraisal reduce internal and external failures, resulting in lower costs and less rework. The importance of Quality Costs as a management tool has been recognized by the military, who included use of Quality Cost data in MIL-Q-9858A in 1963.

Quality Program Preparation

Through the incorporation of appropriate features of the various quality concepts at the Quality Program planning stage, top management establishes a management system that stresses prevention of quality problems, active involvement of all project personnel, efficient and economical use of inspection, and utilization of factual performance data to continuously improve performance throughout the project.

The description of the managerial and administrative controls to be used for attaining and verifying quality during the project needs to clearly identify what is to be done, who is to do it, how it is to be done and documented, and when it is to be done. This description is the Quality Assurance Manual of the organization. Details for implementation of the controls are described in supplemental administrative and technical procedures. Administrative procedures are usually prepared by the Quality department with the assistance of other departments. Technical procedures are usually prepared by other departments in accordance with requirements of the administrative procedures and contain the specific instructions for the performance of specific activities. The Quality Assurance Manual, inspection and test plans, and supplemental procedures constitute the Quality Program and must be as simple as possible to permit their understanding and encourage their use. They must be written for the level of the user, not the writer. Complicated documents which cannot be understood will not be used. Project personnel tend to ignore such documents instead of trying to comprehend and implement them. Many organizations write their Quality Assurance Manual and supplemental procedures using vague, nonspecific terminology such as: when applicable, as appropriate, periodically, frequently, as required, the company, etc., in an attempt to provide flexibility in implementation of their program. Although permitting flexibility, such terminology does not provide a clear description of activities and leaves the interpretation of the terminology open to dispute and to each of those persons performing the activities. Such terminology is often used later as an excuse or justification for not performing an activity as intended.

ORGANIZATION

Organizational Structure

Top management of the organization responsible for a project has the responsibility for establishing an organizational structure which is conducive to maintaining the balance between schedule, cost, and quality. To accomplish this, it is necessary for top management to have a clear understanding of the scope and magnitude of the project and the role of each project organization. Top management should document the organizational structure in organization charts which include the job titles of managers and supervisors responsible for quality-affecting activities and for managing the project, and the major contractors for the project. The organization charts identify the project organizational elements and their basic functions and are to be included in the Quality Assurance Manual.

In establishing the organizational structure, top management is faced with the problem of how to incorporate the quality function.

One approach has been that each organizational element is responsible for attaining quality objectives as well as meeting schedule within cost. Therefore, each organizational element should do what it deems necessary to assure the quality of its work.

Another approach has been that, although each organizational element is responsible for attaining quality objectives as well as meeting schedule within cost, each organizational element is biased and quality might be sacrificed to meet the interests of the element and to maintain schedule within cost. This has often happened in organizations where top management has failed to establish and maintain a meaningful balance between schedule, cost, and quality.

Many regulations, codes, and standards contain Quality Program requirements which stipulate a separation of quality-attaining functions from quality assurance functions. The quality-attaining functions are those of defining requirements to be met, translating those requirements into working documents, and performing project activities in accordance with the requirements of the working documents. The quality assurance functions are typically those of planning a Quality Program and checking, reviewing, and verifying that the program is implemented and the desired quality is attained. Personnel performing quality assurance functions are required to have sufficient authority, organizational freedom, and independence from cost and schedule considerations to carry out their functions. Unfortunately, this has often resulted in a perception that quality is the responsibility of the quality assurance function instead of the attainers of quality. As a result, an adversarial role has often developed between personnel performing quality-affecting activities and personnel verifying attainment of quality and implementation of the Quality Program.

In view of the above, where should the quality function be located in an organization? Both approaches have been used with varying amounts of success. Where the performance and management of quality assurance functions have been delegated to each organizational element, there has been a tendency for each element to do as it pleases, resulting in inconsistent, and often inadequate, controls. To prevent this from occurring, it is necessary to coordinate the quality-related activities of each organizational element. The Quality Department accomplishes coordination of activities by establishing management and administrative control guidelines to be followed by each organizational element in establishing their controls, by reviewing the controls and procedures established by each element for their adequacy and completeness, and by performing surveillances and audits of each organizational element's implementation of their controls and procedures. The Quality Department must report to an organizational level and have sufficient independence from schedule and cost considerations which permits it to carry out these functions. Where an adversarial role has developed between personnel performing and verifying quality-affecting activities, top management must reemphasize that quality is everyone's responsibility.

The organizational structure selected and the location of the Quality Department within the organization is often dependent upon the size of the organization and its role in the project. Caution must be taken to assure that multiple layers of management does not result in the filtering of information as it is passed from one level to another, both upward and downward. Such filtering of information results in incomplete information being received by top management for decision-making purposes and by lower-level personnel for carrying out desired actions. Because many project activities involve more than one organizational element, good communication between elements, or horizontally, must also be established and maintained.

Regardless of the organizational structure selected and the location of the quality function, it must be conducive to obtaining and maintaining the balance between schedule, cost, and quality.

Responsibilities, Authorities, and Interfaces

While establishing the organizational structure for the project, top management must clearly define and document the functional responsibilities, levels of authority, and interfaces of both the organizational elements within its organization and any key contractors. In many projects, activities are contracted to other organizations. Because of the reputation of the organization to perform the activities, top management of the project assumes that organization will properly perform their activities and produce the required quality. Top management does not require controls over the contractors to the degree that would be exercised if the activities were to be performed by its own organization. Without such controls, top management becomes aware of major problems only after they have occurred and recognizes, too late, that had they known the status of the situation earlier, they could have taken responsible action to correct the situation and minimize its effects. The organization responsible for a project is ultimately responsible for all project phases and activities, whether it performs the activities itself or has them performed by contractors or suppliers. Only by clearly defining the responsibilities, authorities, and interfaces can top management provide for adequate control over the contractor activities and stay up-to-date with the status of the project.

Key Project Personnel

Top management of the organization responsible for a project is responsible for assuring that qualified personnel are assigned to project activities. To accomplish this task, top management must carefully select key project personnel based upon their expertise and experience. The key project personnel are responsible for assuring that their subordinates are qualified for their areas of activity based upon expertise, experience, and training. Effective selection and training of project personnel can help to minimize the levels of supervision and number of personnel required.

QUALITY PROGRAM IMPLEMENTATION

A well-planned and documented Quality Program is useless if it is not understood and effectively implemented. Top management must provide active support and leadership to assure Quality Program understanding and implementation by project level management, first-line supervision, and all project personnel.

Indoctrination and Training

The key to Quality Program understanding is indoctrination and training of personnel. Personnel performing quality-affecting activities must have indoctrination and training in the Quality Program and the activities they are to perform. Capabilities should be determined by evaluation of education, experience, and training, or by examination or capability demonstration. Performance should be regularly evaluated and additional training performed or reassignment made, as appropriate. Most Quality Programs require indoctrination and training schedules and records. By looking at the schedules and records, one can determine that the indoctrination and training were performed. However, this does not assure that the indoctrination and training were adequate. The effectiveness of the indoctrination, training, and motivation have major impacts on performance of an activity. Do the personnel know what is to be done and how to do it? Are they capable of doing it? Do they want to do it? It is imperative that personnel comprehend that the purpose of the Quality Program is to assure that activities are properly performed and the desired quality is attained. Unfortunately, personnel in many organizations lose sight of the purpose of the program and concentrate on complying with the words of the program. For example, the purpose of reviewing specifications, drawings, procedures, and instructions is to assure their completeness and adequacy. The purpose of signing and dating the document, or a review record for the document, is to provide objective evidence that the review was performed and the document is complete and adequate. When pressured with a backlog of documents to review, a multitude of other demands for the time of the reviewer, and expressed urgency for release of the document to production, the reviewer may sign and date the document to release it, justifying his action on either his confidence in the preparer of the document or on the urgency of the need for the document. As a result, evidence exists for the review of the document as required by the Quality Program, but the document was not properly reviewed to assure its completeness and adequacy. Project personnel must clearly understand the importance of the responsibilities of their positions.

Encouragement of Quality

Top management can provide support and leadership by creating an atmosphere for the project that encourages quality. Emphasis should be placed on preventing, identifying, and correcting problems instead of hiding them and accepting them as a cost of doing business. Measures should be established to prevent the harassment and intimidation of personnel who identify and report problems. Top management should include quality performance in the performance evaluation of all project personnel and as a topic in all Project Review meetings.

Top management can also provide support and leadership for the Quality Program by providing clear, consistent direction to the project; establishing a firm, expeditious decision-making process; providing the necessary instructions, equipment, and materials; having regular assessments performed of the program adequacy and effectiveness; and assuring prompt and effective corrective action for problems. Failure to provide active support results in the perception by project personnel that top management is not really concerned about quality. If top management is not concerned, why should they be?

Compliance with Quality Program

It is the responsibility of all project personnel to implement quality-affecting activities in accordance with the requirements of the Quality Assurance Manual, administrative and technical procedures, drawings, specifications, and instructions, or to cause the requirements of these documents to be reviewed and changed, if necessary. When activities cannot be performed as specified, project personnel are responsible for so notifying their supervisors, who are responsible for resolving the issue or initiating a change to the requirements. Permitting activities to be performed contrary to requirements, without causing the requirements to be changed, results in a perception by project personnel that the requirements are not important. Soon, other activities will also be performed contrary to the requirements, without the project personnel even bothering to notify their supervisors.

Top management should establish a Change Committee to review proposed changes and to minimize the impact of changes on schedule, cost, and quality.

FEEDBACK OF QUALITY-RELATED INFORMATION

Although Quality Program planning is performed at the beginning of a project, the necessary level of control is not always appropriately assigned to each activity and item. Establishing a Quality Program and providing the necessary support for its implementation does not assure that the program will be implemented or is adequate and effective in attaining quality. Top management must establish measures for feedback of quality-related information as well as schedule and cost information so it can effectively manage, coordinate, and control the project. The information must pertain to the quality performance of each organizational element of the project, including suppliers and contractors; must be factual; and must be provided frequently. Such information can be provided through written reports to top management and through the inclusion of quality-related information as a topic at all Project Review meetings. Meeting notes must clearly identify actions to be taken and responsibility for the actions to enable follow-up at later meetings. Management of each organizational element implementing the program should also regularly assess the adequacy and effectiveness of the program as it applies to their quality-affecting activities and recommend any appropriate changes to enhance the program. Quality problems seldom happen overnight. An effective feedback system will promptly identify problems and their causes so corrective action can be taken. Audits and Trend Analysis are two methods frequently used for providing feedback of quality-related information to top management.

Audits

Audits are an organized method of finding out how business is being conducted and comparing the results with how business should have been conducted. How business should have been conducted is described in the Quality Assurance Manual and administrative and technical procedures, specifications, drawings, and instructions identified in the process control documents. Audits determine if personnel know their responsibilities, verify whether required activities are being properly performed, and identify specific instances of deficiencies so that causes can be determined and corrective action taken. They are performed by interviewing personnel, observing operations, checking computer systems and records, and reviewing documentation, records, and completed work. Audit programs include the use of audit schedules, checklists for items and activities to be audited, and audit reports. However, the existence of such documents does not always assure that the intent of the audit was achieved. Audits should be performed by trained personnel who do not have responsibility in the areas audited. Personnel are not likely to find or report problems in their own area of responsibility. Further, audits should be performed using detailed checklists which identify specific requirements. Checklists are often not specific enough to verify compliance with requirements and to identify instances of deficiencies. Unidentified requirements are usually not audited and often show up later as major deficiencies. Two common problems with audits performed during a project are that the audit is either programmatic and based upon documentation only, or that the audit is hardware or technically oriented with a failure to recognize that the deficiencies are but symptoms of larger problems in system controls. Audits need to strike a balance between programmatic and hardware and technical orientation to get a true picture of the Quality Program implementation and effectiveness. Audits of Quality Program implementation are usually included as a method of control in the Quality Assurance Manual. Such audits are typically performed by personnel within the project organization, usually by personnel in the Quality department. In addition to such audits, top management can arrange for an evaluation or audit of the Quality Program by personnel who are independent of the project. Such evaluations and audits are commonly called management audits and eliminate organizational bias, cut through organizational barriers, and objectively report the Quality Program's deficiencies and effectiveness.

Trend Analysis

Trend analysis involves reviewing data and determining if any trends exist of conditions adverse to quality. It is normally performed by reviewing nonconformance reports, inspection reports and logs, audit reports, corrective action reports, and quality cost data. It helps focus attention on repetitive deficiencies so that their cause can be determined and corrective action taken.

CORRECTIVE ACTION

Top management is responsible for establishing measures for prompt and effective corrective action to project problems. The identification of problems and conditions adverse to quality normally occurs during the performance of reviews, inspections, surveillances, tests, audits, and trend analyses. Corrective action consists of four phases. The first phase, the fix, involves fixing or correcting the specific deficiency that was identified. The second phase, the purge, involves reviewing similar documents and activities to determine the extent of the deficiencies and correcting deficiencies in those documents and activities. The third phase, preventive action, is to determine the cause of the deficiencies and take corrective action to prevent recurrence of the deficiencies. The fourth phase, the close-out, is to verify that the corrective action taken was adequate and effective. Corrective action consisting of just the fix, or the fix and purge, is not effective. Without identification of the cause of the problem and the taking of action to eliminate the cause, the problem will reappear and much time and expense will be expended in repeatedly fixing the same problem. Corrective action consisting of just the fix, purge, and preventive action will also not be effective. Without verification that the corrective action taken was adequate and effective, there is no assurance that the same problem will not recur.

Top management must also assure that corrective action is taken for problems reported through the feedback of quality-related information. One approach is for top management to receive audit and trend analysis reports and to initiate corrective action through project management personnel responsible for the area of activity pertaining to the problem. Another approach is for top management to initiate corrective action during Project Review meetings and to follow up on completion of the corrective action at future meetings. Prompt and effective corrective action is a key factor in managing for quality.

SUMMARY

Achieving quality is as important as completing a project on time and within cost and involves all project organizations and personnel performing quality-affecting activities. Quality problems are the result of breakdowns in the overall management of a project and can be prevented through the implementation of a comprehensive Quality Program. A Quality Program is a systematic approach to planning and controlling quality through the use of good business practices. Quality Program management is the element of project management that is designed to assure the attainment of quality. It accomplishes its goal by utilizing basic elements of good management: planning, organization, implementation, feedback, and corrective action. The top management of the organization responsible for a project must provide for project management integration of schedule, cost, and quality planning, control, and performance data throughout all project phases. Through incorporation and implementation of the appropriate features of quality concepts into a comprehensive Quality Program, which integrates the concepts into the activities of each organizational element, quality can be achieved, productivity can be increased, and overall project costs can be reduced. The Quality Program should stress prevention of problems, active involvement of all project personnel, efficient and effective methods of control, and the utilization of factual performance data to continually improve performance throughout the project.

22. The Legal Standards for Prudent and Efficient Project Management

Randall L. Speck*

In our increasingly disputatious society, the project manager has become the focus of ever-closer scrutiny and occasional opprobrium. Although most projects are completed successfully to resounding kudos, some have suffered serious calamities—skyrocketing costs, repeated delays, and unreliable quality. The most notorious examples have occurred in the construction of state-of-the-art nuclear power plants where tenfold cost increases, oft-postponed completion dates, and massive rework have been commonplace. In some of those cases, utility company stockholders have been penalized to the tune of several hundred million dollars for their project managers' apparent lapses. Every project manager is vulnerable to censure, however, whenever the project falls short of its goals and in the process injures a third party (e.g., consumers, owners, contractors, the government, or even stockholders). This chapter reviews the legal standards that have evolved over the last decade to measure project managers' performance and offers a few practical guidelines that may help to fend off unwarranted criticism.†

In the legal vernacular, a project manager's conduct is usually acceptable if his or her performance is considered "prudent" and "reasonable." Obviously, such directives make poor guideposts for the manager about to embark on a project that may be fraught with risks and uncertainties.

---

* Randall L. Speck has been lead attorney and project manager in several major legal proceedings to determine whether particular projects were managed prudently. Most notably, he represented the State of Alaska in the seven-year litigation to set the tariff for the $8 billion Trans Alaska Pipeline System. Mr. Speck is Managing Director in the law firm of Rogovin, Huge & Schiller in Washington, D.C.
† This brief primer on the putative standards for prudent project management is not intended as a substitute for legal advice that has been tailored to the circumstances of a particular project. The law varies by jurisdiction, and, as noted below, the touchstone for acceptable behavior is often elusive. It is advisable, however, to solicit anticipatory counsel rather than waiting until misfortune has become reality.

These nebulous terms have been infused with a modicum of meaning, however, based on the very large, analogous body of negligence law. Under those hoary principles, unattainable perfection is not required. The law in most state and federal jurisdictions merely prescribes the actions that a "reasonable person" would take under similar conditions, but several states have recently adopted more rigorous criteria in specified regulatory contexts. Even though those standards are not yet well defined, they seem to demand project management techniques that will produce the most efficient performance possible. Project managers should certainly be aware of the tests that will be used to evaluate their actions and adjust their behavior accordingly.

Given an environment in which day-to-day decisions made under the pressures of a dynamic project may be strictly scrutinized, the project manager should be prepared to document the reasonableness of his or her choices. Managers are normally given substantial latitude in running a project, and courts are loathe to second guess a supervisor's judgment. Nevertheless, the project manager may, as a practical matter, be forced to explain cost, schedule, or quality deviations in some detail, and the consequences of inadequate data could be extremely costly. Again, forewarned is forearmed. Thorough contemporaneous documentation (as opposed to explanations constructed after the fact) can provide a palpable defense to charges of mismanagement.

There is no facile recipe for prudent management. The other chapters in this *Handbook* cover the range of issues that are likely to arise in any challenge to management's performance, and there are a myriad of subissues that could loom large in litigation over a major project. There are three critical aspects of the project manager's responsibilities, however, that are the most likely candidates for probing review: (1) planning, (2) organization, and (3) control. A brief case study of the New York Public Service Commission's evaluation of the construction of the Shoreham Nuclear Generating Facility provides a good framework for analyzing the substantive requirements for prudent project management.

Finally, claims of unreasonable management will inevitably be predicated on some form of monetary loss—for example, excessive cost of the final product, inadequate performance that requires expensive repairs, or lost profit attributable to delays. If there is evidence of management shortcomings, the court or regulatory agency will be required to reconstruct the project as it would have unfolded if management had performed prudently. Of course, that exercise tempts the protagonists to flights of imagination and to hypotheses of an aerial project that has no relevance to reality. Judges are commonly called upon, however, to weigh models or estimates of what would have happened if the facts had been different.

Thus, with appropriate data derived from the project itself, the parties can formulate a reasonable assessment of the cost consequences of any management dereliction.

CONTEXTS FOR CHALLENGES TO THE REASONABLENESS OF PROJECT MANAGEMENT

Almost any project may be subjected to a reasonableness review whenever a service or product is to be produced for a third party based on a specified standard, with a specified time for completion, or for a specified price. If those expectations are frustrated, the injured party is likely to seek redress, particularly where the stakes are large. The most common forum for examination of project management is in regulatory proceedings to set the rates that a utility will be allowed to charge. Very similar issues arise, however, in the execution of government contracts and in disputes between owners and contractors over performance under the terms of the contract.

Regulation as a Substitute for Competition

It is a basic premise of most regulatory policy in the United States that the regulator serves as a surrogate for competition. In theory, the marketplace and the profit motive provide the impetus for unregulated enterprises to operate efficiently, and no external controls are necessary or desirable. For certain natural monopolies (e.g., electric utilities), however, there is no realistic opportunity for competition. Thus, a governmental watchdog is designated to act on behalf of the consumer and the public interest to monitor the company's performance against the standards that would be expected in a competitive environment. As the Federal Energy Regulatory Commission (FERC) has held:

[m]anagement of unregulated business subject to the free interplay of competitive forces have no alternative to efficiency. If they are to remain competitive, they must constantly be on the lookout for cost economies and cost savings. Public utility management, on the other hand, does not have quite the same incentive. Regulation must make sure that the costs incurred in the rendition of service requested are necessary and prudent. [*New England Power Company*, 31 F.E.R.C. ¶ 61,047 at 61,083 (1985) (quoting *Midwestern Gas Transmission Co.*, 36 F.P.C. 61, 70 (1966), *aff'd*, 388 F.2d 444 (7th Cir.), *cert. denied*, 392 U.S. 928 (1968) (cited herein as ''NEPCO'')]

Similarly, the New York Public Service Commission concluded that "[t]he prudence rule is a regulatory substitute for the discipline that would be imposed by a free, competitive market economy where the penalty for mismanagement and imprudent costs is a loss of jobs, profits or business failure" (*Long Island Lighting Co.*, 71 P.U.R. 4th 262, 269 (1985) (cited herein as "LILCO"). Finally, the Iowa State Commerce Commission articulated its regulatory duty as follows:

> to maintain surveillance over costs associated with a particular decision, and in the absence of the kind of incentive provided by a competitor, the responsibility falls upon us to provide the requisite incentives. We do not believe we are unduly interfering with management prerogatives when we attempt to distinguish between reasonable and unreasonable [management] decisions. We believe such an inquiry is required of us by the legislature's directive that rates we allow be reasonable and just. [*Iowa Public Service Co.*, 46. P.U.R. 4th 339, 368 (1982)]

The basic principle of regulatory review of utility expenditures is at least 60 years old. The U.S. Supreme Court in 1923 held that a regulated company is entitled to a return on its investment that is "adequate, under efficient and economical management," to enable the utility "to raise the money necessary for the proper discharge of its public duties" (*Bluefield Waterworks & Improvement Co. v. Public Service Commission*, 262 U.S. 679, 693 (1923)). Justice Brandeis elaborated on this precept in his oft-quoted definition of "prudent investment."

> The term prudent investment is not used in a critical sense. There should not be excluded from the finding of the [capital] base [used to compute rates], investments which, under ordinary circumstances would be deemed reasonable. The term is applied for the purpose of excluding what might be found to be dishonest or obviously wasteful or imprudent expenditures. Every investment may be assumed to have been made in the exercise of reasonable judgment, unless the contrary is shown. [*Missouri ex rel. Southwestern Bell Telephone Co. v. Public Service Commission*, 262 U.S. 276, 289 (1923) (Brandeis, J. concurring)]

In recent years, regulatory bodies have used these principles to deny recovery to utilities for very significant portions of their expenditures related to major projects. For instance, the New York Public Service Commission disallowed $1.395 billion of the cost of the Shoreham Nuclear Project based on its findings of unreasonable project management,

LILCO, supra, and subsequently denied recovery of approximately $2 billion of the capital cost of the Nine Mile Point 2 nuclear project, *Re Nine Mile Point 2 Nuclear Generating Facility,* 78 P.U.R. 4th 23, 41 (N.Y. 1986); the Missouri Public Service Commission excluded $384 million for imprudent management in constructing the Callaway Nuclear Point, *Re Union Electric Co.,* 66 P.U.R. 4th 202, 228 (Mo. 1985); the Iowa State Commerce Commission excluded $286 million of the costs for the same plant, *Re Union Electric Co.,* 72 P.U.R. 4th 444, 454 (Iowa 1986); the Michigan Public Service Commission rejected $397 million of the Femi 2 capital expenditures as imprudent, *Re the Detroit Edison Company,* Case No. U-766 [Mich. P.S.C., April 1, 1986); the Kansas State Corporation Commission denied recovery of $244 million of the costs of the Wolf Creek Nuclear Generating Facility, *Re Wolf Creek Nuclear Generating Facility,* 70 P.U.R. 4th 475, 508 (Kan. 1985); the New Jersey Board of Public Utilities reduced the rate base for the Hope Creek nuclear plant by $432 million based on unreasonable management, *Re Public Service Electric and Gas Co.,* No. ER8512116 (N.J. Bd. of P.U., April 6, 1987); the Illinois Commerce Commission disallowed $101 million of the Byron 1 Nuclear plant costs, *Re Commonwealth Edison Co.,* 71 P.U.R. 4th 81, 98 (Ill. 1985); and the California Public Utilities Commission refused to permit Southern California Edison to include $330 million of the plant costs for San Onofre-2 and -3 because it had been imprudently spent, 80 P.U.R. 4th 148, 153 (Calif. 1986).

Most of these dramatic deductions were related to nuclear plants, but the same maxims have been used to deny cost recovery for projects involving traditional fossil power plants, a synthetic natural gas plant, oil pipelines, and the management of scheduled outages for nuclear power plants. As regulatory commissions become more comfortable with their role as sentinel against unreasonable costs, they are likely to expand their inquiries to include any significant utility expenditure that might have been controlled more effectively by management. Thus, the project manager for any regulated entity or its contractors should expect his or her decisions to be subjected to microscopic attention.

The Prudent Project Management Standard for Contract Disputes

The measure of performance under many contracts is almost identical to the prudent management standard that has been applied in the regulatory context. In fact, by statute, contracts for some defense projects are subject to renegotiation if the contractor earns "excessive" profits, but

[i]n determining excessive profits, favorable recognition must be given to the efficiency of the contractor or subcontractor, with particular regard to attainment of quantity and quality production, reduction of costs, and economy in the use of materials, facilities and manpower. [50 U.S.C., App. § 1213(e)]

Thus, a project manager who can demonstrate his project's efficiency may be able to retain profits that would otherwise be returned to the government.

Virtually any project-related contract could also be the subject of litigation focusing on the manager's performance. In a very typical case, a subcontractor may claim that it lost profits on a project when the prime contractor or the owner failed to integrate all of the project elements efficiently and caused a delay in the subcontractor's work. Similarly, an owner may sue its services contractor for failure to manage a project component prudently so that it would satisfy the owner's requirements (e.g., failure to debug computer software adequately or on time to permit initiation of a new manufacturing process). Occasionally (and preferably) the performance standard is spelled out in sufficient detail in the contract itself, but much more frequently, the parties are relegated to presenting evidence on the reasonableness of project management under the particular circumstances of that contract.

STANDARDS FOR PRUDENT PROJECT MANAGEMENT

The Reasonable Project Manager

The Reasonable Person Test.   The Federal Energy Regulatory Commission (FERC) concluded in its seminal *New England Power Co.* decision that "the most helpful test" in resolving issues of "prudent investment" is the "reasonable person" test, which the Commission defined as follows:

In performing our duty to determine the prudence of specific costs, the appropriate test to be used is whether they are costs which a reasonable utility management . . . would have made, in good faith, under the same circumstances, and at the relevant point in time. [*NEPCO, supra,* at 61,084]

This "reasonable person" test has been consistently applied by state public service commissions in evaluating the prudence of costs incurred by utilities under their jurisdictions and has been applied as well in other areas of law involving regulated companies, including occupational safety and health, banking, and government contracting.

The "reasonable person" is widely accepted as a standard in large part because it is an *objective* test that avoids the adverse policy implications of alternative legal criteria such as strict liability or "guilty knowledge." A strict liability approach would deem a project manager imprudent whenever a management decision produced harm significantly greater than its benefits. Under that analysis, however, regulatory bodies would undoubtedly be inundated with requests by public utilities for advance approval of projects before they undertake substantial capital investments. A "guilty knowledge" approach would consider management imprudent only when the manager acted with a conscious apprehension that his or her conduct was wrongful or otherwise faulty. That standard tends to exculpate irresponsible management, however, because it would be virtually impossible to prove that management acted with conscious knowledge of its wrongdoing. The "reasonable person" standard avoids these legal pitfalls and provides an appropriate level of regulatory or judicial scrutiny.

The "reasonable person" in the project management context draws its meaning from an extensive body of tort cases involving issues of negligence. It is clear from these well-established principles of tort law that the "reasonable person" standard is, above all, an objective standard, not dependent on individual judgment:

> The standard which the community demands must be an objective and external one, rather than that of the individual judgment, good or bad, of the particular individual. [*Restatement (Second) of Torts* § 283 comment c, at 12 (1965)]

Thus, the "reasonable person" standard does not depend on what a particular person considers reasonable under the circumstances, but rather on a standard of reasonableness imposed by the community. Indeed, the courts have gone to great lengths to emphasize the abstract and hypothetical character of the reasonable person:

> The reasonable man is a fictitious person, who is never negligent, and whose conduct is always up to standard. He is not to be identified with any real person; and in particular he is not to be identified with the members of the jury, individually or collectively. [*Restatement, supra,* § 283 comment c, at 13]

Community Standards. Community standards as a measure of the reasonable person's behavior may be established in a variety of ways, not the least of which are published treatises by respected project managers such as those included in this *Handbook*. Professional codes such as the Project Management Institute Code of Ethics (e.g., requiring application of state-of-the-art project management tools and techniques to ensure that schedules are met and that the project is appropriately planned and coordinated) and the Canons of Ethics of the American Society of Civil Engineers may also help define the parameters of prudent project management. In some cases there may even be a statute or regulation mandating a particular level of project management attention. For example, the Department of Interior Stipulations that governed construction of the Trans Alaska Pipeline project dictated that the owners should "manage, supervise and implement the construction . . . to the extent allowed by the state of the art and development of technology" (Agreement and Grant of Right-of-Way for Trans Alaska Pipeline, January 23, 1974). The U.S. Department of Defense also established very clear community standards for high-technology projects in its "Cost/Schedule Control Systems Criteria, C/SCSC Joint Surveillance Guide," initially issued in the late 1960s and periodically updated. Courts and regulatory agencies have used these external measures to assess project managers' performance.

Internal Project Standards. In some instances, however, the most relevant criteria for evaluating project management's prudence may not be set by the community, but by the managers themselves. Certainly the most applicable estimates, schedules, or quality norms are those that were tailored to the particular project at issue. Project management presumptively considered all pertinent constraints when they set those benchmarks, and it is reasonable to apply those standards to assess project execution. The New York Public Service Commission followed that approach in the Shoreham case. The company argued that it would be more appropriate to compare the procurement cycle actually achieved at Shoreham with those achieved at other nuclear construction projects. The Commission concluded, however, that:

> such a comparison would not be germane. This is because the cycles planned but unachieved at Shoreham were those that [the utility's] management considered essential if the procurement function was to succeed in supporting the engineering and construction schedules. A cycle short enough to support construction in some other plant's schedule might nevertheless have been too lengthy to achieve that same objective at Shoreham. Conversely, the failure of procurement to sup-

port construction at another plant would not establish that Shoreham was prudently managed despite such failures. [*LILCO, supra,* at 286]

Similarly, the Missouri Public Service Commission used the definitive estimate for the Callaway Project as "the proper starting point for an investigation of cost overruns and a determination as [to] whether cost[s] incurred on the project are reasonable" (*Re Union Electric Co., supra,* at 229).

Internally approved project standards have an initial attractiveness that has seduced some fact finders to divine imprudence whenever project goals are not met. That conclusion is clearly inappropriate. Project objectives may be set for a variety of purposes—for instance, to provide an ambitious target that will always be just beyond the reach of all but the most capable managers. Moreover, the project managers may simply have erred and established standards or procedures that are impractical. Finally, circumstances may have changed so that the norms conceived at the beginning of the project no longer have any relevance. Thus, judges and commissioners should not blithely adopt the project's standards as coincident with prudent management without first testing the objective reasonableness of those criteria within the framework of the conditions that actually existed.

Standards That Exceed Common Practice.   Even compliance with an established precedent—whether set by the community or by project management internally—may not be sufficient, however, to demonstrate prudence. The reasonable person standard applied by courts and juries reflects an observation made by Judge Learned Hand more than half a century ago in his opinion in *The T. J. Hooper:* "in most cases reasonable prudence is in fact common prudence" (60 F.2d 737, 740 (2d Cir.), *cert. denied,* 287 U.S. 662 (1932)). Thus, evidence of the usual and customary conduct of others under similar circumstances is normally relevent and admissible as an indication of what the community of project managers regards as proper.

Proof that project management practices and organizational structures consistently fell short of contemporaneous industry standards and practices serves a particularly useful function for the trier of fact:

Proof that the defendant took less than customary care has a use different from proof that the defendant followed business usages: Conformity evidence only raises questions, but subconformity evidence tends to answer questions. If virtually all other members of the defendant's craft follow safer [or more efficient] methods, then those methods are practical; the defendant has heedlessly overlooked or consciously failed to adopt common precautions. [Morris, *Custom and Negligence,* 42 Colum. L. Rev. 1147, 1161 (1942)]

It should be emphasized that although failure to conform to industry standards establishes imprudence, proof of limited conformity to the practices of others does not carry the same weight in establishing prudence. Consequently, even if one or more specifically identifiable "real-world" project managers would have acted in a particular fashion, such evidence of limited conformity would not establish prudence. For unlike the fictional "reasonable manager" of the law, "real-world" managers, even though they are generally considered "reasonable" by their peers, sometimes act unreasonably or imprudently.

Because even people who are generally reasonable may sometimes act negligently, it is not surprising that the law refuses to allow any one individual to set the standard of prudent behavior by his or her conduct alone. Indeed, the courts have consistently held that even adherence to an industry-wide custom or practice will not insulate a defendant from liability, because an entire industry may be negligent. This principle was perhaps most eloquently articulated by Judge Hand in his oft-cited opinion in *The T. J. Hooper:*

[I]n most cases reasonable prudence is in fact common prudence; but strictly it is never its measure; a whole calling may have unduly lagged in the adoption of new and available devices. It never may set its own tests. . . . Courts must in the end say what is required; there are precautions so imperative that even their universal disregard will not excuse their omission. [*The T. J. Hooper, supra,* 60 F.2d at 740]

The New York Public Service Commission applied a similar analysis to the Shoreham nuclear project and found that "if gross inattention to cost and schedule control was typical of the industry, industry practices on their face would be unreasonable and could not excuse [the utility] from its responsibility to act reasonably" (*LILCO* at 278). Indeed, commissions have also found that utilities are not necessarily prudent simply because they produced project results that were better than the norm. The Illinois Commerce Commission found that although the Byron nuclear power plant was:

one of the cheaper plants to be built recently, that certainly does not preclude investigation into particular aspects of the project to determine whether there were reasonably avoidable diseconomies . . . . The favorable plant cost comparisons do, however, help to prevent the Commission from inferring mismanagement simply from cost increases, or increased project ratios, or other such simple arithmetical comparisons. [*Re Commonwealth Edison Co., supra,* at 101]

Requirement for Expert Project Management.   The common use by commissions and courts of a reasonable manager standard implies application of the qualifications required from a specialist, which differs substantially from the criteria applied to the ordinary person engaged in ordinary activities. This expert standard, again, is a familiar facet of negligence law, which has traditionally demanded more than ordinary care from those who undertake any work calling for unique skill. Specialists have always had a duty to display "that special form of competence which is not part of the ordinary equipment of the reasonable man, but which is the result of acquired learning and aptitude developed by special training and experience" (*Restatement (Second) of Torts,* § 299A comment a).

An expert generally is held to "the standard of skill and knowledge required of the actor who practices a profession or trade"—the "skill and knowledge," in other words, "which is commonly possessed by members of that profession or trade in good standing" (*Id.* § 299A comment e). Thus, as members of a particularly skilled group, project managers will normally be held to a standard based on the distinctive skill and knowledge commonly possessed by members of the profession they undertake to practice.

The level of expertise demanded by the courts will be commensurate with the complexity and challenge of the project. For instance, significantly greater talent and experience will be expected from the manager of a multibillion-dollar nuclear power plant project than from the project manager responsible for the addition to a residential home. In general, the greater the risk of calamitous outcomes (e.g., runaway costs or injury to the environment or populace from quality shortcomings), the greater the burden that will be imposed on the project manager.

Reasonable Project Management "Under the Circumstances"

Hindsight Prohibited.   Courts and regulatory agencies have uniformly applied the criteria for prudent project management applicable at the time decisions were made based on the facts that were available to the decision maker at that time. For instance, in adopting a reasonable utility manager standard in *NEPCO,* the FERC remarked that while in hindsight it may be clear that a management decision was wrong, our task is to review the prudence of the utility's actions and the costs resulting therefrom based on the particular circumstances existing . . . at the time the challenged costs were actually incurred. [*NEPCO, supra,* 31 F.E.R.C. ¶ 61,047, at 61,084]

Thus, the Commission made it clear that the standard to be used is not one of perfection, that is, judging the reasonableness of management decisions with the benefit of hindsight. Instead, management conduct must be evaluated according to the circumstances that existed at the time the relevant decision was made.

Some project managers have attempted to invoke severe time constraints as a mitigating circumstance that might justify less than optimal procedures. The courts, however, have imposed two important limitations on the rule that an actor's conduct must be evaluated according to the circumstances (including "crisis circumstances") that existed at the time of the challenged conduct. First, crisis conditions are not considered as a mitigating circumstance when the actor's own negligence creates the crisis. "The fact that the actor is not negligent after the emergency has arisen does not preclude his liability for his tortious conduct which has produced the emergency" (*Restatement, supra,* § 296(2), at 64). Thus, an individual may be held liable in a situation in which he acts "reasonably in [a] crisis which he has himself brought about" (*Id.* § 296 comment d, at 65). Second, an actor who engages in an activity in which crises arise frequently is required to anticipate and prepare for those situations. In particular, experts or professionals who perform work that is characterized by frequent crises (i.e., most project mangers) are required to have particular skill and training to deal with those situations (*Restatement, supra,* § 296 comment c, at 65).

As part of the "reasonable person" standard, the FERC has expressly held that "management must operate its systems to avoid circumstances that give rise to emergencies." In *Texas Eastern Transmission Corp.,* 2 F.E.R.C. ¶ 61,277 (1978), the FERC precluded the gas company from recovering the costs of emergency gas purchases because the commission found that the company imprudently operated its system so as to create a situation in which emergency purchases were necessary. The commission emphasized that it was not judging the company's behavior with the benefit of hindsight; rather, it found that, based on information available to the company at the time, it was imprudent in failing to take steps early in the year that would have eliminated the need for later emergency gas purchases (*Id.* ¶ 61,277, at 61,617–18).

The "Large Complex Project." A few commentators have argued that some projects (which they dub "large complex projects" or LCPs) are *sui generis* and that their peculiar circumstances (e.g., size, complexity, application of new technology) make it impossible to define meaningful management criteria for assessing performance. This position has been soundly rejected. In the proceeding before the New York Public Service Commission to establish the allowable costs for the Shoreham nuclear project, the utility advocated a "theory which suggests that large-scale complex projects are inherently unmanageable" and a standard of conduct that "would insulate [the utility's] management from a finding of imprudence short of outright fraud, self-dealing, blatant carelessness, or gross negligence" (*LILCO, supra,* at 269). The Commission disdained this approach because "[t]he public is entitled to expect that such undertakings by public utilities are controllable" (*Id.*) The development of the project management discipline over the past 25 years would appear to confirm the commission's judgment. Project managers are unlikely to be able to hide their failures behind rationalizations that their projects were somehow unique and not amenable to standard project management techniques.

Project Managers' Responsibility for Agents' Actions

In most instances, the focus of any judicial inquiry will be on whether the project manager acted prudently. Of course, that investigation should include an examination of the project manager's role in selecting contractors, defining the scope of their work, supporting their efforts, and monitoring performance. Any dereliction in these duties would obviously be the project manager's direct responsibility.

According to some regulatory commissions, however, the project manager may also be vicariously liable for the imprudent conduct of his or her agents. For example, the Maine Public Utility Commission found that under its regulatory scheme, the ratepayers should "pay no more than the reasonably necessary costs to serve them. Any other reading [of the statute] is likely to lead to economic inefficiency, to excess costs, and sometimes to dubious practices between utilities and their suppliers" (*Re Seabrook Involvements by Maine Utilities,* 67 P.U.R. 4th 161, 168–69 (Me. P.U.C. 1985)). The Maine Commission held explicitly that "a supplier's unreasonable charges, even when not found to have been imprudently incurred by the utility, cannot be passed on to the utility's ratepayers" (*Id.*). Similarly, the Pennsylvania Public Utility Commission found that because the project manager, not the ratepayers, chose the contractor, the risk of performance failures should be borne by the stockholders.

It must be recognized that the basic question is who should pay for the cost of the improper design and manufacture of the Salem 1 generator. . . . Including these costs in [the utility's rates] means that all ratepayers are charged for [the contractor's] actions. This insulated both [the utility] and [the contractor] from responsibility for the generator failure. Conversely, denying . . . recovery places the costs on the party most capable of pursuing legal remedies and negotiating future contractual protections, [the utility]. Only [the utility] can structure its operations in such a fashion as to minimize the costs of contractor error or pursue damages should errors occur. [*Re Salem Nuclear Generating Station,* 70 P.U.R. 4th 568, 606–07 (Pa. P.U.C. 1985)]

Although these cases ostensibly hold the project manager responsible for contractor negligence, regardless of his or her own fault, reality may not dictate so harsh a result. The fundamental premise underlying the commissions' holdings is an expectation that the project manager can control the contractor's performance, either through negotiation of strict contract terms that make the contractor accountable for any mismanagement or through careful monitoring and direction of the contractor's work. The project manager's reasonable steps to preclude contractor misfeasance should provide an adequate defense, particularly if the contractor withheld material information about its failures from the project manager. The manager should be penalized only if there were steps that he or she could have taken to avoid or mitigate the contractor's imprudence.

An Alternative Standard: Efficient Project Management

In some jurisdictions, regulated companies should anticipate being held to a somewhat more rigorous performance standard if they expected to obtain full recovery for their project costs. In Texas, for instance, the legislature has determined that a utility seeking to include an allowance for construction work in process (CWIP) in its rate base must show that a project has been managed "prudently" *and* "efficiently" (Texas Public Utility Regulatory Act, § 41(a)). Under the most likely interpretation of this statute, utilities will have to show more than the reasonableness of their conduct; they will have to show that the project used "the most effective and least wasteful means of doing a task or accomplishing a purpose" and performed in "the best possible manner" (*Houston Lighting & Power,* Docket No. 5779, Examiner's Report (December 20, 1984) at 17, *aff'd* (January 11, 1985)). Similarly, the Illinois Commerce Commission has held that its statute requires a demonstration of more than mere reasonableness before a utility can recover its project costs:

> In addition to prudency, considered narrowly, the act now directs the commission to consider efficiency, economy, and timeliness, so far as they affect costs. [*Re Commonwealth Edison Co., supra,* at 94]

These seemingly broader mandates for project review have not been fully tested in the courts, but they appear to imply a greater focus on the results that are actually achieved. All projects are plagued with niggling inefficiencies, and management's task is to minimize them to the extent possible. Rigid application of the efficiency standard, however, might mean that no project, no matter how well managed, would be able to demonstrate absolute efficiency and recover 100% of its costs, at least in the context of extraordinary rate relief such as CWIP. In these cases, there will be an even greater premium on the project manager's competence.

THE BURDEN OF PROVING PRUDENCE

Courts and regulatory agencies have long recognized the importance of giving managers relatively free reign to run projects as they see fit and to avoid second guessing managers' decisions. Thus, absent a significant showing to the contrary, they have presumed that managers act reasonably. The FERC has formulated the following general rule:

> Utilities seeking a rate increase are not required to demonstrate in their cases-in-chief that all expenditures were prudent. . . . Where some other participant in the proceeding creates a *serious doubt* as to the prudence of an expenditure, then the applicant has the burden of dispelling these doubts and proving the questioned expenditure to have been prudent. [*Minnesota Power and Light Co.,* 11 F.E.R.C. ¶ 61,312 (1980) (emphasis added)]

Several states have concluded that a "serious doubt" is raised about management's prudence whenever the final project costs materially exceed the originally estimated costs, thus shifting the burden to the company to show that it acted reasonably and that all costs were justified (*Re Union Electric Co., supra* at 212; *Houston Lighting & Power Co.,* 50 P.U.R. 4th 157, 187 (Tex. P.U.C. 1982); *Consumers Power Co.,* No. U-4717, slip op. at 8 (Mich. P.S.C. 1978)). Other factors that might create a "serious doubt" include performance that deviates significantly from the industry average, a major accident or component failure, or a fine imposed by a regulatory body for violation of statutes or regulations (e.g., an OSHA or Nuclear Regulatory Commission fine for safety infractions). If any of these tokens is present, the project manager may be called upon to marshal evidence to defend his or her administration.

This allocation of accountability is consistent with the basic legal maxim that the party having best access to the relevant information must normally carry the initial burden of proof. The project manager, with intimate knowledge of project planning, organization, and control, should be in the preeminent position to vindicate his or her prudence. Such proof should be straightforward for a meticulously run project that pays assiduous attention to documentation. Many managers have been rudely surprised, however, by their inability to demonstrate their project's good health to an outsider despite hale and hearty prognoses throughout the project's life. The project manager must be able to point to contemporaneous documentation (not "post-hoc rationalizations") to confirm management's prudence.

Two recent decisions illustrate the weight courts and commissions have given to data that was created as a routine part of the project. In *Long Island Lighting Co.*, the New York Public Service Commission was faced with a contradiction between a very critical report prepared by the architect/engineer during the project and the owners' later disclaimers. The commission found that:

> [t]he company's reconstructed version of the facts is not plausible. [The A/E's] report identified a significant problem in need of correction when the construction effort was under way and when [the A/E] was intimately familiar with the problem by virtue of its role as architect/engineer. The Judges had a choice between [the A/E's] contemporaneous analysis or an analysis prepared by [the owner] in 1984 for purposes of this proceeding. Thus, they quite reasonably attached more credence to the former. . . . [I]f the report were faulty, [the owner's] management failed to discern its alleged infirmities back in the 1970's when it was important that the design change process be carefully appraised and effectively managed. [*LILCO, supra,* at 290]

Similarly, the Missouri Public Service Commission in *Re Union Electric Co., supra,* relied on reports generated by the utility, its consultants, and its contractors during the course of the project in finding that the utility imprudently managed the Callaway nuclear project.

In evaluating after-the-fact explanations of events, courts have long recognized "the familiar phenomenon of post-hoc reconstruction." This phenomenon refers not to deliberately false testimony, but rather to "the often-encountered tendency, though unintentional, to testify to what one believes 'must have happened' and not to what did happen" (*United States ex rel. Crist v. Lane,* 577 F. Supp. 504, 511 n. 11 (N.D. Ill. 1983), *rev'd on these grounds,* 745 F.2d 476 (7th Cir. 1984), *cert. denied,* 105 S.Ct. 2146 (1985)). Because "post-hoc reconstruction" is so familiar, courts traditionally give greater weight to contemporaneous statements or documents than to later explanations of events offered by witnesses at trial. Moreover, it is well established that business records have special indicia of reliability based on the fact that managers relied on them in making decisions in the ordinary course of the project.

The prudent project manager, anticipating the possibility of a subsequent challenge, should pay particular attention to documentation as the project progresses. Ordinarily, the same records that should be used to plan and control the project will also be most useful in championing it through later trials. One of the most glaring weaknesses in the defenses mounted to date has been the project manager's inability to demonstrate the specific causes for major cost increases. The shibboleths of "regulatory interference" or "changed conditions" as justifications for broken budgets have not been adequate when millions of dollars are at stake. As knowledgeable project managers are well aware, however, a rudimentary configuration management system enhances rational decision making to accommodate change during the project and at the same time creates a concrete record that can justify cost increases in any later proceedings. Some companies (notably Southern California Edison) now prepare a "pedigree" for each design change that includes a definition of the source of the design requirements, an evaluation of alternatives, a cost/benefit analysis, and steps taken to monitor expenditures versus the estimate. This data will be invaluable for managing the project, but will also demonstrate the reasonableness of the design change should there be a future interrogation. The most crucial lesson of the last decade of prudence proceedings is the absolute necessity for comprehensive record keeping.

SUBSTANTIVE STANDARDS FOR PRUDENT PROJECT MANAGEMENT

It is impossible to prescribe the unassailable tenets of project management that, if followed, will always invoke the imprimatur of prudence. Standards will evolve as the discipline develops, and courts may be more or less tolerant of shortcomings based on the need to meet other societal goals (e.g., an energy crisis may cause a temporary relaxation of efficiency standards in order to meet the immediate demand). Nevertheless, a few basic principles can be adduced from recent cases. This section reviews some of the illustrative holdings from the New York Public Service Commission's Shoreham prudence proceeding in three critical areas: planning, organization, and control.

Planning

Planning is the essence of prudent management. Every element of a project demands foresight and a design for realizing goals. Planning is even more essential as the tasks become larger and more complex. Specialized expertise must be marshaled to anticipate technical specifications, lead times, potential impediments, and control requirements. Moreover, all of the parts must mesh to enable the owners and senior managers to assign priorities, assess risks, define the organization, and measure performance. Prudent planning minimizes foreseeable risks and therefore becomes more crucial as predictable risks increase. Precautions that might arguably be optional become obligatory when the peril of inaction is grave.

The New York Commission identified planning as the lynchpin for a prudent project.

> Reasonable management would have foreseen the need for a systematic approach to this large-scale construction project and would, therefore, have exercised its responsibilities by formulating a plan to achieve its objectives. [The owner] failed to commence this project with a baseline plan defining what was to be built; how the work would be performed, and by whom; how changes would be incorporated into the plans if necessary; and, most critically, how the status of the project would be monitored and kept on schedule. This failure resulted in numerous problems throughout the project's history, including an inability to perform cost and schedule monitoring; confusion over roles and areas of responsibility among the project participants; low labor productivity; and the absence of a mechanism for providing the Board of Directors with sufficient, timely information to form a basis for providing guidance and making policy decisions. Accordingly, [the utility's] planning failure not only constituted imprudence, . . . but it also had direct and foreseeable adverse consequences on the course of the project. . . .
> [*LILCO, supra,* at 275–76]

Any prudence review will focus first on the adequacy of project planning.

Organization

Four basic premises guide a prudent project organization: (1) clearly defined roles and responsibilities for all of the parties at the project's inception; (2) delegated responsibility and authority based on the project's plan; (3) a relatively stable organizational structure for the project's duration; and (4) experience as the basis for building an organization. Conversely, an imprudent project organization is typically characterized by duplication, poorly defined roles, antagonism among the parties, delayed decision making, and instability.

Organizational flaws were at the heart of many of the problems pinpointed by the New York Commission on the Shoreham project.

> The Judges found that the lack of comprehensive, adequately explicit planning at the inception of the project laid the groundwork for serious conflicts and confusion over the respective roles of the various participants in the construction effort. They found that the failure to define discrete areas of responsibility led to a situation in which [the utility's] own project manager interfered with [the A/E's] managers,
>> producing friction, resentment and antagonism between [sic] [the A/E, utility] and the major contractors. Because of these interferences and poorly defined authority, major tasks of planning, supervision and coordination were not performed. Construction was adversely affected.
>> . . . [T]he record evidence establishes that in 1975 [the utility's project manager] began allowing contractors to submit problems to him instead of to [the A/E]. This was interference with [the A/E's] construction management authority, which undermined [the A/E's] control over contractors and engendered antagonism between [the utility] and its architect/engineer. [The utility's] interference is also evidenced by contemporaneous documentation describing confusion over who, as between [the utility] and [the A/E], was in charge of construction management. [*LILCO, supra,* at 276]

A common problem on many projects has been the absence of a clearly designated project manager who could coordinate all elements of the project. An astonishing number of major projects in the 1970s attempted to function without a distinct focus for management authority. The result was predictable confusion and inattention to crucial problems.

Control

Prudent project controls must be commensurate with management's experience and the nature of the contractual relations. For instance, inexperienced managers should be given a shorter reporting leash so that corrective action can be taken at an appropriate stage before the project gets out of hand. Similarly, the owner's control under a cost-plus contract must be substantially more stringent than with fixed-price contracts where the contractor has an incentive to control its own costs. Fundamentally, controls must be tailored to fit project conditions. Regulatory bodies have expressed a strong preference, however, for formal controls over ad hoc, informal mechanisms, and some form of network analysis has become virtually *de rigueur*.

The New York Commission found that controls on the Shoreham project were sadly deficient and that the utility "never instituted a reporting system adequate to enable management to discern problem areas and to make well-informed decisions about possible corrective action" (*LILCO, supra,* at 293). The Commission pointed to evidence that there were "no genuinely informative field reports"; that due to understaffing, the reports to the project manager on construction problems lacked substance and were frequently inaccurate; that reporting problems persisted; and "generally that the reporting system was misleading and difficult to interpret" (*Id.*). The Commission concluded that the utility "failed to establish a monitoring and reporting system capable of providing the information that it needed for the purpose of making intelligent decisions about Shoreham's course and progress" (*Id.* at 294). Without these controls, the Commission found, the project could not be managed prudently.

CALCULATION OF PRUDENT PROJECT COSTS

Once there has been a determination that a project suffered from some imprudence, the fact finder must determine whether this imprudence increased the project's costs, and if so, by how much. Causation is a factual question, and again there is no simple formula for whether particular consequences are sufficiently connected to the underlying management misconduct to warrant some form of penalty. Generally, courts and commissions have relied on expert testimony to establish a "clear causal connection" between management imprudence and resulting excess project costs (*LILCO, supra,* at 316; *Re Union Electric Co., supra,* at 228).

At first blush, the task of sorting prudent from imprudent project costs would seem quixotic. The courts have recognized, however, that reconstruction of the expenses that would have been incurred if management had acted differently is an extraordinarily imprecise art, and mathematical precision cannot be attained. This principle is not unique to the regulatory arena. Courts have long held in numerous substantive contexts that damages are at best approximations and can only be proved with whatever definiteness and accuracy the facts permit. One of the most frequently cited cases is the United States Supreme Court's decision in *Story Parchment Co. v. Paterson Parchment Paper Co.,* 282 U.S. 555, 563 (1931) (an antitrust case), in which the Court held that

[w]here the tort itself is of such a nature as to preclude the ascertainment of the amount of damages with certainty, it would be a perversion of fundamental principles of justice to deny all relief to the injured person, and thereby relieve the wrongdoer from making any amend for his acts. In such case, while the damages may not be determined by mere speculation or guess, it will be enough if the evidence shows the extent of the damages as a matter of just and reasonable inference, although the result be only approximate. The wrongdoer is not entitled to complain that they cannot be measured with the exactness and precision that would be possible if the case, which he alone is responsible for making, were otherwise.

In three recent cases examining the prudence of nuclear power plant construction, state utility commissions have addressed the question of how to quantify the costs that should be disallowed as a result of imprudent management. In each, the commissions relied where possible on specific data tracing the cause of cost overruns. When this information was not available, the commissions adopted reasonable estimates to establish the cost of imprudence.

In *LILCO*, the New York Commission first concluded that the utility's management of the Shoreham nuclear project was imprudent in several respects. The Commission rejected the utility's argument that the staff was required to quantify the effect of each discrete instance of imprudence in order to show that alleged acts of mismanagement directly caused specific costs (*LILCO, supra,* at 316–17). The Commission concluded that the staff's methodology, which compared Shoreham cost data in four categories (engineering and construction man-hours, schedule delay costs, and diesel generator problems) with cost data of other nuclear power plant construction projects was "logical and rational" and reached "a just and reasonable result" (*Id.* at 317). Based on these approximations, the Commission disallowed $1.395 billion in costs (*Id.* at 326).

In *Re Union Electric Co.,* the Missouri Public Service Commission addressed the issue of whether the utility had prudently managed construction of the Callaway nuclear project. The Missouri Commission concluded that, as a general matter, the utility "failed to meet the prudence standard," and that this imprudence "require[d] significant disallowances in order to establish 'just and reasonable rates' " (*Re Union Electric Co., supra*).

To quantify the imprudent costs, the Missouri Commission compared the actual cost of construction with a definitive cost estimate generated by the utility during the early stages of construction. The Commission rejected the utility's argument that it should not be "held" to the definitive estimate, stating that "the definitive estimate is the proper starting point for an investigation of cost overruns and a determination as [to] whether cost[s] incurred on the project are reasonable" (*Id.*). With respect to particular quantification methodologies, the Commission acknowledged that the staff's calculation "represent[ed] an approximation," but concluded that the staff's model "allow[ed] a reasonable estimate of these costs" (*Id.* at 243).

Finally, the Kansas State Corporation Commission, in *Re Wolf Creek Nuclear Generating Facility,* found that:

> lack of management attention coupled with the lack of efficient effective management on the part of the owners, resulted in schedule delays and increased costs that could have been mitigated by strong management action earlier in the project. [*Re Wolf Creek Nuclear Generating Facility, supra,* at 495]

To quantify those increased costs, the Kansas Commission adopted two approaches. First, it relied on the owners' definitive estimate of costs, their reconciliation of those projections with final costs, and the staff's independent estimates of specific costs. Second, the Commission estimated the delay in the critical path that was caused by imprudent management and quantified the effect of that delay.

All of these approaches to calculating the costs of a prudently managed project have potential drawbacks or inequities. Great care must be exercised, for instance, in choosing an appropriate baseline cost and schedule for the project. As noted above, estimates and schedules may have been devised for a variety of objectives and may not accurately reflect realistic project goals. Comparisons with costs and schedules on other projects also present significant pitfalls because no two projects are exactly comparable, and it is difficult to make fair adjustments between projects. The basic admonition to project managers, however, is a familiar refrain in this chapter—be prepared with contemporaneous data to justify the costs that were incurred. Deviations from previous projections or from experience on other projects should be explained. To the extent that there are justifications for cost increases, a prudent project manager should be able to document them.

CONCLUSION

The last decade has been both the boon and the bane of the project manager. The higher profile of megaprojects has generated intense postmortems that have focused on project managers' behavior. A shadowy profile of the "reasonable project manager" has emerged from these reviews, but it does not yet offer a model that can be easily emulated. In order to toe the line of prudence, managers must be constantly aware of the most sophisticated techniques and alert to document their reasonable efforts to apply those strategies in their projects. The law should serve the salutary purpose of enhancing and improving project efficiency, and the growing body of cases addressing prudent project management will almost certainly have that effect.

Section VII
Project Control

This section focuses on the project control process that complements project planning.

In Chapter 23, James A. Bent develops the project control concept as it relates to project planning. He emphasizes project control ideas in the construction context, but his ideas are widely applicable in other situations as well.

In Chapter 24, Mr. Bent presents 'project control basics' in the form of a briefing that could be provided to familiarize management with some of the fundamental historical statistical relationships that drive a typical project. He has selected those 'rules of thumb' which, although developed in the construction context, he believes apply to many industries.

Kenneth O. Chilstrom provides in Chapter 25 the framework for the management of audit of projects—a diagnostic tool that can serve important control objectives.

In Chapter 26, Harold Kerzner presents various techniques for assessing the performance of project personnel. Project control is thereby conceived as not only involving *project* assessments, but also assessments of people.

In Chapter 27, John Tuman, Jr., discusses the development and implementation of an effective system for the control of a project. He relates the control function to the information that is necessary if control is to be exercised and provides information flow models and modular configurations for a project management information and control system. (The systems development methodology that he prescribes is related to that described in terms of the linear responsibility chart in Chapter 16.)

'Computers in project management''—the subject of Chapter 28—ties together the planning techniques of Section V with the control ideas of this section. Most modern organizations use the computerized project planning and control software that is discussed by Harvey A. Levine to support their project management efforts.

23. Project Control: An Introduction

James A. Bent*

SECTION 1.

General

Philosophical discussions on defining "control" are never ending. There is the long-stated opinion that actual control is only exercised where the right of decision is vested—in this case, the decision making of the project manager, line supervisors, and design engineers.

It is stated that cost and schedule engineers only provide information and, therefore, have no exercise of control. This is partly true. Often, a staff function does become one of reporting and accounting. However, reporting, trending, and analysis are essential ingredients for forecasting which, in turn, is an essential ingredient of control.

It is also true that control is minimal where there is little creative analysis and only reporting and accounting.

The fundamental elements of control are the cost estimate and project schedule.

Planning the Project

One of the most important functions in the life cycle of a project is project planning, especially in the preliminary phases when basic decisions are being made that will affect the entire course of the project. The purpose of project planning is to identify the work that must be done, to gain the participation of those best qualified to do the work, and to develop appro-

---

* James A. Bent has been a consultant in project management since 1980. Previously, he worked more than 30 years for owners/contractors, such as Mobil and M. W. Kellogg. Mr. Bent's experience covers both onshore plants and offshore platforms, with project assignments in the United States, United Kingdom, Australia, Netherlands, Germany, Norway, and Italy. He is an author and presents training courses (3 days–3 weeks) in project management, scheduling, estimating, cost control, contracting, claims/management/negotiating, and shutdowns/turnarounds. These training assignments take Mr. Bent to the United States, United Kingdom, Norway, Europe, Japan, South America, and South Africa.

priate project cost and schedule objectives. Sound planning will minimize lost motion and clearly define for all participants—owner, contractor, associated corporate departments, and outsiders—their role in the project. Sound planning will also provide adequate consideration of all project elements, and will ensure a proper effort to meet the completion date. Figure 23-1 illustrates the major elements of project planning.

The project manager should personally supervise this effort with the support of business, cost, and schedule specialists. Project planning should consider such items as organization, communication channels, personnel skills, client requirements, business-political environment, and project execution strategy, and a plan should be drawn up to set in motion these operations. The project manager should develop a *Project Coordination Procedure,* after consulting with client and others, as necessary. This document will identify all principals concerned with the project, define their functions and responsibilities, and indicate appropriate con-

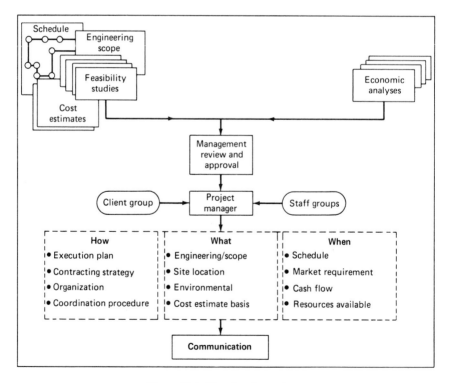

Figure 23-1. Planning the project.

tacts for each. The purpose of the document is to provide an effective basis for coordinating company activity and communications on the project, especially in the early stages of project execution when project scope and other elements are being defined. *Effective communication channels are essential for successful control.*

Who determines the organization, control systems, and resource requirements?

Too often, project managers will set up projects without seeking the support, advice, and assistance of staff personnel. On large projects this can be disastrous, particularly for the project control and estimating function. Resource requirements, control systems, and organizational arrangements should be matters of consultation and discussion with staff groups prior to decision by the project manager. This will also ensure that anticipated manpower requirements and resources are adequately reflected in the early conceptual estimates.

Apart from project size, the proposed execution plan and contracting strategy are the most significant elements for determining the control basis and associated organizations for the project. Figure 23-2 shows the typical phases of a project from an owner's feasibility and front-end studies to full implementation by a prime contractor. This typical life cycle is for a large process plant and shows durations of 8 months for a Phase I and 33 months for a Phase II operation. The durations for the front end vary widely.

There are many possible variations of project life cycles, this particular configuration is a typical routine of large oil corporations. Many owners use a phased approach, rather than a straight-through approach. This provides the owner with less risk on capital investment and also the ability to fully investigate the feasibility and financial viability of multiple projects at the same time.

A phased approach, particularly of large projects, also provides for more control by corporate management as the project is being developed in the feasibility, scoping, and design phase. However, it may add costs and will increase the overall project duration.

The following brief explanations cover the various phases as illustrated in Figure 23-2.

Owner front end is the feasibility stage when a design specification is produced by engineering, economic and market evaluations by the affiliate, and capital cost estimate and schedule by the cost group. The design specification is sometimes produced by a contractor, in greater detail than an owner-engineered design specification, but not to the detail of a Phase I operation. The control basis will be set by overall corporate objectives, mainly in the form of a development budget.

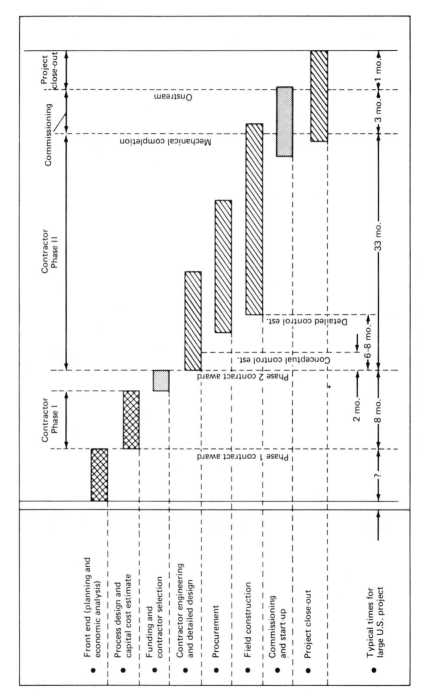

Figure 23-2. Project life cycle—typical.

562

Phase I generally covers conceptual design, process selection, optimization, upgrading of estimate/schedule, environmental/governmental studies, and finalization of the process design. The "authorization for funds" for the Phase II work is then prepared and presented, and, when approved, a contractor is selected to carry out the work. The Phase I work is carried out by a contractor, normally on a reimbursable basis with a small Owner Project Task Force (PTF) in attendance. There are two basic objectives for a Phase I operation. For large projects and revamps, it provides greater definition of scope, schedule, and cost. On small projects, it provides a design package suitable for lump sum bids. An important element of a Phase I operation is to provide an execution plan for Phase II. The control basis will be the expenditure and cost of the contractor man-hours and a milestone project master schedule.

Phase II is full execution of the project by a contractor. The normal project philosophy is that of a prime contractor with single responsibility for engineering, procurement, and construction. Most large projects are executed on a reimbursable basis with an Owner PTF directing/monitoring the work. This will require a complete project control system.

There are variations of a Phase II, where engineering and construction responsibilities are split and awarded to different contractors. This is the method usually adopted by utility companies where architect-engineers provide the design and construction contractors manage the field work on a subcontract basis. This approach does not provide a single responsibility and the designer and constructor can blame each other for errors of design and installation.

As outlined, the phased approach requires different control methods for each phase. A front end (feasibility study), usually carried out within the owner's organization, is authorized by an operating affiliate from its own development budget. As these budgets are developed in one-year and five-year cycles, there is rarely a need for detailed cost and schedule control at this stage. Expenditures can range from $100,000 for a small project, to $5 million for a very large project.

A contractor Phase I, on a reimbursable basis, requires a monthly monitoring of engineering man-hours and associated costs. Controls will be manual expenditure curves and progress measurement of engineering design. Expenditures can range from $1 million for small projects to $20 million for very large projects.

A contractor Phase II will require full schedule control for reimbursable and lump sum bases, but minimal cost control if on a lump sum basis.

A further variable on control requirements is the question of technology. New technology, such as synthetic fuels and offshore facilities, will generally require additional controls due to the lack of an existing data base. The past decade of the Alaska Pipeline, nuclear power plants, and North Sea platforms has clearly shown that prototype engineering, project size, hostile environments, and lack of data have produced poor cost estimates and schedules. This type of project will generally require a phased approach in order to develop data for a detailed project execution plan.

It cannot be emphasized too strongly that poor cost estimates and unrealistic project schedules can only result in an "out of control" project.

Project Execution Plan

Figure 23-3 shows major elements of a project execution plan. This plan is developed during Phase I and covers all aspects of scope, associated services, infrastructure, approach to engineering-procurement-construction (EPC), resources, organization structure, and project control requirements.

This detailed execution plan is essential for developing a quality control estimate and project schedule. Large overseas projects with remote job sites require that the execution plan consider logistics and material han-

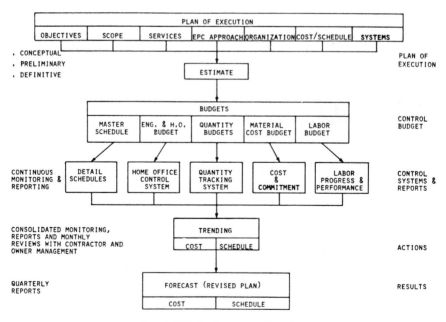

Figure 23-3. Project execution plan.

dling, local infrastructure and resources, camp facilities, training, expatriate conditions, and national and governmental requirements. A quality execution plan will provide a good estimate, control budgets, detailed schedules, and a breakdown of the project into controllable areas and cost centers. The project organization will be similarly structured, as will trending, control, and reporting systems.

Key Items of Execution Plan (this list is not all-inclusive):

- *Objectives*—reach agreement with owner on broad objectives.
  - —National engineering and construction content.
  - —Limits of authority.
  - —Community responsibility/town planning.
  - —Public relations. T.V., press, job site tours.
  - —Contractual relationship/responsibilities.
- *Scope*
  - —Process decisions/engineering specifications.
  - —Capacity/feed stock and product slate.
  - —Owner products for use during construction.
- *Services*—contractor and owner responsibilities.
  - —Subcontracts.
  - —Procurement.
  - —Commissioning and start-up assistance.
  - —Training. Management and craft labor.
- *Engineering-Procurement-Construction (EPC) Approach*
  - —Licensors and other third parties.
  - —Location of design offices.
  - —Purchasing, procedures and practices.
  - —Infrastructure. Local area and job site interface.
  - —Project procedures.
  - —Work week for engineering and construction.
  - —Contractor employee conditions and procedures.
  - —Preassembly/modularization.
  - —Constructability analysis.
  - —Labor relations and recruiting strategy.
  - —Construction equipment plan/rigging studies.
  - —Construction preplanning. Path of construction, field facilities.
- *Infrastructure*
  - —Camp. Messing and personnel facilities.
  - —Local resources. Banks, postal, religious, etc.
  - —Transportation. Job site and local area.
  - —Rest and recreation.
  - —Security.

- *Organizations*
  - —Size and complexity. Integration and project management.
  - —Breakdown of project. Cost and management.
  - —Engineering and construction management.
  - —Third party integration.
  - —Owner organization. Relationship with contractor.
  - —Organization development (OD).
  - —Communication system.
  - —Matrix, task force, and functional considerations.
  - —Decision process. Delegation, strategic, tactical.
- *Cost and Schedule*
  - —Resource evaluation. Manpower and manufacturing.
  - —Control estimate/work breakdown structure.
  - —Project control system.
  - —Trending systems/quantity control.
  - —Schedule milestones and owner interfaces.
  - —Long-lead items.
  - —Logistics and material handling.
  - —Environmental, governmental regulations and permits.
- *Systems*
  - —Manual versus computer.
  - —Owner requirements.
  - —Level of detail and distribution.
  - —Flexibility requirements. Contraction and expansion.
  - —Frequency of reports.
- *Auditing System*
  - —Terms of reference.
  - —Evaluations and reports.
  - —Procurement and financial.
  - —Documentation.
- *Procurement*
  - —World-wide operation.
  - —National requirements.
  - —Purchasing procedures and strategy.
  - —Centralized buying/field purchasing.
  - —Owner approvals.
  - —Negotiation practices.
- *Subcontracting*
  - —Content. Work category and contract type.
  - —Organization and control requirements.
  - —Prequotation meetings.

- *Material Control*
  —Material take off. Control and reporting.
  —Freight consolidation.
  —Marshalling yards.
  —Job site controls.
  —Weather protection and maintenance.
  —Documentation.
- *Project Run-Down and Demobilization*
  —What to control and at what point.
  —Level of control and reporting.
  —Personnel demobilization.
  —Material surplus program.

Contract Strategy

The current market environment plus the project cost and schedule objectives will generally determine the contracting strategy. Lump sum work is generally the most efficient method; however, a well-defined engineering package and stable market conditions are essential. There are several alternatives for the reimbursable project, and a phrased approach, though lengthy, can reduce the financial risk of a "straight-through" project.

Lump sum (fixed price) bids are expensive to produce and contractors are not anxious to pursue this course without a reasonable expectation of success. A poor owner definition can cause a low contractor estimate, resulting in continuous claims and extras by the contractor. It can also result in a large contingency being applied by the contractor.

Under lump sum contracts, control of time and money is the primary concern of the contractor, as his performance directly affects his profits. Here, the owner is concerned with checking contractor's compliance with project requirements, with evaluating cost extras, and with periodic analyses of the project schedule.

Under most cost-plus contracts, however, the contractor has limited incentive for controlling time and money beyond professional responsibility. In such cases, the owner is more deeply involved in the project control function than on lump sum projects. Here, owner personnel must supervise closely contractor's preparation of the definitive cost estimate and control system. This is necessary to ensure that the estimates and evaluations are prepared for facilities that are adequate for owner's needs, and to provide the owner with a better insight and understanding of the reliability and accuracy of the contractor estimates.

Target cost and schedule incentives can produce improved performance. However, the owner thereafter faces a contractor program to inflate the cost target with high estimates of engineering changes and extras.

A fixed fee, based on a percentage of the total cost, can reward poor performance. The higher the cost, the greater the fee.

Omnibus-type fees for portions of engineering and construction can result in the lack of necessary services. A fee for engineering can result in lack of optimization, poor design, overgenerous specifications, and poor equipment engineering, resulting in high-priced equipment. Material costs are reimbursable. Similarly, a fee for construction equipment can result in excessive use of labor, leading to higher labor costs and schedule extension. Labor costs are reimbursable. A fixed fee for construction management can result in lack of supervision and services, particularly if construction conditions change from those anticipated.

The above problems can be magnified with projects on a "fast-track" approach where there is a greater element of the unknown.

The Control Estimate

Most owners develop an estimate at the front-end and feasibility stage. This conceptual estimate would generally fall in the ±30% accuracy level and would be based on cost-capacity curves or equipment and bulk ratio breakdowns.

This estimate could be updated as the design is developed, or the control could be transferred to the contractor's estimate, which is probably being developed on a different basis. Using the contractor's estimate will generally produce a greater sense of commitment and responsibility by the contractor. Whichever estimate is used to control the project costs, it is not recommended that the contractor be forced to structure his estimate to the work breakdown and account codes of the owners.

The Project Schedule

In addition to a conceptual estimate, an overall schedule is developed by the owner at the front end of a project. This schedule is developed on a summary basis as scope and execution plans are still in a preliminary stage. As the project develops, it is recommended that daily control and detailed planning be transferred to the contractor's scheduling operation. The owner should maintain overall monitoring of the contractor's schedules and planning operation.

This early schedule provides the time basis for the estimate and presents to management an overall program showing the major decision points. At this stage, it is vital that this information be easily and clearly communicated to management.

The best format for this summary schedule is a time-scaled network. It will provide an excellent picture of time and the major phases and dependencies of the project. From a technical viewpoint, time-scaled networks are inefficient as they can require considerable rework and redrafting, but from a communication viewpoint, they are outstanding.

Figure 23-4 is a typical example of a summary schedule. This schedule, of a synthetic fuel plant, shows a phased approach, the major scope elements of a process plant and a coal mine, environmental requirements, contracting decision points, mechanical completion, and plant start-up.

With an adequate scheduling data base, the following significant information can be easily developed with this schedule:

- Escalation midpoints for material and labor.
- Progress curves for engineering and construction (Phase II).
- Manpower histograms for engineering and construction (Phase II).
- Owner manpower and project team requirements.

Activity durations are determined by judgment, past experience (data base), or a combination of both.

A Project Control Organization

Figure 23-5 illustrates a typical organization for project control. It is recommended that the project control section be part of the project management division, whereas estimating and its associated functions can be a separate group.

The project control section would have three main project support groups and one staff support group: cost control and scheduling support groups organized on a geographic or manufacturing basis; a central group for methods development, training, manpower planning; and a specialist group to handle subcontract administration and construction management.

Rotational assignments and career development objectives should ensure the movement of personnel through the project control and project management groups. This would improve manpower utilization, provide greater training opportunities and increasing individual skill levels.

Personnel in the cost and schedule support groups should be developed to handle both cost and schedule work. Capability in both functions would be beneficial for providing home office "suitcase" services and also personnel for control manager positions.

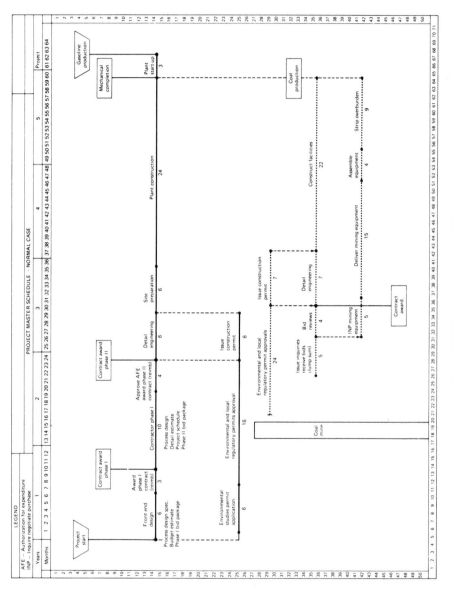

Figure 23-4. Project master schedule.

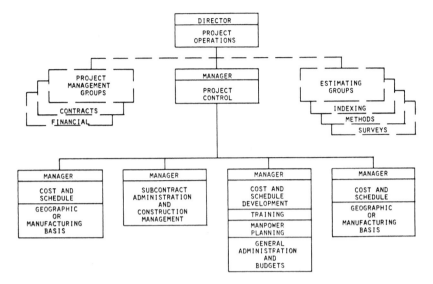

Figure 23-5. A project control organization.

Due to high work load, large projects would require separate functions of cost and scheduling.

A significant organization problem of project management and a staff project control group is the "we and they" attitude. When the project control group is part of the project management division, the "we and they" attitude is greatly reduced. In addition, the "audit image" is also reduced.

Alignment in project management divisions can sometimes stifle independent and adverse evaluations by project control personnel.

SECTION 2. A CONTROL ENVIRONMENT

General

Without question, *it is the project manager's responsibility to create an environment which will enable "control" to be exercised.* This means he will seek counsel, accept sound advice, and stretch control personnel to the extent of their capability.

A key element for effective control is timely evaluation of potential cost and schedule hazards and the presentation of these evaluations with recommended solutions to project management. This means that the control engineer must be a skilled technician and also be able to effectively communicate to management level. Sometimes, a skilled technician's performance is not adequate because he is a poor communicator. *Technical expertise will rarely compensate for lack of communication skills.* As in all staff functions, the ability to "sell" service can be as important as the ability to perform the service. Project teams are mostly brought together from a variety of "melting pots," and the difficulty of establishing effective and appropriate communications at all levels should not be underestimated. In this regard, the project manager is responsible for quickly establishing a positive working environment where the separate functions of design, procurement, construction, and control *are welded into a unified, cost-conscious group.* Project managers who relegate the control function to a reporting or accounting function are derelict in their duties.

Project control can be defined as the process which:

- Forecasts and evaluates potential hazards prior to occurrence so that preventive action can be taken.
- Reviews trends or actual situations to analyze their impact and, if possible, proposes action to alleviate the situation.
- Provides constant surveillance of project conditions to effectively and economically create a "no-surprise" condition.

Task Force versus Functional Organization

The question of a functional organization versus a task force approach is a much debated subject. It is the writer's opinion that a task force approach is more efficient for large projects, whereas the functional organization can be adequate for small projects. The task force approach brings a greater concentration of resources and fewer levels of management as the reporting line to the functional departments becomes one of personnel allocation and advice, rather than direction.

Many owners now use task forces to monitor contractor performance. Some contractors are of the opinion that this approach increases schedule durations and project costs. However, in today's volatile marketplace with associated contractors' reluctance to bid on a lump sum basis, owners believe that task forces are necessary and that they make a clear, positive contribution to meeting owner objectives. In addition, owner's project control expertise, in many instances, is equal to contractor's capability.

Figure 23-6 illustrates a typical owner task force organization. This shows an owner operation with a central engineering department having responsibility for the corporation capital project program. The operating company, or client group, is responsible for funding the project and, in a

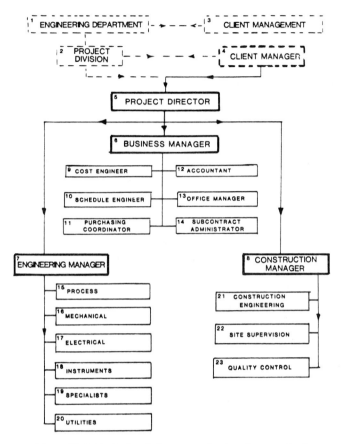

Figure 23-6. Typical task force organization (large project).

sense, hires the central engineering department to manage the project. This requires that the project director have two reporting lines: a functional line to the engineering project division and a financial line to the client manager.

The dual relationship can cause conflict. This mostly occurs when the client manager attempts to manage the project director in functional project business. The most common situation of conflict is when the client manager works directly with the contractor.

The focal point for instructions to the contractor must be through the project director and then flow from the owner task force to the contractor organization. Owner and contractor must structure their task force organizations to harmonize. The better the coordination and communication of owner and contractor personnel in this joint task force operation, the greater the prospect for successful project execution. *Systems and procedures do not build projects—people do.*

Owner-Contractor Relationships

A significant feature of a successful project control operation is the relationship between contractor and owner personnel. One item in the initial phase of a capital project is the "screening and qualifying" of contractors prior to contract award. During this activity, owner control requirements can be clearly explained and an implementation program obtained from the contractors can be evaluated. Some owners have a formal system for evaluating contractors.

After contract award, the reality of the implementation program will be tested during detailed discussions in setting up a mutually acceptable system. These should be conducted in a spirit of equal partnership. *The owner control specification will be the basis of discussions on control organization, procedures, systems, and controls.* These early reviews can prevent later system changes, costly reorganizations, and personnel reassignments. Such discussions should be promptly followed by meetings with the contractor's engineering, procurement, construction, and project services groups to verify mutual understanding and acceptance of a common approach to planning, scheduling, and cost control. At this stage, the discussions must necessarily be brief and to the point. Everybody is busy. But they are essential to ensure that contractor's control system meets owner's requirements.

Detailed planning, scheduling, and cost control are the contractor's responsibility, and it is his responsibility to see that they are efficient operations, effectively utilized. This is an equal partnership operation.

Apart from estimating systems, many owners have established control data such as the following:

- Engineering man-hours per piece of equipment and man-hours per drawing.
- Construction man-hours per work category.
- Standard engineering and construction productivity profiles.
- Standard engineering and construction progress profiles.
- Overall milestone durations and dependent relationships.
- Standard procurement and subcontract relationships.
- Typical man-hour expenditure curves.
- Typical material commitment curves.
- Standard engineering discipline relationships.

- Home office and construction indirect relationships.
- Standard engineering and construction rate profiles.
- Typical breakdown of engineering by discipline and section.
- Typical breakdown of construction by craft and prime account.
- Domestic and worldwide productivity factors.
- Typical manpower buildup and rundown.
- Construction manpower density/productivity curves.
- Domestic and worldwide labor and material escalation rates.

Data, as indicated above, enables owners to check contractors' estimates and continuously monitor performance through all phases of a project. Many contractors have invested heavily in the development of PERT, CPM techniques and control systems*. In spite of this investment, and resulting sophisticated systems with their associated heavy running costs, owners continue to comment on poor execution of the contractor project control function. In turn, contractors complain that owners do not clearly identify their project objectives, change their minds on scope causing costly recycles of engineering, and are often disorganized. A major complaint by contractors is that owners monitor their activities too closely. It is essential that the owner's cost and schedule representatives refrain from continuously getting into "too much detail." This, invariably, causes an adverse relationship. Contractors should be allowed freedom of action and an occasional error.

There are two significant procedures which attempt to clearly establish the detailed working relationship of owner and contractor: the coordination procedure, outlined earlier, which covers organizational and functional relationships, and a "document action schedule" which specifies the owner involvement in all documents produced by the contractor. This covers engineering drawings, specifications, inquiry packages, bid tabulations, purchase orders, subcontracts, and all control and reporting documents.

When too tight a level of approval is imposed by the owner, it can result in additional costs and lengthening of the schedule.

A major complaint by owners is in contractor scheduling. Rarely does the owner encounter a contractor's performance where the planning, scheduling, and control of engineering, procurement, and construction phases are effectively bound into one system. Too often, rigid departmentalization of contractors has forced owners' representatives to act as catalysts and coordinators to achieve efficient execution.

See Chapter 15 for a detailed discussion of PERT, CPM and other network planning techniques.

Overdepartmentalization is evident when separate groups of a contractor's organization operate to an appreciable degree to the exclusion of the interests of associated groups and departments. In particular, owners experience too many instances where engineering, design, procurement, project, and construction departments act as separate companies. Corporate politics sometimes are allowed to override project objectives and the true long-range objectives of the engineer-contractor. Unless engineering, procurement, and construction groups operate as a team, with differing functions but common objectives, project execution will be inefficient and costly.

All contractors emphasize in sales presentations the unified application of their resources to the owner's project. Departmental flexibility and coordination are stated as being strengths of the company organization. In practice, the owner too often finds that planning, scheduling, and control are exercised only within compartmented contractor departments. While it is highly desirable that individual departments and departmental sections participate in the setting of schedules, and in controlling to these schedules, overall progress scheduling and control are the owner's prime concern. For this reason, final schedule authority must rest in a strong, active project management, supported by adequate staff schedule personnel.

Alternatively, owners sometimes find scheduling operations consolidated in autonomous groups, the output of which is voluminous, but unused. If the engineer-contractor is to meet the owner's objectives, and in the long run, his own objectives, the output of planning and scheduling groups must be both usable and used by the project team.

An Integrated System

Like any control function, effective project control requires that all efforts be fully integrated; that status be fully and accurately reported; that costs, programs, and engineering scope be compared against budget estimates, schedules, and specifications (the norms); and that the loop be closed either by modifying and correcting the control system, or by changing the control methods. This cycle of events is necessary, and should be continual for successful project execution. The owner's interest and participation in these events will vary from project to project and depend primarily on the type of project contract. In short, for effective project control, a project team (not an individual) must concentrate on anticipating and detecting deviations from project norms, and then take full and timely action to handle such deviations. Project norms should only be revised when it is absolutely certain that they are beyond achievement; *however, prompt reports should indicate deviations as they become apparent,* even though no immediate action is taken.

Figures 23-7 and 23-8 illustrate major elements of integrated scheduling and cost control systems.

Figure 23-7 is a flowchart indicating the elements necessary for an integrated schedule system. It is the writer's opinion that owners and contractors need to achieve fully integrated and coordinated control sys-

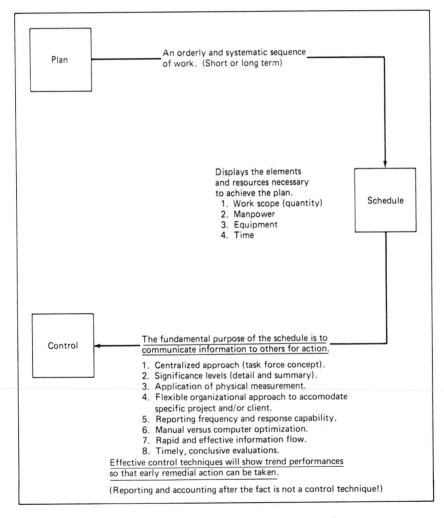

Figure 23-7. Planning/scheduling/control—an integrated system.

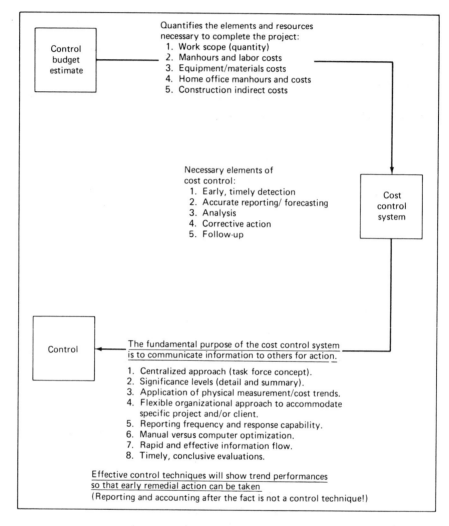

Figure 23-8. Project cost control—an integrated system.

tems along these general lines. To do so will require, in many instances, a thorough rethinking of schedule-related operations, and upgrading of personnel. In some instances, judicious "headknocking" is going to be required to call attention to outmoded practices and attitudes, and failures to conform to stated management policies.

Figure 23-8 is a flowchart indicating the elements necessary for an integrated cost control system. The major items are a quality estimate, based on quantities, an effective trending system, and qualified personnel working on a task force basis.

Communication—Manual or Computer

Figure 23-9 is a flowchart of a typical management information system, or, in other words, the operating levels of the project control system.

Again, the key word is communication.

The project control system must generate summary and detailed information for different levels of management. Information must be current, timely, and accurate. This flowchart shows four levels of detail, which are typical for most large projects.

Information is generally a combination of computer programs and manual reports. It is difficult to conclude that computer programs are better than manual systems. There are obvious advantages with the computer, but many systems prove ineffective due to the tremendous level of detail.

Scheduling systems with tens of thousands of activities are rarely effec-

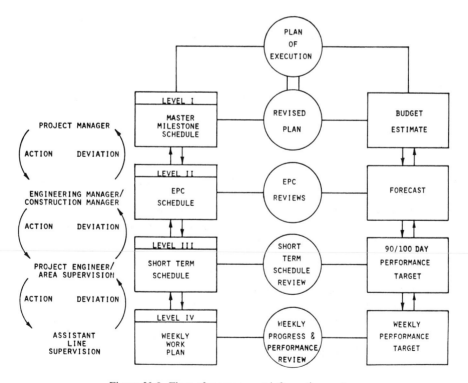

Figure 23-9. Flow of management information system.

tive. Alternatively, it is very time-consuming to produce a detailed field progress report without a computer program.

Each project and each contractor operation should be thoroughly investigated for application of a computer approach to project control. (See Chapter 28 for a discussion of the use of computer software in project management.)

As most owners work in a monitoring role, it is unlikely that owners would need their own extensive computer programs for control purposes.

Owner Review of Contractor Control System

On large projects, early after contract award, a team should be established to review, in detail, the contractor's cost and schedule system, organization, and assigned personnel. The purpose is to recommend to the project manager a complete project control system for the project. The team should be led by a senior member of the home office control group and consist of task force and staff cost and schedule personnel. As this review will take four to six weeks, the addition of home office personnel is generally necessary as the work load of the project-assigned personnel is very heavy at this time. The team leader must be very experienced in order to understand and handle the complete range of a contractor's project control operation. Hence, a supervisor from the home office is generally required.

Personnel should be nominated by the manager of project control, and a timed execution plan presented to the project manager for approval prior to commencement of the work.

Specific objectives of this review are listed below:

- To investigate the project control systems and organization of prime contractor, joint venture or management contractors and prepare a recommended total project control system. *The investigation should be based on maximizing the use of existing contractor systems and resources. Changes should be minimal and only significant deficiencies should require modification.*

  Should a contractor system or organization have significant deficiencies, it is recommended that the contractor modify his system by supplementing it with the appropriate owner procedure and formats. However, it is important that changes be kept to a minimum and the contractor be permitted full use of procedures and methods with which he is familiar.
- To prepare a detailed report covering the investigation and recommendation.
- To prepare a schedule for the implementation of the above recom-

mendations, extending to the point where the control system is fully operational.

- To present the plan and recommendation to the owner and contractor executive management to obtain full understanding and endorsement by management at an early stage in the project.

Implementation Schedule—Project Control System

It is essential to establish a quality Project Control System at the earliest possible date. As an aid to meeting this objective, it is recommended that a detailed "Implementation Schedule" be prepared showing the completion dates agreed to with the contractor. This schedule should be developed in summary and detailed form and will outline all facets of the proposed control system, showing deadlines for completion and personnel allocations for the work.

Contractor should list and provide "duration estimates" for all procedures, such as Schedules, Reports, Estimates, Computer Programs and Organization Charts, etc., which constitute the overall Project Control System. It is suggested that a flowchart(s) showing the major elements of the system be prepared by the contractor.

The contractor should provide schedules and details of resource for completion of the Project Control System.

This owner review and preparation of associated implementation schedule can be a frustrating time for contractors. It can be doubly so if owner personnel lack experience and the contractor has to spend considerable time in education as well as explanation. The process is time-consuming and may require the time of the key contractor control personnel who are already heavily engaged in the project.

However, this is the time for contractors to fully explore owner control requirements, provide effective and detailed explanations of their systems, accept obvious improvements, and defend "poor" programs which they believe are effective and which they have proved out on projects.

Owners should have a "minimal change" policy and contractors should encourage owner personnel to live up to this policy.

Figure 23-10 illustrates a segment of a typical implementation schedule.

This schedule should cover major categories of procedures, schedules, cost, computer, measurement, and reporting. It should be updated weekly or biweekly for progress and status.

Jumbo Projects

A significant aspect of project work in the 1970s was the increasing size and complexity of projects.

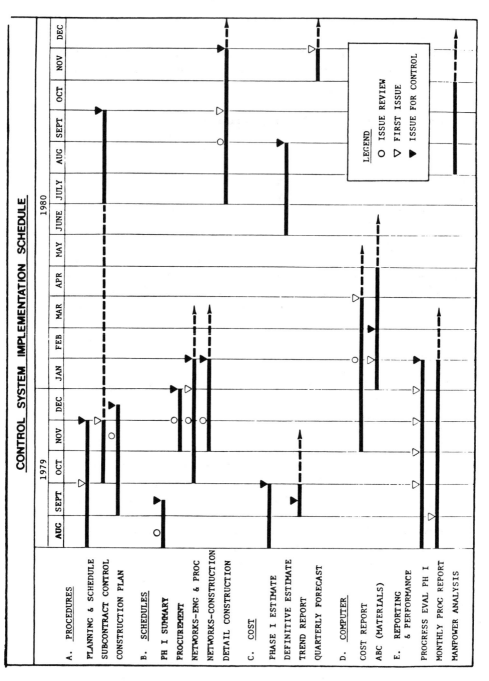

Figure 23-10. Segment of a typical implementation schedule.

Major examples are the Trans-Alaska pipeline, offshore platforms in the North Sea, gas-gathering facilities in the Middle East, the Sasol synthetic fuel plant in South Africa, and the Syncrude Tar Sands plant in Alberta. These are termed jumbo or mega projects.

New and changing technology, a hostile environment (Alaska and the North Sea), construction on a massive scale, plus the minimum of experience and data, provided the background to estimating, planning, and scheduling of these facilities.

The oil industry was breaking new technological barriers in terms of size and complexity of production facilities. The resultant first-generation jumbo projects experienced a considerable degree of last-minute innovation, and were built without full scope definition and little appreciation of offshore construction. Because of the urgent need to bring these facilities on stream, companies were tackling many of the problems during the construction and installation stages. Therefore, cost and schedule overruns were common occurrences.

It was not until about 1976 that realistic criteria and appropriate techniques had been developed to control these very large and complex projects. It was discovered that current concepts and practices of functional and task force organizations were not very effective. In particular, a task force with centralized decision making was not adequate. Management layers stretched out communication channels and decision making.

The following size parameters give a general breakdown of projects into small, medium, large, and jumbo:

		SMALL	MEDIUM	LARGE	JUMBO
(a)	Engineering Manhours	100,000	600,000	1,500,000	6,000,000
(b)	Engineering manpower	100	200	400	1,000
(c)	Construction man-hours	500,000	400,000	8,000,000	50,000,000
(d)	Construction	400	1,500	3,000	10,000
(e)	Construction staff	50	150	500	1,000
(f)	Schedule (months) (Detailed engineering to completion of construction)	25	30	35	50/60

Comparing the jumbo projects of the 1970s with conventional plants, the major lessons learned were:

- The desirability of a decentralized approach to place decision making as close to the work as possible.
- The need to combine owner and contractor project teams into one operating unit.

- The need to reduce management layers so that decentralized project teams could communicate quickly with overall project management.
- The increased effect that basic organization changes can have on a very large project.
- The importance of leadership, as opposed to managerial skills, in an effective project management organization.
- The increased importance of a quality execution plan prior to the start of detailed engineering, procurement, and construction (Phase II). The execution plan is to provide a base for the estimate, as well as a plan for executing the project.
- The significance of greatly increased influence of governmental agencies and joint venture partners.
- The inadequacy of existing data base and assumptions of size effect. It is possible that the traditional "scale effect," where increased size and units reduce unit costs, does not apply on jumbo projects. Pioneer projects are likely to experience unit-cost increases as their technology advances. Extreme caution must be exercised in scaling up capacity-cost ratios of conventional plants for jumbo projects requiring new technology and prototype engineering.

The following comments further amplify a new approach to a jumbo project.

Decentralization. During Phase II, the project should be divided into major cost centers, to an approximate value of ±$200MM, each with its own budget, schedule, and complete project organization. Jumbo projects would then have 15–20 of such individual cost centers.

Decision making should be by the individual project organization, constrained only by its budget and schedule and objectives set by the central project management group. The central project group would be responsible for coordination of resources and common services, overall cost and schedule objectives, and interfaces with client, corporate, and government groups.

Cost, schedule, procurement, and engineering specialists of the individual project group would report directly to their project manager and functionally to the specialist manager of the central group. They would receive their day-to-day direction from their project manager and technical guidance from the functional manager of the central group.

Phase I (conceptual process design) and the commissioning and start-up phases should be organized on a central project group basis. As the major decisions of a Phase I operation are comparatively few, mainly process design and selection, execution plan, and contracting strategy, the decision-making process should be in the hands of a few people. Similarly, construction at the 95–98% point will move into the commissioning and start-up phase. This requires the reuniting of the individual projects for a common approach to start-up and operations.

Owner-Contractor Partnership.   An adversary or stand-alone relationship between owner and contractor will add costs and extend the schedule on jumbo projects. The amounts of money are large. Decision making requires greater evaluation and analysis. Fast decision making requires that owner and contractor work as a team during the evaluation process to prevent loss of time with major reviews and presentations.

As most jumbo projects are built on a "fast-track" basis, fast decision making is essential if the schedule is to be achieved.

Continuous agreement at working levels between owner and contractor will generally require owner personnel additional to the traditional levels of the past.

Even though there will be a united team approach, it is vital that the contractor be allowed to freely operate at the daily working level.

A new concept is the completely integrated owner-contractor project team, where owner personnel may have supervisory and subordinate roles. The major problems of this approach are questions of contractor responsibility, professional pride, personnel relationships, and proprietary information.

The concept has much to offer and is one that deserves considerably more study, analysis, and development.

Organization Changes.   The need for organizational and procedural changes can be recognized and the problem reduced with an organization development group.

The O.D. Group.   This group would be established to unblock decision-making bottlenecks and improve inadequate procedures. Its objectives would be to constantly monitor and evaluate organization, communications, procedures, and methods. This function requires specialized personnel with experience to cover all phases and functions of the project.

Due to the wide range of experience required, it is probable that two groups will be required: one group for the home office covering engineering and procurement, the second group for the field covering construction. About four to six personnel, at peak, would be required for an effective O.D. group.

Leadership Versus Managerial Skills. People skills are essential in the management and control of jumbo projects. With task forces ranging in size from 500 to 1000, the importance of people skills cannot be overemphasized.

It is possible that leadership skills are more important than managerial skills. Personnel motivation is an essential ingredient of a successful project team.

Control Estimate. As a quality estimate is vital to the project control effort, an owner-contractor team should be established to develop the estimate. This will provide continuous working agreement on such significant elements as escalation, productivity levels, unit rates, work breakdown structure, control areas, and individual cost centers.

A detailed estimate could be produced about 12–16 months after Phase II contract award and would probably require 40 contractor and 10 owner personnel. With this approach, management review and approval could take one week instead of the months of review and reconciliation, which is the more normal case.

Planning and Scheduling. The size of the activity network is not the major consideration. The quality of the weekly construction program is the main concern. Construction man-hours will be in the range of 40MM–100MM. With peaks of 10,000–15,000 men, a quality weekly work program is absolutely essential.

It is likely to be a manual system and should be based on quantities, unit man-hour rates, and varying productivity adjustments and be reconciled against the objectives of the overall schedule. Productivity goals should be preplanned and then reported against on a weekly basis.

Quantity Control. This technique is rarely used. On jumbo projects, where the amounts of money are so large, a quantity tracking system is essential for effective cost control.

Appropriate "bulk quantities" (earth, concrete, piping, etc.) should be selected and tracked, by a random sampling technique, from the process design of Phase I through detailed engineering of Phase II.

Rundown Control. This method is rarely used in present-day project work. Again, due to size, this is an essential technique for jumbo projects.

As engineering and construction commence their rundown (about 80% complete), individual budgets, schedules, and manpower histograms should be developed to separately control the remaining work.

Governmental Agencies and Joint Venture Partnerships.   Many of today's jumbo projects have governments as partners. Governmental regulations and agencies, partner and joint venture relationships add a further dimension that must be recognized by the planning, scheduling, and cost effort.

Governmental energy companies may require "preferred purchasing" (buying in the host country), extensive training programs for supervisory staff and craft labor, and the development of an infrastructure local to the project job site.

Joint venture partners require a vote in major decisions. This takes time. Major purchases can require approval of partners prior to purchase. Again, this takes time. Periodic reviews and presentations can be required by partners. This takes effort and costs money.

All of the above aspects should be carefully considered when developing the project execution plan and schedule.

Figure 23–11 vividly illustrates the effects of problems outlined in the opening paragraph of this subsection. This study (R-2481-DOE) by the Rand Corporation for the Department of Energy shows final costs versus initial feasibility estimates for many jumbo projects. As can be seen, the cost growth is 200–300%. This is caused by either bad estimates, poor performance, or a combination of both. Major changes causing significant

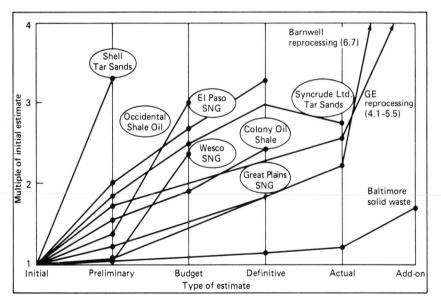

Figure 23-11. Cost growth in pioneer energy process plants (constant dollars).

cost additions can be classed as poor performance. Concern is being expressed that current estimates for jumbo synthetic fuel projects will follow the same patterns as the chart in Figure 23-11.

Project Levels of Control and Reporting

Levels of control and reporting vary widely in the industry. They can be dependent on:

- Recognition, understanding, and need for control.
- Company commitment to control.
- Personnel resources and capability.
- Size and complexity of projects.
- Owner/contractor contractual arrangements.
- Owner/contractor control relationship/expertise.
- Acceptance of cost control.
- Cost effectiveness of control.

Most major contractors have comprehensive project control systems. However, very few owners have a similar capability, or even detailed control specifications which would enable contractors to thoroughly understand the owner's project control requirements.

As already outlined, an early, effective project control program is an essential requirement. It is difficult to achieve this objective on reimbursable projects if owners are not able to specify, in detail, their requirements. Even on lump sum projects, a similar approach is necessary, as effective planning, scheduling, and progress measurement should be an owner requirement. Apart from an adequate change order procedure, cost control reporting is the contractor's sole responsibility on lump sum projects.

Figure 23–12 lists typical project control requirements for the following project categories:

- Feasibility Study (0–10,000 engineering hours).
- Small Project (10,000–100,000 engineering hours).
- Medium Project (100,000–500,000 engineering hours).
- Large Project (500,000–1,500,000 engineering hours).

In an attempt to quantify project size, engineering man-hours have been allocated to these categories. *This can only be a guide as project size is dependent on the size of the company.*

It is generally recognized that as project size increases, additional con-

				JAMES BENT ASSOCIATES, INC.	DATE

PROJECT LEVELS OF CONTROL & REPORTING — REIMBURSABLE PROJECTS

For the designated project size, the outlined techniques, reports and procedures are additive to the previous level lump sum projects would require most of the scheduling procedures. See project control manual for details of method and procedure.

PROJECT	OVERALL	ENGINEERING	PROCUREMENT	CONSTRUCTION	SUBCONTRACTS
1. FEASIBILITY (10,000 eng. hours)	Summary schedule	Project master schedule	Delivery lead times	Site survey	Licensor packages
	Execution plan		Logistics evaluation	Soil report	
	Estimate	Manhour curve			
	Cost report	Manhour rate curve			
	Monthly report	Manpower histogram			
2. SMALL PROJECT (100,000 eng. hours)	Trend report	Discipline schedule (milestones)	P.O. commitment register	Pre-planning program	Overall schedules (by subcontract)
	Project status report • Engineering • Material commitment • Construction	Engineering manhour curve	Material status report	Manforce report	
			Overall commitment curve ($)	Three month schedules	Progress/status report (by subcontract)
		Home office manhour curve	Vendor dwg. report	Construction progress barchart (overall)	Summary cost report
	Contingency rundown curve	Bid evaluation program		Manpower histogram	
	Cash flow curve			Overall manhour curve	
				Overall rate curve	
3. MEDIUM PROJECT (500,000 eng. hours)	Contractors evaluation program	Engineering change log	Equipment commitment curve ($)	Field estimate (quantities)	Subcontract commitment curve ($)
		Material requisition curve	Bulk material commitment curve ($)	Construction area progress barcharts	Subcontract preparation schedule
	Detailed control specs.	Document and action schedule	Material requisition curves	Weekly work program	Unit price subcontracts • Cost report • Quantity report • Performance evaluation • Progress curve • Manpower histogram
	Task force approach	Progress measurement program (discipline) • Quantities/hours • Progress curves • Manpower curves • Productivity curves	Inspection — expediting reports	Progress measurement program • Quantities/hours • Progress curves • Manpower curves • Productivity curves	
	Computer scheduling program				
	Coordination procedure				
	Extra work/change order procedure			Status report • Progress • Productivity • Manpower	
		Front end schedules (3 mo.)			
		Dwg. schedules		Indirects expenditure curve ($)	
		H.O. Expense expenditure curve ($)		Staff schedule	
				Equipment schedule	
				Backcharge register	
				Cost report	
4. LARGE PROJECT (1,500,000 eng. hours)	Contractors screening program	Account requisition curves	Account commitment curves ($)	Work lint tracking curves • earthwork • concrete • piping	Independent bid analysis program
	Project control implementation schedule	Piping design program	Account requisition report		Sensitivity analysis
		Drawings tracking curves (P&I's) (foundations) (isometrics)	Critical purchasing list	Area status reports	Performance curve and report
	Weekly manforce report		Material delivery histogram	Staff manhour & rate curve	
		Quantity tracking program	Surplus material report	Equipment manhour rate profile	
		Rundown control program • Drawings • Manhours • Dates • Manpower • Progress • Productivity		Field office expense expenditure curve ($)	
				Indirect manhour and rate curve	
				Rundown control program • Manhours • Manpower • Progress • Productivity	
		Punch lists		Punch lists	

Figure 23-12. Project control requirements.

589

trol procedures are necessary. Obviously, control for control's sake should be avoided. Typical examples of costly and inefficient control systems are very large activity network programs, duplication of effort by owner and contractor on reimbursable projects, and some governmental reporting procedures.

The outlined control procedures are divided into the major phases of a project. They are additive as the project category increases in size. A small project would require the items listed in categories 1 and 2. Similarly, a large project would require all the listed items.

Manpower Planning—Engineering Department

One of the more difficult areas of project control is in-house company planning of engineering personnel. The major uncertainty, causing difficulty, is forecasting the amount and type of future project work. The difficulty is usually greater for owners.

The contracting industry has two major considerations: an annual estimate of the owner's capital projects program and an assessment of their ability to obtain a share of that work.

The owner's engineering department can face the following:

- Amount of feasibility studies.
- Technical service requirements.
- Methods development and technical research.
- Actuality of probable or anticipated projects.

Many owner central engineering departments act as a nonprofit service company to operating divisions of the corporation. As such, their work load is largely dependent on the capital projects program of the operating divisions. It is not too difficult to assess technical service requirements, methods development, and technical research based on past experience. But assessments of feasibility studies and capital projects depend on factors often outside the control of the engineering department:

- Quality of corporate strategic planning program.
- Corporate financing.
- Project economic viability.
- Communication channels with operating divisions.
- Relationships with operating divisions.
- "Project charter" of engineering department.
- Image/credibility/capability of engineering department.

Even though there can be many uncertainties in work load, one thing is certain: Quality evaluations of work load and associated manpower planning are essential—particularly with the typical shortfall of engineers and the industry prediction that the shortfall will increase for the long term.

The following exhibits outline a systematic approach to engineering manpower planning.

Planning by Individual. Individual planning is the lowest level of detail. Not only does it provide an assessment of manpower needs to meet a projected work load, it also provides a program of career development for each engineer.

Figure 23–13 illustrates a three-year plan for project services personnel (estimating, cost control, scheduling). This shows feasibility work, project assignments (home office and task force), methods development, rotational assignments, transfers, replacements, and recruiting requirements. This should be a "dynamic document" as conditions/requirements can quickly change. The control sheet should be constantly updated and issued monthly.

It is recommended that all section personnel "plans" be evaluated and summarized by the project services group into a monthly engineering department manpower report. It is probable that this would be a computer-based program so as to provide overall manpower reports by individual listing, project assignments, feasibility work, sections, etc.

As manpower plans are only as good as assessments of work load, it is vital that work projections be evaluated each month. This requires close liaison/coordination between project, engineering, construction, and project services groups to ensure that current and future work assessments are adequate.

Planning by Project. The following report format is mostly used by contractors as it concentrates on project manpower allocations.

Figure 23-14, usually a computer report, assesses manpower allocations and requirements based on budget man-hours, forecast, man-hours to date, schedule, and man-hour allocations for the past six weeks. Only three months of the schedule are shown and continuation sheets would provide requirements for the complete schedule. The past six weeks show current trends and also a base to assess the viability of future requirements. The computer program will take the man-hour forecast, to-date man-hours, schedule, and hourly workweek assessment and forecast the weekly scheduled manpower requirement.

The bottom two lines show men required against men available, and the difference provides the necessary recruiting program.

COLOR CODE:	HOME OFFICE	PROJECT ASSIGNMENT	TRANSFER OUT	
Activity PROJECT SERVICES		Staff Assignments and Personnel Planning		PAGE ——— DATE ———
NAME	SCHEDULE			REMARKS
ESTIMATING				
1. EVANS	GEN. | ABC PHASE I | XYZ FEASIBILITY | TASK FORCE (XYZ) COST CONTROL		GENERAL EST'G	
2. DAVIES	GENERAL ESTIMATING | • BUDGETS • FEASIBILITY			
3. JONES	A.F.E. ESTIMATING			
4. WILLIAMS	METHODS DEVELOPMENT | PRODUCTIVITY FACTORS | LABOR & MATERIAL ESCALATION		TRANSFER TO SCHEDULING	
COST CONTROL				
5. PRICE	TASK FORCE | TRANSFER TO PROJECTS			
6. BENNETT	"SUITCASE" PROJECTS 103|201|430 | XYZ PROJECT TASK FORCE			
7. GRAHAM	"SUITCASE" PROJECTS 120|150|250|310			
SCHEDULING				
8. ROBERTS	FEASIBILITY SCHEDULES & "SUITCASE" PROJECTS		TRANSFER TO DESIGN	
9. JENKINS	FEASIBILITY SCHEDULES & "SUITCASE" PROJECTS | XYZ PROJECT TASK FORCE			
10. LONGDEN	METHODS DEVELOPMENT | FEASIBILITY SCHEDULES			
RECRUITING				
11. COST ENGINEER	RECRUIT | TRAINING | GENERAL COST CONTROL (SUITCASE) | TASK FORCE			TO REPLACE PRICE
12. ESTIMATOR	RECRUIT | TRAINING | GENERAL ESTIMATING			TO REPLACE WILLIAMS
13. SCHEDULER	RECRUIT | TRAINING | GENERAL SCHEDULING			TO REPLACE ROBERTS
14. ESTIMATOR	RECRUIT | TRAINING | GENERAL ESTIMATING			TO REPLACE EVANS
	JAN. FEB. MAR. APR. MAY JUN. JUL. AUG. SEPT. OCT. NOV. DEC.	JAN. FEB. MAR. APR. MAY JUN. JUL. AUG. SEPT. OCT. NOV. DEC.	JAN. FEB. MAR. APR. MAY JUN. JUL. AUG. SEPT. OCT. NOV. DEC.	
	1980	1981	1982	

Figure 23-13. Project services—personnel.

Use continuation sheet for rest of schedule ⟶

Engineering Department — Manpower Planning

Project number	Manhours			Manhours for past six weeks						Men weeks to go	Weekly scheduled men			
	Budget	Forecast	To date								Jan	Feb	Mar	
1	2	3	4	5	6	7	8	9	10	11	12	13	14	
Total above projects														
Miscellaneous projects														
Development work														
Total manhours														
Total men available														
Total men required														

Figure 23-14. Manpower planning.

ENGINEERING DEPARTMENT – MANPOWER PLANNING – WORK CATEGORY

NOTES:
1. DRAFTING IS OUTSIDE CONTRACT.

CODE	WORK CATEGORY	%	ANNUAL PLAN						% FIGURES ARE AS OF MIDYEAR AS OF MARCH					
			J	F	M	A	M	J	J	A	S	O	N	D
	TECHNICAL PERSONNEL													
	CURRENT AFE PROJECTS	48	188.7	197	197	192.1	188.6	180.4	184.1	183.3	181.1	179.4	159.6	159.6
	PROBABLE PROJECTS	5	0	0	0	1	3.3	18.6	26.6	35.3	41.8	44.3	55.4	55.6
	FEASIBILITY STUDIES	12	43.2	43	43	43.5	44.6	44.8	45.8	46	46.1	46.1	45.3	44.9
	TECHNICAL SERVICE	4	14.2	14.2	14.2	14.2	14.2	14.2	14.2	14.2	14.2	14.2	14.2	14.2
	TECHNICAL METHOD DEVELOPMENT	12	42.8	42.8	43.8	43.8	43.3	43.4	43.6	43.5	43.5	43.5	43	43
	START UP/OPERATIONS	1	2	2	2	2	2	2	2	2	2	2	2	2
	SUB TOTAL TECHNICAL	82	290.9	299	300	296.6	296	303.4	316.3	324.3	328.7	329.5	319.5	319.3
	MANAGERS & SECRETARIES	7	27.2	27.2	27.2	27.2	27.2	27.2	27.2	27.2	27.2	27.2	27.2	27.2
	OTHER INDIRECTS (SERVICES ETC.)	11	42.9	42.9	42.9	42.9	42.9	42.9	43	43	43	43	43	43
	MISCELLANEOUS	0	0	0	0	0	0	0	0	0	0	0	0	0
	REQUIRED TOTAL	100	361	369.1	370.1	366.7	366.1	373.5	386.5	394.5	398.9	399.7	389.7	389.5
	ACTUAL PAYROLL		319	327											

Figure 23-15. Manpower planning—work category.

ENGINEERING DEPARTMENT – MANPOWER PLANNING – BY SECTION

NOTES:
1. DRAFTING IS OUTSIDE CONTRACT.

% FIGURES ARE AS OF MIDYEAR

CODE	SECTION	%	ANNUAL PLAN						AS OF MARCH					
			J	F	M	A	M	J	J	A	S	O	N	D
	EMPLOYEE RELATIONS	1	4.5	4.5	4.5	4.5	4.5	4.5	4.8	4.9	4.9	5	5	5
	PROCUREMENT	1	4.2	4.4	5	5.3	5.7	4.8	4.7	4.8	5.4	5	5.2	5.4
	PROJECTS – U.S. REFINING & CHEMICAL	5	14.6	15.9	15.9	16.7	17.3	19.7	19.8	20.1	21.4	20.8	19.7	20.1
	– OVERSEAS R & C	6	17.6	18.3	17.6	17.4	17.3	21.7	23.4	24.7	24	23.2	23.2	22.6
	– MIDDLE EAST	3	9.5	9.5	9.5	9.5	9.5	9.5	9.5	9.5	9.5	9.5	9.5	9.5
	– OFFSHORE/SYNFUELS	12	45.2	45.2	45.2	46	45.8	46.2	46.1	45.2	44.3	44.3	44.3	44.3
	PROJECT SERVICES (EST'G./COST & SCHED.)	11	40	40	40.5	40.5	40.5	40.5	42.5	44.3	46	47	45	4.5
	CONTRACTS	1	4.5	4.5	4.5	4.5	4.5	4.5	5.5	5.5	5.5	5.5	5	5
	GENERAL SERVICES (NON TECH.)	5	22.4	22	21.9	21	21	20.2	22.4	23.5	21.6	21	21	21
	PROCESS ENGINEERING	14	52.6	55.8	55.8	54.5	52.7	53.2	48.8	49.2	48.3	48.7	46	45
	FACILITIES ENGINEERING	26	93.3	96.1	98.2	94.8	94.7	97	104.5	108.8	114.1	115.6	111.2	112.3
	OFFICE & PLANT SERVICES	5	17.7	17.7	17.7	17.7	17.7	17.7	17.8	17.8	18	18.1	18.2	18.3
	OVERSEAS ENGINEERING OFFICES	10	34.9	35.2	33.8	34.3	34.9	34	35.7	36.6	35.9	36	36.4	36
	REQUIRED TOTAL	100	361	369.1	370.1	366.7	366.1	373.5	386.5	394.5	398.9	399.7	389.7	389.5
	ACTUAL PAYROLL		319	327										

Figure 23-16. Manpower planning—by section.

This particular report illustrates an overall engineering manpower report. A similar report could be produced for each section.

Planning by Work Category.   Figure 23–15 illustrates a report format generally used by owners. It is similar to the previous contractor project report, but has additional categories: probable projects, feasibility studies, technical service, etc. Also, it separates technical from nontechnical and managers/secretaries. Obviously, some managers are technical. But this provides a continuous assessment of number of managers to engineers and relationship of technical to nontechnical. Both relationships need to be evaluated for an efficient operation. This report shows an annual plan. Additional years could be developed based on the quality of the individual plan cycle.

As previously stated, assessments for feasibility studies and probable projects can be difficult.

The outlined numbers illustrate a large, international operating company having a central engineering department of some 300 engineers. Evaluation of these manpower relationships should bear in mind that detail drafting and other services can be outside contracts. A typical relationship of draftsmen to engineers can be about 3.5 to 1.

This report should be issued monthly and would undoubtedly be derived from a computer program.

Planning by Section.   Figure 23–16 is a report for the same company, as previously illustrated. Whereas the previous report showed manpower by work category, this report shows manpower by section. The construction group is part of the project management groups.

Individual section reports would clearly indicate a "shortfall" or "overmanning" of personnel by engineering classification. Adequate recruiting and training programs could be developed from this information.

Manpower requirements based on physical assessments can only be made for design groups where drawing/document take-offs and man-hour assessments can be made. Historical relationships, engineering department "character"/responsibilities, control requirements, and company policy can determine allocations of service personnel to project work.

Chapter 24 deals with control techniques that are useful to the project manager.

24. Project Control: Scope Recognition

James A. Bent*

PRACTICAL PROJECT CONTROL—BASIC SCOPE APPRECIATION

The use of historical data, typical relationships, statistical correlations, and practical "rules of thumb" can greatly add to the effectiveness of a project control program. Such information can provide guidance, in:

- Developing/evaluating schedules.
- Assessing manpower requirements.
- Determining appropriate productivity levels.
- Improving cost/schedule assumptions.
- Carrying out trend analysis.
- Establishing the cost of the project.
- Evaluating the status and performance of the work.
- Recognizing the scope of work, at all times.

It is this last item that really highlights the key to effective project control. That key is *SCOPE RECOGNITION*. This equates to the ability to properly establish the scope in the first place, through a good estimate, and thereafter to constantly recognize the true scope of the work as the project develops and is executed. The "testing" and measuring of actual performance against past experience can be a valuable source of verifying status, determining trends, and making predictions. Naturally, the appli-

---

* James A. Bent has been a consultant in project management since 1980. Previously, he worked more than 30 years for owners/contractors, such as Mobil and M. W. Kellogg. Mr. Bent's experience covers both onshore plants and offshore platforms, with project assignments in the United States, United Kingdom, Australia, Netherlands, Germany, Norway, and Italy. He is an author and presents training courses (3 days–3 weeks) in project management, scheduling, estimating, cost control, contracting, claims/management/negotiating, and shutdowns/turnarounds. These training assignments take Mr. Bent to the United States, United Kingdom, Norway, Europe, Japan, South America, and South Africa.

cation of historical data to a specific project must always be carefully assessed.

The following figures represent historical and typical cost/schedule "rules of thumb" that can assist in the establishment and development of scope during the execution phase of a project. This information is especially useful at the front end of a project when engineering is at a low percentage of completion, resulting in a broad and preliminary cost estimate and overall schedule.

Figure 24-1 shows the scheduling relationship of engineering and construction for a project on a fast-track program, with the full scope of engineering, procurement, and construction (EPC). Such a project is often referred to as an EPC project. The schedule relationship/duration only covers the execution phase. This phase is sometimes referred to as Phase 2, where the earlier Phase 1 covers the conceptual design studies of process/utility alternatives and case selection.

It should also be noted that the "schedules" are illustrated as trapezoids. This concept is extremely important, as it shows that all "complex" work is executed with:

- A buildup.
- A peak period.
- A rundown.

This concept, *this fact,* then forms the basis of quality scheduling and manpower assessment. It is only "simple" work, where the task is performed by a single crew or squad, that has no buildup or rundown.

It should also be noted, and such a note is found on the figure, that the ratio breakdowns of the buildup, peak, and rundown have been rounded off to whole numbers. The historical numbers are slightly different, but at this overall level of scheduling, such minor numerical differences are of little consequence. However, further reference to the writer's historical data base would show slightly different numbers. For example, the engineering buildup, shown as 20%, is 22%, and the construction buildup, shown as 50%, is 57%.

Figure 24-2 shows the trapezoidal technique for the construction phase. The calculation procedure shows two formulas.

Formula 1 is used to determine the peak duration, shown as X, on the basis that the following information is known, or assumed:

- Scope, in man-hours.
- Effective monthly hours per man.
- Buildup, usually developed from standard schedules.

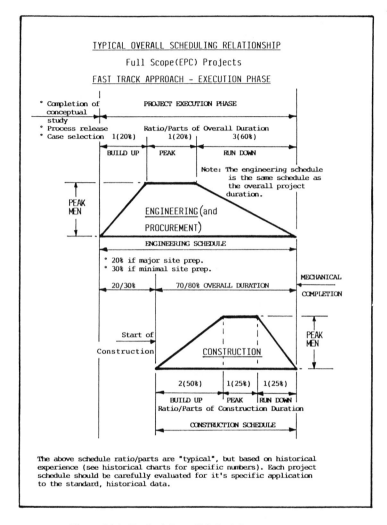

Figure 24-1. Typical Overall Scheduling Relationship.

- Rundown, half of buildup.
- Peak men, as per formula 2.

Formula 2 covers the calculation of the peak men, if the battery limits area (plot plan) is known. By evaluating a labor density level (usually in the range of 150–300 square feet/man), one can determine the peak number of men. (See Figure 24-3 for information on labor density.)

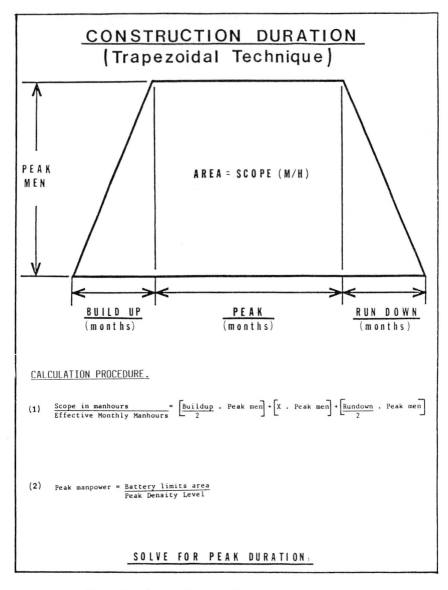

Figure 24-2. Construction Duration—Trapezoidal Technique.

This schedule/manpower evaluation technique is a very powerful program for developing or checking an overall construction duration. The key assumption, requiring good judgment, is the assessment of the labor density level. If this assessment is good, then the resulting scheduling evaluation is of a high quality.

It is emphasized that the peak manpower/density level application can only be used on single process units. The calculation process does not always work for smaller areas of work.

Figure 24-3 shows a working example of the trapezoidal density method when applied to an FCC unit. As noted in the figure, the density level of 250 square feet/man was too optimistic for such a complex unit as an FCC plant.

The first step in the calculation process is to properly assess the man-hour scope. As shown, allowances have been made for indirect labor working in the same area as direct labor and for the estimating allowance. An allowance for better subcontract productivity has been made. Assessing the density/level is extremely important. A 12% absenteeism allowance has been made.

The buildup duration was determined from a standard schedule that showed that the peak labor period would be reached at 30% of the piping duration. This activity was preceded by foundation and equipment installation work, 3 months and 2 months, respectively. The total piping duration was 15 months.

For the subcontract labor case, the man-hours are reduced to reflect a better productivity than with the direct-hire case, possibly a 10% improvement.

In the case of engineering, manpower density is not a consideration. Figure 24-4, therefore, shows the calculation of peak manpower rather than the calculation of the duration.

The same routine can be carried out for construction, if the duration is known.

This figure also shows the calculation formula for a simple piece of work, the 400-hour task, and the error of applying the "simple formula" to a complex task, the 20,000-hour task. As shown, the calculation error of 25 men, instead of 41 men, is significant.

An alternative method to the trapezoidal calculation for complex work is to use the "simple formula" and multiply the result by a "peak factor" (usually 1.6/1.7). The resulting solution is adequate.

The specific factors, based on historical data, are:

Engineering peak factor—1.65.
Construction peak factor—1.45.

EXAMPLE

Refinery FCC unit:

- Plot area = 320 ft × 200 ft = 64,000 ft^2
- Scope (direct hire) = 445,000 man-hours
- Allowance for indirect
  labor in area + 10% = 44,500 man-hours
- Estimating allowance + 15% = $\underline{66,700}$

  556,200 total scope for evaluation

Consider two cases: Case 1, direct-hire labor, and case 2, subcontract labor.

ASSUMPTIONS:

- Due to "criticality", use Density of 250 (but 300 more probable)
- Allow 12% absenteeism for "effective manhours"
- "Buildup" duration from standard schedule (fdns+eqpt+piping buildup)

Case 2: Subcontract Labor. The project strategy, based on experience, is that local subcontractors are more productive than prime contractors (direct hire).

Scope = 556,200 man-hours for direct hire
less 10% productivity adjustment for local subcontractor labor
- 55,600
= 500,600 man-hours

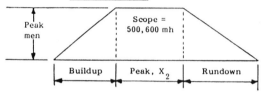

1. Labor availability: No restraint, no adjustment to manpower level.
2. Peak density level: U.S. large project, subcontract labor (from curves) = 250 ft^2/man.
3. Peak manpower = $\dfrac{64,000 \text{ ft}^2}{250 \text{ ft}^2/\text{man}}$ = 256 men.
4. Effective man-hours per man-month = 40 × 88% × 4¼ = 153 h.
5. Buildup (by judgment) = 3 + 2 + 5 = 10 months.
6. Rundown (by judgment) = 6 months.

Solve for peak, X_2:

$$\frac{500,600}{153} = \left(\frac{10}{2} \times 256 \right) + \left(X_2 \times 256 \right) + \left(\frac{6}{2} \times 256 \right)$$

$X_2 = 4.8$ (say 5 months)

Therefore

Total construction duration (subcontract labor) = 10 + 5 + 6 = $\underline{21 \text{ months}}$

This confirms that a subcontract operation, even though more productive, will generally take longer than one on a direct-hire basis.

Figure 24-3. Worked Example—Trapezoidal/Density Method.

SCHEDULE BASIC

1. A SMALL ENGINEERING TASK - 400 HOURS - IS REQUIRED TO BE

    COMPLETED IN 2 WEEKS

    ### HOW MANY MEN ARE REQUIRED?

2. CALCULATION METHOD IS $\dfrac{\text{MANHOURS}}{\text{MANHORS/WEEK x No WEEKS}}$ = No MEN

    $$= \dfrac{400}{40 \text{ X } 2} = 5\text{MEN}$$

3. TASK INCREASES 50 TIMES IN SIZE -20,000HOURS - IS NOW REQUIRED

    TO BE COMPLETED IN 20 WEEKS

    CALCULATION $\dfrac{20,000}{40 \text{ X } 20} = 25 \text{ MEN}$

    ### IS THIS CORRECT ?   NO

4. CALCULATION PRINCIPLE - TRAPEZOIDAL TECHNIQUE FOR SIMPLE TO
        COMPLEX TASKS

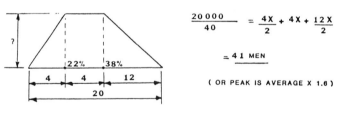

$$\dfrac{20\,000}{40} = \dfrac{4X}{2} + 4X + \dfrac{12X}{2}$$

$$\approx 41 \text{ MEN}$$

(OR PEAK IS AVERAGE X 1.6)

Figure 24-4. Worked Example—Engineering Trapezoid.

But the common use of 1.6/1.7, for either category of work, is a practical approach.

Figure 24-5 shows the construction indirect and direct costs in the "true" trapezoidal configuration. The "trapezoidal reality" is extremely important for the development of construction claims. As the majority of

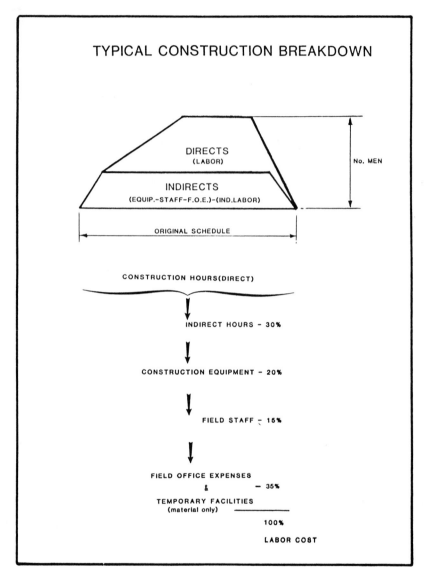

Figure 24-5. Typical Construction Cost Breakdown.

construction claims are time/schedule related, the understanding of the trapezoidal reality is vital. In fact, quality assessments of claims cannot be made without this application.

A typical breakdown of the major indirect costs is also shown. Individual companies might allocate their indirect costs slightly differently, but there is a high degree of conformity to this direct/indirect allocation within the process industry.

Figure 24-6 takes the information in Figure 24-5 a stage further, by adding some engineering information to the construction data. Again, it is emphasized that the stated information only applies to a "full EPC" project.

The emphasis of this figure is on the engineering/construction man-hour relationship. This is shown as the ratio of 1 : 6. In other words, one engineering man-hour "automatically" generates six direct construction man-hours. This is a very useful "rule of thumb" and, of course, the ratio does vary a little as the design complexity varies.

This relationship highlights the need for design engineers to *fully* realize that as they are designing, they are also generating the construction man-hours. Full realization of this fact should lead the designers to more carefully consider the question of *constructability*. This is the design process of working to construction installation considerations as well as working to standard design specifications. Constructability considerations can result in significant savings in construction labor. Such considerations are essential in the following types of construction:

- Heavy lifts.
- Prefabrication and preassembly.
- Modularization.
- Offshore hookup work.
- Site problems of limited access.

The relationship between home office support services (project management, project control, procurement, computer, clerical, etc.) and engineering is also shown, at 40%. This relationship is in man-hours.

Figure 24-7 shows a typical relationship between construction complexity and labor density. Judgment is required in assessing the appropriate density level for the specific project.

Complexity (Man-hours/Square Foot). Complexity is "automatically" generated by the design specifications. This statistic is based on the number of direct construction man-hours (within the plot) divided by the plot area (battery limits.) As noted, this assumes that there is no preinvestment in the design basis. Preinvestment is a fairly common practice and is

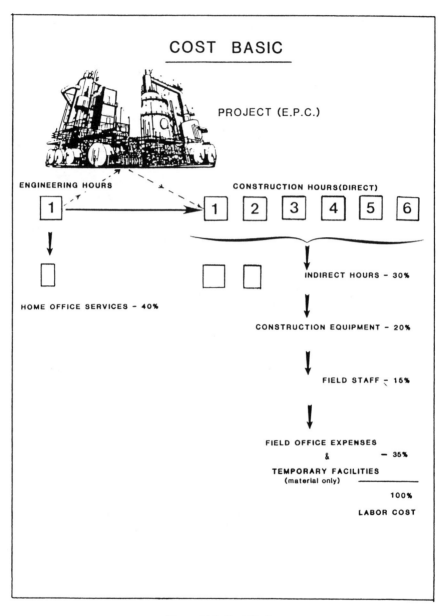

Figure 24-6. Cost Basic.

CONSTRUCTION COMPLEXITY AND LABOR DENSITY

° Only applicable to complete Process Units(small or large)

° Assumes an economic design - no "Preinvestment"

° Based on "average" US labor productivity(Calif./Union)

COMPLEXITY (direct manhours/sq.ft.)

Manhours/sq.ft.

    ° SIMPLE UNIT........................... 4/5
    ° AVERAGE UNIT.......................... 6/7
    ° COMPLEX UNIT......................... 8/10

LABOR DENSITY (sq.ft./man)

Sq.ft./man

Tied to above Complexity Data.

    ° SIMPLE UNIT(4/5 mh./sq.ft.)........ 150/180
    ° AVERAGE UNIT(6/7 mh./sq.ft.)....... 180/250
    ° COMPLEX UNIT(8/10 mh./sq.ft.)...... 250/300

Density data is based on a Prime EPC Contractor/reimbursable
contract. For fixed or unit price contracts, density numbers
should be increased by about 50sq.ft./man. This reflects the
need for lower numbers of men to achieve higher productivity
to meet "hard money" financial requirements.

Figure 24-7. Construction Complexity and Labor Density.

carried out when forward company planning has determined that the plant
will need to be expanded within a few years. At the moment, the planned
(design) capacity is sufficient. The design preinvestment, therefore, usually includes extra area in the plot for future installation of equipment.
This "extra" area, open at the moment, would give "false" complexity
numbers and density levels.

Density (Square Feet/Man). This statistic is based on the "economic"
total number of craftsmen working at peak (supervision is not included).
The data is based on historical experience and is tied to the complexity of
the area. The more complex, the lower the number of men that can work
in the area. In practical terms, this means that greater complexity has

more equipment (more man-hours) per square foot, thus taking up space for the men to work in.

The chart in Figure 24-8 enables an overall schedule to be instantly generated, if the construction man-hours are known. The result is not of high quality, but is intended to provide a preliminary schedule during the early development or feasibility stage of a project.

The chart provides "add factors" for straight-through and overseas projects. Also shown are curves for projects that were built in the 1950s and 1960s, and for Norwegian-based projects. Curves can be developed for most overseas locations.

It is interesting to note that the project durations of the past (1950s and 1960s) cannot be repeated today. The major reasons are as follows:

- Productivity reduction—engineering and construction—(cannot always be compensated for by increased men).
- Greater complexity for same capacity (higher temperatures and pressures).
- Increased environmental/regulatory engineering.
- Increased management/approval time.
- Poor project management/poor planning.
- Fast-track approach.
- Longer equipment delivery times (1970–1983).
- Lack of manpower (1970–1983).
- Increased use of the reimbursable-type contract.

Figure 24-9 provides general guidelines for establishing a direct-labor productivity profile for the construction phase. These guidelines cover incremental and cumulative profiles. As bad weather can have a significant impact on productivity, separate guidelines are provided.

This profile should be developed as soon as the physical site conditions are known and a detailed construction schedule is available. The horizontal axis should be translated from percent complete to a calendar time frame.

As direct construction labor can be 20% of total project costs, it is important that labor productivity be tracked as early as possible. Productivity can only be properly measured if construction progress is evaluated with physical quantities and associated work measurement units.

Application.   These guidelines show incremental productivity for the major phases of construction.

The mobilization phase (first 15%) is shown with a reduced productivity of 10% from the construction estimate. It then improves with phases of

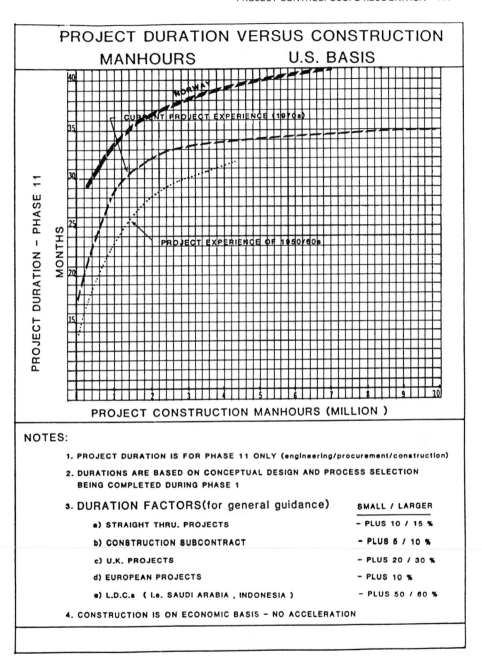

Figure 24-8. Project Duration Chart.

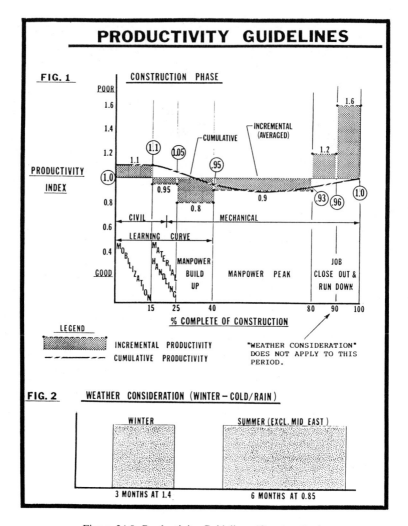

Figure 24-9. Productivity Guidelines (Construction).

5% and 20% for the material handling and manpower buildup phases. At manpower peak (40% of construction), the incremental productivity is shown to be still good at 0.9. Thereafter, for the last 20% of construction, it is shown as rapidly deteriorating.

The cumulative curve is calculated and is shown as tracking from poor to good and ending at 1.0. Additional factors for weather would be superimposed on the top profile. If the winter occurred at 40% of construction, the 0.9 could be multiplied by 1.4, resulting in a projection of 1.3 for the period. If the other periods were as shown on the chart, then the overall productivity of 1.0 would not be achieved. The "weather consideration" does not apply during the last 20% of the job.

This evaluation can be made early in the project, and these guidelines and this method can greatly assist in monitoring and forecasting productivity levels.

The "Poor" Rundown Productivity. Based on historical experience, the reasons for the last 20% "poor" productivity are as follows:

1. The major work during this period is punch list/check out type of work. Such work has low budget value, hence the earned value system "measures" low productivity.
2. This is also the stage of remedial work and changes, mostly required by the operational and maintenance staff. This work does not usually fall into the class of official change orders that would result in increased budget.
3. Labor has a poor attitude. The work is drawing to a close and the on-site labor may not be eager to go to a new job. In fact, there may be no other work available in the area.
4. Management/planning is poor. There is, sometimes, the tendency for the construction manager to order the work to be executed on a "crash basis" so as to finish quickly and get to the next job. This can result in significant overmanning and poor work. Costs can increase drastically.

Figure 24-10 is a typical breakdown of total home office man-hours for a "full scope" project. It is based on historical data for small-to-medium-sized projects engineered on a reimbursable basis and executed during the period 1955–1975.

Application. This information can be used to check an estimate or a contractor proposal of home office man-hours. It can be used for early evaluations of home office manpower and schedules when only total costs or man-hours are available.

Example.
1. For a typical project we can assess the percent piping man-hours. This is derived by summing the hours required for piping engineering activities (plant design, 16.4%; piping engineering, 2.1%; bill of materials, 2.1%; and model, 0.4%, for a total of 21%).
2. As a percent of engineering only, piping becomes 21%/0.67 = 32%.

Home Office Man-hour Breakdown

Description		% Man-hours
Design & Drafting	*Full-Scope (%)*	
Civil & structural	25.00	10.000
Vessels	7.50	3.000
Electrical	15.00	6.000
Plant design (piping)	41.00	16.400
Piping engineering	5.25	2.100
Bill of material	5.25	2.100
Model	1.00	0.400
	100.00	40.000
Administration—indirect drafting		4.000
Engineering		
Instrument (engineering & drafting)		3.000
Mechanical (rotating machinery, plant utilities, metallurgy, etc.)		3.000
Mechanical (consultants)		0.200
Project management		7.500
Project engineering		6.000
Project (operating expenses, services administration)		0.200
Process design		3.000
Process technology services		0.100
Project services	67%	*Engineering*
Estimating & cost control		4.000
Proposals		—
Computer control		—
Computer systems		1.000
Initial operations—office		0.200
Technical information		0.200
Scheduling		2.000
Procurement		
Purchasing		5.000
Inspection and Expediting		5.000
General office		
Stenographic		4.500
Accounting		7.000
Office services		2.000
Labor relations		0.100
Construction (office)		2.000
	Total	100.000

Figure 24-10. Home Office Man-hour Breakdown.

As overall engineering and piping design are often on the critical path, individual evaluations are frequently required. Where information is lacking, use the following:

- Engineering man-hours as a percent of total home office: 65%.
- Piping man-hours as a percent of engineering: 35%.

Figure 24-11, an overall breakdown of project cost, is based on historical data for projects built in the United States on a prime contract basis during the period 1955–1975.

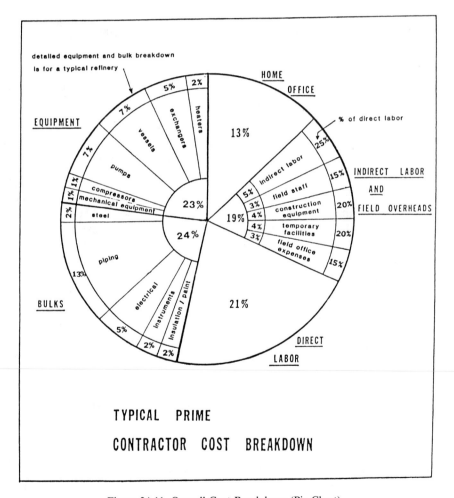

Figure 24-11. Overall Cost Breakdown (Pie Chart).

Application.   When only an overall cost is known, this breakdown can be useful in providing overall data for a quick evaluation of engineering and construction schedules.

Example.   Assume that a project has an estimated overall cost of $100 million.

1. From the diagram, home office costs are roughly 13%, or $13 million. By a further assumption that the contractor home office all-in cost is $30/hour, we can derive a total number of home office man-hours:

$$\text{No. of man-hours} = \frac{13,000,000}{30} = 433,000$$

   Thus, a gross schedule and manpower evaluation can now be made.
2. From the chart, direct field labor costs are roughly 21%, or $21 million. By a further assumption that the direct field labor payroll cost is $10/hour:

$$\text{No. of man-hours} = \frac{21,000,000}{10} = 2,100,000$$

   Applying known and historical relationships allows gross evaluations for engineering and construction durations to be made. These in turn can be used to prepare manpower histograms and progress curves.

NOTE: For larger projects, the percent of home office and field overheads increases.

Figure 24-12 compares the breakdowns (%) of overall costs and construction man-hours for large, grass roots projects against small, revamp projects. The data for the large, grass roots breakdown is based on historical experience, whereas the small, revamp breakdown is typical only. As there are wide variations in the EPC makeup of small projects, the "typical breakdown" should be examined very carefully for its application to a specific project.

As with the previous figure, these breakdowns/relationships, can be helpful in evaluating man-hours, schedules, and manpower requirements. The data for Figure 24-13 has been compiled from historical experience. This figure shows that the indirect curves are essentially constant throughout the execution of a project. Early buildup for field organization and installing temporary facilities is matched by a late buildup for final job cleanup and demobilization.

```
                TYPICAL PROJECT COST BREAKDOWN
                (CONTRACTOR - TOTAL SCOPE PROJECT)


GRASS ROOTS-LARGE               ITEM              SMALL REVAMP
      %                                                 %
     10 · - - - - - - ENGINEERING (D&D)- - - - - - -20
      3 - - - - - - - HOME OFFICE (SUPPORT) - - - - -5
     47 - - - - - - -MATERIAL (DIRECT) - - - - -40
     21 - - - - - -CONSTRUCTION DIRECT - - - - -17
     19 - - - - - CONSTRUCTION INDIRECT - - -18
     ____                                            ____
    100%                                            100%


                DIRECT CONSTRUCTION LABOR HOURS
     10 - - - - - - SITE PREPARATION - - - - - - 1
     12 - - - - - - FOUNDATIONS/UNDERGROUNDS - - - 8
      7 - - - - - STRUCTURAL STEEL/BUILDINGS - - 5
     10 - - - - - EQUIPMENT - - - - - - - - -12
     35 - - - - - PIPING - - - - - - - - - 48(INCL.FAB)
     11 - - - - - -ELECTRICAL - - - - - - - -10
      6 - - - - - INSTRUMENTS - - - - - - - 8
      4 - - - - - PAINTING - - - - - - - - 3
      4 - - - - - INSULATION - - - - - - - 3
      1 - - - - - HVAC/FIREPROOFING - - - - 2


     ____                                            ____
    100%                                            100%
     ____                                            ____
```

Figure 24-12. Typical Project Cost Breakdown.

The purpose of this figure is to illustrate a typical relationship between *direct work* and *indirects*.

Direct-work progress is a measure of physical quantities installed, and, as shown, the direct-work curve is identical to the historical construction curve included in the writer's data base.

Indirect construction progress cannot be assessed by measuring physical quantities and is usually measured in man-hours. This typical curve shows the rate at which these man-hours would normally be expended.

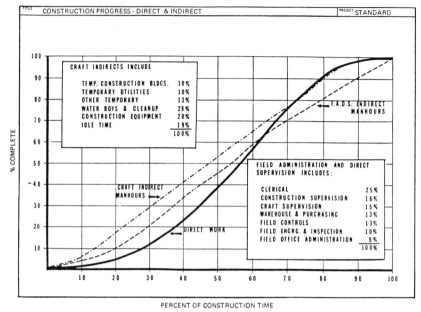

PERCENT OF CONSTRUCTION TIME

Chart of construction indirects—craft and staff.

Figure 24-13. Construction Progress—Direct and Indirect.

Indirect and direct construction curves for a project could be compared with the curves in this exhibit. During construction, actual performance should be compared with these profiles. This can provide an early warning that the expenditure of man-hours is deviating from the norm.

The percentage breakdowns for craft indirects and field administration and direct supervision can be used to check estimates and performances of individual categories.

On megaprojects, individual control curves could be developed for individual categories.

There are occasions when a project is placed on extended overtime to shorten the schedule. In many cases, productivity will be reduced and costs will increase. If this condition was not part of the original estimate, an assessment of the increased cost, as well as the schedule advantage, should be made. The schedule evaluation should recognize increased man-hours in the duration calculation. It is also possible that absenteeism will increase, sometimes to an extent that there is no schedule advantage for the increased workweek.

Figure 24-14 presents data compiled from the sources indicated on the chart. It plots labor efficiency against overtime hours worked, based on

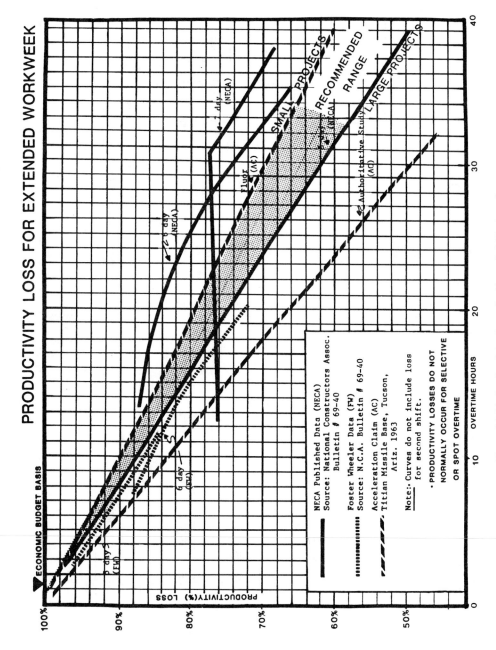

Figure 24-14. Productivity Loss for Extended Workweek.

ACCOUNT	CODE	%	BOIL	BRICK	CARP	ELEC	LAB	% INSUL	OPER	MILL	PAINT	PIPE	IRON	TEAM
SITE PREPARATION		9												
FOUNDATIONS		10			37		47		4			8	10	2
BUILDINGS		3		9	24	1	26		3				27	2
STRUCTURAL STEEL		5	27		4		4		12	1		4	47	1
SPECIAL EQUIPMENT		1	14		11	6	5		6	25		22	9	2
HEATERS		4	43	7	7		23	5	5			6	2	2
EXCHANGERS		1	17		6		6		14	5		44	7	1
VESSELS		2	64		3	1	14	1	7			4	4	2
TOWERS		2	80		3		4		8			1	2	2
TANKS		1	61		5		9		10	2		10	3	
PUMPS-COMPRESSORS		2	2		5	3	8		4	56		16	6	
PIPING		32			2		5		9			82	1	1
ELECTRICAL		7			4	86	8		1				1	
INSTRUMENTS		6			1	45	1		1			51	1	
PAINTING-INSULATION		9	2		7		10	59	1		16	2	2	1
TEMPORARY CONSTRUCTION		5	3		30	18	21		5			20	3	

Figure 24-15. Craft Mix by Account.

5-, 6-, and 7-day workweeks. These data apply only to long-term extended workweeks. Occasional overtime can be very productive with no loss of efficiency. The exhibit shows a recommended range of productivity loss by project size (small to large.)

Application. This chart can be useful in an overall evaluation of the impact of overtime hours on schedule and cost. It can establish an increase in total labor hours required for a loss in efficiency due to an extended workweek. However, judgment should be used on an individual location basis. Some areas, particularly less developed countries (LDCs), work 60-hour weeks which are as productive as 40-hour weeks.

Example. Assume that a project has a total construction scope of 1 million man-hours and is based on a 5-day, 40-hour workweek. If the same workweek were increased by 8 hours to 48 hours, look to the chart for 8 hours of overtime and, using the (NECA) 5-day (large-project) curve, read across to an efficiency of 90%. This indicates that 10% more hours will be required to accomplish the same amount of work due to a loss in efficiency. Thus, we estimate that the total man-hours will be 1 million × 1.10 = 1,100,000. man-hours. Schedule and cost evaluations can now be made for an additional 100,000 man-hours but at an increased level of work. Obviously, there is a schedule advantage.

NOTE: These curves do not include efficiency losses for a second shift, which can be about 20%. However, shift work losses depend on the type of work, company organization, and experience. In the offshore industry, where shipyards traditionally work on a shift basis, losses can be minimal, or zero.

Most construction estimates are prepared on an account basis. Scheduling manpower resources at a detailed level would, therefore, require a craft breakdown of labor by account.

Figure 24-15 shows a typical breakdown of craft labor by major account for the United States. Overseas labor practices will often not conform to this mix of labor.

25. Project Needs and Techniques for Management Audits

Kenneth O. Chilstrom*

A periodic checkup has become routine for determining an individual's well-being and for early diagnosis of physical problems. Similarly, we wouldn't permit the operation of complex equipment such as airplanes or nuclear power stations without performing periodic inspections to ensure safe and proper performance. Applying this logic during the management of projects is just as appropriate in order to determine the health of the organization and its performance in meeting all objectives.

Management's knowledge of the actual status of a project varies with the frequency of reporting and the credibility of the data. It is also recognized that most organizations have a "velvet curtain" which frequently shields the manager's vision and hearing, thereby limiting his ability to take early corrective action. It is generally true that there is a reluctance to tell the boss the bad news, thereby delaying an early recovery plan with a minimum impact. Another factor which can be expected with a highly professional group of seasoned experts is overconfidence coupled with complacency that contributes to a false sense of security. For many people, there is a danger that experience is no more than doing today what was thought of yesterday, either in the same old way or in a slightly modified manner. The black book of failure is filled with the stories of people who have had experience. Experience should be a servant, not a handicap. Unfortunately, the aftermath of the Shuttle Challenger disaster in January 1986 indicated that conditions mentioned above were all prevalent in a very mature project.

---

* Kenneth O. Chilstrom's management auditing experience has been extensive in both government and industry. Early assignments in the Air Force as an experimental test pilot, R&D Staff Officer, and Program Manager led to later assignments in charge of management surveys of programs. His industrial experience includes program management surveys within the General Electric Company, and the auditing of projects and functional areas. He was an industry consultant to the GAO on a special study to determine the management "Lessons Learned" on what makes projects successful since then, he has had assignments with Science Applications, Inc., and Pratt & Whitney, United Technologies Corporation.

The periodic audit of a project is yet another tool that assists management in maintaining effective control.

AUDIT POLICY

Authority Established

Every business has corporate policies formally established in writing for essential business functions. It is also necessary that audit policy be established at the company level. This identifies the technique and use of audits with the boss—the President or General Manager. Unless this occurs, the likelihood of having the support required to conduct successful audits will be greatly reduced. The policy should be adequate in scope to cover responsibilities and the general approach for conduct of project audits. This would include how projects are selected for audit, who selects the projects and the audit team, the support responsibilities of the project team and functional organizations, and how the audit team will report their findings.

Process for Selection of Project Audits

Audit policy established at the corporate level should identify the President or General Manager as the final authority in the selection of a project for audit. He may choose to make his own selection; however, the approach found most successful is when he and his immediate subordinates mutually agree as to which projects need an audit and when best to accomplish this. This procedure then commits these individuals to the support of the audit since they have agreed to its necessity. Support from the functional organization is absolutely essential to the successful conduct of an audit. When this does not exist, the individuals involved will clam up, compromising the availability of facts, and thus extend the time required to complete the audit.

PLANNING FOR THE AUDIT

Scope and Subject Areas Defined

At the time the decision is made to have a management audit of a project, there is usually a reason why top management has selected the particular project. This reason or purpose will most often establish the scope of the audit. Since this indicates the area of major concern, it generally is not necessary to accomplish a full-scale review of all areas of project management. However, if it is early in the schedule, such as six months from go-ahead, it is usually considered necessary to examine all areas. The most important factor is to have the areas of audit, which may limit the scope, well defined and understood at the beginning. Then there can be no misunderstandings about the objective and expectations of top management and what the audit team members will concentrate on. An example which may typify a very limited scope audit would be a project in early qualification testing of the hardware which is experiencing some failures although other areas of technical, schedule, and cost performance are in good control. Experience of many companies has shown that most new projects deserve a thorough review of all technical and nontechnical areas in their first year. It should be obvious that the early phase of a project is where weaknesses will show up in estimating, scheduling, interface relationships, and cost control. Also, the more complex the project, the more people involved and, where past experience is limited, the greater the opportunity for management problems in all areas.

Organization of Audit Team

In a majority of companies which have 1000 employees or more, there is often a staff function of internal management specialists who form the nucleus of the audit function. In large companies there may exist a good-size office of 10 persons or more whose sole activity is operational auditing of projects, or reviews/surveys of special subject areas.

It is desirable and recommended that a professional staff be responsible for the organization and planning of audits, and then augmented with other specialists as required to conduct the audits. These full-time management auditors would be experienced specialists in functional areas as well as seasoned operational auditors, and would individually complement and supplement each other. It is the team chief/chairman who must decide on the makeup of the team. The number of persons required to cover the areas of the audit and the technical or nontechnical expertise and experience required are critical considerations bearing on the audit success. Criteria in the selection process would generally include but not be limited to the following:

- Specialist versus generalist (need good mix).
- Must have professional acceptance at all levels.
- Technical competence in specialized areas.
- Analytical mind, articulate, and personable.
- Writing ability.
- Listening ability.
- Maturity and adaptability.

- Line, staff, supervisor experience.
- No project involvement—increasing objectivity.
- Enthusiasm and support of audit assignment.

The results of the audit will always be compared to the caliber of the team and its individual members. As is true in other tasks—one should not send out a boy to do a man's job. The audit payoff will always be directly relatable to the qualifications of the audit team.

Development of Audit Plan

Preparing a plan for the conduct of a project audit not only assists the audit team members, but helps the project team and functional areas in knowing what the audit team needs and where the audit will concentrate its attention. The audit plan should not be a detailed voluminous coverage of how to do an audit, but rather a detailed outline of the subject areas to be covered. The audit team members who have not had recent experience in the actual conduct of the audit should be coached in the technique prior to the auditing phase by the team chief and other members who have had past experience.

In the development of an audit plan, the problems and shortcomings of other projects can provide an insight or a yardstick to judge the project performance. These "lessons learned" are worth identifying in order to determine if they are being repeated and are the source of problems or a successfully applied benefit. It is also important to identify, during the course of the audit, those activities that are performing well. Too often audits concentrate solely on the trouble areas, which may compromise the true perspective in judging the overall health of the project and the performance of the project team. However, as an example of where many projects incur pitfalls, the experience of others may identify such typical deficiencies as these:

- Techniques of estimating are poorly developed. They reflect an un-voiced assumption which is quite untrue—that all will go well.
- Estimating techniques confuse effort with progress, hiding the assumption that men and months are interchangeable.
- Schedule progress is poorly monitored.
- When schedule slippage is recognized, the natural response is to add manpower. This can make matters worse, particularly for the budget.
- Planners are optimists, so the first false assumption that underlies the scheduling of projects is *that all will go well, that each task will take only as long as it ought to take.*

The plan for a project audit that includes all areas of project management should include the following:

- Organization of project team.
- Functional support and relationships.
- Master plan.
- Contract committments.
- Work definition and assignment.
- Work progress reporting and control.
- Technical plan and capabilities.
- Manufacturing plan and capabilities.
- Product integrity/quality control.
- Logistic support plan.
- Customer relationships.
- Company/corporate policies and procedures applicable.

Initial Data Review

Upon completion of preparing the audit plan and selection of the full audit team, the team chief should conduct an initial meeting with the project manager. This will enable the project manager to understand the scope of the project and the subject areas to be covered, and would identify the first need and request for the audit team. The team chief, with the assistance of the project manager, can then develop a listing of project data to be provided for the audit team as soon as possible. This data package, which would include such items as the contract, project operating plan, technical and management progress reports, etc., would provide the audit team background information in order to get well acquainted with the details of the project. This step is essential in order to avoid going in cold when starting the interviews with the project team. An adequate understanding about the project, its status, customer, etc., is important for the audit team member to prepare himself for the interviews and further pursuit of data. The ability to ask the right question, to find the trail, to penetrate to the right depth, is a measure of the auditor's effectiveness, and to a great extent will depend upon the amount of preparation given before the actual auditing begins.

GAINING ACCEPTANCE FOR THE AUDIT

Establishing the Environment

Audits of a project, or any area of an organization, can be accomplished either by an internal team or by an outside management consultant firm.

In most cases, an internal team should have advantages since they have the benefit of inside knowledge of why things are the way they are, including organization politics and personalities. However, in some situations, an outside person or team can be more effective for not having any bias and for being able to see the issues or reasons for problems in better focus. However, regardless of the use of either approach, it is essential that the organization know that top management is supportive of the audit and should make it known both in writing and vocal opportunities. When this is done, the individuals at working levels should be more willing to recognize and accept the audit in a constructive way than judging it to be an investigation or a witch hunt. When audits are seldom used, they will be more suspect and people less cooperative than if routinely used on all projects and looked upon as a normal way of business.

Top Management Support

In those instances in which outside auditors are hired, it is usually undertaken by top management. When this is done, the reasons for the audit should be made known and may include an explanation for the advantages of having an outside group. In addition to this expressed support at the beginning, it may require frequent assessments to ascertain the progress of the audit team and those factors which may be hindering their activity. The success of an audit team can be severely handicapped if it finds an environment which is relating the way things should be done rather than what is actually being done, or only answering Yes or No without offering any information. In most cases the responsiveness of the working levels will depend upon the support that supervision and top management provide the audit on a day-by-day basis.

In the situation where a business routinely has internal auditors review all projects and functional areas for management effectiveness and efficiency, the problem of top management support is minimized. When audits have become a way of life, the reason for their being has been overcome and generally accepted. Although top management support is a continuing requirement, the communication problem is less in this circumstance.

Again experience has proven that in most cases management auditing is a tool for the boss and his top management team and requires their support.

Team Credentials

There is a distinct difference between the known credentials of an auditor who is hired from an outside firm as compared to those persons assigned to auditing from within the organization. As expected, the outside person is only known by his written resume of experience along with the reputation of his company, and this must be sufficient to impress management However, when persons from internal resources are assigned either full-time or temporarily to an audit team, then everyone judges them on many years of personal observations and assessments of character as well as job performance It is well known that it may be easier to accept a person that you do not know too well. When this situation is recognized it, becomes most important that the best people with related experience be selected for audit team assignments. Some companies have a small permanent audit staff who provide the nucleus of the team and who are augmented on a temporary assignment with others from within the organization. It is normally the responsibility of the team chief to identify his team needs and then recommend individuals from throughout the organization who could meet the requirements. It is very important that not only the best-qualified people are identified but that they are recognized by top management as having the needed qualifications and have top management's approval.

If top management does not select and approve the audit team, then their confidence in the team's findings will not exist and the final payoff may be drastically affected. The criteria for individual selection must always recognize the need for specialists in functional or technical fields. However, other factors are equally important in selecting those who are broad thinkers, but still analytical, and who understand the human behavioral aspects of job performance. Too often, managers are guilty of giving ad hoc or other than normal assignments to those persons who are more available rather than selecting individuals on a criteria basis. There must be a general consensus that the findings of an audit team will generally reflect the qualifications of the auditors. If significant results are needed and expected, then the quality of the audit team is essential; therefore each individual's qualifications are important.

Announcements

Communication of audit activity from the top down is an essential factor influencing the success of an audit. Usually the President or General Manager of the company should sign the internal memorandum which announces the audit, the reason for it, and the support required, and identifies the team members. In addition, verbal announcements should follow from the President to his staff, and from each level down to that of first supervision. It is hoped and desired that discussions at each organizational level will be an affirmation that all will cooperate and support the audit, and that there will not be any negative expressions which will promote withholding of information or foot dragging. People at the working levels can usually discern the true feelings of those providing direction and may then exercise a choice of full, some, or no support to the auditors.

It cannot be overemphasized that when top management decides to have an audit they select the best audit team possible, and provide evidence of their support in written and vocal form to all within the organization.

CONDUCTING THE AUDIT

Protocol

It is very important, as a step toward gaining further acceptance for the audit team, that normal protocol be observed in the early phase of interfacing with the project team and the supporting functional areas. The initial point of contact and arrangements for interviews must start with the project manager, and it is most appropriate to have the entire team meet with the project manager, his deputy, and other key staff members. Such a meeting should include the discussion and outline of the contact plan for the individual interviews to follow. The best procedure is to have a member of the project team assigned to the task as the interface or focal point for arranging all interviews. This has several advantages in that it allows the project team to exercise their prerogative in identifying the sequence of audit areas, provides an organized approach for each day's activities, and ensures that each individual is notified in advance that an interview has been scheduled.

Audit interviews should generally follow the organization structure, starting at the top and proceeding to lower levels. This gives those in charge the first opportunity to provide data which they view as important, and to point out areas which they judge as impacting the success or failure of project activities; therefore, talking to a subordinate should not occur before talking to the subordinate's boss. Since auditors are outsiders to the project team, but are having an opportunity to observe the inside operation, they must observe ethics and politeness. If an auditor disregards this approach and instead acts as a privileged superior who barges in whenever and wherever he pleases, then the doors will be hard to open, and data and knowledge will be difficult to obtain.

A rule for an auditor's conduct is to treat each person the way one would like to be treated if the roles were reversed.

Team Operation

The results of a project audit are the accomplishments and product of the individual auditors; however, their performance can best be directed by the team chief/chairman. He shoulders the ultimate responsibility for the audit success; therefore his involvement in the planning and the conduct of the audit is absolutely essential. Once the scope of the audit is decided, the plan outlined, and area assignments made, then the team chief becomes a manager of the audit team to make sure that they are ready for the job at hand and that daily performance is as a team rather than a mix of individual efforts. There must be a close working relationship between audit team members during the interview phase. Often the findings of one auditor overlap into another auditor's area and may have an unforeseen impact. A sharing of knowledge and data is needed on a daily basis; therefore "end-of-day" meetings pay off and the audit team chief will ensure that communications occur for mutual benefits. As the audit progresses, the individual auditors begin to arrive at preliminary conclusions or findings. These need to be identified as the interview phase continues for each major subject area that is being reviewed. Once they surface, they need to be challenged and discussed by the audit team to ascertain the validity and sufficiency of data. This will assist the auditor in writing his portion of the report.

Since audit teams may have persons with experience in both auditing and specialized areas, it stands to reason that individual capability is enhanced. The team achieves the most benefit when these areas complement and supplement each other. At the start of an audit, it is often best to have a person who has never conducted an audit interview get his feet wet by accompanying an experienced auditor. Although the audit team chief continually works to get the working interface established early, experience has revealed that the individual auditors are so preoccupied with their own areas that during the early phase they fail to see the need for exchange. As the audit progresses, this attitude usually changes and each auditor becomes a better team player.

Selection of Audit Areas

The development of an audit plan, regardless of the amount of detail contained in the plan, is essential at the start. The team chief will have a general agreement with those in authority who have directed that an audit be performed. The scope, along with the reason or purpose of the project audit, has been included in the initial announcement which sets the stage for outlining the audit plan. The contents of this plan should include, but need not be limited to, the following subject areas:

Audit Plan for Project XX

I. Purpose
II. Scope
III. Approach for Conduct
   A. Team Assignments
   B. Schedule/Itinerary
IV. Audit Areas
 V. Interview Questions by Area

In the case of a new project, an audit plan is usually developed to cover all management areas that could affect the success of the project. In this event, a typical plan would include the following areas to be audited: Example:

IV—Audit Areas for Project XX

A. Organization
B. Policies and Procedures
C. Master Planning and Control
D. Work Authorization
E. Contract Administration
F. Engineering
G. Manufacturing
H. Quality Control
 I. Test
J. Logistics Support
K. Customer Requirements
L. Vendor Support

The assignment of individual auditors to specific areas is usually done according to the background and experience of the auditor. On a large-scale project it may be necessary to have more than one auditor per area, and whenever possible this is desirable since the combined talents of two may be needed. The scope, size, and sophistication of the project will dictate the number and assignment of auditors to review the many subject areas involved.

Interview Techniques

Interviews for the auditors should be made at least one day in advance. As discussed above, this is best accomplished by having one person arrange all interviews for the project team. Schedules always require some negotiating and last-minute changes may occur; however, it is expected that people will make themselves available when the auditors request.

The time scheduled for an interview should usually be not less than one hour and not more than two. In many cases the best practice is to have a return interview rather than extend the time to a half a day. Auditors often need time to assess the information and data provided or to confer with other members of the audit team before deciding what additional data is needed.

Prior to the actual interview, the auditor should make preparations by familiarizing himself with both background data and information on the responsibilities of the individual involved. In addition, it is necessary to be aware of the status of progress in the area as well as any known problems. The auditor, of course, will only have enough knowledge to be conversant during the early interviews; however, as time goes by, he will be continually adding to his own knowledge and his proficiency at interviewing will improve. For those auditors who are interviewing for the first time, the development and use of a list of interview questions are a must. As expected for those persons who have been auditing projects for several years, their need of a checklist of questions is more for reminders than being dependent upon the use of such a tool. The following examples of checklists of interview questions are presented only to encourage their development by the audit team members before the interviews.

Example: Interview Questions
for: *Organization and Management*

1. Request organizational charts for the project, delineating relationships between operations.
   a. Clearly indicate who reports to whom.
   b. How does structure reflect department management emphasis on the project?
   c. Where and how are project management responsibilities defined?
   d. How many people are actually managing the project effort, and what authority and responsibilities are delegated to each?
2. Does the project have its own policies and procedures for assignment of responsibilities and work accomplishment?

Example: Interview Questions
for: *Logistics Support*

1. What method is used to assure the timely delivery of spare parts?
2. What method is used to assure that instructions in manuals will allow the accurate operation and maintenance of equipment?

During the interview the auditor is a listener, asking only those questions necessary to keep the discussion on track. Requesting copies of a document needed is the best approach rather than taking time to write lengthy descriptions. The use of a list of interview questions will enable the auditor to keep the interview moving along a logical path, and will permit the taking of short notes on the replies to questions asked. In addition to the modus operandi of the auditor in pursuing the subject material, the auditor's style is important. Since he is not an investigator looking for violation of law, it is essential that the tenor of the conversation be friendly. When a healthy rapport develops between the auditor and interviewee, the likelihood of productive results increases dramatically. In contrast, an adversary situation will make it difficult to get the data needed and will also be a mutually unpleasant experience. If at all possible, it pays to be a nice guy.

Development/Preparation of Findings

As the interviews are completed, and data are assembled and analyzed, the auditor will have reached conclusions which can then be identified as Findings. This represents the culmination of the auditor's work and requires concerted effort to ensure that each Finding is accurately stated, is fully supported, and will stand up to challenge. The format for documenting the Findings is simple and provides the framework to report the auditor's efforts. This approach and format have been used by many auditors.

FINDINGS

Subject: (Use a short descriptive title)

Finding No.: (Number by subject area)

State the Finding briefly but include a statement that describes the problem or outstanding condition, the cause, and the effect.

Discussion: Present as thorough and comprehensive an analysis of the condition as is necessary to prove the statements in the Finding. Include corrective actions at end.

Recommendations: State what action must be taken and by what office or position in the organization.

This phase of analyzing and writing the Findings often requires as much time as was spent in the planning, preparation, and undertaking of the interview. Seldom is an initial draft of a Finding adequate in statement of the problem or in the supporting evidence of the discussion. This is not a quick and easy task and deserves whatever time it takes to do it justice. The involvement of other team members is a good practice, for the view and perspective should help in the writing and the final acceptance by the team chief and other members.

Validation of Findings

In the preparation of the Findings, and before they are finalized, it is good to go back and discuss them with those individuals directly involved. Most frequently the people involved and concerned the most are really the first to realize what may have gone wrong and what is necessary to correct the situation. In addition, since the individuals involved have had a hand in revealing the situation, they are more willing to accept the Findings, and may assist in determining what the recommended solutions should be. There may be times when it seems impossible to discuss the Findings without a confrontation; but this is usually the exception. In most instances, all levels of management will cooperate and appreciate a postmortem critique. This has a double effect, for if they accept the Findings, they have now become a part of the solution—which you want them to be. Taking the Findings and achieving confirmation of them on up to the project manager is the goal, and it will mean more when the complete audit results are presented to general management.

REPORTING RESULTS OF THE AUDIT

Report Preparation

A report is the end product of the combined efforts of the audit team. The payoff of the audit effort and the effectiveness of follow-up actions will depend upon the manner in which the report is written and presented. Findings must be clearly stated, and discussions must contain only factual information to support each Finding. Avoid lengthy philosophies, opinions, and observations. Where credit is deserved it should be recognized and receive equal treatment in comparison to problem areas and deficiencies. The team chairman should hold frequent coordination meetings to review progress and accomplish the interexchange of information. Drafts of Findings should be made as early as possible since considerable review is usually necessary to get agreement within the team, accomplish validation with those involved, and finally satisfy the team chairman. Experience has shown that preparing the audit results in report and briefing form will take as many or more hours as conducting the interviews and analysis. Another rule of thumb when writing the Findings is that most often it may take five iterations before achieving the final version for use in the report. There is a natural tendency to rush this final phase of the audit since those on temporary assignment will be anxious to return to their regular jobs. At this point, it is the team chairman who must hold to accepting nothing less than a well-expressed, accurate, and complete report that all can be proud of.

Report Format

The results of the project audit must be presented to the person or persons who originally directed and requested its accomplishment. This usually requires a verbal briefing/presentation and a written report. Typically, the briefing would be a summary of the written report. The following outline is recommended for a project audit report:

AUDIT REPORT FORMAT

PART I—INTRODUCTION
  Section I—Purpose
   (Give a brief explanation of any special reasons that audit is being conducted.)
  Section II—Scope
   (Give a description of scope of audit including limitations imposed.)
  Section III—Audit Team
   (List team membership by name, title, and organization.)
  Section IV—Audit Interviews
   (List all persons interviewed, by name, title, and organization.)
PART II—AUDIT RESULTS
  Section I—Summary and Recommendations
   The summary of results will be a one-page abstract of the major findings and recommendations. Following each specific recommendation will be the action office responsible for that recommendation.
  Section II—Findings, Discussion, Recommendations
   This portion of the report will contain the detailed Findings, discussion, and recommendations that pertain to the program.
   1. Subject: Use a short descriptive title, e.g., "Overtime."
   2. Finding: The Finding should be brief but include (1) a statement that describes the condition, i.e., problem or outstanding condition; (2) the cause or reason for this condition or problem; and (3) the effect or impact resulting from the condition. *Summarized, the Finding should reflect a condition, a cause, and the effect.*

3. Discussion: Mention the pertinent factors collected during discussion with others or revealed through your personal investigations. Present as thorough and comprehensive an analysis of the condition as necessary to prove the statements in your Finding.

4. Recommendations: If corrective action(s) are suggested by the Finding, they should be recorded at the end of the discussion. Following each recommendation, note the action assignments.

PART III—SUPPLEMENTARY DATA

Note: The appendices listed are for guidance only and will not necessarily apply to each audit report. Conciseness should be employed. As an example, data under appendices for program history and description of system should not normally exceed one page each.

Appendix A—Project history

B—Description of system

C—Documentation and reporting

D—Programming and funding history

E—Customer organization

F—Program organization and management controls

Briefings to Management

This is another time for respecting protocol and recognizing prerogatives. Just as it was important during the audit to start at the top and work down, it is now important to start at the bottom and work up. Early discussion of Findings with the working persons involved will establish credibility and ensure that data is accurate and complete. When the report is essentially complete and a briefing structured, there may be an opportunity to have a dry run with a second level of the project team which could provide a shakedown and then the chance for a final tune-up before a more formal review with the project manager and his staff. At this preview, the report should be 98% solid, with no holes or obvious shortcomings, and hopefully the project manager will not only endorse the report but say it's a job well done.

Since project managers seldom have all the resources under their control, the need to reach top management is absolutely necessary. It is most likely that a majority of the Findings will require decisions and actions by the functional managers. Further, it is the man at the top who can make sure it all happens—if he is convinced of the project's needs. A good briefing is the best way to get the audit results to the top management team. The team chairman may elect to do the entire briefing or to include members of the audit team to cover their specialized areas. If at all possible, members of the audit team should be included for it provides them an opportunity for recognition which is due. Copies of the briefing charts should be provided to all recipients of the report for they serve as good summaries and ready references. This last step of the audit process which requires effective written and verbal communication becomes the final measure for judging the degree of success of the entire audit effort.

FOLLOW-UP ACTIONS

Responsibilities

The auditor, in the recommendations for the Findings, should make every effort to determine the organization and person responsible for taking corrective action. In some instances there may be shared assignments; in others assignments may not be absolutely clear-cut. Experience has shown that final assignment of responsibilities for each and every recommendation may occur during the briefing to management. This level makes the final decisions, and their acceptance and involvement are an important step to the follow-up activity to the project audit.

It has been known that some audit operations report only the conditions and are not required to make recommendations or identify responsibilities for corrective actions. As a general practice, this is not recommended for it does not take full advantage of the audit team's capabilities and tends to shackle their initiative and limit their contribution.

Closeout of Report

The audit team, as a part of the audit plan, should present a follow-up and closeout plan at the time of final briefings. This provides an organized means to get actions under way by the responsible individuals. When top management accepts the plan requiring a 30-day report and a 90-day final report from all involved in action assignments, then management direction has occurred and there is a control system to ensure response. At the time of these two reports to management, the audit team chairman and other appropriate team members should be present. This has several benefits, for if actions described are not adequate to correct the condition entirely, then the audit team member should have the opportunity to express his concern. Also this enables him to see the completion of his efforts, and to see a job completed is a part of the final reward.

EVALUATION OF AUDIT FUNCTION

Management Assessment

Since the use of the audit function of projects or other specialized subject areas is a tool that best serves the interests of management, it stands to reason that they should periodically question the value it serves. In the event that the audit results are not sufficient to warrant the use of this tool, management should determine what is required to make it more effective or do away with it. Experience has shown that the audit tool has been successful when top management has actually used it and supported it. This is also true for other internal management consultant functions which are staff support activities. A good example of the right environment was the approach used by a top executive of a high-technology firm who immediately after winning a new contract would assess past performance for needed improvements. Sometimes he would ask for an assessment by his entire team so that the next project could benefit from the lessons learned. The alternative is to continue either getting by or even repeating the same mistakes.

Applying "Lessons Learned"

The greatest opportunity for payoff from project management auditing may often occur for the next project in order to avoid early shortcomings in applied manpower, policies, and procedures on the next project. The results of a project audit during any phase will reveal problems which, if given visibility and understanding, can assist the next project manager and top management to avoid or reduce the probability of similar deficiencies occurring again. Although there is universal lip service in recognizing the potential of lessons learned, the action needed to correct such conditions is too often lacking. Here is where top management can take direct action and change people, resources, policies and procedures, and their own involvement. For example, the lessons learned from one project audit could provide the basis for the following plan to be required on the management of new projects:

- More frequent management reviews in the first year of the project.
- More careful selection of key people with proven experience.
- Early assessment of customer satisfaction.
- Early assessment of test results.

As can be expected, people and methods are slow to change; therefore it is the responsibility of management to make changes happen. Results of each project audit will enable the project manager to better see himself and his team and determine the immediate needs and changes to be initiated. Response to such needs may work best when self-initiated, so top management should permit and encourage corrective actions whenever possible. However, there are other times when only management direction gets things done.

Whereas the impatience and daring of a new project manager are often to be admired, it is concluded that as a great philosopher—George Santayana—said, "Those who cannot remember the past are condemned to repeat it."

26. Evaluating the Performance of Project Personnel

Harold Kerzner*

In most traditional organizations, the need for project management is first recognized by those functional, resource, or middle managers who have identified problems in allocating and controlling resources. The next step is the tedious process of trying to convince upper-level management that such a change is necessary. Assuming that upper-level management does, in fact, react favorably toward project management, the next step becomes critical. Many upper-level managers feel that project management can be forced on lower-level subordinates through simple directives together with continuous upper-level supervision.

This turns out to be a significant turning point in the implementation phase. Upper-level management must obtain functional employee support before total implementation can be achieved. Functional employees have two concerns. Their first concern is with their evaluation. Who will evaluate them? How will they be evaluated? Against what standards will they be evaluated? Who will help them put more money into their pockets through merit increases or promotions?

The employee's second concern is centered about the resistance to change. Functional employees, especially blue-collar workers, have a strong resentment to changing their well-established occupational life styles. They must be shown enough cases (i.e., projects) in order to be convinced that the new system will work. This could easily take two to

---

* Dr. Harold Kerzner is Professor of Systems Management and Director of The Project/ Systems Management Research Institute at Baldwin-Wallace College. Dr. Kerzner has published over 35 engineering and business papers, and ten texts: *Project Management: A Systems Approach to Planning, Scheduling and Controlling; Project Management for Executives; Project Management for Bankers; Cases and Situations in Project/Systems Management; Operations Research; Proposal Preparation and Management; Project Management Operating Guidelines; Project/Matrix Management Policy and Strategy; a Project Management Dictionary of Terms; Engineering Team Management.*

three years to accomplish. It is therefore imperative that the first few projects be successful. Most upper- and middle-level managers agree to the necessity for initially demonstrating success, but often forget about the importance of looking at the evaluation procedure problems.

UNDERSTANDING THE NATURE OF THE PROBLEM

In most project situations, the functional employee reports to at least two bosses: a functional manager and a project manager. If the employee happens to be working on three or four projects simultaneously, then he or she can have multiple project managers to whom they must report, either formally or informally. This concept of sharing functional employees is vital if project management is to be successful because it allows better control and use of vital manpower resources by allowing key functional personnel to be shared.

In almost all cases, the relationship between the employees and their superior is a "solid" line where the manager maintains absolute employee control through the use of promotions, job assignments, merit and salary increases. The ability of the manager to motivate personnel is easily achieved through the use of the employee's purse strings.

The project manager, on the other hand, will probably be in a "dotted" line relationship and be less able to motivate temporarily assigned project personnel by using monetary rewards. Therefore, what types of interpersonal influences can a project manager use to motivate people who are assigned temporarily for the achievement of some common objective and who might never work together again? The most common interpersonal influence styles used by project managers are:

- Formal authority.
- Technical expertise.
- Work challenge.
- Friendship.
- Rewards (and punishment).

Formal authority is the ability to gain support from the functional employees because they respect the fact that the project manager has been delegated a certain amount of authority from upper-level management in order to achieve a specific objective. The amount of delegated authority may vary with the amount of risk that the project manager must take. Formal authority is not a very effective means of motivating and controlling employees because all the employees know that they have come to the project recommended by their managers.

Technical expertise is the ability to gain support because employees respect the fact that the project manager possesses skills which they lack or because he or she is a recognized expert in their field. If a project manager tries to control employees through the use of "expert power" for a prolonged period of time, conflicts can easily develop between the project and functional managers as to who is the "true" expert in the field.

Work challenge is an extremely effective means of soliciting functional support. If the employees find the work stimulating and challenging, they tend to become self-motivating with a strong desire for achievement in hopes of attaining some future rewards.

Friendship, or referent power, is a means of obtaining functional support because the employee feels personally attracted to either the project manager or the project. Examples of referent power might be when:

- The employee and the project manager have strong ties, such as being in the same foursome for golf.
- The employee likes the project manager's manner of treating people.
- The employee wants specific identification with a specific product line or project.
- The employee has personal problems and believes that he can get empathy or understanding from the project manager.
- The employee might be able to get personal favors from the project manager.
- The employee feels that the project manager is a winner and that the rewards will be passed down to the employee.

Rewards, or reward power, can be defined as the ability to gain support because the employee feels that the project manager can either directly or indirectly dispense those rewards which employees cherish. If the employee is assigned directly to the project manager, such as project office personnel, the project manager has the same direct rewarding system as does a functional manager. However, the project manager may have only indirect reward power with regard to the employees that are assigned to the project but are still attached administratively to a functional department. This chapter focuses on those problems of rewarding the temporary functional employees. The last two items under friendship are examples of reward power as well as referent power. Project managers prefer work challenge and rewards as the most comfortable means for soliciting functional support. Unfortunately, project managers are somewhat limited as to what rewards they can offer directly to the employee. What commitment should or can the project manager make in the way of:

- Salary?
- Grade?
- Responsibility?
- Evaluation for promotion?
- Bonus?
- Future work assignment?
- Paid overtime?
- Awards?
- Letters of commendation?

The major problem with project management is that, in theory, the project manager can *directly* provide only paid overtime rewards, and even this can be questionable. If the project manager cannot directly provide the necessary organizational rewards in order to motivate temporary employees, then what inducement is there for the employee to do a good job? Employees believe in the equity theory, which states that a fair day's work should receive a fair day's pay. The difficulty lies in the fact that employees occasionally perceive themselves as working for a project manager who cannot guarantee them any of these awards.

A special note need be mentioned concerning a project manager's ability or authority to provide an employee with additional responsibility. Most companies that adopt project management have rather loose company policies, procedures, rules, and guidelines. To illustrate this point, a functional employee can be performing the same task on three separate projects, yet his responsibilities might be quite different.

The problem appears when the project manager attempts to upgrade an employee. As an example, a Grade 7 employee does a good job on a Grade 7 task and receives an excellent evaluation. The project manager, having established a good working relationship with this employee, and not wanting to see it end, decides to let this employee assume the responsibilities of a Grade 8 on a follow-on task. The employee again performs above average and receives an outstanding evaluation by the project manager. The employee then demands that his manager promote him since he has now successfully performed the work of a Grade 8. The manager now becomes overly upset and claims that the project manager had no right to upgrade an employee without prior approval from the manager.

THE INDIRECT REWARDING PROCESS

Under the definition of rewards, we stated that the project manager could either directly or indirectly dispense the valued organizational rewards.

Each project, although considered as a separate entity within the company, is still attached administratively to the company through policies and procedures. These policies and procedures dictate the means of administering the wage and salary program. It is operationally disastrous for the project manager and functional manager to be administering different wage and salary policies at the same time.

When employees are assigned to a new project, their first concern is with the identification of the mechanism by which they can be assured that their manager will be informed if they perform well on their new assignment. A good project manager will make it immediately clear to all new employees that if they perform well on this effort, then he (the project manager) will inform their manager of their progress and achievements. This assumes that the manager is not providing close supervision over the employee and is, instead, passing on some of the responsibility to the project manager. This is quite common in project management organizational structures. Obviously, if the manager has a small span of control and/or sufficient time to monitor closely the work of subordinates, then the project manager's need for indirect reward power is minimal.

Many good projects as well as project management structures have failed because of the inability of the system to properly evaluate the employee's performance. This problem is, unfortunately, one of the most often overlooked trouble spots in project management.

In a project management structure there are basically six ways that an employee can be evaluated on a project.

- *The project manager prepares a written, confidential evaluation and gives it to the functional manager.* The line managers will evaluate the validity of the project manager's comments and prepare their own evaluation of the employee. The employee will be permitted to see only the evaluation form filled out by the line manager.
- *The project manager prepares a nonconfidential evaluation and gives it to the functional manager.* The project manager prepares his own evaluation form and both evaluations are shown to the functional employee. This is the technique preferred by most project and functional managers. However, there are several major difficulties with this technique. If the employee is an average or below-average worker, and if this employee is still to be assigned to this project after the evaluation, the project manager might rate the employee as above average simply to prevent any repercussions or ill feelings downstream. In this situation the manager might want a confidential evaluation instead knowing that the employee will see both evaluation forms. Employees tend to blame the project manager if they receive a

below-average merit increase, but give credit to the manager if the increase is above average. The best bet here is for the project manager to periodically inform the employees as to how well they are doing, and to give them an honest appraisal. Of course, on large projects with vast manpower resources, this approach may not be possible. Honesty does appear to be the best policy in project management employee evaluation.

- *The project manager provides the functional manager with an oral evaluation of the employee's performance.* Although this technique is commonly used, most functional managers prefer documentation on employee progress.
- *The functional manager makes the entire evaluation without any input from the project manager.* In order for this technique to be effective, the functional manager must have sufficient time to supervise each subordinate's performance on a continual basis. Unfortunately, most functional managers do not have this opportunity because of their broad span of control.
- *The project manager makes the entire evaluation for the functional manager.* This technique can work if the employee is assigned to only the one project or if the project is physically located at a remote site where he cannot be observed by his functional manager.
- *The project and functional managers jointly evaluate all project functional employees at the same time.* This technique may be limited to small companies with less than fifty or so employees; otherwise the evaluation process might be time consuming for key personnel. A bad evaluation is known by all.

In five of the above six techniques the project manager has either a direct or indirect input into the employee's evaluation process.

WHEN AND HOW TO EVALUATE

Since the majority of the functional managers prefer written, nonconfidential evaluations, we must determine what the evaluation forms look like and when the employee will be evaluated. The indirect evaluation form should be a relatively simple tool to use or else the indirect evaluation process will be time consuming. This is of paramount importance on large projects where the project manager may have as many as 200 employees assigned to various activities.

The evaluation forms can be filled out either when the employee is up for evaluation or after the project is completed. If the evaluation form is to be filled out when the employee is up for promotion or a merit increase, then the project manager should be willing to give an *honest* appraisal of the employee's performance. Of course, the project manager should not fill out the evaluation form if the employee has not been assigned long enough to allow a fair evaluation.

The evaluation form can be filled out at the termination of the project. One problem with this technique is that the project may end the month after the employee is up for promotion. One advantage of this technique is that the project manager may have been able to find sufficient time both to observe the employee in action and to see the complete output.

Performance factors	Excellent (1 out of 15) Far exceeds job requirements	Very good (3 out of 15) Exceeds job requirements	Good (8 out of 15) Meets job requirements	Fair (2 out of 15) Needs some improvement	Unsatisfactory (1 out of 15) Does not meet minimum standards
Quality	Leaps tall buildings with a single bound	Must take running start to leap over tall building	Can only leap over a short building or medium one without spires	Crashes into building	Cannot recognize buildings
Timeliness	Is faster than a speeding bullet	Is as fast as a speeding bullet	Not quite as fast as a speeding bullet	Would you believe a slow bullet?	Wounds himself with the bullet
Initiative	Is stronger than a locomotive	Is stronger than a bull elephant	Is stronger than a bull	Shoots the bull	Smells like a bull
Adaptability	Walks on water consistently	Walks on water in emergencies	Washes with water	Drinks water	Passes water in emergencies
Communications	Talks with God	Talks with angels	Talks to himself	Argues with himself	Loses the argument with himself

Figure 26-1. Guide to performance appraisal.

EMPLOYEE'S NAME			DATE	
PROJECT TITLE			JOB NUMBER	
EMPLOYEE ASSIGNMENT				
EMPLOYEE'S TOTAL TIME TO DATE ON PROJECT		EMPLOYEE'S REMAINING TIME ON PROJECT		

TECHNICAL JUDGEMENT:

☐ Quickly reaches sound conclusions   ☐ Usually makes sound conclusions   ☐ Marginal decision making ability   ☐ Needs technical assistance   ☐ Makes faulty conclusions

WORK PLANNING:

☐ Good planner   ☐ Plans well with help   ☐ Occasionally plans well   ☐ Needs detailed instructions   ☐ Cannot plan at all

COMMUNICATIONS:

☐ Always understands instructions   ☐ Sometimes needs clarification   ☐ Always needs clarifications   ☐ Needs follow-up   ☐ Needs constant instruction

ATTITUDE:

☐ Always job interested   ☐ Shows interest most of the time   ☐ Shows no job interest   ☐ More interested in in other activities   ☐ Does not care about job

COOPERATION:

☐ Always enthusiastic   ☐ Works well until job is completed   ☐ Usually works well with others   ☐ Works poorly with others   ☐ Wants it done his/her way

WORK HABITS:

☐ Always project oriented   ☐ Most often project oriented   ☐ Usually consistent with requests   ☐ Works poorly with others   ☐ Always works alone

ADDITIONAL COMMENTS: _____

_____

_____

Figure 26-2. Project work assignment appraisal.

Figure 26-1 represents a rather humorous version of how project personnel perceive the evaluation form to look. Unfortunately, the evaluation process is very serious and can easily have a severe impact on an individual's career path with the company even though the final evaluation rests with the manager.

Figure 26-2 shows a simple type of evaluation form where the project manager identifies the box that best describes the employee's performance. The project manager may or may not make additional comments. This type of form is generally used whenever the employee is up for evaluation, provided that the project manager has had sufficient time to observe the employee's performance.

	Excellent	Above average	Average	Below average	Inadequate
EMPLOYEE'S NAME				DATE	

EMPLOYEE'S NAME   DATE

PROJECT TITLE   JOB NUMBER

EMPLOYEE ASSIGNMENT

EMPLOYEE'S TOTAL TIME TO DATE ON PROJECT   EMPLOYEE'S REMAINING TIME ON PROJECT

	Excellent	Above average	Average	Below average	Inadequate
Technical judgement					
Work planning					
Communications					
Attitude					
Cooperation					
Work habits					
Profit contribution					

Additional comments

Figure 26-3. Project work assignment appraisal.

Figure 26-3 shows a typical form that can be used to evaluate an employee at project completion. In each category the employee is rated on a scale from one to five. In order to minimize time and paper work, it is also possible to have a single evaluation form at project termination for all employees (Figure 26-4). As before, all employees are rated in each category on a scale of one to five. Totals are obtained to provide a relative comparison between employees.

Even though the project manager fills out an evaluation form, there is no guarantee that the functional manager will give any credibility to the project manager's evaluation. There are always situations where the project and functional managers disagree as to either quality or direction of work. This can easily alienate the project manager into recommending either a higher or lower evaluation than the employee's work justifies. If

EMPLOYEE'S NAME	DATE
PROJECT TITLE	JOB NUMBER
EMPLOYEE ASSIGNMENT	
EMPLOYEE'S REMAINING TIME ON PROJECT	EMPLOYEE'S TOTAL TIME TO DATE ON PROJECT

CODE:

Excellent = 5
Above average = 4
Average = 3
Below average = 2
Inadequate = 1

NAMES	Technical judgement	Work planning	Communications	Attitude	Cooperation	Work habits	Profit contribution	Self motivation	Total points

Figure 26-4. Project work assignment appraisal.

the employee spends most of his time working alone, then the project manager may have difficulty appraising quality and give an average evaluation when in fact the employee's performance is superb or inferior. There is also the situation where the project manager knows the employee personally and may allow personal feelings to influence the evaluation.

Another problem situation is where the project manager is a "generalist," say at a Grade 7 level, and requests that the functional manager assign his best employee to the project. The functional manager agrees to the request and assigns his best employee, a Grade 10. Now, how can a Grade 7 generalist evaluate a Grade 10 specialist? The solution to this problem rests in the fact that the project manager might be able to evaluate the expert only in certain categories such as communications, work habits, problem solving, and other similar topics but not upon his technical expertise. The functional manager might be the only person qualified to evaluate personnel on technical abilities and expertise.

It has been proposed that employees should have some sort of reciprocal indirect input into a project manager's evaluation. This raises rather interesting questions as to how far we can go with the indirect evaluation procedure.

From a top management perspective, the indirect evaluation process brings with it several headaches. Wage and salary administrators readily accept the necessity for utilizing a different evaluation form for white-collar workers as opposed to blue-collar workers. But now, we have a situation in which there can be more than one type of evaluation system for white-collar workers alone. Those employees who work in project-driven functional departments will be evaluated directly and indirectly, but based upon formal procedures. Employees who charge their time to overhead accounts and nonproject-driven departments might simply be evaluated by a single, direct evaluation procedure.

Many wage and salary administrators contend that they cannot live with a dual white-collar system and therefore have tried to combine the direct and indirect evaluation forms into one, as shown in Figure 26-5. Some administrators have gone so far as to utilize a single form company-wide, regardless of whether an individual is a white- or blue-collar worker.

The last major trouble spot is the design of the employee's evaluation form. The designs must be dependent upon the evaluation method or procedure. Generally speaking, there are nine methods available for evaluating personnel:

- Essay Appraisal
- Graphic Rating Scale
- Field Review
- Forced-Choice Review
- Critical Incident Appraisal
- Management by Objectives (MBO)
- Work Standards Approach
- Ranking Methods
- Assessment Center

Descriptions of these methods can be found in almost any text on wage and salary administration. Which method is best suited for a project-driven organizational structure? To answer this question, we must analyze the characteristics of the organizational form as well as those of the

I. Employee information

  1. Name _____ 2. Date of evaluation _____

  3. Job assignment _____ 4. Date of last evaluation _____

  5. Pay grade _____

  6. Employee's immediate supervisor _____

  7. Supervisor's level: ☐ Section ☐ Dept. ☐ Division ☐ Executive

II. Evaluator's information:

  1. Evaluator's name _____

  2. Evaluator's level: ☐ Section ☐ Dept. ☐ Division ☐ Executive

  3. Rate the employee on the following:

	Excellent	Very Good	Good	Fair	Poor
Ability to assume responsibility					
Works well with others					
Loyal attitude toward company					
Documents work well and is both cost and profit conscious					
Reliability to see job through					
Ability to accept criticism					
Willingness to work overtime					
Plans job execution carefully					
Technical knowledge					
Communicative skills					
Overall rating					

  4. Rate the employee in comparison to his contemporaries:

Lower 10%	Lower 25%	Lower 40%	Midway	Upper 40%	Upper 25%	Upper 10%

  5. Rate the employee in comparison to his contemporaries:

Should be promoted at once	Promotable next year	Promotable along with contempories	Needs to mature in grade	Definitely not promotable

  6. Evaluator's comments: _____

_____

                                         Signature _____

III. Concurrence section:

  1. Name _____

  2. Position: ☐ Department   ☐ Division   ☐ Executive

  3. Concurrence   ☐ Agree   ☐ Disagree

  4. Comments: _____

_____

                                         Signature _____

IV. Personnel Section: (to be completed by the Personnel Department only)

	Lower 10%	Lower 25%	Lower 40%	Midway	Upper 40%	Upper 25%	Upper 10%
6/79							
6/78							
6/77							
6/76							
6/75							
6/74							
6/73							
6/72							
6/71							
6/70							

V. Employee's signature _____ Date: _____

Figure 26-5. Job evaluation.

personnel who must perform there. As an example, project management can be described as an arena of conflict. Which of the above nine evaluation procedures can best evaluate an employee's ability to work and progress in an atmosphere of conflict? Figure 26-6 compares the above nine evaluation procedures against the six most common project conflicts. This type of analysis must be carried out for all variables and characteristics which describe the project management environment. Many compensation managers would agree that the MBO technique offers the greatest promise for a fair and equitable evaluation of all employees. Unfortunately, MBO implies that functional employees will have a say in establishing their own goals and objectives. This might not be the case. In project management, the project manager or functional manager might set the objectives and the functional employee is told that he has to live with it. Obviously, there will be advantages and disadvantages to whatever evaluation procedures are finally selected.

Having identified the problems with employee evaluation in a project environment, we can now summarize the results and attempt to predict the future. Project managers must have some sort of either direct or indirect input into an employee's evaluation. Without this, project managers may find it difficult to adequately motivate people with no upward mobility. The question is, of course, how this input should take place. Most wage and salary administrators appear to be pushing for a single procedure to evaluate all white-collar employees. At the same time, however, administrators recognize the necessity for an indirect input by the

	Essay appraisal	Graphic rating scale	Field review	Forced-choice review	Critical incident appraisal	Management by objectives	Work standards approach	Ranking methods	Assessment center
Conflict over schedules	•	•		•	•		•	•	
Conflict over priorities	•	•		•	•		•	•	
Conflict over technical issues	•			•			•		
Conflict over administration	•	•	•	•			•	•	•
Personality conflict	•	•		•			•		
Conflict over cost	•		•	•	•		•	•	•

Figure 26-6. Rating evaluation techniques against types of conflicts.

project manager and, therefore, are willing to let the project and functional managers (and possibly personnel) determine the exact method of input, which can be different for each employee and each project. This implies that the indirect input might be oral for one employee and written for another, with both employees reporting to the same functional manager. Although this technique may seem confusing, it may be the only viable alternative for the future. A process of good employee evaluations is essential to project success.

27. Development and Implementation of Project Management Systems

John Tuman, Jr.*

As we move forward toward the twenty-first century, project managers in all fields of endeavor will be called upon to accomplish their responsibilities in an increasingly complex technical, social-economic, and political environment. Thus, project managers will deal with a broad range of issues, requirements, and problems and make decisions which involve complexities and risk well beyond anything experienced in the past. Yet the project manager will still be expected to be the focal point for planning, scheduling, measuring, evaluating, informing, and directing a myriad of organizations, complex tasks, and valuable resources to accomplish some specific technological or business undertaking.

As always, the project manager's situation will be doubly demanding because he functions for the most part outside the traditional organizational structure. He must complete a difficult job by certain dates with limited resources, and in most cases he must accomplish his goals with people and organizations who do not work for him. In addition, the project manager is considered to be the fountainhead of knowledge and information about every aspect of the project. In this type of setting it goes without saying that the project manager's only hope for survival rests with some type of well-developed system for the systematic management of project information and action. Without such a system, the project

---

* John Tuman, Jr., is a Senior Consultant with Gilbert/Commonwealth, Inc., a major U.S. engineering and consulting firm. Mr. Tuman has been involved in all aspects of project management for more than 25 years. He has been a project manager and a program manager on several major military, aerospace, and R&D programs for the General Electric Company and the AVCO Corporation. In recent years he has directed the development of advanced computer-based project management systems as well as providing consulting expertise to major companies in the United States, the Middle East, and Asia. He has given numerous presentations and seminars on project management and has written extensively on project management methods, techniques, systems, and problems. Mr. Tuman is a registered professional engineer; he has a M.S. degree in Computer Science and B.S. degree in Mechanical Engineering.

manager and the project participants will soon be lost in a quagmire of conflicting plans, schedules, reports, activities, and priorities.

Experience has shown that as projects become large, or more numerous, the work environment becomes more complex, and the number of people, organizations, functions, and activities involved become increasingly interdependent. As this happens, the project manager tends to become further and further removed from the total day-to-day project requirements and problems, and his ability to deal with real-time issues begins to be seriously diminished. In short, the effectiveness of the project manager and the project participants tends to be inversely related to the size and/or complexities of the project. However, this process can be minimized if we provide the project manager with "systems" which are specifically designed to increase his range of control and effectiveness over project activities. Thus, in the following we will discuss why it is necessary to design unique systems for project management, how to actually design and develop these systems, and finally, how to implement these systems to ensure that they perform as intended.

WHY DEVELOP A SYSTEM?

Before we consider the approach to defining, designing, and developing a system we must clearly establish that there is a need for such a system. In view of the large investments that have been made by corporations in the development of management information systems in recent years, one would question the need for development of yet another system within the corporate environment. And yet, this is exactly what is proposed here. The soundness of our rationale becomes evident if we examine the role of the project manager and his function within the traditional corporate hierarchical structure.

Traditionally, management information systems have been designed primarily to support functional units within the corporate structure. The computerized accounting system, the payroll system, the general ledger system, and so on provide systematized approaches to handling the corporate financial functions. In similar fashion, computer-supported systems for marketing and sales exist to aid and improve the efficiency of these functions, and personnel subsystems have been developed to aid the human resource functions of the corporation. In the operational or production areas (manufacturing, construction, services, tests, etc.) there are a myriad of computer-supported systems available to aid the product/service-producing end of the business. By and large, all of these systems have been designed to perform as efficiently as possible to collect and process data to produce information for their respective organizational functions. In more advanced management information systems designs, we see the utilization of the Data Based Management System (DBMS), which is designed to efficiently share information between functions. However, for the most part management information systems in today's corporate environment are designed to support decision making in the traditional hierarchical organizational structure.

Unfortunately, by the very nature of project management, the project manager must cut across functional organization lines to accomplish his goal of integrating and directing specific resources of the organization(s) toward a particular goal. The question naturally arises, can he do this effectively utilizing the traditional available management information resources?

In the earlier days of project management, and in fact, even today, for relatively small projects, the project manager acts either in a staff capacity to top management or in a line capacity within a functional organization. As a staff function, the project manager strives to coordinate in the name of top management certain capabilities of the functional organization. In this role, the project manager relies on the functional departments for the detailed planning, scheduling, budgeting, and control of their specific tasks. The project manager's information needs are limited and, generally, are of a summary nature. Even in the line function, the project manager is working in an environment where he can rely on the information system already in place.

However, as projects become larger and more complex, companies have established large project organizations which are functioning either deliberately or indirectly in a matrix fashion with the total organization. In this environment project managers have attempted to carry out their responsibilities utilizing the information systems already in place. However, for the most part these project managers have found that their information resources were severely limited. Some of the more typical problems encountered by project managers in trying to do their job while relying on existing or the traditional management information systems resources of the corporation are listed below:

1. *Usefulness*—Existing corporate management information systems do not generate the specific information required by the project manager and other project participants. The needed information is not generally available in a useful form, and it requires considerable time and money to revise the existing systems to get the needed data in a timely manner.
2. *Quality Versus Quantity*—Too much detailed information is generated. It is necessary to pour through reams of computer printouts to

extract the required data. It is difficult to get exception reports, especially when several functions may be involved.

3. *Integration*—There is little uniformity between corporate systems. Hence, it is difficult to develop a total project picture where several different companies are involved. Even within one organization's management information system it's difficult to reconcile information between diverse functions like finance, personnel, and operations to develop an integrated project status report.

4. *Responsiveness*—Whenever top management requests an answer to a specific question or problem, it initiates a mad scramble to obtain the required data. The existing information systems are not structured to integrate across functions to produce timely exception reports.

The essence of all of the above problems is that the traditional corporate management information systems cannot be efficiently and effectively used by the project manager simply because these systems were designed for another purpose, namely, that of enabling the functional organizations to efficiently carry out their responsibilities. This is now a fairly well recognized fact. Many companies with formalized project management organizations are now making the effort to design and implement computer-based project information and control systems specifically suited to their *unique* project management requirements.

CHARACTERISTICS OF THE PROJECT MANAGEMENT SYSTEM

Before getting into the methodology of building a project management system, it is necessary to examine some of the basic characteristics of these systems. For, in order to design a system which is truly effective, we must have a clear idea of what these systems should do for the project manager, executive management, and the total organization at large.

Let us begin by examining the basic concept of the project. A project is an organization of people dedicated to a specific purpose or objective. Projects may be large, expensive, unique, or high-risk undertakings; however, all projects have to be completed by a certain date, for a certain amount of money, within some expected level of performance. At a minimum, all projects need to have well-defined objectives and sufficient resources to carry out all the required tasks. The important elements of a project can be depicted by the simple cybernetic diagram shown in Figure 27-1.

As shown in Figure 27-1, the project is responsible for accomplishing certain specific objectives or outputs. Those outputs can be defined in

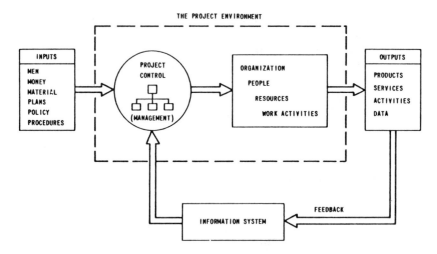

Figure 27-1. The total project management process.

terms of activities, products, services, or data generated by the project. In order to accomplish these objectives (outputs), the project needs appropriate inputs or resources. These can be defined as men, money, or material which the project will expend in the process of accomplishing its objectives.

The control function in this process is management. Management's responsibility is to allocate to the project only those resources required to do a good job, no more and no less. And, of course, management is also concerned that these resources are used in an optimum manner. The question is, how does management determine the quantity of resources to allocate to the project and decide whether or not these resources are being used effectively in terms of the project goals and accomplishments? The answer is, through the information system. The primary function of the information system is to enable management to assess how the project is performing against its established goals and thereby formulate timely decisions for the effective utilization of valuable resources.

This simplified view of the project is useful to highlight two important elements which must be carefully considered in the design of any project management system. These two elements are (1) the information system, and (2) the control system. It is particularly important to note that these two distinct and different elements are mutually related and dependent on each other. The reasons for this are obvious if we examine Figure 27-2. Note that the *information* element of the system concerns itself primarily

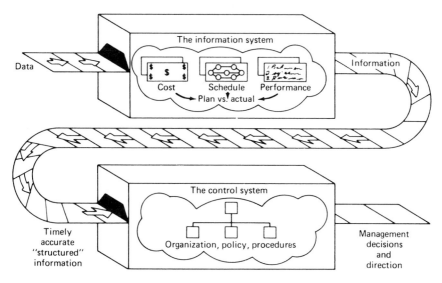

Figure 27-2. Information and control. The information system must be designed and matched to the control system such that management decisions are a natural output of the process. This means that the right kinds of information must go to the appropriate levels of management at the right time and the decision-making process must be initiated as a direct result of established procedures and routines.

with the task of processing data to produce timely, accurate, structured information regarding the cost, schedule, and performance aspects of the project. On the other hand, the *control* element of the system is concerned primarily with using the information supplied to formulate decisions and give direction relative to future utilization of resources and/or resolution of problems. Unless the control element and the information element are designed to be mutually compatible and dependent on each other, they will not function as an integrated system.

With this brief view of the "system" we can define the "project management" system as the people, policies, procedures, and systems (computerized and manual) which provide the means for planning, scheduling, budgeting, organizing, directing, and controlling the cost, schedule, and performance accomplishments of a project. Implicit in this definition is the idea that *people plan and control projects,* and *systems serve people by producing information.* The design and implementation of the procedures and methodologies which integrate people and systems into a unified whole is both an art and a science. Some of the more pragmatic aspects of these procedures and methodologies are considered next.

GETTING STARTED

Once the need to develop a system has been established, there is generally a great temptation to make an industry-wide survey to find out what everyone else is doing. These whirlwind tours usually result in a mind-boggling collection of facts and philosophy on computer hardware, data base management systems, CPM packages,* classification schemes, programming concepts, etc. At best, a survey of other systems will give the uninitiated a feel for the magnitude and complexities of the undertaking.

The other extreme is to call in the computer or systems consultants who, in most cases, recommend the purchase of a particular set of software packages. Unfortunately, instant implementation of these packages is generally not possible. Extensive customizing may be required to enable usage of the system for a particular project. Also, software packages are designed for specific purposes and unless the buyer knows exactly what he is going to do with these packages, they are unlikely to be used to their fullest potential.

The only sure way to develop a project management system that fits a particular business environment is to first formulate a step-by-step system program plan. This master plan or program plan should fulfill two needs. First, it should be sufficiently detailed to serve as a long-range blueprint for the total program, and second, it should serve as a mechanism for obtaining continued top management support. The development effort will have a much greater chance of survival if top management has more than just a vague understanding of what the system will eventually do for the organization.

The system program plan should be a living document which is updated frequently and circulated to those who are involved in or provide support to the program. At a minimum, the system program plan should contain the following:

1. *System Objectives*—System objectives should give a concise description of what the system is supposed to accomplish, and for whom. The system objectives should define the functions, disciplines, and levels of management to be served by the system, as well as the types of information to be provided. One reason for establishing system objectives is to determine the scope and complexity of the system to be developed. It is especially important to avoid glittering generalities

---

* See Chapter 15 for a discussion of CPM and Chapter 28 for a discussion of computer software that is useful in project management.

such as, "The system will provide management with all the information necessary to carry out their responsibilities." In some instances it is valuable to define the areas that *will not* be served by the system. This will help avert potential misunderstandings in the future, especially with organizational entities not directly involved in the project.

2. *The System Criteria*—Fairly comprehensive criteria must be established to define the system parameters. All the disciplines to be included in the system (i.e., planning, scheduling, estimating, accounting, cost management, material management, etc.) should be defined, as well as the level of detail of information that will be addressed by these disciplines. In effect, the system criteria establish the philosophy by which the projects will be managed and define, or provides boundaries for, the information and level of control needed to effectively manage these projects. *These criteria should accurately reflect the project management environment in which the system will operate.*

3. *The Work Plan*—The basic segments of work related to the design, development, implementation, and maintenance of the system should be spelled out in broad terms. Also, the organizational groups responsible for doing the work must be identified.

   In the early stages of conceptualizing the system, development of a detailed work plan is of little value. This can be done after a comprehensive study is made to identify the system resources that currently exist in the organization and the new ones that must be developed.

4. *Schedule and Budget*—A general phasing schedule covering the major blocks of work and a gross overall budget should also be included in the system program plan. Here again, the main emphasis should focus on establishing the time and cost boundaries for the total program. Attempting to define more detailed schedules and budgets at this stage would be, for the most part, an exercise in wishful thinking.

It cannot be overstated that the most important step in the successful development of an effective information and control system is defining the nature of the system itself and the environment in which it must operate. Establishing the program plan, as outlined above, is a good start in this direction; however, the real effort required to develop a comprehensive set of system objectives and system criteria will begin following a thorough study and analysis of the organization's *existing* system resources and project management methodology. This type of study will set the stage for development of the detailed work plans, budgets, and schedules that will be used to carry out the program through actual system design, development, and implementation.

PROGRAM SCOPE

A typical program for the development of a new or improved computer-based project management system will involve three distinct phases of work including:

- Phase I —Study and Analysis (Determine what we have now and what we need for the future.)
- Phase II —Design, Development, and Implementation (Specify the system, build it, and actually apply it to a project.)
- Phase III—Documentation, Training, Test, and Support (Ensure people know how to use the system; make it work using actual project data; and improve it as needed.)

The first phase of effort involves a study of the organization's existing information and system resources to determine what is presently available for use in building a computer-based project information system. Out of this analysis should come a list of systems and procedures that will need to be procured or developed. In addition, the project management approach or mode of operation for management of future projects should be established to identify the types of information resources that must be made available. This analysis must produce very comprehensive system criteria, as well as a preliminary description of the total project information system concept. The final output of the Phase I study and analysis effort should be the action plan which specifies how the recommendations should be carried out, by whom, when, and at what approximate cost. The flowchart given in Figure 27-3 shows the major activities and accomplishments to be realized in the three phases of the program. These will be discussed in detail later.

In the second phase of the program, efforts will concentrate on design, development, and implementation of the software, hardware, and related procedures for the total system. Typically, during this phase of the program, studies are made of commercially available software and hardware which will meet specific project requirements. Appropriate analyses and cost trade-off studies will be made to select those systems which lend themselves to the total project system concept. Or, in the situation where the management systems of several organizations or firms may be integrated to produce a composite management system, the focus of the study will be on selecting the best elements of the individual systems and integrating them in as needed. Specific software packages will be defined and the related programming and coding will be accomplished. To the maximum extent possible, new systems will be operated in parallel with exist-

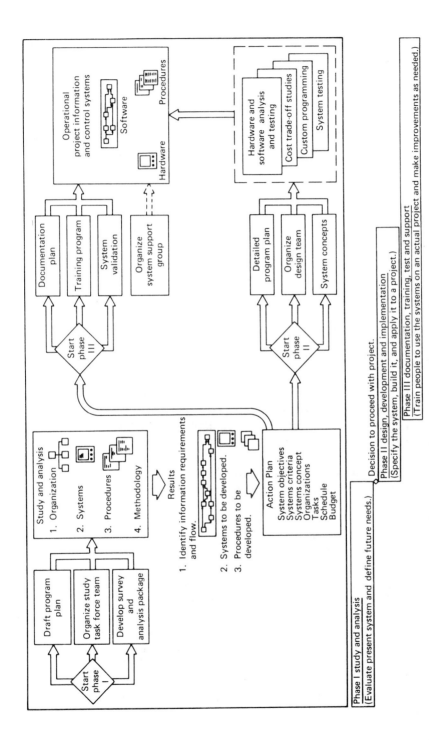

Figure 27-3. Major phases in development of a project information and control system.

661

ing systems in order to subject them to real-life project environments. Generally, all new systems are tested in parallel with existing systems until such time as these systems are debugged and documented and the results verified. Only then will the systems be formally turned over to the using project organizations.

The third and final phase of the program, which will overlap the second phase, involves training all personnel who will use or be served by the system. Appropriate training sessions must be organized and seminars scheduled for all levels of management. In addition, all documentation should be finalized as each element of the system completes it validation test. Once the user's organizations are satisfied that the system fulfills their needs, the development team will phase out of the program.

This is a brief overview of the total program scope; however, to get a feel for the problems that must be faced in actually carrying out such an undertaking, it will be necessary to examine each program phase in some detail.

PHASE I—STUDY AND ANALYSIS

The Study Team

Determining the extent and value of the organization's existing systems and defining the system requirements in detail requires that personnel be designated to organize, direct, and accomplish this effort. Obviously, a team of some type is in order. In most companies this assignment falls upon a committee which is organized for that specific purpose. This committee is most often comprised of part-time members from various departments including engineering, data processing, finance, and the project office.

Almost without exception, this committee will do a poor job, and for good reason! They have other, more immediate responsibilities, and are generally unschooled in the art of making a system survey and analysis. Experience has shown that the most successful approach is to organize a full-time task force team dedicated specifically to making a study, and providing recommendations and a proposed implementation plan. A typical team (see Figure 27-4) would include a program manager, who is specifically *responsible* for the work of the team, and several specialists with expertise in systems analysis, planning, scheduling, estimating, cost management, material management, etc. The size of the team can vary as new members are added to focus on specific topics; but, at a minimum, a core group of individuals should be identified as part of the project team until the study is completed. The team's program manager should report

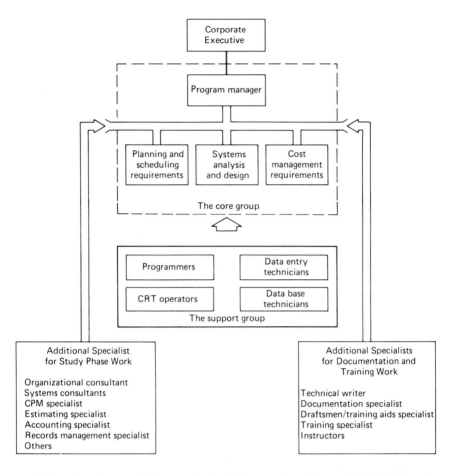

The Core Group is responsible for carrying the total program through to completion. This group is augmented by various specialists during all phases of the program. In addition, a support staff is organized to bring the system into actual operation. Selected members of the core group and the support group can be designated to maintain the system once it becomes operational.

Figure 27-4. The program team organization.

to a high level of management, in most large companies a senior vice president. The senior vice president should, in turn, be held *accountable* for the work of the study team.

Study Methodology

Once a program team is organized and committed to making the study, preparatory work is needed to ensure that the team will make an objective

evaluation and collect the required information in an organized, systematic manner. To this end, the team will need to map out the organizational
elements to be included in the study, develop appropriate interview and
questionnaire forms, and establish a mechanism for sorting out and evaluating all the information that will be collected. As shown in Figure 27-3, in
Phase I the team's study and analysis work will focus on the organization,
systems, procedures, and methodologies now in place to support project
management.

A well-organized survey plan would include the following:

1. *Memo of Introduction*—A brief memo should be directed to all those
   to be included in the study to advise them of the purpose of the study,
   the topics to be covered, and the length of time required. The memo
   should advise all participants of the importance of the effort and should
   be signed by top management.
2. *Survey Questionnaire*—A well-designed questionnaire is invaluable
   for ensuring that all the appropriate topics are covered consistently
   from one interview to the next interview. The interviewers can utilize
   an outline or checklist (see Figure 27-5) to keep the conversation flow-
   ing along the required topics. The questionnaire can be completed after
   the meetings and, if necessary, follow-up discussions can be held to fill
   in the gaps.

The questionnaire should be designed to capture information on the
following topics from the individual being interviewed:

- Responsibilities and functions of the unit.
- Interfaces with the unit.
- Primary work tasks.
- Data inputs needed to perform these tasks.
- Data outputs generated as a result of performing these tasks.
- Problems, requirements, and suggestions.*

In addition, the questionnaire should investigate at least three major
aspects of the organization including: (a) information requirements and
information flow, (b) methods and procedures, and (c) systems used by
the organization. For all three of these major areas, specific questions
should be developed. Since the project management system is concerned to a large degree with the information that a unit needs in order

---

* Chapter 16 describes the way in which a linear responsibility chart may be used as a basis
for obtaining this information in the systems design process.

INTERVIEWER		
NAME _____		WORK ORDER _____
DEPT. _____	PROJECT _____	FILE NO. _____
DATE _____		PAGE _____ OF _____
TIME START _____	CLIENT _____	
TIME STOP _____		

SURVEY OUTLINE & INSTRUCTIONS
(CHECK BLOCKS TO MONITOR PROGRESS OF THE DISCUSSION)

I. ORGANIZATIONAL ANALYSIS & INFORMATION FLOW

☐1. IDENTIFY ORGANIZATIONAL LEVEL & LOCATION

☐2. PRIMARY RESPONSIBILITIES OF THIS ORGANIZATION AS UNDERSTOOD BY THE INTERVIEWEE.

☐3. STRONGEST CAPABILITY AND/OR TALENT OF THIS ORGANIZATION

☐4. INTERFACES (INTERNAL & EXTERNAL)

☐5. ROUTINE TASKS PERFORMED (LIST)
      SPECIAL ASSIGNMENTS (WHAT AND HOW OFTEN)

☐6. PROBLEMS

☐7. INPUTS (DATA/INFO) REQUIRED

☐8. OUTPUTS (DATA/INFO) PRODUCED

☐9. NEW IDEAS – PROBLEM SOLUTIONS

☐10. OTHER AREAS TO LOOK INTO

II. PROCEDURES ANALYSIS

☐1. WHAT PROCEDURES ARE USED (FORMAL AND/OR INFORMAL) HOW CLOSELY UTILIZED

☐2. EFFECTIVENESS OF THESE PROCEDURES

☐3. PROBLEMS

☐4. ADDITIONAL PROCEDURES REQUIRED (IDENTIFY)

☐5. IDEAS & SUGGESTIONS

III. SYSTEMS & METHODOLOGY

☐1. DEFINE SYSTEMS NORMALLY USED – COMPUTER BASED
                                   – MANUAL SYSTEMS

☐2. SYSTEMS UNDER DEVELOPMENT OR BEING CONSIDERED

☐3. MAJOR PROBLEM AREAS

☐4. IDEAS & SUGGESTIONS FOR SYSTEMS

IV. SPECIFIC QUESTIONS (SEE ATTACHED LIST)

Figure 27-5. Survey questionnaire.

to carry out its function, much effort must be devoted to mapping out this requirement. Simple input/output charts (see Figure 27-6) can be developed for each of the organizational units surveyed. These charts can then be connected (since the information outputs of one unit become the inputs of another unit) to develop a composite system information flow (see Figure 27-7). This total system information flowchart will then become an excellent tool for designing the total system logic.

3. *Survey Timetable and Score Card*—Every individual and/or area to be covered in the study should be identified and a fairly comprehensive timetable developed to be sure that the survey effort does not exceed the time allotted. It is important that the study team talk to everyone while management's interest in the project is still strong. Also, it is equally important that the results of the survey be catalogued while still fresh in the interviewers' minds. Thus, a simple matrix will not only ensure that all required areas are covered, but will also provide an evaluation of the effectiveness of the coverage.

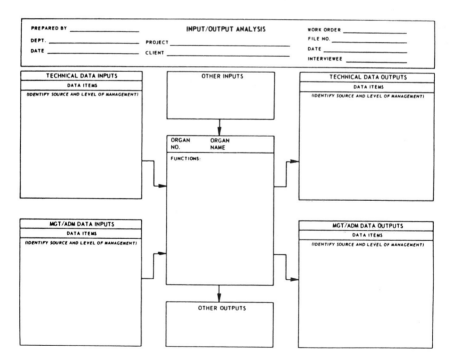

Figure 27-6. Input/output chart.

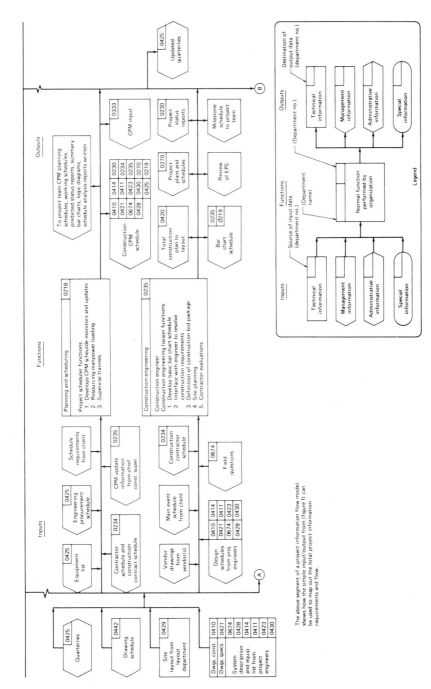

Figure 27-7. Constructing an information flow model for the project.

Compiling the Findings

Armed with a well-organized survey plan, the study team can proceed to conduct their interviews and review the organization's current systems, procedures, and methodology for managing projects. As might be expected, information or systems studies are, at best, very subjective. The problem will be to separate facts from opinions. To have some degree of confidence in the final results, efforts must be directed at evaluating all interview data on a consistent basis; otherwise, the investigators will fall into the trap of devising systems which respond to what the interviewers think people said, and not what the people actually did say. The following approach will help to minimize the subjective influences:

1. *Compile and Structure the Findings*—To ensure a high degree of consistency in evaluating information collected, the information should first be compiled by discipline and then by level of management. Once this is done, the information requirements should be further subdivided according to technical, management, and administrative types of information needed to support each level of management and each discipline.
2. *Categorize the Results*—It is especially important to categorize the inputs obtained during the study to make a clear distinction between those things which are applicable to management information system (MIS) requirements and those which are not. The following three categories are suggested:
   a. Problems and requirements for the information system.
   b. Problems and requirements which are procedural in nature.
   c. Problems and requirements which are managerial or organizational in nature.
3. *Analysis*—After compiling the information and carefully categorizing all the facts, the study team should perform an analysis from two distinct viewpoints: first, from the viewpoint of the organizational element (and the disciplines within these elements) and second, from the viewpoint of the different levels of management. The results of these two analyses should be consolidated to identify all common requirements that must be addressed by the system to be developed. From this, a priority list can be developed to specify the system development sequence.

Making Recommendations

If the study team has carefully organized and documented their efforts as outlined above, the team should be in a position to define the concept for a project management system which reflects the personality and unique requirements of their company. At a minimum, the study recommendations should identify:

1. The specific information resources required by
   a. Each organization or function involved in the project.
   b. Each level of management within the company that will contribute to, or be affected by, the project.
2. The new systems (hardware and software) that may have to be developed or procured.
3. The existing systems that may have to be modified.
4. The existing systems that will be utilized.
5. The organizations that must contribute to the development effort.
6. The timetable for developing the total system.
7. A budget estimate.
8. An overview (pictorial flowchart) of the system concept.

The final recommendations should include some discussion of what the system will do to increase the effectiveness of the project management organization. Often there is an attempt to identify cost savings as a means for justifying system development. However, the value of a good project management system lies in its ability to enable a small team to manage something large, complex, or very important to the organization. Unfortunately, this is extremely difficult to quantify in terms of dollar savings.

From the foregoing it should be obvious that the Phase I Study and Analysis is the key to the eventual development of a truly effective project management system. Successful development of these systems can be assured to a large degree if the study team follows a well-established approach of the type outlined here. Equally important, however, is the need to have a team composed of people who have worked in the project environment and know from experience the value and need for systems. These types of individuals, armed with a structured study and analysis methodology, should be able to produce the detailed information and plans necessary to start the actual design of the proposed project management system.

PHASE II—DESIGN, DEVELOPMENT, AND IMPLEMENTATION

In the first phase of our program considerable effort has been expended to carefully establish parameters for a project management systems which will effectively function within a particular organizational environment. In addition, we have inventoried the existing systems and procedures and have attempted to evaluate these in terms of their effectiveness in supporting present and future project management requirements. Thus, we have developed a fairly detailed blueprint of what the future system will look like, what it will do for management, and how long and how much it will take to get there. To the system analyst, most of this work would be categorized under the heading of the functional specification. Regardless of what it is called, the purpose is the same, namely to spell out as meticulously as possible all of the user requirements prior to actually designing the system. These user requirements should identify the particular features and capabilities of the systems which must function within a given industry, organization, and management environment. However, in spite of the wide range of applications for these systems, all project management systems should have the capabilities to support the basic requirements given in Figure 27-8.

It should be noted that the requirements identified in Figure 27-8 hold true for large sophisticated computer-based systems as well as simple

PROJECT MANAGEMENT FUNCTIONS		BASIC ACTIVITIES INVOLVED IN THESE PROJECT MANAGEMENT FUNCTIONS
1. Project Objectives	—	Define the cost, schedule and performance goals for the project.
2. Work Definitions	—	Define work task to be done and the organizations responsible.
3. Scheduling	—	Define the sequence for doing the work and the time constraints.
4. Budgeting	—	Define the resources (men, money, material available for doing the work.
5. Baseline	—	Define the parameters for measuring cost, schedule, performance accomplishments.
6. Monitoring/Reporting	—	Define how progress will be tracked (the events and level of detail) and how this will be reported.
7. Analysis	—	Define how and who will assess progress against plans.
8. Corrective Action	—	Define who is responsible for corrective action, how it is to be implemented and when.

The Project Management System must provide the people, policies, procedures, systems (manual and computer) to accomplish the basic task involved in each of the eight Project Management functions.

Figure 27-8. Minimum requirements for project management systems.

manual systems. Irrespective of the degree of sophistication of the system, it must be designed to support the project management process.

Design Concepts for Project Management Information and Control Systems

As noted earlier, the "systems" discussed here involve people, procedures, and computer software and hardware integrated into a unified approach to processing data to produce information to effect a timely management decision process. Note that we do not merely talk about generating information to support the decision-making process, but rather we infer that the decision-making process must be forced to take place as a result of the systems information outputs. The implication here is quite important, because for the system concept to truly work for the project management process, the people involved in the process must be an integral part of the input, output, feedback cycle depicted in the cybernetic diagram shown back in Figure 27-1. This means that our project management system must include, in addition to the procedures and systems for generating information, procedures and systems which ensure that decisions or actions are generated as a result of the information inputs. A general concept for doing this is depicted in Figure 27-9.

The system concept for project management information and control given in Figure 27-9 utilizes a one-for-one modular concept to integrate information and management control. That is to say, for every specialized module we create (computer-based or manual) to process data and generate information relative to a specialized discipline or topic, we also create a module for project control action. These control modules identify the people (organizational functions) involved and the process that must be initiated as a result of the outputs of the information module. Thus, in designing our "systems" we must focus on the two unique requirements of information and control. Some suggestions for the methodology to follow in designing these elements of our system are discussed in the next section. However, an advantage of using a modular approach to our design is that we can build a system which can eventually support a wide range of project management requirements.

The system shown in Figure 27-10 addresses a wide range of project management requirements. These include the technical requirements (Group I Module); the usual cost, schedule, and performance requirements (Group II Module); and the predictive requirements (Group III Module) of a project. In this example we show the type of system which might need to be developed for a project environment dealing with large scale, high risk, high cost, or unusual technical or business development

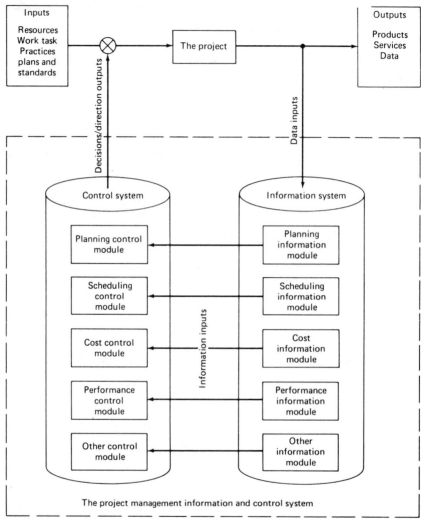

The information system receives data from the project and evalutes the plans, schedules, cost, and performance of the project against established plans and goals. Information is developed relative to the variance between what the project planned to do and what it has actually done. This information is fed to the control system. The control system evaluates the variances for various project parameters against established standards to determine if progress to date is acceptable. The outputs of the control system are decisions/directions which redirect resources, work task, practices and plans and standards of the project.

Figure 27-9. Project information flow.

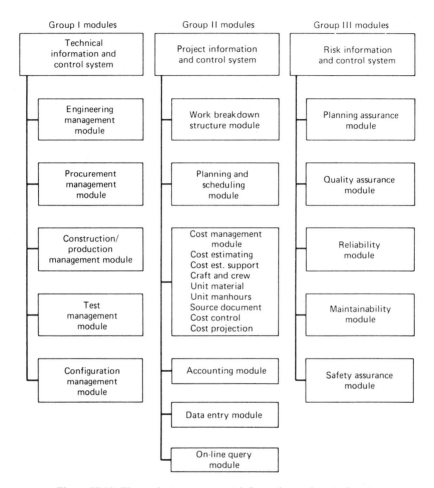

Figure 27-10. The project management information and control system.

requirements. By utilizing the modular building block approach, the design effort can focus on the priority areas and make these operational in tune with management's needs and availability of resources. The point that needs to be stressed here is that it is extremely important to conceptualize the total system in the beginning, before starting actual design; otherwise there is a high possibility that the resulting product will be a hodge-podge of poorly related systems. The design process should begin only when the objectives and the design concepts have been carefully defined, understood, and agreed to by all.

Design of the Information System

A modern management information system normally consists of two major elements (see Figure 27-11). The first is a data management system, which is the heart of the system, and is comprised of a series of data base-related software packages which "manage" (store and retrieve) the project's data on an integrated and logical basis. The second major element of the system consists of a series of computer software packages, or modules, which provide the means for generating information on specific functions of the project. For a project management application these modules will typically address planning, scheduling, estimating, cost management, project accounting, and so on. Additional modules can be utilized to produce information on almost any aspect of the project that management may wish to control. The primary objective of the information system module is to organize, collect, store, and process data quickly and effi-

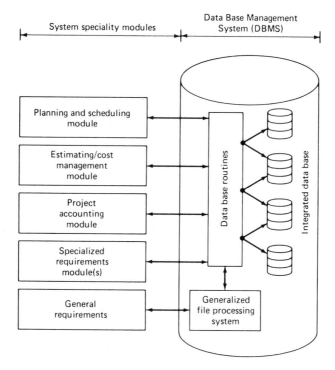

Figure 27-11. Project information system concept. The DBMS provides a convenu method for managing all project data on a logical basis. The individual application programs process the data to produce "information" or new data. This "information" is directed to management and/or to the DBMS for use by other modules.

ciently to produce meaningful information which will advise management on the project's status, trends, and potential problem areas.

Elements of the Information System

For project management some of the basic elements of the information system that will need to be designed are described as follows:

1. *Planning and Scheduling Module*—Effective management of a large or complex project calls for a systematic method of depicting the time-sensitive relationships and the interdependency between such functions as engineering, design, procurement, operations, testing, and so on. Normally, the Planning and Schedule Module utilizes Critical Path Method (CPM)* scheduling techniques with resource leveling and target scheduling to provide the tools for planning and monitoring the project. The information generated by the project CPM also provides the keys for more detailed monitoring and analysis of subtasks within various disciplines. This is done by creating data base files for specific work tasks or requirements of individual project disciplines. Because of the integrated nature of the data base files themselves, the information can be used to support other modules. Thus, drawing lists, specification lists, purchasing schedules, and all types of cost information can be interrelated and used by all the project's organizations (engineering, purchasing, operations, tests, etc.) to manage their specific tasks as well as by the project management organization to overview the total effort.
2. *Project Accounting Module*—The project will require a formalized method to monitor, record, and report all costs, and to develop the final cost records upon completion of the project. In the Project Accounting Module this is accomplished through computer-based systems which, together with predefined operating procedures, produce periodic reports and provide for development of actual cost records as the project progresses. Typical outputs for this type of module might be
   a. *Commitments and Invoice Record of Purchase Orders and Contracts*—Used to determine the cost status of each purchase order and contract, and through appropriate coding techniques, to keep track of change orders against these orders.
   b. *Statement of Commitments and Recorded Expenditures*—Provides a quick reference to the status of all purchase orders and contracts

---

* See Chapter 15.

including base amounts, change orders, recorded cost, remaining commitments, and retentions.

    c. *Project Ledger*—Detailed cost record for the project.

    d. *Change Order Status Reports*—Provide information relative to all change orders associated with each purchase order and contract.

    e. *Statement of Recorded Expenditures by Account*—A list, at the account code level, of all actual expenditures, current estimates, and current balances for the project.

3. *Estimating/Cost Management Modules**—Effective cost management for the project requires that the system provide an efficient method for making comparisons between current and budget estimates and scheduled and actual cash flow. This is accomplished through the computer-based Estimating/Cost Management Modules and the interface which this module maintains through data base with the Accounting and Planning and Scheduling Modules. Typical outputs of the Estimating/Cost Management Modules are

    a. *Detailed Estimates*—Detailed estimates in account code sequences.

    b. *Summary Estimates*—Detailed estimates summarized into work packages.

    c. *Updated Estimate/Cost Report*—Updated estimate, at the account level, providing a comparison of the new estimate with the previous estimate for each account.

    d. *Functional Cost Report*—Cost reporting by major functional categories, i.e., material purchase orders, installation purchase orders, field purchase orders, etc.

    e. *Outstanding Commitments Report*—A comprehensive profile showing the total, actual, and outstanding commitments against each purchase order.

    f. *Forecast of Cash Requirements (Summary and Detail)*—Cash forecast reports at various levels and detailed at monthly, quarterly, and yearly increments.

In addition to the above basic modules, many other modules may be developed to address specialized needs of a project, such as labor resources, materials inventory and controls, document indexing and retrieval, health, safety, and environmental records, etc. Any requirement that can be defined by tangible data elements can be designed and integrated into the total system in building block fashion. Since a data base management approach is at the heart of the system, the system designers

---

* See Chapter 19.

can address all future project needs with relative ease, once these needs are identified.

At this point, it is important to note that the amount of design and development work that will be required to develop a specific project management system will depend on the complexity of the system (which should be dictated by the needs of the project), the time and money available to develop the system, and the knowledge and experience of those responsible for getting the system up and running. Obviously, trade-offs must be made when all the factors are taken into consideration; however, three fundamental strategies and combinations thereof can be used to obtain the desired results. These are listed below:

1. *Specialized Design and Customizing*—For projects which are unique, large, or complex it may be necessary to design and program specialized modules or application programs from scratch. It may even be appropriate to procure commercially available software packages and customize them to meet specific user needs. Specialized design and customizing may represent a sizable investment; however, the investment may be well justified if the final system supports the management style of the project participants and enables them to manage a high-value or high-risk undertaking at a reasonable cost.

2. *Procurement of Project Management Packages*—Projects with routine or straightforward requirements may be satisfied by one of the many commercially available project management packages. Within recent years there has been a virtual explosion of new products for project management. Commercially available software packages range from the relatively simple and inexpensive package which is designed to run on the personal computer, very sophisticated systems which run on powerful minicomputers, and the most comprehensive project management system which takes full advantage of the speed and capacity of the large mainframe computer.

   Selection of a commercially available or canned project management package may be quite difficult and time consuming in view of the large number of systems now available. Nevertheless, the problem can be managed if the user follows the procedure prescribed in our Phase I—Study and Analysis—and uses the results to specify and evaluate the candidate project management packages.

3. *System Integration*—The strategy here is to devise a project management system by integrating major elements of the information and control systems that the project participants have in place. This strategy may be quite suitable for very complex undertakings or superprojects where the contributions of many diverse firms and highly special-

ized organizations are required. Building the actual system involves assessing the internal systems that the project participants have in place and carefully selecting and integrating elements of the system into a composite system. This approach is possible where the participants' technologies are compatible and where their respective project responsibilities can be segmented by discrete or unique information boundaries and work tasks.

Regardless of the strategy employed, the fundamental problem is to ensure that the systems which are devised support the specific project-related requirements and are compatible with the control procedures and philosophy of the management environment where they are being applied. For projects of any significance it is paramount that the system be able to collect, process, and present information in a form which will support the diverse range of organization, management, and technical needs which are unique to the project environment. Thus, for most project management system development efforts, the logical starting point will be the selection of a data base management system.

There are a number of excellent data base management systems (DMBS) currently available on the market.* The goal is to select the one most suited to the user's needs. To this end, the user will have to develop some type of evaluation criteria. At a minimum, these criteria must address in detail the following:

1. *Technical Capabilities and Requirements of the DBMS*—core requirements, interfaces, security, performance statistics, editing features, utilities available, batch/on-line, maintenance, etc.
2. *Flexibility of the DBMS*—control feature, data access, languages supported, data storage devices, linkage capabilities, search capabilities, etc.
3. *Standardization*—comply with various standards that have been developed for data bases.
4. *Resource Support Requirements*—internal and external support requirements, documentation, etc.
5. *Design Features*—data levels, indexing techniques, networking features, etc.

It is strongly recommended that the user carefully establish his criteria prior to consulting with vendors or other users. Otherwise, the user will be barraged by bewildering terminology and an array of philosophies on DBMS. It is difficult to provide specific guidelines in this area because individual needs vary so widely. However, common sense dictates that

---

* See Chapter 28.

the user should not purchase a DBMS more sophisticated than he needs or has the *capability* to use and maintain.

The same situation is true with respect to development of the Planning and Scheduling Modules. For large projects involving design, procurement, and construction, CPM (Critical Path Method) networks are a very popular (and very effective) way of depicting all of the project's major requirements. For large research and development projects involving activities whose outcomes are doubtful, PERT (Program Evaluation and Review Technique) can be utilized most effectively. Since PERT can establish the probability of meeting deadlines, it can be helpful in the development of alternative plans. Fortunately, there are many excellent CPM/PERT software packages on the market today to satisfy a variety of requirements*. Here again, the goal is to define the needs of the individual project, develop an appropriate criterion, and begin an investigation to choose the package which offers the features, options, and capabilities most closely suited to management's needs.

The decision to procure and modify software packages to meet a project's individual requirements versus the prospect of developing a system from scratch will depend on the uniqueness of the system requirements and the availability of system design and programming support. Certainly, it does not pay to design a DBMS or a CPM/PERT software package, in view of the number of well-designed systems currently on the market. But, by the same token, it may not be practical to try to modify someone else's estimating system to suit a particular project's cost control requirements.

Design of the Control System

The design of the information modules for our system essentially involves the development of procedures for collecting, storing, and processing data to produce useful information in a timely manner. Many of these procedures will be instructions for the computer (programs). Hence, a good portion of our information system design efforts deal with selecting the appropriate software packages or designing new packages. Unfortunately, when it comes to the control element of our system, there are few in the way of "canned" packages that are available for our use, primarily because it is generally assumed that if managers are given the information they need, they will automatically initiate the appropriate action to "control" the situation. If we are going to devise a project management system which informs and controls as an integral part of the total project function, we cannot rely on a tacit understanding of what management is expected to do. The mechanism for control must be built into the system

---

* See Chapter 28.

and it must be activated automatically by the appropriate system stimuli. To establish the parameters for design of the control modules of our system, it is necessary to define exactly what we mean by control.

Control

The purpose of control is to ensure that events conform to plan. Controlling involves locating or identifying deviations from plan and taking appropriate action to ensure desired results. Furthermore, control is concerned with the present and involves regulation of what is happening *now*. In a large measure we are concerned with regulating present activities in order to influence future outcomes.

For a project manager, the importance and the need to control are quite clear. The project manager is the one individual totally responsible for accomplishing project objectives on time and within budget. However, to be able to control, the project manager must have some frame of reference to measure against and he must have some way of determining when he deviates from this reference. This brings us to the essential elements of control.

Elements of Control

There are four essential elements involved in control, and these provide the framework for any good project control system. These elements of control are:

1. Setting objectives.
2. Reporting.
3. Evaluating.
4. Taking corrective action.

Obviously, when we talk of controlling something we assume that we have some predefined target or goal. For a project these targets or goals are usually defined in terms of schedule, cost, and technical and quality objectives or requirements. Certainly, the project manager must know what he is trying to accomplish (i.e., get a power plant designed and constructed, design and implement an MIS system, etc.). His problem is to regulate the activities, resources, and events to accomplish the technical, cost, and schedule goals defined in the project plan. This can be done with appropriate status visibility and timely feedback. Thus, he needs an information system which reports on all the important facets of a project, which brings us to the second element of control: reporting.

Since the act of controlling is concerned with the present, the project manager needs a reporting system which is time sensitive. That is, the reporting system must identify problems and requirements in a manner which enables the project manager to make decisions and given direction while there is still time to make a positive change. If the reporting system can only provide feedback considerably after the fact, as a matter of history, then the project manager cannot control his project. Thus, at the heart of control is an information system which gives timely visibility to significant project events. This is why it is so important to have an information system specifically for the project management process.

The third essential element of control is the interpretation and evaluation of the information generated by the information system. This is extremely important because it is the basis for taking corrective action. We know from experience that problems in their early stages of development are seldom black or white. Thus, careful evaluation of indicators, or trends, in project cost, schedule, or technical parameters is extremely vital to the whole process of control. Here again a comprehensive project information system can provide the project manager with a powerful tool for spotlighting early problem areas and requirements. Of course, once having identified a problem, the project manager must take prompt corrective action. This is the fourth and final element of control.

Corrective action means that the project manager has identified a situation which is going to cause a deviation from a desired goal and does something about it. Thus, the project manager must develop a number of alternative approaches to solving the problem and he must select the best approach. In effect, the project manager will examine his options and implement a course of action that best utilizes the resources at his command.

Our interest in designing the control system is to ensure that we have established the appropriate interface between the information modules and those who control and that we have put into place the procedures which will ensure that appropriate action is taken as a result of the information process.

Overview of the Control System

A general scheme for the control element of our system is given in Figure 27-12. The basic function of the control module is to receive inputs from the information system relative to the current status of project activities and accomplishments. Generally, these inputs will be in terms of the cost, schedule, and performance aspects of the project. Each discrete status input is measured against the previously established project goal, for that

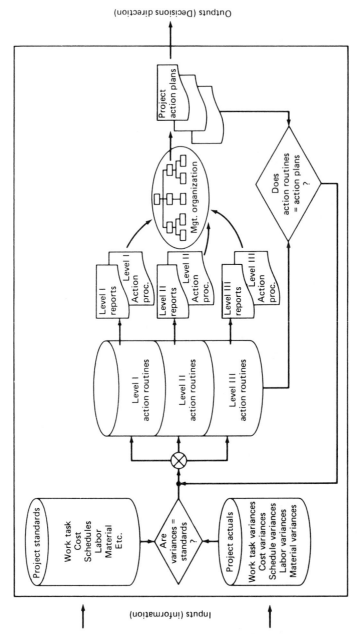

Figure 27-12. Project control system concept.

measurement period, to determine if a variance exists. In simple terms the control module is asking: "How well are we doing against what we had planned to do?" When deviations are identified they are compared against standards which have been established by management. Again, a new set of deviations are identified. We shall call these deviations "action level deviations." That is, the magnitude of the deviations from our standards will automatically identify the level of management responsible for taking corrective action and the time available for initiating this action. Routines are built into the control module so that, if action is not taken, or is not satisfactory by the next reporting period, the module automatically triggers the problem up to the next level of management. The whole process is repeated until the problems are resolved or the problem reaches the highest level of management.

The tangible actions that can be initiated by a project manager to change the course of events of his project are surprisingly few. Basically, these actions involve manipulating or controlling the following:

1. *Resources*—The allocation of resources (men, money, material, facilities, and time) to the project participants (a powerful mechanism for control).
2. *Scope of Work*—Increasing or decreasing the amount of work or the type of work to be done.
3. *Practices*—Establishing or changing the methods, techniques, policies, procedures, systems, or tools used on the project.
4. *Plans and Standards*—The degree and level of effectiveness of control is determined by the project plans and standards established. These may be changed or modified during the life of the project.

Thus, the final outputs of the control module are decisions by project mangement (at all levels) which essentially deal with one or more of the above four factors.

Once the information modules and the control modules have been designed so that they contain the systems and procedures which enable them to function as a unified system within a specific project environment, consideration must be given to the methodology for implementation.

Implementation

Management information system textbooks offer a variety of schemes for putting a new system into operation. These include (a) running parallel systems, (b) operating a pilot system, (c) using the phase-in/phase-out technique, or (d) employing the cut-off method (burning the bridges). In most project environments, it is usually a matter of operating parallel systems until the new system proves itself. If no computer-based system presently exists, the other alternative is to run a pilot system until all the refinements are made. This then becomes the real system.

In any event, the system must be implemented in a real project environment and the test of the system effectiveness is whether or not management is able to use it to *make decisions*. Unfortunately, experience has shown that this has not been the case for most new systems. And this is why the next phase of the program is the most important of all.

PHASE III—DOCUMENTATION, TRAINING, TEST, AND SUPPORT

Documentation Requirements

One task generally disliked by system designers is documentation. Yet, in terms of the effective utilization of the total system, this is probably the most important task to be accomplished. It is especially important that proper system documentation be developed to meet the needs of the system users and those who will maintain and, more than likely, eventually enhance the system. In this regard, four distinct levels of documentation have been identified as follows:

1. *System Documentation*—These documents are designed to provide management with an understanding of how the computer system works at all levels. It will summarize all interfaces, files, and the logic connecting all jobs, providing an overview of the general concepts, features, capabilities, and constraints.
2. *Program Documentation*—Program Documentation provides the programmers and analysts with an understanding of the relation between their own work and the entire effort. This procedure provides a definition of the step-by-step logic developed within each program.
3. *Operations Documentation*—The Operations Documentation dictates the relationship between the functional tasks and the procedures, and establishes a time sequence. It dictates the responsibility for each task, providing a procedure to determine all action taken following a request. This procedure must contain the necessary information to process job steps.
4. *User Documentation*—This section provides a formal description of all functions necessary to input data into the system. Relevant information for the control and processing of source documents and reports should be described.

Actual development of the above required documentation should start quite early in the design effort. In fact, documentation should be a mandatory effort in parallel with system design and development. Ideally, the program manager should devise a documentation checklist which specifies the four levels of documents associated with each major system element or module and provides a timetable for the rough draft, final draft, and fully released documents. Generally speaking, the rough draft documents, which may consist of simple outlines, will suffice throughout the early design effort. However, by the time the systems are fairly well defined (during the program development and implementation stages), this documentation should begin to evolve into descriptive manuals. Once the validation and demonstration tests of the systems have been completed, the revision and publication of final system documentation manuals should be a routine, straightforward task.

A special note of caution is in order relative to documentation. In any program requiring a year or more to complete, it is highly unlikely that the original team will remain intact. Personnel turnover is inevitable; therefore, it is absolutely vital to maintain a consistent, strong documentation trail throughout the project.

Training Considerations

In similar fashion, training should start very early in the program. A common error is to wait until all the bugs are totally out of the system before attempting to train system users. The system will have greater acceptance and be utilized more effectively if all levels of management are gradually made to understand the philosophy and mechanics of the system. This can be accomplished by handling the training program in stages as follows:

- *1st Stage Training—System Philosophy.* A series of orientation seminars should be planned to explain to management the role of computer-based information and control systems in the management of large projects. These seminars should focus on the types of information that can be provided to all levels of management and dwell on how the system is used to tie together all the project functions. It is particularly appropriate to organize workshop sessions to get the various levels of management to critique prototype reports and system approaches. This feedback can be used to enhance the actual system design work.
- *2nd Stage Training—System Capabilities.* This stage of training will

discuss the "nuts and bolts" of the system and focus on middle management and project specialists. Training will deal with specifics and should address such items as development of the CPM network schedule and the report outputs of the Planning and Scheduling Module, Estimating Module, and so on. Those organizations that will depend on the system for regular data and reports must be made to understand what type of information they can and cannot get from the system.

- *3rd Stage Training—System Operations.* Formalized training must be provided to those who will operate and maintain the system. Generally, this type of training is directed to technicians and system engineers and will include specialized courses offered by equipment manufacturers and software vendors. This portion of the training program should also focus on standard operational procedures associated with the system that may be developed by the in-house MIS organization.
- *4th Stage Training—System Utilization.* This stage of training should be a natural follow-up from the first stage or System Philosophy training discussed above. A very strong attempt should be made to get project management, selected middle management, and top management involved in seminar-type sessions to give them an opportunity to see firsthand how the system can be used to enhance their functions and capabilities. Very carefully structured "what if" type problems can be used to illustrate use of the computer-based information system in the quick evaluation of a number of alternatives or options to arrive at practical project decisions.

Obviously, the scope and level of the training to be provided will be somewhat dependent on budget restrictions and time availability. Nevertheless, money spent for training purposes will help to dispel the mystique surrounding the computer-based system and increase the likelihood that the system will be implemented and utilized successfully.

System Validation

The last major milestone in the project information and control system development should be a validation test. This test should not be confused with the unit test that system designers or programmers will perform to check out the software packages. A validation test should cover all aspects of the system operation and utilization in a real-life project environment. This includes everything from data collection, receipt and utilization of the final output report, and subsequent management action. A formal test plan should be written and, at a minimum, this test plan must address all of the system criteria defined in the system program plan. If the program manager has been conscientiously keeping his program plan up to date, this should be a fairly straightforward effort.

Actual formal validation testing may be spread over a long period of time, especially if the system is developed and brought into actual use one module at a time. The program manager and system designers must objectively assess the results of each test and determine if they are within the established criteria. Obviously, there will always be some revisions and improvements that are desirable, but the program manager must be resolute and selective and ensure that the system is usable in a timely manner.

System Support

A final word is in order relative to the long-term use of computer-based project information and control systems. While these systems are complex and costly to develop, this cost is small in comparison to the cost of the projects to be managed and the benefits to be derived from proper use of the systems. To ensure that the system is used effectively, management must take an additional step and provide a full-time staff of personnel dedicated totally to maintaining, supporting, improving, and constantly educating the user with regard to system capabilities. Otherwise, the system's effectiveness will diminish and reams of unread computer reports will begin to pile up on the corner of the project manager's desk.

FUTURE DEVELOPMENTS

Truly useful information and control systems for project management have become a reality in recent years primarily because of the advancements in computer hardware and software. Computer speed and capacity have increased dramatically while cost has declined substantially. Innovative software programs have been devised while computer literacy has become commonplace. Yet we have barely tapped the potential of technology to devise more powerful tools for project management. The next generation of systems for project management will capitalize on the maturing techinques in communication, hardware for workstations, and system software for problem solving and decision making. The fundamental job of project management to plan and direct organizations and resources to accomplish a specific objective will be enhanced by tools for communication which can integrate organization and function over widely separated areas. Thus, satellite communication, electronic conferencing, local area network, electronic mail, and the automated office or workstation will be fundamental to any project management system. In addition, the ability to process information—that is, the receipt, storage, manipulation, organization, and presentation of information in a form that is useful to the user—is now possible because of advancements being made in computers, data base systems, and software. Because these systems can be integrated to form networks, we can devise project management systems in which the project participants can share information on a real-time basis and where detailed planning and control is performed at the level where the work is done (see Figure 27-13).

However, the most exciting potential for project management is the field of Artificial Intelligence (AI). Advancements in AI software and computer workstations are contributing to the development of so-called expert systems for planning, scheduling, monitoring, analysis, and decision making for a wide range of management and technical problems. The potential of AI in devising so-called expert systems is to enhance the ability of the user by providing him with tools that not only access a vast range of information quickly, but provide the means to interpret this information through some rational process much in the fashion as an expert would. The specific applications of AI are well beyond the goals of this chapter; however, the potential for providing very powerful tools for

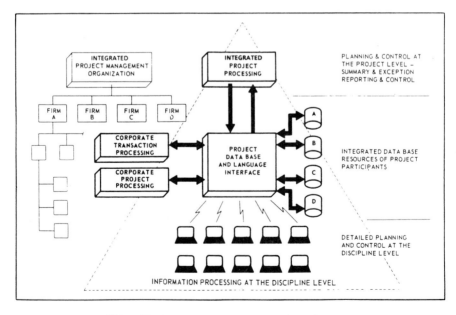

Figure 27-13. Integrated planning and control system.

project management must be recognized and accepted with an open mind. For it is only by visualizing the potential for applying these new tools to project management problems that will we be able to bring order and direction to an increasingly complex environment.

SUMMARY

As projects become more numerous, larger, and more complex, the need increases for systems which provide for the systematic management of project information and action. These systems should be designed to function within a particular organizational environment and must reflect the unique project management requirements of that organization.

It is important to address the information system and the control system as two separate but highly dependent components of a total integrated computer-based project management system. In the design of the information system, the focus is on the procedures and techniques for collecting, storing, and processing data to produce information concerning project plans, schedules, cost, and performance parameters. In the control system the goal is the development of procedures and routines for evaluating plans against actuals to define the deviations or variances in plans, schedules, cost, and performance; the assessment of the acceptability of these variances (evaluated against some predefined standards); and the systematic development and implementation of action plans by the appropriate organizational units to produce decisions and/or directions which attempt to correct the project's deviations from plan.

Actual design, development, and implementation of an integrated system should follow a well-defined project methodolgy. The first step in this process involves making a comprehensive analysis of what is required in the way of information resources and control procedures to make project management function successfully within a particular organization environment. Once this analysis is completed, the actual design and development of the system(s) can be initiated. Design and development involves procurement of specialized software packages and/or design of new packages, as well as the development of the procedures for management action. The eventual success of the new systems will depend to a large degree on how accurately they meet the requirements specifications (as defined in the initial study), how well the systems have been documented, and how adequately the using organizations have been trained to apply these systems to the actual project environment. The true value of a project information and control system will be realized only when it enables a relatively small project management organization to successfully plan, direct, and control a complex, expensive, high-risk undertaking.

BIBLIOGRAPHY

Articles

Baugh, Eddie W. and Scamell, Dr. Richard W. "Team Approach to Systems Analysis." *Journal of Systems Management*, 32–35 (April, 1975).

Brown, Foster. "The Systems Development Process." *Journal of Systems Management*, 34–39 (December, 1977).

Chapman, Charles H. et al. "Project Cost Controls for Research, Development and Demonstration Projects." *PMI Proceedings*, 53–63 (October, 1979).

Clarke, William. "The Requirements for Project Management Software: A Survey of PMI Members." *PMI Proceedings*, 71–79 (October, 1979).

Cullingford, Graham, Mawdesley, Michael J. and Chandler, Robert L. "Design and Implementation of an Integrated Cost and Schedule System for the Construction Industry." *PMI Proceedings*, 390–397 (October, 1977).

Finneran, Thomas R. "Data Base Systems Design Guidelines." *Journal of Systems Management*, 26–30 (March, 1978).

Gildersleeve, Thomas R. "Optimum Program Structure Documentation Tool." *Journal of Systems Management*, 6–11 (March, 1978).

Herzog, John P. "System Evaluation Technique for Users." *Journal of Systems Management*, 30–35 (May, 1975).

Mattiace, John M. "Applied Cybernetics Within R&D." *Journal of Systems Management*, 32–36 (December, 1972).

Miller, Earl J. "Chapter 9—Project Information Systems and Controls." In *Planning, Engineering, and Construction of Electric Power Generation Facilities*, Jack H. Willenbrock and H. Randolph Thomas, ed. Wiley, New York, 1980.

Niwa, Kiyoshi et al. "Development of a 'Risk' Alarm System for Big Construction Projects." *PMI Proceedings*, 221–229 (October, 1979).

Ramsaur, William F. and Smith, John D. "Project Management Systems Tailored for Selective Project Management Approach." *PMI Proceedings*, IV-A.1–IV-A.7 (October, 1978).

Ross, Ronad G. "Evaluating Data Base Management Systems." *Journal of Systems Management*, 30–35 (January, 1976).

Tuman, John, Jr. "The Problems and Realities Involved in Developing an Effective Project Information and Control System." *PMI Proceedings*, 279–293 (October, 1977).

Wilkinson, Joseph W. "Guidelines for Designing Systems." *Journal of Systems Management*, 36–40 (December, 1974).

Books

Archibald, Russel D. *Managing High-Technology Programs and Projects*. Wiley, New York, 1976.

Ashby, W. Ross. *An Introduction to Cybernetics*. Methuen, London, 1964.

Carlsen, Robert D. and Lewis, James A. *The Systems Analysis Workbook: A Complete Guide to Project Implementation and Control*. Hall, New Jersey, 1980.

Cleland, David I. and King, William R. *Systems Analysis and Project Management*. 3rd ed. McGraw-Hill, New York, 1983.

Fuchs, Walter Robert. *Cybernetics for the Modern Mind*. Translated by K. Kellner. Macmillan, New York, 1970.

Katzan, Harry, Jr. *Computer Data Management and Data Base Technology*. Van Nostrand Reinhold, New York, 1975.

Kerzner, Harold. *Project Management: A Systems Approach to Planning, Scheduling and Controlling. Van Nostrand Reinhold, New York, 1979.*

Martin, Charles C. *Project Management: How to Make It Work.* AMACOM, New York, 1976.

Murdick, Robert G. and Ross, Joel E. *Information Systems for Modern Management.* Prentice-Hall, Englewood Cliffs, N.J., 1971.

Myers, Glenford J. *Reliable Software Through Composite Design.* Petrocelli/Charter, New York, 1975.

O'Brien, James J. *Scheduling Handbook.* McGraw-Hill, New York, 1969.

Orlicky, Joseph. *The Successful Computer System Its Planning, Development, and Management in a Business Enterprise.* McGraw-Hill, New York, 1969.

Prothro, Vivian C. *Information Management Systems Data Base Primer.* Petrocelli/Charter, New York, 1976.

28. Computers in Project Management*

Harvey A. Levine†

Project management can be a very involved process, requiring a great deal of expertise in many disciplines. It requires that these processes be very structured and organized. It requires the development and processing of large volumes of data. It requires frequent reporting of plans and progress.

While the complete scope of project management requires much more than planning and scheduling, tracking and control, it is these specific functions that can be so effectively helped by the use of computers. It was 30 years ago that the old lumbering mainframes were put into service to support project management. For most of those years, access to computerized project management was reserved for the large organizations: those that had management information system operations, an army of dedicated project control specialists, and barrels of money to spend on hardware and software. But because of the computer technology changes during the first half of this decade, the benefits of computerized project management have been put within the reach of any potential user, for any project application.

During the past few years, the world of automation has been turned

---

* Chapter material used with permission from Osborne/McGraw-Hill, CA.

† Harvey A. Levine is the founder and principal of The Project Knowledge Group, Clifton Park, New York, a consulting firm specializing in project management software selection and evaluation, project management training, and project management using microcomputers. Mr. Levine is the author of the book *Project Management Using Microcomputers* (Osborne/McGraw-Hill), 1986. Mr. Levine provided project management applications, systems design, and consulting services to the General Electric Company for 24 years, has written several articles on project management, and has taught project management in both business and university environments. He is past Chairman of the Board of the Project Management Institute.

inside out by the fantastic success of the microcomputer and the acceptance of the microcomputer in the business community. With that acceptance has come the development of computer programs for use in solving business problems. Now, with a minimum investment, and bypassing the MIS bureaucracies, the doors to computer utilization in the business place have been opened to all of us.

Who would have believed, just a few years ago, that we would have this abundance of project management software available for the casual, as well as the serious, user, and at prices that are enticingly low. The microcomputer has given us accessibility to sophisticated programs that only recently were the private domain of the information systems gurus. The nature of project management systems, a combination of simple algorithms, calculations, and data base management, is a natural for computers. The need to do "what if" analyses, in the typical project management environment, was an additional driver of the microcomputer explosion.

These products address the entire range of the project management marketplace. There are programs for the local theater group that can help with the planning of their next production. There are programs for bankers, and programs for researchers. Programs exist at every level for the assignment and tracking of resources, and for cash flow planning and monitoring. Even formal project management organizations, with mainframe computer systems, are finding it advantageous to supplement, or even replace, their expensive batch systems with some of the very sophisticated professional-level project management software programs that are available for the microcomputer.

This chapter fully explains the planning and control process, while discussing why computers are a useful—almost necessary—tool for the performance of project management. It begins with a definition of what gets managed, and a list of typical project planning and control functions and phases.

Next, we invite you to follow the typical process, in detail, starting with establishing project objectives, defining the work, and developing the baseline schedule; then on to the development of resource plans and budgets; to the tracking of schedule, resources, and costs; and finally to a review of reporting and graphics for displaying the results of the project control efforts.

Throughout these discussions, we will define the functions themselves and then provide information relative to the support for these functions that is available through the various commercial microcomputer-based software packages, and furnish guidance on how to specify and evaluate such software for your applications and needs.

PROJECT MANAGEMENT: A DEFINITION

It is important to understand the specific characteristics of a project if we are to understand the functions of project management. Furthermore, if we cannot recognize the differences between the management of a project and the management of the day-to-day business functions, then why should we acquire and learn new software? This is one of the fastest-growing segments of the software industry. There must be something significantly different in these two management areas, and indeed there is!

An underlying factor in general management is that one is dealing with a long-term, continuing business, with many of the measurements being associated with current performance as compared to prior performance as well as annual or other time-phased objectives.

In a nonproject environment, this management would concentrate on productivity-oriented and time-phased measurements. How many widgets did we manufacture this week? How does this compare to last week? How does this compare to the same week, last year? What were profits, or sales, or orders this week, as compared to whatever? What were our applied hours for this week versus last? Or more important, what were our unapplied hours? What were our expenditures for the last quarter versus our budget for that quarter? What is our staffing level in Department A versus our plan for this date? How is product A doing against product B? How is our product A doing against our competitor's product A?

Quality and human resource factors are, of course, also measured. What is our reject trend? Has our employee satisfaction index improved? What is the trend in customer satisfaction? Are we meeting our equal opportunity employment goals? The industry does not matter here. We can ask these questions about a construction firm. We can equally apply them to a library, a manufacturing firm, or a fast-food chain. The underlying factor is that one is dealing with a long-term, continuing business, with many of the measurements being associated with current performance as compared to prior performance, as well as annual or other time-phased objectives.

Keep this definition of general management in mind as we define the characteristics of a project and see that those characteristics demand that we use a different basis for project management.

A *project* is a group of tasks, to be performed in a definable time period, to meet a specific set of objectives. In general, a project will exhibit most of the following conditions:

- It is likely to be a unique, one-time program.
- It will have a life cycle, with a specific start and end.

- It will have a work scope that can be broken up into definable tasks.
- It will have a budget for its execution.
- It may require the utilization of multiple resources. Many of these resources may be in short supply and have to be shared with other projects.
- It may require the establishment of a special organization for its execution or require the crossing of traditional organizational boundaries.

While some of the general business measurements can apply to a projects situation, the project measurement framework will be primarily structured so that budgetary and manpower control is based on the accomplishment of the defined work rather than time frames. Also, reporting and measuring will be categorized by the various sections of the work (deliverables, physical areas, cost accounts) as well as by the traditional functional divisions (responsible areas).

It is these differences, this different measurement framework, that generated the need for the development of separate project management software for planning and control.

Project management software supports the planning and control of such elements as the work scope, or contents, of a project; the project timing; human and nonhuman resources; budgeting and costs, and communications.

What Gets Managed

According to a definition developed by the Project Management Institute, in the managing of projects we will normally be involved in the following:

- Scope management.
- Time management.
- Human resource management.
- Cost management.
- Quality management.
- Communication management.

For each of these functions, it is necessary to plan, organize, direct, and control. Every project must have a plan. And it is this plan that becomes the basis for control. As this chapter addresses the utilization of microcomputers in project management, we will concentrate on the planning and control aspects of project management.

THE TYPICAL PLANNING AND CONTROL FUNCTIONS

The following is an listing of the typical functions involved in planning and controlling projects:

- Establish the project objectives.
- Define the work.
- Determine the work timing.
- Establish the resource availability and requirements.
- Establish a cost baseline.
- Evaluate the baseline plan.
- Optimize the baseline plan.
- "Freeze" the baseline plan.
- Track work progress.
- Track actual costs.
- Compare progress and costs to the baseline plan.
- Evaluate performance.
- Forecast, analyze, and recommend corrective action.

A flowchart of these functions is presented in Figure 28-1. Each of these functions will be discussed in detail later in this chapter.

PHASES OF PROJECT MANAGEMENT

Before we leave this description of project management, let's go back to the project management definition statement again. We said that project management is the planning, organizing, directing, and controlling of resources for a specific time period to meet a specific set of one-time objectives. That specific time period generally consists of three primary phases:

- Proposal phase.
- Implementation Phase.
- Closeout phase.

The implementation phase really consists of two distinct subphases:

- Planning phase.
- Execution phase.

In Figure 28-1, we can see the functions associated with these two implementation phases. Those items leading to the development of the

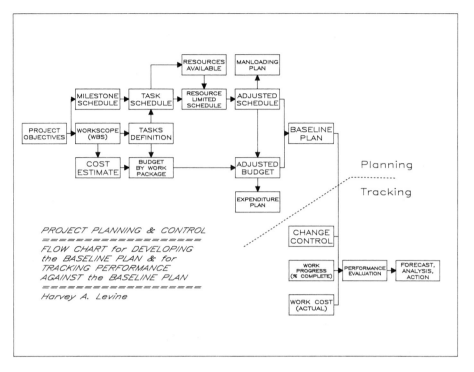

Figure 28-1. Project planning and control—flowchart.

baseline plan are associated with the planning phase. The remaining functions are part of the execution phase.

It is extremely important to recognize the impact of these phases on your choice of a planning and control system. If you only need to support the development of proposals or baseline plans, then you can utilize software that only does *planning*. On the other hand, if you are to *control* a project, you will need software that provides for progress tracking and comparison to the plan.

When many of the PC-based project management software programs were first introduced, several of them did not have the capability to retain a baseline plan. In such programs, the entry of any current data obliterated the original data, thereby prohibiting the direct use of the project data base for the comparison of actual to plan—a necessary ingredient for project control. Mention of the lack of these functions is also often missing in the magazine reviews of software. Today, there are very few programs that do not have some means of comparing the current status to the plan, but they vary considerably.

Below are listed the necessary features for project control.

**Necessary Features for
Project Control**

- The ability to save a version of your data base as a baseline or target plan, or to be able to freeze a set of data within your project data base for comparison to current status and actual expenditures.
- The ability to enter actual start and finish dates without having those entries override the plan dates.
- The ability to revise task durations or remaining durations without having those entries override the plan dates.
- The ability to enter actual costs incurred, for comparison to the budget.
- The ability to record actual resource use.

THE TYPICAL PLANNING AND CONTROL FUNCTIONS AND THE ROLE OF THE COMPUTER

Getting back to the list presented earlier in this chapter, let's complete this overview of project management with a closer look at those primary functions and a look at how the computer can be effectively used to aid the project manager in the execution of these functions.

Establish the Project Objectives

The Function.   It is strange, perhaps even annoying, that this first item is most often missing from the discussion of project planning and control. But isn't this the very reason for having project planning and control? The plan must be developed to support a set of objectives. These objectives should be defined in the general terms of time objectives, budget objectives, technical, etc. But, also, they should be defined, where possible, in the terms of deliverable end items. The definition of the project objectives should also be related to the overall organization objectives and to the organization's policies.

Where Does the Computer Fit In?   This first set of project planning tasks sets the stage for work that will eventually be processed on the computer.

This setting of the objectives, and associated strategizing and organizing, cannot be helped much by the computer. Don't look to the computer to do the front-end thinking and decision making that must be the responsibility of the project manager and top management. There are several software packages that provide some guidance for this function in their users' manuals.

Define the Work

The Function.　To develop a baseline plan, you will push forward in three parallel paths, with considerable crosstalk between them. You will be defining the work to be done, the resources and budget for that work, and the timing for that work. Obviously, the whole thing is dependent upon the quality of the work scope definition.

A popular and useful approach toward defining the work scope is called the *Work Breakdown Structure* (WBS). In this approach, the project objectives are placed at the top of a diagram as deliverable end items. Each top-level segment of the project is then subdivided into smaller groups, in a manner similar to typical organization charts. The work breakdown continues until you have groups of activities (or tasks) that would comprise a natural set of work. These smallest groups are often called *work packages*. Several other names have been given to this approach, all of which also are descriptive of the technique. These include *tree diagram, hierarchical chart, top-down planning,* and *gozinto chart*. In all cases, the lower elements go into the next higher level. A hierarchical numbering system is generally used to facilitate the rolling-up (or summarization) of data to the various levels of the WBS. A multipart numbering system can be used to also include codes for roll-up in other categories, such as department codes, accounting codes, etc. Figure 28-2 illustrates such a WBS.

Each of the work packages is reviewed to establish a set of task definitions. There are many ways to get to this necessary list of tasks. The WBS approach has many advantages, including better organization of the work, elimination of "reinventing the wheel," and use of the WBS as a checklist. The WBS also facilitates summarization and reporting. The list of the tasks will be used as a basis for scheduling, resource planning, and budgeting.

Where Does the Computer Fit In?　Most of this portion of the project planning process is *not* done by the computer. A few of the vendors, notably ViewPoint and Harvard Total Project Manager II, have incorporated a top-down planning or WBS feature in their software. In these

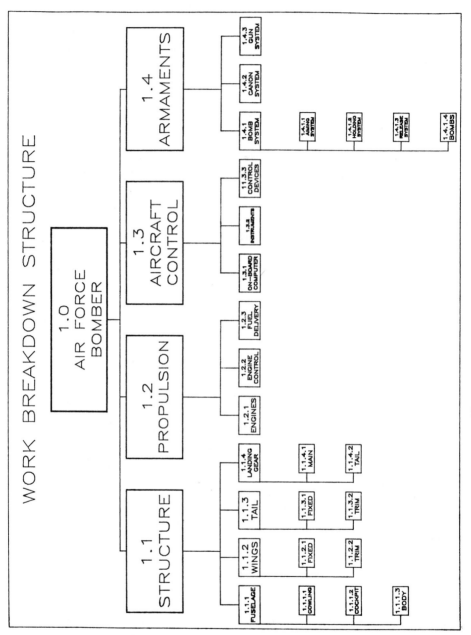

Figure 28-2. Work breakdown structure.

programs, the user can define the WBS to the system, which then automatically uses that definition as a hierarchical structure for the project data. While certainly useful, the important thing is that the program that you select have the facility to allow the defining of a coding structure for the WBS and other selection/summarization criteria. You should opt for at least three code fields for you to enter WBS codes, responsibilities, cost account codes, phase codes, and so forth. The system, of course, should allow you to sort and select on any of these codes.

A potentially helpful feature of the aforementioned ViewPoint program is that the plans developed for each of the WBS sections can saved as a "region" in a "library." These library regions can be recalled when a new schedule is being developed and inserted into the new network.

Define the Work Timing

The Function.   Part of the definition of project objectives will be the establishing of the overall timing parameters of the project. These timing objectives and assumptions should be first processed into a project milestone schedule (see Figure 28-3). The milestone schedule provides guidance by defining the time windows into which the task scheduling will attempt to fit.

Now, with the list of tasks and the milestone schedule in hand, you can take a first cut at developing the task schedule.

The detailed schedule can be either duration driven or resource driven. The more common basis is the duration-driven approach. Working with your list of tasks, you will add the expected time duration for the execution of each task. Next, identify the relationship of each task to each other task in the project, that is, develop the precedence rules for each task. Methods of doing this are numerous, although they all aim at the same objective—to enable the computation of the earliest start and finish times for each task.

The assignment of task durations and relationships would produce a schedule that assumed that there were no other factors that dictated when an activity could start or must be finished, except those two components. Yet, we know that there are times when even if an activity's predecessors are complete, the activity cannot be started until other, external conditions are satisfied. For instance, you may not want to plant grass in Wisconsin in January, even if the preceding landscaping has been completed. Or you may want to force the completion of the roof of a building before the snow falls, even though the network logic may dictate that the roof need not be completed until February to support the successor tasks.

Therefore, the last element of determining the work timing is to identify

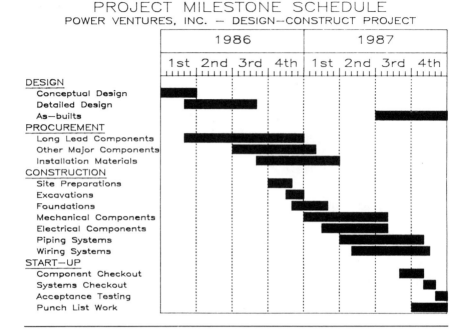

Figure 28-3. Project milestone schedule.

all activities that require imposed date constraints, often referred to as "start no earlier than" and "finish no later than" constraints.

In a resource-driven task schedule, the precedence relationships are still required. But, instead of single task durations, one identifies the labor resources required. This entails the quantification of the total man-hours (for each resource) required to do the task, and the allowable crew sizes. The scheduler (computer) can then determine the task durations. The overall result is the same as above. It is a common practice to do a duration-driven schedule first so as to get an idea of the best schedule attainable without resource limit considerations.

Where Does the Computer Fit In?   Essentially, at this point you have built a model of the project work. This is called a *critical path network*. The computation of the early start and finish is usually performed by a computer and is referred to as the *network analysis*. Once the latest task is identified, via the forward pass of the network analysis, a backward computation can be made to determine the latest that each activity can start

and finish without delaying the overall project. You will also have identified the relative time priority of each activity, because the difference
between the early dates and the latest dates indicates the *float* or *slack* for
each task.

The task schedule can be displayed in three typical formats: a tabular
listing (see Figure 28-4), a bar (Gantt) chart (see Figure 28-5), and a
network diagram. The network diagram can be presented in two formats.
The simple flowchart style, as shown in Figure 28-6, depicts only the
relationships between activities without a graphic reference to the time

```
Schedule Name:   PROJECT SPLASH
Project Manager: Esther Williams
As of date:      29-May-86  1:31am   Schedule File: C:\TLDATA\POOL529
```

Task	How Long	Early Start		Early End		Late Total Start		Late Total End	
Decide To Do	2 days	31-Mar-86	8:00am	1-Apr-86	5:00pm	31-Mar-86	8:00am	1-Apr-86	5:00pm
Gather Info	8 days	2-Apr-86	8:00am	11-Apr-86	5:00pm	2-Apr-86	8:00am	11-Apr-86	5:00pm
Concept	5 days	14-Apr-86	8:00am	18-Apr-86	5:00pm	14-Apr-86	8:00am	18-Apr-86	5:00pm
Establish Program	3 days	28-Apr-86	8:00am	30-Apr-86	5:00pm	28-Apr-86	8:00am	30-Apr-86	5:00pm
Estimate Costs	2 days	1-May-86	8:00am	2-May-86	5:00pm	1-May-86	8:00am	2-May-86	5:00pm
Apply For Permit	3 days	1-May-86	8:00am	5-May-86	5:00pm	27-May-86	8:00am	29-May-86	5:00pm
Issue Permit	15 days	6-May-86	8:00am	26-May-96	5:00pm	30-May-86	8:00am	19-Jun-86	5:00pm
Apply For Loan	3 days	5-May-86	8:00am	7-May-86	5:00pm	7-May-86	8:00am	9-May-86	5:00pm
Issue Loan	10 days	8-May-86	8:00am	21-May-86	5:00pm	12-May-86	8:00am	23-May-86	5:00pm
Price Fencing	5 days	21-Apr-86	8:00am	25-Apr-86	5:00pm	21-Apr-86	8:00am	25-Apr-86	5:00pm
Order Fencing	2 days	5-May-86	8:00am	6-May-86	5:00pm	16-May-86	8:00am	19-May-86	5:00pm
Fencing Delivered	15 days	7-May-86	8:00am	27-May-86	5:00pm	20-May-86	8:00am	9-Jun-86	5:00pm
Erect Fence	5 days	10-Jun-86	8:00am	16-Jun-86	5:00pm	10-Jun-86	8:00am	16-Jun-86	5:00pm
Price Patio Kits	5 days	21-Apr-86	8:00am	25-Apr-86	5:00pm	21-Apr-86	8:00am	25-Apr-86	5:00pm
Patio Detailed Plans	5 days	5-May-86	8:00am	9-May-86	5:00pm	16-May-86	8:00am	22-May-86	5:00pm
Obtain Support Material	2 days	21-May-86	8:00am	22-May-86	5:00pm	23-May-86	8:00am	26-May-86	5:00pm
Dig Holes	1 day	27-May-86	8:00am	27-May-86	5:00pm	27-May-86	8:00am	27-May-86	5:00pm
Form	3 days	28-May-86	8:00am	30-May-86	5:00pm	28-May-86	8:00am	30-May-86	5:00pm
Pour	1 day	2-Jun-86	8:00am	2-Jun-86	5:00pm	2-Jun-86	8:00am	2-Jun-86	5:00pm
Cure	3 days	3-Jun-86	8:00am	5-Jun-86	5:00pm	3-Jun-86	8:00am	5-Jun-86	5:00pm
Strip & Backfill	1 day	6-Jun-86	8:00am	6-Jun-86	5:00pm	6-Jun-86	8:00am	6-Jun-86	5:00pm
Order Patio Kit	2 days	5-May-86	8:00am	6-May-86	5:00pm	7-May-86	8:00am	8-May-86	5:00pm
Deliver Patio Kit	14 days	9-May-86	8:00am	28-May-86	5:00pm	20-May-86	8:00am	6-Jun-86	5:00pm
Erect Patio Base	4 days	9-Jun-86	8:00am	12-Jun-86	5:00pm	9-Jun-86	8:00am	12-Jun-86	5:00pm
Erect Patio Rails	2 days	13-Jun-86	8:00am	16-Jun-86	5:00pm	13-Jun-86	8:00am	16-Jun-86	5:00pm
Finish Patio	2 days	17-Jun-86	8:00am	18-Jun-86	5:00pm	17-Jun-86	8:00am	18-Jun-86	5:00pm
Get Pool Quotes	5 days	21-Apr-86	8:00am	25-Apr-86	5:00pm	21-Apr-86	8:00am	25-Apr-86	5:00pm
Order Pool	2 days	5-May-86	8:00am	6-May-86	5:00pm	5-May-86	8:00am	6-May-86	5:00pm
Pool Delivered	18 days	7-May-86	8:00am	30-May-86	5:00pm	7-May-86	8:00am	30-May-86	5:00pm
Install Pool	10 days	2-Jun-86	8:00am	13-Jun-86	5:00pm	2-Jun-86	8:00am	13-Jun-86	5:00pm
Fill Pool	3 days	16-Jun-86	8:00am	18-Jun-86	5:00pm	17-Jun-86	8:00am	19-Jun-86	5:00pm
Clean-up	2 days	17-Jun-86	8:00am	18-Jun-86	5:00pm	17-Jun-86	8:00am	18-Jun-86	5:00pm
Send Invites	1 day	16-Jun-86	8:00am	16-Jun-86	5:00pm	18-Jun-86	8:00am	18-Jun-86	5:00pm
Get Party Supplies	1 day	17-Jun-86	8:00am	17-Jun-86	5:00pm	18-Jun-86	8:00am	18-Jun-86	5:00pm
Hold Pool Party	1 day	19-Jun-86	8:00am	19-Jun-86	5:00pm	19-Jun-86	8:00am	19-Jun-86	5:00pm

Figure 28-4. Tabular schedule (Time Line).

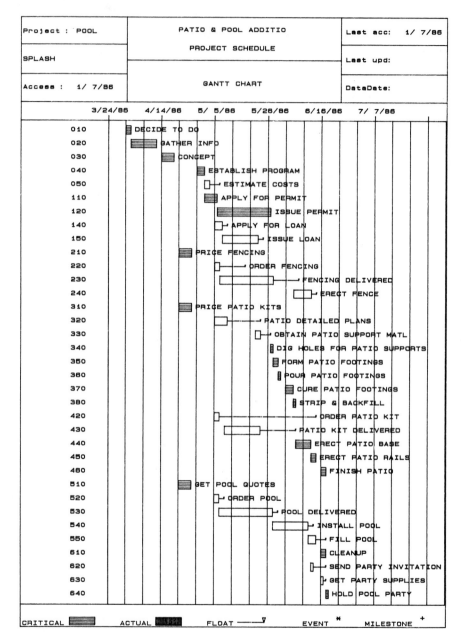

Figure 28-5. Bar (Gantt) chart schedule (PROMIS).

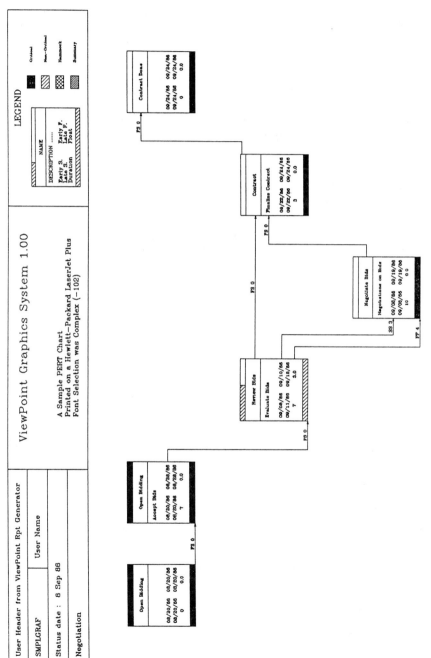

Figure 28-6. Network diagram—node format (ViewPoint).

duration of each task. Eash task is usually drawn in a box describing the task and its duration, schedule dates, and float. A more cogent format is the time-phased logic diagram (see Figure 28-7), which plots the activities against a time scale, thereby depicting both the relative time and dependencies of each task. While the latter style is more informative, we usually pay a price in loss of clarity in presentation. As task placement is now controlled by task duration and schedule, the time-phased network logic diagram can become very busy and difficult to read. This is controlled by careful selection and grouping of activities, assuming that your software will allow you to have such control over the diagramming process.

The mass market media and software vendors appear to have developed their own language to define these two network diagram formats. A common, but erroneous, term for the simple network logic diagram is "PERT chart." On occasion you will also see the time-phased logic diagram referred to as a "CPM diagram." PERT and CPM refer to the two original computerized scheduling protocols, developed in the late 1950s,

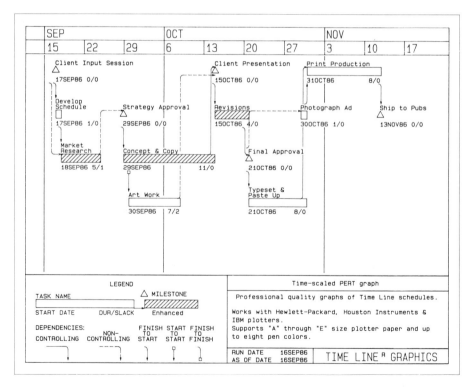

Figure 28-7. Network—time-phased logic diagram format (Time Line).

that form the basis for today's popular project management programs. Most of today's programs use the activity-on-the-node format rather than the event-oriented PERT format or the activity-on-the-arrow CPM format.

Establish the Resource Availability and Requirements

The Function. Your needs in resource allocation and costing will determine how you look at the resource and cost functions of project management software. Resources include both manpower and materials. There is a tremendous range of capabilities for resource planning. It is important, then, to take a look at the levels of detail that can be addressed in resource planning and to determine what capabilities you will need for the level of planning and control that you will need to exercise on your projects. Beginning at the lowest end of the detail range, you may wish to:

- Assign task responsibility to an individual.
- Assign more than one individual to a task.
- Assign multiple resources (manloading) to a task from groups of pooled resources, without identifying a specific, named individual for a specific task.
- Define a *constant* limit for any pooled resource and have the scheduling system show the demand against the availability (resource indication).
- Define a *variable* limit for any pooled resource and have the scheduling system show the demand against the availability (resource indication).
- On a person-to-person basis, have the system reschedule tasks so that an individual is not working on more than one task at any time (simplified version of resource allocation).
- On a person-to-person basis, define the man hour availability (per day or week), and have the system reschedule tasks so that an individual is not working on a task load that exceeds that availability (another simplified version of resource allocation).
- Define a limit (single or variable) for any pooled resource and have the scheduling system reschedule tasks to hold the resource demand to that availability (resource/limited-resource allocation).
- Define a desired limit for any pooled resource, and a must-hold end date, and have the scheduling system reschedule tasks to attempt to stay within the resource limits, but only if the rescheduling does not violate the required (latest) dates (time/limited-resource allocation).

- Define a desired limit for any pooled resource, and a must-hold end date, and have the scheduling system reschedule tasks, *and availability,* to level the resource demand and hold the end date (resource leveling).

Even within these definitions, there are finite differences than can be important to the user. For instance, if you are assigning multiple resources to a task, do all of the assigned resources have to be assigned for the full duration of the task? In the real world, it is likely that some resources will only have to be applied for parts of certain tasks. But in most programs, especially at the mass market ($395–$495) level, you cannot define this criterion.

Where Does the Computer Fit In?   As you can see, the variations on a resource theme are almost without limit and cannot be determined by a simple review or specification statement that such-and-such a program has resource leveling. Your selection of a project management software program will have to take into consideration which of the levels of detail you need, based on the preceding listing.

Regardless of the level of detail used, the process essentially calls for you to work with the list of tasks, itemizing the resources (labor, materials, services, etc.) required for each task. If you have developed a schedule for these tasks, you can now get an indication of the total resources required to execute the job on a period-by-period basis. Computers are very good at producing *resource histograms.* If you can define the desired or mandated resource availability, you should be able to note and evaluate when the required resources exceed these limits. This function (see Figure 28-8a) is called *resource aggregation* or *resource indication.*

If you require both resource allocation and leveling capabilities, how likely are you to get efficient utilization of available resources from your program? Well, that depends on the algorithms programmed into that software, and how finite the work resource parameters can be defined. A major cause of peaks and valleys (after leveling), is the inability to "split" activities. The assumption, by most programs, is that once a task has been started (or allocated resources), it must be scheduled to completion without interruption. There are a few sophisticated programs (MicroPlanner, for one) that allow the user to state whether a task can be split, and if so, what the minimum split duration is. SuperProject is another.

Once again, when it comes to evaluating programs against your resource criteria, you will first have to clarify those criteria per the above variations, and then actually use the candidate programs to see if they do what you need them to.

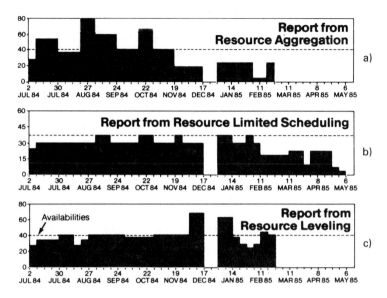

Figure 28-8. Resource histograms. (Courtesy of Computerline, Inc.)

Before we leave the area of resource planning, let's dwell a moment on the concepts of the smoothing of peaks and valleys, and staying within resource limits. While we can use the common labels of "resource leveling" and "resource allocation," the terms are not always clear, and, as usual, there can be variations to the basic concepts. Many programs give you more than one option, all of which have valid applications. These include

1. Resource-Limited Scheduling:
   Activities are scheduled when resources are available. Resource availability is not exceeded. When many activities vie for scarce resources, the resources are assigned to those activities that are more critical (or possibly by other priority schemes), and the other activities are forced to slip to later dates. The overall project schedule may slip because of resource shortages. See Figure 28-8b.
2. Time-Limited Scheduling:
   As above, activities will be scheduled according to the availability of resources. However, activities must be scheduled within the total float. Prescribed resource limits can be exceeded in order to hold the overall project schedule. See Figure 28-8c. This is often called resource leveling.

3. Time/Resource Limited Scheduling:
This is a combination of the two above. The user can define a secondary resource level which can be invoked when the target end date cannot be held with the base resource availability. Or, the user may specify a date that the schedule can slip to if the original, non-man-loaded date cannot be met with the available resources. Optimizing the schedule/resource plan is usually achieved via trial and error computations with various resource levels and target dates.

Establish a Cost Baseline

The Function. To control costs, you will want to establish a work scope-oriented budget. This can be done at the task level, or at the next higher level, the work package level. At the task level, the budget can be established by determining the resources for each task, the cost rate for each resource, the duration for each task, and the fixed costs and other expenses. Let's look at this function further as we examine the various approaches that are possible with the computer.

Where Does the Computer Fit In? With most computer programs, a table of resources and resource costs is established, so that much of the budget process is automatic. With the entering of task durations, resources, and fixed costs, the budget is created. As with the resource area, costing can be approached at various levels of detail.

Actually, there are two primary ways that project management programs address cost planning. We initiated this topic by describing the preferred way to deal with costs for each activity, which is on the basis of the specific resources that are used and the resource rates. This we can call resource-driven costing. If you cannot define the costs and other variables for each resource in a resource definition table or library, then you are limited to define all costs for a task as if they were fixed costs. Since, in reality, they are not fixed but affected by hourly rates, duration of the activity, and quantity of resources assigned, you will have to calculate these costs manually and input them yourself. If you do have a resource-driven program, you should be able to define both resource-generated and fixed costs. In that case, the computer will do your calculating for you, a decided advantage.

In the nonresource (fixed-cost) environment, the variations of detail could be as follows:

- Define a cost (budget) for each task.
- Establish a cost library (cost categories) and assign a series of "fixed" costs to each task.

- Assume all costs to be apportioned evenly across the duration of the task.
- Specify whether each cost item is to be allocated evenly or at the start of the task or at the end of the task.
- Report on task budgets by task.
- Report on task budgets by task and by cost categories (summary).
- Calculate and/or plot a project expenditure schedule (cash flow plan).

In the *resource-driven costing system* it gets much more involved. Here is a list of the possible variations (in addition to those above):

- Define a resource library with a single cost rate for each resource.
- Define a resource library with a multiple cost rate for each resource (standard time, overtime, etc.).
- Define a resource library with a stepped cost rate for each resource (escalation, union rate changes, etc.).
- Enter task costs by resource, by fixed cost, and by overhead or G&A categories.
- Allocate costs by four modes: even distribution, all at start, all at end, and at the resource library *rate* for the specified resource duration, for that task.

Evaluate the Baseline Plan

The Function. At this time, having done all of the above, you have a baseline plan. But is it the one that you want? Does it meet the project time, cost, and resource objectives? Chances are that it will require some "adjustment."

You will want to evaluate how the schedule of the individual tasks, with their durations and relationships, correlates with the milestone schedule. This is probably the first opportunity to validate the earlier assumptions. Will you need additional resources, more work hours per week, or adjusted relationships in order to meet the overall timing objectives?

Where Does the Computer Fit In? The computer is an excellent tool for performing the "what if" processing required to evaluate and optimize the baseline plan. First, in its scheduling mode, the computer will trace the logic from project start to finish, calculating the earliest start and finish dates for each activity. After completing this "forward pass," the computer makes a "backward pass" to determine the latest dates that any activity can start and finish to meet the target end dates. The difference between the early dates and the late dates is the "float" or "slack" for each activity. Those that have more float are easily noted, and one's attention can be given to those activities with the least float (the most critical activities).

The other major area to evaluate will be the resource loading and distribution. It is very likely that your first cut of the schedule will produce a resource utilization profile having significant peaks and valleys, such as in Figure 28-8a. This is, at the least, an inefficient and costly condition and, in fact, may not be supportable by your labor sources. You will want to attempt to smooth the resource profiles out, which means rescheduling activities that can be moved without creating delays to the overall project milestones.

Look to your project management software to help you get at the specific information you need to evaluate the baseline plan. How well will your software allow you to sort and select records and fields from your data base? You don't want to sift through 50 pages of reports where just a page or two will focus in on the specific areas that are outside of your desired schedule and resource targets. Look for software that will allow you, the user, to pull out just the information that you need, in the formats that you want. Schedule reports should be retrievable by total float (critical path) and by key interest groups, such as area, responsibility, WBS, and so forth. Resource reports should be retrievable by specific resource and by time periods, in both resource quantity and cost formats.

Optimize the Baseline Schedule

The Function. If the overall duration of the project computes to a longer—and unacceptable—time than specified, you will want to reexamine the task durations, and especially the task relationships. We often define more stringent relationships between activities than actually exist in our project. For instance, if we have three tasks, consisting of digging 300 feet of trench, laying 300 feet of pipe, and backfilling the trench, we may schedule them as three sequential activities, each with a finish-to-start relationship. Yet, in reality, we can start to lay the pipe at one end of the trench while we are still digging further along the path. Likewise, we can be backfilling at the first end while completing the pipe laying at the other end.

Where Does the Computer Fit In? If your software package allows the use of overlapping dependencies (start-to-start and finish-to-finish), you can redefine some of the finish-to-start relationships to shorten the schedule (see Figure 28-9). This should only be done to reflect actual overlap situations. Misuse or abuse of this feature to arbitrarily shorten the schedule will only come back to haunt you later.

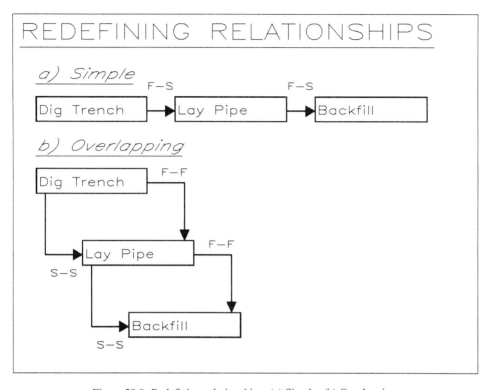

Figure 28-9. Redefining relationships. (a) Simple. (b) Overlapping.

As we stated earlier, your computer can help you in this schedule adjustment quest by organizing your data. Use your exception reporting capability to call for the longest path through the project, the "critical path," by asking the computer to sort the activities by *least float*. This will produce an analysis report (see Figure 28-10) with the activities listed in the order in which you will want to review their durations and relationships.

To the extent that you can reasonably do so, evaluate your critical activities and adjust durations and relationships. Reschedule and rerun your least float reports and continue to adjust until you have a realistic schedule that supports your objectives, if possible.

Optimize the Resource Plan

The Function.   If you have resource peaks and valleys, you may wish to "level" the resources, by moving the more highly loaded tasks, that have

```
-------------------------------------------------------------------------------------------------
My Humble Hacienda                    PRIMAVERA PROJECT PLANNER              PROJECT SPLASH

REPORT DATE 29MAY86  RUN NO.    7                                    START DATE 31MAR86  FIN DATE

TABULAR SCHEDULE REPORT - Sorted by Criticality                     DATA DATE 31MAR86  PAGE NO.    1
```

ACTIVITY NUMBER	ORIG DUR	REM DUR	PCT	CODE	ACTIVITY DESCRIPTION	LEVELED START	LEVELED FINISH	LATE START	LATE FINISH	TOTAL FLOAT
10	2	2	0		DECIDE TO DO	31MAR86	1APR86	31MAR86	1APR86	0
20	8	8	0		GATHER INFO	2APR86	11APR86	2APR86	11APR86	0
30	5	5	0		CONCEPT	14APR86	18APR86	14APR86	18APR86	0
210	5	5	0		PRICE FENCING	21APR86	25APR86	21APR86	25APR86	0
310	5	5	0		PRICE PATIO KITS	21APR86	25APR86	21APR86	25APR86	0
510	5	5	0		GET POOL QUOTES	21APR86	25APR86	21APR86	25APR86	0
40	3	3	0		ESTABLISH PROGRAM	28APR86	30APR86	28APR86	30APR86	0
110	3	3	0		APPLY FOR PERMIT	1MAY86	5MAY86	1MAY86	5MAY86	0
120	15	15	0		ISSUE PERMIT	6MAY86	26MAY86	6MAY86	26MAY86	0
340	1	1	0		DIG HOLES FOR PATIO SUPPORTS	27MAY86	27MAY86	27MAY86	27MAY86	0
350	2	2	0		FORM PATIO FOOTINGS	28MAY86	29MAY86	28MAY86	29MAY86	0
360	1	1	0		POUR PATIO FOOTINGS	30MAY86	30MAY86	30MAY86	30MAY86	0
370	3	3	0		CURE PATIO FOOTINGS	2JUN86	4JUN86	2JUN86	4JUN86	0
380	1	1	0		STRIP & BACKFILL	5JUN86	5JUN86	5JUN86	5JUN86	0
440	4	4	0		ERECT PATIO BASE	6JUN86	11JUN86	6JUN86	11JUN86	0
450	2	2	0		ERECT PATIO RAILS	12JUN86	13JUN86	12JUN86	13JUN86	0
460	2	2	0		FINISH PATIO	16JUN86	17JUN86	16JUN86	17JUN86	0
610	2	2	0		CLEANUP	16JUN86	17JUN86	16JUN86	17JUN86	0
640	1	1	0		HOLD POOL PARTY	18JUN86	18JUN86	18JUN86	18JUN86	0
240	5	5	0		ERECT FENCE	6JUN86	12JUN86	9JUN86	13JUN86	1
630	1	1	0		GET PARTY SUPPLIES	16JUN86	16JUN86	17JUN86	17JUN86	1
50	2	2	0		ESTIMATE COSTS	1MAY86	2MAY86	5MAY86	6MAY86	2
520	2	2	0		ORDER POOL	5MAY86	6MAY86	7MAY86	8MAY86	2
140	3	3	0		APPLY FOR LOAN	5MAY86	7MAY86	7MAY86	9MAY86	2
530	15	15	0		POOL DELIVERED	7MAY86	27MAY86	9MAY86	29MAY86	2
150	10	10	0		ISSUE LOAN	8MAY86	21MAY86+	12MAY86	23MAY86	2
330	2	2	0		OBTAIN PATIO SUPPORT MATERIAL	21MAY86	22MAY86	23MAY86	26MAY86	2
540	10	10	0		INSTALL POOL	28MAY86	10JUN86	30MAY86	12JUN86	2
550	3	3	0		FILL POOL	11JUN86	13JUN86	13JUN86	17JUN86	2
620	1	1	0		SEND PARTY INVITATIONS	12JUN86	12JUN86	17JUN86	17JUN86	3
220	2	2	0		ORDER FENCING	5MAY86	6MAY86	15MAY86	16MAY86	8
230	15	15	0		FENCING DELIVERED	7MAY86	27MAY86	19MAY86	6JUN86	8
320	5	5	0		PATIO DETAILED PLANS	5MAY86	9MAY86	16MAY86	22MAY86	9
430	10	10	0		PATIO KIT DELIVERED	9MAY86	22MAY86	23MAY86	5JUN86	10
420	2	2	0		ORDER PATIO KIT	5MAY86	6MAY86	21MAY86	22MAY86	12

Figure 28-10. Critical path report (Primavera).

positive float, to periods of lesser demand for that resource. You may also wish to reset the maximum limit on certain resources and recalculate a revised schedule and project completion date.

At this point, you are involved in an iterative process, aimed at balancing the various means at hand to come as close as possible to establishing a baseline plan that meets the project overall objectives, that is consistent with organizational policies and guidelines, and that can be lived with by the project team.

Where Does the Computer Fit In?   Obviously it would be most difficult and tedious to do this iterative process by hand. The computer becomes virtually a necessity if you are to attempt to perform this optimization. With today's programs, there should be no reason why you cannot have this capability. Most of the programs will provide some degree of resource allocation, of course, within the variations discussed earlier.

"Freeze" the Baseline Plan

The Function.   If you are going to exercise project control, you have to be able to compare the project progress to the plan. Therefore, once you have developed an acceptable project plan you will want to save it for further reference.

Where Does the Computer Fit In?   Some programs allow you to label one or more "target" schedules. Others allow you to save the baseline plan and do your updates on a copy of that plan. I find the first approach to be preferable. In these programs, the target and current schedules reside in the same data base and the program provides prestructured reporting functions to allow the users to compare the two schedules. These reports may be either tabular formats with variance indication and/or Gantt charts with separate bars for each schedule. Although target schedule capabilities have been recently added to a few of the lower-priced programs that did not have that capability in earlier versions, most have still not provided formats that are as practical and readable as the programs at the higher end. In any event, as stated in the introduction, if you do not have some way to compare your current status to the baseline plan, your program will be of limited use in the execution of project control.

Track the Work Progress

The Function.   Now we are in the execution phase. Tracking entails the recording of how much work has been done, what resources were utilized, and what costs were incurred. In tracking the work progress, you will want to note when any task started and was finished. In addition, at any update or measurement point, usually at regular intervals, you will need to record the current status of in-progress activities. This may be noted in terms of remaining duration, expected completion, or percent complete.

Tracking the work progress also entails keeping track of the work scope changes and amending of the network plan and budgets to account for such scope changes.

Where Does the Computer Fit In?   We've already discussed the difference between a planning-only program and a planning/tracking program. Here we will concentrate on variations within the latter group: those that allow us to enter current status for eventual comparison to the baseline. While the basic elements all fall within the three data items listed above—remaining duration, expected completion, or percent complete—they can be approached in different ways. These subtle variations can affect your satisfaction with the software.

Remaining duration is usually the time, from the data date, for an activity in progress to be completed. The *data date* is a very important element of the project progressing process. It is the reference point for many of the calculations, including remaining duration and earned value. When using the remaining duration technique of defining progress, you must first decide on the as-of date for your update. If you decide to change the as-of date (data date), you may have to revisit the remaining duration entries to evaluate them against the new data date. Most programs will not let you input an actual date that is later than the data date, or an imposed date that is earlier than the data date. Figure 28-11 illustrates the effect of the data date. In this example, the remaining duration of five days is figured from the data date of 6/10. The system assumes that, even though the task started a week ago, it is 38% complete (five of eight days remaining to be done).

Some programs, like QWIKNET, have an auto-progress setting. When in auto-progress mode, the system assumes that any activity that was scheduled to start prior to the data date has actually progressed as planned, although no progress has been entered. For instance (see Figure 28-12), with a data date of 4/9/86, a four-day activity that was scheduled to

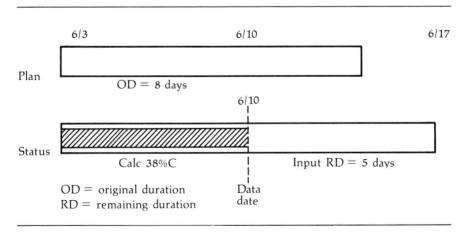

Figure 28-11. Effect of data date on remaining duration.

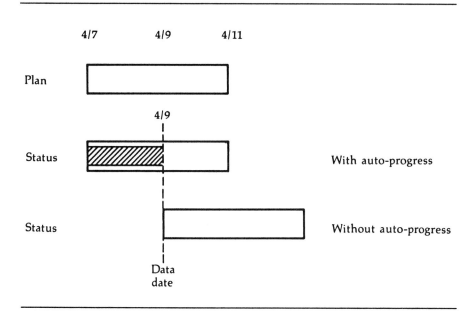

Figure 28-12. Effect of auto-progress mode on remaining duration.

start on 4/7/86 will be shown to be 50% complete and have a two-day remaining duration. Without the auto-progress mode invoked, the system will assume no progress unless reported. In this case, the preceding example would be slipped to start no earlier than the data date. The user is advised to use the auto-progress feature, if available, with judicious constraint. There is a tendency to reduce one's diligence toward quality updating when each and every in-progress activity does not have to be specifically addressed. In updating progress in ViewPoint, if you indicate that a duration-driven activity is 100% complete and do not enter actual start and finish dates, the system assumes that the task took place as scheduled, saving the user from unnecessary inputting. User override is possible, however, by just entering any dates that are different from the plan dates.

Activity percent complete reporting, when available, represents the percent of the activity duration that is complete. In other words, the system will calculate a remaining duration by subtracting the percent complete, times the planned duration, from that planned duration. In Figure 28-13, we show an eight-day task that is only 50% complete five days after it started. The system will assume a remaining duration of four

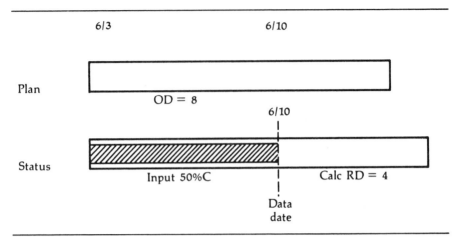

Figure 28-13. Effect of percent complete data on remaining duration.

days (50% of the eight day OD). The activity percent complete will be taken, by most systems, to also mean the resource and cost percent complete, although that may not be the specific case in all instances. Some programs will allow the user to specify resource and cost percent complete separately. The Primavera approach toward this methodology is defined later in this chapter (under resource status). Also, while some programs tie the percent complete and remaining duration figures together, interlocking those two data items, other programs provide a user option as to whether these measurements are linked or untied.

Expected completion is not available as an input option in all programs, and it is just as well, as many people tend to misuse this field as a scheduling option rather than for inputting status on tasks in progress. Abuse of this feature, when available, can result in degradation of the network logic. When an expected completion field is not available, the user is forced to calculate the remaining duration, so that the computer can tell you what you already know about that activity. Therefore, when used properly, the expected completion field can be helpful.

One other variable to consider is how any program deals with *out-of-sequence activity progress*. Remember that the activity logic and durations, which were defined in establishing the baseline plan, were only a best guess at how the work would be done. Remember, also, that these critical path project management techniques are used primarily for work that is unique in nature, and, therefore, the plans do not have the benefit of previous experience or hindsight. In practice, we could expect that the actual durations will vary and that some of the planned logical constraints will be violated.

There are great variations as to how the various programs deal with this phenomenon. Some will flag an out-of-sequence progress as an error and require the user to correct the status or the logic. Many will reduce the duration of the statused activity to the remaining duration, but leave it in the existing logical path (see Figure 28-14). A few may give the user an option to ignore the predecessor constraints for any activity with progress. In this "logic override" mode, the subject activity is processed as if all its predecessors had been completed, and all its successors may be scheduled to follow the new completion of that activity.

Track Actual Resource Usage

The Function. In resource tracking, we will be interested in similar data as in the task tracking, except in this case we will address the status of specific resources for each task. Of course this assumes that we were able to input data for specific resources in our baseline plan. If we can, we will address the actual work performed by each resource in such quantifications as actual units used, estimated units remaining, and/or percent re-

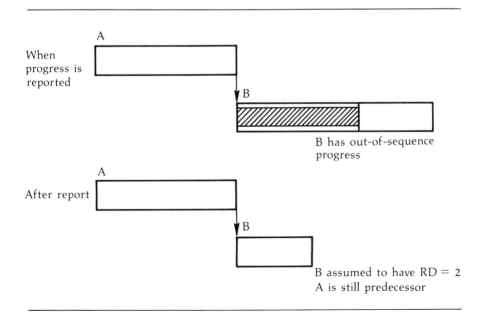

Figure 28-14. Effect of out-of-sequence progress.

source used. If your baseline plan dealt with delayed and partial duration application of the resources, then you would probably wish to further address these specifications during the project update.

If your task durations are resource driven, then you will have to reexecute your schedule computation after entering the resource usage data.

Where Does the Computer Fit In?   Some of the software packages do not have the facility to enter actual resource usage. That is, they allow you to define resource requirements, in the planning stage, to establish resource-driven budgets, and to support resource aggregation and allocation functions. However, you may not enter data relative to the resources actually used. With these programs, you can show the effect of resource usage only by entering the *cost* of the actual resources used. This does permit analysis of the project cost performance, and may be satisfactory in many project control situations. The negative aspects are that (1) you have to figure out the costs (resource usage times resource rate); (2) if the rates have changed from the plan, you lose accuracy of any resource usage measurement; and (3) it is difficult to perform any resource productivity measurements.

Several programs allow you to enter actual resource utilization experience, for each activity, and to provide data as to the resource percent complete (which may be different from the activity percent complete) and the estimate to complete. Such programs, Primavera for example, will also usually have the facility to report these resource performance and productivity data. Figure 28-15 illustrates the entry of resource data for an activity which is in progress. Here we show that, although we are one day into this two-day task, we estimate that it will take another two days to complete. We enter the data that indicates that we have spent two man-days, to date, of the resource "Carpenter," and that we estimate that four additional man-days are required. The system calculates the forecast at completion, which is six, and the variance, which is -2.

We can observe the aggregate results of the resource statusing, in such reports as shown in the next two figures. Figure 28-16 reports the budget, actual, estimate to complete, forecast at completion, and variance for each resource, with the details for each activity for that resource. Figure 28-17 is a current versus target resource report, by week, for the resource "Carpenter."

With the rescheduling resulting from the entering of schedule progress, we may find that we no longer have a schedule that respects our resource limits. If there has been a schedule slippage, in all likelihood we have lost some of the float that was used to level critical resources. Therefore, as part of the resource tracking and analysis function, we will have to review

```
                         ACTIVITY DATA                         POOL
Activity number:     350                                    TF:  -1
          Title:  FORM PATIO FOOTINGS                       PCT:  33

     ES:           EF: 30MAY86  Orig, duration   2   Actual start: 28MAY86
     LS:           LF: 29MAY86  Rem,  duration   2   Actual finish:

Activity Codes:  P1
```

RESOURCE SUMMARY:	Resource 1	Resource 2	Resource 3
Resource code	C		
Cost acct code/type	21L		
Units per day	2.00	0.00	0.00
Budget quantity	4	0	0
Resource Lag/Duration	0 0	0 0	0 0
% Complete	0	0	0
Actual qty this Period	0	0	0
Actual qty to date	2	0	0
Quantity to complete	4	0	0
Quantity at completion	6	0	0
Variance (units)	-2	0	0

```
Commands:Add Delete Edit Help More Next Return autoSort Transfer View Window
Windows :Act,codes Blank Constraints Dates Financial Log Resources Successors
```

Figure 28-15. Entering resource usage data (Primavera).

the current resource aggregation and, if unsatisfactory, rerun the resource leveling.

Track Actual Costs

The Function. Once the work is initiated, you will need to track the actual costs incurred (see Figure 28-18). Ledgers should be set up both for the incurrence of cost commitments (as in purchase orders or labor contracts), and for actual (invoiced) costs. The tracking of committed costs against the budget permits an early warning system for cost overruns. Unfortunately, most systems track only actual costs, which may provide you with cost performance data too late for corrective action.

In the planning phase, we showed how you can tie the projected resource and fixed expense data to your activities and develop a time-phased budget for the project, and each of its parts. We said that by having this activity level cost plan, we would be able to measure cost performance against this plan and be able to best forecast the probable project cost performance, based on the experience to date. The activity-

My Humble Hacienda				PRIMAVERA PROJECT PLANNER			SPLASH			
REPORT DATE 23NOV85 RUN NO. 38				RESOURCE CONTROL REPORT			START DATE 31MAR86 FIN DATE 18JUN86			
RESOURCE CONTROL REPORT - by RESOURCE							DATA DATE 29MAY86 PAGE NO. 1			

ACTIVITY NO	RESOURCE CODE	ACCOUNT CODE	ACCOUNT CATEGORY	UNIT MEAS	BUDGET	PCT CMP	ACTUAL TO DATE	ACTUAL THIS PERIOD	ESTIMATE TO COMPLETE	FORECAST	VARIANCE
	C	- CARPENTER					UNIT OF MEASURE = MD				
350 C		21L	LABOR	MD	4	33	2	0	4	6	-2
380 C		21L	LABOR	MD	2	0	0	0	2	2	0
440 C		21L	LABOR	MD	8	0	0	0	8	8	0
450 C		21L	LABOR	MD	4	0	0	0	4	4	0
TOTAL C					18	10	2	0	18	20	-2
	L	- LABORER					UNIT OF MEASURE = MD				
240 L		22L	LABOR	MD	15	0	0	0	15	15	0
340 L		21L	LABOR	MD	2	100	2	0	0	2	0
380 L		21L	LABOR	MD	2	0	0	0	2	2	0
440 L		21L	LABOR	MD	2	0	0	0	2	2	0
610 L		1 L	LABOR	MD	4	0	0	0	4	4	0
TOTAL L					25	8	2	0	23	25	0
	M	- CONCRETE WORKER					UNIT OF MEASURE = MD				
360 M		21L	LABOR	MD	3	0	0	0	3	3	0
TOTAL M					3	0	0	0	3	3	0

Figure 28-16. Resource control report (Primavera).

oriented project budget therefore was used to establish a framework for the inputting and analysis of cost performance.

In this tracking and analysis phase, we will be interested in seeing how we are doing, cost-wise, against the budgets for each activity, and, perhaps, in summarizing and evaluating cost performance by resource, cost account, or work breakdown structure grouping. We may also wish to review the cost experience against the cash flow plan, and, using a process called "earned value analysis," we can look at the cost performance against the value of the work actually performed. Next, we may want to estimate the costs for the remaining work (selective override of the uncompleted budget), generating forecast at completion data and variances from the plan. Last, having inputted the project experience to date and analyzed the results against the budget plan, we will need to evaluate

PERIOD ENDING	NORMAL	MAXIMUM	USAGE	AVG.DAILY	CUMULATIVE	USAGE	AVG.DAILY	CUMULATIVE	USAGE	AVG.DAILY	CUMULATIVE
				—EARLY SCHEDULE—			—LATE SCHEDULE—			—TARGET 1 SCHEDULE—	
C		- CARPENTER				UNIT OF MEASURE = MD			EARLY		
4APR86	0	0	0	.0	0	0	.0	0	0	.0	0
11APR86	0	0	0	.0	0	0	.0	0	0	.0	0
18APR86	0	0	0	.0	0	0	.0	0	0	.0	0
25APR86	0	0	0	.0	0	0	.0	0	0	.0	0
2MAY86	0	0	0	.0	0	0	.0	0	0	.0	0
9MAY86	0	0	0	.0	0	0	.0	0	0	.0	0
16MAY86	0	0	0	.0	0	0	.0	0	0	.0	0
23MAY86	0	0	0	.0	0	0	.0	0	0	.0	0
30MAY86	0	0	6	1.2	6	0	.0	0	4	.8	4
DATA DATE											
6JUN86	0	0	2	.4	8	0	.0	0	4	.8	8
13JUN86	0	0	10	2.0	18	0	.0	0	10	2.0	18
20JUN86	0	0	2	.4	20	0	.0	0	0	.0	18
27JUN86	0	0	0	.0	20	0	.0	0	0	.0	18
4JUL86	0	0	0	.0	20	0	.0	0	0	.0	18

Figure 28-17. Resource usage report—current vs. target (Primavera).

ACTIVITY DATA   **POOL**

Activity number: **430**   TF:
      Title: **PATIO KIT DELIVERED**   PCT: **90**

ES: EF: Orig. duration   **10**   Actual start: **9MAY86**
LS: LF: Rem. duration   **1**   Actual finish:

Activity Codes: **P2**

FINANCIAL SUMMARY:	Resource 1	Resource 2	Resource 3
Resource code	M$		
Cost acct code/type	21M		
Budgeted cost	350.00	0.00	0.00
Actual cost this period	0.00	0.00	0.00
Actual cost to date	192.50	0.00	0.00
Percent expended	55	0	0
Percent complete	50	0	0
Earned value	175.00	0.00	0.00
Cost to complete	192.50	0.00	0.00
Cost at completion	385.00	0.00	0.00
Variance	-35.00	0.00	0.00

Commands :Add Delete Edit Help More Next Return autoSort Transfer View Window
Windows :Act.codes Blank Constraints Dates Financial Log Resources Successors

Figure 28-18. Entering actual cost data (Primavera).

possible corrective action or changes in the remaining plans to try to achieve the original project objectives.

It's important to note that cost tracking and analysis are a crucial and often neglected part of project management. All too often, we collect tons of data, calculate, process, and massage the data until we produce more tonnage of output, and then do nothing. There are many reasons (or excuses) for this. One is the proverbial "we're too busy putting out fires to bother with planning to correct for future potential problems." Another is that to consider corrective action requires one to admit that there may, indeed, be some problems. Many project managers will wait until the problem is absolutely undeniable or uncorrectable before acceding to the long-projected facts. Yet another is that the project manager does not understand the project cost performance data reported by the system.

A final, and very prevalent, reason is that the cost-tracking framework was not set up in such a manner as to match the tracking and analysis needs for the project. This latter item, while being a major cause of project control failures, is actually the easiest to rectify. The problem is often manifested by the setting up of tracking categories (cost accounts) to one structure, and then collecting data to a totally different structure. The "baseline" is therefore no longer usable for tracking, and there is no target against which to compare the actual experience. The message here, of course, is to think very carefully about how you are going to collect your actual cost data, before you structure your cost account system.

Where Does the Computer Fit In?   The data considerations and options for cost tracking are similar to the ones discussed under resource tracking. The most essential data item to enter is actual costs to date. If we have a resource-tracking system then this data item should be automatically calculated from the resource usage data. Of course, we will want to have a user override for those instances where the actual costs deviated from the direct resource usage times resource rate computation.

If there is one piece of information that top management most often wants to have (in addition to the project completion date), it is the project forecasted cost at completion. Many systems can provide that data for you, essentially by computing the estimated cost for the uncompleted work and adding that value to the actual costs to date. Here again, the user will want to be able to get at these data elements to override the default calculations when the current estimate to complete is no longer reflective of the baseline plan. There are several minor variations in how each program addresses these functions, and they are constantly changing as the vendors respond to techniques preferred by their users. These requests have indicated that there are multiple preferred approaches, all of which are perfectly valid. One vendor, Primavera, responded to this dilemma by providing a user-selectable resource/cost rules screen. You may work with a set of system defaults, or a set of project-specific defaults, and further selectively override the rules that you have selected, for any activity.

Compare Progress and Costs to the Baseline Plan

The Function. Tracking progress and cost do not constitute control. Project control consists of many steps, leading to the taking of corrective action directed at achieving the project objectives. In this progressive action, the first step, following the collection of progress data, is to examine that progress against the target schedule. There are two measurements that should be monitored. The most obvious is the project end date that was calculated by the network critical path. If there have been any delays to activities on or near the critical path, they will generate a schedule delay. One should also observe the general progress of the noncritical activities. If enough of these fall behind, you can assume that the lower production rate will eventually impact on the critical schedule dates. Project control systems that provide measurement of production rates and earned value will facilitate this appraisal of *schedule variance*.

In the case of completed activities, it is satisfactory to compare the actual cost to the budget, for each activity. However, for in-progress tasks, the measurement of actual costs and comparison to the budget can only be effective if based on the *"earned value"* principle. The earned value, for any activity, is simply the activity budget times the activity percent complete. The biggest advantage of the earned value method is that it reduces all data to a common denominator of dollars. This facilitates the roll-up (summarization) of performance data to any level, and by any coded grouping.

Where Does the Computer Fit In? We've already discussed some of the attributes of computers in presenting a comparative analysis of baseline and current schedule data, namely the tabular listings and Gantt charts. For a comparison of resource and cost performance to the baseline, we will use an entirely different set of reporting structures. Let's look at these in detail as part of the next topic: performance evaluation.

Evaluate Performance.

The Function. As noted earlier, there are two primary measurements that will be watched by the people whose careers may depend on the success of a project. One, of course, is the project completion date. The other is the project margin. These measurements are a composite of individual task measurements. While the specific period data is the basis for the measurement of performance, the most revealing data will generally be the *trends* that are indicated by tracking that performance over several periods. A dip in production rate, or a spike in costs, for a particular period may only be a matter of measurement fidelity or timing, and should not be a cause for alarm. But to ignore such perturbations over an extended period is certainly courting disaster.

The most important condition for performance evaluation and trend analysis is consistency. Hence, again, the computer is a major aid to that end.

In general, when evaluating resource and cost performance, we are interested in comparing the actual resource usage and costs to the budget. We may want to perform that comparison by activity, by resource, or by each resource within each activity. We may also wish to perform that comparison at the detailed level (each task and resource) or at various summary levels based on WBS, responsibility, phase, cost accounts, and what have you.

In any of these modes, comparing actual to budget is only helpful for work that has been completed. As we noted earlier, for work that is in progress, we need to compare the actuals to the value of the work that has been accomplished. This "earned value" is the percent complete of the item times the budget for the item. An alternate reporting mechanism is to compare the budget to the forecast at completion, which is the sum of the actual to date plus the estimate to complete.

Both of these approaches overlap greatly and have generated a common language and set of acronyms. They are also the basis for the two well-known government protocols. The Department of Defense uses an instruction known as DODI 7000.2, also known as Cost/Schedule Control System Criteria (C/SCSC). A similar protocol, developed by the Department of Energy, goes by the name of Performance Measurement System (PMS).

The overall objective of the performance measurement approach is to measure progress and cost against the same definition as the baseline, and to measure this performance in comparable units. Another important facet is to conduct these measurements periodically. Certainly it is essential to good project control that performance be measured while there is still time to take corrective action, and that the effect of the periodic review and corrective actions can be revealed by the trend data coming out of these periodic measurements and reviews.

In a performance measurement system, therefore, we will want to have data pertaining to the schedule and budget, both expressed in comparable units (usually dollars, and sometimes man-days). We will want to have this data for the entire duration of the project, and for specified periods during the project. We will need to be able to project (estimate or forecast) the results at the end of the project, and to express the variance of current and/or projected status against the plan.

The language in these PMS protocols is very descriptive of the data items that are used in the system. Table 28-1 lists and defines the common acronyms used in PMS.

Where Does the Computer Fit In?   This is where the computer really earns its keep. All of the expressions described in Table 28-1 are easily programmed into the project management software systems, and many of the vendors, but not all, have chosen to do so. Hence, if the user wishes to have reports that present this kind of data, the choices are certainly there. Look for programs that provide reports that actually use this terminology. They are likely to provide the types of analytical data that you will need to evaluate and report project performance. A good example of such is the newly released QWIKNET Professional, which supplies the data item and computation formats, and allows the user to select the terms to be used for the field headers. See Figure 28-19.

Look for systems that will allow you to select, sort, and summarize based on your WBS, responsibility, phase, cost account, and other codes. Depending on your needs, ascertain whether the program can arrange these data by activity, by resource, by cost account, by time period, or any combination of these. Check into how the program deals with actuals and forecast to complete. It should either match your mode of progress tracking or permit you to set to criteria to meet your needs.

REPORTING AND EXPORTING DATA

The real test of program functionality will be not only if the data formats match your environment and needs, but also whether the program will give you the control over the preparation of hard copy (reports and graphics) for presentation to the various project stakeholders.

Perhaps the most noticeable differences between the mass market and higher end programs will be in the reporting and graphics area. In general, the lower end programs (primarily those in the $395 to $695 price class) will emphasize on-screen graphics and ease of use, as opposed to an emphasis on functionality and hard-copy reporting, which are featured in

Table 28-1. PMS Terms and What They Mean.

ACRONYM	STANDS FOR	MEANING
BAC	budget at completion	The budget for an entire item or any group of items, or roll-up (summary) of the entire project.
BCWS	budgeted cost of work scheduled	At any specified point in time the percent complete that the item is scheduled to be at that time, times the BAC, for that item. (Item Planned %C × BAC = BCWS)
BCWP	budgeted cost of work performed	At any specified point in time, the actual percent complete, times the BAC, for that item. This is the earned value of the work performed. (Item Actual %C × BAC = BCWP)
ACWP	actual cost of work performed	At any specified point in time the actual cost incurred for the work. The timing of the actual cost measurement should be the same as the %C progress measurement so that you can compare actual cost to earned value (BCWP).
ETC	estimate to complete	An estimate of the cost to be incurred to complete the remaining work.
EAC	estimate at completion	The sum of the actual cost to date, plus the estimate to complete. (ACWP + ETC = EAC)
FTC	forecast to complete	A forecast of the cost to be incurred to complete the remaining work. In some applications the FTC and FAC are synonymous with the ETC and EAC. In others the *forecast* refers to a computerized extrapolation of the performance to date, based on a built-in forecast algorithm, and *estimate* refers to a judgmental expression of the cost for the remaining work.
FAC	forecast at completion	The sum of the actual cost to date plus the forecast to complete. (ACWP + FTC = FAC)
CV	cost variance	The difference between the value of the work performed and the actual cost for that work. (BCWP − ACWP = CV)
SV	schedule variance	The difference between the value of the work performed, and the value of the work that had been planned to be performed, at the measurement time. The schedule variance is expressed in dollars, so that the same measurement units are used as in the cost variance and so that both the cost and schedule variance can be plotted on the same graph. (BCWP − BCWS = SV)

```
My Humble Hacienda                        EARNED VALUE REPORT                                         Page
Jose Doe                                                                           Project Start   31Mar86
Project Name  POOL    PROJECT SPLASH                                               Project Finish  19Jun86
Run Date    21Dec86 22:16                                                          Data Date        29May86
```

Activity ID	DESCRIPTION	TO DATE					AT COMPLETION		
		BCWS ($$)	BCWP (EV) ($$)	ACWP ($$)	SV ($$)	CV TODATE ($$)	BAC ($$)	EAC ($$)	CV AT END ($$)
230	FENCING DELIVERED	250.00	250.00	250.00	0.00	0.00	250.00	250.00	0.00
240	ERECT FENCE	0.00	0.00	0.00	0.00	0.00	1200.00	1200.00	0.00
330	OBTN PATIO SPRT MATL	150.00	150.00	150.00	0.00	0.00	150.00	150.00	0.00
340	DIG HOLES	160.00	160.00	160.00	0.00	0.00	160.00	160.00	0.00
350	FORM	200.00	133.32	200.00 -	66.68 -	66.68	400.00	600.00 -	200.00
360	POUR	0.00	0.00	0.00	0.00	0.00	288.00	288.00	0.00
380	STRIP & BACKFILL	0.00	0.00	0.00	0.00	0.00	360.00	360.00	0.00
430	PATIO KIT DELIVERED	350.00	350.00	425.00	0.00 -	75.00	350.00	425.00 -	75.00
440	ERECT PATIO BASE	0.00	0.00	0.00	0.00	0.00	800.00	800.00	0.00
450	ERECT PATIO RAILS	0.00	0.00	0.00	0.00	0.00	400.00	400.00	0.00
460	FINISH PATIO	0.00	0.00	0.00	0.00	0.00	160.00	160.00	0.00
530	POOL DELIVERED	6000.00	0.00	0.00 -	6000.00	0.00	6000.00	6000.00	0.00
540	INSTALL POOL	0.00	0.00	0.00	0.00	0.00	4000.00	4000.00	0.00
550	FILL POOL	0.00	0.00	0.00	0.00	0.00	75.00	75.00	0.00
610	CLEAN-UP	0.00	0.00	0.00	0.00	0.00	320.00	320.00	0.00
TOTALS		7110.00	1043.32	1185.00 -	6066.68 -	141.68	14913.00	15188.00 -	275.00

Figure 28-19. Earned value report with user-selected headers (QWIKNET Professional).

most of the higher end programs ($1495 and up). Given my choice, and assuming that I need and can operate the more functional systems, I would opt for the latter group.

Look for your system to provide schedule reports in three formats, tabular, bar charts, and network diagrams. The bar charts and network diagrams, as produced on most printers, are of dubious quality. Look for those products that include or offer optional graphics functions to produce bar charts and network diagrams on plotters or laser printers. A compromise capability, to print these diagrams on a printer in a graphics mode, is a questionable compromise because of the usual slowness of that process. Plotter graphics capabilities are included in Scitor Project Scheduler Network, SuperProject EXPERT, Open Plan, PROMIS, Plantrac, ARTEMIS Project, Project Workbench (partial, and ViewPoint. Optional

```
                RESOURCE  ACCOUNT   ACCOUNT   UNIT           PCT  ACTUAL     EARNED
ACTIVITY NO     CODE      CODE      CATEGORY  MEAS   BUDGET  CMP  TO DATE    VALUE    VARIANCE
-----------     --------  --------  --------  ----   ------  ---  --------   ------   --------

         L    - LABORER                              UNIT OF MEASURE = MD

    240 L                 22L LABOR   MD     1200.00   0      .00      .00      .00
    340 L                 21L LABOR   MD      160.00 100   160.00   160.00      .00
    380 L                 21L LABOR   MD      160.00   0      .00      .00      .00
    460 L                 21L LABOR   MD      160.00   0      .00      .00      .00
    610 L                 1 L LABOR   MD      320.00   0      .00      .00      .00

  TOTAL L                                    2000.00   8   160.00   160.00      .00


         C    - CARPENTER                             UNIT OF MEASURE = MD

    350 C                 21L LABOR   MD      400.00  33   200.00   132.00   -68.00
    380 C                 21L LABOR   MD      200.00   0      .00      .00      .00
    440 C                 21L LABOR   MD      800.00   0      .00      .00      .00
    450 C                 21L LABOR   MD      400.00   0      .00      .00      .00

  TOTAL C                                    1800.00  10   200.00   132.00   -68.00


         M    - CONCRETE WORKER                       UNIT OF MEASURE = MD

    360 M                 21L LABOR   MD      288.00   0      .00      .00      .00

  TOTAL M                                     288.00   0      .00      .00      .00


        M$    - MATERIAL COST                         UNIT OF MEASURE = $

    230 M$                22M MATERIAL $     250.00 100   250.00   250.00      .00
    330 M$                21M MATERIAL $     150.00 100   150.00   150.00      .00
    430 M$                21M MATERIAL $     350.00 100   425.00   350.00   -75.00
    530 M$                1 M MATERIAL $    6000.00   0      .00      .00      .00

  TOTAL M$                                   6750.00  12   825.00   750.00   -75.00


        S$    - SUBCONTRACTOR COST                    UNIT OF MEASURE = $

    540 S$                1 S SUBCONTR $    4000.00   0      .00      .00      .00
    550 S$                1 S SUBCONTR $      75.00   0      .00      .00      .00

  TOTAL S$                                   4075.00   0      .00      .00      .00


                REPORT COST TOTALS          14913.00   8  1185.00  1042.00  -143.00
```

Figure 28-20. Earned value report—by resource by activity (Primavera).

plotter graphics programs are offered with Time Line, MicroTrak, and Primavera.

Look for your system to provide resource and cost performance data in several ways. Graphically you will want to see incremental resource and cost histograms, and cumulative resource and cost curves. While these diagrams are very graphic, they do not provide specific quantities. These are best obtained from a tabular presentation of the resource and cost data.

The most revealing information relative to resource and cost performance is presented in the aforementioned earned value type reports. A good example of these resource and cost reports can be seen in Figures 28-20 and 28-21, featuring Primavera's approach. Similar reports can be

```
-------------------------------------------------------------------------------------------------------
My Humble Hacienda                          PRIMAVERA PROJECT PLANNER              SPLASH

REPORT DATE  29MAY86  RUN NO.   15          COST CONTROL ACTIVITY REPORT          START DATE 31MAR86  FIN DATE 18JUN86

COST CONTROL REPORT - by ACTIVITY by Resource                                     DATA DATE 29MAY86   PAGE NO.   1
-------------------------------------------------------------------------------------------------------
             RESOURCE  ACCOUNT   ACCOUNT  UNIT           PCT    ACTUAL    ACTUAL   ESTIMATE TO
ACTIVITY NO  CODE      CODE      CATEGORY MEAS  BUDGET   CMP    TO DATE  THIS PERIOD COMPLETE  FORECAST     VARIANCE
-----------  --------  --------  -------- ----  -------  ---   --------- ---------- --------- ----------   ----------
      330 OBTAIN PATIO SUPPORT MATERIAL
          RD    0 AS 21MAY86 AF 22MAY86

          M$              21M MATERIAL $   150.00 100   150.00       .00       .00   150.00        .00
                                         ----------- ---  --------- ---------- --------- ----------  ----------
                                          150.00 100   150.00       .00       .00   150.00        .00

      340 DIG HOLES FOR PATIO SUPPORTS
          RD    0 AS 27MAY86 AF 27MAY86

          L               21L LABOR   MD   160.00 100   160.00       .00       .00   160.00        .00
                                         ----------- ---  --------- ---------- --------- ----------  ----------
                                          160.00 100   160.00       .00       .00   160.00        .00

      350 FORM PATIO FOOTINGS
          RD    2 AS 28MAY86 EF 30MAY86      LF 29MAY86  TF   -1

          C               21L LABOR   MD   400.00  33   200.00       .00    400.00   600.00    -200.00
                                         ----------- ---  --------- ---------- --------- ----------  ----------
                                          400.00  50   200.00       .00    400.00   600.00    -200.00

      360 POUR PATIO FOOTINGS
          RD    1 ES  2JUN86 EF  2JUN86 LS 30MAY86 LF 30MAY86  TF   -1

          M               21L LABOR   MD   288.00   0      .00       .00    288.00   288.00        .00
                                         ----------- ---  --------- ---------- --------- ----------  ----------
                                          288.00   0      .00       .00    288.00   288.00        .00

      380 STRIP & BACKFILL
          RD    1 ES  6JUN86 EF  6JUN86 LS  5JUN86 LF  5JUN86  TF   -1

          C               21L LABOR   MD   200.00   0      .00       .00    200.00   200.00        .00
          L               21L LABOR   MD   160.00   0      .00       .00    160.00   160.00        .00
                                         ----------- ---  --------- ---------- --------- ----------  ----------
                                          360.00   0      .00       .00    360.00   360.00        .00

                                         ----------- ---  --------- ---------- --------- ----------  ----------
                  REPORT COST TOTALS     1358.00  38   510.00       .00   1048.00  1558.00    -200.00
```

Figure 28-21. Cost control report—by activity by resource (Primavera).

produced by programs such as PROMIS, QWIKNET Professional, View-Point, and PMS-II. Some of the other programs can be made to produce such reports, but only by using supplementary programs or report writers. Some of the mass market programs can also produce earned value and PMS type reports, but with a lesser degree of detail and user control. Time Line, Microsoft Project, and QWIKNET Professional also offer a matrix type of reporting (as illustrated in Figures 28-22 through 28-24), a different and interesting way of presenting resource and cost data.

Regardless of how varied and thorough a package's reporting capability may be, many users will want to do more with the data than can be provided in a general-purpose program. One need may be to develop one's own computation algorithms for forecasting. Another may be to feed selected data to other data bases. Many vendors are providing export capabilities. These fall into three general categories: export to a mainframe, export to other non-project management programs on the micro, and, lately, export to other microcomputer-based project management programs. Export to the mainframe can be product specific, such as PS-

```
Schedule Name:   PROJECT SPLASH
Project Manager: Esther Williams
As of date:      29-May-86 12:31am   Schedule File: C:\TLDATA\POOL529


This is a selective report.  All items shown
(Additionally, some tasks were manually selected or excluded.)

TASK                            C          L          M          M$         S$            TOTAL
----------------------------    ---------  ---------  ---------  ---------  ---------  ---------------
Fencing Delivered                                                250                            250
Erect Fence                               1,200                                               1,200
Obtain Support Material                                          150                            150
Dig Holes                                   160                                                 160
Form                           600                                                              600
Pour                                                   288                                       288
Strip & Backfill               200          160                                                 360
Deliver Patio Kit                                                425                            425
Erect Patio Base               800                                                              800
Erect Patio Rails              400                                                              400
Finish Patio                                160                                                 160
Pool Delivered                                                 6,000                          6,000
Install Pool                                                               4,000              4,000
Fill Pool                                                                     75                 75
Clean-up                                    320                                                 320
============================    =========  =========  =========  =========  =========  ===============
TOTALS                         2,000      2,000        288      6,825      4,075           15,188
```

Figure 28-22. Matrix type cost report—activities vs. resource (Time Line).

PROJECT SPLASH

Project: POOLMP			Date: Dec 15, 1985 12:11 PM	
Timescale: Month				

Period ending	May 1, 1986	June 1, 1986	July 1, 1986
1 LABORER	$0.00	$160.00	$1840.00
2 CARPENTER	$0.00	$400.00	$1400.00
3 CONCRETE WORKER	$0.00	$288.00	$0.00
4 MATL-PAT/FNC	$0.00	$750.00	$0.00
5 MATL-POOL	$0.00	$6000.00	$0.00
6 SUBCON-POOL	$0.00	$4000.00	$75.00
Total:	$0.00	$11598.00	$3315.00

Figure 28-23. Matrix type cost report—resource vs. time (Microsoft Project).

```
J. L. GRAPHICS and PRINTING              ACTIVITIES VS. TIME REPORT                        Page   1.1
Prj Mgr: Joseph Leahy                                            Units ($$)    Project Start   15Jun87
Project Name  BROCHURE  Brochure section of CURE-ALL product                   Project Finish  20ct87
Run Date    30-Jul-86 15:05                                                    Data Date       15Jul87
--------------------------------------------------------------------------------------------------------
Activity ID   15-jun-87 To  29-jun-87 To  13-jul-87 To  27-jul-87 To  10-aug-87 To  24-aug-87 To  :
Project ID    29-jun-87     13-jul-87     27-jul-87     10-aug-87     24-aug-87     7-sep-87     :   Totals
--------------------------------------------------------------------------------------------------------
ART               0.00          0.00          0.00          0.00          0.00          0.00    :     0.00
BROCHURE
ART-PREP          0.00       2049.75       4571.75          0.00          0.00          0.00    :  6621.50
BROCHURE
PASTEUP           0.00          0.00          0.00          0.00          0.00          0.00    :     0.00
BROCHURE
PLAN-ART       2763.63        363.63        872.72          0.00          0.00          0.00    :  3999.99
BROCHURE
OTHER             0.00          0.00          0.00          0.00          0.00          0.00    :     0.00
BROCHURE
SETCOPY           0.00          0.00          0.00          0.00          0.00          0.00    :     0.00
BROCHURE
SCHED-PROJ     1200.00        150.00          0.00          0.00          0.00          0.00    :  1350.00
BROCHURE
PRINTING          0.00          0.00          0.00          0.00          0.00          0.00    :     0.00
BROCHURE
WRITE             0.00          0.00          0.00          0.00          0.00          0.00    :     0.00
BROCHURE
REVIEW2           0.00          0.00          0.00          0.00          0.00       1475.00    :  1475.00
BROCHURE
DRAFTFINAL        0.00          0.00          0.00          0.00          0.00       1156.50    :  1156.50
BROCHURE
DRAFT2            0.00          0.00          0.00       1156.50       2313.00        385.50    :  3855.00
BROCHURE
DRAFT1            0.00       2056.50       3384.00       1342.00          0.00          0.00    :  6782.50
BROCHURE
OUTLINE        1217.65       1685.31        168.53          0.00          0.00          0.00    :  3071.50
BROCHURE
REVIEW1           0.00          0.00          0.00       3277.50          0.00          0.00    :  3277.50
BROCHURE
--------------------------------------------------------------------------------------------------------
TOTALS  ($$)   5181.29       6305.19       8997.00       5776.00       2313.00       3017.00    : 31589.49
```

Figure 28-24. Matrix type cost report—activities vs. time (QWIKNET Professional).

DI's QWIKNET to PROJECT/2, or can be in ASCII. The most popular export function is to produce files, containing selected project data, in formats that can be accessed by other microcomputer programs. Initial capabilities centered on the more universal ASCII, DIF, and CSV formats. While these files could eventually be read by most other programs, an intermediary conversion step was necessary. The trend lately is to write files directly in spreadsheet and data base formats, with .WKS (Lotus 1-2-3) and .DBF (dBASE) formats being the most popular. If you have an extensive need to add supplementary data items to your project data base, you will want to look into one of the programs that is written in an easily user-accessable data base language such as Open Plan (dBASE III) or the new Artemis Project (Artemis 2000). These programs actually allow the user to modify the project data base structure, as well as to add extensions to that structure.

CONCLUDING COMMENTS

All of the functions described in the past several pages are of little value unless they contribute to the attainment of the project objectives. Good plan development, coupled with accurate, dependable progress tracking, and followed up by truthful forecasting and analysis are the necessary ingredients to a successful project planning and control endeavor. Being able to develop alternatives for corrective action, and being able to back up any recommendations with a presentable project story, are equally essential. It has been generally found that the discipline of a computer-based project planning and control system leads to more cohesive and supportable project management and reporting. The general acknowledgment of this condition has helped project managers to be more respected and, in turn, to get better support from their contributors and management.

TRADEMARKS

The following names are trademarked products of the corresponding companies.

Artemis 2000® and Artemis Project®	Metier Management Systems Limited
dBASE II®	Ashton-Tate
dBASE III®	Ashton-Tate
Harvard™	Software Publishing Corporation
Lotus®	Lotus Development Corporation

Micro Planner®	Micro Planning Software, USA
Microsoft®	Microsoft Corporation
MicroTrak®	SofTrak Systems, Inc.
1-2-3®	Lotus Development Corporation
Open Plan™	Welcom Software Technology
PLANTRAC®	Computerline, Inc.
PMS-II	North America Mica, Inc.
Primavera Project Planner®	Primavera Systems, Inc.
Project Scheduler Network™	SCITOR Corporation
PROJECT/2®	Project Software & Development, Inc.
Project Workbench®	Applied Business Technology Corporation
PROMIS™	Strategic Software Planning Corporation
QWIKNET®	Project Software & Development, Inc.
QWIKNET Professional	Project Software & Development, Inc.
SuperProject® EXPERT	Computer Associates International
Time Line®	Breakthrough Software Corporation
ViewPoint	Computer Aided Management, Inc.

Section VIII

Behavioral Dimensions and Teamwork in Project Management

In the first chapter in this section (29) Dennis Slevin and Jeffrey K. Pinto discuss the important intangible elements of the project manager's job—leadership and motivation. They include diagnostic tools that project managers, or aspiring project managers, will find to be useful in assessing themselves for this role.

Teams and teamwork are so important to project management that three chapters are devoted to these topics in this section.

In Chapter 30, Raymond E. Hill and Trudy Somers treat the management of the social conflict that inherently arises in the project context. They prescribe how, in the team context, this conflict may be managed constructively.

Teamwork is also the key to Chapter 31 by Thomas E. Miller. He shows how failure in teamwork creates resistance to change using a clinical case study from a large urban fire department to illustrate and underscore his diagnosis.

Hans J. Thamhain, in Chapter 32, characterizes an effective team and delineates barriers and drivers of effective team performance. He discusses the organization of the project team, examines team building as an ongoing process, and presents recommendations for effective team management.

In Chapter 33, David L. Wilemon and Bruce N. Baker discuss some major research findings regarding the human element in project management. This chapter is particularly useful to the project manager who is experiencing some problems managing this aspect of the project.

29. Leadership, Motivation, and the Project Manager*

Dennis P. Slevin†
Jeffrey K. Pinto‡

INTRODUCTION

The project manager typically works through a project team consisting of individuals with diverse backgrounds, education, experiences, and interests. One secret to successful project implementation is the project manager's ability to get this diverse set of actors performing at maximal effectiveness. Consequently, the project manager must be both a *leader* and a *motivator* of the members of the project team. He or she is often required to work through others while possessing minimal legitimate line authority over their actions. Consequently, the techniques of effective leadership and motivation become very important in the project management context.

* Portions of this chapter are adapted from *Executive Survival Manual,* by Dennis P. Slevin, Innodyne: Pittsburgh, 1985. The authors are indebted to Dr. Thomas V. Bonoma for the development of the Bonoma/Slevin Leadership Model and to Dr. S. Lee Jerrell for the development of the Jerrell/Slevin Management Instrument.
Copyright © 1987 by Dennis P. Slevin and Jeffrey K. Pinto
† Dennis P. Slevin is an Associate Professor of Business Administration at the University of Pittsburgh's Joseph M. Katz Graduate School of Business. He holds a B.A. in Mathematics from St. Vincent College, a B.S. in Physics from M.I.T., an M.S. in Industrial Administration from Carnegie-Mellon, and a Ph.D. from Stanford University. He has had extensive experience as a line manager, including service as the CEO of four different companies, which qualified him as a member of the Young Presidents' Organization. He presently serves as a director of several corporations, and consults widely. He publishes in numerous professional journals, and is co-editor of *Implementing Operations Research Management Science, The Management of Organizational Design, Volumes I and II,* and *Producing Useful Knowledge.* He has written the pragmatic *Executive Survival Manual* for practicing managers.
‡ Jeffrey K. Pinto is Assistant Professor of Organization Theory at the College of Business Administration, University of Cincinnati. He received his B.A. in History and B.S. in Business from the University of Maryland, M.B.A. and Ph.D. from the University of Pittsburgh. He has published several papers in a variety of professional journals on such topics as project management, implementation, instrument development, and research methodology.

This chapter is intended to assist the project manager in these two important areas. First, a contingency model of leadership is presented along with an instrument to aid the project manager in diagnosing his or her leadership style. The emphasis is on the conscious selection of a leadership style contingent upon the varying parameters of the project situation. Second, the issue of motivation is addressed both from the conceptual standpoint of motivating others and from the standpoint of diagnosing one's internal motivational structure and determining if it is appropriate for the project management situation. This chapter is intended to give the reader both a conceptual grounding in leadership and motivation issues along with diagnostic techniques to determine appropriate actions with regard to these concepts in varying project management situations.

LEADERSHIP DEFINED

Leadership is a complex process that is crucial to successful management. Behavioral scientists have been studying the leadership problem over the past half century in an attempt to better understand the process and to come up with prescriptive recommendations concerning effective leader behaviors. Years of careful research have generated a variety of findings that at best are sometimes confusing to the practicing manager and at worst are at times internally inconsistent. For example:

- Leaders will be most effective when they show a high level of concern for both the task and the employees (1).
- Leaders should be task-oriented under conditions where they have either high or low control over the group. When there is moderate control over the group, leaders should be people-oriented (4).
- Leaders will be effective to the extent that they assess the required quality of the decision to be made in relation to the required level of acceptance by subordinates and seek participation by subordinates in decision making accordingly (25).
- Leaders will be accepted and will motivate employees to the extent that their behavior helps employees progress toward valued goals and provides guidance or clarification not already present in the work situation (11).
- A participative approach to leadership will positively influence employees' morale and increase their commitment to the organization (5).
- Under stressful conditions (e.g., time pressure) an autocratic leadership style will lead to greater productivity (6). A minimum level of friendliness or warmth will enhance this effect (24).

- Even when a leader has all the needed information to make a decision and the problem is clearly structured, employees prefer a participative approach to decision making (8).
- Effective leaders tend to exhibit high levels of intelligence, initiative, personal needs for occupational achievement, and self-confidence (21, 7).
- Effective leadership behavior may be constrained by the organizational setting so that similar behaviors may have different consequences in different settings (2, 20).
- Leadership behavior may not be important if subordinates are skilled, if tasks are structured, if technology dictates actions, and if the administrative climate is supportive and fair (12).
- Leadership behavior can be divided into task behavior (one-way communication) and relationship behavior (two-way communication). An effective leadership style using these behaviors can be selected according to the maturity level of subordinates relative to accomplishing the task (9).

These principles of leadership present a variety of sometimes conflicting premises which make it difficult to select appropriate behaviors in practice. Some of the work suggests that a participatory style is best in all situations, while other work suggests that a participatory style is more effective in some situations than in others. Some of the work suggests that the traits of the leader determine effectiveness, while other work shows that the dynamics of the interaction of the leader with subordinates or the interdependency with other organizational factors determines effectiveness. Still other work suggests that, under some conditions, leadership style is not important at all.

What is needed for the practicing executive is a conceptual model that clarifies some aspects of the concept of leadership, suggests alternative leadership styles that may be used, and provides normative recommendations on conditions under which alternative styles might be used. One of the purposes of this chapter is to describe a *cognitive* approach to leadership that will help the practicing executive consciously select the leadership style correct for alternative situations.

A DIAGNOSTIC

Before continuing, the reader may wish to develop a diagnostic on his or her leadership style without being biased by the conceptual discussion. Respond to the questions in the Jerrell/Slevin management instrument in Figures 29-1, 29-2, and 29-3. This instrument has been used effectively

LEADERSHIP 1

JERRELL/SLEVIN MANAGEMENT INSTRUMENT

Complete this instrument by circling the number for each item that represents your best estimate.

	Strongly Disagree	Disagree	Neutral	Agree	Strongly Agree
1. I don't like it when others disagree with me.	1	2	3	4	5
2. I like quick results.	1	2	3	4	5
3. I find it hard to accept others decisions.	1	2	3	4	5
4. I have a strong ego.	1	2	3	4	5
5. Once I make up my mind I stick to it.	1	2	3	4	5
6. I enjoy giving orders.	1	2	3	4	5
7. The work group should determine its own vacation schedule.	5	4	3	2	1
8. The work group should determine its own work schedule.	5	4	3	2	1
9. I feel comfortable being placed in a powerful position.	1	2	3	4	5
10. I like working in a group situation.	5	4	3	2	1
Total your D score (Items 1–10 above)		D = _____			
11. It is easier to make a decision in a group.	1	2	3	4	5
12. Groups usually take up more time than they are worth.	5	4	3	2	1
13. I often ask for information from subordinates.	1	2	3	4	5
14. Groups give a deeper analysis of a problem.	1	2	3	4	5
15. I often use what subordinates have to say.	1	2	3	4	5
16. No one else can know as much about the problem as I do.	5	4	3	2	1
17. I usually make my decision before calling a staff meeting.	5	4	3	2	1
18. Better decisions are made in group situations.	1	2	3	4	5
19. A group is no better than its best member.	5	4	3	2	1
20. Group decisions are the best.	1	2	3	4	5
Total your I score (Items 11–20 above)		I = _____			

Copyright © 1984 S. Lee Jerrell & Dennis P. Slevin   Used with permission

Figure 29-1. A leadership assessment instrument.

LEADERSHIP 1

JERRELL/SLEVIN MANAGEMENT INSTRUMENT
(Continued)

Scoring Instructions

1. Record your D score (the sum of the answers to items 1–10 on the previous page)

   D = _____

2. Record your I score (the sum of the answers to items 11–20 on the previous page)

   I = _____

3. Determine your percentile score from the table below

Raw Score	D Percentile	Raw Score	I Percentile
19	1	22	1
20	1	23	1
21	1	24	1
22	3	25	2
23	5	26	2
24	6	27	4
25	9	28	6
26	12	29	7
27	15	30	8
28	22	31	15
29	27	32	18
30	37	33	26
31	42	34	39
32	53	35	48
33	64	36	56
34	72	37	69
35	81	38	78
36	85	39	84
37	91	40	87
38	94	41	92
39	97	42	96
40	98	43	98
41	99	44	99
42	99	45	99
43	100	46	100

4. Plot yourself on the grid on the following page

Percentiles are estimates based on data collected from 191 American managers.

Figure 29-2. A leadership assessment instrument. (*continued*)

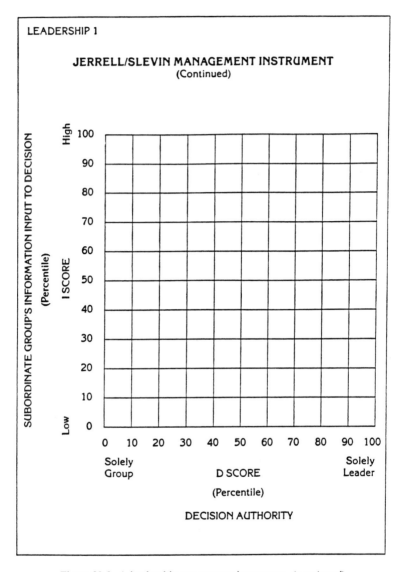

Figure 29-3. A leadership assessment instrument. (*continued*)

with thousands of managers in both explaining the theory and providing them with a diagnostic on their particular style.

THE BONOMA/SLEVIN LEADERSHIP MODEL

Suppose that you are the leader of a group of five immediate subordinates. You are faced with a problem that is complex and yet a decision must be made. From the standpoint of leadership, before you make the decision, you must answer two "predecisional" questions:

1. *Where will you get the information input?* (Whom do you ask?)
2. *Where should you place the decision authority for this problem?* (Who makes the decision?)

The first question asks which members of the group you head will furnish information about a particular decision. The second asks to what extent you maintain all the decision authority and make the decision yourself or to what extent you "share" your decision authority with members of your group and have them make the decision in more or less democratic fashion.

The first dimension is one of information, the second one of decision authority. These two critical dimensions are essential for effective leadership and they have been plotted on the graph in Figure 29-4. As a leader you may request large amounts of subordinate information input into a decision or very small amounts of input. This is the vertical axis—information input. As a leader you may make the decision entirely yourself or you may share power with the group and have the decision made entirely as a group decision. This is the horizontal axis—decision authority. If we use percentile scores, any leadership style may be plotted in the two-dimensional space. For convenience we will refer to the horizontal axis (decision authority) first, and the vertical axis (information) second in discussing scores.

FOUR LEADERSHIP STYLES

Using this plotting system, we can describe almost any leadership style. Refer to Figure 29-4. The four extremes of leaders you have known (depicted in the four corners of the grid) are the following:

1. *Autocrat (100, 0).* Such managers solicit little or no information input from their group and make the managerial decision solely by themselves.

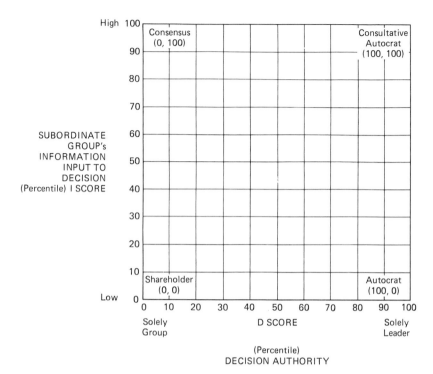

Figure 29-4. Bonoma/Slevin leadership model.

2. *Consultative Autocrat (100, 100)*. In this managerial style intensive information input is elicited from the members, but such formal leaders keep all substantive decision making authority to themselves.

3. *Consensus Manager (0, 100)*. Purely consensual managers throw open the problem to the group for discussion (information input) and simultaneously allow or encourage the entire group to make the relevant decision.

4. *Shareholder Manager (0, 0)*. This position is literally poor management. Little or no information input and exchange takes place within the group context, while the group itself is provided ultimate authority for the final decision.

The advantages of the leadership model, apart from its practical simplicity, become apparent when we consider three traditional areas of leadership and managerial decision style:

- Participative management.
- Delegation.
- Personal and organizational pressures affecting leadership.

PARTICIPATIVE MANAGEMENT

The concept of "participation" in management is a complex one with different meanings for different individuals. When the construct of participation is discussed with practicing managers in a consulting setting, the following response is typical:

"Oh, I participated with my subordinates on that decision—I asked each of them what they thought before I made the decision."

To the practicing manager, participation is often an *informational* construct—permitting sufficient subordinate input to be made before the hierarchical decision is handed down.

When the construct of participation is discussed with academics, the following response is typical:

"Managers should use participation management more often—they should involve their subordinates in consensual group processes."

To the academic, the concept of participation is often an issue of *power*, that is, a moving to the left on the Bonoma/Slevin model such that decision authority is shared with the group.

In actuality, participation is a *two-dimensional* construct. It involves both the solicitation of information and the sharing of power or decision authority. Those familiar with the Vroom-Yetton model might be interested that this conjecture is reinforced by their five positions as well. The first four positions of the Vroom-Yetton model (A1, A11, C1, C11) can be plotted vertically on the Bonoma/Slevin model as one moves from autocrat (100, 0) to consultative autocrat (100, 100), as shown in Figure 29-5 and Table 29-1. The final Vroom-Yetton position (G11) can be consigned to the consensus manager position (0, 100) on the Bonoma/Slevin model. The authors have found in a number of consulting situations that the Vroom-Yetton style selected by practitioners for a given situation is quite consistent with the position taken for the same situation on the Bonoma/ Slevin model.

DELEGATION

A good manager delegates effectively. In doing so he negotiates some sort of compromise between the extreme of "abdication"—letting subordinates do everything—and "autocratic management"—doing everything himself. When you have a task that might be delegated, you may wish to

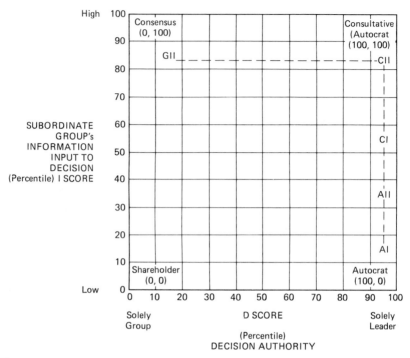

Figure 29-5. Bonoma/Slevin leadership model showing the Vroom-Yetton leadership decision styles.

ask yourself these questions which recent research has shown to relate to delegation (13):

1. How capable are my subordinates?
   (Capable subordinates make delegation more likely.)
2. How important is the decision?
   (Important decisions are less likely to be delegated.)
3. How large is my work load?
   (High supervisor work load increases delegation.)

Once you have decided to delegate a task, you may wish to use the leadership model explicitly. We have found the model useful for managers as they delegate work to their subordinates. After exposure to the model, managers are more likely to be more explicit about the informational and decision authority requirements of a delegated task. For example, the practitioner might say to his subordinate, "Get the information that you need from my files and also check with marketing [information]. You

Table 29-1. Decision Styles For Leadership: Individuals and Groups.[a]

AI.	You solve the problem or make the decision yourself, using information available to you at that time.
AII.	You obtain any necessary information from subordinates, then decide on the solution to the problem yourself. You may or may not tell the subordinates what the problem is in getting the information from them. The role played by your subordinates in making the decision is clearly one of providing specific information that you request, rather than generating or evaluating solutions.
CI.	You share the problem with the relevant subordinates individually, getting their ideas and suggestions without bringing them together as a group. Then *you* make the decision. This decision may or may not reflect your subordinates' influence.
CII.	You share the problem with your subordinates in a group meeting. In this meeting, you obtain their ideas and suggestions. Then *you* make the decision, which may or may not reflect your subordinates' influence.
GII.	You share the problem with your subordinates as a group. Together, you generate and evaluate alternatives and attempt to reach agreement (consensus) on a solution. Your role is much like that of chairman, coordinating the discussion, keeping it focused on the problem, and making sure that the critical issues are discussed. You do not try to influence the group to adopt "your" solution, and you are willing to accept and implement any solution that has the support of the entire group.

[a] From Gibson, James L., John M. Ivancevich, James H. Donnelly, Jr., *Organizations, Behavior, Structure, Processes,* Business Publications, Inc. Plano, Texas, 1985 Fifth Edition. Adapted from Vroom, Victor H. and Philip W. Yetton, *Leadership and Decision Making,* University of Pittsburgh Press, 1973.

make the decision yourself [decision authority], but notify me in writing as soon as you have made it so that I am kept informed." Thus the subordinate understands both the information and decision authority aspects of the delegated tasks. Delegation often fails when the communication is unclear on either or both of these dimensions.

PRESSURES AFFECTING LEADERSHIP

As a manager, you may act differently as a leader under different conditions, depending on three kinds of pressure:

1. Problem attributes pressures.
2. Leader personality pressures.
3. Organization/group pressures.

Think of the leadership model in terms of a map of the United States. Table 29-2 summarizes these pressures on leadership style in terms of geographical direction (for example, a movement "north" is a movement upward on the vertical axis of the leadership model, and so on).

Table 29-2. Three Leadership Style Pressures.

1. PROBLEM ATTRIBUTE PRESSURES	DIRECTION OF PRESSURE ON LEADERSHIP MODEL
• Leader lacks relevant information; problem is ambiguous	North: more information needed
• Leader lacks enough time to make decision adequately	South and east: consensus and information collection take time
• Decision is important or critical to organization	North: information search maximized West: if implementation is crucial
• Decision is personally important to leader	North and east: personal control and information maximized
• Problem is structured or routine	South and east: as little time as possible spent on decision
• Decision implementation by subordinates is critical to success	West and north: input and consensus required

2. LEADER PERSONALITY PRESSURES	DIRECTION OF PRESSURE ON LEADERSHIP MODEL
• Leader has high need for power	East: personal control maximized
• Leader is high in need for affiliation; is "people oriented"	North and west: contact with people maximized
• Leader is highly intelligent	East: personal competence demonstrated South: if leader lacks trust in subordinates
• Leader has high need for achievement	East: personal contribution maximized

3. ORGANIZATION/GROUP PRESSURES	DIRECTION OF PRESSURE ON LEADERSHIP MODEL
• Conflict is likely to result from the decision	North and west: participative aspects of decision making maximized
• Good leader/group relations exist	North and west: group contact maximized
• Centrality, formalization of organization is high	South and east: organization style matched
• Highly participative culture—strong norm for power sharing	North and west: consensus maximized
• High level of intergroup conflict	South and west: Communication between groups break down (North and west preferred as a solution to conflict)

Problem Attributes

Problem attribute pressures generate eastward forces in the leader. This is especially true when problems are characterized as:

- Time-bound.
- Important.

- Personal.
- Structured and routine.

In such cases, it is very tempting to take "control" over the decisional process personally and "get the job done."

However, northward pressures can occur too, given:

- Important decisions.
- Ones in which you as the leader lack the resources to make the decision yourself.
- Problems in which subordinate implementation is critical to success.

In these cases, information input and exchange will be maximized.

Leader Personality

Some managers tend to be inflexible in their leadership style because of who they are and how they like to manage. Such managers have at least one of the following characteristics:

- Have a high need for power.
- Are task-oriented.
- Are highly intelligent.

They will make many decisions themselves that might otherwise be left to subordinates, and they also may make decisions without acquiring information from the group. These managers typically see the sharing of the decision-making authority with subordinates as an abdication of power, or "selling out." Further, if they are highly task-oriented, their motivation is simply to get the job done or make the decision, with little thought given to the feelings of subordinates. A third characteristic, high intelligence, can often have the effect of influencing more autocratic decisions in the belief that they are more intellectually capable of arriving at the "best" decision.

People-oriented leaders, on the other hand, will act to maximize information inputs from their subordinates and to share their decision authority as well. Both activities are people processes.

Organizational/Group Pressures

If conflict is likely to result from any decision made, effective managers are most likely to want their subordinates as involved as possible in both the input (northward) and authority (westward) dimensions, so as to help manage the potential conflict. Should good leader/group relations exist, pressure northward (but *not* necessarily westward) will be felt. The leader will feel great pressures to fit into the "culture" of the organization. The R&D lab expects a consensual approach; most business groups expect a consultative autocrat approach; the factory floor may expect an autocratic approach. It is important to match your style to the norms, needs, and expectations of your subordinates.

Flexibility

The key message here is that this is a contingency model of leadership. No one style is best for all situations. Rather the successful manager is flexible and moves around the model as appropriate to the given situation. If time pressures are overwhelming, autocrat decisions may be appropriate. For a majority of management decision making, the consultative autocrat may be appropriate. And in dealing with high-tech professionals, the manager may choose to use a more consensual style. The key to success is *to match your leadership style to the situation and people involved.*

FINDINGS FROM THE FIELD

Based on the presentation and discussion of this model with thousands of practicing managers, we would like to share with you our conclusions concerning important principles.

1. *You're more autocratic than you think.*
   In the eyes of your subordinates you are probably closer to the autocrat on the graph than you are in your own eyes. Why? Because you're the boss and they are the subordinates. No matter how easygoing, friendly, participative, and supportive you are, you are still the boss. There is almost always difference in leadership style as perceived by supervisor and subordinates.
2. *But it's O.K.*
   Often, when you ask subordinates where they would like their boss to move, they respond, "Things are O.K. as they are." Even though there are perceptual discrepancies concerning leadership style, there may not necessarily be a felt need or pressure for change. The status quo may be O.K.
3. *It's easy to move north and south.*
   It's easy to move vertically on the graph. Why? Because management is a job of communications. It's easy to collect more informa-

tion or less information before you make the decision. The information dimension is the least resistant to change.

4. *It's hard to move west.*

Most managers of our experience find it quite threatening to move westward too quickly. Why? Because a westward movement upsets the basic power realities in the organization. If your head is in the noose, if things don't work out, then it is hard to turn the decisions totally over to your subordinates.

5. *If subordinates' expectations are not met, morale can suffer.*

What would you expect to be the consequences if your subordinates expected you to use a (50, 90) process and instead you made the decision using a (90, 10) style? Very likely the result would be dissatisfaction and morale problems. As mentioned before, decision process can be as important as decision outcome, especially from the standpoint of motivating subordinates.

6. *Be flexible.*

A successful manager is autocratic when he needs to be, consultative when necessary, and consensual when the situation calls for it. Move around the leadership space to fit the needs of the situation. Unsuccessful managers are inflexible and try the same style in all situations. Most managers feel that their score on the Jerrell/Slevin management instrument is a function of the particular job they have been in over the last few months. Be flexible and match your leadership style to the job.

LEADERSHIP CHECKLIST

Let us now see how well your leadership style squares with your organization.

	Yes	No
1. *Dominant Leadership Style*		
Should I try to change my own style?	☐	☐
Should I become more autocratic?	☐	☐
Or more consensual?	☐	☐
2. *Fit*		
Is my leadership style inappropriate for my organization?	☐	☐
Am I an autocratic peg in a participative hole?	☐	☐
3. *Flexibility*		
Do I fail to move my leadership style around the graph to match the different problems that I face?	☐	☐
Am I sometimes too inflexible for the responsibilities that I have?	☐	☐

4. *Subordinate Fit*
   Do my subordinates have expectations and needs that are
   not in line with my leadership style? ☐ ☐
   If so, do I need new subordinates? ☐ ☐
5. *Information*
   Do I receive insufficient information for decision making? ☐ ☐
   Do my subordinates fail to regularly send me meaningful
   reports? ☐ ☐
6. *Decision Authority*
   Do I fail to share decision authority appropriately? ☐ ☐
   Am I stifling my subordinates by not letting them partici-
   pate in decisions affecting them? ☐ ☐

If you answered "no" to all of the questions, you're O.K. in all six
areas and are in excellent shape. If you answered "yes" to any questions,
these are your problem areas and you should examine them. For example,
if your subordinates don't seem to fit your own leadership style, maybe
you need some new subordinates. Or you need to change. Or, if you just
don't seem flexible enough to take on the broad range of problems you
face, maybe you need to reexamine your leadership style. If you have
three or more problem areas, it's undoubtedly time to give that corporate
headhunter a call. (Or maybe you'd better engage in a serious high-priority program of leadership therapy.)

AN EXAMPLE

Does the leadership model really work? We have applied it in a number of
research, training, and field management settings. Here's an example of
the sorts of results that might be forthcoming.

Production Supervisor, Polyurethane Division, Large Chemical Corporation

This manager kept a running diary over a three-week period of 41 decision
situations he faced on the job. Later he plotted them on the model. He
found a strong divergence between the way he thought he behaved and
the way he actually behaved in most leadership situations. It became
obvious to him that his dominant leadership style was not that of a consensus manager but more that of a consultative autocrat, for when he
plotted his flexibility space on the basis of actual behavior, he found that
the only direction in which he was flexible was vertical (that of allowing
increased information input from subordinates). In no case did he behaviorally allow any decision authority sharing, as he had previously supposed he did. He concluded:

The merit of the Bonoma-Slevin Leadership Model was in its simplicity, since it uses only two dimensions to describe alternative leadership styles. The model confirmed that my actual leadership style was inconsistent with my preconceived image of leadership style. It presented a visual conception of changes necessary for me to alter my present leadership style as that of a Consultative Autocrat to become a Consensus Manager.

My recommendation for anyone wanting to use the Leadership Model for self analysis would be to keep a diary of decisional situations faced over a period of time.

Vice President, Division of International Manufacturing Firm

This manager supervises approximately five other managers and five people not holding managerial status. He asked each of his subordinates, first, to estimate his dominant decision style over the last 12 months, and, second, to recommend how he should change. As a result, he learned that his subordinates rated him approximately 20% more autocratic than he had rated himself. However, he also found that his subordinates were quite happy with his leadership style, and desired only slightly less autocratic decisions and slightly more information input.

CONCLUSION: ORGANIZATIONAL IMPLICATIONS OF LEADERSHIP

The leadership framework presented in our model forces the manager to ask two key questions concerning decision making:

- Whom do I ask?
- Who makes the decision?

Obtaining accurate information input from one's subordinate group is crucial to effective management. Similarly, decision-making authority must be located in the right place vis-à-vis the leader's group.

In addition, this model might be broadened to apply to even more fundamental questions of your managerial job. Forgetting for a moment that you are a leader of a subordinate group, answer the following questions by considering both vertical and horizontal relationships in your organization:

1. *Where do I get my information?*

Every manager needs accurate information to make effective decisions. Do you get sufficient information:

- From your boss?
- From your peers?
- From the formal information system?
- From all sources in the organization that can aid you in your job?

2. *Who makes the decisions?*

Is the decision authority vested in the right people, not just concerning your subordinates but also upward and laterally? Should other departments be making decisions that you now make or vice versa?

The answers to these questions have broad implications for the management information system and the power structure of your organization. If you are not getting necessary information, perhaps the management information system should be modified to provide it. If you have a problem of misplaced decision authority (downward or upward), this problem should be addressed. If the answers to these fundamental questions are satisfactory, then only one important question remains, which cannot be addressed here: are the decisions good ones?

MOTIVATIONAL ISSUES

Motivation is important to the project manager from two perspectives. First, the individual must be motivated to *be* a project manager. If one does not have sufficient intrinsic motivation to take the types of managerial steps required, then one is not likely to succeed at the project management task. Second, the project manager must be able to motivate others. For this it is crucial that the project manager have an adequate understanding of motivation and techniques for motivating others. This section is intended to provide the reader with the ability to diagnose his or her intrinsic motivation to manage and also the ability to understand better the motivational structures that others bring to their work settings and ways to utilize them for an effective performance.

MOTIVATION TO MANAGE DEFINED

Do you have the necessary internal motivation to be an effective project manager? Many people who find themselves in project management situations are technically skilled and analytically oriented. Consequently, they often feel uncomfortable in assuming the managerial role which requires numerous interventions into the work of other people. The construct of Motivation to Manage (17) can be a useful tool for the current or prospective project manager.

According to research conducted over the past two decades, the Motivation to Manage and its associated attitudes and motives are likely to cause one to:

- Choose a managerial career.
- Be successful in a managerial position.
- Move rapidly up the managerial ladder.

In other words, the Motivation to Manage is essential for managerial success. The six components included in the Motivation to Manage, outlined by John B. Miner, follow.

The manager should have:

1. Favorable Attitude Toward Authority—Managers are expected to behave in ways that do not provoke negative reactions from their superiors; ideally, they elicit positive responses. Equally, a manager must be able to represent his group upward in the organization and to obtain support for his actions at higher levels. This requires a good relationship between a manager and his superior.
2. Desire to Compete—There is, at least insofar as peers are concerned, a strong competitive element built into managerial work; a manager must compete for the available rewards, both for himself and for his group. Certainly, without competitive behavior, rapid promotion is improbable. On occasion a challenge may come from below, even from among a manager's own subordinates.
3. Assertive Motivation—There is a marked parallel between the requirements of the managerial role and the traditional assertive requirements of the masculine role as defined in our society. Although the behaviors expected of a father and those expected of a manager are by no means identical, there are many similarities: both are supposed to take charge, to make decisions, to take such disciplinary action as may be necessary to protect the other members of their group. . . . when women are appointed to managerial positions, they are expected to follow an essentially assertive behavior pattern, at least during the hours spent in the work situation.
4. Desire to Exercise Power—A manager must exercise power over his subordinates and direct their behavior in a manner consistent with organizational (and presumably his own) objectives. He must tell others what to do when this becomes necessary and enforce his words through positive and negative sanctions. The individual who finds such behavior difficult and emotionally disturbing, who does not wish to impose his wishes on others or believes it wrong to do so, probably cannot be expected to meet this requirement.

5. Desire for a Distinctive Position—The managerial job tends to require a person to behave differently from the ways his subordinates behave toward each other. He must be willing to take the center of the stage and assume a position of high visibility; he must be willing to do things that invite attention, discussion, and perhaps criticism from those reporting to him; and he must accept a position of considerable importance in relation to the motives and emotions of others.

6. A Sense of Responsibility—The managerial job requires getting the work out and staying on top of routine demands. The things that have to be done must actually be done; constructing budget estimates, serving on committees, talking on the telephone, filling out employee rating forms, making salary recommendations, and so on. To meet these requirements, a manager must be capable of dealing with this type of routine and, ideally, of gaining some satisfaction from it.*

RESEARCH RESULTS

Can you predict your degree of success and job satisfaction by knowing your Motivation to Manage? It appears that you can. Research has compared the initial Motivation to Manage with subsequent promotions over a five-year period in two departments. The results are presented below:

Motivation to Manage

Initial Motivation to Manage and Number of Subsequent Promotions over Next 5 Years in the R&D Department of an Oil Company

Motivation to Manage	No Promotions	One Promotion	Two or More Promotions
High	3(25%)	6(38%)	15(71%)
Low	9(75%)	10(62%)	6(29%)

Initial Motivation to Manage and Rate of Subsequent Promotion over Next 5 Years in the Marketing Department of an Oil Company

Motivation to Manage	No Promotions	Slow Promotion Rate	Fast Promotion Rate
High	13(32%)	14(64%)	16(89%)
Low	28(68%)	8(36%)	2(11%)

Source: Miner (17), pp. 28–29.

---

* (Copyright © 1973 by the President and Fellows of Harvard College; all rights reserved. Reprinted by permission of *Harvard Business Review.* "The Real Crunch in Managerial Manpower," by John B. Miner, Vol. 51, No. 6, 1973, p. 153.

Numerous other results have suggested the basic premise:

- To be a successful manager you must have the Motivation to Manage.

What is the relevance of this for you? Many project managers evolved into their managerial positions out of areas of technical expertise such as accounting, finance, marketing, and engineering. It is not uncommon to have highly qualified individual contributors promoted to the managerial ranks. The change is dramatic. In the previous roles they communicated primarily with things. They now must communicate primarily with people. Previously they could spend long uninterrupted hours reading, reflecting, collecting data, and working on technical projects. They now must spend large amounts of time in group meetings, talking on the telephone, being interrupted by subordinates, and doing the other frenetic activities that encompass a typical manager's day. Before, they could self-actualize by coming up with good technical solutions. Now they must engage in the sometimes unpleasant process of exercising power over others and engaging in competition for key resources.

Management is recognized as a step up in the career ladder. It is noted as a logical progression in one's professional advancement. Nevertheless, for the talented specialist with a low Motivation to Manage, it may be a traumatic metamorphosis indeed. A crucial question every manager should ask himself is: "Do I have sufficient Motivation to Manage to ensure that I will be satisfied and successful in this position?"

DIAGNOSING YOUR MOTIVATION TO MANAGE

Now it's time to give you an opportunity to see where you stand on Motivation to Manage (MTM). Complete the Motivation to Manage Audit (Motivation 1, Figure 29-6). This is a subjective assessment and you may have some error, but at least it will sensitize you to the key variables and encourage you to think about these issues.

MTM AND PREFERRED JOB CHARACTERISTICS

Activities that are preferred and enjoyed are very different for the person with a high versus a low Motivation to Manage. Jobs with given characteristics are better and less well suited to each managerial type. Table 29-3 indicates those job characteristics that are best matched with people with high MTM and low MTM.

MOTIVATION 1

MOTIVATION TO MANAGE AUDIT

How motivated to manage are you?

Complete this instrument by circling the number for each item that represents your best estimate of your current level.

	Well Below Average	Average	Well Above Average

1. Favorable attitude toward authority   0 1 2 3 4 5 6 7 8 9 10

2. Desire to compete   0 1 2 3 4 5 6 7 8 9 10

3. Assertive motivation   0 1 2 3 4 5 6 7 8 9 10

4. Desire to exercise power   0 1 2 3 4 5 6 7 8 9 10

5. Desire for a distinctive position   0 1 2 3 4 5 6 7 8 9 10

6. A sense of responsibility   0 1 2 3 4 5 6 7 8 9 10

TOTAL MOTIVATION TO MANAGE = _____

Now place a check mark next to the number for each item that represents your best estimate of where you would *like to be*. The difference between your *desired* and *actual* score for each item is your Motivation to Manage deficit on that factor. It will be used in completing your Motivation to Manage Action Plan (Motivation 2).

Figure 29-6. Instrument for assessing the motivation to manage.

Table 29-3. Job Characteristics Associated with Motivation to Manage (MTM).

LOW MTM	HIGH MTM
Relatively small span of control	Large span of control
Small number of subordinates	Large number of subordinates
High technical/engineering component	High people/budgetary component
Maintain "hands-on" expertise	Surround oneself with technical experts
Limited number of activities per day	As many as 200 activities per day
Few interruptions	Many interruptions
Time for reading, analyzing	Time for interactions
Serve as facilitator to staff	Serve as "boss" to staff
Career progression = increase in technical expertise	Career progression = managerial advancement
Little exercise of power required	Much intervention in lives of others
Lower stress position	Higher stress position

MTM/JOB FIT

In order for you to be satisfied and successful in an organizational role, you must first attempt to match your basic motivation to the job. Does your job fit your Motivation to Manage? Different jobs require different levels of MTM. Look at Table 29-3 and try to determine if you are in a high or low MTM job. Suppose that you have just concluded that you have low Motivation to Manage? What should you do?

You have two alternatives:

1. Select jobs that are more appropriate to your MTM.
2. Attempt to change your MTM.

In order for you to be happy, fulfilled, and successful in your job, you must fit the job requirements. There must be a match between your motivation and the characteristics of the job, the activities you like to perform and those demanded by the job. Thorough and accurate self-assessment regarding your Motivation to Manage can present you with very important information as you make career choices.

CHANGING YOUR MOTIVATION TO MANAGE

It is generally accepted in psychology that a certain amount of motivation is learned. McClelland (15) has claimed the ability to teach people to increase their need for achievement. He has also concluded that successful managers have a higher need for power than their need for affiliation

(16). This seems compatible with the MTM in that one must be prepared to exercise power over others in order to succeed as a manager.

Is it possible to increase a person's Motivation to Manage? We think so. Little research has been done in this area. There are no figures to cite. However, look at the six components of Motivation to Manage. They are learned motives. Therefore one should be able to change them. Is it possible to change your Motivation to Manage? Definitely! If you want to.

Do you want to change your Motivation to Manage? If yes, you will need to formulate an action plan for changing each of the components of managerial motivation.

Go back to the Motivation to Manage Audit (Figure 29-6). Look at your desired level for each of the factors in the Motivation to Manage in your present position. The difference between the desired level and your actual level provides a managerial motivation deficit for each factor. List on the Motivation to Manage Action Plan (Motivation 2, Figure 29-7) the specific steps that you might take to increase your MTM on each factor to remove the deficit.

MOTIVATING OTHERS

So far we have focused on what motivates you, on diagnosing your internal motivational structure. As a successful manager you must be able to effectively motivate others. We have attempted here to provide you with a pragmatic approach to the problem of motivating others. In the old days this was easier, or it at least appears to have been from today's perspective. To dramatize this, let's go back to the Bethlehem Steel Company labor yard in Bethlehem, Pennsylvania, in the spring of 1899. Frederick Winslow Taylor, the father of scientific management, comes over to the laborer Schmidt whose job it is to load pig iron onto gondola cars. (His real name was Henry Noll, but Taylor thought "Schmidt" sounded better in his historical record.) Schmidt's job was quite simple: pick up a 91-pound pig of iron, walk horizontally across the yard with it, up an inclined ramp, and deposit it in the gondola car. He then returned to the pile for another pig of iron and continued to do this throughout the day. During a typical day, Schmidt would load between 12 and 13 tons (long tons = 2240 pounds each) of pig iron per day. For doing this he earned his daily wage of $1.15. Taylor studied him "scientifically." He carefully timed how long it took to pick up a pig, the speed with which one could walk horizontally up the incline with a load, back down the ramp unloaded, etc. He then made Schmidt a proposition: "Follow my instructions and increase your output and pay." Schmidt agreed, since he was put on a piece-rate system under which he could now earn $1.85 per day provided he reached his

MOTIVATION 2

MOTIVATION TO MANAGE ACTION PLAN

Record your Motivation to Manage deficit (desired - actual) for each factor below. Then specify appropriate action steps you might take to increase your Motivation to Manage on each factor and remove the deficit.

1. Favorable Attitude Toward Authority   Deficit: _____
    Action Plan: _____
    _____
    _____ Probability of Success: _____

2. Desire to Compete   Deficit: _____
    Action Plan: _____
    _____
    _____ Probability of Success: _____

3. Assertive Motivation   Deficit: _____
    Action Plan: _____
    _____
    _____ Probability of Success: _____

4. Desire to Exercise Power   Deficit: _____
    Action Plan: _____
    _____
    _____ Probability of Success: _____

5. Desire for Distinctive Position   Deficit: _____
    Action Plan: _____
    _____
    _____ Probability of Success: _____

6. A Sense of Responsibility   Deficit: _____
    Action Plan: _____
    _____
    _____ Probability of Success: _____

Figure 29-7. Motivation to manage action plan.

target. His target amounted to 45–48 tons of pig iron per day. According to Taylor (22), Schmidt reached his target and continued to perform at this rate on a regular basis.

The enormity of his task is hard to contemplate in today's world. To accomplish his 45 tons per day, Schmidt had to walk the equivalent of 8 miles each day with a 91-pound pig of iron in his arms. He then had to run 8 miles back to the pile (23). According to Taylor's reports, Schmidt was not a large man, weighing about 130 pounds, but was particularly suited to his work. Based on discussions that we have had with the Human Energy laboratory at the University of Pittsburgh, one can conclude that Schmidt's caloric energy output amounted to at least 5000–6000 calories per day. The poor man would have had to spend much of his waking hours eating just to keep from slowly disappearing over time.

As an interesting human interest side of this story, although Taylor reported Schmidt as happy with his work, later reports indicate that Henry Noll became an excessive drinker and lost both his home and his job. Also, although Taylor's self-reports seem to indicate great success and relative ease of implementation, such was not the case. The excellent history written by Daniel Nelson (19) demonstrates some extremely difficult problems such as worker resistance, lack of cooperation from top management, political infighting, and other problems reminiscent of the difficulties of implementation of modern-day organizational change.

The moral of this story is that it is much easier to motivate an extremely deprived and hungry worker. Taylor's writings include stories of tremendous accomplishments with his "first-class men," individuals who were willing to work at extremely high physical rates. He was able to accomplish these feats because the workers were at near subsistence levels and were willing to work quite hard to get that potential 60% increase in pay. Imagine the difficulties that Taylor might have in a modern-day steel yard!

MASLOW'S HIERARCHY OF NEEDS

One very useful model for explaining the changes that have occurred in human motivation over the years is that developed by Abraham Maslow (14). Maslow's hierarchy argues that man's needs come in an ordered sequence that is arranged in the following five need categories:

1. Physical needs: the need for food, water, air.
2. Safety needs: the need for security, stability, and freedom from threat to physical safety.
3. Love needs: the need for friends with whom one may affiliate.
4. Esteem needs: the need for self-respect and esteem of others. This includes recognition, attention, and appreciation from others.

5. Self-actualization needs: the need for self-fulfillment to be able to grow and learn.

Maslow argued that these needs were arranged on a "hierarchy of prepotency." In other words, they must be fulfilled in sequential fashion starting with the lower-order needs first and progressing up the need hierarchy. One who is dying of dehydration in the desert is not interested in esteem needs; one who is being threatened by a criminal is not interested in self-actualization, etc. Substantial follow-up research (and even Maslow's original speculations) indicate that the needs do not always have to be fulfilled in a lock-step fashion. At times the artist may be willing to starve in order to create, etc. But, in general it is a useful managerial model when we consider the problem of how to motivate workers. Over the eight decades since Taylor's initial success, society at large has moved dramatically up the need hierarchy. It would be quite difficult today to get a worker to triple output in return for a 60% increase in wages.

The manager of today must be able to assess where each of his subordinates and co-workers are on the hierarchy and attempt to appeal to the appropriate needs. Some people crave status and recognition. Others want strongly to be a member of a cohesive team and "to belong." Others have a tremendous need to be creative, innovative, and learn new skills. If you have a motivational problem with a worker, attempt to answer these three questions:

1. Where is he or she on Maslow's Need Hierarchy?
2. What needs will motivate him or her?
3. How can I help him or her to satisfy these needs?

The key point for you as manager and potential motivator of your subordinates is this: individuals are driven by differing sets of needs and, consequently, must be motivated individually. In other words, the manager who supposes that one motivation style will work for all employees (e.g., Taylor, who thought all workers were motivated solely by the need for more money) greatly oversimplifies his or her job in attempting to motivate subordinates. Adequate time must be spent up front with subordinates, in getting to know them and understand those drives on which their needs are based.

HERZBERG'S MOTIVATION HYGIENE THEORY

Herzberg (10) has suggested that there are two types of motivational factors: hygiene factors and motivators. He suggests that the hygiene factors are necessary conditions for a satisfied worker, but do not guarantee satisfaction. If they are absent, you will have an unhappy worker; but their presence does not guarantee contentment. The hygiene factors include:

- Company policy and administration.
- Supervision.
- Relationship with supervisor.
- Working conditions.
- Salary.
- Relationship with peers.
- Personal life.
- Relationship with subordinates.
- Status.
- Security.

Table 29-4. Herzberg and Maslow Compared.[a]

NEED THEORY		TWO-FACTOR THEORY
Self-actualization and fulfillment	Motivational	Work itself Achievement Possibility of growth
Esteem and status		Advancement Recognition Status
Belonging & social needs		Relations with supervisors Peer relations Relations with subordinates Quality of supervision
Safety & security	Maintenance	Company policy and administration Job security Working conditions
Physiological needs		Pay

[a] Keith Davis and John W. Newstrom, "Human Behavior at Work," *Organizational Behavior,* New York; McGraw-Hill, 1985, p. 77. Used with permission.

In other words, the hygiene factors satisfy the lower-level Maslow needs. On the other hand, there are motivators which are factors that account for satisfaction in the worker. The motivators include:

- Achievement.
- Recognition.
- Work itself.
- Responsibility.
- Advancement.
- Growth.

In other words, the motivators are found at the higher levels of Maslow's Hierarchy (see Table 29-4).

Herzberg's model has been challenged on both empirical and conceptual grounds. However, it has been demonstrated to be quite powerful as a general guide to the process of "job enrichment." The basic philosophy is that you can enrich someone's job and induce that individual to work harder by making the work more interesting and satisfying.

If you would like to explore the possibility of job enrichment, perform the following steps:

1. Remove serious dissatisfiers. For example:
   - Make sure working conditions are pleasant:
     Be sure pay is equitable, make supervision fair.
2. Vertically load the job content on the satisfiers. For example:
   - Push responsibility downward,
   - Push planning upward,
   - Provide meaningful modules of work.
   - Increase job freedom.
   - Introduce new and difficult tasks.

It is well known that individuals tend to do what is satisfying to them. They are more likely to repeat behaviors that result in rewards and to not repeat behaviors that do not. Consequently, if you can design a work environment in which individuals are reinforced by the work itself, you will experience much greater effectiveness as a manager.

IN CONCLUSION: MOTIVATING YOURSELF AND OTHERS

You have now had an opportunity to assess in a personal way your Motivation to Manage. The logical steps in this assessment are portrayed in the flowchart shown in Figure 29-8. Try to accomplish this in as perceptive a way as possible. It's fun to consider your own personal motivational structures and to talk to others about career, job, and personal needs. If you can better understand where you are concerning your Motivation to Manage, you will be in a better position to perform your job at peak efficiency. If your Motivation to Manage is insufficient for your current or future job prospects, then you must seriously consider chang-

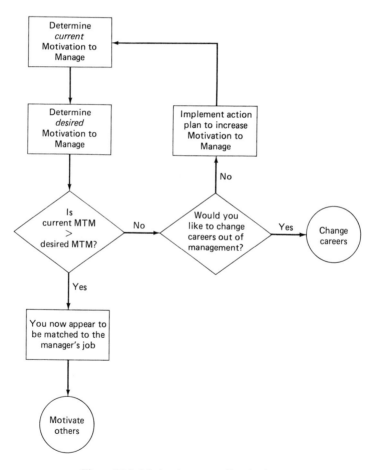

Figure 29-8. Motivating yourself and others.

ing these needs or changing your career. Millions of people get matched to millions of jobs through ad hoc and almost accidental sequences of events. In this chapter you are provided with a framework for consciously and analytically attempting to assess the match between your motivation structure and the manager's job.

The second point of this section consists of attempting to motivate others. Remember that different people have different motivational needs. You may have to respond in a very contingent manner to individuals on your team. Entire books have been written on this topic, and human motivation is indeed a complex area. In brief, you should try to assume the role of a facilitator that links up need satisfactions with desired job performances. If you can structure an environment in which diverse individual needs are being met through job performance, you will find yourself with a more cohesive and dedicated work group. If you can master these techniques, you will be well on your way to becoming a highly effective and successful project manager.

SUMMARY

A good project manager is a capable leader. You must be able to lead the project team—often under conditions of minimum legitimate power. The leadership model presented here should enable the project manager to select leadership styles consciously, based on the parameters of the situation. A good project manager similarly must be able to motivate the project team. The models presented here should enable the project manager to assess his or her own internal motivation and also help in the selection of strategies for the motivation of others. These two skills, leadership and motivation, are important tools for the successful project manager.

REFERENCES

1. Blake, R. R. and Mouton, J. *The Managerial Grid* (Gulf Publishing. Houston, 1964).
2. Dansereau, F., Green, G. and Haga, B. "A Vertical Dyad Linkage Approach to Leadership Within Formal Organizations: A Longitudinal Investigation of the Role Making Process." *Organizational Behavior and Human Performance*, Vol. 13 (1975), pp. 45–78.
3. Davis, K. and Newstrom, J. *Human Behavior at Work*, 7th Ed. (McGraw-Hill. New York, 1985).
4. Fiedler, F. E. "Contingency Model and the Leadership Process," in *Advances in Experimental Social Psychology*, Vol. 11, ed. Berkovitz, L. (Academic Press. New York, 1978).
5. Fleishman, E. A. 1973, "Twenty Years of Consideration and Structure," in *Current Developments in the Study of Leadership*, ed. Fleishman, E. A. and Hunt, J. G. (Southern Illinois University Press. Carbondale, 1973).

6. Fodor, E. M. "Group Stress, Authoritarian Style of Control, and Use of Power." *Journal of Applied Psychology,* Vol. 61 (1976), pp. 313–318.
7. Ghiselli, E. *Exploration in Managerial Talent* (Goodyear. Santa Monica, Calif., 1971).
8. Heilman, M. E., Hornstein, H. A., Cage, J. H. and Herschlag, J. K. "Reactions to Prescribed Leader Behavior as a Function of Role Perspective: the Case of the Vroom-Yetton Model." *Journal of Applied Psychology,* Vol. 69 (1984), pp. 50–60.
9. Hersey, P. and Blanchard, K. H. *Management of Organizational Behavior: Utilizing Human Resources,* 3rd Ed. (Prentice-Hall. Englewood Cliffs, N.J., 1977).
10. Herzberg, Frederick. "One More Time: How Do You Motivate Employees?" *Harvard Business Review,* Vol. 46(1) (1968), pp. 53–62.
11. House, R. J. "A Path-Goal Theory of Leader Effectiveness." *Administrative Science Quarterly,* Vol. 16 (1971), pp. 321–333.
12. Kerr, S. and Jermier, J. M. "Substitutes for Leadership: Their Meaning and Measurement." *Organizational Behavior and Human Performance,* Vol. 22 (1978), pp. 375–403.
13. Leana, Carrie R. "Predictors and Consequences of Delegation." *Academy of Management Journal,* Vol. 29(4) (1986), pp. 754–774.
14. Maslow, A. H. "A Theory of Human Motive Acquisition." *Psychological Review,* Vol. 1 (1943), pp. 370–396.
15. McClelland, David C. "Toward a Theory of Motive Acquisition." *American Psychologist,* Vol. 20 (1965), pp. 321–333.
16. McClelland, David C. and Burnham, David H. "Power Is the Great Motivator." *Harvard Business Review* (March–April, 1976).
17. Miner, John B. *The Human Constraint* (The Bureau of National Affairs, Inc. Washington, D.C., 1974).
18. Miner, John B. "The Real Crunch in Managerial Manpower." *Harvard Business Review,* Vol. 51(6) (1973), pp. 146–158.
19. Nelson, Daniel. *Frederick W. Taylor and the Rise of Scientific Management,* (University of Wisconsin Press. Madison, 1980).
20. Salancik, G. R., Calder, B. J., Rowland, K. M., Leblebici, H. and Conway, M. "Leadership as an Outcome of Social Structure and Process: A Multi-Dimensional Analysis," in *Leadership Frontiers,* ed. Hunt, J. G. and Larson, L. L. (Kent State University, Kent, Ohio, 1975).
21. Stogdill, R. *Handbook of Leadership* (Free Press. New York, 1974).
22. Taylor, Frederick W. "Time Study, Piece Work and the First-Class Man." *Transactions of the American Society of Mechanical Engineers,* Vol. 24 (1903), pp. 1356–1364, Reprinted in Merrill, Harwood F. *Classics in Management* (American Management Associates. New York, 1960).
23. Taylor, Frederick. *The Principles of Scientific Management* Harper & Row. New York, 1911).
24. Tjosvold, D. "Effects of Leader Warmth and Directiveness on Subordinate Performance on a Subsequent Task." *Journal of Applied Psychology,* Vol. 69 (1984), pp. 422–427.
25. Vroom, V. H. and Yetton, P. W. *Leadership and Decision Making* (University of Pittsburgh Press. Pittsburgh, 1973).

30. Project Teams and the Human Group

Raymond E. Hill* and Trudy L. Somers†

A central theme in managing the human side of project teams is the management of social conflict. Conflict in organizations is pervasive, inevitable, and ubiquitous; organizations develop specialized differentiated subunits which then obey many of the principles of general systems theory, not the least of which is the emergence of opponent processes among the differentiated parts. Project teams, by the very act of bringing together representatives of the specialized subunits, become a microcosm of the larger organizational dynamics.

There are a variety of issues around which conflict arises. Thamhain and Wilemon (1)‡ have reduced these issues to seven fundamental areas which include the following: project priorities, administrative procedures, technical opinions and performance trade-offs, manpower resources, cost estimates, scheduling and sequencing of work, and personality conflict. Thamhain and Wilemon found significant variation in intensity of the seven conflict types over the life cycle of a project. Data from one hundred project managers indicated considerable variation over time in the intensity of conflict from almost all sources except personality clashes. Personality conflicts were relatively constant during all phases of a project life cycle including project formation, buildup, main program phase,

* Raymond E. Hill is Associate Professor of Organizational Behavior in the Graduate School of Business Administration, The University of Michigan. He is a member of the American Psychological Association and the Academy of Management. His research interests are focused on project management, with recent interests centered around career choice and development processes, particularly of systems and computer personnel. He has published several articles in professional journals, and has edited a book of readings on Matrix Organization.
† Trudy L. Somers is a Ph.D. student of Organizational Behavior in the Graduate School of Business Administration, The University of Michigan. She is a member of the Academy of Management and the American Psychological Association. Her current research interests arise from years of working experience in computer-related firms and center in strategic human resource management, with special interest in careers.
‡ Numbered references are given at the end of this chapter.

and phaseout. In discussing personality clashes as a source of conflict, Thamhain and Wilemon suggest that while it is not as intense as some other conflict types, it is nevertheless problematical. In particular, they suggest, "Project managers emphasized that personality conflicts are particularly difficult to handle. Even apparently small and infrequent personality conflicts might be more disruptive and detrimental to overall program effectiveness than intense conflict over nonpersonal issues, which can often be handled on a more rational basis" (2).

It is the purpose of this chapter to relate two frameworks for conceptualizing personality conflict, both of which can be diagnosed and assessed using standardized questionnaires, to discuss the relationship of these frameworks to group performance, to report on how differences can be managed for more effective project performance, and to identify additional references for the interested reader. The first framework (MBTI) deals with different problem-solving strategies determined by how the individual (1) gathers and (2) processes information. The second framework (FIRO-B) focuses on emotional dynamics expressed through interpersonal relational styles.

PROBLEM-SOLVING STYLES: THE MBTI FRAMEWORK

This section explores a framework for understanding the cognitive or problem-solving styles of group members, and how these styles influence team functioning. Problem solving can be viewed as involving two dimensions: the process of gathering information, and the process of making evaluations, decisions, or judgments based on that information. Information gathering involves such tasks as finding out about a problem, interpreting the world, and inferring meaning from all the complexity which usually surrounds a given event. As Hellriegel and Slocum (3) note, information gathering also involves rejecting some data and reducing much of it to a manageable, comprehensive form. Judgment, the process by which information is evaluated and decisions are made, is the second important operation in problem solving.

A framework for conceptualizing and assessing problem-solving styles has been developed by Isabel Briggs-Myers based on Jung's theory of psychological types (4). The basic dimension of information gathering is referred to as perception and takes the two opposing forms of either sensing or intuition. Information evaluation, or judgment, takes the opposing forms of either thinking or feeling. The Myers-Briggs Type Indicator (MBTI) is a questionnaire that assesses which type of perception and judgment an individual prefers to use in problem solving. An initial categorization of problem-solving styles can be depicted as the four quadrants of Figure 30-1 (adapted from Hellriegel and Slocum (5)).

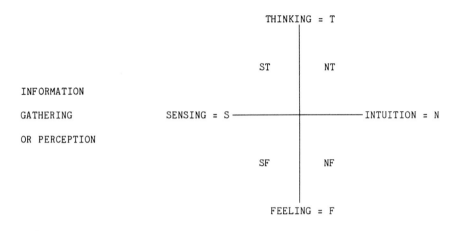

Figure 30-1. Problem-solving styles. (Adapted from Hellriegel, D. and Slocum, J. W., "Preferred Organizational Designs and Problem Solving Styles: Interesting Companions," *Human Systems Management,* 1: 151–158 (1980).

Two Ways of Perceiving: Sensing and Intuition

Sensing types (S) look at the world and see the hard data that is directly available through the senses (i.e., seeing, hearing, touching.) They tend to be realistic, pragmatic, and focused in the here and now. They prefer problems which lend themselves to standardized solution procedures. They prefer routine work and enjoy working in structured settings. They dislike unstructured problems, high degrees of uncertainty and change, and working with "soft data."

Intuitive (N), types on the other hand, look at the world and see not what is "just there," but rather what might be. They see beyond the here and now into the realm of possibilities, implicit meanings, and potential relationships among events. Intuitives often use "soft data," hunches and possibilities which come to them rather spontaneously. They also tend to see the "big picture" or totality rather than the fine print or details, as sensing types do. Intuitive types also enjoy complexity, unstructured problems, and newness, and are burdened by too much routine. Mary McCaulley, president of the Center for Applications of Psychological Type (CAPT, Inc.), who oversees applications and development of the MBTI, suggests that "In a new and complex venture, a team needs more intuitive types; in a venture which requires careful management of many details, a team needs more sensing types" (6).

Two Types of Judgment: Thinking and Feeling

The second dimension in the model involves making decisions, and again there are two opposing approaches. Those who prefer thinking as their favorite judgment process like putting things into a structured format and using cause-effect logic. Thinking types (T) tend to be uninterested in people's feelings and seem "hard-headed" (or hard-hearted) and are able to fire or reprimand people when necessary. They enjoy applying data and formulas to problems, and are particularly attracted to the contributions made by operations research and management science to decisional problems. They like to think of management as a science, not an art. As Hellriegel and Slocum (7) note, there is considerable similarity between thinking types, the scientific method, and work in bureaucratic organizations which emphasize rationality and impersonality in human relations.

Feeling types (F) also make decisions by a rational process. As McCaulley notes, "Feeling does not refer to emotions, but rather to the process of setting priorities in terms of values, weighing their greater or lesser importance to oneself and others" (8). They tend to become sympathetic, are concerned about their own and other's reactions in decision situations, and reflect a concern for the establishment of harmonious interpersonal relations. They do not particularly like to tell others unpleasant things, and often gravitate toward mediator and conciliator roles in team situations. Whereas thinking types approach decisions with abstract true or false judgments and formal logic rules, the feeling type invokes more personalistic judgments of good or bad, pleasant or unpleasant, and like or dislike.

The Composite Styles

Each type of perception can team up with each type of judgment, so that the quadrants of Figure 30-1 represent four basic problem-solving styles. The sensing thinkers (STs) are the traditionalists of organizational life. They can absorb, remember, and manage a large number of facts and details. They strive to create and maintain order, structure, and control; sensing thinkers are realistic, pragmatic, economically motivated. They follow through on assignments and generally represent the "quintessential organization man," in the positive sense of the term. They are good task leaders.

Sensing-feeling types (SFs) also prefer structured organizations and work, but could be characterized as "loyalists," and gravitate toward social-emotional leadership. They tend to accept people as they are, know a lot of personal things about the people with whom they work, and are sensitive to the fit between the person and the job.

Intuitive thinkers (NTs) are visionaries. They are innovative and enjoy creating a new system, rather than maintaining or running an established program. They need to be supported by persons who are good at implementation and maintenance of new programs. They feel burdened by overly structured organizations and jobs, and function best in looser organization designs.

Intuitive-feeling types (NFs) could be considered catalysts in a team setting. They focus on possibilities, and can often get other people excited about new projects, or spark new enthusiasm in the face of obstacles or current problems. They prefer democratic, less structured organizations, and are particularly interested in the quality of working life experienced by both themselves and others. Other people are likely to attribute personal charisma to NFs, because they are popular and tend to become personally involved with those around them. Sometimes, this involvement makes them vulnerable since they prefer positive harmonious relations with others. These four composite styles are shown in Table 30-1, which has been reproduced here from *Introduction to Type* (9).

Other Aspects of the MBTI

The Myers-Briggs Type Indicator output is somewhat more complex than the two-dimensional model shown in Figure 30-1, but the present discussion explicates a central part of the framework. In addition to providing dimensionality to problem-solving strategies, the perception and judging categories are considered as definitions of basic mental functions or processes. The functions serve to provide distinct goals for conscious mental activity. "Sensing (S) seeks the fullest possible experience of what is immediate and real. Intuition (N) seeks the broadest view of what is possible and insightful. Thinking (T) seeks rational order and plan according to impersonal logic. Feeling (F) seeks rational order according to harmony among subjective values" (10). Because these functions aim in different directions, one of them must be dominant for purposeful action by the individual, although all of them are present in any individual to some degree. The dynamic interaction of the functions provides additional substance for the MBTI framework.

Two more bipolar scales are part of the MBTI dimensions. The first is an extraversion-introversion* scale which measures complementary atti-

---

* Extraversion is a Jungian term describing a preference for the outer world as an attitude toward life. It is frequently equated by the layman with the similar concept of extroversion, meaning "not shy." The spelling in this chapter will be extraversion, because most of the references are in the context of the MBTI framework, and therefore refer to the Jungian scale.

Table 30-1. Composite Styles: Effects of the Combinations of Perception and Judgment.[a]

PEOPLE WHO PREFER	ST SENSING + THINKING	SF SENSING + FEELING	NF INTUITION + FEELING	NT INTUITION + THINKING
focus their attention on	Facts	Facts	Possibilities	Possibilities
and handle these with:	Impersonal analysis	Personal warmth	Personal warmth	Impersonal analysis
Thus they tend to become:	Practical and and matter-of-fact	Sympathetic and friendly	Enthusiastic and insightful	Logical and ingenious
and find scope for their abilities in:	Technical skills with facts and objects	Practical help and services for people	Understanding and communicating with people	Theoretical and technical developments
for example:	Applied science Business Production Construction Etc.	Patient care Community service Sales Teaching Etc.	Behavioral science Research Teaching Etc.	Physical science Research Management Forecasts, analysis Etc.

[a] Adapted from Myers, Isabel B. *Introduction to Type,* Gainesville, Florida: Center for Application of Psychological Type, 1976, 2nd ed. and reproduced by special permission of the publisher, Consulting Psychologists Press, Inc., 577 College Ave., Palo Alto, Calif. 94306.

tudes toward life. An extraverted (E) individual prefers to operate primarily in the outer world of people, action, and objects. The following characteristics are typical of the extraverted attitude: "awareness and reliance on the environment for stimulation and guidance; an action-oriented, sometimes impulsive way of meeting life; frankness; ease of communication; or sociability" (11). On the other hand, the introvert (I) operates in a more contemplative, inner world of ideas and concepts. The extrovert experiences an attention flow from the individual to the environment. The intravert concentrates energy from the environment. An introverted attitude is frequently characterized by the following attributes: "interest in the clariy of concepts and ideas; reliance on enduring concepts more than on transitory external events; a thoughtful, contemplative detachment; and enjoyment of solitude and privacy" (12).

The final scale reflects whether a judging or perceiving attitude will be taken toward the outer world. Judging types (J) "tend to live in a planned, decided, orderly way, aiming to regulate life and control it. Perceptive types (P) . . . tend to live in a flexible, spontaneous way, aiming to understand life and adapt to it" (13). (For more detailed descriptions of the MBTI, the reader is referred to References 4, 8, 9, 10, 15, and 16.)

Implications for Team Functioning

Effective team functioning requires that the psychological and intellectual resources of all individuals be utilized. One of the greatest barriers to effectiveness is the truncation of one person's resources by another simply because they perceive and react to problems in quite different ways. Sensing-thinking types, for instance, are inclined to want the facts and an explicit statement of the problem before considering possible solutions. Intuitive-feeling types (the opposite of STs) must first be inspired by interesting possibilities before they will pay much attention to facts. And even then the "facts" seen by the NF will more likely appear as "soft" impressionistic data to the ST.

As Myers (14) notes, problem solving generally could be viewed as a sequential use of the various perception and judgment functions: sensing establishes the facts, intuition suggests possible solutions, thinking establishes the probable consequences of different courses of action, and feeling weighs the likelihood of acceptance among relevant persons. Thus all the psychological functions should ideally be brought to bear on problems, and well-balanced teams which allow broad participation should have greater resources than even the best balanced individual decision maker. In fact, leadership in a team could be defined as insuring that the appropriate functions are brought to bear on problems at the appropriate stage.

The formation of interdepartmental project teams is likely to bring together different types because there is some evidence to suggest type is related to occupational specialization (15,16). Engineering is dominated by thinking types, although the theoretical specialties tend to be more thinking oriented than the applied specialties. McCaulley notes that two important implications flow from this trend (17). First, a team heavily weighted with similar types can develop group "blind spots" characteristic of the dominant type. Thinking types often neglect the human aspect of project work because technical work is more appealing to them. Second, if feeling types are in a minority, they may be undervalued and criticized, which causes them to withdraw their vitality and energy from the team effort. Third, thinking types may be inclined to take a laissez-faire attitude toward persuading others to accept their work, believing, often erroneously, that "the logic will speak for itself," and that high-quality technical work will unquestioningly be accepted by project clients. Fortunately, as McCaulley notes, the engineering professions contain a large number of feeling types who are of great value in gaining acceptance of project work with the client-users. The leadership challenge, however, is to create a climate where thinking judgment can predominate during planning stages and feeling judgment during project implementation.

The type situation does vary quite a bit across the specialties. The *Atlas of Type Tables* (18), compiled from over 60,000 of the records submitted to CAPT for scoring from 1971 through 1982, includes classifications for many standard occupational codes. (See Table 30-2.) Within any engineering project team, and especially for teams that combine specialties, there may be a wide range of types, as indicated in the prior discussion. For the planning stage of a project, it is conceivable to combine engineers from, for instance, mining and mechanical specialties. The typical profile for each field is quite different—in fact, opposite. For mining engineers, the predominant type is ESFP. Mechanical engineers tend to be INTJ. Even within a specialty, there may be various combinations of types of

Table 30-2. Distribution of Type Among Engineers[a]

FIELD	E	I	S	N	T	F	J	P
				PREFERENCE TYPE[b]				
Engineers	47.7%	52.3%	52.6%	47.4%	63.6%	36.4%	60.5%	39.5%
Engineering Specialty								
Aeronautical	50.0%	50.0%	42.6%	57.4%	40.7%	59.3%	53.7%	46.3%
Chemical	50.0%	50.0%	53.9%	46.1%	71.2%	28.8%	78.9%	21.1%
Electrical/								
Electronic	37.0%	63.0%	51.9%	48.1%	66.7%	33.3%	63.0%	37.0%
Mechanical	46.8%	53.2%	58.4%	41.6%	70.1%	29.9%	62.3%	37.7%
Mining	53.2%	46.8%	54.2%	45.8%	25.8%	74.2%	44.2%	55.8%
Engineering and Science Technicians								
General	48.0%	52.0%	55.4%	44.6%	57.1%	42.9%	56.0%	44.0%
Electrical/								
Electronic	42.1%	57.9%	56.1%	43.9%	68.4%	31.6%	63.2%	36.8%

[a] Adapted and compiled from Macdaid, Gerald P., McCaulley, Mary M., and Kainz, Richard I., *Atlas of Type Tables,* Gainesville, Florida: Center for Application of Psychological Type © 1986 (1987) and reproduced by special permission of the publisher, Center for Application of Psychological Type, P. O. Box 13807, Gainesville, Florida 32604.

[b] E = extraversion   I = introversion
  S = sensing   N = intuitive
  T = thinking   F = feeling
  J = judging   P = perceiving

individuals. For example, in an engineering project, there may be all engineers in the planning stage of a project. When the project moves to the implementation stage, technicians may be also a part of the staff. In electrical engineering, these profiles are quite similar. Both groups exhibit dominant preferences for ISTJ. However, for the field of engineering in general, the profile preferences indicate that engineers exhibit a preference for Introversion, while engineering technicians exhibit a preference for Extraversion. This may cause a change in the composition of the group, and alter the ability of the group to function at all. The relationship of type to group development is discussed in a later section of this chapter.

For the past six years, McCaulley and her associates at CAPT have participated in a longitudinal study of a consortium of engineering schools concerned with the constructive uses of individual differences in the educational setting for engineers. Various institutions have different "typical" student profiles. Recent analysis of the panel data indicates that some types of students who initially majored in engineering either transferred to another major or left the institution. McCaulley comments in the six year follow-up:

> Engineering has and will continue to have a challenge to engage students whose minds work in a linear fashion (S) and those who see patterns more easily. You seem to be losing substantial numbers of the types who can do engineering well—the practical, hands-on linear thinkers. . . . Many of [the fast-moving extraverts] are transferring out of engineering. . . . Engineering . . . attracts large numbers of hands-on practitioners and theoretical visionaries. It is essential . . . to develop mutual respect and communication so that the skills of both— who see their world so differently—can be used constructively. (19)

The challenge to institutions which prepare students for engineering continues for the industries in which they will subsequently work. (Additional information about the types in engineering can be found in references 20 through 26.)

In summary, our purpose in this section has been to introduce the MBTI framework in its simpler form and to suggest how it can be useful in understanding conflict between team members. Individual team members must come to see others as sources of differing resources, or "differing gifts," rather than as sources of antagonism. Table 30-3 illustrates how complementary functions can be supplied by opposite types to the benefit of both (adapted from *Introduction to Type*) (27). This process could be greatly facilitated by having either an external or internal organization

Table 30-3. Mutual Usefulness of Opposite Types[a]

INTUITIVE NEEDS A SENSING TYPE	SENSING NEEDS AN INTUITIVE TYPE
To bring up pertinent facts	To bring up new possibilities
To apply experience to problems	To supply ingenuity on problems
To read the fine print in a contract	To read the signs of coming change
To have patience	To have enthusiasm
To keep track of essential details	To watch for new essentials
To face difficulties with realism	To tackle difficulties with zest
To remind that the jobs of the present are important	To show that the joys of the future are worth working for

FEELING NEEDS A THINKING TYPE	THINKING NEEDS A FEELING TYPE
To analyze	To persuade
To organize	To conciliate
To find the flaws in advance	To forecast how others will feel
To reform what needs reforming	To arouse enthusiasms
To hold consistently to a policy	To teach
To weight "the law and the evidence"	To sell
To fire people when necessary	To advertise
To stand firm against opposition	To appreciate the thinker

[a] Adapted from Myers, Isabel B., *Introduction to Type*, Gainesville, Florida: Center for Application of Psychological Type, 1976, 2nd ed. and reproduced by special permission of the publisher, Consulting Psychologists Press, Inc., 577 College Ave., Palo Alto, Calif. 94306.

development specialist administer and conduct educational seminars for teams using the MBTI. It is an instrument which is gaining increasing application in the behavioral sciences to a variety of management problems.

EMOTIONAL STYLES: THE FIRO FRAMEWORK

Whereas the prior section examined a framework for understanding individual problem-solving styles, this section presents a framework for understanding emotional styles in a group. It is important to recognize that the location of the problem in most so-called personality conflicts does not reside solely in one person. Most social conflicts are inherently relational; that is, a problem does not exist until two or more persons have to work together, or live together, etc. The dysfunction then is typically not located in one person or the other, but rather is located in their relationship. Thus any framework which systematically attempts to explain personality conflict must in fact be a theory of interpersonal relationships. The framework used in the present study was developed by Schutz (28), and is both concise and operational in the sense that it provides for a method of assessing the degree of potential interpersonal strife or incompatibility in any relationship.

Three Basic Interpersonal Needs

In the following discussion, interpersonal incompatibility will be used as synonymous with "personality conflict," whereas interpersonal compatibility suggests harmony and lack of conflict. The basis of Schutz's theory is the individual's fundamental interpersonal relations orientation, or FIRO as it is usually abbreviated. One's FIRO is an "interpersonal style" which is hypothesized to be rather stable and to have developed from psychological forces in the person's childhood and developmental history. It reflects a person's central emotional position with respect to other people generally. That is, people learn a way of relating to others along certain dimensions, and they tend to carry that style around with them as a rather stable aspect of their personality which affects their work and social relations. The FIRO is in fact a set of three basic interpersonal needs which are common to all persons in greater or lesser degrees. These three needs (inclusion, control, and affection) are considered to be predictive in a general sense of the fundamental behavior that occurs interpersonally. Inclusion refers to the need to be included in other people's activities, or to include others in one's own activities, and is analogous to the extraversion-introversion dimension of other authors, or to sociability. It entails moving toward or away from people psychologically. Control refers to the need to give and receive structure, directions, influence, power, authority, and responsibility, to the need to engage in leadership or followership. Affection is concerned with emotional closeness to others, friendship, liking, or disliking, and refers to the need to act close or distant toward others.

There are two aspects to each of the three interpersonal needs. One is what we do or have a need to express toward others. The second is how we want others to behave toward us. This is shown schematically in Table 30-4. That is, people have a need to both give and receive in each need area and this forms the basis for interpersonal harmony or strife. Harmony (compatibility) results when one party has a need to give (or express) what the other party is interested in getting (or wants).

Scaling Group Interpersonal Incompatibility

If we symbolize the need to express behavior as "e," the need to receive from others as "w," and the three need areas of inclusion, control, and

Table 30-4. The FIRO Framework.

		NEED AREA	
	INCLUSION	CONTROL	AFFECTION
e^a	eI Need to initiate interaction with others—need to reach out and include others in one's activity	eC Need to assume leadership, responsibility, control and exert influence	eA Need to act close and personal toward others—express friendship
w^b	wI Need to be invited to join others—need to be included in interaction	wC Need to receive directions, guidance, assume followership roles, receive influence	wA Need to be on the receiving end of friendship and personal closeness

[a] What I need to express to others is symbolized by e.
[b] What I need or want from others is symbolized by w.

affection as I, C, and A, then any individual can be characterized by the six scales: eI, wI, eC, wC, eA, wA. Schutz has developed a questionnaire, referred to as FIRO-B, which is designed to measure an individual's need levels in each of the six categories (the "B" indicates the questionnaire is designed to predict behavior). The six categories are measured on a scale from a low of zero to a high of nine. This scaling provides a way of assessing the potential conflict or incompatibility in an interpersonal relationship.

Schutz has developed methods for scaling the degree of potential interpersonal incompatibility in a group by combining the FIRO-B scores of all individuals in the group according to certain formulas. The control dimension will be used to explain these formulas since control is often at the heart of difficulties in work settings. The examples shown below are based on Pfeiffer and Heslin's (29) work with the FIRO-B instrument in human relations training.*

	Supervisor	Subordinates
Need to express (eC)	low score	low score
Need to receive (wC)	low score	high score

* Used with permission and reprinted from J. W. Pfeiffer, R. Heslin and J. E. Jones, *Instrumentation in Human Relations Training* (2nd Ed.) San Diego, Calif.: University Associates, 1976.

Subordinates: "Boss, we're ready to go, tell us what you want us to do."

Supervisor: "Look over the situation, and do whatever you think is best."

Pfeiffer and Heslin report a situation where the physical education department of a college had this constellation of scores. The employees would say, "Fred, what do you think we should do with the intramural program this year?" Fred would usually respond, "I don't care fellows. Do whatever you want." Needless to say, this caused employee frustration and low performance since the employees wanted (and needed) influence from others to be effective.

The reverse case also occurs:*

	Supervisor	Subordinates
Need to express (eC)	high score	high score
Need to receive (wC)	low score	low score

Subordinates: "Boss, let us do it our way and we'll give you the best sales department in the country."

Supervisor: "You'll do things the way I say to do them."

This relational constellation represents competitive, aggressive incompatibility wherein it is difficult for the parties to share control and leadership. Since the supervisor has formal authority and can invoke various forms of punishment for noncompliance, the subordinates often lose interest in work and withdraw their vitality from the job. On the other hand, these subordinates may actively express their anger in the form of sabotage and other counterproductive maneuvers.

Schutz's concept of originator compatibility reflects the degree to which one person's excess of a need to express or receive in a given need area is balanced by the other person's excess in the reverse direction; for example, if one party's e score is greater than the w score, the other party's w score should be greater than the e score so that one difference counterbalances the other. The originator compatibility formula symbolized as OK for person i and person j is given in equation 1.

$$\text{Originator compatibility: } OK_{ij} = (e_i - w_i) + (e_j - w_j) \qquad (1)$$

The score, therefore, would range from 0 to 18. For example, returning to the extreme case illustrated earlier of a competitive, incompatible relationship around control, the two persons, i and j, would be

---

* Ibid.

	i	j
need to express (eC)	9	9
need to receive (wC)	0	0

$OK_{ij} = (9 - 0) + (9 - 0) = 18$, perfect incompatibility

Two persons who are compatible around initiation-reception might be

	i	j
need to express (eC)	7	2
need to receive (wC)	2	7

$OK_{ij} = (7 - 2) + (2 - 7) = 0$, perfect compatibility

Person i's propensity to initiate control is directly counterbalanced by person j's propensity to receive control, and hence they would be compatible with i initiating and j following. There must be some complementarity, reciprocity, or "oppositeness" in the relationship for originator compatibility to exist. Schutz (30) suggests this aspect of relationships reflects the old maxim "opposites attract."

Another maxim seemingly contradictory to the first about interpersonal relationships is that "birds of a feather flock together," or similarity attracts. The second type of compatibility can be used to assess this dimension of relationships. It is called interchange compatibility (symbolized as IK) and refers to whether two persons have a need to be similarly active in a given need area. Incompatibility results where two persons are very different in how much interchange (activity) they prefer in the various need areas.

For inclusion, the typical conflict is between the joiner or participator (high interchange) who likes to be surrounded by people doing things together, and the more withdrawn person who prefers to work alone (low interchange). In the control area, the conflict is between those who like to create a system of rules and clearly delineated roles (high interchange) versus those who prefer to "live and let live" in a more permissive, unstructured atmosphere (low interchange). For affection, interchange incompatibility reflects a conflict between those who want to be close, personal, and confiding versus those who prefer cooler, more distant, and nondisclosing relationships. Interchange compatibility between persons i and j is given by the following formula

Interchange compatibility: $IK_{ij} = [(e_i + w_i) - (e_j + w_j)]$ (2)

Interchange compatibility also ranges from 0 (most compatible) to 18 (least compatible). In our three prior examples, all pairs would be interchange compatible in the sense that within each pair there would be an interest in the same amount of "general control activity" even though not all cases were originator compatible. Thus people may be compatible in one sense, but not the other. Below is an example that would be originator compatible, but not interchange compatible:

	i	j
need to express (eC)	9	1
need to receive (wC)	8	2

$OKij = (e_i - w_i) + (e_j - w_j) = (9 - 8) + (1 - 2) = 0$, compatible

However,

$$IKij = (e_i + w_i) - (e_j + w_j) = 17 - 3 = 15, \text{ incompatible}$$

Thus, person j would usually want to work in an unstructured fashion, whereas person i would be very concerned about establishing order, roles, rules, and leader-follower behavior. Control would be a source of friction for this pair. However, if person j could accept the necessity for leader-follower behavior he or she would likely be the follower in relation to person i. It is no paradox, incidentally, to be high in both expressed and wanted control. The ideal military officer, for instance, must take orders from above (be high on wanted control) and turn around and give orders to those below (be high on expressed control). In short, individual i in the last example would be comfortable both as a leader and as a follower.

There is another type of compatibility, referred to as reciprocal compatibility, which is rather similar to originator compatibility and will not be discussed here. Interested readers are referred to Schutz (31), Pfeiffer and Heslin (32), and Hill (33) for further information on reciprocal compatibility.

The typical data for a group is displayed in the format shown in Table 30-5, where each compatibility type is shown for each need area. In addition, the rows and columns can be averaged to illustrate compatibility by need area or type. Finally, the entire matrix can be averaged to assess the total group compatibility. Inspection of this matrix can signal the source and nature of potential conflicts in a group. Schutz indicates that the most frequently occurring types of incompatibility which affect work group functioning usually center around inclusion interchange, control interchange, and control origination.

Table 30-5. Compatibility Types and Areas.

		AREAS OF COMPATIBILITY		
		INCLUSION	CONTROL	AFFECTION	ROW AVERAGES
Type of compatibility	O[a]	OK(I)	OK(C)	OK(A)	Overall OK
	I	IK(I)	IK(C)	IK(A)	Overall IK
	Column average	Overall K, Inclusion	Overall K, Control	Overall K, Affection	Average K, entire matrix

[a] O = originator compatibility.
  I = interchange compatibility.

Inclusion interchange problems in project teams are usually expressed as conflicts between members who prefer to work in groups (high-inclusion activity) versus those who prefer to work more individualistically (low-inclusion activity). The differences manifest themselves in the group setting, because, whenever a decision must be made, those high on inclusion prefer working it out together, whereas those low on inclusion attempt to go off on their own in pursuit of the decision.

Control interchange problems tend to pervasively affect a group. While high-control group members attempt to create a group structure and definite roles and responsibilities, those low in the control area will be resisting the high-control persons and attempting to create an unstructured group with freedom to play different roles at different times as they see fit.

Control originator compatibility problems, like many interpersonal conflicts, are also expressed through the task all too often. If someone makes a suggestion in a group meeting, it is improbable that someone else would say, "Your suggestion is okay, but I want mine accepted because I want to have the most influence here." The person is more likely to say, "Your idea is okay, but these are its disadvantages, and I think we should do so and so." The merits of suggestions are often secondary to the deeper agenda of who will have how much control over the decision process. This competitive incompatibility often produces a general feeling of struggle and conflict in the group. Apathetic incompatibility, on the other hand, usually produces feelings of emptiness and boredom with the group process.

Affectional conflicts are perhaps less frequently felt in work settings. However, a high-interchange person in a low-interchange group would probably complain of an impersonal group in which there was not enough encouragement and support.

Using the FIRO-B to Enhance Team Performance

The FIRO system then can be used to conceptualize interpersonal strife in any work group or team which must accomplish some objectives. Probably its greatest value lies in diagnosing and defining the kind of conflict likely to occur in a group. If the FIRO-B questionnaire is administered to a project team, a profile can be obtained of the potential points of friction, and the manager as well as the entire team can then be more informed as to the likely origin and nature of conflict in the team. This procedure would probably best be carried out with the assistance of a staff specialist, and in an open manner wherein the results were fed back to the entire team and the meaning and nature of the FIRO system fully explained. In short, all of the usual organizational development group rules regarding survey feedback (i.e., voluntary participation, disclosure of results) would ideally be adhered to, and the feedback effort itself would become an intervention to facilitate team development. The FIRO system has been used to select submarine crews and police teams, and for personnel placement in various industries.

If the FIRO-B instrument is used to help a team see its conflict areas more clearly, and deal with them more constructively, there are several uses which Pfeiffer and Heslin (34) suggest as relevant for group and individual development. These uses are reproduced below:

Generating a Personal Agenda. Giving the FIRO-B scale early in a training session can provide participants with insights into their inclusion, control, and affection desires and behavior which they may wish to modify or change by trying out new behaviors within the group setting.

Sensitization to Interpersonal Dimensions. Scoring and discussing the FIRO-B can make participants aware of dimensions of interpersonal relations with which they will be dealing during a training session. It introduces terminology for understanding inclusion, control, and affection problems.

Checking Self Understanding. Administering the FIRO-B can be preceded by asking members to estimate how they expect to score (high, medium, or low) on each scale. If the group has been in existence long enough, members can also predict how they expect the other members to score on the instrument. FIRO-B is not a deceptively-worded instrument, so pre-awareness should have little effect on the respondent's scores.

Individual Interpretations. The FIRO-B can be given in a group followed by a general discussion of the subscales. Later the facilitator can meet with members individually to interpret each person's pattern of scores in detail and discuss how this feedback affects the individual's understanding of his or her past and future group behavior.

The upshot of most group interventions with the FIRO-B is that it serves to sensitize the members to, and to educate them about, the nature of interpersonal conflict. It also serves as a stimulus for an open discussion of problem areas within the group, which, when attended by a competent facilitator, can enable a group to work through the problem of interpersonal agendas contaminating the productive efforts of the group.

RELATIONSHIPS BETWEEN THEORETICAL FRAMEWORKS

The discussion so far has presented the FIRO-B and the MBTI as separate theoretical frameworks for assessing differences in the human personality, but the two are not unrelated. Indeed, many of the theoretical frameworks used to measure personality differences are related in some ways to each other. They do not measure the same constructs entirely, but the correlated measures, which indicate some overlap, help to illuminate the complexities of the human personality and relationships in the human group. Table 30-6 relates the MBTI and the FIRO-B frameworks to each other. Not surprisingly, the emotional stance measures of the FIRO-B are strongly related to the Feeling preference of the TF dimension of the MBTI, the measure of which kind of judgment to rely upon when making a decision. Also, the high Inclusion scores of the FIRO-B are associated with the Extraversion preference of the MBTI.

Multiple pictures of individuals' personality characteristics can be used together to help group functioning. Obviously, the process is complicated by using multiple frameworks, but the additional information is potentially of great value. The nature of the project and the project team would affect a firm's decision to make the time and money commitment to employ the exploration of multiple personality frameworks to enhance group performance. Such factors as sensitivity to production delays, anticipated disastrous consequences if an intact project team disbands prematurely, or the need for a project planning task force to begin work quickly could make such an investment attractive to a firm. Again, using multiple instruments can be enhanced by having either an external or internal organization development specialist administer and conduct educational seminars for teams using these frameworks. Additional frameworks, some of which require the intervention of a trained psychologist, that might be of use are presented here. Table 30-7 provides correlations between some of them and the MBTI.

Table 30-6. Relationship of MBTI Continuous
Scores with the FIRO-B.[a]

FIRO-B SCALE	EI	SN	TF	JP
Expressed inclusion	E[b]			
Wanted inclusion	E		F	
Expressed affection	E		F	
Wanted affection	E		F	
Expressed control			T	
Wanted control		S		

[a] Adapted and compiled from Myers, Isabel B. and McCaulley, Mary H., *Manual: A Guide to the Development and Use of the Myers-Briggs Type Indicator.* Gainesville, Florida (1985) and reproduced by special permission of the publisher, Consulting Psychologists Press, Inc., 577 College Ave., Palo Alto, Calif. 94306.

[b] The values in the table indicate that the scales are correlated at beyond the .001 level. Since the Jungian preferences are bidirectional, a strong negative correlation is indication of relationship to one preference, a strong positive correlation is indication of relationship to the other. For example, in the FIGO-B comparison, the Expressed inclusion scale is correlated significantly with the MBTI Extraversion scale. Individuals who tend to score high on one of the scales also tend to score high on the other.

Study of Values (35) rank orders the importance of six categories of values (Theoretical, Economic, Aesthetic, Social, Political, and Religious) for the individual. The relationship of this measure to the MBTI is included in Table 30-7.

Edwards Personality Preference Schedule (36) includes measures for such categories as Achievement, Order, and Affiliation.

Vocational Preference Inventory (37) measures six basic vocational interest scales: Realistic, Investigative, Artistic, Social, Enterprising, Conventional. The relationship of selected scales in this measure to the MBTI is included in Table 30-7.

Strong Campbell Interest Inventory (38) provides scales for Holland's scales, 23 general occupational themes and over 200 specific occupations. The relationship of selected scales in this measure to the MBTI is included in Table 30-7.

SYMLOG (39, 40, 41) measures overt group actions as well as individual values along three dimensions: Friendly versus Unfriendly, Emotionally expressive versus Instrumentally controlled, and Dominant versus Submissive.

Table 30-7. Relationship of MBTI Continuous Scores with Other Scales[a]

| | STUDY OF VALUES (35) | | | |
	EI	SN	TF	JP
Theoretical		N[b]	T	
Economic		S	T	
Aesthetic	I	N		P
Social			F	
Political	E	S		
Religious			F	

| | VOCATIONAL PREFERENCE INVENTORY (37) (SELECTED OCCUPATIONAL THEMES) | | | |
	EI	SN	TF	JP
Investigative		N		
Artistic		N		

| | STRONG CAMPBELL INTEREST INVENTORY (38) (SELECTED BASIC INTEREST SCALES) | | | |
	EI	SN	TF	JP
Mechanical Activities			T	
Business Management	E			
Art		N		

[a] Adapted and compiled from Myers, Isabel B. and McCaulley, Mary H., *Manual: A Guide to the Development and Use of the Myers-Briggs Type Indicator*. Gainesville, Florida (1985) and reproduced by special permission of the publisher, Consulting Psychologists Press, Inc., 577 College Ave., Palo Alto, Calif. 94306.

[b] The values in the table indicate that the scales are correlated at beyond the .001 level. Since the Jungian preferences are bidirectional, a strong negative correlation is indication of relationship to one preference, a strong positive correlation is indication of relationship to the other. For example, in the Vocational Preference Inventory comparison, individuals who tend to score high on the Investigative scale also tend to score high on the N dimension of the MBTI scale.

Kolb Learning Style Inventory (42) provides scores along three dimensions of preferred style of learning: Concrete versus Abstract, Experiential versus Conceptual, Reflective versus Active.

California Psychological Inventory (43) measures such traits as Dominance, Tolerance, Flexibility, and Extraversion-introversion.

Omnibus Personality Inventory (44) measures attributes such as Artistic sensitivity, Likes being with people, Impulsive or imaginative, and Likes applied, concrete activities.

Comrey Personality Scales (45) include such measures as Extraversion versus Introversion and Orderliness versus Lack of compulsion.

IMPLICATIONS FOR TEAM BUILDING AND DEVELOPMENT

The discussion thus far has assumed that a group exists, and that understanding the individual differences in a group, the potential for conflict, will help the group to function more efficiently and effectively. Certainly, in industry, the extant group is the norm, but in firms which deal with turbulent environments or deal with rapidly changing production needs or planning duties, the project team may be an ad hoc phenomenon. Further, it may be subject to a matrix organization. These groups need not only to function, but also first to become groups instead of a collection of individuals if they are to perform most effectively and efficiently. As a group moves through various stages of development, from inception through productive functioning to disbandment, different aspects of the individuals involved in the group may variously cause or ease conflict in stage transitions.

As a work group or project team develops, it progresses through several stages: forming, storming, norming, and performing (46, 47, 48, 49). Each stage is typified by a major dilemma to resolve. Appropriate (successful, in some sense) resolution of the dilemma is necessary before moving to the next stage. It is possible for a group to remain plateaued at any of the stages. Not surprisingly, a major factor in group development is the ability to handle conflict generated by the dilemmas. This section discusses each stage and suggests some of the characteristics which might be most relevant, the ones to which a group member or group leader should be most sensitive.

Forming, the initial group stage, includes resolving the conflicting demands of the individual's self versus the external pressures. In the case of the project group, these external demands are often such things as project schedules and deadlines or organizational goals and standards. This dilemma is labeled inclusion and consists of setting group boundaries and goals (50). In this stage, it is common for group members to exchange their opinions of what is expected of them. In the MBTI framework, for example, STs will be impatient to get on with the task in this stage, while NFs will want to explore all the possibilities open to them before taking any action at all. In the FIRO-B framework, as another example, members high on wanted affection will be concerned with first impressions and how people react to each other. On the other hand, project members low on wanted affection will be concerned with getting to the task at hand. See the potential for conflict? Further, if group members who need to have possibilities explored and feelings affirmed are not vocal or strong enough to have these personal needs met, they are unable to progress to the next stage. If the "group" progresses without dealing with these needs, the group is fragmented into subgroups, and effective functioning is impaired.

When the group proceeds to the storming stage, new tasks bring out new aspects of the individuals who make up the group. Determining the authority structure within the group is the major task at this stage (51). If the project team is an ad hoc group, perhaps drawn from different functional specialties, different people will be working from different agendas. In the framework of the FIRO-B, individuals high on expressed control and high on wanted control will want to be in charge, or have the vice president of their own division acknowledged as the real "final authority" on the project. Those who are high on wanted control and low on expressed control will be content as long as somebody is designated "head." In the MBTI framework, SFs are likely to consider the way it was done the last time, while NFs will want to find a new, better way to resolve this authority situation.

Norming, the third stage of group development, is concerned with agreeing on an appropriate level of intimacy for the project group (52). There must be mutual agreement on issues such as the shared level of trust, the mix of personal and professional issues, and whether contributions are to consist of individual effort or of consensualized group work, if the project team is to perform optimally. In this stage, if the norm is set for impersonal, work-only items, individuals who are F in the MBTI preference for TF may experience isolation and complain of a group that is not sensitive to personal needs. On the other hand, T-preference individuals will be delighted with the resolution of the stage dilemma in this "no nonsense" way. The potential for conflict looms large as one remembers that engineering groups are typically split along this dimension, with a mix of T and F types. A similar scenario develops for the FIRO-B scale of expressed affection.

Once these stages have been successfully negotiated, the group is considered a performing group. In the real world, many groups never acknowledge or resolve these early developmental stages, and, consequently, try to perform without successful completion of a prior stage. The project team output may be good, but it could probably be better if these group stage needs were successfully met. The literature suggests a final group stage, that of separation and termination, to provide some sort of closure to the life of the group (53). Without this, some workers are not able to release an involvement in prior group experience and to proceed to the next project group situation. A nagging sense of something left undone may interfere with the ability to engage in the next project for the MBTI J type. Because workers tend to anticipate future group experiences based on their prior project team efforts, an experience in which the stages are not successfully negotiated may make a good engineer reluctant to contribute further in a project team setting.

MANAGING CONFLICT CONSTRUCTIVELY*

The previous discussion of differences in the individuals who work in project teams suggests that moderate levels of conflict are inevitable, and desirable, particularly if people are able to constructively utilize conflict. The key is effective conflict management by supervisors and members of the team. Note the key word here is conflict management rather than resolution. Probably the majority of social conflicts are not amenable to complete resolution, and it is probably more realistic to think in terms of managing conflict for productive purposes rather than resolving it. Hill (54) studied the characteristics of project team leaders employed in a large oil company who were selected by their organization as being outstanding project managers, and compared them to a sample of average managers in terms of the leadership practices which distinguished the two samples. The descriptions below (55) borrow heavily from the results of these interviews.

There seem immediately to be two general aspects in which high-performing managers differed from the lower-performing in terms of responding to internal team conflict. First, the high performers reflected a much larger repertoire of responses. They simply had more ideas and choices about how to deal with conflict generally. Second, they seemed much less afraid of disagreements, and intimated much more willingness to approach conflict rather than avoid it. This latter point is a common theme in management literature and has been noted by other authors as a preference for confrontation rather than withdrawal as a conflict-handling mode. The lower-producing managers had a more prevalent feeling that conflict would "go away" if left unattended. With these general differences in mind, the next question became, "What specific behavior did the higher-performing managers report which distinguished them from their lower-performing counterparts?"

---

* Parts of this section are reprinted from "Managing Interpersonal Conflict in Project Teams" by Raymond E. Hill, *Sloan Management Review*, Vol. 18, No. 2, by permission of the publisher. Copyright © (1977) by Sloan Management Review Association. All rights reserved.

Personal Absorption of Aggression

Being willing to hear subordinates out when they are particularly disturbed by a peer was a common theme. One manager described a situation in which two subordinates were making life rather miserable for a third and had essentially rejected this third subordinate. When confronted about their behavior, one of the two team members launched a brief personal attack on the manager. Instead of counterattacking, the manager simply asked the subordinate involved what was really wrong, as it appeared that some hidden agenda was more responsible for the anger. The subordinate declined to answer, and abruptly walked away. At this point, the manager felt some concern about losing the respect of the two subordinates. However, the next day, they both came to the manager's office, apologized, and explained their feelings that the third subordinate did not take enough initiative and do an appropriate share of work, which subsequently left them carrying most of the load. Whereas the manager had originally feared loss of respect, it now appeared that perhaps the reverse was true. Equally important, the manager had started a process of owning up to interpersonal antagonisms which could then be worked on with future benefits to team functioning.

If a manager does not flinch in the face of negative interpersonal feelings, and accepts them as a normal part of working life, differences between people are viewed as legitimate and their expressions are not inhibited. This is closely related to the next differentiating characteristic.

Encouraging Openness and Emotional Expression

Interpersonal relationships as well as leadership behavior have long been characterized by at least two fundamental dimensions: instrumental and expressive behavior. The higher-performing managers seemed more concerned with how their subordinates felt about work, the organization, their peers, etc., and reported more initiative in attempting to allow expression of those feelings. More of the high-performing managers claimed to have an "open-door" policy in which subordinates were free to speak with them anytime. However, there was much more to the picture than just a manager sitting passively in his or her office with the door open. One manager, who initiated conversation with subordinates "anytime" and frequently, commented, "I don't like to be in the dark about what's going on out there or what people are thinking."

In addition to encouraging expression and being employee-centered directly, a more subtle difference seemed to characterize the high-performing managers as a group. It seemed that they simply enjoyed social interaction more than their less effective counterparts. Although there were exceptions, as a group they talked more enthusiastically, spontaneously, and longer during the interviews. Comparison of the magnitude of the total interpersonal needs on the FIRO-B scale for the high- and low-performing project managers showed that the higher-performing managers averaged 27.2 whereas the lower group averaged 22.9. The scale, a combination of the six subscales, would run from a low of 0 to a high of 54. This difference was not statistically significant at the usual 5% level but was in the direction expected from clinical observation—the higher performers reflected a greater propensity for interpersonal activity.

Norm Setting, Role Modeling, and Counseling

One of the most fascinating aspects of the study involved managers who, in essence, "taught" their subordinates how to cope with interpersonal conflict in productive ways. Several of the high-performing managers felt it was important for them to "set an example" when it came to reacting to personality clashes. They felt it was more legitimate for them to urge a subordinate to listen to his or her emotional rival with more understanding if they in fact did that themselves. One manager noted that "Effective supervisors teach others to listen by doing it themselves. Some analysts have trouble listening . . . they keep talking when it is inappropriate. A good boss will be emulated, though, and find that is one of the best ways to get across an idea on how to behave."

An interesting correlate of this process was the observation that often a peer would intercede and act out a third-party conciliation role much like the manager might normally perform. Thus two parties in conflict would find themselves the target of peer pressure to live up to a norm which involved at least trying to understand the other party's point of view. At the same time, each party would also be likely to find other peers who tried to be impartial, but reassuring that it was okay to feel hostility. The norm seemed to be one of acceptance of conflict rather than suppression, and was apparently felt by members of high-producing groups more often than lower-producing teams.

Other comments which reinforced the idea that supervisors served as role models included the observation that managers set the "climate" in the group, and that if conflict was handled poorly in a group, it was usually because people did not feel free to "open up" in front of the supervisor. In fact, one manager observed that many groups seem to take on the personality characteristics of the supervisors. Of course, it is not the "group" which takes on the manager's characteristics, but rather the individuals who comprise it. Lower-producing managers seemed to verbally encourage openness with admonishments about the value of keeping people informed, but did not report as many instances where they actually practiced it themselves or taught it by example.

Awareness of the Utility of Conflict

The higher-producing managers seemed to more frequently evidence the attitude that conflict could be harnessed for productive ends. One high-producing manager noted that "You have to break people in to the idea that conflict does not have to be personally destructive, but can be important toward task accomplishment. . . . I try to encourage freedom of expression, and consensus on issues with my team." On the other hand, the lower-producing managers seemed to speak more frequently of the disruptive effects of conflict.

Pacing and Control of Potential Conflict

While the prior factors suggested a pattern of high-producing managers confronting differences, they also intimated a sense of when to do just the opposite. There were cases when high-producing managers delayed face-to-face group meetings because they felt two rival members were on the edge of acrimonious outbursts. The higher-producing managers seemed more willing to stop work and to socialize with two or three persons over coffee, and on occasion would take the entire team out to lunch as a way of getting away from work pressures. In fact, it seemed that informal work stoppages were more frequent during periods of high work stress such as deadlines and project phaseout. Sometimes, however, the process was more formal and involved allowing team members time off from work (with no pay penalty) because they had recently put in a large amount of overtime. People were becoming exhausted and tempers were getting short. The extreme of this general containment strategy involved removing people from teams; only one high-producing manager had actually done this, although others reportedly threatened it on rare occasions.

The important aspect of pacing and control of conflict as a coping strategy was that high-producing managers seemed to be in close enough touch with team members that they could judge whether it was appropriate to approach or to avoid conflict. The lower-producing managers did not exude the same sense of relatedness to subordinates and interpersonal sensitivity.

Summary of the Effective Project Manager

The composite picture of a high-producing manager which emerged was one who "came on straight" with subordinates and who was open in dealing with their conflicts, who also encouraged subordinates to express their problems, and signaled to all concerned a tolerance of negative and hostile feelings. High-producing managers also "taught" their team members through example as well as direct counseling how to respond to conflict. This appeared to be a critical phenomenon since it apparently expanded the conflict-managing capacity of the entire team. While exuding a belief in approaching conflict, the high-producing manager also had enough knowledge of subordinates to know when to avoid conflict, and postponed meetings or confrontations when necessary. The higher-producing managers tended to play out a third-party conciliation and interpersonal peacemaking role. It is important to reemphasize, however, that these actions were taken primarily in response to what was perceived to be personality clashes rather than disagreement over substantive issues (even though they are often difficult to separate). As Walton notes:

> The distinction between substantive and emotional issues is important because the substantive conflict requires bargaining and problem solving between the principals and mediative interventions by the third party, whereas emotional conflict requires a restructuring of a person's perceptions and the working through of feelings between the principals, as well as conciliative interventions by the third party. The former processes are basically cognitive; the later processes more affective.(56)

The particular kinds of third-party conciliative roles involved several actions. First, empathic support and reassurances that hostile feelings are accepted in someone's eyes is important in getting parties to express real differences between themselves. Second, helping parties express their differences by patient listening is crucial to the management or resolution of them. As Walton (57) suggests, differentiation puts a certain reality and authenticity into the relationship of the principals to the conflict. In addition, it provides information as to opinions and attitudes in the relationship which can be checked and corrected as to accuracy. In short, an expressional function is critical to interpersonal conflict because a person cannot begin productive resolution of differences until he or she is clear what the real differences in fact are. In addition, under stress one usually has to be emotional before being rational. Third, superior knowledge of the principals' situation and feelings helped the higher-producing managers pace the confrontation of conflict. Confrontation per se is not universally a panacea for conflict management, but rather confrontations in which the principals can exhibit a modicum of rationality and problem-solving behavior are what is needed. Fourth, so-called counseling tended to place the manager in the role of an interpersonal process consultant.

There are some crucial limitations on the effectiveness of organizational superiors as third-party conciliators of subordinate conflict. Walton (58) suggests that effective third-party consultants should not have power over the fate of the principals, and should also be neutral as to the substantive outcome. This is rarely if ever approximated in most organizational settings. However, the fascinating aspect of the study results suggested that team member peers often acted out third-party conciliator roles by modeling and identification with their manager. Peers usually have no formal power over the fate of the principals to the conflict, and are potentially able to be more neutral as to the outcome. Thus, peer members of a conflict pair often supplied a third-party influence which the manager could not. This phenomenon, however, appeared to depend critically on whether subordinates identified with the manager. By creating a more open interpersonal climate, the high-performing managers apparently leveraged their ability to manage personality clashes by stimulating resolution responses from the conflicted parties' peers. This is similar to Likert's (59) observation that participative management systems stimulate leadership behavior from subordinates themselves, or "peer leadership" as he calls it.

A more subtle process may also have been operating through the mechanism of identification with the superior. Heider (60) proposes a "balance theory" of interpersonal conflict which suggests that two parties find it more difficult to maintain negative feelings toward each other when they both feel positively toward a third party. Thus the higher-producing managers who created positive subordinate relations may have ameliorated conflict largely by an unconscious process. Levinson (61) expands on the dynamics of the process by saying that "A generalized process of learning how to behave and what to become occurs through identification. . . . By acting as the focal point of unity—the ego ideal of the group or organization—the leader serves as a device for knitting people together into a social system."

CONCLUSION

If this discussion has served to pique interest in the use of theoretical personality frameworks among project teams, our purpose will have been served. Carl Jung suggested that individual development and maturity involves an integration over time of the four psychological functions of sensing, intuition, thinking, and feeling. A team can similarly develop, given democratic leadership and norms which value the uniqueness and individuality of its members. Orchestrating these unique contributors can provide results beyond that of any single individual contribution.

REFERENCES

1. Thamhain, H. J. and Wilemon, D. L. "Conflict Management in Project Life Cycles." *Sloan Management Review* (Spring, 1975), pp. 31–49.
2. Op. cit., p. 39.
3. Hellriegel, D. and Slocum, J. W. Jr. "Preferred Organizational Designs and Problem Solving Styles: Interesting Companions." *Human Systems Management,* Vol. 1 (1980), pp. 151–158.
4. Myers, Isabel B. *Manual: The Myers-Briggs Type Indicator* (Consulting Psychologist Press. Palo Alto, Calif., 1962, 1975).
5. Op. cit.
6. McCaulley, M. "How Individual Differences Affect Health Care Teams." *Health Team News,* Vol. 1(8) (1975).
7. Op. cit.
8. McCaulley, M. "Psychological Types in Engineering: Implications for Teaching." *Engineering Education,* Vol. 66 (1976), pp. 729–736, p. 732.
9. Myers, Isabel B. *Introduction to Type,* 2nd ed. (Center for Application of Psychological Type. Gainesville, Fla., 1976), p. 3.
10. Myers, Isabel B. and McCaulley, Mary H. *Manual: A Guide to the Development and Use of the Myers-Briggs Type Indicator.* (Consulting Psychologists Press. Palo Alto, Calif., 1985), p. 13.
11. Ibid.
12. Ibid.
13. Myers, Isabel B. *Type and Teamwork* (Center for Application of Psychological Type. Gainesville, Fla., 1974), p. 2.
14. Op. cit., p. 3.
15. Macdaid, Gerald P., McCaulley, Mary H. and Kainz, Richard I. *Atlas of Type Tables* (Center for Application of Psychological Type. Gainesville, Fla., 1987).
16. McCaulley, Mary H. *Personality Variables: Model Profiles that Characterize Various Fields of Science* (Center for the Application of Psychological Type. Gainesville, Fla., 1976).
17. McCaulley, M. "Psychological Types in Engineering: Implications for Teaching," op. cit., p. 732.
18. Macdaid, op. cit.
19. McCaulley, M. H. and Macdaid, G. P. "Results of a Six-Year Study of Retention at Eight Engineering Schools." Paper presented at the 94th Annual Conference of the American Society for Engineering Education, Cincinnati, Ohio (1986), p. 16.
20. McCaulley, M. H., Godleski, E. S., Yokomoto, C. G., Harrisberger, L. and Sloan, E. D. "Applications of Psychological Type in Engineering Education." *Engineering Education,* Vol. 73 (1983), pp. 394–400.
21. McCaulley, M. H., Macdaid, G. P. and Granade, J. G. "ASEE-MBTI Engineering Consortium: Report of the First Five Years." Paper presented at the 93rd Annual

Conference of the American Society for Engineering Education, Atlanta, Georgia (1985).

22. Myers, Isabel B. with Myers, Peter B. *Gifts Differing* (Consulting Psychologists Press. Palo Alto, Calif., 1985).

23. Sloan, E. D. "An Experiential Design Course in Groups." *Chemical Engineering Education,* Vol. 16 (1982), pp. 38–41.

24. Thomas, C. R. "Personality in Engineering Technology." *Journal of Engineering Technology* (March, 1984), pp. 33–36.

25. Thomas, C. R. "Results of an MBTI Utilization in Engineering Technology." *Journal of Psychological Type,* Vol. 8 (1985), pp. 42–44.

26. Yokomoto, C. F. and Ware, J. R. "Individual Differences in Cognitive Tasks." In *Proceedings: 1984 Frontiers in Education Conference* (1984).

27. Op. cit., p 5.

28. Schutz, William C. *The Interpersonal Underworld,* Reprint ed. Science and Behavior Books, Palo Alto, Calif., 1966.

29. Pfeiffer, J. William and Heslin, Richard. *Instrumentation in Human Relations Training* (University Associates. Iowa City, 1973), p. 144.

30. Op. cit., p 118.

31. Op. cit.

32. Op. cit.

33. Hill, R. E. "Interpersonal Compatibility and Workgroup Performance." *The Journal of Applied Behavior Science,* Vol. 11 (1975), pp. 210–219.

34. Op. cit., p. 140.

35. Allport, G. W., Vernon, P. E. and Lindzey, G. *Study of Values: A Scale for Measuring the Dominant Interests in Personality,* 3rd ed. (Houghton Mifflin. Boston, 1960).

36. Edwards, A. L. *Manual for the EPPS* (The Psychological Corporation. New York, 1954).

37. Holland, John L. *Vocational Preference Inventory: Manual* (Consulting Psychologists Press. Palo Alto, Calif., 1978).

38. Campbell, David P. and Hansen, Jo Ida C. *Manual for the SVIB-SCII Strong-Campbell Interest Inventory,* 3rd ed. (Stanford University Press. Stanford, Calif., 1981).

39. Bales, Robert F. and Cohen, Stephen P., with Williamson, Stephen A. *SYMLOG: A System for the Multiple Level Observation of Groups* (The Free Press. New York, 1979).

40. Bales, Robert F. *Personality and Interpersonal Behavior* (Holt, Rinehart and Winston. New York, 1970).

41. Bales, Robert F. *Interaction Process Analysis* (University of Chicago Press. Chicago, 1976).

42. Kolb, David A. *Learning Style Inventory: Technical Manual* (McBer and Company. Boston, 1976).

43. Gough, H. G. *Manual for the California Psychological Inventory* (Consulting Psychologists Press. Palo Alto, Calif., 1975).

44. Heist, P. A., McConnell, T. R., Webster, H. and Yonge, G. D. *Omnibus Personality Inventory* (The Psychological Corporation. New York, 1963).

45. Comrey, A. L. *Manual for the Comrey Personality Scales* (Educational and Industrial Testing Service. San Diego, Calif., 1970).

46. Bennis, Warren F. and Shepard, H. A. "A Theory of Group Development." *Human Relations,* Vol. 9 (1956), pp. 415–437.

47. Davies, D. E. and Kuypers, H. C. "Group Development and Interpersonal Feedback." *Group and Organization Studies,* Vol. 10(2) (1985).

48. Lacoursiere, R. B. *The Life Cycle of Groups: Group Developmental Stage Theory* (Human Sciences Press. New York, 1980).
49. Tuckman, B. W. "Developmental Sequence in Small Groups." *Psychological Bulletin,* Vol. 63 (1965), pp. 384–399.
50. Bennis and Shepard, op. cit.
51. Ibid.
52. Ibid.
53. Ibid.
54. Hill, R. E. "Managing Interpersonal Conflict in Project Teams." *Sloan Management Review,* Vol. 18 (1977), pp. 45–62.
55. Ibid.
56. Walton, Richard E. *Interpersonal Peacemaking: Confrontations and Third Party Consultation* (Addison-Wesley. Reading, Mass., 1969), p. 75.
57. Op. cit.
58. Ibid.
59. Likert, Rensis A. *New Ways of Managing Conflict* (McGraw-Hill. New York, 1976).
60. Heider, F. *The Psychology of Interpersonal Relations* (Wiley. New York, 1958).
61. Levinson, Harry *The Exceptional Executive: A Psychological Conception* (Mentor. New York, 1968), pp. 163–164.

31. Teamwork—Key to Managing Change

Thomas E. Miller*

This new work schedule dreamed up by the experts in city hall is for the birds! The men don't like it and are laying down on the job. A lot of them aren't showing up or they're late, or calling in sick. Injuries are up, equipment gets lost or it's in the repair shop half the time, and we battalion chiefs are spending God knows how many hours detailing men from one fire station to another. We've told city hall about our morale problem, but they say if the men refuse to fulfill the contract agreement, we have no recourse but to reprimand, suspend, and in chronic cases, fire them. But, hell, if any of these steps are taken, we just aggravate the manpower shortage. If you were a seasoned firefighter, how would you like to put your life on the line with a raw young recruit next to you?

I'm swamped with paperwork and I have to go to a training course that's supposed to tell me how to handle the men, but I spend most of my time listening to their complaints. I don't have any time for training, equipment inspection, or fire prevention as the plan says I should. I'm lucky to make it to a fire since I'm usually in a meeting trying to iron out the kinks in this schedule. We chiefs have all complained to city hall, but they argue that the new work schedule is a success. The computer says so. Now, if they can only get the computer to fight the fires, we can all go home.

---

* Dr. Thomas E. Miller is Professor of Administration and Human Relations at the University of Missouri-Kansas City, where he teaches courses in human relations, organizational behavior, and theory of communication. He also taught at Northwestern University and the University of Kansas, and was a training fellow and instructor in human relations at the Harvard Business School. Dr. Miller has been a trainer in the private as well as the public sector, and has authored several case studies and articles on change, teamwork, and management. His current research interests focus on career development, promotions, and leadership, particularly in federal, law enforcement, and fire suppression organizations.

These remarks were made by a middle manager, a battalion chief, some months after a new work schedule had been introduced in his fire department.

Any reader of the organizational behavior literature will quickly recognize in this excerpt many of the familiar "resistance-to-change symptoms," such as restriction of output, sick-outs, work slowdowns as well as some more subtle symptoms—passive indifference, hostility and "rationalizations" on why the changes won't work.*

The "change-resistance syndrome"† has been well documented in the literature.‡ Roethlisberger believes the syndrome has the properties of reciprocalness, similar to the reciprocal relations encountered in mathematical relations.** The reciprocal pattern begins when management introduces a change. Immediately, the workers counter with resistance. Anticipating this resistance, managers resort to stratagems designed to overcome the workers' objections. These approaches can take many forms such as (1) giving elaborate logical explanations as to why the change is necessary; (2) hiring outside consultants to "justify" the change or to help "facilitate" its acceptance; (3) using "feedback" sessions involving managers, union, and/or staff personnel to alert all parties to the "realities" behind the change; and sometimes, as in this case study, (4) sending middle managers, who usually experience the brunt of the change, to training programs to acquire techniques on how to handle resistance.

When all else fails, management proposes *new* (and different) changes to cure the illnesses caused by the original change. Frequently, these new proposals are also resisted, thus reactivating the reciprocal cycle. In frustration and anger, management then forces the change on the workers by

---

* Paul R. Lawrence, "How to Deal with Resistance to Change," *Harvard Business Review*, Vol. 32 (1954), p. 49.
† The phrase is the author's.
‡ For a sampling of classic studies see: Fritz J. Roethlisberger and William J. Dickson, *Management and the Worker* (Cambridge: Harvard University Press, 1949), pp. 657–668 and 579–580; Kurt Lewin, "Group Decisions and Social Change," in G. E. Swanson, T. M. Newcomb, and E. L. Hartley (Eds.), *Readings in Social Psychology*, Rev. ed. (New York: Holt, 1952), pp. 459–473; Lester Coch and John R. P. French, "Overcoming Resistance to Change," *Human Relations*, Vol. 1(4) (1948), pp. 512–532; Alvin Zander, "Resistance to Change—Its Analysis and Prevention," *Advanced Management*, Vol. 15 (1950), pp. 9–11; David Klein, "Some Notes on the Dynamics of Resistance to Change: The Defender Role," in W. G. Bennis, K. D. Benne, and R. Chin (Eds.), *The Planning of Change* (New York: Holt, Rinehart and Winston, 1976), pp. 117–124; Gary Powell and Barry Z. Posner, "Resistance to Change Reconsidered: Implications for Managers," *Human Resource Management*, Vol. 17(1) (1978), pp. 29–34.
** Fritz J. Roethlisberger, *The Elusive Phenomena* (Boston, Mass.: Division of Research, Harvard Graduate School of Business Administration, 1977), pp. 169–170.

utilizing its positional authority. As resistance persists, management punishes the holdouts and rewards the collaborators. This reward-punishment pattern drives wedges among the organizational social groupings and the battle continues until the ringleaders quit or the workers passively accept the change, or management decides to chuck the whole idea. At this point, stability in the organization is restored, except for one major difference: often bitterness and resentment linger between the two parties and make the next innovation and its acceptance that much more difficult. Thus the changes that should be accomplished during the normal day-to-day work routines are avoided, brushed aside, and minimized by management and the worker until external or internal pressures force them to face the change process again.*

In spite of all of our managerial knowledge on how to handle change, the change-resistance syndrome still appears and appears frequently in modern-day organizations.† Some writers believe that the symptom-by-symptom attack that management is prone to take in overcoming resistance does not get below the surface to the human factors involved. By failing to recognize the hydra-headed nature of the social situation with which it is faced when introducing technical innovation, management will cut off one head, only to have two new ones appear.‡ Other writers argue that the whole idea of resistance to change needs reconceptualization since management's anticipation of resistance may lead them to the creation of resistance—a sort of self-fulfilling prophecy.** Whatever the basis, most writers concede that there is a gap between our existing knowledge (theory) and managerial practice (skill) when introducing change.

The purpose of this chapter is to examine once again the causes of the change-resistance syndrome by reporting a clinical case study of change

---

* Larry E. Greiner, "Patterns of Organizational Change," *Harvard Business Review,* Vol. 45 (1967), pp. 119–130.

† Recent publications indicate the "change-resistance syndrome" is still very much with us. See, for example: John P. Kotter and Leonard A. Schlesinger, "Choosing Strategies for Change," *Harvard Business Review* (March–April, 1979), pp. 106–114; Jay W. Lorsch, "Managing Change," in Paul R. Lawrence, Louis B. Barnes, and Jay W. Lorsch, (Eds.), *Organizational Behavior and Administration* (Homewood, Ill.: Irwin, 1976); Gerald Zaltman and Robert Duncan, *Strategies for Planned Change* (New York: Wiley, 1977); Michael Beer, *Organization Change and Development* (Pacific Palisades, Calif.: Goodyear Publ. Co., 1980); Douglas Basil, *The Management of Change* (New York: McGraw-Hill, 1974); E. F. Huse, *Organization Development and Change* (New York: West, 2nd ed., 1980); Rosabeth Moss Kanter, *The Change Masters* (New York: Simon & Schuster, 1983); Arnold Brown and Edith Weiner, *Supermanaging: How to Harness Change for Personal and Organizational Success* (New York: McGraw-Hill, 1984).

‡ Paraphrased from Fritz J. Roethlisberger, "The Foreman: Master and Victim of Double Talk," in *Man-In-Organization: Essays of F. J. Roethlisberger* (Cambridge: Belknap Press of Harvard University Press, 1968), p. 36.

** Powell and Posner, "Resistance to Change Reconsidered," p. 29.

in a large urban fire department. The thesis is that resistance to change is a *failure in teamwork*. Where teamwork exists resistance does not emerge, or if it does, the proactive collaboration between those affected—both managers and workers alike—allows them to develop technical and social skills in handling both their logical and social involvement in the change process. Teamwork gets to the core of resistance by facilitating the cooperative interactions between people, irrespective of their status, in the accomplishment of a common task. This is the basic insight from the relay assembly room of the Western Electric Studies: where teamwork existed, no special resistance was encountered between workers and investigators in spite of the fact that several major technical changes were introduced. "What actually happened," wrote Mayo, "was that six individuals became a team and the team gave itself wholeheartedly and spontaneously to cooperation in the experiment."* The team process held the human situation steady and permitted the participants to develop both technical and social skills in relation to change phenomena.† The workers did not view or experience change as something externally imposed by management; rather, change became a way for them to adapt and experience social complication in their work. Satisfaction came from meeting and coping with the challenge.

More often than not, when teamwork is left to chance, managers do not get teamwork; they get instead the kind of resistance behavior which was described by the battalion chief in the opening paragraphs of this chapter. Resistance is management's external evaluation of the workers' behavior when they do not accept a technical change; opposition to management's change is the workers' internal response in protecting the social character of their world. Teamwork bridges the gap between these internal and external processes during change. However, unless both managers and workers diagnostically understand this process and can behaviorally respond to each other in such fashion as to create cooperation, then teamwork will elude both.‡ Before we explore further the worth of this idea

---

* Elton Mayo, *The Social Problems of an Industrial Civilization* (Boston, Mass.: Division of Research, Harvard Graduate School of Business Administration, 1945), p. 72.
† Ibid.
‡ A recent and widely adopted organizational approach to encourage worker participation is known as quality circles. Many American managers see their utilization as a major breakthrough for encouraging cooperation and shared decision making in a common task. Although teamwork is not specifically mentioned in definitions of quality circles, teamwork would certainly be a major prerequisite to their success. The following are some recent sources on quality circles: Robert I. Patchin, *The Management and Maintenance of Quality Circles* (Homewood, Ill.: Dow Jones-Irwin, 1983); Sud and Nima Ingle, *Quality Circles in Service Industries* (Englewood Cliffs, N.J.: Prentice-Hall, 1983); Laurie Fitzgerald and Joseph Murphy, *Installing Quality Circles: A Strategic Approach* (San Diego, Calif.: University Associates, Inc., 1982).

and its implications, let us give a brief description of the changes so colorfully alluded to in the battalion chief's remarks.

Introduction of a Change in a Fire Department

In a major move from conventional scheduling, the management of a large urban city placed its firefighting personnel on a 40-hour workweek consisting of three eight-hour work shifts. This contrasted with the department's former 48-hour a week schedule of 24 hours on duty and 48 hours off duty. The primary objective of the plan was to maximize the on-duty time of the firefighting personnel, thus providing a better level of fire service to the citizens and taxpayers of the city.

The eight-hour shift was just one component of the city's comprehensive fire protection plan, but was viewed by management as central to the plan and an innovative step forward in fire service. Many advantages seemed to be inherent in the plan: fresh personnel every 8 hours rather than every 24 should reduce life risks due to fatigue; an increase in on-duty productivity and communications should result because the men would work their full shifts instead of sleeping part of them; and last, round-the-clock attention could be given to fire prevention, training, and equipment maintenance. Also management believed that by putting the men on an eight-hour schedule it would be easier to justify raising their pay commensurate with other protective service personnel in the city. The eight-hour shift was thus negotiated as part of a pay package requested by the local firefighters' union. Pay increases in the contract were tied to a "good faith, best effort" on the firefighters' part in carrying out management's plan.

During the three years that the eight-hour shift was in operation, the department was in almost constant turmoil because of the firefighters' steadily mounting resistance to the changes in the work schedule. Management pointed to the many tactics the firefighters were using to resist the plan: slowdowns, work stoppages, sick-outs, and damaging and losing equipment. On their part, the firefighters felt that the city was squandering the taxpayers' money on what was a totally unworkable plan, designed only to "punish" them for their pay demands.

The fire chief and his technical assistants held many meetings with the battalion chiefs in an effort to work out "the bugs" in the plan. Several adjustments were made to the plan as a result of these meetings: 313 persons were promoted; relief companies were formed to provide backup manpower; and a special task force consisting of several senior battalion chiefs was created to "track" the progress of the fire protection plan. But in spite of all of management's efforts, few of the chiefs and even fewer of the rank-and-file firefighters "accepted" the new work schedule. A six-months' evaluation of the plan prepared by the special task force concluded that the eight-hour work shift had failed to achieve management's objective of greater productivity and had been devastating to the morale of the firefighters.

When contract negotiations came due, communication relations between city management and the union were at the boiling point. The union was determined to change the eight-hour workday; management was equally determined to keep the plan intact, but was open to any internal modification to make the work schedule more flexible. When negotiations broke down, the union initiated a massive work slowdown. Management responded by discharging some 40 firefighters for contract violations. Fearing that the discharged firefighters would not be rehired because of the slowdown, the men returned to their jobs and negotiations resumed. When it then became apparent to the union that the city did not intend to rehire the discharged firefighters, the union called a strike, leaving the stations virtually unmanned except for the battalion chiefs. In short order, the city manager called in the police and the national guard to man the fire stations and their presence naturally inflamed the situation. Before the paralyzing strike was over, an international firefighters' union, the governor of the state, the city council, the mayor, and many prominent citizens had become involved in trying to resolve the crisis. Public opinion was divided. Some citizens believed that the firefighters had failed to honor their agreement with the city and were attempting to usurp the city's authority to run the department. Others felt that the city had "forced" an impractical plan on the firefighters and that the latter were justified in their counteractions.

After the strike was settled, the eight-hour shift was replaced by a 10/14-day workweek, a schedule regarded by the firefighters as better than the eight-hour shift but not as desirable as the original 24/48 workweek. The outcome of the situation seemed to be losses for all concerned: the city had spent a great deal of time and money on the innovative plan which they were finally forced to abandon largely due to outside pressures; the firefighters settled for a longer workweek with the same pay and few additional benefits; the fire chief with over 30 years of service resigned; the union president was passed over for promotion although he was more than qualified; and many outstanding firefighters left the department either through early retirement or by seeking employment in other fire departments. These were the immediate and apparent consequences—hundreds of thousands of dollars lost, turnover, lowered morale and motivation, and no noticeable improvement in fire service.

Briefly, then, these are the facts of the implementation of a change in a fire department. We might now ask: how did management and the firefighters evaluate their experiences in the presence of the same concrete phenomena? Needless to say, both managers and firefighters pointed to the technical and organizational alterations as the single cause of their problems, although each group drew very different conclusions from the same events because of their dissimilar organizational and group roles and individual personal needs. However, as we saw it, both top management and the firefighters responded to the change process in the *same* fashion. In other words, both the city manager and his technical support staff as well as the rank-and-file firefighters made the assumption (and this was clearly evident in their behavior) that what was happening in the fire department was strictly a rational-logical experience. Let us explore further the way managers and firefighters alike reasoned about the change.

How Management Reasoned

To management, obviously, there was nothing basically wrong with the plan and any number of adjustments could be made to eliminate the "bugs." The real problem, they concluded, was the firefighters' refusal to carry out the plan in "good faith." Being good logicians, they were at first reluctant to draw this inference (although they felt it in their guts) until more evidence was in. So, to be consistent at all costs, upper management spent innumerable hours and considerable sums of money getting the "bugs" out of the work schedule, in order to allay the complaints of the battalion chiefs and the firefighters. In particular, technical specialists, both inside and outside the department, along with a specially appointed associate city manager and the fire chief, spent endless hours discussing the battalion chiefs' and firefighters' objections to the schedule and making appropriate modifications only to find that each modification required another and yet another until at the end of the first six months, a major adjustment was made approximately once a week: management seemed to be operating on the assumption that the better the firefighters and, particularly, the battalion chiefs, understood the logics of the plan, the more likely it was that they would support it. When this assumption did not come true, upper management then drew the inference that the battalion chiefs and the firefighters were "unreasonable" because of their stubborn refusal to face the facts.

How the Firefighters and Battalion Chiefs Reasoned

In the presence of the same happenings and utilizing the same rational approach, the firefighters, along with the union officers and middle-management battalion chiefs, drew just the opposite inference from that of top management: "The plan is not working because it is not suitable to our work situation, and no amount of propping it up can save it." The battalion chiefs and the union countered logic with, from their point of view, better logic. Like upper management, they produced lengthy reports— filled with facts and figures—to demonstrate how the plan, not they, had failed. As the firefighters never tired of pointing out to city management, "a firefighter's job is unique and will not fit into a nine-to-five work schedule." The battalion chiefs and the union argued that other cities had tried the eight-hour work schedule and had eventually abandoned it as impracticable. The more they talked and tried to explain their position (just like top management), the more they tended to evaluate management as being unreasonable and resisting logic.

A Stalemate Results from the Rational Approach

Because of the circular nature of the rational approach, it is difficult for its practitioner to realize consciously what he is doing at any given point in the reasoning process. Within this framework, the practitioner evaluates as follows: change → causes consequences (both expected and unexpected) → leading to the need for correction. Since the "unexpected" consequences are by definition not anticipated (and therefore not desirable), someone or something is to *blame*. Either the designer of the schedule did not set it up properly, the supervisors did not effectively implement it, or the firefighters did not do what they were told.

In meeting after meeting both city managers and firefighters pointed to the external, technical phenomena and blamed the other party for its failure to comprehend the "facts." Both assumed they were talking only about the technical shortcomings of the plan, when in reality they were responding also to their uncomfortable feelings and disturbed social relationships. Both firefighters and battalion chiefs tried to convey to top management the social confusion which had been brought into their lives by the change, but in management's presence their explanations always came out as logical rationalizations, which management, with a superior set of logic, always succeeded in beating down. Likewise, the chiefs never understood nor were able to accept management's emotional involvement in the change. As one chief put it: "It's the city's plan; let them make it work!" So, in time the positions froze because of a basic misevaluation: that social evaluations and behavior are not involved in technical change.

The conflict between management and firefighters becomes more phenomenologically understandable when viewed through the membership commitments each had to their respective social groups. Social membership roles were manifested in their meetings and discussions, but neither management nor the men understood how they were linked to the success or failure of the work schedule change. It was essentially their *social* world which was threatened by the change, and this factor needs to be placed in perspective along with the technical aspects of the change. Let us now turn first to a description of the fire department as a social system and, second, to an analysis of the four major subgroupings which determined in a large degree the social memberships of both firefighters and battalion chiefs.

A Description of the Fire Department as a Social System

As the writers on social systems have stressed, people who work together over a period of time begin to form into collective configurations or groupings. Because of the formal and logical divisions established in an organization, certain people are brought together more frequently than others. Initially, people interact with one another in certain prescribed ways dictated by the wider society and the formal requirements of the work. But, in time, these prescribed patterns are modified, changed, or adapted to accommodate to individual and group differences and needs. And, gradually, groups form among those who share the same values, the same sentiments, and similar needs. Out of these shared interactions, sentiments, and activities, norms of behavior develop. Group members as a whole develop certain ideas about how they should be treated, what their contributions are worth, and what are proper and improper ways of behaving according to their status and job roles. It is these group processes and evaluations which emerge and feedback on the purposive organization that we point to when we speak of social phenomena.

Although social phenomena are related to technical phenomena, they are also different. Technical phenomena often are created, ordered, modified, and even eliminated without consideration of the feelings of people. Technical phenomena can be talked about, pointed to, diagrammed, and manipulated far more easily than social phenomena. Social phenomena exist at lower levels of abstraction; they are "relations of interconnectedness which exist among persons" and are part and parcel of concrete natural systems.* These phenomena are more difficult to point to, to talk about, and to manipulate. More important, they are *naturally ordered* by individuals and groups to bring stability and meaning to their lives. Technical phenomena are logically ordered to attain the purposes of the organi-

---

* Roethlisberger, *The Elusive Phenomena,* p. 144.

zation. Social phenomena are nonlogical in origin and seldom can be modified by logic alone.

The social interconnectedness among the members of the fire department was "tight." Firefighting is the most dangerous of occupations, and firefighters literally depend upon each other for survival. This fact alone would create the need for cooperation among them. In addition, living together "around-the-clock" in the fire stations increased opportunities for social interactions. The firefighters—from raw recruits to senior battalion chiefs—ate, slept, and fought fires together; occasionally, some died together. They thought of their stations as home; many brought television sets and furniture to make the stations more livable, more like home. The family atmosphere and group loyalty was expressed in the elaborate parties given for those who had retired, the large attendance at funerals for "old-timers," and contributions made toward gifts to fellow firefighters at times of noteworthy occasions in their lives.

To illustrate the deep sense of dedication, loyalty, and friendship that bound them together, here is a typical statement from the casewriter's data:

> Our job is different, it isn't just a nine-to-five kind of job. We actually spend more time with each other than with our families. We have trust because of our work. Remember, when you go out on a run, that man next to you can save your life or let you burn. We are all brothers. This feeling is hard to explain to someone who has never been a firefighter. If you make friends with a firefighter, you make it for life.

These sentiments were expressed by a senior battalion chief nearing the end of his career. Most firefighters would share this viewpoint. However, agreement with these sentiments did not mean that as a consequence all firefighters thought alike, behaved alike, shared the same values, or followed the same norms of social behavior. Depending on their background values, personal needs, and social ranking, some firefighters regarded work as more important than friendship, status more important than group respect, competence more important than seniority, and pleasing the boss more important than conforming to his co-workers' expectations.

Four Natural Groups

The different values brought to the work situation and the values which emerged on the job while they interacted resulted in the formation of several social groups in the fire department. We will briefly describe the four major groups which we delineated from the data, keeping in mind, of course, that not every individual fitted neatly into any one group.*

Technical-Specialist Organizational. As the name suggests, these people are most comfortable relating to technical phenomena and organizational authority. They tend to be "standoffish" in social relations and they are usually regarded by other group members, particularly the social regulars, as isolates, although they may be admired for their technical competence. Their isolation is often self-imposed. If they rise in the management hierarchy—many do because of their performance—their social isolation is reinforced by their becoming organizationals, namely, "boss oriented." Their values: "Technical competence is foremost. My job is to get the work done regardless of whose toes I step on." Technical specialists can be high producers.

Social-Specialist Regular. Feeling lonely, misunderstood, or disliked is the worst thing that can happen to a social regular. Satisfaction is secured not exclusively from doing a good job, but is only secondary to being accepted by one's colleagues. Leaders of this group have great influence with their peers and subordinates because they are people, rather than power, oriented. Their values: "We stick together, and that's how we get the job done. Keep confidences, never hurt a brother." Their production can be on the line or high (never low) depending on how established their group membership is and the way their performance is regarded by their colleagues, not by top management.

Underchosen. These men may truly be unhappy isolates, not self-chosen like the technical specialists. They are underchosen by both the technicals and the socials because of some critical value out-of-lineness such as age, competence, ethnicity, education, or personality. If they rise in the hierarchy, they are seen as sycophants by their colleagues because of their subservience to management. Around their fellow workers they often behave like "good Joes," but their social influence is limited. By "working both sides of the street," they hope to gain acceptance and status. Their values: "Whatever you desire me, I'll be. I've paid my dues and I want what's coming to me." Their production is often minimal and they usually keep a low profile when conflict emerges because of their unstable organizational status and group membership.

---

* For some of the ideas and the distinctions in the social groupings, the author is indebted to David Moment and Abraham Zaleznik, *Role Development and Interpersonal Competence,* Division of Research, Harvard Graduate School of Business Administration, Boston, pp. 122–125.

Power Specialist.   These people seek recognition and acceptance by exercising power. To enhance their standing with the social regulars, with whom they ultimately identify, they openly confront hierarchical authority in the name of a "good cause." Both their organizational status and group membership can be threatened because of their aggressive activities. On the one hand, they are admired by social regulars—never organizationals or the underchosen—for their accomplishments, but on the other hand, they are feared because of their reckless actions. They often have enormous group influence and power, particularly at times of crisis. Their values: "Go for broke, rock the boat, the cause is everything." Their production is variable like their status and group membership. They have many labels—politicos, power-seekers, do-gooders, troublemakers—depending on where you and they identify in the social system.

The Impact of the Social Groups in the Change Process

The delineation of social groupings could be extended or modified in terms of the many existing social patterns in the fire department. These groups were chosen because they provided a comprehensible framework for viewing and understanding the departmental members' behavior during the change.

As the tensions mounted over the work schedule, group membership became a major determinant of the firefighters' evaluations. The technical-organizational group, composed of the fire chief, an associate city manager, and their assistants, clearly identified with the values of upper management. These members experienced no role conflict within their own group; their frustrations and conflict resulted from their inability to enlist many followers. Since upper management had originally entrusted them with the creation and implementation of the plan, these men had to gain the men's acceptance of the work schedule. But because they were identified with upper management's values and goals, they were regarded with suspicion by other group members and their effectiveness was limited. The target of the technical organizationals was, of course, the chiefs who had strong social ties with both the social regular firefighters and the power specialist union members. In time, the only people the fire chief and his group influenced significantly were a handful of the department's staff personnel and some underchosen low producers and "good Joes."

Explicitly opposed to the work schedule was the power specialist group. Headed by the union officers, this group urged all firefighters to resist the work schedule at all costs or run the risk of forfeiting their "social" membership. Paying the price could mean accusations of group disloyalty and weakness at best or group exclusion and loneliness at worst. The pressure of this group was felt by both the social regulars and the underchosen.

Caught between these two groups, which were both vying for their support, were the critical management line supervisors, the battalion chiefs. Over the years most of the chiefs had identified with the values of the social regulars, but a few had split loyalties, partly to upper management and partly to the union of which they had historically been members.

Their organizational role placed them right in the middle of the conflict. On the one hand, the chiefs had to enforce the logics of the change to keep their supervisory positions, while on the other hand, they needed to maintain their group standing in order to sustain the firefighters' cooperation. A decision for management could mean rejection by the men; a decision for the men could mean organizational exclusion by upper management.

The chiefs' role conflict erupted into the open at the time of the six-months' evaluational report presentation. Intentionally or not, upper management evoked the incident when they selected the members of a steering committee to "track" the results of the change and write up a report. Management "bent over backwards" to appoint a fair and equitable representation of the chiefs, knowing full well that many were not sympathetic to the new schedule. In preparing the written report, the committee solicited reactions from all the chiefs and added their own inputs. The report, when completed, was signed by all battalion chiefs.

The Six-Months' Evaluational Report

On the day of the presentation, the committee, chaired by a senior battalion chief, met with the fire chief and his assistants. The chairman and most of the chiefs were social regulars and carried the brunt of the interactions; a few were "underchosens" and remained largely silent during the meeting. The power specialists were present as "spectators" along with several members of the news media. (News had leaked out to the press that the report on the work schedule was unfavorable.)

In a tense atmosphere, the chairman opened the meeting:

Chairman:	The purpose of this meeting is to review the findings of the six months' evaluation of the plan. (He passes out copies of the report.)
Fire Chief:	(Thumbing through his copy.) This is the first time I've seen this report.
Chairman:	No one has seen it but the chiefs. Duplication was just finished yesterday. However, it isn't that long. We can all go through it together.

Fire Chief:	All the chiefs have seen the report since they all signed it. All officers have read the report except the chief officer of this department. Is that correct?
Chairman:	Well, Chief, you were away and. . . .
Associate City Manager:	The report was requested by the city manager's office. Your job was to make an objective appraisal. Just glancing through the report, it seems to contain a number of subjective statements and not much hard data. You must fold into your report the computer data on response times and allocations of equipment and manpower. Your statistics and conclusions must be carefully meshed. We must be guided by the facts in our evaluations.
An Assistant:	Who wrote the report?
Senior Battalion Chief:	We all wrote it. It bears no malice to anyone. We report the concerns of all the chiefs.
Chairman:	The report isn't all that bad. It's written from an operational point of view, it isn't very long, and it has several good things to say.
Fire Chief:	I will make no comments until I have thoroughly studied the report.
Chairman:	(Pause) I accept your decision, of course, but I think it's a sad day when we can't discuss our mutual problems openly.
Firefighter:	(Speaking from the back of the room) I think this report should be gotten out and not buried somewhere. The public should be informed about what kind of fire protection they are or are not getting.
Associate City Manager:	Of course, when everyone has had time to read the report, we'll certainly go through it carefully and consider every recommendation.

At this point, the meeting turned to other matters, and shortly afterwards was adjourned.

Ostensibly, the committee had met to discuss the report, but intergroup relationships and feelings were such that an open discussion was impossible. The report was a "plea for understanding and help," although this was probably an unconscious wish on the part of the chiefs; however, management perceived the report as a "slap in the face." Management reacted only to the "slap" and "slapped back." In fact, all committee participants evaluated what happened in the meeting only from their respective group referents.

These were the reactions after the meeting:

Technical Organizational:	The chiefs are just too close to the men. They should support the city. I told the city manager and fire chief they'd get a bad report from this committee. (He had not read the report.)
Social Regular:	Had the report been given to the city first, all the findings unfavorable to them would just have been buried. There's no way in good conscience we chiefs can ignore the men.
Underchosen:	I didn't want to sign the report, but what else could I do? I was on the spot.
Power Specialist:	After this, maybe the chiefs will come over to our side where they belong.

Subsequent communications within each group and between groups only reinforced these perceptions. Upper management immediately came to the defense of the technical organizationals by verbally reprimanding the chiefs for publicly airing departmental differences. (They believed the chiefs were responsible for the leak to the press.) The city officials felt strongly and, understandably, that they had been "set up" to look bad in the public's eye. The chiefs felt misunderstood, but admitted they had mishandled the presentation of the report. At the next meeting, the committee members apologized to upper management; management reciprocated. Following this exchange, a technical organizational commented: "It's good we got this off our chests; now, we can turn to the real work, the facts of the report." In short, he was saying that now they could dismiss the uncomfortable social dimensions of the situation and return to the only feasible task at hand, the logical implementation of the work schedule change.

In the months ahead, staff meetings were concerned exclusively with the technical problems caused by the work schedule. Upper management met less and less with the battalion chiefs until finally all meetings between them ceased. As time went on, management tended to exclude the chiefs from all major decisions, and thereby, consciously or not, reduced their status and authority. This exclusion by upper management, which was exploited by the power specialists, eventually forced the chiefs to make a choice. In time, they joined the social regulars and the power specialists in their overt opposition to upper management and the technical organizationals. By joining with these groups, the chiefs became ineffective in working out a managerial compromise between the city and the firefighters' union.

The technical organizationals totally understimated the strength of intrinsic group membership values and never really understood how these values were linked to success in achieving extrinsic goals. At least, if they did understand, they were never able to act upon their insights in any effective way. The power specialists learned only to exploit the weaknesses and strengths of the various groups for their own purposes. The social system of the fire department, for all practical purposes, became frozen and the change-resistance syndrome intensified between upper management and the union. At contract negotiation time, when the union was free of legal obligations and all communications had broken down between the city and the firefighters, the union called a strike.

A few months after the strike, the fire chief resigned. In subsequent months, his resignation was followed by that of the associate city manager, all technical specialists who had been connected with the fire protection plan, and eventually the city manager himself. Although these personnel changes cannot entirely be attributed to the upheaval in the fire department, certainly the failure of the fire protection plan was in the picture. In 1985, the union successfully negotiated with the new city manager a return to the *original* 24/48-hour work shift. In addition, by this time, most of the technical innovations introduced with the fire protection plan had been abandoned.

Summary

This case study has illustrated once again a breakdown in communications and cooperation between management and workers during a change process. In the fire department, both upper management and the firefighters were quickly swept up in the vicious cycle of the change-resistance syndrome. Both parties evaluated the technical consequences of the change as the problem; both failed to grasp the impact that the technical change had on their interactions and interpersonal feelings. In their meetings and discussions, they responded to breakdowns in communication as though they were only technical misunderstandings which could be corrected through logical coordination and formal rules. Because only the logical impact of the change was addressed, the vital social group processes which were disturbed by the change went unattended.

This occurred not because one or both parties were power-oriented, stupid, or illogical. Both intuitively understood and responded to their own needs and their own group involvement; less clearly did each understand the impact that their behavior had on each other as they went about satisfying their needs for security, belonging, and status. The fire department situation could be best described not as a battle for power between opposing forces—as both management and the firefighters evaluated it—but rather as a struggle between the logics of change and the sentiments of group membership.

When introducing change, the manager's role becomes crucial. On the one hand, he must determine what changes are necessary for the effective survival of the organization, and on the other, he must secure and maintain the effective cooperation of individuals and groups to insure their acceptance. How is he to achieve this?

Implications for Practice

Diagnostic Skills. It may seem strange today to say that we need to improve our understanding of the dynamics of organizations, but all our clinical research points to this need.* A manager is a practitioner and requires diagnostic skills similar to those of the clinician. Before a physician can act, he must diagnose the sort of illness he is handling—whether it be a case of measles, mumps, or cancer. Managers often behave as if they require no such equivalent skills in diagnosis. Too often, if we are not careful, we try to solve our problems of teamwork and change intellectually, abstractly, and analytically rather than through the diagnostic identification and sizing up of individual values and group norms in relation to organizational requirements.

To become better diagnosticians requires that we understand our own involvement and the impact of our behavior on others. This is particularly true during an introduction of change when actions on the part of both managers and workers are so critical and subject to such easy misunderstanding. A manager is an involved participant and member of his social system, and from this involvement there is no escape. He is both an instrument of change and a recipient of that change; his dilemma is: how can he (a part of a system) effect a change in other parts of the system as a whole of which he is an involved member without destroying cooperative relations in the process? A manager is the bridge between organizational requirements and interpersonal cooperative processes, and how well he understands social processes will largely determine whether his change is accepted or rejected.

Here is an example of a simple social pattern which was unrecognized by upper management. When it was altered, the change led to much bitterness and deepened the chasm between management and firefighters.

---

* For several ideas in this section, the author is indebted to Roethlisberger, *Man-In-Organization,* pp. 65, 139, 169.

The social custom of the "cook shack" was a long established practice in the fire stations under the former work schedule. The fire companies took enormous pride in their food preparation and there was considerable vying among the various stations for a reputation as "best house." Deputies and battalion chiefs were often invited as special guests to share a meal and pass judgment on the "table."

On these occasions, the senior ranking officers sat at the head of the table, while the less senior in rank and age took their respective places around the sides. The conversation was not limited to social matters; often chiefs, captains, and experienced firefighters shared mutual problems about particular fires, equipment, etc., while the younger men listened and added their comments.

According to the "logics" of the new work schedule, firefighters were discouraged from cooking in the stations. They were expected to "brown bag" it or eat at nearby restaurants. Neither the city nor the firefighters properly understood how this alteration in eating habits with the new work schedule impacted upon morale. "Eating together" was a social process which paid off handsomely at the fire site later in terms of strengthening the patterns of company and battalion teamwork.

Distinguishing Fact from Sentiment. Diagnostic understandng and intuitive familiarity with social uniformities deters a skillful manager from making a quick size-up when introducing change. He begins not with a theory or technique but rather, with the slow, laborious task of observing social behavior in relation to technical behavior. By practicing a diagnostic skill, a manager can begin to improve his communications with others; he can become gradually more proficient at promoting cooperation and participation during the change process.*

For example, a skillful manager realizes he cannot express his own feelings without regard to the impact they will have on others, particularly his subordinates, who cannot be expected to distinguish between his expression of feelings and his statements of fact. He must help them to make that distinction. This confusion between fact and sentiment was at the core of the conflict between managers and firefighters.

Basically, the confusion arises when one participant makes a value judgment of another's behavior from the former's point of view. Not only do people make value judgments, but they also insist that the other person

---

* Fritz J. Roethlisberger, "Conversation," in William Dowling, Ed., *Effective Management and the Behavioral Sciences* (New York: AMACOM, A Division of American Management Association, 1978), p. 207.

accept these judgments as correct, factual, and true. When this pattern occurred in the case study, all cooperation ceased. A manager needs to practice a skill of communication which distinguishes between fact and sentiment in his dealings with others. He must learn to identify the values, sentiments, and norms which are important for him and others to maintain in their interactions. Simply put, when people are not kept busy defending their personal feelings, they have more time and *desire* to cooperate.

Utilizing Listening Skills to Facilitate Teamwork.   No group was more critical to the successful introduction of change in the fire department than the middle-management battalion chiefs. Both upper management and the union knew this. As we have stated, the chiefs were caught in a role conflict aggravated by a change which they intellectually understood but emotionally found difficult to handle. Their job organizationally, as seen by upper management, was simply to enforce the change. This placed the chiefs, as they saw it, in the role of being "watchdogs," a role they found personally uncomfortable and virtually impossible to carry out and at the same time maintain their image in the eyes of the rank-and-file firefighters. Time and time again they had to do things that were "disloyal" from upper management's point of view in order to get the work done. On the other hand, with the firefighters in the field, the chiefs frequently had to "distort reality," plead ignorance, or be vague about some happening or regulation in order to maintain their social group standing.

Had upper management recognized the chiefs' role dilemma and responded to it more skillfully by listening, two important processes would have been set in motion. First, upper management would have heard not only the chiefs' *words,* but more important, what these words *pointed to*—the chiefs' role conflict. Listening implies we attend to (1) what people want to tell you, (2) what they don't want to tell you, and (3) what they cannot tell you without help. Listening reduces social distance and softens social status differences between groups. It is a facilitator to understanding and cooperation. By being listened to, the chiefs would have felt more accepted and less defensive in their communications with upper management.

Secondly, the systematic practice of listening gives the manager more phenomenologically relevant data upon which to take action, since such data come to him from an internal as opposed to an external point of view. Had upper management understood that the chiefs' role conflict sprang not from a lack of "management knowledge about logics" but rather from the very nature of the concrete social system of which they were a part, they might have made a more proper evaluation of the chiefs' "double talk" during their meetings. With this insight, management's actions could have been made consistent with the chiefs' internal experiences. This is one of the most important lessons we need to learn when introducing change—that a little difference, such as listening, can make a big difference among organizational members.*

Listening and Teamwork Go Hand in Hand. Although many managers would readily concede the importance of listening, particularly as a tool in creating teamwork, the skill is not widely practiced in organizations, certainly not in the fire department under consideration in this chapter. Generally stated, most of us don't listen because we honestly believe it is a waste of time. We already have our minds made up and all we want from our subordinates and colleagues is acceptance of our point of view. It is much easier, neater, and quicker just to tell people what is expected of them logically and hope for the best. As the city manager remarked in the early stages of the resistance, "In time the firefighters will come to accept the change because they will see the logic in it."

At a deeper and more personal level, the resistance to listening is subtle and difficult to cope with. To this writer, the major barrier to the practice of listening arises from the uncomfortable and insecure feelings which the practice sets up in the practitioner.† These uncomfortable feelings are aroused in the practitioner because listening forces him to be more conscious of his own behavior—his attitudes and feelings—and take responsibility for the consequences of his behavior in relation to others. Listening requires a willingness to see, appreciate, and even accept points of view different from his own.

For most of us these ideas are difficult to accept emotionally. It is not difficult for us to understand intellectually that people are motivated more by feelings and sentiments than by facts and logic. It is not difficult to appreciate that people are members of groups and act in accordance with the sentiments of these groups. Furthermore, it is even obvious to most of us that we do not all perceive the world in the same way. What is important to one person is not important to another. This is a way of saying that we do not respond to reality as it actually is, but rather as we perceive it to be.‡ These matters are all easy to understand intellectually, but to practice this understanding by listening to others is quite another matter.

Time after time, city managers and firefighters ignored nonlogical behavior in their dealings with each other. As a consequence the resistance

---

* Ibid., p. 217.
† For certain ideas in this section, the author is indebted to Roethlisberger, *Man-In-Organization,* pp. 105–106.
‡ For a recent statement on a relativistic view of "reality," see James Burke, *The Day the Universe Changed,* (Boston,: Little, Brown, 1985) pp. 336–337.

between them intensified. Listening requires that we address individual and group sentiments and evaluations in face-to-face interactions, and failure to do so means that teamwork will languish or even worse, atrophy, and the change-resistance syndrome will persist.

Breakdowns in cooperation and communications between management and workers continue to be commonplace. Disillusionment with interpersonal skills such as listening and understanding is also rising among managers, possibly because they expect too much from them too soon. It is only human to want the "quick fix," particularly when we introduce change. There is no magic nor any guarantees of success in the listening process. However, management's recent shift back to reliance on organizational structure as the exclusive change variable may prove, as it did in this case study, costly, disruptive, and self-defeating. Perhaps it is time we take Mayo's admonition of nearly 40 years ago seriously: Teamwork ". . . is the problem we face in the . . . twentieth century. There is no 'ism' that will help us to solution; we must be content to return to the patient, pedestrian work at the wholly neglected problem of the determinants of spontaneous participation.*

---

* Mayo, *The Social Problems,* p. xvi.

32. Team Building in Project Management

Hans J. Thamhain*

Team building is important for many activities. It is especially crucial in a project-oriented work environment where complex multidisciplinary activities require the integration of many functional specialties and support groups. To manage these multifunctional activities it is necessary for the managers and their task leaders to cross organizational lines and deal with resource personnel over whom they have little or no formal authority. Yet another set of challenges is the contemporary nature of project organizations with their horizontal and vertial lines of communication and control, their resource sharings among projects and task teams, multiple reporting relationships to several bosses, and dual accountabilities.

To manage projects effectively in such a dynamic environment, task leaders must understand the interaction of organizational and behavioral variables in order to foster a climate conducive to multidisciplinary team building. Such a team must have the capacity of innovatively transforming a set of technical objectives and requirements into specific products or services that compete favorably against other available alternatives in the marketplace.

A New Management Focus

Building effective task teams is one of the prime responsibilities of project managers. Team building involves a whole spectrum of management skills required to identify, commit, and integrate various task groups from traditional functional organizations into a multidisciplinary task/management

---

* Hans J. Thamhain is Associate Professor of Management at Bentley College in Waltheim, Massachusetts. He has held engineering and project management positions with GTE, General Electric, Westinghouse, and ITT. Dr. Thamhain is well known for his research and writings in project management, which include 4 books and 60 journal articles. He also conducts seminars and consults in all phases of project management for industry and government.

system. This process has been known for centuries. However, it becomes more complex and requires more specialized management skills as bureaucratic hierarchies decline and horizontally oriented teams and work units evolve. Starting with the evolution of formal project organizations in the 1960s, managers in various organizational settings have expressed increasing concern and interest in the concepts and practices of multidisciplinary team building. Responding to this interest many field studies* have been conducted, investigating work group dynamics and criteria for building effective, high-performing project teams. These studies have contributed to the theoretical and practical understanding of team building and form the basis for the discussion of the fundamental concepts in this chapter.

The Process of Team Building

Team building is an ongoing process that requires leadership skills and an understanding of the organization, its interfaces, authority and power structures, and motivational factors. It is a process particularly critical in certain project situations, such as:

- Establishing a new program.
- Improving project-client relationships.
- Organizing for a build proposal.
- Integrating new project personnel.
- Resolving interfunctional problems.
- Working toward major milestones.
- Transitioning the project into a new activity phase.

Team Building is defined as the process of taking a collection of individuals with different needs, backrounds, and expertise and transforming them into an integrated, effective work unit. In this transformation process, the goals and energies of individual contributors merge and support the objectives of the team.

Today, team building is considered by many management practitioners and researchers as one of the most critical leadership qualities that determines the performance and success of multidisciplinary efforts. The outcome of these projects critically depends on carefully orchestrated group efforts, requiring the coordination and integration of many task specialists in a dynamic work environment with complex organizational interfaces. Therefore, it is not surprising to find a strong emphasis on teamwork and

---

* See bibliography numbers 3, 4, 5, 8, 17, 18, 22, 24, and 49

team building practice among today's managers, a trend which, we expect, will continue and most likely intensify for years to come.

A SIMPLE MODEL

The characteristics of a project team and its ultimate performance depend on many factors. Using a systems approach, Figure 32-1 provides a simple model for organizing and analyzing these factors. It defines three sets of variables which influence the team characteristics and its ultimate performance: (a) environmental factors, such as working conditions, job content, resources, and organizational support factors; (b) leadership style; and (c) specific drivers and barriers toward desirable team characteristics and performance. All of these variables are likely to be interrelated in a complex, intricate form. However, using the systems approach allows researchers and management practitioners to break down the complexity of the process and to analyze its components. It can further help in identifying the drivers and barriers toward transforming resources into specific results under the influence of managerial, organizational, and other environmental factors.

CHARACTERISTICS OF AN EFFECTIVE PROJECT TEAM

Obviously, each organization has its own way to measure and express performance of a project team. However, in spite of the existing cultural and philosophical differences, there seems to be a general agreement among managers on certain factors which are included in the characteristics of a successful project team:*

1. Technical project success according to agreed-on objectives.
2. On-time performance.
3. On-budget/within-resource performance.

Further, over 60% of the managers who identified these three measures ranked them in the above order.

When describing the characteristics of an effective, high-performing project team, managers point at the factors summarized in Figure 32-2. These managers stress consistently that a high-performing team not only produces technical results on time and on budget but is also characterized by specific job- and people-related qualities as shown in Table 32-1.

---

* In fact, over 90% of the project managers interviewed during a recent survey (46) mentioned the measures among the most important criteria of team performance.

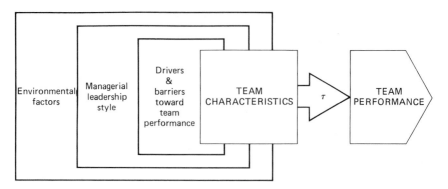

Figure 32-1. A simple model for analyzing project team performance.

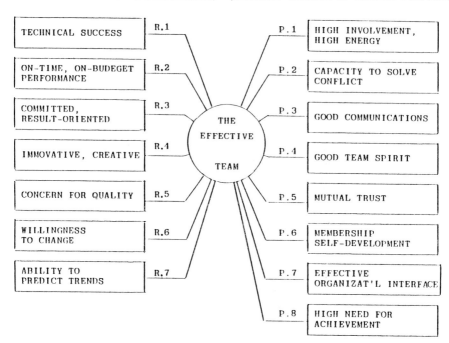

Figure 32-2. Characteristics of an effective project team.

Table 32-1. Qualities Associated with High-Performing Teams.

TASK-RELATED QUALITIES	PEOPLE RELATED QUALITIES
• Committed to the project • Result-oriented attitude • Innovative and creative • Willingness to change • Concern for quality • Ability to predict trends	• High involvement, work interest, and energy • Capacity to solve conflict • Good communication • High need for achievement • Good team spirit • Mutual trust • Self-development of team members • Effective organizational interfacing

In fact, field research shows (41) a statistically significant association between the above team qualities and team performance at a confidence level of $p = 95\%$ or better.*

The significance of determining team performance characteristics is in two areas. First, it offers some clues as to what an effective team environment looks like. This can stimulate management thoughts and activities for effective team building. Second, the results allow us to define measures and characteristics of an effective team environment for further research on organization development efforts, such as defining drivers and barriers toward team performance.

DRIVERS AND BARRIERS OF HIGH TEAM PERFORMANCE

Additonal management insight has been gained by investigating drivers and barriers to high performance.† Drivers are factors associated with the project environment, such as interesting work and good project direction. These factors are preceived as enhancing team effectiveness and correlate *positively* to team performance. Barriers are factors, such as unclear objectives and insufficient resources, that are perceived as impeding team performance and statistically correlate *negatively* to performance.

Studies by Gemmill, Thamhain, and Wilemon (39, 41, 42) into work group dynamics clearly show significant correlations and interdependencies among work-environmental factors and team performance. These studies indicate that high team performance involves four primary fac-

---

* Specifically, a Kendall-Tau rank-order correlation model was used. These measures yielded an average association of $\tau = .37$. Moreover, there appears to be a strong agreement between managers and project team members on the importance of these characteristics, as measured via a Kruskal-Wallis analysis of arience at a confidence level of $p = 95\%$.

† The Kendall-Tau Rank-Order correlation was used to measure to association between these variables. Statistical significance was defined at a confidence level of 95% or better.

tors: (a) managerial leadership, (b) job content, (c) personal goals and objectives, and (d) work environment and organizational support. The actual correlation of 60 influence factors to the project team characteristics and performance provided some interesting insight into the strength and effect of these factors. One of the important findings was that only 12 of the 60 influence factors were found to be statistically significant.* All other factors seem to be much less important to high team performance. Specifically, the *six drivers which have the strongest positive association to project team performance are:*

1+ Professionally interesting and stimulating work.
2+ Recognition of accomplishment.
3+ Experienced engineering management personnel.
4+ Proper technical direction and leadership.
5+ Qualified project team personnel.
6+ Professional growth potential.

The *strongest barriers to project team performance are:*

1- Unclear project objectives and directions.
2- Insufficient resources.
3- Power struggle and conflict.
4- Uninvolved, disintegrated upper management.
5- Poor job security.
6- Shifting goals and priorities.

It is furthermore interesting to note that the six drivers not only correlated favorably to the direct measures of high project team performance, such as the technical success and on-time/on-budget performance, but also were positively associated with the 13 indirect measures of team performance, ranging from commitment to creativity, quality, change-orientation, and needs for achievement. The complete listing of the 16 performance measures is shown in Figure 32-3. The six barriers have exactly the opposite effect. These conclusions provide consistently and measurably support to the findings from a variety of field studies (4, 8, 9, 16, 21, 24, 28, 38, 41).

What we find consistently is that successful organizations pay attention to the human side. They seem to be effective in fostering a work environment conducive to innovative creative work, where people find the as-

---

* The research on team characteristics and drivers versus barriers is based on a field study by H. Thamhain and D. Wilemon, published as ''A High-Performing Engineering Project Team,'' *IEEE Transactions on Engineering Management,* August, 1987.

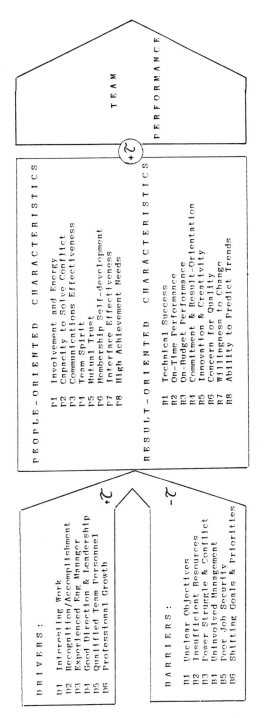

Figure 32-3. Influence factors of project team performance.

signments challenging, leading to recognition and professional growth. Such a professionally stimulating environment also seems to lower communication barriers and conflict, and enhances the desire of personnel to succeed. Further, this seems to increase organizational awareness as well as the ability to respond to changing project requirements.

Secondly, a winning team appears to have good leadership. That is, management understands the factors crucial to success. Managers are action oriented, provide the needed resources, properly direct the implementation of the project plan, and help in the identification and resolution of problems in their early stages. Taken together, the findings support three propositions:

P1 : The degree of project success seems to be primarily determined by the strength of six driving forces and six barriers which are related to (a) Leadership, (b) job content, (c) personal needs, and (4) the general work environment.

P2 : The strongest driver toward project success is a professionally stimulating team environment, characterized by (a) interesting, challenging work; (b) visibility and recognition for achievements; (c) growth potential; and (d) good project leadership.

P3 : A professionally stimulating team environment also leads to low perceived conflict, high commitment, highly involved personnel, good communications, change orientation, innovation, and on-time/on-budget performance

To be effective in organizing and directing a project team, the leader must not only recognize the potential drivers and barriers but also know when in the life cycle of the project they are most likely to occur. The effective project leader takes preventive actions early in the project life cycle and fosters a work environment that is conducive to team building as an ongoing process.

The effective team builder is usually a social architect who understands the interaction of organizational and behavioral variables and can foster a climate of active participation and minimal dysfunctional conflict. This requires carefully developed skills in leadership, administration, organization, and technical expertise. It further requires the project leader's ability to involve top management, to assure organizational visibility, resource availability, and overall support for the new project throughout its life cycle.

It is this organizational culture which adds yet another challenge to project team building. The new team members are usually selected from hierarchically organized functional resource departments led by strong individuals who often foster internal competition rather than cooperation. In fact, even at the contributor level, many of the highly innovative and creative people are highly individualistically oriented and often admit their aversion to cooperation. The challenge to the project manager is to integrate these individuals into a team that can produce innovative results in a systematic, coordinated, and integrated way to an overall project plan. Many of the problems that occur during the formation of the new project team or during its life cycle are normal and often predictable. However, they present barriers to effective team performance. They must be quickly identified and dealt with.

ORGANIZING THE NEW PROJECT TEAM

Too often the project manager, under pressure to start producing, rushes into organizing the project team without establishing the proper organizational framework. While initially the prime focus is on staffing, the program manager cannot effectively attract and hold quality people until certain organizational pillars are in place. At a minimum, the basic project organization and various tasks must be defined before the recruiting effort can start.

These pillars are not only necessary to communicate the project requirements, responsibilities, and relationships to team members, but also to manage the anxiety which usually develops during the team formation. This anxiety is normal and predictable. It is a barrier, however, to getting the team quickly focused on the task.

This anxiety may come from several sources. For example, if the team members have never worked with the project leader, they may be concerned with his leadership style and its effect on them. In a different vein, team members may be concerned about the nature of the project and whether it will match their professional interests and capabilities. Other team members may be concerned whether the project will be helpful to their career aspirations. Furthermore, team members can be anxious about lifeor work style disruptions. As one project manager remarked: "Moving a team member's desk from one side of the room to the other can sometimes be just as traumatic as moving someone from Chicago to Manila to build a power plant" (41).

As the quote suggests, seemingly minor changes can result in sudden anxiety among team members.

Another common concern among newly formed teams is whether or not there will be an equitable distribution of work load among team members and whether each member is capable of pulling his or her own weight. In some newly formed teams, members not only have to do their own work, but they must also train others. Within reason this is bearable, necessary, and often expected. However, when it becomes excessive, anxiety increases and morale can fall.

Make Functional Ties Work for You

It is a mistaken belief that strong ties of team members to the functional organization are bad for effective program management and should be eliminated. To the contrary, loyalty to both the project and the functional organization is a natural, desirable, and often very necessary conditon for project success. For example, in the most common of all project organizations, the matrix, the program office gives operational directions to the program personnel and is responsible for the budget and schedule, while the functional organization provides technical guidance and personnel administration. Both the program manager and the functional managers must understand this process and perform accordingly or severe jurisdictional conflicts can develop.

Structure Your Organization

The key to successfully building a new project organization is clearly defined and communicated responsibilities and organizational relationships. The tools for systematically describing the project organization come, in fact, from conventional management practices:

1. *Charter of the Program or Project Organization.* The charter of the program office clearly describes the business mission and scope, broad responsibilities, authorities, the organizational structure, interfaces, and the reporting relationship of the program organization. The charter should be revised for each new program. For small projects a simple one-half page statement may be sufficient, while larger programs usually require a formal charter supported by standardized company policies on project management.

2. *Project Organization Chart.* Regardless of the specific organizational structure and its terminology used, a simple organizational chart shall define the major reporting and authority relationships. These relationships can be further clarified in a policy directive. (See Chapter   ).

3. *Responsibility Matrix.* This chart defines the interdisciplinary task responsibilities: who is responsible for what. The responsbility matix not only covers activities within the project organization, but also defines the functional relationship with support units, subcontractors, and committees. In a simpler format, a task roster can be used to just list project tasks and corresponding responsible personnel.

4. *Job Description.* If not already in existence, a job description shall be developed for all key project personnel, such as the program managers, system project managers, hardware project managers, task managers, project engineers, plan coordinators, and so on. The job descriptions are usually generic and hence portable from one project to the next. Job descriptions are modular building blocks which form the framework for staffing a project organization. The job description includes (a) the reporting relationship, (b) responsibilities, (c) duties, and (d) typical qualifications.

Define Your Project

In dealing with engineering personnel, there is seldom a problem in finding project managers capable of defining the technical components of the project. The challenge is to convince these project leaders that all four segments of the project management system must be defined, at least in principle, before staffing can begin:

Segment 1.	*The Work:*	● Overall specifications ● Requirements document ● Statement of work ● System block diagram ● Work breakdown structure ● List of deliverables
Segment 2.	*Timing:*	● Master schedule ● Milestone chart ● Interdependencies of interfaces
Segment 3.	*Resources:*	● Budget ● Resource plan
Segment 4.	*Responsibilities:*	● Task matrix ● Task rostes ● Project charter ● Work packages

Regardless of how vague and preliminary these project segments are at the beginning, the initial description will help in recruiting the appropriate personnel and eliciting commitment to the preestablished parameters of technical performance, schedule, and budget. The core team should be formed prior to finalizing the project plan and contractual arrangements. This will provide the project management team with the opportunity to participate in trade-off discussions and customer negotiations leading to technical confidence and commitment of all parties involved.

Staff Your Project

Staffing the project organization is the first major milestone during the project formation phase. Because of the pressures on the project manager to produce, staffing is often done hastily and without properly defining the basic project work to be performed.

The results are often personnel poorly matched to the job requirements, conflict, low morale, suboptimum decision making, and, in the end, poor project performance.

The comment of a project section leader who was pressed into quick staffing actions is indicative of these potential problems: "How can you interview task managers when you cannot show them what the job involves and how their responsibilities tie in with the rest of the project?"

Therefore, only after the project organization and the tasks are defined in principle can project leaders at various levels start to interview candidates. These interviews should always be conducted one to one. *The interview process* normally has five facets which are often interrelated:

1. *Informing the candidate about the assignments.*
   What are the objectives for the project?
   Who will be involved and why?
   Structure of the project organization and its interfaces.
   Importance of the project to the overall organization or work unit; short- or long-range impact.
   Why was the team member selected and assigned to the project? What role will he or she perform?
   Specific responsibilities and expectations.
   What rewards might be forthcoming if the project is completed successfully?
   A candid appraisal of the problems and constraints which are likely to be encountered.
   What are the rules of the road that will be followed in managing the project, such as regulate status review meetings?
   The challenges and recognition the project is likely to provide.
   Why is the team concept important to success and how should it work?
2. *Determining skills and expertise.*
   Probe related experience; expand from resume.
   Probe candidate's aptitude relevant to your project environment: technology involved, engineering tools and techniques, markets and customer involvement, and product applications.
   Probe into the program management skills needed. Use current project examples: "How would you handle this situation . . . ?"

Probe leadership, technical expertise, planning and control, administrative skills, and so on.

3. *Determine interests and team compatibility.*

What are the professional interests and objectives of this candidate?

How does the candidate manage and work with others?

How does the candidate feel about sharing authority, working for two bosses, or dealing with personnel across functional lines with little or no formal authority?

What suggestions does the candidate have for achieving success?

4. *Persuading to join project team.*

Explain specific rewards for joining the team, such as financial, professional growth, recognition, visibility, work challenge, and potential for advancement.

5. *Negotiating terms and commitments.*

Check candidate's willingness to join team.

Negotiate conditions for joining: salary, hired, signed, or transferred, performance reviews and criteria.

Elicit candidate's commitment to established project objectives and modus operandi.

Secure final agreement.

Suggestions for Handling the Newly Formed Project Team

During its formation, the project group represents just a collection of individuals who have been selected for their skills and capabilities as collectively needed to perform the upcoming project task. However, to be successful the individual efforts must be integrated. Even more demanding, these individuals have to work together as a team to produce innovative results which fit together to form an integrated new system as conceptualized in the project plan.

Initially, there are many problems which prevent the project group from performing as a team. While these problems are normal and often predictable, they present barriers to effective team performance. The problems therefore must be quickly identified and dealt with. The following list presents typical *problems which occur during a project team formation:*

- Confusion.
- Responsibilities unclear.
- Channels of authority unclear.
- Work distribution load uneven.
- Assignment unclear.
- Communication channels unclear.

- Overall project goals unclear.
- Mistrust.
- Personal objectives unrelated to project.
- Measures of personal performance unclear.
- Commitment to project plan lacking.
- Team spirit lacking.
- Project direction and leadership insufficient.
- Power struggle and conflict.

Certain steps taken early in the life of the team can help the project leader in identifying the specific problems and dealing with them effectively. These steps may also provide preventive measures which eliminate the potential for these problems to develop in the first place. *Specific suggestions* are made below.

1. *Make Sure the Assignment Is Clear.* Although the overall task assignment, its scope, and objectives might have been discussed during the initial sign-on of the person to the project, it takes additional effort and involvement for new team members to feel comfortable with the assignment. The thorough understanding of the task requirements comes usually with the intense personal involvement of the new members with the project team. Such involvement can be enhanced by assigning the new member to an action-oriented task that requires team involvement and creates visibility, such as a requirements analysis, an interface specification, or producibility study. In addition, any committee-type activity, presentation, or data gathering will help to involve the new team member and to give him or her a better understanding of the specific task and his or her role in the overall team effort.

2. *Make New Team Members Feel Professionally Comfortable.* The initial anxieties, the lack of trust and confidence, are serious barriers to team performance. New team members should be properly introduced to the group, and their roles, strengths, and criticallity to the project explained. Providing opportunities for early results allows the leader to give recognition for professional accomplishments which will stimulate the individual's desire for the project work and build confidence, trust, and credibility within the group.

3. *Be Certain Team Organization Is Clear.* Project team structures are often considered very "organic" and inconsistent with formal chain-of-command principles. However, individual task responsibility, account-ability, and organizational interface relations should be clearly defined to all team members. A simple work breakdown structure (WBS) or task matrix, together with some discussion, can facilitate a clear understanding of the team structure, even with a highly unconventional format.

4. *Locate Team Members in One Place*. Members of the newly formed team should be closely located to facilitate communications and the development of a team spirit. Locating the project team in one office area is the ideal situation. However, this may be impractical, especially if team members share their time with other projects or if the assignment is only for a short period of time. Regularly scheduled meetings are recommended as soon as the new project team is being formed. These meetings are particularly important where team members are geographically separated and do not see each other on a day-to-day basis.

5. *Provide a Proper Team Environment*. It is critical for management to provide the proper environment for the project to function effectively. Here the project leader needs to tell the management at the outset of the program what resources are needed. The project manager's relationship with senior management support is critically affected by his or her credibility and the visibility and priority of the project.

6. *Manage*. Especially during the initial stages of team formation, it is important for the project leader to keep a close eye on the team and its activities to detect problems early and to correct them. The project manager can also influence the climate of the work environment by his of her own actions. The manager's concern for project team members, ability to integrate personal goals and needs of project personnel with the project objectives, and ability to create personal enthusiasm for the work itself can foster a climate which is high on motivation, work involvement, and resulting project performance.

TEAM BUILDING AS AN ONGOING PROCESS

While proper attention to team building is critical during the early phases of a project, it is a never-ending process. The project manager is continually monitoring team functioning and performance to see what corrective action may be needed to prevent or correct various team problems. Several barometers provide good clues of potential team dysfunctioning. First, noticeable changes in performance levels for the team and/or for individual team members should always be followed up. Such changes can be symptomatic of more serious problems, such as conflict, lack of work integration, communication problems, and unclear objectives. Second, the project leader and team members want to be aware of the changing energy level in various team members. This, too, may signal more serious problems or indicate that the team is tired and stressed. Sometimes changing the work pace, taking time off, or selling short-term targets can serve as a means to reenergize team members. More serious cases, however, can call for more drastic measures, such as reappraising project objectives and/or the means to achieve them. Third, verbal and nonverbal clues from team members may be a source of information on team functioning. It is important to hear their needs and concerns (verbal clues) and to observe how they act in carrying out their responsibilities (nonverbal clues). Finally, detrimental behavior of one team member toward another can be a signal that a problem within the team warrants action.

It is highly recommended that project leaders hold regular meetings to evaluate overall team performance and deal with team functioning problems. The focus of these meetings can be directed toward "What are we doing well as a team?" and "What areas need our team's attention?" This approach often brings positive surprises in that the total team will be informed on progress in diverse project areas such as a breakthrough in the technology department, a subsystem schedule met ahead of the original target, or a positive change in the client's behavior toward the project. After the positive issues have been discussed, attention should be devoted toward areas needing team attention. The purpose of this part of the review session is to focus on real or potential problem areas. The meeting leader should ask each team member for his or her observations on these issues. Then an open discussion should be held to ascertain how significant the problems really are. Assumptions should, of course, be separated from the facts of each situation. Next, assignments should be agreed upon how to best handle these problems. Finally, a plan for follow-up should be developed. The process should result in better overall performance and promote a feeling of team participation and high morale.

Over the life of a project the problems encountered by the project team are likely to change, and as the old problems are identified and solved, new ones will emerge.

In summary, effective building is a critical determinant of project success. While the process of team building can entail frustrations and require energy on the part of all concerned, the rewards can be great.

Social scientists generally agree that there are several indicators of effective and ineffective teams. At any point in the life of a team, the project manager should be aware of certain effectiveness-ineffectiveness indicators, which are summarized in Table 32-2.

As we go through the next decade, we anticipate important developments in team building. As shown in Figure 32-3, these developments will lead to higher performance levels, increased morale, and a pervasive commitment to final results that can withstand almost any kind of adversity.

Table 32-2. Project Team Characteristics: Effective Versus Ineffective.

LIKELY CHARACTERISTICS OF EFFECTIVE TEAM	LIKELY CHARACTERISTICS OF INEFFECTIVE TEAM
+ High performance and task efficiency + Innovative/creative behavior + Committed, results oriented + Professional objectives of team members coincide with project requirements + Technically successful + On-time/on-budget performance + Team members highly interdependent, interface effectively + Capacity for conflict resolution, but conflict encouraged when it can lead to beneficial results + Communicates effectively + High trust levels + High achievement needs + Result-oriented + Interested in membership self-development + High energy levels and enthusiasm + High morale + Change-oriented	− Low performance − Activity-oriented − Low level of involvement and enthusiasm − Low commitment to project objectives − Unclear project objectives and fluid commitment levels from key participants − Schedule and budget slips − Uninvolved management − Anxieties and insecurities − Unproductive gamesmanship, manipulation of others, hidden feelings, conflict avoided at all costs − Confusion, conflict, inefficiency − Subtle sabotage, fear, disinterest, or foot-dragging − Frequent surprises − Quality problems − Cliques, collusion, isolating members − Image problems (credibility) − Lethargic/unresponsive

RECOMMENDATIONS FOR EFFECTIVE TEAM MANAGEMENT

Taken together, the project leader must foster an environment where team members are professionally satisfied, are involved, and have mutual trust. As shown in Figure 32-2, the more effective the project leader is in stimulating the drivers and minimizing the barriers, the more effective the manager can be in developing team membership and the higher the quality of information contributed by team members, including their willingness and candor in sharing ideas and approaches. By contrast, when a team member does not feel part of the team and does not trust others, information will not be shared willingly or openly. One project leader emphasized the point: "There's nothing worse than being on a team where no one trusts anyone else. Such situations lead to gamesmanship and a lot of watching what you say because you don't want your own words to bounce back in your own face. . . ."

Furthermore, the greater the team spirit, trust, and quality of information exchange among team members, the more likely the team will be able to develop effective decision-making processes, make individual and group commitment, focus on problem solving, and develop self-forcing, self-correcting project controls. As summarized in Figure 32-2, these are the characteristics of an effective and productive project team. *A number of specific recommendations* are provided for project leaders and managers responsible for the integration of multidisiplinary tasks to help in their complex efforts of building high-performing project teams.

1. *Barriers.* Project managers must understand the various barriers to team development and build a work environment conducive to the team's motivational needs. Specifically, management should watch out for the following barriers: (a) unclear objectives, (b) insufficient resources and unclear funding, (c) role conflict and power struggle, (d) uninvolved and unsupportive management, (e) poor job security, and (f) shifting goals and priorities.

2. *The Project Objectives* and their importance to the organization should be clear to all personnel who get involved with the project. Senior management can help develop a "priority image" and communicate the basic project parameters and management guidelines.

3. *Management Commitment.* Project managers must continuously update and involve their managements to refuel their interests and commitments to the new project. Breaking the project into smaller phases and being able to produce short-range results frequently seem to be important to this refueling process.

4. *Image Building.* Building a favorable image for the project, in terms of high priority, interesting work, importance to the organization, high visibility, and potential for professional rewards is crucial to the ability to attract and hold high-quality people. It is also a pervasive processs which fosters a climate of active participation at all levels; it helps to unify the new project team and minimizes dysfunctional conflict.

5. *Leadership Positions* should be carefully defined and staffed at the beginning of a new program. Key project personnel selection is the joint responsibility of the project manager and functional management. The credibility of project leaders among team members, with senior management, and with the program sponsor is crucial to the leader's ability to manage the multidisciplinary activities effectively across functional lines. One-on-one interviews are recommended for explaining the scope and project requirements, as well as the management philosophy, organizational structure, and rewards.

6. *Effective Planning* early in the project life cycle will have a favorable impact on the work environment and team effectiveness. This is especially so because project managers have to integrate various tasks across many functional lines. Proper planning, however, means more than just generating the required pieces of paper. It requires the participation of the entire project team, including support departments, subcontractors, and management. These planning activities, which can be performed in a special project phase such as Requirements Analysis, Product Feasibility Assessment, or Product/Project Definition, usually have a number of side benefits besides generating a comprehensive road map for the upcoming program.

7. *Involvement.* One of the side benefits of proper project planning is the involvement of personnel at all organizational levels. Project managers should drive such an involvement, at least with their key personnel, especially during the project definition phases. This involvement will lead to a better understanding of the task requirements, stimulate interest, help unify the team, and ultimately lead to commitment to the project plan regarding technical performance, timing, and budgets.

8. *Project Staffing.* All project assignments should be negotiated individually with each prospective team member. Each task leader should be responsible for staffing his or her own task team. Where dual-reporting relationships are involved, staffing should be conducted jointly by the two managers. The assignment interview should include a clear discussion of the specific task, the outcome, timing, responsibilities, reporting relation, potential rewards, and importance of the project to the company. Task assignments should be made only if the candidate's ability is a reasonable match to the position requirements and the candidate shows a healthy degree of interest in the project.

9. *Team Structure.* Management must define the basic team structure and operating concepts early during the project formation phase. The project plan, task matrix, project charter, and policy are the principal tools. It is the responsibility of the project manager to communicate the organizational design and to assure that all parties understand the overall and interdisciplinary project objectives. Clear and frequent communication with senior management and the new project sponsor becomes critically important. Status review meetings can be used for feedback.

10. *Team-Building Sessions* should be conducted by the project

manager throughout the project life cycle. An especially intense effort might be needed during the team formation stage. The team is being brought together in a relaxed atmosphere to discuss such questions as, How are we operating as a team? What is our strength? Where can we improve? What steps are needed to initiate the desired change? What problems and issues are we likely to face in the future? Which of these can be avoided by taking appropriate action now? How can we "danger-proof" the team?

11. *Team Commitment.* Project managers should determine lack of team member commitment early in the life of the project and attempt to change possible negative views toward the project. Since insecurity is often a major reason for lacking commitment, managers should try to determine why insecurity exist, then work on reducing the team members' fears. Conflict with other team members may be another reason for lack of commitment. It is important for the project leader to intervene and mediate the conflict quickly. Finally, if a team member's professional interests may lie elsewhere, the project leader should examine ways to satisfy part of the team member's interests by bringing personal and project goals into perspective.

12. *Senior Management Support.* It is critically important for senior management to provide the proper environment for the project team to function effectively. Here the project leader needs to tell management at the outset of the program what resources are needed. The project manager's relationship with senior management and ability to develop senior management support is critically affected by his or her credibility, visibility, and priority image of the project.

13. *Organization Development Specialists.* Project leaders should watch for changes in performance on an ongoing basis. If performance problems are observed, they should be dealt with quickly. If the project manager has access to internal or external organization development specialists, they can help diagnose team problems and assist the team in dealing with the identified problems. These specialists can also bring fresh ideas and perspectives to difficult and sometimes emotionally complex situations.

14. *Problem Avoidance.* Project leaders should focus their efforts on problem avoidance. That is, the project leader, through experience, should recognize potential problems and conflicts at their onset and deal with them before they become big and their resolutions consume a large amount of time and effort.

A FINAL NOTE

In summary, effective team building is a critical determinant of project success. Building the engineering team for a new technical project is one of the prime responsibilities of the program leader. Team building involves a whole spectrum of management skills to identify, commit, and integrate the various personnel from different functional organizations into a single task group. In many project-oriented engineering organizations, team building is a shared responsibility between the functional engineering managers and the project manager, who often reports to a different organization with a different superior.

To be effective, the project manager must provide an atmosphere conducive to teamwork. Four major considerations are involved in the integration of people from many disciplines into an effective team: (a) creating a professionally stimulating work environment, (b) providing good program leadership, (c) providing qualified personnel, and (d) providing a technically and organizationally stable environment. The project leader must foster an environment where the new project team members are professionally satisfied, involved, and have mutual trust. The more effectively project leaders develop team membership, the higher is the quality of information exchanged, including the candor of sharing ideas and approaches. It is this professionally stimulating involvement that also has a pervasive effect on the team's ability to cope with change and conflict, and leads to innovative performance. By contrast, when a member does not feel part of the team and does not trust others, information will not be shared willingly or openly.

Furthermore, the greater the team spirit, trust, and quality of information exchange among team members, the more likely the team will be able to develop effective decision-making processes, make individual and group commitment, focus on problem solving, and develop self-forcing, self-correcting project controls. These are the characteristics of an effective and productive project team.

The potential gains from increased engineering productivity are great for individuals, organizations, and society as a whole. Such gains are possible only if we can utilize our engineering resources effectively. One such improvement is through effective team building.

Over the next decade we anticipate important developments in team building which will lead to higher performance levels, increased morale, and a pervasive commitment to final results. This chapter should help both the professional in the field of engineering management as well as the scholar who studies contemporary organizational concepts to understand the intricate relationships between organizational and behavioral elements by providing a conceptual framework for specific situational analysis of engineering team-building practices.

BIBLIOGRAPHY

1. Adams, John R. and Kirchof, Nicki S. "A Training Technique for Developing Project Managers." *Project Management Quarterly* (March, 1983).
2. Altier, William J., "Task Forces—An Effective Management Tool" *Sloan Management Review,* Spring 1986
3. Aquilino, J. J. "Multi-Skilled Work Teams: Productivity Benefits." *California Management Review* (Summer, 1977).
4. Aram, J. D. and Morgan, C. P. "Role of Project Team Collaboration in R&D Performance." *Management Science* (June, 1976).
5. Atkins, S. and Katcher, A. "Getting Your Team In Tune" *Nation's Business* (March, 1975).
6. Baler, Kent H. "The Hows and Whys of Teambuilding," *Engineering Management Review* (December, 1985).
7. Barkman, Donald F., "Team Discipline: Put Performance on the Line," *Personnel Journal,* Vol 66, March 1987, p. 58
8. Benningson, Lawrence. "The Team Approach to Project Management." *Management Review, 61:*48–52 (January, 1972).
9. Carzo, R., Jr. "Some Effects of Organization Structure on Group Effectiveness." *Administrative Science Quarterly* (March, 1963).
10. Conover, W. J. *Practical Nonparametric Statistics.* Wiley, New York, 1971.
11. Diliddo, Bart A., James, Paul, C. and Dietrich, Harry J. "Managing R&D Creatively: B. F. Goodrich's Approach." *Management Review* (July, 1981).
12. Ely, D. D. "Team Building for Creativity." *Personnel Journal* (April, 1975).
13. Foster, Richard N. "A Call for Vision in Managing Technology." *McKinsy Quarterly* (Summer, 1982).
14. Galagan, Patricia, "Work Teams at Work", *Training and Development Journal,* Vol 40, November 1986, p. 33
15. Gray, James, "Team Building: Transforming Individuals into Work Groups", *Executive,* Vol 26, Winter 1986, p. 24
16. Harris, Philip R. "Building a High-Performance Team." *Training and Development Journal* (April, 1986).
17. Hayes, J. L. "Teamwork." *Management Review* (September, 1975).
18. Hopkins, D. S. "Roles of Project Teams and Venture Groups in New Product Development." *Research Management* (January, 1975).
19. Howe, R. J. "Building Teams for Increased Productivity." *Personnel Journal* (January, 1977).
20. Huesing, S. A. "Team Approach and Computer Development." *Journal of Systems Management* (September, 1977).
21. Jewkes, John, Sawers, David and Stillerman, Richard. *The Sources of Innovation.* Macmillan, New York, 1962.
22. Katz, F. E. "Explaining Informal Work Groups in Complex Organizations." *Administrative Science Quarterly* (10) (1965).
23. Kidder, John Tracy. *The Soul of a New Machine.* Avon Books, Hearst Corporation, New York, 1982.

24. Likert, Rensis. "Improving Cost-Performance with Cross-Functional Teams." *Management Review* (March, 1976).
25. Maister, D. H. "The One-Firm: What Makes It Successful." *Sloan Management Review* (Fall, 1985).
26. Miller, Donald Britten, "Understanding the R&D Culture," *Management Review*, Vol 75, December 1986, p. 34
27. Pincus, Claudio. "An Approach to Plan Development and Team Formation." *Project Management Quarterly* (December, 1982).
28. Quinn, James Brian. "Technological Innovation, Entrepreneurship and Strategy." *Sloan Management Review* (Spring, 1979).
29. Rantfl, R. M. *R&D Productivity, A Study Report.* Hughes Aircraft Company (1978).
30. Raudsepp, Eugene. "Motivating Engineers." *Engineering Management Review* (March, 1986).
31. Reich, Robert, "Entrepreneurship Reconsidered: The Team as Hero", *Harvard Business Review*, Vol 65, May-June 1987, p. 77
32. Rigby, Malcom J., "The Challenge of Multinational Team Development," *Journal of Management Development*, Vol 6, Fall 1987, p. 65
33. Rogers, L. A. "Guidelines for Project Management Teams." *Industrial Engineering* (December, 1974).
34. Salomon, B. A. "A Plant that Proves that Team Management Works" (Digital). *Personnel* (June, 1985).
35. Senia, Al, "Hewlett-Packards Team Approach beats back the Competition" *Production*, Vol 97, May 1986, p. 89
36. Shea, Gregory P. and Guzzo, Richard A., "Group Effectiveness: What really matters", *Sloan Management Review*, Vol 76, Spring 1987
37. Thamhain, Hans J., *Team Building in Technology-based Organizations*, Addison-Wesley, 1988
38. Thamhain, Hans J. and Wilemon, David L. "Building High Performing Engineering Project Teams." *IEEE Transactions on Engineering Management* (August, 1987).
39. Thamhain, Hans J. "Managing Engineers Effectively." *IEEE Transactions on Engineering Management* (August, 1983).
40. Thamhain, H. and Wilemon, D. "Skill Requirements of Engineering Program Manager." *Proceedings of the 26th Engineering Management Conference* (1978).
41. Thamhain, Hans J. and Wilemon, David L. "Anatomy of a High Performing New Product Team." *Convention Record, 16th Annual Symposium of the Project Management Institute*.
42. Thamhain, Hans J. and Gemmill, Gary R. "Influence Styles of Project Managers: Some Project Performance Correlates." *Academy of Management Journal* (June, 1974).
43. Tichy, N. "Analysis of Clique Formation and Structure in Organizations." *Administrative Science Quarterly* (June, 1973).
44. Watson, D. J. H. "Structure of Project Teams Facing Differentiated Environments: An Exploratory Study in Public Accounting Firms." *Accounting Review* (April, 1975).
45. Ward, Brian K. and Hardaker Maurice, "How to make a Team Work", *Harvard Business Review*, Vol 65, November-December 1987
46. Wilemon, David L. and Thamhain, Hans J. "Team Building in Project Management." *Project Management Quarterly* (July, 1983).
47. Wilemon, D. L., et al. "Managing Conflict on Project Teams." *Management Journal* (1974).

48. Wilemon, David L. and Thamhain, Hans J. "A Model for Developing High-Performance Teams." *Proceedings of the Annual Symposium of the Project Management Institute,* Houston, (1983).
49. Zenger, J. H. and Miller, D. E. "Building Effective Teams." *Personnel* (March, 1974).
50. Ziller, R. C. "Newcomer's Acceptance in Open and Closed Groups." *Personnel Administration* (September, 1962).

33. Some Major Research Findings Regarding the Human Element in Project Management

David L. Wilemon*
Bruce N. Baker†

One of the most significant developments in management practice during the past two decades has been the accelerated emphasis on project management in administering complex tasks. Project management is a widely utilized management system. The early project management literature tended to be oriented around the development and explanation of the tools and techniques of the project manager (1).‡ More recently, however, increased research attention has been placed on the behavioral and organizational dimensions of project management. This research has resulted in a growing body of knowledge which helps explain the myriad of complex human factors which contribute to project management effectiveness. This chapter summarizes the mainstream of research in the human factors of project management. This review should help users better understand the numerous interpersonal forces found in project organizations.

Although the authors reviewed dozens of articles, some important research may have been omitted. Space limitations preclude a complete coverage of all the relevant research. In some areas, pertinent research dealing with general management problems has been cited to further con-

* Dr. David Wilemon is a professor and director of the Innovation Management Program in the Graduate School of Management at Syracuse University. He is widely recognized for his work on conflict management, team building, and leadership skills in project-oriented work environments. He has studied various kinds of project management systems in the United States and in several foreign countries.

† Dr. Bruce N. Baker is Program Manager of Information and Computer Security at SRI International. He conducts project management seminars and is a frequent speaker on the topics of improving teamwork and success in project management environments. He received his A.B. degree from Princeton University, his M.B.A. degree from Stanford University, and his D.P.A. degree from The George Washington University.

‡ Numbered references are given at the end of this chapter.

tribute to the understanding of the interpersonal dimensions of project management.

Five major areas were selected for a review of key research contributions. These areas include (a) leadership styles/interpersonal skills; (b) conflict management; (c) decision-making styles and team-building skills; (d) organizational design and project manager authority relationships; (e) communications in project management; and (f) project team relationships with the parent, client, and other external organizations.

LEADERSHIP STYLES/INTERPERSONAL SKILLS

The leadership abilities and interpersonal skills of the project manager are critical to effective project management performance. While there has been much discussion on the role of leadership in project management, only recently has there been a growing interest in empirical investigations of some of the determinants of effective project management leadership.

Lawerence and Lorsch investigated the differences between effective and ineffective integrators (managerial positions like project managers) in terms of their behavioral styles in dealing with others in their organizations (2). Ten integrators were rated as "effective" and ten were evaluated as "less effective" (superiors' ratings were utilized). It was found that:

- Effective integrators had a significantly higher need for affiliation than the integrators rated as less effective. Differently put, the effective integrators had higher needs for interpersonal involvement, interactions, and demonstrated empathy in dealing with others.
- No statistically significant findings were found between the effective and less effective integrators in their need for achievement. A tendency, however, did emerge which seemed to indicate that the more effective integrators had a lower need for achievement than their counterparts.
- The need for power was rated approximately the same for the effective and the less effective integrators.
- Integrators rated as effective "prefer to take significantly more initiative and leadership, they are aggressive, confident, persuasive, and verbally fluent. In contrast, less effective integrators avoid situations that involve tension and decisions"(3).
- Effective integrators also were more ambitious, forceful, and effective in communications than those rated as less effective.

Hodgetts empirically addressed the means of overcoming the "authority gap" in project management (4). Researching project management in aerospace, construction, chemicals, and state government environments, he found the following:

- Negotiation skills were important in aerospace and construction project environments.
- Personality and/or persuasive ability was considered important in all the project management situations.
- The project manager's competence was considered important in aerospace, construction, and chemicals.
- Reciprocal favors were noted as important as a surrogate for authority in aerospace and construction.
- The combined sample of firms (aerospace, construction, chemicals, and state government) rated the four authority supplements as "very important" or "not important." The following represents the significance of each technique as rated by the project managers in overcoming authority deficiencies. (Percentages are for those authority surrogates rated as either very important or important.)

  —Competence   98%
  —Personality and/or Persuasive Ability   96%
  —Negotiation Ability   92%
  —Reciprocal Favors   47%

Gemmill and Wilemon's exploratory research on 45 project managers and supporting project team members focused on identifying several influence bases utilized by project managers in eliciting support (5). Their research suggested the following:

- Authority, reward, punishment, expertise, and referent power are sources of influence frequently utilized by project managers in gaining support. Each influence mode can have different effects on the climate of the project organization.
- Two fundamental management styles used by project managers were identified. The first style relied primarily on the project manager's authority, ability to reward, and ability to "punish" those who did not furnish needed support. The second relied on an expert and referent power influence style.

Gemmill and Thamhain's empirical research of 22 project managers and 66 project support personnel addressed the relationship of the project manager's utilization of interpersonal influence and project performance (6). Their research revealed the following:

- Support project personnel ranked the eight influence methods as follows (1 is most important, 8 is least important):

Influence Method	Mean
Authority	3.0
Work Challenge	3.2
Expertise	3.3
Future Work Assignments	4.6
Salary	4.6
Promotion	4.8
Friendship	6.2
Coercion	7.8

- Project managers who were perceived to utilize expertise and work challenge as influence modes experienced higher levels of project performance.
- Project performance was positively associated with high degrees of support, open communication among project participants, and task involvement by those supporting the project manager.
- The use of authority by project managers as means to influence support personnel led to lower levels of project performance.

The work of Fiedler has been a catalyst to the research and literature concerning effective leadership styles under various levels of authority and for various task situations (7). Space limitations preclude describing his model which supports a contingency-oriented approach to leadership, but one of his major findings is that:

Both the directive managing, task-oriented leaders and the nondirective, human relations-oriented leaders were successful under some conditions. Which leadership style is the best depends on the favorableness of the particular situation and the leader. In very favorable or in very unfavorable situations for getting a task accomplished by group effort, the autocratic, task-controlling, managing leadership works best. In situations intermediate in difficulty, the non-directive, permissive leader is more successful [8]. This corresponds well with our everyday experience. For instance:

- Where the situation is very favorable, the group expects and wants the leader to give directions. We neither expect nor want

the trusted airline pilot to turn to his crew and ask, "What do you think we ought to check before takeoff?"
- If the disliked chairman of a volunteer committee asks his group what to do, he may be told that everybody ought to go home.
- The well-liked chairman of a planning group or research team must be nondirective and permissive in order to get full participation from team members. The directive, managing leader will tend to be more critical and to cut discussion short; hence he or she will not get the full benefit of the potential contributions of group members.

The varying requirements of leadership styles are readily apparent in organizations experiencing dramatic changes in operating procedures. For example:

- The manager or supervisor of a routinely operating organization is expected to provide direction and supervision for subordinates to follow. However, in a crisis the routine is no longer adequate, and the task becomes more ambiguous and unstructured. The typical manager tends to respond in such instances by calling the group together for a conference. In other words, the effective leader changes his or her behavior from a directive to a permissive, nondirective style until the operation again reverts to routine conditions.
- In the case of a research planning group, the human relations-oriented and permissive leader provides a climate in which everybody is free to speak up, to suggest, and to criticize. Brainstorming can help institutionalize these procedures. However, after the research plan has been completed, the situation becomes more structured. The director now prescribes the task in detail, and he specifies the means for accomplishing it. Woe betide the assistant who decides to be creative by changing the research instructions! [9].

Other research findings also support a contingency-based view of project management organization design.

CONFLICT MANAGEMENT

It is widely accepted that project environments can produce intense conflict situations (10). The ability of project managers to handle conflict is a determinant of successful project performance. Researchers have addressed the causes of disagreements in project management as well as the means by which conflict is managed.

Determinants of Conflict

Wilemon's study on delineating fundamental causes of conflict in project management revealed that (11):

- The greater the diversity of expertise among the project team members, the greater the potential for conflict to develop.
- The lower the project manager's power to reward and punish, the greater the potential for conflict.
- The less the specific objectives of a project are understood by project team members, the more likely that conflict will occur.
- The greater the ambiguity of roles among the project team members, the more likely conflict will develop.
- The greater the agreement on superordinate goals (top management objectives), the lower the potential for detrimental conflict.
- The lower the project manager's formal authority over supporting functional and staff units, the higher the probability of conflict.

Butler also developed a number of propositions on the primary causes of conflict in project management (12). Many of his propositions are supported by prior research on conflict in various organizational settings—not exclusively project management. A few of the propositions advanced by Butler may be summarized as follows:

- Conflict may be either functional (beneficial) or dysfunctional (detrimental).
- Conflict is often caused by the revised interaction patterns of team members in project organizations.
- Conflict can develop as a result of the difficulties of team members adapting their professional objectives to project work situations and requirements.
- Conflict often is the result of the difficulties of diverse professionals working together in a project team situation where there is pressure for consensus.
- Role ambiguity and stress by the project managers and supporting functional personnel are more likely to occur when project authority is not clearly defined.
- Competition over functional resources, especially functional personnel, is likely to produce conflict.
- Conflict may develop over the lack of professional incentives derived from functional specialists participating in project-oriented work.

Thamhain and Wilemon's research focused on the causes and intensity of various conflict sources (13). Utilizing a sample of 100 project managers, their study measured the degree of conflict experienced from several variables common to project environments which were thought particularly conducive to the generation of conflict situations.

- The potential sources of conflict researched revealed the following rank-order for conflict experienced by project managers:
  1. schedules
  2. project priorities
  3. manpower resources
  4. technical conflicts
  5. administrative procedures
  6. cost objectives
  7. personality conflicts
- The most intense conflicts occurred with the supporting functional departments, followed by conflict with personnel assigned to the project team from functional departments.
- The lowest degree (intensity) of conflict occurred between the project manager and the immediate subordinates.

Thamhain and Wilemon followed their 1974 research with a study focused on measuring the degree of conflict experienced in each of the four generally accepted project life-cycle phases, namely, project formation, buildup, main program, and phaseout (14). Results reported from this research include the following:

- Disagreements over schedules result in the most intense conflict situations over the entire life cycle of a project.
- The mean conflict intensities over the four life-cycle stages reveal the following rank order:
  Project Formation
  1. Project priorities.
  2. Administrative procedures.
  3. Schedules.
  4. Manpower resources.
  5. Cost.
  6. Technical conflicts.
  7. Personality.
  Buildup Phase
  1. Project priorities.
  2. Schedules.
  3. Administrative procedures.

4. Technical conflicts.
5. Manpower resources.
6. Personality.
7. Cost.
   Main Program Phase
1. Schedules.
2. Technical conflicts.
3. Manpower resources.
4. Project priorities.
5. Administrative procedures, cost, personality.
   Phaseout
1. Schedules.
2. Personality.
3. Manpower resources.
4. Project priorities.
5. Cost.
6. Technical conflicts.
7. Administrative procedures.

Conflict-handling Methods

If recognizing some of the primary determinants of conflict is a first step in effective conflict management, the second step is understanding how conflictful situations are managed in the project environment. Lawrence and Lorsch examined the methods that "integrators" used in handling conflicts (15). The following items from their study are considered pertinent:

- The uses of three conflict-handling modes were examined, namely, the confrontation or problem-solving mode, the smoothing approach, and the forcing mode. The utilization of forcing often results in a win-lose situation.
- The most effective integrators relied most heavily on the confrontation approach.
- Functional managers supporting the integrators in the most effective organizations also relied more on the confrontation approach than the other two modes.
- Functional managers in the highly integrated organizations employed "more forcing, and/or less smoothing behavior" than their counterparts in less effective organizations.

Building on the methodologies of Lawrence and Lorsch (16), Blake and Mouton (17), and Burke (18), Thamhain and Wilemon examined the effects of five conflict-handling modes (forcing, confrontation, compromising, smoothing, and withdrawal) on the intensity of conflict experienced (19). They found:

- When interacting with personnel assigned from functional organizations, the forcing and withdrawal methods were most often associated with increased conflict in the project management environments.
- Project managers experienced more conflict when they utilized the forcing and confrontation modes with functional support departments.
- The utilization of the confrontation, compromise, and smoothing approaches by project managers were often associated with reduced degrees of conflict in dealing with assigned personnel.
- The withdrawal approach was associated with lower degrees of conflict. (This of course may be detrimental to overall project performance.)

To determine the actual conflict-handling styles utilized by project managers, research was conducted by Thamhain and Wilemon in conjunction with their study on conflict in project life cycles (20). The results reported included:

- The problem-solving or confrontation mode was the most frequently utilized mode of project managers (70%).
- The compromising approach ranked second, with the smoothing approach ranking third. The forcing and withdrawal approaches ranked fourth and fifth.
- Project managers often use the full spectrum of conflict-handling modes in managing diverse personalities and various conflict situations.

Several suggestions for minimizing or preventing detrimental conflict were also provided by the study.

First, conflict with supporting functional departments is a major concern for project managers. Within the various categories of common conflict sources (schedules, project priorities, manpower resources, technical opinions, administrative procedures, and cost objectives), the highest conflict intensity occurs with functional support departments. The project manager frequently has less control over supporting functional departments than over his assigned personnel or immediate team members, which contributes to conflict. Moreover, conflict often develops due to the functional department's own priorities which can have impact on any of the conflict categories, that is, manpower resources and schedules.

Minimizing conflict requires careful planning. Effective planning early in the life cycle of the project can assist in forecasting and perhaps minimizing a number of potential problem areas likely to produce conflict in subsequent project phases. Consequently, contingency plans should be developed early in the life of a project. Senior management involvement in and commitment to the project may also help reduce some of the conflicts over project priorities and needed manpower resources and administrative procedures. In the excitement and haste of launching a new project, good planning by project managers is often insufficient.

Second, since there are a number of key participants in a project, it is important that major decisions affecting the project be communicated to all project related personnel. When project objectives are openly communicated there is a higher potential for minimizing detrimental, unproductive conflict. Regularly scheduled status review meetings, for example are for communicating important project-related issues.

Third, project managers need to be aware of their conflict resolution styles and their potential effect on key interfaces. Forcing and withdrawal modes appear to increase conflict with functional support departments and assigned personnel, while confrontation (problem-solving) and compromise can reduce conflict. Again, it is important for project managers to know when conflict should be minimized and when it should be induced. In some instances project managers may deliberately create conflict to gain new information and provoke constructive dialogue. Creating an open dialogue can produce positive results for the decision-making process.

Fourth, a definite relationship appears to exist between the specific influence mode of project managers and the intensity of conflicts experienced with interfaces. For example, the greater the work challenge provided by a project manager, the less conflict experienced with assigned project personnel. Thus, project managers need to consider the importance of work challenge not only in eliciting support but also in assisting in the minimization of conflict. One approach is to stimulate interest in the project and to match the professional needs of supporting personnel with the task requirements of the project.

Conflict with functional departments also can develop if the project manager overly relies on penalties and authority. The overuse of these power sources can have a negative effect in establishing a climate of support, cooperation, and respect.

Thus, project managers not only must be aware of the approaches they use in eliciting support but also of the effect of the conflict resolution approaches they employ. For the project leader each set of skills is critical for effective performance. If a project manager, for example, is initially skillful in gaining support but cannot manage the inevitable conflict situations which develop in the course of a project, then his or her effectiveness as a manager will erode.

DECISION-MAKING STYLES AND TEAM-BUILDING SKILLS

The degree of participative decision making and esprit de corps have considerable impact upon not only the human aspects of the project environment but also upon the perceived success of projects.

Baker, Murphy, and Fisher, in their study of over 650 projects, including over 200 variables, found that certain variables were significantly associated with the perceived failure of projects, others were significantly associated with the perceived success of projects, and still others were linearly related to failure/success (21), for example:

- Lack of project team participation in decision making and problem solving, lack of team spirit, lack of sense of mission within the project team, job insecurity, and insufficient influence of the project manager were variables significantly associated with perceived project failure.
- In contrast, project team participation in setting schedules and budgets was significantly related to perceived success.
- The relative degree of goal commitment of the project team and the degree to which task orientation (with a backup of social orientation) was employed as a means of conflict resolution were linearly related to project success.*

Kloman's study contrasting NASA's Surveyor and Lunar Orbiter projects revealed that several elements contributed to the higher levels of actual and perceived success associated with the Lunar Orbiter project:

- Lunar Orbiter benefited from a strong sense of teamwork within both the customer and contractor organizations and in their relations with each other. Surveyor was handicapped by a lack of teamwork, particularly in the early years of the program.
- Senior management was committed to full support of the Lunar Orbiter project and was personally involved in overall direction at both

---

* These findings are discussed in detail in Chapter 35.

the NASA field center and in the prime contractor's organization. There was far less support and involvement in the case of Surveyor (22).

There has been an accelerated use of team building in project management in the last few years. Varney suggests that there are three primary reasons for the increasing interest in team building (23). First, there are more specialists/experts within organizations whose talents need to be focused and integrated into the requirements of the larger task. Second, many organizational members want to become more involved in the overall project rather than just perform narrowly defined roles. Third, there is ample evidence that people working well together can create synergy and high levels of creativity and job satisfaction.

In a recent exploratory research study with over 90 project managers, Thamhain and Wilemon identified some of the major barriers project leaders face in their attempts to build effective teams (24). The results of the exploratory field probe revealed the following barriers to team building:

- Differing priorities, interests and judgments of team members
  A major barrier is that team members can have different professional objectives and interests. Yet project accomplishment can require team members to place "what's good for the project" above their own interests. When team members are reluctant to do so, severe problems can develop in building an effective team. This problem is further compounded when the team relies on support groups which have widely different interests and priorities.
- Role conflicts
  Team development efforts are thwarted when role conflicts exist among the team members. Role conflicts are most likely to occur when there is ambiguity over who does what within the project team and between the team and external support groups. Overlapping and ambiguous responsibilities are also major contributors to role conflicts.
- Lack of team member commitment
  Lack of commitment to the project was cited as one of the most common barriers. Lack of commitment can come from several sources, such as: the team members' professional interests lying elsewhere; the feeling of insecurity sometimes associated with projects; the unclear nature of the rewards which may be forthcoming upon successful project completion; and intense interpersonal conflicts within the team.
  Other issues which can result in uncommitted team members are

suspicious attitudes which may exist between the project leader and a functional support manager or between two team members from two warring functional departments. Finally, it was found that low commitment levels were likely to occur when a "star" on a team "demanded" too much deference or too much pampering from the team leader.

- Communication problems
  Not surprisingly, poor communication was a major barrier to effective team development efforts. The research findings revealed that communication breakdowns could occur among the members of a team as well as between the project leader and the team members. Often the problem was caused by team members simply not keeping others informed on key project developments. The "whys" of poor communication patterns are far more difficult to determine than the effects of poor communication. Poor communication can result from low motivation levels, poor morale, or simply carelessness. It was also found that poor communication patterns between the team and support groups could result in severe team-building problems, as did poor communication with the client. Poor communication practices often led to unclear objectives, poor project control and coordination, and uneven work flow.

- Project objectives/outcomes not clear
  One of the most frequently cited team-building barriers was unclear project objectives. As one project leader in the study remarked:

  How can you implement a team building program if you're not clear on what the objectives of the project are? Let's face it, many teams are muddling along on fifty percent of their potential because no one is really clear on where the project should be headed.

  Thus, if objectives are not explicit, it becomes difficult, if not impossible, to clearly define roles and responsibilities.

- Dynamic project environments
  A characteristic of many projects is that the environments in which they operate are in a continual state of change. For example, senior management may keep changing the project's scope, objectives, and resource base. In other situations, regulatory changes or client demands for new and different specifications can drastically affect the internal operations of a project team. Finally, the rate by which a team "builds up" to its full manpower base may present team-building barriers, e.g., not fully sharing "the vision" of the project.

- Credibility of the project manager
Team-building efforts also are hampered when the project leader suffers from poor credibility within the team or with important managers external to the team. In such cases, team members are often reluctant to make a commitment to the project or the leader. Credibility problems may come from poor performance skills, poor technical judgments, or lack of experience relevant to the project.
- Lack of team definition and structure
One of the most frequently mentioned barriers was the lack of a clearly delineated team. The study found this barrier to be most likely to occur among computer system managers and R&D project leaders. A common pattern was that a work unit (not a project team) would be charged with a task but no one leader or team member was clearly delegated the responsibility. As a consequence, some work unit members would be working on the project but not be clear on the extent of their responsibilities.

  In other cases, a poorly defined team will result when a project is supported by several departments but no one person in these departments is designated as a departmental coordinator. Such an approach results in the project leader being unclear on whom to count on for support. This often occurs, for example, when a computer systems project leader must rely on a "programming pool."
- Competition over team leadership
This barrier was most likely to occur in the early phases of a project or if the project ran into severe problems and the quality of team leadership came into question. Obviously, both cases of leadership challenge can result in barriers (if only temporary) to team building. These challenges were often covert attacks on the project leader's managerial capability.
- Project team member selection
This barrier centered on how team members were selected. In some cases, project personnel were assigned to the teams by functional managers, and the project manager had little or no input into the selection process. This, of course, can impede team development efforts especially when the project leader is given "available personnel" versus the best, hand-picked team members. The assignment of "available personnel" can result in several problems, for example, low motivation levels, discontentment, and uncommitted team members. As a rule, the more influence the project leader has over the selection of his or her team members, the more likely team-building efforts will be fruitful.

ORGANIZATIONAL DESIGN CONSIDERATIONS IN PROJECT MANAGEMENT

Several research studies have investigated the impact of organizational arrangements and the authority of the project manager. Baker, Murphy, and Fisher found that with respect to organizational and authority arrangements:

- Excessive structuring within the project team and insufficient project manager authority were significantly related to perceived project failure.
- Adequate and appropriate organizational structures and effective planning and control mechanisms were significantly related to perceived project success. (Note that no particular type of organizational structure or particular type of planning and control mechanism was associated with success. This finding supports the contingency theory of management.)
- Degree of bureaucracy and degree of spatial distance between the project manager and the project site were linearly related to success/failure; that is, the greater the bureaucracy and the greater the spatial distance, the more likely the project was perceived as a failure (25).*

Marquis and Straight studied approximately 100 R&D projects (mostly under one million dollars) and found that:

- Projects in which administrative personnel report to the project manager are less likely to have cost or schedule overruns (26).
- Projects organized on a functional basis produce better technical results.
- Matrix organizations in which there is a small project team and more than half of the technical personnel remain in their functional departments are more likely to achieve technical excellence and, at the same time, to meet cost and schedule deadlines, than purely functional or totally projectized organizations (27).

Baker, Fisher, and Murphy also found that insufficient project manager authority and influence were significantly related to cost and schedule overrun. Chapman found that:

---

* These findings are discussed in greater detail in Chapter 35.

- A matrix structure works best for (a) small, in-house projects, where project duration is two years or less; (b) where assignments to technical divisions are minimal; and (c) where a field installation has substantial fluctuation in the amount of project activity it is handling.
- A matrix structure begins to lose its flexibility on large, long-duration projects, and therefore a more fully projectized structure is appropriate in these circumstances (28).

In contrasting functional organizations with project organizations, Reeser found some unique human problems associated with projectized organizations:

- Insecurity about possible unemployment, career retardation, and personal development is felt by subordinates in project organizations to be significantly more of a problem than by subordinates in functional organizations.
- Project subordinates are more frustrated by "make-work" assignments, ambiguity and conflict in the work environment, and multiple levels of management than functional subordinates.
- Project subordinates seem to feel less loyal to their organization than functional subordinates (29).

COMMUNICATIONS IN PROJECT MANAGEMENT

Increasingly, effective interpersonal communication is being recognized as a critical ingredient for project success. A study by Tushman, for example, clearly illustrates the role and managerial consequences of effective communication networks within R&D-oriented project work environments (30). He notes that for complex problem solving, "verbal communication is a more efficient information medium than written or more formal media (e.g., management information systems)."

Tushman found the following communication patterns existing for complex research projects conducted in a large corporate laboratory:

- There were high degrees of problem solving and administrative communication within the high-performing teams. Further, the frequency of these two types of communication were positively associated with performance.
- The high-performing project teams relied more on peer decision-making interaction than on supervisory direction.
- Communication to provide feedback and technical evaluation to areas outside the project but within the host organization tended to be

highly specialized for the more effectively managed research projects.

- The high-performing research teams made effective use of "gate-keepers" to link with expertise external to the project team, for example, universities and professional societies.

From his major findings Tushman developed an information-processing model to help plan and manage communication requirements for complex projects and programs.

RELATIONSHIPS OF THE PROJECT TEAM WITH THE PARENT ORGANIZATION, THE CLIENT, AND THE EXTERNAL WORLD

The patterns of relationships among the project team, the parent, the client, and other external organizations are highly important to the perceived success of projects. Baker, Murphy, and Fisher found that:

- Coordination and relation patterns explained 77% of the variance of perceived project success. (Stepwise multiple regression analysis with perceived success as the dependent variable; perceived success factor included satisfaction of all parties concerned and technical performance.)
- Success criteria salience and consensus among the project team, the parent, and the client also significantly contributed to perceived project success (second heaviest factor in the regression equation).
- Frequent feedback (but *not* meddling or interference) from the parent and the client, a flexible parent organization, lack of legal encumbrances or governmental red tape, and a minimal number of public governmental agencies involved with the project were pertinent variables significantly related to perceived project success (31).*

These findings supported Kloman's earlier study:

- From a management viewpoint, the greatest contrast between the Surveyor and Lunar Orbiter projects was the nature of the relationships of participating organizations, or what might be called the institutional environment. For Surveyor, there was an unusual degree of conflict and friction between Headquarters, JPL, and the prime contractor. For Lunar Orbiter, harmony and teamwork prevailed. Institutions and people worked together in a spirit of mutual respect (32).

---

* These findings are discussed in Chapter 35.

CONCLUSIONS

Research regarding the human element in project management has enabled practitioners to formulate strategies which can not only improve the behavioral aspects of project management (the climate) but which also results in more effective project performance. The many research projects are relatively consistent with each other. Some of the principal findings which should be consistently stressed are:

- There is no single panacea in project management; some factors work well in one environment while other factors work well in other environments.
- It is important to vest a project manager with sufficient authority; once vested with authority, the project manager is well advised to also utilize his expertise and work challenge as major influence modes.
- The problem-solving approach is more successful than the smoothing or the forcing mode of conflict resolution.
- Participative decision-making styles are generally more successful than other styles; commitment, teamwork, and a sense of mission are important areas of attention in project management.
- Project organizational design must be tailored to the specific task and the environment, but higher degrees of projectization and higher levels of authority for the project manager result in less probability of cost and schedule overruns.
- To attain high levels of perceived success (including not only adequate technical performance but also satisfaction of the client, the parent, and the project team), effective coordination and relations patterns are important; also, success criteria salience and consensus among the client, the parent, and the project team are crucial.

Fully understanding the complexity of the interpersonal network in project management requires an ongoing research effort. We hope that research on this crucial area of project management will continue to produce new knowledge in the future.

REFERENCES

1. Such a focus is a natural development in the life cycle of many management concepts. In the area of systems analysis, for example, the early literature centered on the hardware, software, and technical information handling processes. An earlier version of this paper appeared in the *Project Management Quarterly* (March, 1977), pp. 34–40.

2. Lawrence, Paul R. and Lorsch, Jay W. "New Management Job: The Integrator." *Harvard Business Review* (November-December, 1967), pp. 142–151.

3. Ibid., p. 150.

4. Hodgetts, Richard M. "Leadership Techniques in the Project Organization." *Academy of Management Journal*, Vol. 11 (1968), pp. 211–219.

5. Gemmill, Gary R. and Wilemon, David L. "The Power Spectrum in Project Management." *Sloan Management Review* (Fall, 1970), pp. 15–25.

6. Gemmill, Gary R. and Thamhain, Hans J. "Influence Styles of Project Managers: Some Project Performance Correlates." *Academy of Management Journal* (June, 1974), pp. 216–224. Also see Gemmill, Gary R. and Thamhain, Hans J. "The Effectiveness of Different Powerstyles of Project Managers in Gaining Project Support." *IEEE Transactions on Engineering Management* (May, 1973), pp. 38–43.

7. Reprinted by permission of the *Harvard Business Review*. Excerpt from "Engineer The Job To Fit The Manager" by Fred E. Fiedler (September/October 1965). p. 119 Copyright 1965 by the President and Fellows of Harvard College; all rights reserved.

8. Ibid.

9. Ibid.

10. Gaddis, Paul O. "The Project Manager." *Harvard Business Review* (May-June, 1959), pp. 89–97; Goodman, Richard M. "Ambiguous Authority Definition in Project Management." *Academy of Management Journal* (December, 1967), pp. 395–407; Steward, John M. "Making Project Management Work." *Business Horizons* (Spring, 1967), pp. 63–70.

11. Wilemon, David L. "Project Management Conflict: A View from Apollo." *Proceedings of the Project Management Institute* (1971).

12. Butler, Arthur G. "Project Management: A Study in Organizational Conflict." *Academy of Management Journal* (March, 1973), pp. 84–101.

13. Thamhain, Hans J. and Wilemon, David L. "Conflict Management in Project-Oriented Work Environments." *Proceedings of the Project Management Institute* (1974).

14. Thamhain, Hans J. and Wilemon, David L. "Conflict Management in Project Life Cycles." *Sloan Management Review* (Summer, 1975), pp. 31–50.

15. Lawrence, Paul R. and Lorsch, Jay W. (same reference as footnote 2), pp. 148–149.

16. Lawrence, Paul R. and Lorsch, Jay W. (same reference as footnote 2).

17. Blake, R. R. and Mouton, Jane S. *The Managerial Grid* (Gulf Publishing Company. Houston, 1964).

18. Burke, Ron J. "Methods of Resolving Interpersonal Conflict." *Personal Administration* (July-August, 1969), pp. 48–55.

19. Thamhain, Hans J. and Wilemon, David L. (same reference as footnote 13).

20. Thamhain, Hans J. and Wilemon, David L. (same reference as footnote 13).

21. Murphy, David C., Baker, Bruce N. and Fisher, Dalmar. *Determinants of Project Success*. Springfield, Va. 22151; National Technical Information Services, Accession number: N-74-30392, 1974, pp. 60–69.

22. Kloman, Erasmus H. *Unmanned Space Project Management—Surveyor and Lunar Orbiter*, a Report Prepared by the National Academy of Public Administration and sponsored by the National Aeronautics and Space Administration, Washington, D.C.; U.S. Government Printing Office, 1972, p. 14.

23. Varney, Glenn H. *Organization Development for Managers* (Addison-Wesley. Reading, Mass., 1977), p. 151.

24. Thamhain, Hans J. and Wilemon, David L. "Team Building in Project Management." *Proceedings of the Project Management Institute,* Atlanta (1979).

25. Murphy, Baker, and Fisher (same reference as footnote 21).

26. Marquis, Donald G. and Straight, David M. *Organizational Factors in Project Performance*. Washington, D.C.: National Aeronautics and Space Administration, July 25, 1965.

27. Marquis, Donald G. "A Project Team + PERT = Success or Does It?" *Innovation* (5) (1969), pp. 26–33.

28. Chapman, Richard L. *Project Management in NASA,* a report of the National Academy of Public Administration Foundation (January, 1973).

29. Reeser, Clayton."Some Potential Human Problems of the Project Form of Organization." *Academy of Management Journal* (December, 1969), p. 467.

30. Tushman, Michael L. "Managing Communication Networks in R & D Laboratories." *Sloan Management Review* (Winter, 1979), pp. 37–49.

31. Murphy, Baker, and Fisher (same reference as footnote 21).

32. Kloman (same reference as footnote 22), p. 17.

Section IX

The Successful Application of Project Management

This section deals with successful applications of project management in the sense of both contextual applications and "success factors" that contribute to project success.

In Chapter 34, Michael K. Gouse and Frank A. Stickney provide an overview of a wide range of project management applications. Their annotated bibliography is an excellent guide to the broader literature describing various such applications.

In Chapter 35, Bruce N. Baker, David C. Murphy, and Dalmar Fisher discuss "project success and failure factors"—those factors that have been demonstrated to affect the perceived success or failure of projects. Such factors can provide the project manager with insight into those characteristics that might influence the eventual degree of success that his project is perceived to have achieved.

In Chapter 36, Baker, Fisher, and Murphy present a comparative analysis of public- and private-sector projects in terms of their success and failure patterns.

In Chapter 37, Laura C. Leviton and Gordon K. MacLeod discuss the successful application of project management in the health care sector.

In the concluding Chapter 38, David I. Cleland discusses the cultural ambience of the matrix organization—those "climatic" or cultural factors that appear to be associated with successful matrix organizations.

34. Overview of Project Management Applications

Michael K. Gouse*
Frank A. Stickney†

This chapter updates material included in the first edition of *Project Management Handbook*. It also identifies and discusses more recent applications of project management in specific contexts including health care management, research and development, government/defense, construction, and business and industry. The continued and increased use of the project management concept further convinces the authors that project management is the most effective approach to the management of multiple tasks, projects, programs, and products in many contemporary organizational situations. A major factor contributing to the increased use of project management has been the rapid development of computer software packages devoted to simplifying the process of implementing and executing a project management program. These recent innovations in computer applications to project management and their impact will also be analyzed.

Over the past 25 years, many contemporary organizations have adopted and implemented the project management concept for improving planning and control of their multiple tasks, projects, programs, and products. Project management should not, however, be considered a panacea for every organization encountering problems in multiple task manage-

---

* Michael K. Gouse is pursuing a Masters of Business Administration degree from Wright State University, Dayton, Ohio. His field of specialization is financial management.
† Frank A. Stickney is a Professor of Management at Wright State University. He received his Ph.D. from The Ohio State University in 1969. In addition to his academic research activity and consulting, he has extensive work experience in project management and related activities. His primary areas of research interest are organizational design, job satisfaction, the supervisory process, and strategic management.

ment. Project management is not relevant to all organizational situations because the implementation and execution of project management requires the use of additional resources and creates strains on the traditional roles and relationships within an organization. It should be considered only when the benefits derived from its use outweigh these additional costs. The authors propose that any organization considering the adoption and implementation of project management should follow the contingency approach; that is, if any organization is designed and operating under the traditional functional structure, without project management, and is achieving its objectives satisfactorily, then the adoption of project management may be unnecessary.

Project management received its strongest and earliest stimulus in organizations functioning in the aerospace, communications, and electronics technologies. The technologies involved in these industries are very dynamic and are characterized by rapid and continuous change. However, these conditions of technological change are rapidly spreading to organizations with historically stable technological environments. Organizational growth, complexity, and change in this environment are evident in the various applications presented in this chapter. These organizational changes, coupled with the impact of recent innovations in computer applications on the project management process, are also discussed.

The following structure will be used to present and review these applications:

1. A definition of project management and the circumstances under which it should be used.
2. A brief review and analysis of project management applications cited in the first edition of the handbook.
3. Description and analysis of recent project management applications.
4. The impact and use of the computer in project management.
5. Summary and conclusions.

A DEFINITION OF PROJECT MANAGEMENT AND THE CIRCUMSTANCES UNDER WHICH IT SHOULD BE USED

Project management is the application of the systems approach to the management of technologically complex tasks or projects whose objectives are explicitly stated in terms of time, cost, and performance parameters. A project is, in reality, one of several subsystems in an organization. All of these subsystems must be managed in an integrative manner for the effective and efficient accomplishment of organizational objectives. Project management provides an interfunctional structure for a specified project and has a primary management orientation. It involves a project manager who, through funding allocation and control, obtains the required resources from the various functional departments: engineering, marketing, production, etc. This project manager should be proactive on tasks, as compared with the functional manager who is proactive on functional specialization, but reactive on tasks. Through the process of planning, organizing, directing, and controlling, the project manager coordinates the application of these resources to a given project with specific objectives providing the primary focus. The project manager should be evaluated on the successful completion of the project in terms of timeliness, budgetary constraints, and task performance.

The project organization is the focal point for all activities on a given project and provides total project visibility. It is integrative in nature and becomes the hub of all activities, both internal and external, which affect the project. It is a management mechanism and supplements, rather than replaces, the functional activities of the various departments. It is again emphasized that project management is not applicable to every task, project, product, or program. It is not an organizational panacea.

Many organizations employing project management use a "team or task-force approach," "matrix structure," "program structure," or "product structure." Not all of these approaches/structures fully qualify as pure project management applications, but all contain some characteristics of the project management concept. Specifically, the differences among these recognized subsets of the general project management approach are simply a matter of emphasis (1).* For example, the task-force approach is interdisciplinary, but does not have a finite termination date. The term "program" structure is usually used to define a multi-"project" structure (basically similar, but more complex).†

The authors consider project management a means of managing technological change when organizations are engaged in multiple tasks. It provides the organizational structure necessary for the successful management of these efforts relative to organizational and functional as well as task/project objective achievement. Several criteria have been developed to be used in evaluating the applicability of project management. The

---

* Numbered references are given in a bibliography at the end of the chapter.

† For a more thorough discussion of the forms of project management, please refer to Adams, John R., Barndt, Stephen E. and Martin, Martin D., *Managing by Project Management* (Dayton, Ohio: Universal Technology Corp., 1979) pp. 1–14.

following organizational conditions should exist when considering the applicability of project management:

- An objective-oriented work allocation structure is required.
- Identifiable product and/or task with a distinct life cycle (as well as performance, time, and cost objectives) are the primary outputs.
- The environment is highly uncertain and dynamic.
- Complex short- and long-run products are the organization's primary output.
- Complex and functionally integrated decisions are required with both innovation and timely completion.
- Several kinds of sophisticated skills are required in designing, producing, testing, and marketing the product.
- A rapidly changing marketplace requires significant changes in products between the time they are conceived and delivered.
- There is a stream of projects, some of which are not achieving project objectives.
- A task/project or other organizational activity requires simultaneous coordination of two or more departments (interdisciplinary) (11).

The above are the major factors which an organization should consider in determining whether to implement project management. The organization should ensure that the benefits of better project planning, control, and performance outweigh the additional costs required by the implementation of project management. The examples cited in the first edition of the handbook and the more recent project management applications reviewed in this chapter appear to have benefits which exceed additional costs.

Figure 34-1 is a model illustrating the interaction between the organizational (system) objectives, project/product objectives, and functional objectives. Notice that a system of "checks and balances" must be in effect to preclude the enhancement of one set of objectives to the detriment of the others. This figure is a conceptual model introduced to analyze and understand the project and functional management relationships and does not represent an actual organizational design.

A REVIEW AND ANALYSIS OF PROJECT MANAGEMENT APPLICATIONS CITED IN THE FIRST EDITION OF THE HANDBOOK

These previously cited project management applications are presented by type of technology. The references are indexed to the bibliography for more complete information.

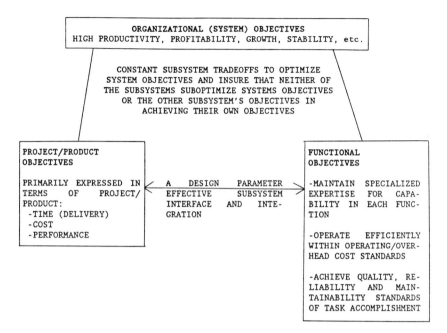

Figure 34-1. System and subsystem objectives. (From Frank A. Stickney and William R. Johnston, "Communication: The Key to Integration," *1980 Proceedings of the Project Management Institute* (The Project Management Institute. Drexel, Pa., 1980), p. I-A.7.

Research and Development

The Searle Laboratories Division of G. D. Searle and Company, Chicago, Illinois, is involved in drug development. As such, it operates in a complex, ever-changing environment requiring a dynamic system of operations. To meet this challenge, Searle has utilized a "collateral" project structure for achievement of both its research and organizational objectives. This structure includes the following groups:

1. A corporate *Pharmaceutical R and D Group* has goal-setting responsibilities and interfaces primarily with the Action Council in a strategic administrative capacity.
2. The *Action Council* is an interfunctional group employing worldwide technical personnel; this group has responsibility for product selection and prioritization and for selection and evaluation of project leaders.
3. *Core Committees* are interfunctional groups interfacing with the Action Council, project teams, and project task forces; they are

responsible for needed resources, and project sites, and for determining the nature of worldwide technical inputs.

4. *Interfunctional Task Forces* consist primarily of members from the Core Committees; they are responsible for project planning.

5. *Project Leaders* are responsible for managing the projects and *Project Management Consultants* are responsible for monitoring the project progress. Project leaders have personnel assigned based on skill assessment requirements determined by the interfunctional task forces; this comprises the basic management team.

All of the above groups are in continuous interaction by organizational/ system plan, and their specific roles and relationships are explicitly defined. The task of these groups is made extremely difficult by government regulation and monitoring, by frequent changes and modifications, and by the nature of basic research. The project structure, although seemingly complex, appears to be conducive to achievement of objectives in these types of environment (22).

Battelle Pacific N. W. Laboratories (BNW), a division of Battelle Memorial Institute, has project contracts from both government and industry (national and international) which are extremely broad in scope, with their size and complexity ranging from the small single-discipline type to the large multimillion-dollar, multidisciplinary type. A Research Project Management System (RPMS) was established which supports a work environment conducive to the creative and innovative output expected from researchers with functional/specified discipline orientations. It also provides for effective performance of the firms' many projects.

BNW maintains a "functional" structure with an implied "project" structure. Project managers report to functional managers but maintain the flexibility for temporary assignment to other functional managers within the organization. The project organization is not reflected in the formal organizational chart but is created when needed (35).

Construction

The James H. Campbell Plant #3 is a coal-fired power plant designed and constructed near Grand Haven, Michigan. This project was under the direction of Consumers Power Company (CPCo), plus two separate organizations, Townsend and Bottam Engineers and Contractors, the contractor, and Gilbert/Commonwealth, the engineer. These two autonomous organizations joined together in providing the single responsibility and interdisciplinary focus CPCo required. This effort was carried out by integrated project teams (utilizing the expertise of both companies) with a single project manager as the individual with key responsibility to CPCo. Complex channels of communication, distance, and a lack of understanding among the different groups of the companies were dealt with through weekly management meetings. Progress reviews were held first for each functional discipline, and then followed by a project group meeting where open communication and constructive criticism was the mode. In addition, "Team Building Sessions" were held to promote cooperation between and among all groups. The success of this project is attributable to the project management approach and the resulting integration of effort (40).

Another construction organization where project management was applied is the Los Angeles County Flood Control District, a system of flood control and water conservation facilities (i.e., dams, major channel improvements, spreading grounds, etc.) for Los Angeles County. In 1966, a small program management effort was adopted and implemented consisting of two people and a secretary, with mainly a facilitating responsibility for recommending change. The program management function grew from that state, continuing to solve problems despite encountering resistance to change. Several years later, program/project managers were directly assigned to projects and a management Systems Division was formed. This change in organizational structure is believed by many within the Flood Control District to be an appropriate vehicle for dealing with complex management problems. It clearly indicates the use of project management as an integrating mechanism for diverse activities required for achievement of common objectives (17).

Government/Defense

NASA's space shuttle program is an immense undertaking. The complexity of this program necessitates a tremendously dynamic system structure. A structure has been developed consisting of the following four levels:

- Level I: NASA Headquarters in Washington, D.C., which interfaces directly with Congress and other government agencies. It is responsible for provision of major program direction and planning, basic performance requirements, and control of funding allocations to NASA field centers.
- Level II: the Space Shuttle Program Office, which has major interfunctional project management responsibilities.
- Level III: the actual projects, which are managed through project offices at NASA.

- Level IV: the level where contractors carry out operational duties (37).

This structure facilitates smooth communication flows and processing of information to key decision centers within the constraints of the program.

The Naval Air Systems Command uses project management in its defense weapon systems acquisition process. Project offices are formed for the weapon systems requiring large outlays of R&D and/or production dollars, and project managers are assigned overall project responsibility. The technical and administrative experts from the functional departments are assigned to projects to provide the specialized expertise on an as-needed basis. The Command's contractors (suppliers) also use the project management concept for managing their portion of the project and for interfacing with the project manager in the Command. With the complexities and interdependencies inherent in major weapon systems development and acquisition, the project management structure utilized in this situation has worked well (38).

Business and Industry

By the end of 1973, the business environment in the automobile industry had become increasingly complex and uncertain. General Motors management determined that conditions were appropriate for project management, and in 1974 the project center concept was implemented to coordinate the efforts of GM's five automobile divisions. These project centers were temporary in nature and were formed whenever a major effort requiring interfunctional specialties was required. Work in the project centers focused on problems common to all divisions (i.e., frames, electrical systems, steering gear, and brakes). The implementation of this concept speeded new technological ideas onto the production line and utilized resources to their best advantage, eliminating much redundancy in efforts.(7)*

At the Inland Division of General Motors, a "team approach" was implemented to minimize the suboptimization of organizational objectives that often occur in complex organizations. This approach consists of interfunctional teams working on one or more major projects, rotating team chiefs with differing technical specialties, and a "board" to oversee the

---

* See the Business and Industry Section, page 32, Recent Project Management Applications, for more recent information on G.M.

team operations and to provide strategic management direction. Although the situation does not meet the exact criteria for a project office, it is another illustration showing positive results of the project management approach (12).

The management of Standard Steel Company of Burnham and Latrobe, Pennsylvania, a traditionally functional organization, made the decision to implement project management. This structure was integrated with the functional structure, and teams of specialists (production, finance, metallurgy, etc.) jointly managed a product line or geographic area. The approach worked well at Standard Steel, although other companies in the metals industry may not find this application of project management applicable to their situations (9).

Health Care Management

The British National Health Service was reorganized in 1974, involving the overlapping of the functional hierarchical organization with various lateral relationships, some permanent, some ad hoc. The lateral groupings were tasked with a variety of responsibilities ranging from direct provision of services by health service professionals to developing policies and/or plans for use by both in-house personnel and non-health agency personnel. In addition, this organizational form has a synergistic effect upon the health service. When those with technical expertise are brought together to solve problems, learning from the knowledge and experience of one another is inherent in the interactions, resulting in greater optimization of organizational goals (16).

In 1976, the Westside Community Mental Health Center was a traditional functional organization. Problems existed because a limited number of services were offered and service areas exhibited varying degrees of productivity. Coordination among service areas was increasingly complex, communications were poor. Often, patients were discharged from the Inpatient Department with no follow-up arrangements made with the Outpatient Department; a systems perspective among personnel was almost nonexistent. The conditions were conducive for change. A matrix project management structure was adopted and major improvements in operations were observable within two years. In 1978, there were five additional service programs offered employing seven less staff personnel than in 1976. The adoption and implementation of the project management organizational form was highly conducive to increased communication, coordination, control, and achievement of organizational objectives (44).

DESCRIPTION AND ANALYSIS OF RECENT PROJECT MANAGEMENT APPLICATIONS

Research and Development

Groups involved in research and development are basically concerned with turning intangible concepts, ideas, and theories into specifications, tangible products, and processes. Consequently, these groups are different from other subsystems within an organization and often require a different structure (24).

Several recent drug development successes in the Medical Research Division (MRD) of American Cyanamid are credited to a systems and project management organizational perspective. There are two main factors in this R&D success story: one, participative management in the form of interdisciplinary teams focused on project planning at the mid-management level of detail; and, two, the teams continuously evaluated project specifications which are constantly changing in the R&D projects.

Cynamide utilizes a "platoon" approach project structure for achievement of its research and organizational objectives. Project managers are selected from the ranks of the functional organizations, spending about 20% of their time as the project team leader. It is the project manager's responsibility to lead the project team members in preparation of a project plan, and the tracking, reporting, and adjusting of that plan through project conclusion. Representatives from each of the functional groups are on the project teams. The marketing representative has been identified as one of the most critical on the team. Constant assessment of any changes in project specifications must be made vis-à-vis market potential at projected product launch time.

Three basic guidelines for project management success have been derived from this experience:

- *Focus:* Because project objectives will change, focus on, and continuous reassessment of, these objectives is imperative. Exceptions and changes to the project are analyzed and coordinated at status review meetings.
- *Communication:* The project reporting system should be kept relatively simple; it should be objective-oriented. Members of the R&D functional organizations, such as the Regulatory and Marketing departments, should be on the project team. A formal and timely mechanism must be available to distribute information to those who need to know.

- *Team Leadership:* The team leader should be both a good manager and a good scientist because the project decisions need to be based on both scientific and managerial factors.

Basic project management concepts have been applied to the pharmaceutical R&D environment, and success in these endeavors is attributed to utilization of these concepts. Clearly defined project specifications and the availability of automated project management systems for project planning, evaluation, and control are required (23).

The Tri University Meson Facility (TRIUMF), located at Vancouver, B.C., Canada, is the only meson factory in Canada and is one of three intermediate-energy nuclear physics laboratories in the world. More than 500 people from different disciplines, countries, and cultures conduct both basic and applied research at this facility. On the average, 10 to 20 projects are active at any one time, each involving 10 to 30 people and total costs ranging from $500,000 to $2,500,000 (Cdn.). Two typical projects were both completed within two to three weeks of the projected project duration of approximately 15 months and within 10% of the budget. Such notable success is attributed to utilization of CAMS (Computer Aided Management System), timely project progress reviews, and remarkable team effort (43).

In such a dynamic, complex environment, the planning process is extraordinarily important. In 1978, the National Research Council (NRC) of Canada asked TRIUMF to submit its future plans and related budgetary proposals. The plans and budgets were divided into three categories consistent with TRIUMF organizational objectives:

- *Basic Support* covering the maintenance, repair, and operation of all commissioned facilities, general and technical services, and administration.
- *Facility Development* involving the requirement to increase the scope and capabilities of TRIUMF, including the upgrading and/or extension of existing facilities and construction of new facilities.
- *Experimental Support* including site standard instrumentation, services, and equipment required to carry out the experiments.

The above reflects the functional activities/capabilities required to support TRIUMF's projects. Each major project has a project description serving as a guideline to conceptually define and plan the project. Both the total project cost and estimated cash flows are defined. These estimates are improved as the project progresses. One of the effective keys to successful project management at TRIUMF is an effective review process which continues throughout the project life cycle. A well-designed review process is important because of the need for interactive communication and interdisciplinary expertise. At TRIUMF, the regular weekly or bi-weekly meeting could be classified as one of information, analysis, evaluation, design, and/or decision making. However, the amount of time and effort expended on reviews should not outweigh their potential benefits.

At TRIUMF, successful project management is based on user participation, feedback, and coordinated team efforts. This is an outstanding example of project management implemented with creativity in team formulation, resulting in more effective communication, integration, and interface management between project and functional support activities (43).

Goodyear Tire and Rubber Company, Akron, Ohio, has an R&D philosophy based on the premise that innovation involves taking an idea and translating it into a more efficient manufacturing process and/or a more marketable product. Basic research is constantly monitored to ensure that it supports other key activities of the organization such as distribution, marketing, and manufacturing (6).

Goodyear utilizes a project matrix management structure that works closely with R&D organizations for project planning and control. Project managers organize teams that are interfunctional and interdisciplinary in nature. A typical project team might consist of a research scientist, a development engineer, and a marketing specialist. One of the key responsibilities of these project management teams is to terminate a project when it is no longer useful. These teams have proven to be very effective in expediting a project toward either completion or termination. Departing from the traditional approach to product design and manufacture, the corporation now utilizes a systems approach that emphasizes basic scientific knowledge by simultaneously looking at all elements involved and their interdependencies, that is, the product itself, materials, and relevant manufacturing processes, etc. Goodyear has found project management an effective approach to accomplishment of its organizational objectives (6).

Stuart Pharmaceuticals is the U.S.-based operation for the research-intensive pharmaceuticals division of Imperial Chemical Industries PLC of London, England. Since 1977, the company has introduced several new products as a result of extensive research. In order to attain organizational objectives, the company has implemented project management in two areas: research development and commercial development. The following are the major project management activities in their research function:

- *Predevelopment activities* culminate with identification of the best chemical compound which has the potential to become a drug. The project manager begins coordinating the compound through the rigors of predevelopment to compound proposal and selection.
- *Compound selection and development strategy* involves the project manager editing the scientific information into a document. This document is used by an international research management team to determine whether funds are allocated for further development of this compound. If the project is funded, the project manager selects appropriate team members and convenes team meetings to ensure completion of documents.
- During the *progressive development* phase, a large percentage of the project manager's time is devoted to managing the preclinical and early clinical aspects of development with computerized monitoring of these developmental activities. The project manager summarizes team proposals and recommendations for international research management team consideration. The resulting decision is communicated to the team by the project manager, who coordinates the decision and its implementation.

After the drug is submitted for approval, research development is replaced by commercial development and the research team manages these activities to the market.

Project management at Stuart blends proven managerial techniques with the technical expertise necessary in dynamic research processes. Stuart has discovered that project management focuses upon the task/project at hand, de-emphasizing the "star" syndrome and potentially destructive infighting. The sources of project management at Stuart Pharmaceuticals are one of the primary reasons Stuart is a leader in the industry (8).

Inherent in these studies of project management application in research and development environments is the strong project/team leader. This individual must possess excellent managerial skills combined with technical expertise. The findings of Katz and Allen suggest a separation of roles between project and functional managers of R&D professionals, although these roles can never be completely separate (25).* A project management structure has been identified in this research which utilizes functional managers as project leaders on a part-time basis. This, however,

---

* For a more thorough discussion, please refer to Ralph Katz and Thomas J. Allen, "Project Performance and the Locus of Influence in the R&D Matrix," *Academy of Management Journal* (March 1985), pp. 67–87.

may be the exception rather than the rule. Management must consider the specific aspects of the organizational environment as a prerequisite to project management implementation and execution. R&D organizations that survive and prosper in today's dynamic, high-tech environment will be those that successfully combine functional expertise and the strategic and operational management of research projects.

Construction

Construction projects requiring interdisciplinary efforts from two or more separate technologically oriented organizations by nature necessitate a project structure. An example is the expansion of Texaco's Louisiana refinery, located at Convent, about 50 miles north of New Orleans on the east bank of the Mississippi River. The overall success of the project was attributed to careful selection of contractors. Texaco contracted with Fluor Engineers, Inc., for engineering and procurement, and with Brown and Root, Inc., for construction. This was the first time Texaco had utilized separate contractors for engineering and construction. The intent was to allow Texaco to concentrate its efforts in other critical areas and to allow the contractors to work in their areas of expertise with minor Texaco input (4).

To satisfy organizational objectives in engineering, procurement, and construction, Texaco determined that an integrated schedule was necessary. To accomplish this, Texaco and contractor personnel developed an overall critical path method (CPM) schedule*. Contractor personnel reported directly to the Texaco project manager, but were never considered Texaco personnel by either contractor. Additionally, Texaco used its own personnel to consolidate cost information from both contractors to develop the current control budget.

In any project of this magnitude, communication is a critical and monumental task. At its peak, over 5000 people were working on the project and 12 groups had to interface with each other. Each company had a staff at the construction site as well as at each organization's project offices. Information between the three companies was expedited more quickly and reliably and problems were identified and solved faster. In an effort to reduce paperwork on the project, meetings were held on an "as-needed" basis, and the co-location of all three organizations' personnel facilitated timely integration (4).

Another application was the CRS Group of Houston, Texas, who are specialists in project design, development, and construction. They were faced with the formidable task to plan and implement a massive irrigation project in the remote deserts of Saudia Arabia. Using project manage-

---

* See Chapter 15.

ment, CRS completed the project on time. A key to the successful completion of this project was breaking it down from a large, unwieldy entity into smaller, more manageable parts. CRS had been hired by Lindsay International, a Houston manufacturer of irrigation equipment, to build and install systems at four locations within eight months. The four sites to be irrigated were at different locations in Saudia Arabia and each site had unique problems. CRS turned each site into a separate subproject, with Riyadh, the Saudi capital, as the coordination point for the four subprojects. With one microcomputer being used for each project, the subprojects were compared with one another on an ongoing basis. CRS credits use of the computerized project management packages with the success of the project (42).*

The Piper Jaffray Tower, a 42-story office building in downtown Minneapolis, is a $90 million project completed within the time schedule and budget that was established before final design was started. The success of this endeavor is attributed to the project manager's striving for excellence in teamwork with open and continuous communication. The project was entirely a local effort: the general partner and developer, the architect and engineers, and the construction manager/general contractor are all local Minneapolis/St. Paul firms. Most of the subcontractors that were used on the project were also local.

On-site project managers were designated and involved in all phases of the project, including these key phases:

Postdesign Development

- Preconstruction and major construction phases scheduled.
- Bid packages selected.
- Monthly construction phase expenditures estimated.
- All involved participants, including owners, lenders, and potential subcontractors, made aware of the overall schedule.

Prebid

- General strategy and construction sequence finalized.
- Comprehensive plan established to be used as a benchmark for controlling progress.
- Subcontractors encouraged to participate in plan refinement.

Preconstruction

- Teamwork attitude developed.
- Schedule plan refined with subcontractor assistance.

---

* See Chapter 28.

Construction

- Attainable short-term progress goals established.
- Plans established for smooth transition from one construction phase to another.
- Schedule problems resolved upon occurrence.
- Schedule modified as necessary.

These areas were integrated by the master project office. Emphasis was placed on all phases of construction activity with timely information flow and communication between all project participants. It is this constant coordination and project commitment by the projects' managers that enabled the project to be completed on schedule and within budget (27).

In the past three years, Paragon Engineering Services, Inc., has had the project engineering and construction supervision responsibility for at least six separate shallow-water oil and gas facilities. Project management techniques which were successfully employed onshore or in water depths greater than 50 feet had to be altered for these shallow-water projects. Paragon developed an approach which has enabled each of these projects to be built in three to six months from well completion and at cost 20% to 40% less than identical "turnkey" projects. A turnkey project is one where the contractor completes all building and installation to the point of readiness for operations, at which time it is sold to the customer at a prearranged price. This "modified turnkey" approach to project organization maintains operator control over quality while providing the shortest project schedule at least cost (5).

A project schedule or plan of project execution is prepared to monitor progress. When this schedule is set, the separate contract or engineering activities whose progress is necessary to assure start-up are identified. Progress toward attaining preset intermediate goals is reviewed weekly to identify problem areas. In the "modified turnkey" approach to project management, the activities of the operator and all vendors are continuously coordinated. Inspection and expediting are greatly simplified compared to other project organizations where the contractor has many subcontractors. This approach allowed major problems to be identified early so that they would not affect the overall project schedule (5).

One of the major considerations in any construction project is the transition period which involves training the operators and maintenance personnel so that the new facility start-up and operation is safe and efficient. Project managers from Standard Oil Company faced such a task in the planning, development, and construction of the Trans Alaska Pipeline (TAPS). The design of this project extended over a long time period because of the size of the project and environmental problems. The owner companies formed a separate organization (corporation) for the construction and operation of the pipeline. In essence, this organization had two major subsytems (groups) whose activities were integrated on a continuous basis: one for construction and one for operation.

The smooth transition of TAPS from construction to operation resulted from the formation of these two primary groups. The following are the critical elements in the operating subsystem which directly contributed to this success:

- It was established early in the design phase of the project.
- It functioned independently and had responsibility for commissioning the new facility.
- It and the project management subsystem worked on an integrated basis with continuous communication.

Separate but integrated organizations for construction and facility operations are recommended so that the demands of construction do not dilute the preparations necessary for operations. The project organization was the primary integrator between these two major functions.

The first person assigned to the operating organization should be the one who will manage the facility after start-up. This person's responsibility is to plan and to organize both the start-up and the permanent operations. The organization of the start-up manager has several overall responsibilities which include reviewing design plans to ensure the facility can be operated, preparing operational manuals and start-up procedures, planning the start-up and training personnel, and commencing operations with timely resolution of all start-up problems.

The major phases of activity for the operating group include design review, start-up planning, and start-up. During these phases, the start-up manager chairs a committee that includes all operating managers (operations, maintenance, technical, administrative) and a high-level manager from the construction project management group. One of the primary functions of this committee is to provide a formal interface between the two groups.

Health Care Management

It has often been suggested that hospitals can be more effectively administered by a product management structure. Rather than operating hospital activities primarily along traditional functional departments such as laboratory, radiology, internal medicine, etc., specific product categories focus on specific areas such as orthopedics, obstetrics, neurosciences, urology, etc. With the advent of diagnosis-related group (DRG) prospective payment systems, discussions of product-managed administration have dramatically increased. With DRG, payments are made based on the number of patients in specific diagnostic/treatment categories rather than on allocated costs from functional departments. DRG is forcing hospitals to think in terms of product line management (30).

Organizational objectives for Miami Valley Hospital (MVH) in Dayton, Ohio include cost management and increased market share. Hospital administration felt that product line management would afford MVH an opportunity to meet those objectives by more appropriately matching products to target market segments (46).

The key to successfully implementing this structure is the selection of an appropriate product manager who possesses skills that are interdisciplinary in nature. The role of this person is significantly different from that of the functional manager. It is critical, however, to recognize that both types of managers are necessary. The organization must gradually transition into the situation where the relationship between the product and functional managers is accepted. The issue of "turf" is a difficult obstacle to overcome in product line management, but the organization must make a concerted effort to effectively organize teams at all levels for product groups.

Product line management is also utilized at Health and Hospital Services in Bellevue, Washington. Management has identified three basic elements in the administration of health care project management; they are *planning, cost control,* and *marketing.* The *planning* stage involves making decisions about what services to offer, how, and to whom; and it is based on hospital activities in terms of its products and product lines. Effective planning is reflected in end results; how well do the sets of products which the hospital offers enable the hospital to achieve its objectives? Product line *cost control* works primarily by influencing how physicians manage their patients; this technique is unlike traditional management efforts to control costs by controlling functional departments. Successful product line cost control management requires the hospital to organize, direct, and control its operations by product line categories. The product line *marketing* effort is concerned with identifying, achieving, and sustaining a specific market position for each product line. The objective should be a position in which a significant number of end-users (physicians, patients, employers) consider the hospital to be the best facility for all products in a specific product line. Marketing effectiveness can be measured by such criteria as patient volumes and mix and their effects on productivity, efficiency, and financial performance (30).

A survey was conducted of U.S. hospitals by Swedish Health Services in August, 1985, to determine which hospitals were utilizing product lines and product line management. The results were significant. Of 47 respondent hospitals, 26 (55%) were using some type of product line management, with length of use up to ten years. Six other hospitals (13%) are considering implementing the method. Some hospitals started with just one product line and added slowly, while others started with as many as 16. Product line managers share areas of responsibilities with other functional segments of the organization. These responsibilities include budgeting, staff supervision, equipment acquisition, market research, and promotional activities. The ultimate organizational objective for product line managers is for them to have complete responsibility for specified product lines (14).

Health care service institutions are complex social and technological organizations existing in a continuously changing and now highly competitive environment. As such, they require a dynamic system of operations to survive and prosper. Product line management, with its myriad uses, purposes, and design is one structure appropriate for dealing with this health care environment.

Government/Defense

The Department of Defense (DOD) has used program/project management for the acquisition of large defense weapon systems for many years. The Polaris submarine project was managed and acquired by a formal project management office. Other major programs such as the B-1 bomber, the Phoenix missile, the F-14, F-15, F-16, and F-18 aircraft, the Apache, Cheyenne, and Blackhawk helicopters, the Trident submarine, and the M-1 tank have all been acquired through the process of project management. Smaller systems and subsytems are also routinely acquired utilizing program/project management. In fiscal year 1983, DOD spent $140.5 billion for the acquisition of defense weapon systems, much of it managed by project managers (26).

In an analysis of the successful completion of a number of these projects, several key factors were identified. These factors for success differ from project to project, but there are some basic themes. Project managers interviewed cited these success factors most often: good staffs, good contractor project managers, realistic requirements, a good contractor or manufacturer, and stability factors (personnel, funding, and product stability). The skill and ability of the project manager is also a vital factor for success. The operational background, leadership ability, education, and project management experience are critical factors. Project managers must be able to communicate well with all types of audiences (26).

In every project analyzed, the project manager was clearly the driving force; personal attributes were clearly important to the success of the project. The project staff gradually assumed the personality of the project manager; enthusiastic and hard-charging, low key, etc. The project became the project manager. The following are several of the key personal attributes which were identified:

- *Experience* in acquisition; decisions are based on judgment gained through experience.
- *Leadership* which instills loyalty and motivates team members.
- Ability to *communicate* with all segments impacting upon the project.
- Willingness to *accept responsibility* and *execute authority*.

These are general attributes which correspond to civilian projects as well as military (26).

Costs overruns still plague the defense procurement system even with attempts by Congress and the Defense Department to improve project management. Much of this problem is traced to military and civilian project managers who have limited training or experience in running large programs that deal with the research, development, and production of defense weapon systems. These people are highly capable, highly motivated individuals trained in the government system of procedures and regulations. However, their formal training often does not equip them with the negotiating skills necessary to deal with contractors. More effort is being made to develop career project managers through training and experience. Outstanding military and civilian personnel should be offered project management as an attractive career opportunity. Project managers who complete acquisition programs on time and within budget should be rewarded with promotion, recognition, and more responsible future assignments. Project management is working in the Defense Department, but improvement continues to be the challenge (19).

Business and Industry

For an organization to survive, prosper, and grow, it must continuously be in interaction with its environment; the technological, political, social, and economic forces are vital factors in decision making. Those organizations which have not maintained this interaction have suffered. Implementation of the project management structure has allowed many organizations to work effectively within their environment.

In a 1984 reorganization, General Motors replaced its decades-old structure of seven divisions and a major subdivision with two super-groups—Buick-Oldsmobile-Cadillac (BOC) and Chevrolet-Pontiac-GM of Canada (CPC). While the five auto divisions continue to exist, they essentially have become marketing arms of the two supergroups. This move involved more than an organizational change; GM also implemented a strategy matrix form of project management. This form of project management was introduced to alleviate the frustrations traditional functional organizations experience in handling interdependent business segments. GM's decision to implement project management was prompted by increasing difficulty in planning, organizing, and controlling the traditional organizational structure. This highly centralized system couples functional lines with matrix management to provide open lines of communication between functions (45).

Another effective project management application is illustrated by an approach taken by BellSouth, Inc., one of the seven regional holding companies formed by the divestiture of American Telephone and Telegraph (AT&T). BellSouth is a holding company that owns two operating companies—South Central Bell and Southern Bell. These two operating companies jointly own BellSouth Services Company, which provides services to both operating companies. Information System Services (ISS) coordinates project management systems development for BellSouth, Inc. ISS utilizes what is termed "centralized project management," a form of project management that is a significant departure from textbook organizational designs. At ISS this approach explicitly recognizes the central role of the project manager in the success of a project throughout its life cycle.

Centralized project management is not suited for organizations with occasional demands for information systems; however, it is a good model for organizations that face continuing demands for the development, implementation, and maintenance of changing information systems. In the ISS approach, a specialized and permanent organization is established that is dedicated to systems planning, design, application, and operation. A significant part of the responsibility of three of the six vice presidents within ISS is project management, an indiciation of the organizational commitment.

The following are the benefits of centralized project management practiced by ISS:

- Projects are managed by professional, experienced project managers, eliminating the beginning-of-project lag that often occurs because a project manager selected from the user organization does not have the proper skills and experience.

- Standards for the development and maintenance of documentation and system interface are determined.
- The integration of information systems throughout the organization is guaranteed; system priorities and possible overlaps are more readily recognized; and work duplication is eliminated.
- There is no split loyalty exhibited between a project and a functional unit, which can occur with project managers in a decentralized approach.

The implementation of centralized project management represents a significant commitment of organizational resources. However, the reduction in the time and expense of developing large-scale systems under this project management structure is more that adequate reward for this commitment (15).

In 1968 Dow-Corning introduced a strategy matrix project management structure in an effort to resolve two specific issues: one, the multidimensional nature of the company's planning, budgeting, and implementation activities, and two, the extreme interdependence of the company's product divisions. This strategy matrix project management structure facilitates the involvement of both business (project) and functional managers in the formulation of organizational objectives and in the implementation of actions for their achievement. Unlike typical hierarchical organizations, decision making is deeply decentralized in the organization, allowing more people to participate in the process. A style of management is encouraged that is characterized by cooperation, trust, and team building among managers (34).

Each business within Dow-Corning is a profit center, although they are not operated as "stand-alone" divisions. A business is managed like a project. The functional managers control the company's scarce resources, while the businesses compete for a share of these pooled resources. Each profit center has its own full-time manager responsible for short-term profitability and long-term performance. Among other responsibilities of these business managers is assessment of product line, development of five-year objectives and strategies, and proposal of specific operating plans and budgets for implementing strategies.

The planning process at Dow-Corning involves the following three major activities within the strategy matrix:

1. The business managers develop one-year business targets, along with five-year objectives.
2. Functional managers allocate resources to the business plans based on the objectives.

3. Detailed cost-center budgets for the coming year are developed from these plans.

Dow-Corning's executive committee carefully reviews these activities at each stage of the planning process. These reviews serve to reconcile the business and integrate functional dimensions.

Since Dow-Corning's successful implementation of strategy matrix project management in 1968, several other major companies have introduced the concept. These companies include IBM and Shell Oil (1972), Velsicol Chemical and Westinghouse (1979), and Citibank and Federal Express (1984) (34).

Although not as dynamic as organizations in rapidly changing technological environments, the banking industry also faces environmental changes in technology, regulation, and competition. In order to adapt to and manage these external forces, banks are using project management more frequently as an administrative tool. The objectives of project management in banking are to provide senior management visibility of major projects and to assign designated project managers responsibility for project cost, time, and performance objectives (18).

Security Pacific Bank of Los Angeles effectively used project management in its automated loan collection system. Under the old system, debt collections were handled manually at each of Security Pacific's 600 loan offices and at collection centers. The bank decided to centralize all collections to six regional adjustment centers in northern and southern California and to a charge card center. Utilizing project management, the $2.3 million development project was completed on time and within budget. Security Pacific estimated it would save $4 million by the end of the first full year of the system's operation (18).

The project management structure implemented was conventional in nature. A project manager was selected and made responsible for overall results and performance. The project manager selected a team comprised of people from the different functional departments involved. This approach provided not only interdisciplinary expertise, but also made better decisions possible when time, cost, or performance trade-offs were necessary. The project team formulated its objectives, financial plan, and schedule. The team met on a regular basis until successful completion of the project. Several distinct phases in the evolution of this project were recognized:

- *Concept phase:* identification of the need was established.
- *Preliminary study:* technical, operational, and economic bases for the project were developed through feasibility studies.

- *In-depth study:* project characteristics were defined. This includes extensive study and analysis and a detailed design and evaluation of alternative solutions.
- *Project development and implementation:* development, procurement, and deployment of all required resources was made.
- *Postproject evaluation:* a written comparison between planned and actual results was made.

Each phase had a distinct beginning and end, but realistically they frequently overlapped. The more they overlapped, the less likely the project objectives were met. Because of the importance of these events in a project life cycle, it is important that senior management formally review each phase upon completion (18).

FACILITATION OF PROJECT MANAGEMENT VIA COMPUTER APPLICATIONS*

The use of computer software to effectively implement and operate project management of complex tasks is commonplace at this time. The software aids project managers in focusing on and controlling criticial segments of the project. Project management software applications range from maintenance of simple bookkeeping systems to multimillion-dollar defense projects. Time, money, and other resource savings may be significant by using project management software.

One reason for this transition from traditional to computerized project management procedures is the increasing power of microcomputers which caused the recent proliferation of project management software packages for personal computers. This trend toward the smaller computer systems facilitates integration from project concept to completion. As these small computers become more powerful and programmers more sophisticated, a full range of project management software will be available for microcomputers (39). Additionally, costs for these software packages continue to decrease due to user demand and intense vendor competition. Original mainframe versions are being scaled down for use on smaller computers, and current packages are offered with more functionality than previously available. Although project managers using these more powerful project management packages may have to invest time in learning the new process, the result is a more effective project management operation (33).

Computer applications are possible in six generic areas in the basic scope and responsibility of a typical project manager. The following are these responsibilities and project management software applications:

---

* See Chapter 28 for a detailed discussion of computer software for project management.

1. *Financial Analysis* - involves planning a project budget, including cost estimates, and resource alloction during the life cycle of the project. Accounting and forecasting programs may be utilized, along with more generalized spreadsheets and data base management messages.
2. *Production Management*—includes planning the production effort of the project, scheduling project milestones, and controlling inventories by determining what resources are needed and scheduling deliveries to interact effectively with the project schedule. Specialized software programs and data base management will meet this requirement.
3. *Forecasting*—involves predicting the future events, requirements, and activities of the project with some degree of accuracy. The project manager will extensively use electronic spreadsheets and computer programs that perform mathematical calculations based on quantitative data.
4. *Report Preparation*—includes all documentation, studies,and reports needed during the project life cycle. Word processing and graphics will be used in this area.
5. *Personal Schedule*—involves the project manager effectively managing his or her time during the project. Specialized programs can be developed to manage the daily and routine matters, while word processing and data base management programs are used to generate necessary lists and documents.
6. *Office Administration*—involves normal office tasks including secretarial work such as typing, generating mailing lists, and personal administration. Word processing and data base management programs will meet these needs (2).

Project managers face myriad responsibilities and details in managing a project to its successful completion. The vast amount of project management software packages available today allows the project manager to fit programs to his or her specific needs. The successful project manager of the present and future must use the computer to the fullest extent possible (2).

In each of the application areas discussed earlier in the chapter (R&D, construction, health care, government/defense, and business and industry) project management is being coupled with computer applications. As software packages become more affordable and projects become more complex in nature, project managers will increasingly adopt and apply computer-aided project management techniques.

In R&D, Goodyear is successfully using a computer-aided design linked to computer-aided manufacturing (CAD-CAM) system. In the technical departments, every professional is given a terminal and access to necessary data bases, which enables them to achieve the highest degree of technological proficiency. CAD-CAM, finite element analysis, and statistical process control are tools Goodyear uses to help reduce testing requirements. These computer uses allow projects to be completed in a shorter life cycle and with less budgetary requirements (6).

One of the earliest uses of project management software was in the construction industry. Computer-aided construction management (CM) was born in the late 1960s when large firms began experimenting with mainframe-based CPM software and automated accounting procedures. Many CM packages are now on microcomputer versions and include scheduling, estimating, job costing, materials handling, equipment inventory, and accounting functions (13).

Management of the Red River Construction Co., Dallas, Texas, measures success by being awarded a bid and then making a profit from the contract. Since adding a computer to its project estimating procedures in 1984, Red River has had a 40% to 50% increase in productivity. In making the estimate, the computer is given the following essential information: manpower requirements, current labor rates, materials required and material costs, subcontract work requirements, and total man-hours anticipated. The company plans to expand the system to include word processing and documentation/report development (3).

Construction firms involved in offshore or arctic activities often face uncertainties due to unpredictable weather conditions. Conventional project management tools are often inadequate in managing weather-sensitive projects. Important issues such as weather downtime and the risk of not completing the project in the limited weather window often cannot be addressed satisfactorily. However, an offshore project simulation program is now available for microcomputers. This program answers "what if" questions in a fast turnaround time, allowing project managers to supplement their own expertise with computer output to make more rational decisions; the results are increased productivity and successibility to weather (10).

When TRW initiated plans to construct a new corporate headquarters in 1979, they utilized computerized facilities design to develop a detailed program which explored several growth scenarios over the anticipated 50-year life of the facility. The needs of the functions to be housed in the corporate headquarters were clearly defined prior to designing the shell of the building. The factors evaluated were:

- The building's design concept and unique design aspects.
- The ongoing assets management needs.
- The facility management process, including planning and design.

The design of the building constructed will allow TRW flexibility at its headquarters for decades (32).

Hospitals using a product management structure are finding they must put a priority on the quality of medical records and the coding of diagnoses and procedures. Administrators making decisions on expanded product lines and services must have access to timely patient data base information. Successful hospital product and data management requires the following:

- Satisfying the information needs for all staff and functional departments.
- Implementing procedures to collect, process, store, retrieve, collate, and distribute the data.
- Evaluating data quality (input and output).
- Assisting data end-users in obtaining and analyzing reports.
- Ensuring that system design objectives are being met.

The basic tenets of hospital record keeping have not changed; they have been improved and expanded by computer technology to enhance product management administration (20).

The Westinghouse Marine Division, a prime contractor to the U.S. Navy, has applied project management microcomputer technology to the Trident II Missile Launching and Handling (ML&H) system being developed for the government. Westinghouse has found the microcomputer useful for many aspects of this project. More daily uses are found as the staff becomes more familiar with the system. Administrative functions are performed in a more efficient manner, and communications have been enhanced. Specific areas of project management that have been improved in this application include planning and scheduling, organizational information lists, budget sheets, scope of work documents, and manpower planning (29).

The military is currently using computerized project management in some areas. For example, the U.S. Marine Corps' Central Design and Programming Activity in Albany, Georgia, has been effectively using project management software for years. However, this use is not mandatory on all military hardware projects. Mandatory computerized project management would provide Congress and other interested agencies a review process to ensure that projects/programs are proceeding according to budget and schedule. Pentagon officials would be more accountable on a "real-time" basis for these multibillion-dollar budgets and projects. Cost overruns and scheduling problems could be identified earlier and resolved more quickly (31).

Iowa Beef Processing, Inc. (IBP) has in-house construction and engineering departments for building and maintaining their plants and offices. These functional departments fluctuate between 100 and 300 employees and are accountable for $40 million to $80 million a year in capital expenditures. Large-volume materials as well as specialized equipment are purchased. To keep track of the many ongoing projects, IBP uses a Capital Project Management System (CPMS) software package from Data Design Associates. In order to get the right information to the right people on a timely basis, CPMS uses a three-tier, hierarchical reporting system. At the project level, reports provide an overview for top-level management and others not involved in the daily operation. At the work unit level, reports are geared to the project managers in the field. Finally, the detail level reports are used by functional specialists such as engineers, accountants, and others responsible for the daily operation of the Engineering and Construction groups. These reports ensure that projects are proceeding in a timely and cost-effective manner, as well as providing needed accountability (28).

The fifth-generation computer systems now being developed will have capabilities from those now used. These Knowledge Information Processing Systems (KIPS) will select, interpret, and adapt huge amounts of information, giving the system the ability to reason. Their artificial intelligence will enable them to learn, make inferences, and reach decisions. The impact of these systems will be significant in many areas, but especially so in project management which involves the interaction of several different disciplines simultaneously. This vast storage of information, combined with superfast processing speeds and reasoning ability, will allow these machines to operate like thousands of experts functioning as one entity. Should only a part of the promise of these machines become reality, project management will experience revolutionary changes (35).

SUMMARY AND CONCLUSIONS

This chapter has reviewed several project management applications and the characteristics of organizations that have utilized project management systems. The ultimate product of these organizations may be an advanced weapon system, automobiles, an offshore oil rig, steel, national defense, or improved health care. The major determinants in considering the implementation and operation of a project management system include such factors as a technologically dynamic and highly uncertain environment, an organizational structure enabling rapid response to change, identifiable performance and cost objectives, and simultaneous coordination of two or more functional departments (interdisciplinary tasks).

In order to evaluate an organization from a system perspective, one is required to consider the organizational structure as a totality with input, transformation, and output processes functioning within greater environmental systems. Two major points must be understood: one is the nature of the interface of the system with its environmental systems; the other is the nature of the complex interdependencies of parts within the system itself. Although organizations vary greatly in their inputs, transformation mechanisms, and output components, they are strikingly similar with respect to the nature of the external environmental forces impacting on them. The organizational structure chosen to manage such diverse projects, tasks, programs, and products must not only be adaptable to internal and external environmental forces, but also provide for a degree of stability. The project management applications reviewed illustrate that it is meeting these requirements.

It is the authors' belief that organizations with varying technologies and differing organizational objectives may still benefit from the implementation of project management. The many well-documented cases cited here and in other literature reinforce this contention. However, organizations contemplating the adoption of project management must consider the specific aspects of its internal and external environments previously described. It has been observed that coordination costs increase as organizations strive to increase specialization to cope with rapidly advancing technology. This implies that the strategic and competitive health of an organization is contingent upon a systems perspective. This perspective allows the organizational design to be an effective trade-off between the cost and benefit factors inherent in the processes of growing specialization and more complex coordination requirements.

Project management was determined to have wide application to research and development organizations because of structural similarities: technologically complex environments, large specialized staffs requiring interfunctional integration, and differentiated outputs. Resistance to change in organizations can be a common problem among specialized professionals in these organizations. Competition among R&D groups in similar industries is critical in the contemporary environment, and those who become most successful will do so by efficiently managing their resources and evolving new products needed and wanted by their customers. Project management has proven to be effective in these roles.

The implementation of project management in the construction field resulted from the need for communication and information flows, interdisciplinary efforts, cost containment, time management, and complexities involved in the materials ordering and handling process. The construction projects cited are similar in that they all involve large numbers of employees with a wide variety of expertise and specialization. They are subject to varying environmental pressures requiring interfunctional integration for specific output with time, cost, and performance parameters inherent in the process.

Organizations in highly uncertain, dynamic environments, which must function for rapid response to internal and external changes, and those organizations with tasks requiring a high degree of reciprocal interfunctional coordination are also prime candidates for project management. Because their services and/or products require an integrated interfunctional orientation, more contempory service organizations are adopting and implementing project, program, team/task force, or product management because the project structure is appropriate and contributes to the more effective achievement of organizational goals and objectives.

Conclusions

This chapter provides a working definition of project management including general guidelines for use in evaluating its applicability; it also familiarizes the reader with recent project management applications and pertinent special factors involved. The bibliography enables the reader to go directly to the source should more in-depth information be required.

The emergence of computer applications to the field of project management has had far-reaching implications. With these innovations, more and more contemporary organizations are determining that some form of project management is applicable to their situation. As these programs become more sophisticated, they will become more readily available to smaller-size organizations; indeed, these programs are being increasingly designed for microcomputers. Computer-managed project management applications will make project management more attractive as implementation and maintenance costs decrease. Organizations already utilizing project management will also benefit from this technology because it helps managers to perform more accurate and reliable planning, coordination, and control of their project/task.

Project management has the potential for contributing to more effective achievement of organizational objectives if internal and external environmental forces justify its use. However, project management cannot, and should not, be considered a panacea for all organizational tasks. It is the authors' contention that the increasing complexity and dynamism of to-day's organizational environment reflected in this review, coupled with innovative computer technology, enable growing applications of project management. The "networking" of microcomputers with each other and with mainframes will give the project and functional managers previously unavailable capability to achieve the required interfaces and integration necessary for project, interfunctional, and interorganizational task success.

The applications discussed and reviewed in this chapter illustrate that there is no one best way to apply and implement project management. Inherent in the concept of project management is the capability to be adaptive to varying organizational and environmental situations; it clearly indicates the essence of the contingency approach to management. The authors forecast that the applications of project management, undoubtedly with many modifications from the traditional applications, will increase significantly since the power and capability of the microcomputer (personal computer) will be readily available at the operating management levels in most organizations.

BIBLIOGRAPHY

1. Adams, John, R. Barndt, Stephen E. and Martin D. (eds.). *Managing by Project Management* (Universal Technology Corp. Dayton, Ohio, 1979), pp. 1–14.
2. Adams, John R. and Morris, Jackelyn Kelley. "Microcomputer Usage for Project Management." *1984 Proceedings of the Project Management Institute* (The Project Management Institute. Drexel Hill, Pa., 1984), pp. 296–304.
3. Adams, John R. and Morris, Jackelyn Kelley. "A Farewell Bid." *Infosystems* (January, 1985), p. 102.
4. Alvi, Akhtar A. and Methven, Andrea L. "Project Management of a Billion Dollar Refinery Expansion." *1985 Proceedings of the Project Management Institute* (The Project Management Institute. Drexel Hill, Pa., 1985), Track 1.
5. Arnold, Kenneth E. "Modified Turnkey Approach Can Cut Cost of Marsh and Shallow-water Projects." *Oil and Gas Journal* (December 17, 1984), pp. 71–77.
6. Barrett, Tom H. "Research and Manufacturing Share a Common World." *New Management* (March–April, 1986), pp. 23–25.
7. Burck, Charles G. "How G. M. Turned Itself Around." *Fortune* (January 16, 1978), pp. 87–96.
8. Byers, Luanne. "The U.S. Pharmaceutical Industry—A Standard for Success." *1985 Proceedings of the Project Management Institute* (The Project Management Institute, Drexel Hill, Pa., 1985), Track 3.
9. Cathey, Paul. "How Metals Industry Uses Management Tools." *Iron Age* (November 20, 1978), pp. 38–41.
10. Chen, Henry. "Computer Program Uses Simulation Method to Help Manage Weather-Sensitive Projects." *Oil and Gas Journal* (June 24, 1985), pp. 80–86.
11. Cleland, David I. and King, William R. *Systems Analysis and Project Management*, 3rd Ed. (McGraw-Hill. New York, 1983), pp. 187–265.

12. Cobbs, John L. (ed). "G.M.'s Test of Participating." *Business Week* (February 23, 1976), pp. 89–90.
13. Cobbs, John L. "Contractors Wrangle with Planning." *Engineering-News Record* (May 31, 1984), pp. 54–58.
14. Craig, Carol. "Hospital Product Line Survey." Swedish Health Systems, August, 1985.
15. Dilworth, James B., et al. "Centralized Project Management." *Journal of Systems Management* (August, 1985), pp. 30–35.
16. Dixon, Maureen. "Matrix Organization in Health Services," in *Matrix Management— A Cross-Functional Approach to Organization,* ed. Knight, Kenneth (Gower Press. Great Britain, 1977), pp. 82–90.
17. Easton, James. "Long-Term Effects of Project and Project Management on a Large Public Works Organization." *1978 Proceedings of the Project Management Institute* (The Project Management Institute. Drexel Hill, Pa., 1978), pp. IVG.1IV19.
18. Einstein, Harold B. "Project Management: A Banking Case Study." *Magazine of Bank Administration* (April, 1982), pp. 36–40.
19. Fox, J. Ronald. "Revamping the Business of National Defense", *Harvard Business Review* (September-October, 1984), pp. 63–70.
20. Fox, Leslie Ann and Tucker, Jeanne. "Product Management Spurs Emphasis on Medical Records." *Hospitals* (March 1, 1985), pp. 92–94.
21. Fraylick, J. R. "How to Start Up Major Facilities (Trans Alaska Pipeline)." *Oil and Gas Journal* (December 3, 1984), pp. 112–115 and (December 10, 1984), pp. 92–94.
22. Gallagher, Susan C. "The Management of World-Wide Pharmaceutical Development Utilizing Geographically Spread Resources." *1975 Proceedings of the Project Management Institute* (The Project Management Institute. Drexel Hill, Pa., 1975), pp. 143–145.
23. Grudzinshas, Charles V. "Change + Communication = Challenge (Management of Pharmaceutical R & D Projects)." *1985 Proceedings of the Project Management Institute* (The Project Management Institute. Drexel Hill, Pa., 1985), Track 3.
24. Gung, H. P. and Pearson, A. W. "Matrix Organization in Research and Development," in *Matrix Management—A Cross-Functional Approach to Organization,* ed. Knight, Kenneth (Gower Press. Great Britain, 1977), pp. 23–44.
25. Katz, Ralph and Allan, Thomas. "Project Performance and the Locus of Influence in the R & D Matrix." *Academy of Management Journal* (March, 1985), pp. 67–87.
26. Kelley, P. A. "Success for Defense Projects." *1985 Proceedings of the Project Management Institute* (The Project Management Institute. Drexel Hill, Pa., 1985), Track 4.
27. Knudson, Robert E. "Case Study of the Successful Development of a Real Estate Project." *1985 Proceedings of the Project Management Institute* (The Project Management Institute. Drexel Hill, Pa., 1985), Track 2.
28. Kohlowski, David. "Capital Project Management System." *Management Accounting* (March, 1986), pp. 69–70.
29. Kohrs, Robert H. "Implementation of the Microcomputer in a Project Management Environment." *1984 Proceedings of the Project Management Institute* (The Project Management Institute. Drexel Hill, Pa., 1984), pp. 311–318.
30. MacStravic, Robin Scott. "Product-Line Administration in Hospitals." *HCM Review* (Spring, 1968), pp. 35–43.
31. Mandrell, Mel. "Budget-Balancing Computers." *Computer Decisions* (February 25, 1986), p. 12.
32. Mayne, Alfred P., Jr. and Wade, A. Dale. "Computerizing Facilities Design." *Industrial Development* (July/August, 1984), pp. 4–8.
33. Morrison, David. "High-Power Project Management." *Computer Decisions* (January 14, 1986), pp. 39–42.

34. Naylor, Thomas H. "The Case for the Strategy Matrix." *New Management* (Summer, 1986), pp. 38–42.

35. Pandia, Rafeev M. "Impact of Super-Computers on Project Management." *1984 Proceedings of the Project Management Institute* (The Project Management Institute. Drexel Hill, Pa., 1984), pp. 374–383.

36. Patrick, Miles G. "Implementing a Project Management System in a Research Laboratory." *1979 Proceedings of the Project Management Institute* (The Project Management Institute. Drexel Hill, Pa., 1979), pp. 243–252.

37. Peters, Frederick. "NASA Management of the Space Shuttle Program." *1975 Proceeding of the Project Management Institute* (The Project Management Institute. Drexel Hill, Pa., 1975), p. 154.

38. Robinson, Clarence A., Jr. (ed.) "Matrix System Enhances Management." *Aviation Week and Space Technology* (January 31, 1977), pp. 41–58.

39. Robbins, Clarence A., Jr. "Scouting the Management Trail." *Engineering-News Record* (May 31, 1984), pp. 45–53.

40. Schrontz, M. P., Porter, G. M. and Scott, N. C. "Organization and Management of a Multi-Organizational Single Responsibility Project—The James H. Campbell Power Plant—Unit #3." *1977 Proceedings of the Project Management Institute* (The Project Management Institute. Drexel Hill, Pa., 1977), pp. 258–264.

41. Stickney, Frank A. and Johnson, William R. "Communication: The Key to Integration." *1980 Proceedings of the Project Management Institute* (The Project Management Institute. Drexel Hill, Pa., 1980), p. I-A.7.

42. Trembly, Ara C. "Getting More From Your Key Resources." *Computer Decisions* (September 15, 1984), pp. 89–94.

43. Verma, Vijay, K. "Achieving Excellence Through Project Management in R&D Environments." *1985 Proceedings of the Project Management Institute* (The Project Management Institute. Drexel Hill, Pa., 1985), Track 3.

44. White, Stephen L. "The Community Mental Health Center as a Matrix Organization."' *Administration in Mental Health* (Winter, 1978), pp. 99–106.

45. Whiteside, David E. "Roger Smith's Campaign to Change the F.M. Culture." *Business Week* (April 7, 1986), pp. 84–85.

46. Wood, William R., et al. "Product-Line Management: Final Report and Recommendations." Miami Valley Hospital, April, 1985.

35. Factors Affecting Project Success*

Bruce N. Baker†
David C. Murphy
Dalmar Fisher

Why are some projects perceived as failures when they have met all the objective standards of success:

- —completed on time,
- —completed within budget,
- —all technical specifications met?

On the other hand, why are some projects perceived as successful when they have failed to meet two important objective standards associated with success:

- —not completed on time,
- —not completed within budget?

* The study reported in this chapter was conducted under the sponsorship of the National Aeronautics and Space Administration, NGR 22-03-028. The complete report is entitled, *Determinants of Project Success,* by David C. Murphy, Bruce N. Baker, and Dalmar Fisher. It may be obtained from the National Technical Information Services, Springfield, Va. 22151, by referencing the title and the Accession number: N-74-30392, September 15, 1974.

† Dr. Bruce N. Baker is Program Manager of Information and Computer Security at SRI International. He conducts project management seminars and is a frequent speaker on the topics of improving teamwork and success in project management environments. He received his A.B. degree from Princeton University, his M.B.A. degree from Stanford University, and his D.P.A. degree from the George Washington University.

David C. Murphy is an Associate Professor at the Boston College School of Management. His research and publications have been concerned with project and program management, strategy and policy formulation, environmental analysis, and organizational decentralization. He has served as editor of *Project Management Quarterly,* and is an active member of several professional societies including the Project Management Institute. He received the D.B.A. degree from Indiana University.

Dalmar Fisher is Associate Professor of Organizational Studies at the Boston College School of Management, where he teaches courses in organizational behavior and administrative strategy. He has authored several articles and books in the areas of organizational communication, project management, and managerial behavior, and has served as associate editor of *Project Management Quarterly.* He received his D.B.A. degree from Harvard Business School.

WHAT CONSTITUTES SUCCESS FOR A PROJECT?

If project success cannot be considered simply a matter of completing the project on schedule, staying within the budget constraints, and meeting the technical performance criteria, then how should project success be defined?

The research conducted by the authors on some 650 projects supports the following definition of success:

If the project meets the technical performance specifications and/or mission to be performed, and if there is a high level of satisfaction concerning the project outcome among key people in the parent organization, key people in the client organization, key people on the project team, and key users or clientele of the project effort, the project is considered an overall success.

Perceptions play a strong role in this definition. Therefore, the definition is more appropriately termed, "perceived success of a project." What types of variables contribute to perceptions of success and failure? One would certainly assume that good schedule performance and good cost performance would be key ingredients of the perceptions of success and failure. But note that schedule and cost performance are not included in the above definition.

How do cost and schedule performance relate to the perceived failure and success of projects? It was found that cost and schedule overruns were not included in a list of 29 project management characteristics significantly related to perceived project failure. See Table 35-1. Conversely, good cost and schedule performance were not included in a list of 23 project management characteristics significantly related to perceived success, Table 35-2. Nor were cost and schedule performance included in the list of ten project management characteristics found to be linearly related to both perceived success and perceived failure, Table 35-3. If the study had been conducted solely on aerospace projects, this might not have been too surprising, but aerospace projects represented less than 20% of the responses. For project managers and project personnel who have constantly lived with heavy emphasis upon meeting schedules and staying within budgets, this finding may be difficult to swallow. A partial explanation may be as follows: the survey was concerned only with *completed* projects. As perspective is developed on a project, the ultimate satisfaction of the parent, the client, the ultimate users, and the project team is most closely related to whether the project end-item is performing as desired. A schedule delay and a budget overrun may seem somewhat

Table 35-1. Project Management Characteristics Which Strongly Affect the Perceived Failure of Projects (The absence of these characteristics does not ensure perceived success).

- Insufficient use of status/progress reports.
- Use of superficial status/progress reports.
- Inadequate project manager administrative skills.
- Inadequate project manager human skills.
- Inadequate project manager technical skills.
- Insufficient project manager influence.
- Insufficient project manager authority.
- Insufficient client influence.
- Poor coordination with client.
- Lack of rapport with client.
- Client disinterest in budget criteria.
- Lack of project team participation in decision-making.
- Lack of project team participation in major problem solving.
- Excessive structuring within the project team.
- Job insecurity within the project team.
- Lack of team spirit and sense of mission within project team.
- Parent organization stable, non-dynamic, lacking strategic change.
- Poor coordination with parent organization.
- Lack of rapport with parent organization.
- Poor relations within the parent organization.
- New "type" of project.
- Project more complex than the parent has completed previously.
- Initial under-funding.
- Inability to freeze design early.
- Inability to close-out the effort.
- Unrealistic project schedules.
- Inadequate change procedures.
- Poor relations with public officials.
- Unfavorable public opinion.

The lists in Tables 35-1, 2, and 3 are based on statistical tests in which data about each project management characteristic were grouped according to whether the project's success was rated in the upper third (successful), middle third, or lower third (unsuccessful).

unimportant as time goes on, in the face of a high degree of satisfaction and a sound foundation for future relationships. Conversely, few can legitimately claim that "the operation was a success but the patient died." If the survey had been conducted on current, ongoing projects only, the management emphasis upon meeting schedules and staying within budgets would undoubtedly have been reflected more heavily in the research results. Moreover, good cost and schedule performance *were* correlated with success but to a lesser degree than the items listed in Table 35-2.

Table 35-2. Project Management Characteristics Stongly Associated with Perceived Success. (The following were found to be necessary, but not sufficient conditions for perceived success.)

- Frequent feedback from the parent organization.
- Frequent feedback from the client.
- Judicious use of networking techniques.
- Availability of back-up strategies.
- Organization structure suited to the project team.
- Adequate control procedures, especially for dealing with changes.
- Project team participation in determining schedules and budgets.
- Flexible parent organization.
- Parent commitment to established schedules.
- Parent enthusiasm.
- Parent commitment to established budget.
- Parent commitment to technical performance goals.
- Parent desire to build-up internal capabilities.
- Project manager commitment to established schedules.
- Project manager commitment to established budget.
- Project manager commitment to technical performance goals.
- Client commitment to established schedules.
- Client commitment to established budget.
- Client commitment to technical performance goals.
- Enthusiastic public support.
- Lack of legal encumbrances.
- Lack of excessive government red tape.
- Minimized number of public/government agencies involved.

Table 35-3. Project Management Characteristics Strongly Linearly Related to Both Perceived Success and Perceived Failure. (The presence of these characteristics tends to improve perceived success while their absence contributes to perceived failure.)

- Goal commitment of project team.
- Accurate initial cost estimates.
- Adequate project team capability.
- Adequate funding to completion.
- Adequate planning and control techniques.
- Minimal start-up difficulties.
- Task (vs. social) orientation.
- Absence of bureaucracy.
- On-site project manager.
- Clearly established success criteria.

ANALYSIS OF VARIABLES ASSOCIATED WITH PERCEIVED SUCCESS AND VARIABLES ASSOCIATED WITH PERCEIVED FAILURE

The listings of variables associated with perceived success and failure, Tables 35-1, 35-2, and 35-3, are much lengthier than anticipated. For a project to be perceived as successful, many, if not most, of the variables associated with success must be present. The absence of even one factor or inattention to one factor can be sufficient to result in perceived project failure. Similarly, most, if not all, of the variables associated with perceived failure must be absent. To add to the fragility of perceived success, the variables must be present or absent in the right degree. For example, project management is closely associated with the use of PERT and CPM networking systems.* So much so, that many managers consider project management and networking systems as synonymous terms.

Is the use of PERT-CPM systems the most important factor contributing to project success?

No. PERT-CPM systems *do* contribute to project success, especially when initial overoptimism and/or a "buy-in" strategy has prevailed in the securing of the contract, but the importance of PERT-CPM is far outweighed by a host of other factors including the use of project tools known as "systems management concepts." These include work breakdown structures, life-cycle planning, systems engineering, configuration management, and status reports. The overuse of PERT-CPM systems was found to hamper success. It was the *judicious* use of PERT-CPM which was associated with success. An important military satellite program was actually hampered by early reliance upon a network that covered four walls of a large conference room. The tool was too cumbersome and consumed too much time to maintain it. Fortunately, someone decided that the network was a classified document and ordered curtains to be placed over the walls. Once the curtains were up, they were never drawn again and the project proceeded as planned. More often than not, however, networking *does* contribute to better cost and schedule performance (but not necessarily to better technical performance).

GENERAL STRATEGIES FOR DIRECTING PROJECTS

Based upon the factors associated with success and the factors associated with failure, a set of general strategies can be developed for directing projects. Some of the strategies tend to be counterintuitive or counter to traditional practice. The somewhat controversial general strategies are

---

* See Chapter 15.

presented in the form of statements which the reader is asked to indicate as true or false.

A matrix form of project organizational structure is the least disruptive to traditional functional organizational patterns and is also most likely to result in project success. True or false?

False. Although there are no clear definitions of the different forms of project organizational structures which have attained widespread acceptance, there are some terms which imply certain patterns. The matrix form of organization is well understood by experienced project management personnel, but the authority which goes with such a matrix form of structure varies considerably. In order to provide a spectrum of choices which attempted to avoid preconception of terms, the following organizational patterns were presented for describing the organizational structure of the project team as it existed during the peak activity period of the project:

- Pure Functional—Project manager, if any, was merely the focal point for communications; he had no authority to direct people other than by persuasion or reporting to his own superior.
- Weak Matrix—Project manager was the focal point for controls; he did not actively direct the work of others.
- Strong Matrix or Partially Projectized—Project manager was the focal point for directions and controls; he may have had some engineering and control personnel reporting to him on a line basis, while remainder of the project team was located administratively in other departments.
- Projectized—Project manager had most of the essential elements of the project team under him.
- Fully Projectized—Project manager had almost all of the employees who were on the project team under him.

Each of these organizational arrangements was associated with perceived success in certain situations, but an F-test of these different forms of organizational structure compared with perceived project success revealed that the projectized form of organizational structure is most often associated with perceived success. In general, it is important for the project manager of a large, long-duration project to have key functions of the project team under him.

In the early days of the Ranger and Surveyor lunar research programs, the project managers had only a handful of people reporting to them on a line basis. Both of these programs were relatively unsuccessful as compared to the Lunar Orbiter program, which employed a projectized organization from the start.*

The question remains, however, how should the decision-making authority of the project manager relate to the decision-making authority of the client organization (the organization which sponsored, approved, and funded the effort), and the parent organization (the organization structure above the level of the project manager but within the same overall organization)?

When a project is critical to the overall success of a company and/or it is critical to the client organization, the parent organization and/or the client organization should take a strong and active role in internal project decision making. True or false?

False. It is important for the client organization to establish definitive goals for a project. Similarly, especially for in-house projects, the parent organization must also establish clear and definitive goals for the project. When there is a good consensus among the client organization, the parent organization, and the project team with respect to the goals of a project, then success is more readily achieved. A path analysis revealed that success criteria salience and consensus are especially important for:

- Projects with complex legal/political environments.
- Projects which are relatively large.
- Projects undertaken within a parent organization undergoing considerable change.

Once success criteria have been clarified and agreed upon by the principal parties involved with a project, that is, the client, the parent, and the project team, then it is essential to permit the project team to "carry the ball" with respect to internal decisions.

Because some decisions require the approval of the client organization, it was found that the authority of the client contact should be commensurate with the authority of the project manager. Projects characterized by strong project manager authority and influence and strong client contact authority and influence were strongly associated with success. Unfortunately, many client organizations and parent organizations tend to believe that the more closely they monitor a project and the more intimately they enter into the internal project decision process, the more likely the project

---

* Many comparisons between the Surveyor program and the Lunar Orbiter program support the findings of this chapter. See Erasmus H. Kloman, *Unmanned Space Project Management—Surveyor and Lunar Orbiter,* a report prepared by the National Academy of Public Administration and sponsored by the National Aeronautics and Space Administration, Washington, D.C.: U.S. Government Printing Office (1972).

is to be successful. Close coordination and good relations patterns were found to be the most important factors contributing to perceived project success. Nonethelesss, there is a very important distinction between "close" and "meddling" and there is just as important a distinction between "supportive" and "interfering" relationships. Many factors and relationships pointed to the need for the client and the parent organization to develop close and supportive working relationships with the project team but to avoid meddling or interfering with the project team's decision-making processes. The lesson is clear: the project manager should be delegated sufficient authority to make important project decisions and sufficient authority to direct the project team. In the case of the Polaris program, for example, the head of the Special Projects Office of the U.S. Navy had extensive authority with respect to contracting arrangements. This level of authority, combined with strong levels of authority for the project managers in the contractors' plants, was a major factor contributing to the success of that program. Once given this authority, how should the project manager arrive at decisions and solve problems?

Because participative decision making and problem solving can tend to slow up the decision-making and problem-solving processes, these approaches should not be employed on complex projects having tight schedules. True or false?

False. First of all, participative decision making and problem solving within the project team was highly correlated with success for the total sample of projects. Second, a path analysis* revealed that under some conditions of adversity, such as a highly complex project, or one where initial overoptimism prevailed regarding the time and cost for completing the project, it was especially important to employ participative approaches to overcome these adversities.

If this pattern is successful, should the public also participate in project decisions affecting the public interest?

Public participation is an essential ingredient of success for projects affecting the public interest. True or false?

Mostly false. Although the trend of the past two decades has certainly been in this direction, that is, to encourage, or at least to facilitate, public participation in the decision-making process for public projects, and although value judgments may lean heavily toward this approach, the facts are that public participation often delays and hampers projects and reduces the probability of success.

Therefore, from a management standpoint (not from a value judgment standpoint), public participation should be minimized, avoided, or cir-

---

* A statistical procedure. Path analysis is explained on pp. 928–929.

cumvented as much as possible. Public participation is, of course, a legal requirement for most public projects but there seems to be little reason for overdoing it.

If too much public participation hampers success, can the cooperation and participation of several agencies help to safeguard the public interest and result in a more successful overall effort than a project undertaken by a single agency?

Public projects involving the cooperation, funding, and participation of several governmental agencies are more likely to be successful than projects undertaken by a single agency. True or false?

False. Again, the trend is certainly in this direction. There has been a great deal of emphasis upon:

- Interagency cooperative efforts, for example, Departments of Labor, Commerce, and Transportation.
- Intergovernmental cooperative efforts, for example, federal, state, and local jointly funded efforts.
- The creation of new, integrative agencies, for example, regional commissions combining the efforts of several states, counties, or cities to attack common problems.

Although the creation of these jointly funded, jointly managed organizational mechanisms may be desirable from the standpoint of integration of efforts, they tend to result in less successful projects as compared to projects undertaken by a single source of funding and authority. Such cooperative efforts often result in the creation of elaborate bureaucratic structures, decision delays, red tape, and relatively diminished success. The New England Regional Commission is an example of an agency which consumed millions of dollars for its own bureaucracy but failed to accomplish much of anything for New England.

Many discussions of project management focus upon qualities of an ideal project manager.

It is much more important for a project manager to be an effective administrator than to be a competent technical person or to possess good human relations skills. True or false?

Mostly false. All three types of skills (technical skills, human skills, and administrative skills) were found to be important but technical skills were found to be most important, followed by human skills, and then by administrative skills.

It is true that technically oriented scientists and engineers who are placed into project manager positions often perform poorly from an administrative and human relations standpoint but, on the other hand, some of the most costly blunders have been made by administrators of proven competence who ventured into unfamiliar areas. During the past two decades, much progress has been made in training technical people to acquire effective human relations and administrative skills.

Leadership style has been the subject of a great deal of research.

The most effective project managers are nondirective, human rela- tions-oriented leaders as opposed to directive, managing, task-oriented leaders. True or false?

Mostly false. Fiedler, for one, conducted extensive research on this subject, finding that, "In very favorable or in very unfavorable situations for getting a task accomplished by group effort, the autocratic, task- controlling, managing leadership works best. In situations intermediate in difficulty, the nondirective, permissive leader is most successful."*

The research described in this chapter supports the concept of a leader who is task-oriented with a backup social orientation for *most* project efforts. Does this contradict Fiedler's research and the previous state- ment that project team participation in decision making and problem solv- ing is important to project success? The authors believe that there is no contradiction. An effective project manager is generally one who is com- mitted to the goals of the project and constantly stresses the importance of meeting those project goals. Yet, he calls upon key project team mem- bers to assist with problem solving and decision making. In *some* very straightforward or very chaotic settings, a project manager may find an autocratic style to be most effective. And, as Fiedler's research suggests, a project manager may need to employ different leadership styles at dif- ferent times during the project effort.

More recent writers on leadership have argued that the effective leader not only responds to settings and situations that present themselves, but shapes and transforms the circumstances by reframing problems and goals in insightful ways that sharpen task definitions and arouse height- ened levels of commitment by team members†. Our data support this concept of the effective project manager as one who can respond to realities "incrementally," but who can also define general strategies and spark others' commitment to them.

A comprehensive list of general strategies is shown in Table 35-4. Strat- egy guidelines are presented for the client organization, the parent organi-

* Fred E. Fiedler, "Engineer the Job to Fit the Manager," *Harvard Business Review* (Sep- tember–October, 1965), p. 18.
† Christ Argyris and Donald A. Schon, *Organizational Learning* (Reading, Mass.: Addison- Wesley, 1978); and Bernard M. Bass, *Leadership and Performance Beyond Expectations* (New York: Free Press, 1985).

Table 35-4. General Strategies for Directing Projects.

	CONCEPTUAL PHASE (BEFORE THE INVITATIONS FOR BID)	BID, PROPOSAL, CONTRACT DEFINITION, AND NEGOTIATION PHASE (BEFORE CONTRACT AWARD OR GO-AHEAD)	IMPLEMENTATION PHASE (AFTER CONTRACT AWARD OR GO-AHEAD)
The Client Organization and/or Principal Client Contact	Encourage openness & honesty from the start from all participants.		Develop close, but not meddling, work relationships with project participants.
	Create an atmosphere that encourages healthy, but not cutthroat, competition or "liars' contests." Plan for adequate funding to complete the entire project.	Reject "buy-ins."	Avoid arms-length relationships.
		Make prompt decisions regarding contract award or go-ahead.	Do not insist upon excessive reporting schemes.
	Develop clear understandings of the relative importance of cost, schedule, and technical performance goals.		
	Seek to minimize public participation and involvement. Develop short and informal lines of communication and flat organizational structures.		
	Delegate sufficient authority to the principal client contact and let him promptly approve or reject important project decisions.		

The Parent Organization and/or Principal Parent Contact

- Select, at an early point, a project manager with a proven track record of technical skills, human skills, & administrative skills (in that order) to lead the project team.
- Develop clear and workable guidelines for your project manager.

  → Do not exert excessive pressure on the project manager to win the contract.

  → Do not slash or balloon the project team's cost estimates.

  → Avoid "buy-ins."

- Delegate sufficient authority to your project manager and let him make important decisions in conjunction with his key project team members.

  → Develop close, but not meddling, working relationships with the principal client contact and the project manager

- Demonstrate enthusiasm for and commitment to the project and the project team.
- Develop and maintain short and informal lines of communication with the project manager.

- Insist upon the right to select your own key project team members

  → Call upon key project team members to assist in decision-making and problem solving.

  → Employ a workable and candid set of project planning and control tools.

Table 35-4. General Strategies for Directing Projects (*continued*)

	CONCEPTUAL PHASE (BEFORE THE INVITATIONS FOR BID)	BID, PROPOSAL, CONTRACT DEFINITION, AND NEGOTIATION PHASE (BEFORE CONTRACT AWARD OR GO-AHEAD)	IMPLEMENTATION PHASE (AFTER CONTRACT AWARD OR GO-AHEAD)
The Project Manager and/or the Project Team	Select key team members with proven track records in their area of expertise.	Develop realistic cost, schedule, and technical performance estimates & goals.	Avoid preoccupation with, or over-reliance upon, one type of project control tool.
	Develop commitment and a sense of mission from the outset among project team members.	Develop back-up strategies and systems in anticipation of potential problems.	Constantly stress the importance of meeting cost, schedule and technical performance goals.
	Seek sufficient authority and a projectized form of organizational structure.	Develop an appropriate, yet flexible and flat, project team organization structure.	Generally, give highest priority to achieving the technical performance mission or function to be performed by the project end-item.
	Coordinate frequently and constantly reinforce good relationships with the client, the parent, and your team.	Seek to maintain your influence over people and key decisions even though your formal authority may not be sufficient.	Keep changes under control.
	Seek to enhance the public' image of the project.		Seek to find ways of assuring the job security of effective project team members.
			Plan for an orderly phase-out of the project

zation, and the project team for three distinct phases of a project. It is important to note (1) the interlocking and interdependent relationships among the three organizational groups involved, and (2) that two of the three phases leading to overall perceived success occur before contract award or go-ahead. Although different combinations are needed for success in various situations and environments, these general strategies seem to apply to most situations.

KEY FACTORS TO MAXIMIZE POTENTIAL OF PERCEIVED PROJECT SUCCESS

Up to this point, the ingredients to assure success and to avoid failure have been somewhat overwhelming. This portion of the chapter will attempt to focus in on the key factors which appear to be most important for achieving high levels of perceived success.

In reexamining Table 35-1, one can see that a large number of the variables associated with perceived failure center about poor coordination and human relations patterns. Therefore, in order to minimize the chances of perceived failure, project managers are well advised to put heavy emphasis on establishing good, effective patterns of coordination and human relations. Such emphasis may eliminate failure but may not necessarily promote success. Table 35-2 sheds light on the need for good, tight controls and commitment to the goals that have been established for a project in order to achieve high levels of perceived success.

Tables 35-1, 35-2, 35-3, and 35-4 also point to another important strategy: effective project planning is absolutely essential to project success. Of the 29 items listed in Table 35-1, over half the variables associated with perceived failure can be avoided through effective project planning. The role of project planning is even more apparent in Table 35-2. Almost every one of the variables associated with success is determined by, or can be significantly influenced by, effective project planning. Finally, every one of the items listed in Table 35-3 is intimately related to the project planning process. As stated previously, two of the three phases of strategies shown in Table 35-4 occur before actual work on the project end-item begins. Therefore, effective project planning is very important to project success.

In addition to the analyses summarized to this point, stepwise multiple regression analysis was conducted to determine the independent contribution of some 32 factors to Perceived Success. It should be re-emphasized that technical performance was integrally associated with success and was part of Perceived Success itself. Beyond technical performance, however, what are the principal factors contributing to project success?

Table 35.5 The Relative Importance of the Factors Contributing to Perceived Project Success.

DETERMINING FACTORS	STANDARDIZED REGRESSION COEFFICIENT	SIGNIFICANCE	CUMULATIVE R^2
Coordination and Relations	+.347	p<.001	.773
Adequacy of Project Structure and Control	+.187	p<.001	.830
Project Uniqueness, Importance, and Public Exposure	+.145	p<.001	.877
Success Criteria Salience and Consensus	+.254	p<.001	.886
Competitive and Budgetary Pressure	−.153	p<.001	.897
Initial Over-Optimism, Conceptual Difficulty	−.215	p<.001	.905
Internal Capabilities Buildup	+.084	p<.001	.911

Table 35-5 shows that the strongest seven of the determining factors explained 91% of the variance in Perceived Success. The makeup of these seven factors is shown in Table 35-6. Note the extremely important impact of coordination and relations patterns (77% of the variance). Success Criteria Salience and Consensus and avoidance of Initial Over-Optimism, Conceptual Difficulty were the next two heaviest weighted factors in the regression equation. Note also that although the factor, Adequacy of Project Structure and Control, is included in the seven principal factors contributing to Perceived Success, no particular tool, as such, is included in the factor. In other words, PERT and CPM are *not* the be-all and end-all of project management.*

Occasionally, project management personnel adopt a defeatist attitude about a project. One hears such comments as, "The project was doomed to failure from the start," or "There was no way we could make them happy on that project." Table 35-5 does not lend credence to such an attitude. An analysis of Table 35-5 reveals that a very high proportion of the key factors associated with success are within the control of the project manager and the project team. The project manager *can* help to achieve effective coordination and relations; the project manager *can*

---

* See Chapter 15.

Table 35-6. Items Included in the Seven Factors of Table 35-5.

Coordination & Relations Factor.
    Unity between project manager and contributing department managers.
    Project team spirit.
    Project team sense of mission.
    Project team goal commitment.
    Project team capability.
    Unity between project manager and public officials.
    Unity between project manager and client contact.
    Unity between project manager and his superior.
    Project manager's human skills.
    Realistic progress reports.
    Project manager's administrative skills.
    Supportive informal relations of team members.
    Authority of project manager.
    Adequacy of change procedures.
    Job security of project team.
    Project team participation in decision making.
    Project team participation in major problem solving.
    Parent enthusiasm.
    Availability of back-up strategies.
Adequacy of Project Structure and Control Factor.
    Project manager's satisfaction with planning and control.
    Team's satisfaction with organization structure.
Project Uniqueness, Importance and Public Exposure Factor.
    Extent of public enthusiasm.
    Project larger in scale than most.
    Initial importance of state-of-art advancement.
    Project was different than most.
    Parent experience with similar project scope.
    Favorability of media coverage.
Success Criteria Salience and Consensus Factor.
    Importance to project manager—budget.
    Importance to project manager—schedule.
    Importance to parent—budget.
    Importance to parent—schedule.
    Importance to client—budget.
    Importance to client—schedule.
    Importance to client—technical performance.
    Importance to parent—technical performance.
    Importance to project manager—technical performance.
Competitive and Budgetary Pressure Factor (Negative Impact).
    Fixed price (as opposed to cost reimbursement) type of contract.
    Highly competitive environment.
    Parent heavy emphasis upon staying within the budget.
    Project manager heavy emphasis upon staying within the budget.
    Client heavy emphasis upon staying within the budget.

Table 35-6. (continued)

Initial Over-Optimism, Conceptual Difficulty Factor (Negative Impact).
    Difficulty in meeting project schedules.
    Difficulty of staying within original budget.
    Original cost estimates too optimistic.
    Difficulty in meeting technical requirements.
    Project was more complex than initially conceived.
    Schedule overrun.
    Difficulty in freezing design.
    Unrealistic schedules.
    Project was different than most.
Internal Capabilities Build-up Factor.
    Extent to which project built up parent capabilities.
    Original total budget.
    Total cost of project.

---

make certain that there are adequate project structure and control systems; the project manager *can* help to achieve success criteria salience and consensus; the project manager *can* help to avoid initial overoptimism and conceptual difficulty; and, the project manager *can* have some impact upon internal capabilities buildup, the atmosphere of competitive and budgetary pressure, and the project uniqueness, importance, and public exposure.

Therefore, the project manager *can* control the destiny of the project and the perceptions others will have of him or her. Even under extremely adverse circumstances, a project manager can be perceived as doing the best job possible under the circumstances.

CONCLUSIONS

The following conclusions seem to be warranted from the research:

1. Project success cannot be adequately defined as
    - Completing the project on schedule.
    - Staying within the budget.
    - Meeting the technical performance specifications and/or mission to be performed.
2. Perceived success of a project can best be defined as
    - Meeting the project technical specifications and/or project mission to be performed.
    - Attaining high levels of satisfaction from:
        - The parent.

- The client.
- The users or clientele.
- The project team itself.

3. Technical performance is integrally associated with perceived success of a project, whereas cost and schedule performance are somewhat less intimately associated with perceived success.

4. In the long run, what really matters is whether the parties associated with, and affected by, a project are satisified. Good schedule and cost performance mean very little in the face of a poorly performing end product.

5. Next to technical performance and satisfaction of those associated with, and affected by, a project, effective coordination and relation patterns are the most important contributors to perceived project success.

6. Project managers can attain high levels of perceived project success even under adverse circumstances.

36. Project Management in the Public Sector: Success and Failure Patterns Compared to Private Sector Projects*

Bruce N. Baker†
Dalmar Fisher
David C. Murphy

INTRODUCTION

How do public sector projects differ from private sector projects? Most people have definite preconceptions about the two. Some of these preconceptions may be summarized by the types of contrasting characteristics listed in Table 36-1. A number of studies have been made of public sector projects which tend to support some of these types of preconceptions. For example, a number of studies regarding cost growth and cost overrun

*The study reported in this chapter was conducted under the sponsorship of the National Aeronautics and Space Administration, NGR 22-03-028. The complete report is entitled, *Determinants of Project Success,* by David C. Murphy, Bruce N. Baker, and Dalmar Fisher. It may be obtained from the National Technical Information Services, Springfield, Va. 22151, by referencing the title and the Accession number: N-74-30392, September 15, 1974.

† Dr. Bruce N. Baker is Program Manager of Information and Computer Security at SRI International. He conducts project management seminars and is a frequent speaker on the topics of improving teamwork and success in project management environments. He received his A.B. degrees from Princeton University, his M.B.A. degree from Stanford University, and his D.P.A. degree from George Washington University.

Dalmar Fisher is Associate Professor of Organizational Studies at the Boston College School of Management, where he teaches courses in organizational behavior and administrative strategy. He has authored several articles and books in the areas of organizational communication, project management, and managerial behavior, and has served as associate editor of *Project Management Quarterly*. He received his D.B.A. degree from Harvard Business School.

David C. Murphy is an Associate Professor at the Boston College School of Management. His research and publications have been concerned with project and program management, strategy and policy formulation, environmental analysis, and organizational decentralization. He has served as editor of *Project Management Quarterly,* and is an active member of several professional societies including the Project Management Institute. He received the D.B.A. degree from Indiana University.

Table 36-1. Some Preconceptions Regarding Private Sector Projects vs. Public Sector Projects.

Private	Public
Efficient	Inefficient
Effective	Ineffective
On schedule	Behind Schedule
Within budget	Overrun of budget
Well planned	Poorly planned
Competitive	Non-Competitive
Capable managers	Incapable managers
Competent workers	Incompetent workers
Free of Politics	Encumbered by politics
The end-product "works"	The end-product doesn't "work"
Minimum paperwork	Excessive paperwork
Definitive goals	Nebulous goals
Feelings of satisfaction	Feelings of dissatisfaction
People seem to care	People don't seem to care
Good team spirit	Lack of team spirit
Incompetent people are fired	Incompetent people can't be fired
Good performance is rewarded	Good performance is not rewarded

of federal government projects have been conducted during the past two decades.

The most sophisticated studies of actual cost performance on Department of Defense programs as compared to original cost estimates were the Merton J. Peck and Frederic M. Scherer studies* and several Rand Corporation studies.

Peck and Scherer analyzed 12 typical weapon systems programs of the 1950s. All 12 systems employed cost-plus-fixed-fee contracts. The average cost growth was found to be 220% beyond original target cost.†

Almost identical results came from a later study of 22 Air Force weapon systems programs involving 68 estimates. The study, entitled *Strategy for R&D: Studies in the Microeconomics of Development,* by Thomas Marschak, Thomas K. Glennan, Jr., and Robert Summers of Rand Corporation, showed an average cost growth of 226% beyond original estimated cost.‡ These programs involved mainly the cost-plus-fee contracts of the late 1950s.

---

* Merton J. Peck and Frederic M. Scherer, *The Weapons Acquisition Process—An Economic Analysis* (Boston: Graduate School of Business, Harvard University, 1962).
† Ibid., p. 429.
‡ (New York: Springer-Verlag New York Inc., 1967), p. 152.

In the 1960s, incentive contracts, rather than cost-plus-fixed-fee contracts, were used for most engineering development efforts in the Department of Defense. One might therefore expect actual program costs to be closer to original cost estimates. Two such studies of the 1960s were undertaken by Rand personnel.

Robert Perry et al. reported in a study of 21 Army, Navy and Air Force system acquisition programs that " . . . [O]n average, cost estimates for the 1960s were about 25% less optimistic than those for programs for the 1950s. Thus, if reduction in bias (or reduced optimism) is a realistic index of 'better,' there is evidence of improvement in the acquisition process."* Even such a statement as this must be hedged considerably as Perry et al. were careful to do: "Still, the model has little explanatory power (in a statistical sense), and it does not indicate *why* improvements have occurred.†

Rand studies of defense procurement in the 1970s showed less cost and schedule overrun than in the 1960s, and studies of the 1980s conducted to date show improvement over the 1970s. Procurement of weapons systems that has gone through one or more production runs have shown minimal cost overrun, except those contracts which were subjected to stretch-out of deliveries.‡ All in all, cost and schedule performance on procurement of weapons systems has improved steadily from the 1950s to the 1980s, if one defines improvement in terms of final cost and schedule performance as compared to original cost and schedule estimates.§

The problems of cost and schedule overruns have not been unique to the Defense Department within the federal sector. Environmental projects, transportation projects, federal housing projects, and space projects, to name a few, have all experienced overrun problems. In many cases, the interactions of federal, state, and local governmental agencies create their own set of inherent problems in addition to the obstacles and setbacks encountered on the actual project work itself. Nuclear plant construction, freeway construction, subway systems, and environmental cleanup efforts entail interaction of many governmental agencies, many types of

---

* *System Acquisition Experience,* Memorandum RM-6072-OR prepared for United States Air Force Project Rand (Santa Monica: The Rand Corporation, November, 1969), p. 6.
† Ibid.
‡ For an excellent analysis of the program stretch-out problem, see Jacques S. Gansler, "Defense Program Instability: Causes, Costs, and Cures," *Defense Management Journal,* Vol. 22, No. 2, Second Quarter, 1986, pp. 3–11.
§ E. Dews, G. K. Smith, A. A. Barbour, E. D. Harris, M.A. Hesse, *Acquisition Policy Effectiveness: Department of Defense Experience in the 1970s,* Report R-2516-DRE (Santa Monica: The Rand Corporation, October, 1979); M. D. Rich, E. Dews, C. L. Batten, *Improving the Military Acquisition Process: Lessons from Rand Research,* Report R-3373-AF/RC (Santa Monica: The Rand Corporation, February, 1986).

business entities, and numerous public interest groups in ways that create a nightmare from a management standpoint. The public has been demanding more of a voice in all of these areas. Housing and Urban Development, for example, does not "control" housing as much as it tries to cope with the special interests it encounters wherever it turns. Projects in some of these areas encounter obstacles and setbacks that the Defense Department never dreamed of.

Personal experience often reinforces the preconceptions of public sector efforts through one's dealings with the U.S. Postal Service, governmental social service agencies, regulatory agencies, etc.

The United States does not have a monopoly on public sector project difficulties. A.P. Martin notes that Canada has experienced a plague of failures of large-scale public sector projects to reach their targets.* He cites the Panartics, James Bay, the Gentilly nuclear reactors, the NORAD defense network renewal, and the Montreal Olympics.

Very few studies have been conducted of private sector projects. For example, cost overrun data is generally not available or at least not publicized by independent sources. Yet, the cost overrun records and fiascos of some major private sector projects are comparable to many public sector projects. For example, cost overruns of pioneer process plants have averaged about 200%.† A list of private sector fiascos is shown in Table 36-2.

Although good data may not be available for a comprehensive comparison of actual cost overrun and actual schedule overrun for private sector projects versus public sector projects, the authors conducted a study which compares these dimensions as well as overall perceived project success for the two sectors. The study was designed to detail the relationships among situational, structural, and process variables as they related to project effectiveness.

The study is believed to be the largest and most comprehensive investigation to date on the subject of project management effectiveness. A sample of 646 responses to a 17-page questionnaire represented a variety of industries (34% manufacturing, 22% construction, 17% government, and 27% services, transportation, and others). Most of the respondents themselves had been directly involved in the particular project they chose to describe in their questionnaire. Of the total sample, 50% had been the project manager, 31% had been in other positions on the project team, and

---

* A. P. Martin, "Project Management Requires Transorganizational Standards," *Project Management Quarterly,* Vol. X, No. 3, 1979, pp. 41–44.

† E. Merrow, K. E. Phillips, C. W. Myers, *Understanding Cost Growth and Performance Shortfalls in Pioneer Process Plants,* Report R-2569-DOE (Santa Monica: The Rand Corporation, September, 1981).

Table 36-2. Some Notable Failures Among Private
Sector Projects.

Ford	The Edsel
Proctor and Gamble	Rely Brand Tampons
General Dynamics	Convair 880 and 990
Lockheed	L-1011 Airbus
Four Seasons	Chain of Nursing Homes
John Hancock Mutual	Windows in Boston Office Building
Polaroid Corporation	Polavision
Firestone	Radial Tires
Dupont	Korfam
Gillette	Digital Wristwatches
Dansk Designs, Ltd.	Gourmet Product Line
BIC Pen Corporation	Fannyhose
General Foods	Burger Chef Restaurants
A & P	WEO Price Reduction Program
National Semiconductor	Consumer Products

another 10% had been the project manager's direct superior. About one-third of the projects were described as being public in nature, the remaining two-thirds being in the private sector. The types of contracts or agreements involved included cost plus fixed fee (32%), in-house work orders (28%), fixed price (21%), and fixed price with incentives (14%). The major activity or end product involved in the projects included construction (43%), hardware or equipment (22%), new process or software (14%), and studies, services and tests (11%).

DETERMINANTS OF COST AND SCHEDULE OVERRUN

The study revealed the principal determinants of cost and schedule overrun for both public and private sector projects. Cost overruns were found to be highly correlated with the size of the project and the difficulty of meeting technical specifications. However, schedule difficulties and resulting schedule overruns were the primary causal factors leading to cost overruns. Schedule overruns were, in turn, caused by the variables listed on Table 36-3.

In order to prevent schedule and cost overruns, or to minimize the amount of schedule and cost overrun when initial overoptimism or a "buy-in"* has occurred, the research points to the need for employing

---

* A "buy-in" is an intentional underestimation of costs in order to obtain a contract or to obtain approval to proceed on an effort with the hope that follow-on contracts, changes, or additional funding will compensate for the original low estimate.

Table 36-3. Determinants of Cost and Schedule Overruns.

- Cost underestimates.
- Use of "Buy-in" strategies.
- Lack of alternative backup strategies.
- Lack of project-team goal commitment.
- Functional, rather than projectized, project organization.
- Lack of project team participation in setting schedules.
- Lack of team spirit, sense of mission.
- Inadequate control procedures.
- Insufficient use of networking techniques.
- Insufficient use of progress/status reports.
- Over-optimistic status reports.
- Decision delays.
- Inadequate change procedures.
- Insufficient project manager authority and influence.
- Lack of commitment to budget and schedule.
- Overall lack of similar experience.

networking techniques, systems management approaches, participative approaches to decision making within the project team, and a task-oriented style of leadership, with a backup relationship-orientated style.

COMPARISONS BETWEEN PRIVATE SECTOR AND PUBLIC SECTOR PROJECTS

The comparisons between the private sector projects (⅔ of the sample) and public sector projects (⅓ of the sample) were extremely intriguing. Although many of the characteristics may seem intuitively obvious and may concide with our preconceptions, some of the findings appear to be counterintuitive. Moreover, some of the characteristics commonly attributed to public sector projects do not appear on the listings of items that statistically differentiate public from private sector projects. The variables which were found to be highly related to public sector projects are shown in Table 36-4.

Of course, the bulk of the items coincide with our preconceptions and experiences. Such items as red tape, overcontrol, overinvolvement of the public, politics, paperwork, the ratio of parent managers to total employees, the number of staff-type project team members, etc., coincide well with our beliefs and experiences.

As indicated by the asterisks, however, there are at least 13 variables on the list which may not concide with our preconceptions or our intuition. We may tend to believe that the private sector has greater latitude in replacing project managers, but the survey clearly shows that project

Table 36-4. Variables Significantly Associated with Public Sector Projects.†

Delays caused by governmental red tape	(P < .001)
Government overcontrol	(P < .001)
Difficulty in obtaining funding to complete the project	(P < .001)
Length of project	(P < .001)
Scheduled length of project	(P < .001)
Multi-funding	(P < .001)
Percent of R&D budget to the total parent budget	(P < .001)
*Number of times the project manager was replaced	(P < .001)
The extent of use of work breakdown structures	(P < .001)
The extent of use of systems management concepts	(P < .001)
The extent of use of operations research techniques	(P < .001)
*The project manager's authority over merit raises	(P < .001)
*The client contact's influence in relaxing specifications	(P < .001)
*The client contact's authority in relaxing specifications	(P < .002)
*The job insecurity of project team members	(P < .002)
The number of governmental agencies involved with the project	(P < .002)
*The legal restrictions encumbering the project	(P < .002)
The need for new forms of government-industry cooperation	(P < .002)
Overinvolvement of the public with the project	(P < .003)
Total project team personnel	(P < .004)
The value of systems management concepts	(P < .004)
*The project manager's authority to select project team personnel	(P < .005)
The amount of politics involved in the contract award	(P < .006)
*The importance to the client of staying within the budget	(P < .006)
The importance to the project manager of obtaining follow-on work	(P < .007)
The difficulty of obtaining funding from the client	(P < .008)
The excessive volume of paperwork	(P < .009)
*The availability of back-up strategies	(P < .010)
The travel time between the project manager and the client	(P < .011)
The importance of state-of-the-art advancement	(P < .012)
The difficulty of keeping competent project team members	(P < .015)
*The degree to which competition was considered cutthroat	(P < .018)
The value of operations research techniques	(P < .020)
The extent to which problems arose because the project was different	(P < .024)
The ratio of the number of parent managers to total employees	(P < .024)
The number of staff-type project team members	(P < .027)
*The influence of the project manager over the selection of project team personnel	(P < .029)
*The client satisfaction with the outcome of the project	(P < .037)
The extent to which bar charts or milestone charts were used	(P < .041)
*The extent to which the project team participated in major problem solving	(P < .043)

* Indicates probable counter-intuitive relationships.

---

† This list is based on statistical tests in which data about each project were grouped according to whether the project was a private or a public sector project.

managers on public sector projects are replaced much more often than their private sector counterparts. We may tend to believe that project managers of private sector projects have much greater authority and influence in selecting project team personnel and in determining their raises, but the study shows just the opposite. We may tend to believe that client contacts for private sector projects have greater influence and authority in relaxing specifications, and greater satisfaction with the outcome of the project, but the study shows just the opposite. We may tend to believe that the legal restrictions resulting from OSHA, EPA regulations, etc., result in greater legal encumbrances over private sector projects as compared to public sector projects, but the study shows just the opposite. We may tend to believe that greater emphasis is placed on the availability of backup strategies for private sector projects, but the study shows just the opposite. And we may tend to believe that cutthroat competition is more prevalent among private sector projects but, again, the study shows just the opposite.

Table 36-5 indicates the variables which are significantly uncharacteristic of public sector projects. As might be expected, unity between the project manager and public officials involved with the public sector effort is generally not high, and the parent organization places little importance upon achieving the technical performance goals of the project (as opposed to staying within the budget and meeting the schedule). Also, the project manager's influence in selecting subcontractors and his authority to permit subcontractors to exceed original budgets or schedules are very low.

Of greater interest than the preceding lists are the characteristics which did *not* show up as significantly different between public sector and private sector projects. Table 36-6 lists some items which did not show statistically significant differentiation. *Note particularly that actual cost and schedule overrun were not found to be significantly different.* Also, satisfaction of the parent organization, the project team, and the ultimate

Table 36-5. Variables Significantly Uncharacteristic of Public Sector Projects.

The degree of unity between the project manager and the principal public officials involved with the effort	(P < .001)
The project manager's authority to permit subcontractors to exceed original budgets or schedules	(P < .009)
The importance to the parent organization of achieving the specified technical performance goals	(P < .016)
*The difficulty in freezing the design	(P < .025)
The project manager's influence in selecting subcontractors	(P < .042)

*This characteristic may be considered counter-intuitive.

Table 36-6. Some Variables Which Did Not Differ Significantly Between
Private Sector and Public Sector Projects.

Actual cost overrun.
Actual schedule overrun.
Extent of use of networking systems.
Advance in state-of-the-art required.
Difficulty in defining the goals of the project.
Difficulty in meeting the technical requirements of the project.
Satisfaction of the ultimate users, recipients, or clientele with the outcome of the project.
Satisfaction of the parent organization with the outcome of the project.
Satisfaction of the project team with the outcome of the project.

users did not differ significantly. In fact, client satisfaction tends to be *higher* for public sector projects, as indicated in Table 36-4.

In general, the comparisons between private sector projects and public sector projects do not support many of our preconceptions. Public sector projects certainly have their share of problems, but they have been maligned more than the evidence of this study warrants.

STRATEGIES FOR OVERCOMING SOME OF THE PROBLEMS FACING PUBLIC SECTOR PROJECTS

Many of the characteristics which distinguish public sector projects from private sector projects can be considered adverse in nature. These adverse conditions make the probability of success less likely for public sector projects as compared to private sector projects. Should those involved with public sector projects therefore accept their fate and be content with very low levels of relative success? The findings of this study do not support such a defeatist approach to the management of public sector projects.

Instead, several strategies have been derived from the research findings which can maximize the success potential of public sector projects. Even when combinations of adversities exist, moderate success levels can be achieved if heavy emphasis is placed upon appropriate strategies for the situation and the environment as well as upon diligent pursuit of the project goals. The strategies which follow are based upon a path analysis diagram which was derived from a series of multiple regressions. Path analysis is a relatively new analytic technique and is not to be confused with networking techniques such as PERT and CPM. The result of a path analysis is a model which explains the interaction of a large number of variables. Such a model illustrates the causal relationships contained in a series of relationships. The strengths of these relationships are measured by path coefficients. These coefficients are standardized measures which can be compared to determine the relative predictive power of each independent variable with the effects of the other variables held constant. The particular value of path analysis is that it illustrates the working relationships of many variables in a network of relative predictive powers, thus allowing one to understand the relationships among variables in a systematic manner. The strategies derived from the path analysis are summarized in Figure 36-1, contingent strategies for successful projects.

The most significant conclusion to be derived from Figure 36-1 is that a *project manager faced with one or more adversities need not and should not adopt a defeatist approach to the management of the project.* Even when combinations of adversities exist, moderate success levels can be achieved if heavy emphasis is placed upon appropriate strategies for the situation and the environment as well as upon diligent pursuit of the project goals.

A project manager can thus use Figure 36-1 as a basis for developing contingent strategies to overcome or circumvent certain adversities. The path analysis diagram was derived from the complete sample of private and public sector projects, but two of the adversities which often face managers of public projects will be analyzed:

- Legal-political difficulties.
- Large projects.

The reader can examine Figure 36-1 to see the basis for the strategies designed to overcome these adversities. Although most of these strategies can be considered general strategies, they should receive added emphasis for public projects facing one or both of these adversities. In situations where these adversities do not exist, these strategies can be played down.

Strategies for Overcoming Legal-Political Difficulties

1. *Encourage openness and honesty from the start from all project participants and specifically seek to avoid and reject "buy-ins."*
When legal-political difficulties surround a project, these difficulties can only be compounded in the long run by permitting "buy-ins" to occur. In the short run, it may appear advantageous to secure initial program funding and initial contracts in order to enable "the camel's nose to enter the

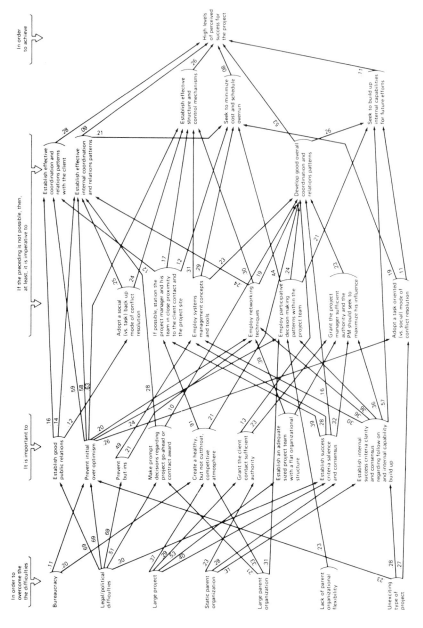

Figure 36-1. Contingent strategies for successful projects.

tent,'' but in the long run such a strategy and/or acquiescence to such strategy results in:

- Inefficient use of resources.
- Panic reprogramming of public funds.
- Diminished reputation of the agencies and contractors involved with the project.
- Loss of credibility regarding future efforts.
- Poor relations with legislative bodies.
- Poor relations with the public.

In view of these factors, the recommended strategy seems best suited to public sector projects in both the short run and the long run. Such a strategy entails planning for and securing adequate funding commitments to complete the project. If the funding is considered excessive in relation to other deserving projects, then the project may be shelved or rejected, but is not this also the best strategy and the fairest in the long run for all competing interests? The parent organization must also refrain from placing excessive pressure on the project manager to win the contract and avoid slashing or ballooning the project team's cost estimates.

2. *Develop realistic cost, schedule, and technical performance estimates and goals.*

This strategy is closely related to the first strategy. It is sometimes difficult to distinguish when intentional overoptimism (or buy-in) has occurred, rather than unintentional overoptimism. Buy-in (or intentional optimism) and unintentional overoptimism were two of the biggest factors contributing to project failure. Cost realism can best be determined by means of an independent cost estimate conducted by a truly independent organization. In most cases, so-called independent government cost estimates can hardly be considered independent because of the vested interests of the agencies involved. In practice, the "independent" government cost estimate may be known by the contractors, and conversely, earlier contractor estimates may be known by the independent cost-estimating team. When they are not known, the government cost estimates may vary over 100% higher or 50% lower than the dollar figures proposed by contractors for cost reimbursement contracts. As a result, contracting officers usually ignore the independent government cost estimates. Even if a truly independent cost estimate could be performed by a disinterested party, the question remains how accurate is such an estimate and how far can a contractor's estimate vary from such an estimate to be considered "realistic"?

The answers do not rest in some rules-of-thumb or complicated formulas. The answers rest in the creation of an appropriate atmosphere and checkpoints to catch unintentional overoptimism and the creation of severe sanctions for intentional overoptimism (buy-in).

3. *Seek to enhance the public's image of the project.*

Project initiators generally are required and/or encouraged to obtain public participation during the planning and approval phases of most types of projects affecting the public interest. Some people believe that the more the public participates in these processes, the more successful the project will be. Although this concept may be appealing in the context of one's value judgments, it is not conducive to project success in a management context. High levels of public participation often result in a "tempest in a teapot." Project delays, poor public relations, and diminished project success are the results of excessive public participation. The most successful strategy from a project management success perspective is to create a good public relations image with only the minimal required levels of public participation. This is not an opinion. It is derived from the study of the hundreds of projects described in this chapter.

4. *Make prompt decisions regarding project go-ahead or contract award.*

This strategy is obviously directed to the client organization. There is nothing wrong with providing sufficient time for studies, planning, definition, etc., before seeking bids on a contract effort. But, once bids are sought, the schedule of contract award or go-ahead should be adhered to. Otherwise morale of the project team cadre deteriorates, to say nothing of the added costs of the delays.

5. *Seek to establish definitive goals for the project and seek to establish a clear understanding and consensus among the principal project participants (client organization, parent organization, and project team) regarding the relative importance of these goals.*

Although this factor was not quite as important as the previous four in overcoming legal-political difficulties, it was, nonetheless, an important factor on the road to project success.

Strategies for Overcoming the Disadvantages of Large Projects

1. *Establish a project team of adequate size but with a flexible and flat organizational structure.*

Obviously, the larger the project, the larger the project team must be, but this does not necessarily entail the creation of excessive levels of organizational structure. Flexible and flat organizational structures were found to be an essential ingredient for project success.

2. *Seek to establish definitive goals for the project and seek to establish*

a clear understanding and consensus among the principal project partici-
pants regarding the relative importance of these goals.

Success criteria salience and consensus was found to be an important factor on both paths discussed here, but it was especially important for large projects.

3. *Create an atmosphere that encourages healthy, but not cutthroat, competition or "liars' contests."*

The larger the project, the more likely there will be many contractors who will be anxious to obtain the contract. It is sometimes tempting for a public agency to take advantage of this situation by creating a cutthroat competitive atmosphere, or even a subtle form of auction. In the long run, such a strategy works to the detriment of all parties concerned. A public agency and public officials must be especially careful to support the healthy aspects of the free enterprise system.

4. *Delegate sufficient authority to the principal client contract and let him or her promptly approve or reject important project decisions.*

The best way to overcome the sluggishness of a large organization and the traditional red tape associated with public projects is to delegate a high level of authority to the principal client contact.

Difficulties that Come in Bunches

Unfortunately, when trouble occurs, it does not occur in just one dimension. The expression "a bag of snakes" is commonly heard in meetings involving public projects. In many cases, as Figure 36-1 allows, a project manager is faced not only with legal-political difficulties but also with a buy-in situation, initial overoptimism, poor public relations, delays in contract award go-ahead, and/or lack of success criteria clarity and consensus. Similarly, a project manager confronting the inherent difficulties of a large project cannot always avoid additional major obstacles such as an inadequately sized project team, heavy budgetary pressure, etc. Figure 36-1 points the way to strategies for overcoming such combinations of adversities. For each combination of adversitites toward the left of the diagram, it is possible to achieve improved levels of perceived success by placing heavy emphasis on the related strategies to the right. The reader may undertake similar analyses with the aid of Figure 36-1 for the other major adversities, such as a static or large parent organization, which may face a public sector project.

CONCLUSIONS

In general, the comparisons derived from the research of public sector projects and private sector projects do not support many of our preconceptions regarding public sector projects. For example, the study revealed no significant difference between private sector projects and public sector projects with respect to cost and schedule overrun. It is not only possible, but also very common, to attain high levels of perceived success on public sector projects.

In order to prevent schedule and cost overruns, or to minimize the amount of schedule and cost overrun when initial overoptimism or a "buy-in" has occurred, the research points to the need for employing networking techniques, systems management approaches, participative approaches to decision making within the project team, and a task-oriented style of leadership with a backup relationship-oriented style.

Adverse environmental or "given" conditions do not necessarily affect project success directly, but often may be seen as affecting success through their influence on other intervening conditions and management processes. An adverse environmental or given condition can therefore be avoided or overcome through astute identification of those factors which it tends to affect directly, and through effective management action on those factors.

A project manager cannot afford to set his sights solely on objectively oriented targets, that is, meet the schedule, stay within the budget, and meet the technical requirements. Perceived success is in the eyes of all participants and the parties affected by the project. In the long run, perceived success appears to be more important than the traditional objective measures of success, provided that the project meets the technical performance specifications or mission to be performed.

Although many general strategy guidelines, based upon the study of hundreds of projects, have been developed to assist with improving project management, these guidelines must be tailored to the situation and the environment. Certain strategies must be given added emphasis in order to overcome specific adversities, and some strategies must be played down in order to meet the demands of other environments. Overemphasis or underemphasis of just one strategy can lead to failure. Combinations of multiple strategies can afford more frequent project successes in the public sector.

If public and private officials would pay more attention to what the project management research is trying to tell them, more frequent and higher levels of success could be attained on project efforts. There is room for improvement in both the public and private sectors in the way projects are managed.

37. Health Project Management in an Occupational Setting*

Laura C. Leviton, Ph.D.† Gordon K. MacLeod, M.D.‡

EMPLOYEE HEALTH PROJECTS

Good employee health is a major asset for any organization. The protection and preservation of an employee's health reflect many important objectives for an organization. Yet, assuring good health is no easy matter. The project management approach can assist in this process. A health project involves the development or transformation of worksite health programs. After a general description of worksite health programs, we apply the project management approach to four health projects: (a) modification of health insurance benefits; (b) development of cost-effective health promotion programs for employees; (c) development of Employee Assistance Programs (EAPs); and (d) development of occupational health and safety programs.

Definitions of Health Projects

Modification of Health Insurance Benefits. The traditional way in which health benefits are covered through employer-funded programs is through

* We gratefully acknowledge the comments and suggestions of several individuals in their review of a draft of this chapter: E. C. Curtis, M.D., Corporate Medical Director, Westinghouse Electric Corporation; Bertram D. Dinman, M.D., then Vice President, Health and Safety, Aluminum Company of America; R. L. Gibson, M.D.; Beaufort B. Longest, Ph.D.; William McClellan, M.D., former Medical Director, Gulf Oil Corporation; and Joseph J. Schwerha, M.D., Director, Industrial Medicine, United States Steel Division, U.S.X.

† Laura C. Leviton, Ph.D., is Assistant Professor of Health Services Administration at the University of Pittsburgh. She has written extensively in the area of work-site health programs. She is a former W.K. Kellogg Foundation Fellow and a former policy analyst of the Health Policy Institute of Pittsburgh.
‡ Gordon K. MacLeod, M.D., is Professor of Health Services Administration and Clinical Professor of Medicine at the University of Pittsburgh. He is a former industrial engineer at the Procter & Gamble Company who later served as the founding Director of the HMO Service for the federal government, and as Secretary of Health for the Commonwealth of Pennsylvania.

a health insurance plan that pays costs or charges to health care providers on a per diem, per case, or fee for service reimbursement basis. That is, a hospital, physician or other therapist submits a bill to the insurance carrier which is then paid, no questions asked. This traditional coverage through reimbursement for costs or changes is one of the main factors that has contributed to huge increases in the cost of medical care over the past several decades. One goal of a health benefits project, therefore, is to stimulate competition among alternative provider systems, limiting increases in medical care costs, whether by improving efficiency or by limiting utilization deemed to be unnecessary. Cost containment can be achieved either through the traditional provider system or through an alternative to that system.

Development of Cost-effective Health Promotion Programs. Health promotion involves actions aimed at improving health and the quality of life. Health promotion is therefore aimed at already healthy employees as well as those at risk of a specific illness. The key to health promotion is to provide opportunities for improving health, and to ensure that a high number of employees take advantage of those opportunities. Health promotion is a broader concept than health education because it includes not just information, but also changes in the environment and organizational climate that ultimately facilitate changes in health behavior (25). Health promotion can also include "wellness" activities that are aimed at more than the absence of disease. For the organization, "wellness" means high levels of productivity and morale, while for the employee wellness means minimizing physical limitations as well as enhancing subjective well-being.

Development of Employee Assistance Programs (EAPs). EAPs provide counseling and arrange for treatment and referral of troubled employees to deal with a variety of counseling needs. Alcohol treatment programs organized through work settings have existed for some time, but organizations now tend to expand the focus of those programs to deal with multiple problems. While EAPs are aimed at facilitating rehabilitation or improving the functioning of the employee, they also hope to reduce absenteeism and sick days, to contain utilization of health care benefits, to reduce the incidence of grievances, and thus to increase productivity.

Development of Occupational Health and Safety Programs. These programs focus on the reduction of injuries and on correcting work conditions conducive to injury and illness, such as exposures to hazardous substances. Programs may also include employee health services on site.

Depending on the organization, they may also involve screening for conditions related to occupational exposures, or preemployment screening to facilitate assignment of individuals to tasks most consistent with their capabilities and physical capacities.

Background

At the present time, employee health benefits and programs are undergoing significant change. Guidance and direction are needed to keep health programs and benefits in line with long-term organizational objectives. Some background is essential in order for the reader to avoid many past pitfalls. A central problem in health project management is that the manager needs to exercise control over costs, utilization, and time lost from productive employment, but also needs to avoid the appearance of paternalism. The history of employer-provided health care shows why this is important (55). In the late nineteenth century, the high incidence of industrial injuries motivated companies to hire physicians to treat cases—and to document the injury, often serving as expert witnesses for the company in lawsuits. Some companies provided medical care, employed physicians, and in some cases even built their own hospitals. Many employees resented mandatory payroll deductions for company-provided care and wanted to choose their own doctor. In the early years of this century, occupational physicians were often held in low esteem by workers as well as by their own professional colleagues (18, 55).

Initially, growth of health insurance was stimulated during World War II by the federal government's decision to exclude health insurance premiums from taxation as employee income (10). Provision of such fringe benefits offset to some extent employee dissatisfaction with government-mandated wage and price controls intended to combat wartime inflation. After the war such benefits packages became an important part of collective bargaining. At the same time, the medical profession endorsed hospital and medical care insurance for the first time, so long as no one interfered with the actual practice of medicine or with the free choice of a physician (55). Insurance obtained through employment has become so widespread that in 1981, employers and unions paid the entire premium for 42% of privately insured people, and helped pay it for another 52% (57). Moreover, retirees frequently receive company coverage for health care in addition to Medicare.

However, health insurance with fee for service payments to physicians and lack of controls on hospitals produced increases in the cost of care, most dramatically after the passage of Medicare and Medicaid. Expenditures on health care reached 10.7% of the GNP in 1985 (58). Employers in the 1980s began to take steps to contain costs. Many providers, insurers, employers, and employee groups are concerned that freedom of choice and quality of care may suffer as a consequence.

The areas of EAP, health promotion, and occupational health are changing no less rapidly than is health insurance. EAP providers are in a state of tremendous flux as concepts such as brief psychotherapy come into ascendance (8). Both EAP and health promotion services are being aggressively sold with unprecedented marketing slickness. In the occupational health area, the model of a corporate medical director is being transfigured by several forces such as decentralization of programs, evolution in the area of toxic torts, and demands that government take over some functions that are currently provided by companies. In summary, all these areas may require health project management to meet the challenge of changing times.

DEVELOPING A HEALTH PROJECT

This section outlines the approach to a generic health project for an organization, from planning to implementation, from monitoring to adjustment, and from quality assessment to corrective action.

The Planning Process

The need for short- and long-term planning for health programs and projects flows from an overall statement of organizational philosophy and objectives. Specific goals and strategies are formulated to achieve desired changes. Beginning even before this formulation, consultation with the many stakeholders of such programs and projects is needed, and may have to be repeated several times during the planning process. Through such consultation, the organization will gain an ability to maximize the value and relevance of health programs.

Objectives.   Following the format of this handbook a health project begins with a statement of the overall objectives of an organization. It is important for project managers to clarify these broad objectives at the outset and specify how they relate to specific goals for health programs (19, 27). The stated objectives should include those that benefit the employee and those that benefit the employer. Frequently, employee and employer objectives coincide, especially for preventive programs. Objectives that focus primarily on the employee include:

- Demonstrating commitment to the health of the employee.
- Demonstrating commitment to the quality of work life.

- Aiming at increasing the life span of the employee.
- Maintaining the employee's physical functioning.
- Improving the retention of employees in the organization.
- Improving employee morale and satisfaction.
- Providing a variety of employee benefits.

Objectives that focus primarily on the organization include:

- Increasing productivity.
- Containing health, life, and disability insurance costs.
- Complying with federal and state "right-to-know" laws.
- Recruiting desirable employees with attractive programs.
- Decreasing absenteeism and workdays lost.
- Saving short-term sick pay costs.
- Reducing Workers' Compensation costs.
- Limiting lawsuits about exposure to hazardous substances.
- Improving organizational image.

An additional objective of many companies needs to be discussed here. Decision makers should at least be aware of the possible impacts of their decisions on their communities. On the one hand, employer-sponsored disease prevention programs are good for the community as well as the organization, because they set a good example for other organizations. On the other hand, experience rating of a company's own health insurance impinges upon the societal good of shared risk in insurance. Although companies save money by insuring young, healthy employees, older and sicker community members must then pay more.

Consultation with Stakeholders. Stakeholders for health programs are all those individuals and groups, both in and outside of the organization, that have a stake in the number and types of programs and the ways in which they are offered. Involving stakeholders can facilitate acceptance of change. Among the many stakeholders for health programs are managers, the work force, dependents and retirees, and providers. These groups will not necessarily have uniform views about health programs. For example, top managers themselves can and do disagree about the importance of offering certain health programs, and unionized employees may differ from those not unionized in terms of some goals.

Several advantages can result from consulting various stakeholder groups about health objectives and goals. First, stakeholders may challenge assumptions about health programs that turn out to be false on closer examination. First-dollar coverage, for example, may be less important than management believes. The statement of a health project's purpose or even objectives may have to be reworked when such assumptions are challenged. Another good example is that prevention and rehabilitation activities can really benefit from employee input. With such participation, EAP, health promotion, and safety and health protection programs will get better compliance from employees.

Needs Assessment.   Supplying good information on needs is a first step toward modifying health programs to be more rational and to suit employees, based on prevailing health issues and problems for the work force. Data bases to measure need vary by the type of health project described below.

Specification of Goals.   Once an overall statement of the purpose of health programs has been formulated and discrepancies have been identified between that statement and the existing programs, the next step is to relate specific activities to the overall statement of purpose, and to develop both short- and long-range specific goals and objectives.

A principal goal for the short term in planning for any health project is to enter the networks of employers who are bringing about changes in health care for employees. Business coalitions in many communities are accomplishing this change. A major coordinating body for those coalitions is the Washington Business Group on Health, which publishes the periodicals *Business and Health* and *Corporate Commentary*. Smaller organizations can affiliate with such coalitions, through associations of smaller businesses. These coalitions have had little direct involvement with occupational health, however. Although knowledge in this area is specialized, the employer can gain useful information from the national and regional Safety Councils and from the American Occupational Medical Association.

Establishing long-term goals requires strategic planning about the future of the company and the health system. Assessing potential changes in public programs is essential for all these health projects. For example, if catastrophic health coverage for all Americans is increased, major medical plans will be affected and stop-loss coverage will become less important. On the other hand, keeping the status quo in public medical care programs will mean that an even larger proportion of retirees' health care must be paid by some other source than Medicare or Medicaid.

Insurance practices may also change. For example, insurers could probably increase their profit margin by reimbursement for preventive services. Should the organization therefore aim toward expansion of prevention? Insurers may eventually reimburse new high-technology interventions such as liver transplants or they may perform careful analysis of cost-effectiveness first. What should the organization's response be?

Several worksite policies may impact on both health and legal matters. For example, AIDS and other community health problems should be followed closely, and policy should be discussed today concerning possible workplace problems later. Drug testing may be required in some organizations—but the legal status of such testing is still under debate. Communicating with employees about health risks is a very complex issue in light of right-to-know laws and the uncertain state of toxic torts.

Organizational Constraints on Planning. So far we have discussed health projects and the objectives and goals they address as though there were no organizational constraints on those projects. Yet most projects are embedded in organizations with characteristics that may pose barriers to achieving rational objectives. Most companies have a past history of providing certain benefits, and change does not come easily. Changes in benefits and programs may require protracted periods. However, the cost crisis in health insurance has created an environment in which such changes can occur more quickly, because the need is more apparent to stakeholders.

The role of top management is crucial in each of the four project areas. The high cost of care has made many businesses fearful that a new benefit could result in the same overutilization they feel has occurred in hospitals. For example, some business leaders are open to inclusion of a mental health benefit, except that they see no effective controls on utilization. Also, a firm commitment from top management is essential to make prevention activities work. Without a commitment, safety and health will be relegated to a marginal status, and health promotion activities will wither (4, 40).

Unions have frequently supported cost containment efforts, unless the efforts represent give-backs. Unions understandably tend to be much more concerned with occupational hazards than with health risks based on individual lifestyle. They also tend to be wary of alcohol, drug abuse, and mental health programs offered by management, because of perceived dangers of paternalism. Cooperation with unions usually produces valuable and effective prevention programs. For example, hypertension control programs have been jointly sponsored by Ford and the United Auto Workers, and by the Storeworkers Union and Gimbel's in New York. These programs are exemplary models for such cooperation (2, 11).

Implementing Health Projects

Organization. One issue in health projects involves whether health programs should be centralized in one department of an organization or decentralized into several departments. Frequently, responsibilities for

health programs are divided among such departments as personnel benefits (for health insurance), human resources (for EAP), and a medical
department (for occupational safety and health). Health promotion is sort
of a free-floater—it is sometimes implemented by a medical department,
but just as often is a sideline for a middle-level manager or committee who
merely have an interest in health and fitness.

Yet for effective project management, coordination among the various
departments is essential. In fact, we would argue for centralized planning
and implementation of all health-related programs. Figure 37-1 presents
an organizational chart for an ideal configuration, for very large organizations. In smaller organizations, much of the service delivery could be
provided by outside consultants, but overall administration might be the
same. A vice president for health programs can supervise both a corporate medical director and a manager of occupational health and safety.
Health data management is a separate independent office that assists the
vice president in policy and planning decisions. Laboratory services are
in a swing position, relating to both employee health and occupational
health and safety.

This type of organization is not common. It is more common, in fact,
for several of these functions to be subsumed under a personnel or human
resources department. Even where our ideal configuration is not possible,
however, it may be feasible for conducting a time-limited health project.
Our proposed organization has some advantages over others for coher-
ently planning health programs and projects.

This configuration permits health specialists to complement each other.
A medical director may deal primarily with an employee health clinic, but

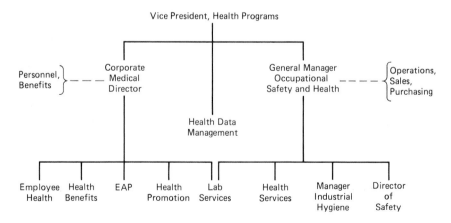

Figure 37-1. Model table of organization.

clinical training also puts him or her in a unique position to identify an individual employee's need for EAP, to suggest health promotion activities designed to lower risk of disease, and to advise health benefits managers about quality assurance in community health care programs. An EAP director frequently implements health promotion activities, and when referring employees for long-term treatment, needs the same kind of utilization review system that the benefits office may be implementing for other health problems. Occupational health nurses see a variety of substance abuse and lifestyle problems. Centralized planning and implementation of health project management are more likely to retain their focus upon and relation to organizational objectives than are fragmented efforts.

Staffing. Selection of personnel to administer health programs for employees will depend on the size of the organization and on the extent to which activities are conducted in-house. The staffing of benefits departments outlined by Griffes (19) applies to some extent: in small organizations, there will usually be a single manager of health benefits, who will also probably be the manager of other insurance benefits as well. In small organizations, this manager is usually a generalist with a background in benefits administration, personnel, and human resource issues. Some familiarity with EAP, health promotion, and occupational health and safety issues is also desirable. He or she is dependent on other departments or on outside consultants for medical, legal, financial, actuarial, investment, communications, accounting, and record-keeping tasks, as well as services in the areas of insurance and occupational health and safety. Health promotion and EAP will usually be provided to individual employees by outside professionals and voluntary organizations as needed.

The health project of a larger organization can administer more services and functions in-house, involving specialists in record keeping, financial management, communications, and planning and design. A part-time medical consultant, an occupational nurse, or some other in-house health-related professional may be a useful addition to administer occupational health and safety, health promotion, and EAP referrals.

The largest organizations have the fewest outside dependencies. If they self-insure for medical care, they may even choose to administer the program in-house, as opposed to giving its administration to an insurer. A medical director or vice president for medical or health affairs is highly desirable for large organizations, since he or she can relate to multiple health programs. Other health-related professionals are also desirable, such as occupational health nurses, industrial hygiene specialists and safety professionals to monitor workplace hazards, psychologists and social workers to administer EAP programs, and exercise physiologists to launch health promotion activities and maintain employee interest in those activities.

The importance of relying on professionals for the provision of health services and programs cannot be overemphasized. Today's market for health care services is extremely competitive. A department which administers health benefits and programs has an obligation both to the organization of which it is a part and to employees to choose services wisely.

Choice of Cost-effective Services.   Cost effectiveness is defined as meeting objectives to the extent possible within the limits of the budget for a health program. There is more than one way to achieve organizational objectives, and they are not all equally effective nor equally costly. Decision makers frequently exhibit a bias that more expensive programs will produce better results. This is not always the case for health benefits, especially for prevention programs. Effectiveness and cost-effectiveness data are not always available, but as organizations gain experience, health projects can be monitored as shown below.

Contracting with Providers.   The choice of services, providers, and benefits should reflect organizational objectives, needs of the employee population, and stakeholder positions. Services to be delivered must be specified. Moreover, contractors should provide some assurances to the organization about performance and safeguards regarding patient care.

Outside consultants may not have the same sensitivity to organizational goals that an insider would have. They may apply the "one size fits all" approach to employees in widely different organizations. This may or may not make a difference, but the situation should be monitored.

It is reasonable to hold service providers and consultants to standards of performance. Cost containment consultants should be able to describe their standards for utilization review and preadmission certification. In health promotion and EAP, providers should be able to specify expected outcomes. Consultants on safety should be able to explain the rationale for suggested changes in the workplace.

For all types of health services, assuring confidentiality is a major concern. Service providers must give assurances that employee names will not be associated with any reports to the organization about alcohol, drug abuse and mental health services. The perception of anonymity is essential to participation in many health programs, especially those that the employer recognizes as essential to health, well-being, and continued productivity on the job.

To the extent possible, providers must guarantee both a high level of quality and a high degree of access. Quality is somewhat difficult to assure directly, since it is difficult to define and monitor. However, the choice of reputable providers should contribute to quality. Access can be assured through rapid feedback on complaints, satisfaction, and utilization of health programs.

Employee Communications. Health program changes or additions may cause some confusion. Surveying a sample of employees from time to time may help reveal the extent to which employees understand their benefits and programs. Communications should be relatively simple and easy to understand (19). Information should be disseminated to employees through multiple channels such as pamphlets, newsletters, bulletin boards, in pay envelopes, and any other means available. In many cases, however, there is no substitute for personal contact when employees have questions.

Monitoring Health Projects and Programs

Use of Data. Once a health project or program is in place, the project manager will want to monitor its progress in two ways. First, he or she will look for any overall changes in trends compared to the past experience of the organization. Second, the manager will want to examine data on individual services to spot significant deviations from the norm that need closer inspection. If, for example, the project manager spots excessive utilization of services, then he or she may want to examine utilization by those providers more closely. This second method of monitoring acts as a filter to direct the attention of the manager toward potential sources of trouble.

Corrective Actions. These occur in several stages. If the employer sees potential problems or deviations from the norm, then the first stage of action is verification of a problem through more intensive study. If problems do emerge, then corrective actions may include negotiating with the existing provider, choosing another provider or system, or better communication with employees.

A PROJECT TO MODIFY HEALTH INSURANCE BENEFITS

Planning

Objectives. Decision makers most frequently say that the objectives of revising the health benefits package are to contain the cost of medical care while continuing to assure quality of care and access. In addition, an attractive benefits package could assist in recruiting desirable employees into the organization (19).

Consultation with Stakeholders.   Not all employees will share the same view about the importance of particular goals of the health benefits package. For example, unmarried employees may have different views from those who are married and have to pay an additional fee for family coverage. Also, those who are young and generally healthy may have different opinions from older employees about the scope of coverage, deductible, and coinsurance. Views on cost sharing by retirees may differ depending on whether they are recently retired and relatively healthy, or beginning to experience more serious chronic ailments.

When choosing among methods of containing costs, the employer will want to know about the acceptability of cost containment approaches to employees. For example, the general trend toward encouraging outpatient procedures has not been popular with surveyed employees (20). Both management and unions have expressed reservations about second surgical opinion programs (20). Unions also oppose increases in cost sharing by employees (5). Access to high-quality tertiary care providers must be considered. In some communities alternative provider systems are fragmented or inaccessible, because complex health care centers are competing to be the sole providers of care (32).

Needs Assessment.   Employee demographics are helpful to the health project manager in assessing the need for the form of the health benefits package. Younger workers are less likely to have serious and costly debilitating illnesses than older workers. Health care utilization experience of the employee group helps to describe health needs. Physician practice patterns, when subjected to small-area analysis (61), can tell the health benefits manager whether to focus first on unnecessary surgery, hospital admissions, or length of stay.

Cost containment methods should be geared to problems revealed in utilization data and surveys of employee attitudes. Are there too many hospital admissions, suggesting the need for preadmission screening? Or is length of stay too long in comparison to the national average, requiring concurrent review? Likewise, the level of employee knowledge of changing patterns of health insurance coverage should be considered. How difficult is it to explain the rules of a second surgical opinion program? How many mistakes are likely to be made by employees? What will be the level of employee dissatisfaction over the consequences?

Specification of Goals.   In the short term, managers of health projects should specify how they intend to deal with changes in governmental programs that will affect employees. For example, Medicare has never covered the full cost of medical care for the elderly (62). A goal for the short term is therefore to establish whether and how an organization will contribute to the ever-widening medigap coverage for retirees. Trends and directions of new governmental programs, such as catastrophic care coverage, warrant consideration.

Changes in the demographic makeup of the country dictate some of the long-term goals that will be set by health benefits planners. With the graying of the population, a vastly greater proportion of retirees will be supported by a reciprocally smaller work force. The retirement age is likely to increase, especially as debilitating chronic conditions in the elderly are delayed or prevented (14, 19). Creation of long-term care alternatives and effective means of coping with the cost of medical care will assist the demographic transition for both the organization and retirees.

Implementation

Organization and Staffing.   Staff should have substantial familiarity with the methods of cost containment described below. Consultants or staff are needed for tax, accounting and auditing, and legal services, as well as direct administration of benefits. If outside consultants are permitted a free hand with limited oversight by the organization itself, there might be negative consequences for both employee and employer. Decisions about admission, length of stay, and surgery are not always clear-cut; if they were, then cost containment might have happened years ago. The organization, not the consultant, has the responsibility to determine how far to pursue cost containment goals.

Choice of Cost-effective Services.   Not much is known yet about the cost-effectiveness of some methods. Even for established methods, the scene is changing so rapidly that information is outdated. What follows is the best available assessment of cost effectiveness of provider systems.

FEE-FOR-SERVICE WITH INDEMNITY INSURANCE. Even with the traditional reimbursement system for health care services, the health benefits manager has some tools to limit unnecessary utilization and therefore limit costs. By requiring deductibles and copayments from employees, a health insurance plan can limit unnecessary utilization and thus control costs. A variety of studies, including a large-scale experiment conducted by the Rand Corporation, have demonstrated that increasing the cost sharing of patients from 0% to 25% can bring about a reduction in medical care expenditures of between 17% and 24% (17, 37). The Rand study also found that quality does not suffer, but this finding is somewhat controversial (20).

Self-insuring employers can also hire consultants or insurers to perform several tasks designed to limit unnecesary utilization of hospitals. One such task is preadmission review of hospital admissions, in which qualified professionals review patient records to determine whether admission is needed. Concurrent review of length of stay is a second task that contributes to hospital cost control; professionals determine whether the patient needs to remain in the hospital beyond a certain time period. Retrospective or claims review of hospital stays is a third task, primarily used to detect and correct accounting errors, rather than to encourage efficiency in hospital care (20). Second surgical opinions provide a fourth approach for controlling utilization and therefore costs. In such programs, employees are required to seek a second opinion for certain elective surgical procedures—the second, and even a third, opinion are reimbursed by the insurance plan, and in some cases employee travel time and time lost from work may be reimbursed as well. While mandating second opinions may well be cost effective (e.g., reference 43), the evidence is still controversial; large employers who have tried the method express the least satisfaction with it compared to other strategies (20).

Case management is a newer concept intended to affect both utilization and costs. It involves arranging for the organization and sequence of medical and social services for an individual. Case management may include elements of utilization review, but also involves a variety of steps to ensure good-quality and appropriate care. Case management is especially appropriate when a health condition is complicated and requires the services of several specialists, or when social and rehabilitative needs also exist, as in the case of the elderly or persons with AIDS.

HEALTH MAINTENANCE ORGANIZATIONS (HMOs). The search for responsible cost containment strategies has given rise to several alternative provider systems. Health maintenance organizations (HMOs) are in fact as old as Blue Cross and Blue Shield plans, but the early 1970s saw federal support for expansion and creation of new HMOs (30, 31, 55). An HMO is a direct service plan which combines per capita prepayment for hospital care along with physician services at a minimum to a voluntarily enrolled population on a contractual basis (31). Mental, dental, drug, and other services are often included. The feature of prepayment alters the usual incentives to the provider. Where fee for service practice may encourage overuse of hospital and medical services, physicians in an HMO need to minimize care that is not needed (17). Preventive medicine, which is seldom reimbursed by insurers under a fee for service system, is a central focus, though often not fully achieved in HMOs (31). Although patient waiting time for a nonurgent appointment may be used as a means to ration services in HMOs, the patient may utilize services as often as required for no additional or only minimal registration fees (17). Thus delays in seeking needed care should be minimized.

Two models of HMO, the prepaid group practice (PGP), and the individual practice association (IPA), are easily distinguishable. In the PGP model, physicians are either employees (staff model), or members of a partnership or corporation and related to the plan through an exclusive contractual arrangement (group model). In the IPA model, physicians and physician groups in independent practice agree to form an association to share financial risk in providing prepaid care to a voluntarily enrolled population, usually on a fee for service basis or on a capitated basis (network model). The IPA service agreement may specify fee levels and degree of risk sharing (30).

PGPs studied in the 1960s and 1970s have been found to result in 10% to 40% lower health care costs in terms of premiums plus out-of-pocket expenses, compared to the traditional fee for service care and indemnity insurance coverage (30). There is no evidence that quality of care in HMOs is different from that of fee for service care (30). Although PGP patients may be somewhat different from the general population in terms of health status or condition, the difference is probably not responsible for the superior performance of PGPs in age, sex, and occupationally adjusted populations (17). Relatively few IPA model HMOs have been studied, but existing IPA's are less effective in lowering health costs, compared to PGP's (30).

PREFERRED PROVIDER ORGANIZATIONS (PPOs). The expansion of another alternative provider system, the PPO, started up in the mid-1980s (46). PPOs are contractual arrangements with a defined group of providers, usually calling for discounted medical care services to be offered to a firm's employees or to retirees. Although patients are not required to use designated providers, incentives are provided for them to do so. These incentives are usually a lower deductible or copayment for medical care (46). PPOs must generally employ all the cost containment strategies outlined for fee for service practice, unless providers are exposed to financial risk factors similar to those used in HMOs. Although charges are discounted, providers have an incentive to contract with PPOs because they hope to get a substantial number of patients in a competitive market for health care. Also, PPOs usually promise rapid response to submitted claims. PPOs may be formed and marketed by insurers, employers, community groups, independent entrepreneurs, or providers themselves, often in a medical staff and hospital (MESH) joint venture (22).

In the mid-1980s PPOs vary greatly, but the majority share certain characteristics. In a survey conducted by Rice et al. (46), discounts by PPOs average 10% to 15% less than the usual charges by hospitals. Physicians are paid on a fee schedule or their usual fees are discounted, often as much as 20%. PPOs employ utilization review as the major way in which costs are controlled within a hospital. Unlike HMOs, relatively few PPOs utilize the case management approach or use networks of primary care physicians as gatekeepers for medical care. In addition to savings in out-of-pocket costs, incentives to use the PPO often include the provision of additional benefits, such as well-baby care. The organization of PPOs may produce some inherent conflicts that may not be to the advantage of employers or employees (46). PPOs formed by hospitals themselves face a conflict between health care cost containment opposed to the need to fill their beds. Thus discounts for services may be swallowed up in extra utilization. Also, a recent survey showed that insurers tend to form PPOs in order to increase their market share, and are not selective in terms of the physicians included in the contractual arrangement (46). This is also said to be true for IPAs. Until PPOs have established a track record that can be demonstrated to purchasers of care, uncertainties about quality and cost-effective performance are likely to persist.

Distinctions among HMOs, PPOs, and any other alternative may become less sharp in future, as principles behind cost-effective care become more prevalent and familiar to purchasers of medical care. With likely deregulation of the health care industry in the future, it is possible that marketplace competition may be used to further contain costs.

NEW DEVELOPMENTS. Two of these are worth mentioning. First, "cafeteria" benefits plans, also known as "flexible spending arrangements," are becoming more common. Under cafeteria plans, employees can choose from among several possible benefits at different levels of coverage. The IRS has ruled that these plans qualify for exclusion of income from taxation. Such plans permit employees to choose how much of their fringe benefits they wish to allocate to health, life, and disability insurance, for example.

Enthoven (10) has been a consistent advocate for a voucher system as an alternative to this development. In a voucher system, individual patients could seek their own source of care, within the limits of the voucher, or could supplement vouchers with their own funds when desired. For this arrangement to work well, consumers must be informed enough to make good choices—and frequently they are not well informed.

Contracting with Providers and Consultants. Providers and consultants for health benefit programs must be chosen with care. For example, consultants may or may not be vigorous in reviewing claims, certifying admissions, and monitoring length of stay. Even if they are vigorous, they may not give sufficient attention to access and quality of care. Likewise, many new HMOs are being formed. Yet not all these organizations will be federally qualified. Many HMOs claim to provide utilization controls, yet show no evidence of having such a system (20). Similarly, all PPOs will not be equally discriminating about the choice of practitioners to be involved, nor about quality control, nor about the kinds of discounts they will give (13).

It is said that the only thing worse than a bad doctor is a bad group of doctors. Organizations must become sophisticated in selecting alternative provider systems with good management and financial skills. The aggressive marketer and deep discounter may not be providing really adequate care, and complaints may surface. In general, discounts will probably turn out to be less important than controls on excess utilization. The early experience of some IPAs as well as prepaid group practices provides evidence of deficiencies in such skills (13).

The health benefits manager will also want to know the HMO's or PPO's track record on quality of care. Satisfactory information is generally not available from hospitals, and even less so from physicians. Hospital quality assurance programs vary in part due to the types of patients seen and the severity of their illnesses. The federal government has developed a system for comingling cost and quality assessment which is monitored by Peer Review Organizations (PROs) for the Medicare population. In some states this process is now spreading to all hospitalized patients. Information on physicians' practice patterns can be obtained through utilization profiles developed by third-party payors for the Medicare program. Thus some data are available for analysis of the numbers and costs of certain procedures attributed to individual hospitals and to groups of physicians.

Contracts for the delivery of hospital and physician care should specify which party will bear the risk of large medical bills. Some PPOs are now more akin to hybrid HMOs in that they receive prepayment and bear the risk of utilization that exceeds the prepayment amount. The contract should specify the basis for charges—will they be based on diagnosis related groups (DRGs)? A discount might be specified, but some analysts have warned that providers might "churn" an excessive number of patients through their facilities, or raise their prices and then offer a discount that is meaningless (13). The contract should guarantee a discount for at least a set period of time. It should also specify which forms of utilization review will be used, and the qualifications of the personnel doing the review. Ready access to second surgical opinion programs means that less travel time to designated physicians is required.

Employee Communications. Employees can misunderstand their benefits, so that medical services rendered to them will not be reimbursed. This is especially the case when there is no gatekeeper mechanism to control the use of medical care. In particular, mandatory second surgical opinion programs run the risk of employees' misunderstanding of the procedures and failing to obtain the required opinion prior to elective surgery.

A benefits information center may be desirable in larger organizations (19). Employees can then direct their questions to a centralized location whose sole function is to answer questions clearly and in a helpful tone. This should be advantageous to benefits managers as well, since their duties will not be interrupted by constant inquiries. In smaller organizations, a single individual might be designated to answer such questions, or the firm might contract with providers for this feature. Some hospitals, for example, now have specialists whose duty is to contact patients prior to admission and to explain what their benefits packages cover.

Monitoring

Use of Data: Utilization and Charges. Information about utilization and charges should be available from the insurer for aggregates of employees. In the future, it will be available from PPOs and HMOs. In smaller employee groups, however, the manager should be aware that the overall level of these indicators is likely to fluctuate from year to year, since the medical care experience of only a few seriously ill employees may skew utilization data and charges for any given year. For this reason, it is important that the employer compare charges and utilization to age-adjusted charges and utilization of the population in the region as a whole, as well as to the past experience of the employee group.

Providers may attempt to reclassify patients into categories of care for which utilization and charges are higher. The Medicare program has developed some methods for dealing with such potential overall changes in classification, through the use of the PROs.

The benefits manager usually does not have access to the same resources as the federal government, but there are still steps that he or she can take to assure that providers do not reclassify of patients. First, the manager should track the regulatory activities of the PRO. Second, if the PRO determines that some providers are changing the classification of patients toward diagnoses that allow more liberal utilization and charges, then the manager might have to consider canceling contracts with those providers or else negotiate new health benefit arrangements with insurers or alternative provider systems.

Use of Data: Quality and Access.   The manager who is concerned about medical care quality should keep his or her eye on certain indicators. Specifically, the manager will want to know about provider licensure, reports by the Joint Commission on Accreditation of Health Care Organizations (JCAHO), and, for HMOs, whether they are federally qualified. The manager may also want to track the proportion of employees admitted to the hospital subsequent to outpatient surgery. If this proportion is too high in comparison with past experience or with the overall experience of the region, then decisions of preadmission assessors may be overly biased against admission for procedu.es. This is not to say that numerous mistakes are occurring or that quality of care *is* deteriorating, but rather, that a closer look at aggregate data over time is in order. The confidentiality of individual records must be respected by the organization itself. Finally, the manager can rely on decisions made by the PROs regarding quality, although in most states these organizations monitor Medicare patients exclusively.

Access to care, patient satisfaction, continuity of care, and perceived quality should continue to be of concern to management and employees alike. Lower performance on these indicators will defeat the purposes of business in offering health benefits. In the past, the employer had to rely on the marketplace to dictate satisfaction and quality. Under new arrangements such as PPOs, the marketplace may not function so well, or so quickly. Periodic sample surveys of employees and monitoring of complaints by those employees should provide indicators of access, satisfaction, and perceived quality. An appeals process is highly desirable, to minimize actual mistakes in denial of benefits and to provide employees with opportunity to air their complaints in an appropriate manner.

DEVELOPMENT OF COST-EFFECTIVE HEALTH PROMOTION PROGRAMS

Planning

Objectives.   Health promotion and disease prevention programs have emerged as a means to improve health of employees; at the same time it is hoped that these programs will help employers meet their own objectives for cost containment, increased productivity, and reduced absenteeism, among others. In this section we explore the extent to which employee and employer objectives are achieved by these programs.

Some health promotion activities have been clearly linked to improving quality of life, health, and increased life span of the employee. Others have not, although they may be regarded as "promising". Still others have not been demonstrated to be beneficial for health although they may be useful in meeting other objectives. But part of health maintenance for the employees is, in principle, to provide guidance concerning effective preventive efforts and protection from marketers of useless fads.

Primary, secondary, and tertiary disease prevention have important financial implications for businesses. Primary prevention by immunization and lifestyle modification activities avoid illness before it begins. They are relatively low-cost, potentially high-yield activities. Use of seat belts does a great deal to prevent later physical impairment (35). Flu shots and pneumovax are particularly beneficial for older employees and those at high risk of respiratory infections. Secondary prevention activities help avoid serious consequences of a condition. Activities such as smoking cessation, hypertension control, and cholesterol reduction can mitigate or reverse the progression of heart disease; in their absence, the employee may become disabled (39, 60). Premenstrual stress is a major cause of work loss; many cases now respond to short-term therapy. Tertiary prevention is primarily a medical matter intended to avoid chronic complications or limit disability from existing diseases. Handicapped employees can benefit greatly from tertiary prevention. Diabetics who learn important self-care skills suffer fewer complications, such as blindness, and require less medical care for problems such as amputation (56).

These activities could have positive effects on health and life insurance premiums, especially as the retirement age increases. Lowering long term disability costs may be especially important, for example, in avoidance of back injuries by matching employees to jobs or by redesigning the work. Savings should be greatest in companies in which the turnover rate is low and tenure long (40). However, savings from these health promotion and disease prevention activities are likely to be modest in most cases (28). Moreover, illnesses avoided will not result in reduced health insurance premiums unless a company self-insures, unless its own experience rating is used in setting premiums, or unless insurers begin to give discounts to companies where employees are willing to participate.

Achievement of higher productivity has not yet been well measured in the literature on health promotion. At present, it can only be inferred that productivity would increase if employee behavior were more consistent with a healthful lifestyle.

Health promotion can potentially reduce liability from occupational exposures, because those linked to cancer are often made worse by smoking. Diseases from tobacco along with exposure to other carcinogens will not become evident for many years. The employer can be held liable for the effects of both smoking and worksite exposures.

Recruitment of desirable employees, increase in morale, and improvement of company image are also frequently mentioned as objectives of health promotion. Indeed, recruitment appears to motivate many companies to provide the trendier health benefits, such as stress reduction, exercise, and weight loss programs (59). Some organizations use health promotion programs to enhance their identification with health, sports, or innovation. Also, managers may see the focus on health as fitting into their overall philosophy or style. Team activities such as bowling and softball are loosely health-related and also promote such an image.

Consultation with Stakeholders.   In health promotion programs it is essential to consult all stakeholders in an organization. Employee interest must be ascertained in order to gain good participation. Employee suspicions about confidentiality must be allayed for activities such as hypertension counseling. At present, health promotion is the least accepted of the health projects described in this chapter. As such, it may have different meanings and relate to different objectives among various stakeholders at the workplace.

Needs Assessment.   Demographic information assists in the planning of health promotion activities, as well. Younger workers are raising families, often with both parents in the work force. They may need information on parenting and preventive health care for children. Also, younger workers are more prone to experience automobile accidents, and seat belt campaigns are important interventions for them. Older workers are more prone to cardiovascular ailments; they may be nearing retirement, and need to know about self-care for the elderly. Women are entering the work force in increasing numbers and are being subjected to many of the same stresses once thought to be exclusively a male domain. This is likely to increase the importance of interventions to prevent cardiovascular disease for both sexes.

Another way to get information on needs for health promotion in the work force is to conduct health screenings and administer health risk appraisals (2, 40). In addition, screening is useful to the employer who wants to be protected from allegations of problems due to worksite exposures to hazardous substances. Health risk appraisals are not just a data collection tool. By themselves, they can be used to educate and motivate employees to make changes in their lifestyle (47).

Specification of Goals. For the short term, health promotion efforts should be aimed at maximizing participation by employees at risk of health problems that can be prevented or improved, minimizing drop-outs from any treatment or intervention, and assisting the maximum number of participants to adhere to lifestyle changes. It is only by these three indices that an organization can hope to improve the health of entire work forces, and only in this way can intervention be made truly cost effective. A special goal for the short term is to ensure that activities are targeted especially to those who can benefit: for example, exercise programs for sedentary people, first, and then perhaps expansion to everyone.

Statements about short-term goals should use action verbs, specify a time frame for accomplishment, and specify outcomes in measurable terms. A very immediate goal for hypertension control might be: "by one year from today, the health promotion program will identify the majority of hypertensives in the work force by screening at least 75% of employees for high blood pressure." Another, longer-term goal might be the following: "by two years from today, the health promotion program will recruit and retain at least 80% of known hypertensives into a worksite hypertension counceling program." Longer-term goals relate to maintaining positive health behavior and gaining a substantial cumulative impact on employees' health.

Implementation

Organization and Staffing. Two models of organization for health promotion are frequently seen. In one model, health professionals such as the medical director take a leadership role in programs. This model has the advantage that health professionals are familiar with the idea of needs assessment and are likely to focus programming onto those activities for which a health benefit can reasonably be expected. In the other model, leadership comes from a committee made up of participants from various parts of the organization. This model has the advantage that organizational members feel ownership of the program; the belief is that they are therefore more likely to participate. However, such committees are sometimes more likely to choose activities without respect to health or other needs, and without a critical appraisal of likely benefits for the organization or for the work force. Combining the two models may incorporate their best elements. Staffing of health promotion efforts does not have to be expensive, since outside consultants and volunteer organizations provide a rich resource. Occupational nurses, health educators, and exercise physiologists frequently supply health promotion services in-house.

Choice of Cost-effective Services. In the area of health promotion, it is fairly clear that some activities (outlined above) are more effective than others in lowering the risk of disease. Some health promotion activities simply do not produce permanent lifestyle changes. Weight reduction for obese employees is not effective because the average reduction across many studies in all settings is only 10 pounds (6). Stress management is useful for specific problems, but when provided to all employees without regard to specified conditions, participation is low and people fail to practice stress-reducing exercises on a routine basis. When stress management is targeted specifically to those who can be expected to benefit, participation and routine practice are much higher. Exercise is linked to lower cardiovascular risk. There is also suggestive evidence of a link to lower absenteeism and higher productivity (53). However, the highest participation rate in worksite exercise to date is 25% (7). Moreover, exercise participation rates frequently fail to take into account people who exercise away from the work setting.

Screening and follow up for hypertension, high cholesterol, and breast cancer are all worthwhile where community services do not pick up these conditions. However, not all screening programs are worthwhile. Also, even good screening programs must be linked to a system to get people under a physician's care. If people are not aggressively guided to a physician's care for problems found in screening, they may take on the "sick role," losing even more workdays and experiencing more anxiety and depression than before they were notified about their condition (44). Excellent health screening programs exist, and they have succeeded in getting many employees under medical care (11). However, many well-intentioned organizations do not understand the importance of aggressively referring people to medical care, and may promote screenings for unselected groups of people without a good understanding of the prevalence of underlying problems, the nature of the test, or the role that the screening information might play in the medical care system.

Even for health promotion activities that are effective in improving health, there are more and less costly approaches. Smoking offers the best example. Most people want to quit on their own (42), and self-help materials are not costly. Even though the percentage of participants who quit is not very great, participation can be so great that the yield is large. Behavioral medicine and commercially marketed programs can be very costly. Although the percent of participants who quit might be higher, such methods might not be warranted until people have tried and perhaps failed through cheaper methods.

Contracting with Providers. Health promotion providers often promise the purchaser more than they can deliver. These providers should be able to present several kinds of information. First, they should be able to tell the purchaser about the extent of participation they can achieve in interventions for smoking, hypertension control, weight reduction, etc. Second, they should project the likely dropout rates from these interventions and explain how they hope to prevent dropouts. Finally, they should project the likely percentage of employees who will sustain behavior changes conducive to health for a year or more. And, they should be able to describe how they plan to help sustain those changes through environmental supports in the workplace, continued contact with participants, etc.

Employee Communications.   Access to health promotion activities means that activities are held at times and in locations that employees deem to be convenient, as ascertained through an employee interest survey. The best means of doing so is to launch an awareness campaign at several levels. Announcements of clinics or classes should appear in multiple locations and through many sources. Feedback to employees about their own Health Risk Appraisals can motivate further interest in participation for at least some activities (47). Several programs have gained good participation by giving small incentives for participation, such as T-shirts, coffee mugs, or apples. Larger incentives for lifestyle change get good participation, but it is still not clear whether lifestyle changes are permanent (28). Changes in employee perception of the corporate culture can also facilitate participation, since employees should perceive that the administration looks with favor on participation and on lifestyle changes.

Monitoring

Use of Data.   To measure the impact of health promotion programs, the employer can use three short-term indicators of lifestyle change: participation in clinics or activities, retention of employees in those activities, and long-term changes in the targeted outcome. For example, it should be relatively easy to track the proportion of smokers who attend a first meeting of a smoking cessation clinic, as well as the number who continue to attend most of the meetings of that clinic. Participants can be contacted one year later and their smoking and health status verified. The use of these three indicators together should give the manager an idea of the performance of the health promotion program. The average experience across many worksites is now available, and the manager can compare the experience of his or her organization to that of many other organizations (28). In general, managers may have an unrealistic idea of what health promotion can accomplish. Only a portion of the at-risk population is likely to participate in health promotion programs, only a portion of those participants will remain in a class or clinic, and only a portion of those retained employees will actually change their behavior. When compared to the results from other companies, however, an organization's health promotion effort may appear quite productive.

Corrective Action. If difficulties do emerge, another survey should be conducted with the object of locating access or interest problems. Participation in health promotion programs can be increased by further attention to employee interest surveys—activities could be made more convenient, occur on company time, with time sharing, or with cost-sharing by the company (28). Also, dropouts could be interviewed confidentially to determine their reasons for quitting the health promotion activity.

A PROJECT TO DEVELOP AN EMPLOYEE ASSISTANCE PROGRAM

Planning

Objectives. EAPs are mostly aimed at helping employees solve personal problems so that productivity can rise or be maintained. Recent data suggest that this is indeed the case, (29). Of special note, alcoholics detected and treated through a worksite program have a much better prognosis than do alcoholics in the community, so limitation in work performance due to alcohol abuse can be reduced or reversed.

EAPs are also aimed at helping employees solve other personal problems, as indicated by the extent to which many EAPs permit self-referrals. Indeed EAPs can be expected to achieve this goal, since counseling is generally found to alleviate anxiety and depression (54).

As a spinoff from the immediate objective, EAPs can also help alleviate several other organizational problems. Since blue-collar workers with alcohol problems are absent from work more frequently than others, EAPs have been demonstrated to lower both absenteeism and workdays lost (51). Alcohol abuse contributes to a variety of health problems, such that rehabilitation should reduce health care utilization (38). Also, there is a consistent relationship found between mental health counseling and lower utilization of medical care services (50). Finally, EAPs give an incentive to employees to deal with drug dependencies, which can prevent involvement of employees with the legal system and help the employer deal intelligently with the issue of drug testing on the job.

Since EAPs are often presented as the only alternative to terminating the employee, they may assist in preventing turnover. However, termination may be more cost-beneficial, depending on the number of years of employment ahead, and the investment in employee training (52).

Consultation with Stakeholders. Some of the decisions made about EAPs really involve organizational values as well as information about program effectiveness. For example, to what extent should self-referrals be permitted? Self-referrals may or may not directly assist the organization in terms of productivity or absenteeism, while referrals from superiors should. Nevertheless, self-referrals may play an important role in prevention of problems, and certainly are in line with providing a benefit to the employee. Along the same lines, counseling for troubles other than substance abuse and mental health may not be essential for productivity or other employee-focused goals. However, such counseling could be of great use to the employee and may benefit the employer indirectly. Organizations must also develop a policy about drug abusers. Is the goal of EAP to detect such drug abusers for possible dismissal? Or is the goal to provide rehabilitation and a warning? What about the role of security and prevention of thefts by hard drug users?

Needs Assessment. The voluntary nature of data collection for preventive activities is especially problematic for alcohol, drug abuse, and mental health programs. The prevalence of substance abuse and emotional problems can never be completely gauged (29). Instead, employers might rely on national data estimates, performance data, health care utilization data, absenteeism data, and other sources that would supply indirect evidence of a general need for an EAP. Some employees may not even admit to themselves that they have a substance abuse problem, and may require constructive confrontation by a supervisor before they are willing to seek treatment. There is often much more substance abuse and emotional disturbance in the work force than people believe.

Specification of Goals. The penetration rate of EAP services is the percentage of troubled employees who receive counseling by the EAP in any given year. Because the prevalence of problems is not known, staff will have to choose an estimate from the population as a whole or from similar organizations in order to plan. For example, they may project a certain number of likely troubled employees based on such estimates, and then set a short-term goal concerning what they hope is a realistic penetration rate. The organization may also wish to set short-term goals for rates of detection and referral by supervisors, as well as rates of acceptance of counseling by employees who are referred. These rates could be based on past experience or the experience of other organizations; some rates are available in the literature (29, 33).

Longer-term goals concerning productivity, absenteeism, and medical care utilization are somewhat easier to quantify, in that information concerning present status of the organization and decrements in performance of individuals can in fact be monitored. Realistic goals for the organization as a whole or for referred individuals can be set in advance.

Implementation

Organization and Staffing. The choice of providers under an EAP, whether full- or part-time physicians, psychologists, social workers, or nurses, will be limited to some degree by the extent to which such services are provided in-house. In-house staff will determine whether employees require referrals for long-term treatment; in this way, EAP staff act in the same way as case managers or "channeling" staff in cost containment strategies for medical care. EAP administrators should be clinically oriented and have good familiarity with the network of providers in a city or region and their practice patterns. A danger in EAP staffing is that low-cost providers with inadequate training will provide the actual counseling. The project manager should make sure that EAP staff can recognize conditions they cannot treat and can make appropriate referrals.

Choice of Cost-effective Services. Services can include treatment for substance abuse, mental health problems, domestic conflict, legal and financial difficulties, etc. They can also include stress management, assistance with housing and daycare problems, gambling, disability counseling, retirement planning, job counseling, assistance in work problems, and counseling on bereavement. Planners for EAPs and similar efforts should ascertain which of the many possible services under an EAP will truly help to achieve organizational objectives. Alcohol abuse programs have been shown to be cost effective, and the likelihood of recovery by employed alcoholics is very high compared to the rest of the population (38). Less information is available concerning drug abuse programs for the working population. Psychotherapy and psychological counseling generally do improve people's self-esteem, decrease anxiety and depression, and permit better job performance (54). For the employer, however, it is important to translate these benefits into quantifiable terms—how much can the person expect to benefit in terms of improved job performance, for example? The majority of troubled employees can benefit from brief psychotherapy and need not undergo long-term treatment (8). Many health benefits managers worry that mental health utilization will expand greatly if benefits are liberalized (8). However, employers should be aware that the EAP itself constitutes a means of referring employees to cost-effective sources of care.

Contracting with Providers.   Outside providers should be able to demonstrate their qualifications. They should also be able to cite average utilization and the types of treatment offered to EAP clients. In addition, they should spell out in writing their means of maintaining confidentiality of records and of reporting progress back to the in-house staff. Access to an EAP would require that employees could refer themselves for counseling, as well as being referred by their supervisors if necessary. In general, case-finding procedures for EAP should be spelled out in writing.

Employee Communications.   For EAP the goal is primarily to motivate at-risk groups to utilize a needed service. For EAP utilization to occur in the manner intended, supervisors must be trained to recognize and refer employees whose performance decrements suggest possible substance abuse or emotional difficulty. Supervisors should not attempt to begin counseling and should limit their confrontation to observed and documented evidence of poor or declining performance. They should leave anything else to the EAP professionals. Many businesses have elected to permit self-referrals to EAP as well. Announcements should be posted with either the phone number or location of the EAP clearly marked. A convenient but private location will help to reduce the stigma of visiting the EAP. Also, the EAP can reduce fears of a stigma by offering other activities, such as smoking cessation or stress management. The employee would not then be identified as visiting the EAP strictly for substance abuse treatment or emotional help.

Monitoring

Use of Data.   Tracking the performance of an EAP is possible at several levels. The manager will want to know about the rate of case finding, types of referrals, utilization, and charges, as well as the proportion of substance-abusing employees who are rehabilitated (33). It will not be possible to know the proportion of troubled employees who are reached by the EAP, however, since all troubled employees are not known to the employer. However, other indicators may be proxies for this aspect of performance, such as the overall rate of absenteeism, performance, accident rates, or utilization of physical health services (29).

Corrective Measures. Improper EAP utilization may require further training or supervising, or new methods of case finding, such as inspection of long-term performance or absenteeism records. Supervisors may need retraining on how to confront employees and how to refer them to the EAP. If a great many EAP clients fail to improve in terms of productivity or absenteeism, decision makers may wish to reconsider whether they have chosen appropriate kinds of people for EAP referral.

A PROJECT TO DEVELOP OCCUPATIONAL HEALTH AND SAFETY PROGRAMS

The motivation for organizations to take action in this area is usually furnished by law, regulation, and economics. Government has mandated much activity, such as the workplace health regulations enforced by the Occupational Safety and Health Administration (OSHA). State and federal "right-to-know" laws require that a company both *obtain* information for its employees concerning the substances with which they come in contact, and must *produce* information for its customers. The danger of liability is very great for any organization that produces materials that could present a health hazard. The importance of high-quality occupational health and safety programs is therefore strongly linked to risk management.

In all probability, more has been written on the subject of occupational health and safety than on our other three projects combined. The reader is referred to texts such as Patty's *Industrial Hygiene and Toxicology* (41), Allen, Ells and Hart (3), Gardner (16), or Hunter (21). We should say at the outset of this brief overview of occupational health and safety that data collection and control are best left to the professionals described below. Nevertheless, the decision to expand, build, or reorient a health and safety program does lend itself to the project management approach, and priorities will still be set by top managers in conjunction with health and safety professionals.

A. Planning

Objectives. Occupational safety and health protection programs are intended to prevent occurrence of work-related injuries and illnesses. The employee benefits from these programs because they improve the work environment, and the employer benefits because these programs first lower premiums on and subsequently control costs for Workers' Compensation insurance. They can also prevent other costs to an organization, such as health care, long-term disability, life insurance, and replacement costs. Although occupational diseases are covered by Workers' Compensation in most states for at least some period of time, lawsuits related to occupational disease that bypass Workers' Compensation are on the increase. Employers who fail to inform workers of hazards are held liable for negligence by the courts. This liability can be avoided if the employer shows that all possible steps were taken to avoid the hazard. Right-to-know laws at federal and state levels make it even more important to demonstrate that the employer has informed its workers.

Consultation with Stakeholders. All literature on occupational safety and health indicates that top management support is crucial to success (4, 36). Top managers set the tone for the rest of the organization and determine whether supervisors and workers will take health and safety seriously. A health and safety committee might be especially helpful for stakeholder consultation. The committee should be made up of representatives from all departments of the organization, and should have rotating membership so that many more individuals can be exposed to the safety and health message (36). Employee health nurses, if present, should sit on this committee, since they are well qualified to speak about the human element in injury or health hazards. Supervisors have the greatest influence over the safety behavior of workers, and should therefore be consulted about any proposed changes in occupational health programs in order to gain their complete support (12). Workers are more likely to cooperate with safety and health measures when they have been consulted first. Also, employees frequently know more about the actual production processes and may have information that challenges preconceptions about problems. Protective equipment can be pilot tested using the committee's judgments concerning comfort and convenience (4).

Certain departments in the workplace should have a special relationship with the occupational health and safety program. The personnel department has a special relevance to occupational safety and health, because it is frequently involved in both training the employee and in employee relations (4). Purchasing should be consulted frequently and the health and safety manager should have input into equipment and chemical product purchasing decisions, to assure that equipment will meet standards and also to assist the organization in meeting "right-to-know" requirements (4, 36). The legal department should consult with the occupational health project manager regarding OSHA rules and possible litigation over worksite exposures. Close collaboration with the operating departments is needed to assure training required by "right-to-know" laws and to plan for the prevention of hazardous exposures and safety risks. When the organization makes certain products, the sales department must also be involved, to assure that valid and accessible "right-to-know" information goes to customers.

Needs Assessment. The nature of the organization and the presence or absence of particular kinds of hazards will dictate certain data needs. Workplaces must keep records of accidents under the Occupational Safety and Health Act (OSHA). OSHA inspections, levels of Workers' Compensation claims, enforcement of "right-to-know" laws, and possible litigation over workplace exposures to toxic substances all could motivate management and employees to cooperate with such a health project.

Beyond routine data collection, industrial hygienists, safety engineers, and toxicologists can provide more detailed analyses of hazardous conditions. Textbooks on occupational safety and health stress the fact that priorities for solving safety and health problems must be set—resources are finite and some hazards are more likely than others to be serious or to cause harm. These priorities must be set by decision makers in consultation with occupational health and safety professionals.

Specification of Goals. Record keeping permits organizations to set realistic goals for any reduction in illness and injuries. Traditionally organizations have set goals for employee compliance with health and safety rules. Setting compliance goals requires a survey of current compliance levels, plus informed judgments about the extent to which compliance can feasibly be increased. Goals can also be set for employee knowledge about hazardous materials in the worksite, so that "right-to-know" requirements can be met. Current knowledge might be assessed via a survey; goals could be expressed in relative terms, such as increases in knowledge, or in absolute terms, such as saying that the "right-to-know" requirements have or have not been met (49).

For the longer term, it is important to recognize that the face of occupational health and safety is changing a great deal. Both large and small organizations are decentralizing programs and are contracting out much of the medical care that was formerly provided by company physicians. Organizations must be aware of the potential for a dangerous fragmented approach, the very opposite of the team approach called for by right-to-know laws, product liability, toxic torts, and other new challenges. Some experts believe that the future holds one of two models for safety and health: either a hospital-based model, or a government-supported model such as those mandated in Europe.

Implementation

Organization and Staffing.   Larger organizations are well advised to have a medical director, while smaller ones with potential safety or health hazards should have a part-time consulting physician with expertise in occupational medicine. Any manager of occupational health and safety should know a great deal about product liability, consumer protection, community protection, toxic torts, and health legislation and regulation.

Other staff are desirable if the size of the organization warrants them. Occupational health nurses are likely to be close to the human element in the analysis of health exposures and safety problems. Safety directors are likely to have some management training and experience-based knowledge, while industrial hygienists have received specialized training in their subject. These two types of specialists are likely to have different viewpoints about the dangers present in the workplace, and these should be resolved (4).

The increasing role of engineering management to control hazardous substances suggests linkage with line and staff operating departments. Some worksites locate occupational health and safety in the legal department, because of the litigation issue. This is a totally inappropriate place for effective protection of employees (4).

Choice of Cost-effective Services.   The major activities of a program include careful analysis of health protection and safety hazards, careful design of equipment and work settings to prevent disease and injury, monitoring of hazards and of compliance with health and safety procedures, and education and training (12). Worksites vary greatly in terms of hazards and feasible solutions. Knowledge in the area of risk assessment is full of gaps (9, 34).

Employee Communications.   Employee education on hazards is required by hazard communication regulations. However, education is not a substitute for careful analysis or for solving a problem through redesign of the work setting (12). Since educational intervention is required, behavioral science offers some means of making it more effective. Rewarding specific behaviors that are conducive to safety seems to make a difference in several diverse settings (12). Although injury events or near misses may be dramatic events that point to the importance of safety, they are also rather infrequent events. It is better to modify behavior by rewarding more frequently occuring behavior that can then be maintained. The role of the supervisor in assisting this process cannot be overstated (12).

Development of educational materials for safety and for employee "right-to-know" purposes does not have to be inordinately expensive. Materials can be purchased from other companies that have already developed them, or they can be developed in-house for the purpose of marketing for use by other organizations (49).

Monitoring

After implementing a project in occupational health and safety, one would expect the rate of accidents to decline or the extent of occupational exposures to be affected. In addition, the organization may wish to monitor employee compliance with safety and health protection measures. Trouble spots could then be reassessed for corrective action, in terms of engineering solutions, employee education solutions, or enforcement by the supervisor.

CONCLUSION

In this chapter we have adapted the project management strategy to four types of health projects normally encountered in organizations. The project management approach is emminently suited to development and change in programs designed to maintain the health of organizational members.

REFERENCES

1. Abraham, J. "A Union's View of Employee Assistance Programs." *Corporate Commentary*, Vol. 1(3) (March 1985) pp. 40–43.
2. Alderman, M. H. and Davis, T. K. "Blood Pressure Control Programs On and Off the Worksite." *Journal of Occupational Medicine*, Vol. 22 (1980), pp. 167–170.
3. Allen, R. W., Ells, M. D., and Hart, A. W. *Industrial Hygiene* (Prentice-Hall. Englewood Cliffs, N.J., 1976).
4. Asfahl, C. R. *Industrial Safety and Health Management* (Prentice-Hall. Englewood Cliffs, N.J., 1984).
5. Bieber, O. F. "Bargaining for Equitable, Cost-effective Health Care." *Business and Health*, Vol. 2(5) (1985), pp. 20–24.
6. Brownell, K. D. "Obesity: Understanding and Treating a Serious, Prevalent and Refractory Disorder." *Journal of Consulting and Clinical Psychology*, Vol. 50 (1982), pp. 820–840.
7. Colacino, D. L. and Gulbronson, C. R. "New Perspectives on Pepsico's Fitness Participation." *Corporate Commentary*, Vol. 1 (1984), p. 36.
8. Cummings, N. A. "The Dismantling of Our Health System." *American Psychologist*, Vol. 41 (1986), pp. 426–431.
9. Dinman, B. "Occupational Health and the Reality of Risk—An Eternal Dilemma of Tragic Choices." *Journal of Occupational Medicine*, Vol. 22 (1980), pp. 153–157.
10. Enthoven, A. "Health Tax Policy Mismatch." *Health Affairs*, Vol. 4(4) (Winter, 1985), pp. 6–13.

11. Erfurt, J. C. and Foote, A. *Hypertension Control in the Work Setting: The University of Michigan–Ford Motor Company Demonstration Program* (University of Michigan. Ann Arbor, 1982) (NIH Publication No. 83-2013).

12. Everly, G. S. and Feldman, R. H. L. *Occupational Health Promotion* (Wiley. New York, 1985).

13. Fox, P. D. and Spies, J. J. "Alternative Delivery Systems: What Are the Risks?" *Business and Health,* Vol. 1(3) (January/February, 1984), pp. 5–10.

14. Fries, J. F. "Aging, Natural Death and the Compression of Morbidity." *New England Journal of Medicine,* Vol. 303 (1980), pp. 130–135.

15. Gallo, P. S. "Meta-analysis—A mixed meta-phor?" *American Psychologist,* Vol. 33 (1978), pp. 515–517.

16. Gardner, A. W. (ed.). *Current Approaches to Occupational Health* (Wright PSG. Boston, 1982).

17. General Accounting Office. *A Primer on Competitive Strategies for Containing Health Care Costs* (GAO. Washington, D.C., 1982) (GAO/HRD-82-92).

18. Goldsmith, F, and Kerr, L. E. *Occupational Safety and Health* (Human Sciences Press. New York, 1982).

19. Griffes, E. J. E. *Employee Benefits Programs: Management, Planning, and Control* (Dow Jones-Irwin. Homewood, Ill., 1983).

20. Herzlinger, R. E. "How Companies Tackle Health Care Costs: Part II." *Harvard Business Review,* Vol. 86 (1986), pp. 108–120.

21. Hunter, D. *Diseases of Occupations* (English Universities Press. London, 1975).

22. Jacobs, P. *The Economics of Health and Medical Care,* 2nd ed. (Aspen. 1987).

23. Jameson, J., Shuman, L. and Young, W. "The Effects of Outpatient Psychiatric Utilization on the Costs of Providing Third Party Coverage." *Medical Care,* Vol. 16 (1978), p. 383.

24. Kannel, W. B. and Gordon, T. *The Framingham Study: An Epidemiological Investigation of Cardiovascular Disease* U.S. Department of Health Education and Welfare, NIH. Washington, D.C., 1974) (NIH) 74-475.

25. Kellogg Foundation. *Viewpoint: Toward a Healthier America* (W. K. Kellogg Foundation. Battle Creek, Mich., January, 1980).

26. Kiefhaber, A. K. and Goldbeck, W. B. "Worksite Wellness." Prepared for the Office of the Assistant Secretary for Planning and Evaluation, U.S. DHHS, in conjunction with the Private Sector Health Care Initiatives Study, contract #100-82-31, n.d.

27. King, W. R. "The Role of Projects in the Implementation of Business Strategy," in *Project Management Handbook,* ed. Cleland, D. I. and King, W. R. (Van Nostrand Reinhold. New York, 1983).

28. Leviton, L. C. "Can Organizations Benefit from Worksite Health Promotion?" *Health Services Research* (in press)

29. Leviton, L. C. "Diversity and Uncertainty in Employee Assistance Programs," in *Mental Health Policy: Patterns and Trends,* ed. Rich R. (Sage, Newbury Park, CA, in press).

30. Luft, H. S. *The Operations and Performance of Health Maintenance Organizations* (NCHSR. Washington, D.C., 1981).

31. MacLeod, G. K. "Health Maintenance Organizations in the United States." *International Labour Review,* Vol. 110(4) (1974), pp. 335–350.

32. MacLeod, G. K. and Schwarz, M. R. "Faculty Practice Plans: Profile and Critique." *Journal of the American Medical Association,* Vol. 256 (July 4, 1986), pp. 58–62.

33. Masi, D. A. *Designing Employee Assistance Programs* (American Management Associations. New York, 1984).

34. Michaels, D. and Zoloth, S. "Occupational Safety: Why Do Accidents Happen?" *Occupational Health Nursing* (October, 1982), pp. 12–16.
35. National Highway Traffic Safety Administration. *Final Regulatory Impact Analysis: Passenger Car Front Seat Occupant Protection* (U.S. Department of Transportation. Washington, D.C., 1984).
36. National Safety Council. *Handbook of Occupational Safety and Health* (National Safety Council. Chicago, 1975).
37. Newhouse, J. P. et al. *Some Interim Results from a Controlled Trial of Cost Sharing in Health Insurance* (Rand Corporation. Santa Monica, Calif., January, 1982).
38. Office of Technology Assessment. *The Effectiveness and Costs of Alcoholism Treatment* (OTA. Washington, D.C., 1983).
39. Oster, G., Colditz, G. A. and Kelly, N. L. *The Economic Costs of Smoking and Benefits of Quitting* (Lexington Books. Lexington, Mass., 1984).
40. Parkinson, R. S. and Associates. *Managing Health Promotion in the Workplace: Guidelines for Implementation and Evaluation* (Mayfield. Palo Alto, Calif., 1982).
41. Patty, F. A. *Patty's Industrial Hygiene and Toxicology,* 2nd ed. (Wiley. New York, 1985).
42. Pechacek, T. F. "Modification of Smoking Behavior," in *The Behavioral Aspects of Smoking,* ed. Krasnegor, N. NIDA Research Monograph 26, Washington, D.C. 1979. DHEW Publication No. (ADM) 79-882.
43. Poggio, E. et al. *Second Surgical Opinion Programs: An Investigation of Mandatory and Voluntary Alternatives* (Abt Associates. Cambridge, Mass., 1982).
44. Polk, B. F. et al. "Disability Days and Treatment in a Hypertension Control Program. *American Journal of Epidemiology,* Vol. 119 (1984), pp. 44–53.
45. Price, D. N. "Income Replacement During Sickness, 1948–1978." *Social Security Bulletin,* Vol. 44 (1981), pp. 18–32.
46. Rice, T., deLissovay, G., Gabel, J. and Erman, D. "The State of PPOs: Results from a National Survey." *Health Affairs,* Vol. 4(4) (Winter, 1985), pp. 26–39.
47. Rodnick, J. E. "Health Behavior Changes Associated with Health Hazard Appraisal Counseling in an Occupational Setting." *Preventive Medicine,* Vol. 11 (1982), pp. 583–594.
48. Russell, L. *Is Prevention Better than Cure?* (Brookings Institution. Washington, D.C., 1985).
49. Samways, M. C. "Cost-effective Occupational Health and Safety Training." *American Industrial Hygiene Association Journal,* Vol. 44 (1983), pp. A-6 to A-9.
50. Schlesinger, H. J., Mumford, E. and Glass, G. V. "Mental Health Services and Medical Utilization," in *Psychotherapy: From Practice to Research to Policy,* ed. Vandenbos, G. (Sage. Beverly Hills, 1980).
51. Schramm, C. J. "Measuring the Return on Program Costs: Evaluation of a Multiemployer Alcoholism Treatment Program." *American Journal of Public Health,* Vol. 7(1) (1977), pp. 50–51.
52. Schramm, C. J. "Evaluating Industrial Alcoholism Programs: A Human-Capital Approach." *Journal of Studies on Alcohol,* Vol. 41(7) (1980), pp. 702–713.
53. Shephard, R. J., Corey, P., Renzland, P. and Cox, M. "The Influence of an Employee Fitness and Lifestyle Modification Program upon Medical Care Costs." *Canadian Journal of Public Health,* Vol. 73 (1982), pp. 259–263.
54. Smith, M. L. and Glass, G. V. "Meta-analysis of Psychotherapy Outcome Studies." *American Psychologist,* Vol. 32 (1977), pp. 752–760.
55. Starr, P. *The Social Transformation of American Medicine* (Basic Books. New York, 1982).

56. Steiner, G. and Lawrence, P., eds. *Educating Diabetic Patients.* (Springer. New York, 1981).
57. U.S. Department of Commerce. *Statistical Abstract of the United States, 1984, 104th Edition* (Washington, D.C., 1983).
58. Waldo, D. R., Levit, K. R., and Lazenby, H. "National Health Expenditures, 1985." *Health Care Financing Review,* Vol. 8(1) (1986), pp. 1–22.
59. Warner, K. E. and Murt, H. A. "Economic Incentives for Health." *Annual Review of Public Health,* Vol. 5 (1984), pp. 107–133.
60. Weinstein, M. C. and Stason, W. B. *Hypertension: A Policy Perspective* (Harvard University Press. Cambridge, Mass., 1976).
61. Wennberg, J. E. "Dealing with Medical Practice Variations: A Proposal for Action." *Health Affairs,* Vol. 3 (1984), pp. 7–32.
62. Wilson, F. A. and Neuhauser, D. *Health Services in the United States* 2nd ed. (Ballinger. Cambridge, Mass., 1985).
63. World Health Organization. "Health Promotion: A Discussion Document on the Concept and Principles." (WHO. Copenhagen, 1984).

38. The Cultural Ambience of the Matrix Organization*

David I. Cleland†

INTRODUCTION

The concept of matrix management has grown beyond the project management context first introduced by John Mee in 1964.‡ Project management has been the precursor of today's matrix management approach found in diverse uses today. In the multinational corporation product, functional, and geographic managers work in a sharing mode of matrix management. Matrix management is found in a wide variety of other contexts: product management, task force management, production teams, new business development teams, to name a few.

In this chapter, I describe the cultural ambience of the project-driven matrix organization.

Culture is a set of refined behaviors that people have and strive towards in their society. Culture encompasses the complex whole of a society which includes knowledge, beliefs, art, ethics, morals, law, custom, and other habits and attitudes acquired by the individual as a member of society. Anthropologists have used the concept of culture in describing primitive societies. Modern-day sociologists have borrowed this anthropolical concept of culture and used it to describe a way of life of a

† David I. Cleland is currently Professor of Engineering Management in the Industrial Engineering Department at the University of Pittsburgh. He is the author/editor of 15 books and has published many articles appearing in leading national and internationally distributed technological, business management, and educational periodicals. Dr. Cleland has had extensive experience in management consultation, lecturing, seminars, and research. He is the recipient of the "Distinguished Contribution to Project Management" award given by the Project Management Institute in 1983, and in May 1984, received the 1983 Institute of Industrial Engineers (IIE)-Joint Publishers Book-of-the-Year Award for the *Project Management Handbook* (with W. R. King). In 1987 Dr. Cleland was elected a fellow of the Project Management Institute.

‡ John F. Mee, "Matrix Organization," *Business Horizons* (Summer, 1964).

people. I borrow from the sociologists and use the term culture to describe the synergistic set of shared ideas and beliefs that is associated with a way of life in an organization.

Nature of a Business Culture

The word culture is being used more and more in the lexicon of management to describe the ambience of a business organization. The culture associated with each organization has several distinctive characteristics that differentiate the company from others. In the IBM Corporation the simple precept, "IBM means service" sets the tone for the entire organization, infusing all aspects of its environment and generating its distinctive culture. At 3M the simple motto "Never kill a new product idea" creates an organizational atmosphere of inventiveness and creativity. In some large corporations such as Hewlett-Packard, General Electric, and Johnson & Johnson, the crucial parts of the organization are kept small to encourage a local culture which encourages a personal touch in the context of a motivated, entrepreneurial spirit of teamwork.

Understanding the culture of the organization is a prerequisite to introducing project management. An organization's culture reflects the composite management style of its executives, a style that has much to do with the organization's ability to adapt to such a change as the introduction of a project management system.

THE ROOTS OF THE MATRIX ORGANIZATION

The cultural ambience of the project-driven matrix organization is unique in many respects. But it should not be strange to us since our first organization, the family, has key features of the matrix design. In the traditional family unit, the child is responsible to, and has authority exercised over him by, two superiors (parents). A perceptive child soon learns that he must work out major decisions and such matters with both his bosses. If his parents have agreed on a "work breakdown structure" where each will exercise authority and assume responsibility over a particular aspect of raising the child, it will make it easier for him to get along with them and his peer group. A child may have to find ways of collaborating with both parents as well as his siblings and peers, adjusting to all groups.

When the child goes to school, another similar matrix design is found. The student is placed in a "home room" with a teacher whose main business is administration, "logistic support," and discipline. The student is taught by other teachers who are the "functional specialists"; thus the student has several more "superiors" to whom he is accountable as well as a larger peer group. If the student is active in extracurricular activities, still more bosses come into his life. Success and acceptance in these activities generally require peer acceptance, teamwork, and an ability to communicate with his "superiors" and his peers.

When the student leaves school and seeks employment, he may find more of a hierarchical structure, yet the new matrix is in many ways similar to those already experienced. If his initial job is on a production line, the production foreman becomes boss number one; yet the quality control specialist can shut down the production line. The perceptive individual finds that certain staff specialists (personnel, finance, maintenance, wage and salary) and even the informal leaders in the peer groups temper the "sovereign domain" of the foreman. He soon finds that certain people in the organization exercise power simply because they have control of information (such as the production control specialist) or have become experts in some areas. People look to the expert to make decisions or take a leadership role in certain matters. The role of the union steward as a tempering influence on production techniques and policies soon becomes obvious to him. If he is active in community affairs he finds many other "bosses" telling (or suggesting to) him what to do. Who's really the boss? Well, it depends on the situation—as it does in the matrix organization.

The sharing context of project management should not be foreign to any of us. Our family life, education, and work experience have given us ample exposure to working for and satisfying several bosses and of learning to communicate and work with peers as well. Then why such resistance to matrix design? I believe the resistance has its roots in several cultural factors. First is the concept that authority flows from the top of the organization down through a chain of command. The foundation of this belief springs from the "divine right" of the king, who is delegated to rule the kingdom by a deity. Historically most social institutions have had a strong vertical structure—a chain of command. Ecclesiastical organizations have contributed much to organization theory; many of these contributions have reinforced the vertical structure. Have we not always assumed that "heaven"—by whatever name it is called—is a higher place or state? The Bible speaks of ascending into heaven. (Why not moving to heaven on a lateral basis?)

A good friend of mine who is a competent minister once delivered a sermon on the theme that "Hell was a state of mind, not a place." After the sermon was over I asked him this question: If hell is a state of mind and not a place, then it follows that heaven is a state of mind and not a place. He said: "Perhaps, but we are not ready for that yet!"

Perhaps, like heaven, the matrix organization is more a state of mind that anything else!

No one would doubt the strong influence the Bible has had on our thinking. Indeed, the words of St. Matthew are familiar to everyone: "No man can serve two masters: for either he will hate the one, and love the other; or else he will hold to the one, and despise the other" (Matthew 6:24).

Part of the rationalization for the principle of "unity of command" may well be traced back to this verse. In managerial theory, this principle and its corollaries "parity of authority and responsibility," "compulsory staff advice," "line commands, staff advises," "span of control," etc., provide the conceptual foundation of the hierarchical organizational form. Indeed, many times managers and professionals have asked, "How can I work for two bosses?"

Yet Matthew also provides us with the basis for doing so: "Render therefore unto Caesar the things which are Caesar's; and unto God the things that are God's (Matthew 22:21).

I contend that in the light of both pragmatic and cultural experience there is as much a basis for the matrix design with its multidimensional sharing of authority, responsibility, accountability, and results, as there is for the hierarchical style of management.

THE MATRIX ORGANIZATIONAL DESIGN

I use the concept of organizational design in a broad context to include organizational structure, management systems and processes, formal and informal interpersonal relationships, and motivational patterns. The matrix design is a compromise between a bureaucratic approach that is too inflexible and a simple unit structure that is too centralized. The design is fluid: personnel assignments, authority bases, and interpersonal relationships are constantly shifting. It combines a sense of democracy within a bureaucratic context.

From an organizational design viewpoint, the entire organization must be psychologically tuned to results: the accomplishments within the organization that support higher level organizational objectives, goals, and strategies. The purpose of a matrix design is not only to get the best from its strong project approach and strong functional approach but to complement these by a strong unity of command at the senior level to insure that the balance of power is maintained in the organization. In some companies only one or a few divisions might require a realignment to the project-driven matrix form; the others might be left in the pyramidal, hierarchical form. Indeed a single organizational chart cannot realistically portray the maze of relationships that exist inside a large organization because some elements select project management, others opt for the conventional line-staff design, and still others choose some hybrid form.

The Design Is Result-Oriented

The matrix design is result-oriented and information-related. The very design itself says that there is need for someone who can manage a process of cutting across the line functions. A compromise results through the bipolarity of functional specialization and project integration. Out of the lateral relations—direct contact, liaison roles, and integration—comes a faculty to make and implement decisions and to process information without forcing an overburden on the hierarchical communication channels. It is the need to reduce the decision process on the hierarchical channels that motivates the formal undertaking of lateral relations through establishing a design which is bilateral:

1. *Project managers* who are responsible for results.
2. *Functional managers* who are responsible for providing resources to attain results.

When implementing a matrix design in the early stages, a poor harmony will usually exist between the behavioral reality and its structural form. It is at this stage that the process of integration become important and a series of critical actions must be initiated and monitored by senior management. Superior-subordinate relationships need to be modified; individual self-motivation leading to peer acceptance becomes critical. The development of strategies for dealing with conflict, the encouragement of participation techniques, and the delineation of expected authority and responsibility patterns are crucial. the complexity of the resulting organizational design, described by Peter Drucker as "fiendishly difficult," reminds us that the matrix design should only be used when there is no suitable alternative. The design lacks the simple model of the conventional hierarchy. The nature of projects each in various stages of its life cycle creates a lack of stability. Key people on the project teams must *not only know* their specialty, but also *how* the specialty contributes to the whole.

The emphasis is on flexibility, peer informality, and minimization of hierarchy. To change an existing design to a fully functioning matrix form takes time—perhaps several years.

The matrix organizational design is the most complex form of organizational alignment that can be used. The integration of specialists along with supporting staff into a project team requires strong and continuing collaborative effort. And the coordination of effort in this kind of design requires a continuing integration of the mutual efforts of the team members. Authority (and consequently power) tends to flow to the individual who has the information that is needed and whose particular skills and knowledge are necessary to make a decision. Many managers are found in the matrix design: project managers, functional managers, work package managers, general managers, staff managers. The greater the number of project teams, the greater the number of managers that will be used. As a result, the management costs in such an organizational approach are increased.

The introduction of project management into an organization tends to change established management practice with respect to such matters as authority and responsibility, procedural arrangements, support systems, department specialization, span of control, resource-allocation patterns, establishment of priorities, evaluation of people, etc. Performance goals within such organizations tend to be assigned in terms of the interfunctional flow of work needed to support a project. In so doing, established work groups within the functional agencies are often disrupted. In addition, there is a potential for the staffing pattern to involve duplication. The functional manager previously had the freedom to manage the organization in a relatively unilateral fashion, for he carried out integration himself or a higher authority handled it. Now he is forced into an interface in an environment which places a premium on the integration of resources through a project team consensus in order to accomplish project results. He must learn to work with a vocal and demanding horizontal organization.

A cultural characteristic of the matrix design causes two key attitudes to emerge: the manager who realizes that authority has its limits and the professional who recognizes that authority has its place.

THE CULTURAL AMBIENCE

In its organizational context, a cultural ambience for matrix management deals with the social expression manifest within the organization when engaged in managing projects. A cultural system emerges which reflects certain behavioral patterns characteristic of all the members of that organization. This system influences the skills, knowledge, and value systems of the people who are the primary organizational clientele. The clientele are a "team" of people who have some vested outcome in the success of an organizational effort.

Thus, project clientele include those in the organizational society who are the managers and professionals collectively sharing the authority and responsibility for completing a project on time and within budget. Superiors, subordinates, peers, and associates are the primary project clientele who work together to bring the project to a successful completion. The cultural ambience that ultimately emerges is dependent on the way these primary clientele feel and act in their professional roles both on the project team and within the larger organizational context. The integration of these clientele results in an ambience which has the following characteristics: Organizational Openness; Participation; Increased Human Problems; Consensus Decision Making; Objective Merit Evaluation; New Criteria for Wage and Salary Classification; New Career Paths; Acceptable Adversary Roles; Organizational Flexibility; Improvement in Productivity; Increased Innovation; Realignment of Supporting Systems; and Development of General Manager Attitudes. These characteristics are discussed below.

Organizational Openness

A propensity toward organizational openness is one of the most characteristic attributes of the matrix design. This openness is demonstrated through a receptiveness to new ideas, a sharing of information and problems by the peer group. Newcomers to a matrix organization are typically accepted without any concern. There is a willingness to share organizational challenges and frustrations with the newcomer. This openness characteristic of project team management is described in one company as "no place to hide in the organization."*

Participation

Participation in the project-driven matrix organization calls for new behavior, attitudes, skills, and knowledge. The demands of working successfully in the matrix design create opportunities for the people as well as for the organization. For the people, there are more opportunities to attract attention and to try one's mettle as a potential future manager. Because matrix management increases the amount and the pattern of recurring contacts between individuals, communication is more intense. The resolution of conflicts is also of a more intense nature than in the traditional organization where conflict can be resolved by talking to the functional boss. In a matrix design, at least two bosses have to become involved—the manager providing the resources and the manager held accountable for results. These two managers, locked in a conflict, may appeal as a last resort to the common line supervisor for resolution. Matrix management demands higher levels of collaboration. But in order

---

* "Texas Instruments Shows U.S. Business How To Survive in the 1980's," *Business Week* (September 18, 1978).

to have collaboration, trust and commitment are needed on the part of the individuals. In order to be committed and to maintain trust, the individuals in the organization must take personal risks in sharing information and revealing their own views, attitudes, and feelings.

There is growing evidence that individuals today wish to influence their work situation and to create a democratic environment at their place of work. People expect variety in their life-style in the organization as well as in their private lives. The flexibility and openness of the matrix design can accommodate these demands.

The degree to which people are committed to participate openly and fully in matrix organization effort can influence results. Murphy, Baker, and Fisher, in a study of over 650 projects including 200 variables, found that certain variables were associated with the perceived failure of projects. Lack of team participation in decision making and problem solving was one important variable associated with perceived project failure. In contrast, project team participation in setting schedules and budgets was significantly related to project success.*

Increased Human Problems

Reeser conducted research to examine the question as to whether project organization might not have a built-in capacity of causing some real human problems of its own. This research was conducted at several aerospace companies. Reeser's research findings suggested that insecurity about possible unemployment, career retardation, and personal development is felt by subordinates in project organizations to be significantly more of a problem than by subordinates in functional organizations. Reeser notes that project subordinates can easily be frustrated by "make-work" assignments, ambiguity, and conflict in the work environment. Project subordinates tend to have less loyalty to the organization. There are frustrations because of having more than one boss. The central implication of Reeser's findings is that although there may be persuasive justifications for using a matrix design, relief from human problems is not one of them.†

Even with formal definition of organizational roles, the shifting of people between the projects does have some noticeable effects. For example, people may feel insecure if they are not provided with ongoing career

---

* D. C. Murphy, Bruce N. Baker, and Delmar Fisher "Determinants of Project Success," Springfield, Va. 22151, National Technical Information Services, Accession No. N-74-30392, 1974, p. 60669. See Chapters 35 and 36.

† Calyton Reeser, "Some Potential Human Problems of the Project Form or Organization," *Academy of Management Journal*, Vol. 12 (December, 1979).

counseling. In addition, the shifting of people from project to project may interfere with some of the basic training of employees and the executive development of salaried personnel. This neglect can hinder the growth and development of people in their respective fields.

Consensus Decision Making

Many people are involved in the making decisions. Members of the matrix team actively contribute in defining the question or problem as well as in designing courses of action to resolve problems and opportunities in the management of the effort. Professionals who become members of a matrix team gain added influence in the organization as they become associated with important decisions supporting an effort. They tend to become more closely associated with the decision makers both within the organization and outside it. Perceptive professionals readily recognize how their professional lives are broadened.

A series of documents which describe the formal authority and responsibility for decision making of key project clientele should be developed for the organization. If a manger is used to a clear line of authority to make unilateral decisions, the participation of team members in the project decision process makes management more complex. However, the result is worth the effort for the decisions tend to be of a higher quality. Also, by participating in the decision process people have a high degree of commitment toward carrying out the decision in an effective manner.

Objective Merit Evaluation

This is an important area of concern to the individual in the matrix design. If the individual finds himself working for two bosses (the functional manager or work package manager and the project manager) chances are good that both will evaluate his merit and promotion fitness. Usually the functional manager initiates the evaluation; then the project manager will concur in the evaluation with a suitable endorsement. If the two evaluators are unable to agree on the evaluation it can be referred to a third party for resolution. For the most part, individuals who are so rated favor such a procedure as it reinforces their membership on the project team as well as ensures that an equitable evaluation is given. A project team member who has been assigned to the project team from a functional organization may find himself away from the daily supervision of his functional supervisor. Under such circumstances a fair and objective evaluation might not be feasible. By having the project manager participate in the evaluation, objectivity and equity are maintained.

New Criteria for Wage and Salary Classification

The executive rank and salary classification of a project manager will vary depending on the requirements of his position, the importance of the project to the company, etc. Most organizations adopt a policy of paying competitive salaries. However, the typical salary classification schema is based on the number and grade of managers and professionals that the executive supervises. In the management of a project, although the project manager may only supervise two or three people on his staff, he is still responsible for bringing the project in on time, at the budgeted cost. In so doing, he is responsible for managing the efforts of many others who do not report to him in the traditional sense. Therefore, new criteria for determining the salary level of a project manager are required. Organizations with successful salary classification schema for project manager's salary have utilitzed criteria such as the following:

- Duration of project.
- Importance of project to company.
- Importance of customer.
- Annual project dollars.
- Payroll and level of people who report directly to project manager (staff).
- Payroll and level of people whom project manager must interface directly on a continuing base with project manager.
- Complexity of project requirments.
- Complexity of project.
- Complexity of project interfaces.
- Payroll and rank of individual to whom project manager reports.
- Potential payoff of project.
- Pressures project manager is expected to face.

In many companies the use of project management is still in its adolesence, and suitable salary criteria have not been determined. In such cases it is not uncommon to find individuals designated as project managers who are not coded as managerial personnel in the salary classification and executive rank criteria. Word of this will get around and the individual's authority may be compromised. The author has found this situation arising usually because of a failure of the wage salary staff specialists to develop suitable criteria for adjusting the salary grade of the project managers. This problem is not as significant in those industries where project management is a way of life, such as in aerospace and construction.

New Career Paths

The aspiring individual typically has two career paths open to him: to remain as a manager in his technical field or to seek a general manager position. Or he may prefer to remain a professional in his field and become a senior advisor, for example, a senior engineer. Project management opens up a third career field in management. The individual who is motivated to enter management ranks can seek a position as a project manager of a small project and use this as a stepping stone to higher-level management positions. It is an excellent way to learn the job of a general manager since the job of project manager is much like that of a general manager except that the project manager usually does not have the formal legal authority of the general manager. This should not deter the project manager; it should motivate him to develop his persuasive and other interpersonal and negotiation skills—necessary skills for success in general management!

Acceptable Adversary Roles

An adversary role emerges in project management as the primary project clientele find that participation in the key decisions and problems is socially acceptable. An adversary role may be assumed by any of the project clientele who sense that something is wrong in the management of the project. Such an adversary role questions goals, strategies, and objectives and asks the tough questions that have to be asked. Such a spontaneous adversary role provides a valuable check to guard against decisions which are unrealistic or overly optimistic. A socially acceptable adversary role facilitates the rigorous and objective development of data bases on which decisions are made. But the prevailing culture in an organization may discourage the individual from playing the adversary role that will help management to comprehend the reality of a situation. This situation is possible in all institutions of a hierarchical character.

An adversary role presumes that communication of ideas and concerns upward is encouraged. As people actively participate in the project deliberations, they are quick to suggest innovative ideas for improving the project or to sound the alarm when things do not seem to be going as they should. If the adversary role is not present, perhaps because its emergence is inhibited by the management style of the principal managers, information concerning potential organizational failures will not surface. An example of the stifling of an adversary role is found in the case of a company in the management of an urban transportation project.

In the late 1960s this company attempted to grow from a $250-million-a-year subcontractor in the aerospace industry into a producer of ground transit equipment. In pursuing this strategy, it won prime contracts for two large urban rail systems. Heavy losses in its rail programs put the company into financial difficulties. What went wrong?

The company got into difficulty in part because the chief executive dominated the other company executives even though he was unable to face overriding practical considerations. When major projects in the rail systems business were in difficulty, the unrealistic optimism demonstrated by the chief executive prevented any executive from doing much about the difficulties. In the daily staff meetings that were held, the executives quickly learned that any negative or pessimistic report on a project would provoke open and sharp criticism from the chief executive. Project managers quickly learned that in the existing cultural ambience the bringing of bad news would not be tolerated. Consequently, they glossed over problem areas and emphasized the positive in order to please the chief executive.

On one of their large contracts they submitted a bid that was 23% below the customer's own estimate, and $11 million under the next lowest competitive bid. The project manager had felt that this estimate was too low but had not argued against it because, "I didn't want to express a sorehead minority view when I was in charge of the program." The cultural ambience within this company during this period might be summarized as follows: Don't tell the boss any bad news, only report good news—if you bring bad news, you run the risk of being sharply criticized.

Members of a project team need to feel free to ask tough questions during the life of the project. When the members of a team can play an adversary role, a valuable check and balance mechanism exists to guard against decisions which are unrealistic. Within Texas Instruments a cultural ambience exists where an adversary role can emerge. Consequently, "It is impossible to bury a mistake in this company. The grass roots of the corporation are visible from the top . . . the people work in teams and that results in a lot of peer pressure and peer recognition."*

Organizational Flexibility

The lines of authority and responsibility defining the structure tend to be flexible in the matrix organization. There is much give and take across these lines with people assuming an organizational role that the situation warrants rather than what the position description says should be done.

---

* "Texas Instruments Shows U.S. Business How To Survive in the 1980's," *Business Week* (September 18, 1978), pp. 66–92.

Authority in such an organizational context gravitates to the person who has the best credentials to make the judgment that is required.

The matrix design provides a vehicle for maximum organizational flexibility; no one has "tenure" on a matrix team. There are variable tasks that people perform, a change in the type of situations they may be working on, and an ebb and flow of work loads as the work of the organization fluctuates. When an individual's skills are no longer needed on a team, that person can be assigned back to his or her permanent functional home.

There are some inherent problems in the flexibility of the matrix organization. The need for staffing tends to be more variable. Both the quantity of personnel and the quality needed are difficult to estimate because of the various projects that are going on in the organization. For example, a structural design group may have a surplus of design engineers at a particular time who are not assigned to any one project. The manpower estimates for oncoming projects, however, may indicate that in several months these professionals will be needed for project assignments. A functional structural design manager has the decision of whether to release the men and reduce his overhead or to assign them to "make-work" for the period and forgo the future costs of recruitment, selection, and training. The same manager may anticipate assigning these professionals to an emerging project yet, if the emerging project is delayed or even canceled, the project manager may not need these people for some time.

As the work effort nears its end, and perceptive individuals begin to look for other jobs, there can be a reduction in their output level. This reduction can damage the efficacy with which the project is being managed. Paradoxically, although morale takes on added significance in the matrix team, the design itself may result in lowering it.

The organizational flexibility of project management does, therefore, create some problems as well as opportunities.

Improvement in Productivity

Texas Instruments credits the use of project teams for productivity improvement in the company. Its productivity improvement over a period of years has slightly more than offset the combined impact of its wage and benefit increases (average 9.2% annually) and its price decreases (averaging 6.4% per unit).*

At Texas Instruments more than 83% of all employees are organized into "people involvement teams" seeking ways to improve their own productivity. The company views its people as interchangeable—"kind

---

* Ibid.

of like auto parts." The culture there is much like the Japanese—a strong spirit of belonging, a strong work ethic, competitive zeal, company loyalty, and rational decision making. The culture of Texas Instruments ". . . has its roots buried deep in a soil of Texas pioneer work ethic, dedication, toughness and tenacity—it (the culture) is a religion. The climate polarizes people—either you are incorporated into the culture or rejected."*

The experience of Litton Industries in its Microwave Cooking Division shows that the use of project teams in the manufacturing function has increased productivity. Since the manufacturing organization was grouped into team units, production increased fourfold in 15 months. Product quality has increased, 1000 new production workers have been added to a base of 400 people, and unit production costs have declined 10–15%.† Some other claims of productivity increases that have come to the author's attention are as follows:‡

- A steel company chief executive states: "Properly applied, 'matrix' management improves profitability because it allows progress to be made on a broader front; with a given staff size, i.e., more programs and projects simultaneously pursued (including those concerning productivity)."
- The chief executive of a company in the microprocessor industry declares that the company's success (15% of the microprocessor market, $1.8 million in revenue, 18.1% ROI) would not be possible without matrix management.
- A chemical company president claims: "Matrix management improves people productivity."

The experiences of these companies suggest that project management techniques can assist in raising productivity.

Increased Innovation

In the private sector in those industries where a fast-changing state-of-the-art exists, product innovation is critical for survival. There is evidence that the use of project teams has helped to further innovation within such organizations. For example, the teams are successfully used in the

---

* Ibid.
† William W. Grove, "Task Teams for Rapid Growth," *Harvard Business Review* (March–April, 1977), p. 71.
‡ These are productivity claims cited to the author in correspondence.

aerospace industry where the ability to innovate is essential, particularly in the development and production of sophisticated weaponry.

Why does the project team seem to foster innovation in organizations? Innovation comes about because an individual has an idea, a technological or market idea, and surrounds himself with some people who believe in the idea and are committed to it. A small team of people is formed, who become advocates and missionaries for the idea. The team of people represents a diverse set of disciplines who view the idea differently. It's difficult to hide anything in such an environment. The openness, the freedom of expression, the need to demonstrate personal effectiveness, all seem to be conducive to the creativity necessary to innovate. Within such organizations, decision making tends to be of a consensus type. An element of esprit de corps exists. The creativity and the innovative characteristics of small teams can be illustrated by the Texas Instruments situation.*

Texas Instruments has been extrememly successful with the use of teams in over 200 product-consumer centers (PCC). In each of these centers, the manager runs a small business of his or her own with responsibilities that include both long-term and short-term considerations. These managers have access to functional groups and are able to utilize the enormous resources that the functional organizations can offer. Indeed, what Texas Instruments has done is to create an organization in which the entrepreneur—the innovator—can flourish by making available to him or her the technical resources that are needed to do the job.

Project teams used effectively can take advantage of the scale economics of large organizations and, by their team nature, the flexibility of a small innovative organization is realized. An early research effort in the use of program (project) organizations noted that such organizations seemed to have been more successful in developing and introducing new products than businesses without program organizations.†

L. W. Ellis, Director of Research, International Telephone and Telegraph Corporation, claims that temporary groups (project teams) that are well organized and have controlled autonomy can stimulate innovation by overcoming resistance to change. Cross-functional and diagonal communication within the project team and with outside interested parties helps to reduce resistance to change.‡

---

* See "Texas Instruments Shows U.S. Business How to Survive in the 1980's," *Business Week* (September 18, 1978), pp. 66–92.
† E. R. Corey and S. H. Star, *Organization Strategy: A Marketing Approach*, Chapter 6, Division of Research, Harvard Business School, Boston, Mass., 1970.
‡ L. W. Ellis, "Effective Use of Temporary Groups for New Product Development," *Research Management* (January, 1979), pp. 31–34.

Jermakowicz found that the matrix design was most effective of three major organizational forms he studied in ensuring the implementation or introduction of new projects, while a "pure" project organization produced the most creative solutions.*

Kolodny, reporting on a study of his own and citing some other studies as well, comments on the effect that matrix organizations have on new product innovation.† Kolodny cites Davis and Lawrence, who point to an apparent high correlation between matrix organization designs and very high rates of new product innovation.‡ In his summary Kolodny notes that there is an apparent relationship between high rates of new product innovation, as measured by the successful introduction of new products, and matrix organizational designs.§

There is no question that an organization whose business involves the work of temporary projects is more anxiety-ridden, tension-filled, and demanding of personal competence and equilibrium than a stable, conventionally organized one. The matrix design is complex, yet its successful operation reflects a complementary mode of collaborative relationships in an open ambience. It is an adaptive, rapidly changing temporary management system that can favorably impact on organizational innovation.

Realignment of Supporting Systems

As the use of project management grows in an organization it soon becomes apparent that many of the systems that have been organized on a traditional hierarchical basis need to be realigned to support the project team. What initially appears to be only an organizational change soon becomes something larger. Effective project management requires timely and relevant information on the project; accordingly, the information systems have to be modified to accommodate the project manager's needs. Financial and accounting systems, project planning and control techniques, personnel evaluations and other supporting systems require adjustment to meet project management needs.

---

* Wladyslaw Jermakowicz, "Organizational Structures in the R & D Sphere," *R & D Management,* No. 8, Special Issue (1978), pp. 107–113v as cited in Kolodny below.
† Harvey F. Kolodny, "Matrix Organization Designs and New Product Success," *Research Management* (September, 1980), pp. 29–33.
‡ Stanley M. Davis and Paul R. Lawrence, *Matrix* (Addison-Wesley Publishing Company, Reading, Mass.), 1977.
§ Kolodny, op. cit., p. 32.

Development of General Manager Attitudes

An organizational culture is in a sense the aggregate of individual values, attitudes, beliefs, prejudices, and social standards. A change for these individuals means cultural changes. The matrix design, when properly applied, tends to provide more opportunity to more people to act in a general manager mode. With this kind of general manager thinking, the individual is able to contribute more to organizational decision making and information processing.

The matrix design with its openness and demands for persuasive skills provides an especially good environment for the manager-to-be to test his ability to make things happen by the strength of persuasive and negotiative powers. A perceptive general manager knows that there is little he accomplishes solely by virtue of his hierarchical position; so much depends on his ability to persuade others to this way of thinking. Exposure to the workings and ambience of the matrix culture brings this point home clearly and succinctly.

Effective collaboration on a project team requires plenty of a needed ingredient—trust. To develop this trust, individuals must be prepared to take personal risks in sharing resources, information, views, prejudices, attitudes, and feelings to act in a democratic mode. Not everyone can do that, yet executives in successful companies are able to do so. For example, in the Digital Equipment Corporation where a matrix environment prevails, the ambience is described as "incredibly democratic" and not for everyone. Lots of technical people can't stand the lack of structure and indefiniteness. In such an organization bargaining skills are essential to survival.* The matrix design is permanent—the deployment of people is changing constantly. In such a transitional situation the only thing that prevents breakdown is the personal relationships as conflicts are resolved and personnel assignments are changed. Communication is continually needed to maintain the interpersonal relationships and to stimulate people to contribute to the project team efforts.

SOME CAVEATS

The matrix organizational design is hard to get started and challenging to operate. The more conventional the culture has been, the more challenges will emerge in moving to the matrix form. A few caveats are in order for those who plan to initiate and use the project-driven matrix design:

---

* Harold Sneker, "If You Gotta Borrow Money, You Gotta," *Forbes* (April 28, 1980), pp. 116–120.

1. Realize that patience is absolutely necessary. It takes time to change the systems and people who make the matrix work.
2. Promote by word and example an open and flexible attitude in the organization. Encourage the notion that change is inevitable, and that a free exchange of ideas is necessary to make project management work.
3. Develop a scheme for organizational objectives, goals, and strategies that will provide the framework for an emerging project management culture.
4. Accept the idea that some people may never be able to adjust to the unstructured, democratic ambience of the matrix culture. For these people a place in the organization must be assured where they can remain insulated from the "fiendishly difficult" surroundings of the matrix organization.
5. Be mindful of the tremendous importance that the team commitment plays in managing the project activities. Make use of the winning football team analogy where the commitment to win is an absolute prerequisite to becoming a championship team.
6. Provide for a forum whereby conflict can be resolved before the conflict deteriorates into interpersonal strife.
7. Realize that project management is not a panacea for organic organizational maladies. In fact, the implementing of a project management system will bring to light many organizational problems and opportunities that have remained hidden in the conventional line and staff organization.
8. Be aware that the particular route that an organization follows in its journey to the matrix design must evolve out of the existing culture.
9. Recognize that senior management support and commitment are essential to success.
10. Work for communication within the company that is uninhibited, thorough, and complete. Information requirements for project management require definition. Those individuals who have a need to know must have access to the information to do their job. Those in key positions have to understand and use the project-generated information.
11. Be aware that shifting to a matrix form is easier for the younger organization. For large well-established companies where a rigid bureaucracy endures, the shift will be quite formidable.
12. Institute a strong educational effort to acquaint key managers and professionals with the theory and practice of project management. Time should be taken to do this at the beginning using the existing culture as a point of departure.

SUMMARY

The real culture of project management refers to actual behavior—those things and events that really exist in the life of an organization. The introduction of project management into an existing culture will set into motion a "system of effects" which changes attitudes, values, beliefs, management systems to a participative, democratic mode. Thus, a new cultural context for the sharing of decisions, results, rewards, and accountability will ultimately emerge as an organization matures in the use of project management.

BIBLIOGRAPHY

Cleland, D. I. and King, W. R. *Systems Analysis and Project Management,* 3rd ed. McGraw-Hill, New York, 1983.

Corey, E. R. and Star, S. H. *Organization Strategy: A Marketing Approach,* Chapter 6. Division of Research, Harvard Business School, Boston, 1970.

Davis, Stanley M. and Lawrence, Paul R. *Matrix.* Addison-Wesley, Reading, Mass., p. 19.

Ellis, L. W. "Effective Use of Temporary Groups for New Product Development." *Research Management* (January, 1979):31–34.

George, William W. "Task Teams for Rapid Growth." *Harvard Business Review* (March-April, 1977):78.

Jermakovicz, Wladyslaw. "Organizational Structure in the R & D Sphere." *R&D Management,* No. 8, Special Issue (1978):107–113v.

Kolodny, Harvey F. "Matrix Organization Designs and New Product Success." *Research Management* (September, 1980):29–33.

Mee, John F. "Matrix Organization." *Business Horizons* (Summer, 1964).

Murphy, D. C., Baker, Bruce N. and Fisher, Delmar. "Determinants of Project Success." National Technical Information Services, Accession No. N-74-30392 (1974), Springfield, Va. 22151, p. 60669.

Reeser, Clayton. "Some Potential Human Problems of the Project Form of Organization." *Academy of Management Journal, 12* (December, 1979).

Seneker, Harold. "If You Gotta Borrow Money, You Gotta." *Forbes* (April 28, 1980):116–120.

"Texas Instruments Shows U.S. Business How to Survive in the 1980s" *Business Week* (September 18, 1978).

Index